COMPUTERS AND COMPUTATION

Readings from
SCIENTIFIC AMERICAN

COMPUTERS AND COMPUTATION

With Introductions by
Robert R. Fenichel
Massachusetts General Hospital

Joseph Weizenbaum
Massachusetts Institute of Technology

W. H. Freeman and Company
San Francisco

Five of the SCIENTIFIC AMERICAN articles in
Computers and Computation are available as separate
Offprints. For a complete list of more than
800 articles now available as Offprints, write to
W. H. Freeman and Company, 660 Market Street,
San Francisco, California 94104.

Printed in the United States of America

Library of Congress Catalog Card Number: 78–170396

Standard Book Number: 0–7167–0937–6 (cloth)
0–7167–0936–8 (paper)

9 8 7 6 5 4 3 2

PREFACE

The time is ripe for this reader. Several dozen articles on computer science have appeared in *Scientific American* in the last few years, and popular interest in the field is increasing.

At the same time, partly because of the recent recession in the American economy, but more for reasons internal to the field, computer science has recently relaxed its pace. Work has not stopped, but that the current mood is one of consolidation can scarcely be doubted. The single exception to this trend is noted in our Introduction to the first section of this book.

Just a few years ago, computer science was moving so swiftly that even the professional journals were more archival than informative. This book could not then have been produced without great risk of misfocus. Today, it is much easier to put the articles that constitute this book—even the most recent ones—into context; we have attempted to do this in our introductions to the five sections into which the book is divided.

We have updated the authors' biographies and bibliographies, generally with the authors' assistance. Few of the bibliographic references are to the nonprofessional literature, but the reader should not be put off. Computer science is sufficiently young that many of its investigations are substantially nontechnical. Much of the professional literature may therefore be read with profit by any determined reader of *Scientific American*.

September 1971

ROBERT R. FENICHEL
JOSEPH WEIZENBAUM

CONTENTS

I FUNDAMENTALS

		Introduction 2
MCCARTHY	1	Information 7
EVANS	2	Computer Logic and Memory 17
RAJCHMAN	3	Integrated Computer Memories 28
SUTHERLAND	4	Computer Inputs and Outputs 42
SUTHERLAND	5	Computer Displays 53
STRACHEY	6	Systems Analysis and Programming 70
FANO AND CORBATO	7	Time-Sharing on Computers 79

II GAMES, MUSIC, AND ARTIFICIAL INTELLIGENCE

		Introduction 90
SELFRIDGE AND NEISSER	8	Pattern Recognition by Machine 95
SHANNON	9	A Chess-Playing Machine 104
BERNSTEIN AND ROBERTS	10	Computer v. Chess-Player 108
HILLER	11	Computer Music 113
MINSKY	12	Artificial Intelligence 123

III MATHEMATICS OF, BY, AND FOR COMPUTERS

		Introduction 134
WANG	13	Games, Logic and Computers 136
WINOGRAD	14	How Fast Can Computers Add? 145
ULAM	15	Computers 151
MCCRACKEN	16	The Monte Carlo Method 162

IV COMPUTER MODELS OF THE REAL WORLD

		Introduction 168
LEVINTHAL	17	Molecular Model-Building by Computer 171
HAMILTON AND NANCE	18	Systems Analysis of Urban Transportation 183
HARLOW AND FROMM	19	Computer Experiments in Fluid Dynamics 192
LEDLEY AND RUDDLE	20	Chromosome Analysis by Computer 199
KEMENY	21	Man Viewed as a Machine 206
SLOTNICK	22	The Fastest Computer 214

V   FOUR ESSAYS ON THE USES OF THE COMPUTER

Introduction   228

COONS   23   The Uses of Computers in Technology   231

GREENBERGER   24   The Uses of Computers in Organizations   243

SUPPES   25   The Uses of Computers in Education   249

OETTINGER   26   The Uses of Computers in Science   261

Biographical Notes and Bibliographies   271

Index   281

Note on cross-references: References to articles included in this book are noted by the title of the article and the page on which it begins; references to articles that are available as Offprints, but are not included here, are noted by the article's title and Offprint number; references to articles published by SCIENTIFIC AMERICAN, but which are not available as Offprints, are noted by the title of the article and the month and year of its publication.

COMPUTERS AND COMPUTATION

I

FUNDAMENTALS

I

FUNDAMENTALS

INTRODUCTION

The articles in this section provide the groundwork on which the remainder of this volume builds. John McCarthy's "Information" is, in fact, a general introduction to the field, and could itself be given no nonredundant introduction.

The reader's first reaction to McCarthy's article may be that it is flawed by an unevenness of depth. McCarthy's discussion ranges from the encoding of alphabetic characters through the social implications of computing. The reader may feel that, whatever the proper level of detail may be, McCarthy has not settled on it.

In fact, there is no best way to describe digital computation. To be sure, any computer behavior can ultimately be described in terms of the underlying circuitry, but this is often no more helpful than it would be to describe a man's behavior in terms of the behavior of the atoms making up his body. The six remaining articles making up this section describe computer behavior at four different levels of abstraction, and most of the articles in the other sections of this reader are still more abstract.

The most fundamental level of description is, as mentioned above, that of the basic electronic circuitry. Computers must store information and perform elementary operations (e.g., addition) on it. Evans ("Computer Logic and Memories") and Rajchman ("Integrated Computer Memories") describe the devices that are used for these purposes.

The transistor is still in its first quarter-century, and most digital devices are even younger. Accordingly, the reader is probably prepared to learn of moderate across-the-board improvements in the various figures cited by Evans and Rajchman. Most digital devices are, indeed, available two to five times cheaper, faster, and/or more capacious than they were four years ago. In particular, batch-fabricated MOS memories, as predicted by Rajchman, have replaced core as the primary memory in at least one line of machines.

These moderate improvements are not the whole story. Since these articles were written, integrated circuitry has dropped in cost by a factor of several *hundred;* the size of feasible integrated-circuit memories has simultaneously risen by a similar factor. These striking trends show no sign of abating.

As Evans predicted, computer designers are scarcely able to deal with this new environment. It is now economically justifiable to build processing units of extreme complexity, if doing so will result in more efficient use of mass memories or other expensive components.

For example, modern processors tend to have many more internal registers than older processors. These registers, which are sometimes so numerous that they require their own sophisticated addressing schemes, would have been prohibitively expensive and unreliable with older technologies. Small content-addressed memories internal to processing units are common. In general, advances in basic digital circuitry are the one exception to the general complacency of the preface to this volume.

Sutherland's article ("Computer Inputs and Outputs") is more abstract than those of Evans and Rajchman. Given that information may be stored for computer reference and manipulated in simple ways, Sutherland describes how this data may be rationally and efficiently transferred from place to place, even when the devices involved in a transfer may be grossly different in their preferred speeds of operation. Here, any discussion of the underlying circuitry would be more obfuscatory than helpful.

Sutherland's other article ("Computer Displays") is yet more abstract. In "Computer Displays," the technology of "Computer Inputs and Outputs" is all assumed to be available, but now new problems must be faced. The human user does not wish to worry about channels, interrupts, and the like. The pictures on his screen depict a universe whose laws these pictures should obey. "Computer Displays" is, as the reader will discover, hardly about cathode-ray tubes at all. Rather, it is about the problems of organizing cathode-ray tubes (and other hardware) to present a usable artifact to an imperfectly predictable human being.

The article by Strachey ("System Analysis and Programming") is about as abstract as "Computer Displays." Strachey describes the means of attack that are used on moderately large, complex problems to prepare them for computer solution. There is a gap here among the articles, for whereas the Evans–Rajchman–Sutherland–Sutherland progression is one of easy steps, the branch from Evans and Rajchman to Strachey begins with a long step indeed.

Strachey limits his attention to the intellectual problems of programming. As he points out, these may all be discussed in the happy context of readable, concise, higher-level languages. Strachey mentions that there exist translating programs to turn such high-level languages into the language directly understood by computers, but he never describes this latter language at all. The following description is misleading for some machines, but it should give the reader a steppingstone in the line of descriptions running from Evans and Rajchman to Strachey. The interested reader should, of course, consult any of the more careful descriptions given in the references.

The elements of any computer's machine language are *instructions*, which the machine interprets one at a time. Each instruction is a bit-string, generally of the same size as a memory word. The bits making up a given instruction tell the machine what operation to perform, what operands (if any) to use, and where to put the result of the operation (if any). A modern machine may have a repertoire of one to two hundred operations, so that typically seven to ten bits of each of its instructions are used to tell which operation is intended.

Since the most natural source of operands and destination of results is the memory, each instruction might have to contain one to three addresses of memory locations. Often, however, the result of one operation is wanted as an operand of an immediately following operation; for this reason, and in order to keep each instruction from being burdened with fifty or sixty bits of addresses, most computers have at least one or two *special registers* that serve as implicit operands and result registers in most operations. Each instruction then carries only a single address, so that some typical instructions might be:

Store zero in memory word 7823.

Load Special Register 1 with the contents of memory word 2486.

Add the contents of memory word 4753 to the contents of Special Register 2; leave the result in Special Register 2.

An important component of the machine is a high-speed register called the Instruction Counter. The Instruction Counter tells the machine the address of the memory word from which its next instruction should be taken. Ordinarily, the Instruction Counter is incremented by one during each instruction execution, so that instructions in successive words in memory are executed consecutively. But certain instructions cause the Instruction Counter to receive wholly new contents, effectively causing the locus of the machine's attention to jump to the specified location. This jump operation may even be performed conditionally, so that additional typical instructions might be:

Set the Instruction Counter to 6427.

If the content of Special Register 2 is zero, set the Instruction Counter to 8453.

These operations all concern such fine detail that short, readable, machine-language programs are almost unknown. For example, Strachey's five-line CPL program on page 71 would involve two or three dozen lines of machine language for most machines. That translators can be written to take the former program into the latter is an impressive fact, discussion of which is unfortunately beyond the scope of this Introduction.

The final article in this section is "Time-sharing" by Fano and Corbató. Time-sharing, the interleaved access to a single computer system by several simultaneous users, logically follows (and chronologically followed) development of the techniques described in "Computer Inputs and Outputs" and "Systems Analysis and Programming." These latter techniques were first developed about fifteen years ago, and they extended the range of feasible programming projects by about an order of magnitude. Time-sharing systems were among the systems made feasible by these developments. As Fano and Corbató point out, the initial goal of time-sharing was to provide an apparent multiplicity of independent, possibly slow, but complete computers.

Soon, however, system designers found themselves caught in a revolution of rising expectations. This revolution continues today. Hardware costs are falling, while social and technological tasks are ever more complex. As Strachey points out, we have nearly reached the limit of present techniques in programming. Certainly each major programming effort of recent times has been much too complex for the compass of any single programmer. The chief concern of today's time-sharing systems is to facilitate cooperation among users; central, shared, file memory has become these systems' most significant feature.

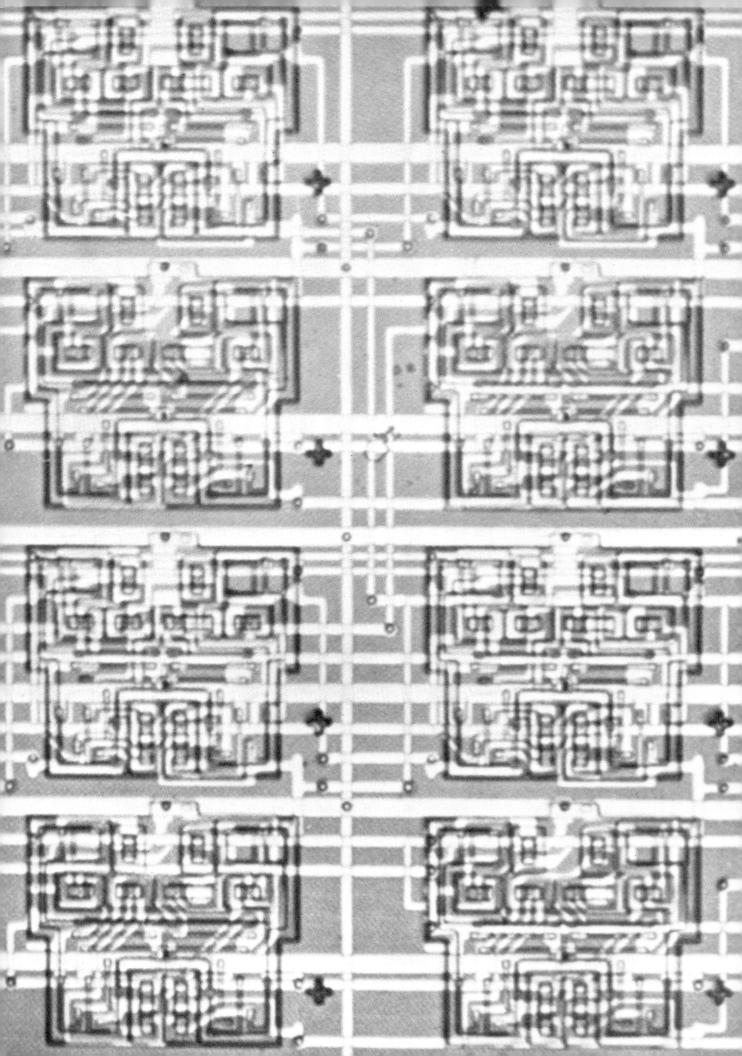

1

INFORMATION

JOHN McCARTHY
September, 1966

The computer gives signs of becoming the contemporary counterpart of the steam engine that brought on the industrial revolution. The computer is an information machine. Information is a commodity no less intangible than energy; if anything, it is more pervasive in human affairs. The command of information made possible by the computer should also make it possible to reverse the trends toward mass-produced uniformity started by the industrial revolution. Taking advantage of this opportunity may present the most urgent engineering, social and political questions of the next generation.

A computer, as hardware, consists of input and output devices, arithmetic and control circuits and a memory. Equally essential to the complete portrait is the program of instructions—the "software"—that puts the system to work. The computer accepts information from its environment through its input devices; it combines this information, according to the rules of the program stored in its memory, with information that is also stored in its memory, and it sends information back to its environment through its output devices.

The human brain also accepts inputs of information, combines it with information stored somehow within and returns outputs of information to its environment. Social institutions—such as the legislature, the law, science, education, business organizations and the communication system—receive, process and put out information in much the same way. Accordingly, in common with the computer, the human brain and social institutions may be regarded as information-processing systems, at least with respect to some crucial functions. The study of these entities as such has led to new understanding of their structures.

The installation of computers in certain organizations has already greatly increased the efficiency of some of the organizations. In the 15 or 20 years that computers have been in use, however, it has become clear that they do not merely bring an increase in efficiency. They induce basic transformation of the institutions and enterprises in which they are installed.

In the first place, computers are a million to a billion times faster than humans in performing computing operations. This follows from the fact that their working parts now change state in a few millionths or billionths of a second. Why should this quantitative change in speed produce a qualitative change in human activities that are facilitated by a computer? It might seem that there is no way to use such speeds outside of the missile business and other exotic undertakings. The answer is that the increase in speed has meant the building of computers with the capacity to handle information on a correspondingly larger scale. The interaction of high-speed, high-capacity computers with their environment is often continuous, with many input and output devices operating simultaneously with the ongoing internal computation.

The computer is, furthermore, a universal information-processing machine. Any calculation that can be done by any machine can be done by a computer, provided that the computer has a program describing the calculation. This was proved as a general proposition by the British mathematician A. M. Turing as early as 1936. It applies to the most rudimentary theoretical system as well as to the big general-purpose machines of today that make it possible, in practice, to write new programs instead of having to build new machines.

MICROELECTRONIC CIRCUITS of the kind shown on the opposite page can be regarded as the nerve tissue of the next generation of computers. The circuits, which are enlarged about 200 diameters, are part of a "complex bipolar array chip" made by Fairchild Semiconductor. Each of the eight complete circuits shown (*dark gray*) is a functional unit consisting of 18 transistors and 18 resistors. These units are connected by a larger microelectronic network (*white*); there are 28 units in the entire chip. Some recent computers incorporate microelectronic circuits, but the circuits are not connected microelectronically. Possibly microelectronic circuits will be used not only as logic elements but also as memory elements.

8

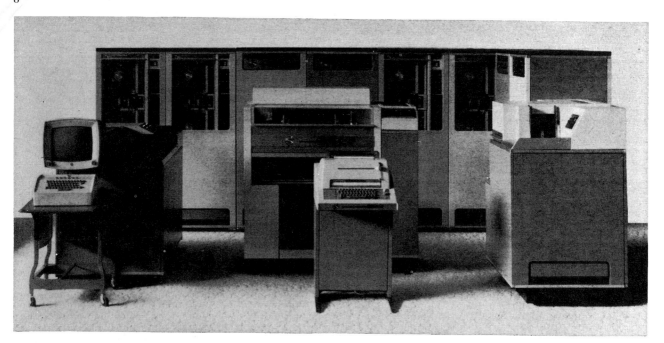

TYPICAL COMPUTER INSTALLATION includes components of the kind shown here in front and top views; the components are identified in the diagram at right. The heart of the system, which is a computer in the Spectra 70 series of the Radio Corporation of America, is the central processor and memory unit; the other units serve for input, output and storage of data. The input devices are

The speed, capacity and universality of computers make them machines that can be used to foster diversity and individuality in our industrial civilization, as opposed to the uniformity and conformity that have hitherto been the order of the day. Decisions that now have to be made in the mass can in the future be made separately, case by case. To take a practical example, it can be decided whether or not it is safe for an automobile to go through an intersection each time the matter comes up, instead of subjecting the flow of automobiles to regulation by traffic lights. A piece of furniture, a household appliance or an automobile can be designed to the specifications of each user. The decision whether to go on to the next topic or review the last one can be made in accordance with the interests of the child rather than for the class as a whole. In other words, computers can make it possible for people to be treated as individuals in many situations where they are now lumped in the aggregate.

The quality of such individual response and attention is another matter. It will depend on the quality of the programs. The special attention of a stupid program may not be worth much. But then the individual can write his own program.

The future that is contemplated here has come into view quite abruptly during the past few years. According to a report published by the American Federation of Information Processing Societies (AFIPS), there were only 10 or 15 computers at work in the U.S. in 1950. Today there are 35,200, and by 1975 there will be 85,000. Investment in computers will rise from $8 billion to more than $30 billion by 1975. Present installations include 2,100 large systems costing about $1 million each; in 1975 there will be 4,000 of these. Even the medium and small systems that are in use today have a capacity equal to or exceeding that of the 1950 generation.

A scientific problem that took an hour on a big 1950 machine at 1,000 operations per second can be run on the fastest contemporary computers in less than half a second. Allowing another 3.5 seconds to transfer the yield to an external storage memory for later printing, it can be said that program running time has been reduced from an hour to three or four seconds. This reflects the impressive recent progress in the design and manufacture of computer hardware.

Big computers are currently equipped with internal memories—the memory actively engaged in the computation under way—that usually contain 10 or 12 million minute ring-shaped ferrite "cores" in three-dimensional crystalline arrays. Each core is capable of storing one "bit" or unit, of information. Along with the replacement of the vacuum tube by the transistor and now the replacement of the transistor by the microelectronic circuit [see illustration on page 6] there has come a steep increase in the speed of arithmetic and control circuits over the past 10 years. The miniaturization of these circuits (from hundreds of circuits per cubic foot with vacuum-tube technology to hundreds of thousands and prospectively millions of circuits per cubic foot with solid-state technology) has speeded up operations by reducing the distance an impulse has to travel from point to point inside the computer.

As increases in speed and capacity have realized the inherent universality of the computer, expenditures for programming have been absorbing an increasing percentage of total installation costs. The U.S. Government, with a dozen or so big systems serving its military and space establishments, is spending more than half of its 1966 outlay of $844 million on software. Without doubt the professions in this field—those of system analyst and programmer—are the fastest-growing occupations in the U.S. labor force. From about 200,000 in 1966 it is estimated that their numbers will increase to 500,000 or 750,000 by 1970. Courses in programming are now offered in many universities and even in some high schools. In a liberal education an exposure to programming is held to be as bracing as an elementary course in mathematics or logic.

Calculating devices have a history that goes back to the ancient Greeks. The first mechanical digital calculators were made by Blaise Pascal in the 17th century. In the mid-19th century Charles Babbage proposed and partially constructed an automatic machine that would carry out long sequences of calculations without human intervention. Babbage did not succeed in making his machine actually work—although he might have, had he used binary instead of decimal notation and enjoyed better financial and technical support.

In the late 1930's Howard H. Aiken of Harvard University and George R. Stibitz of the Bell Telephone Laboratories developed automatic calculators using relays; during World War II, J. Presper Eckert and John W. Mauchly of the University of Pennsylvania developed ENIAC, an electronic calculator. As early as 1943 a British group had an

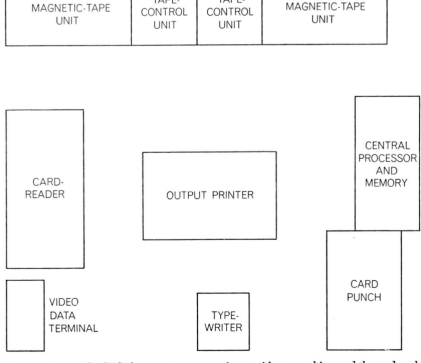

the typewriter, with which the operator communicates with the machine, and the card-reader, for which the card-punch is an adjunct. The main output devices are the printer and the video data terminal, which employs a cathode ray tube. The tape units store data.

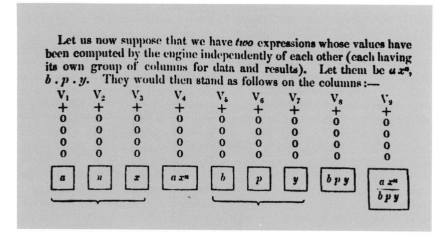

Let us now suppose that we have *two* expressions whose values have been computed by the engine independently of each other (each having its own group of columns for data and results). Let them be ax^n, $b.p.y$. They would then stand as follows on the columns :—

V_1	V_2	V_3	V_4	V_5	V_6	V_7	V_8	V_9
+	+	+	+	+	+	+	+	+
0	0	0	0	0	0	0	0	0
0	0	0	0	0	0	0	0	0
0	0	0	0	0	0	0	0	0
0	0	0	0	0	0	0	0	0
a	n	x	ax^n	b	p	y	bpy	$\dfrac{ax^n}{bpy}$

EARLY PROGRAM was written for Charles Babbage's "analytical engine" by Lady Lovelace, who was the daughter of Lord Byron. She wrote the program, which was for computing the number series known as Bernoulli numbers, to show what the engine could do. The program, of which this is a fragment, was published in 1840 in *Taylor's Scientific Memoirs*.

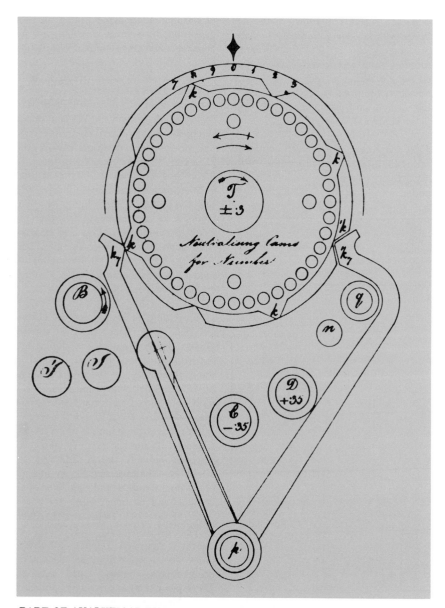

PART OF ANALYTICAL ENGINE was drawn by Babbage. This drawing, one of many that he made for the engine, bears the inscription "Neutralising Cams for Number." Financial and technological difficulties prevented Babbage from completing the machine.

electronic computer working on a wartime assignment.

Strictly speaking, however, the term "computer" now designates a universal machine capable of carrying out any arbitrary calculation, as propounded by Turing in 1936. The possibility of such a machine was apparently guessed by Babbage; his collaborator Lady Lovelace, daughter of the poet Lord Byron, may have been the first to propose a changeable program to be stored in the machine. Curiously, it does not seem that the work of either Turing or Babbage played any direct role in the labors of the men who made the computer a reality. The first practical proposal for universal computers that stored their programs in their memory came from Eckert and Mauchly during the war. Their proposal was developed by John von Neumann and his collaborators in a series of influential reports in 1945 and 1946. The first working stored-program computers were demonstrated in 1949 almost simultaneously in several laboratories in Britain and the U.S. The first commercial computer was the Eckert-Mauchly UNIVAC, put on the market in 1950.

Since that time progress in the electronic technology of computer circuits, the art of programming and programming languages and the development of computer operating systems has been rapid. No small part in this development has been played by the U.S. Government, which is always in the market for the latest and biggest systems available. It is not too much to say that the systems designed for the industry's biggest customer have been the prototypes for each major advance in computer hardware. The creation of the high-speed computer has been as central to the contemporary revolution in the technology of war as the intercontinental missile and the thermonuclear warhead.

The basic unit of information with which these machines work is the bit. Any device that can be in either of two states, such as a ferrite core or a transistor, can store a single bit. Two such devices can store two bits, three can store three bits, and so on. Consider a five-bit register made of five one-bit devices. Since each device has two states, represented, say, by 0 and 1, the five together have 2^5, or 32, states. The combinations from 00000 to 11111 can be taken to represent the binary numbers from 0 to 31. They can also be used to encode the 26 letters of the alphabet, with six combinations left over to represent word spaces and punctuation. This would permit representation

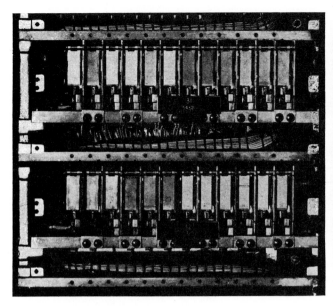 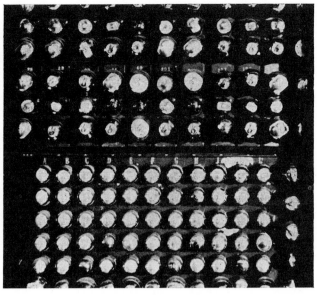

FIRST MODERN COMPUTERS were the Mark I and the ENIAC (Electronic Numerical Integrator and Calculator). The former had electromechanical relays (*left*) as its key parts, the latter vacuum tubes (*right*). A comparison of these parts with the microelectron- ic circuits illustrated on page 64 will indicate how far miniaturization has progressed. Both the Mark I and the ENIAC have been disassembled. The portion of the Mark I shown here is now at Harvard University; panel from ENIAC is at U.S. Military Academy.

of words and sentences by strings of five-bit groups. (Actually, to accommodate uppercase and lowercase letters, the full assortment of punctuation marks, the decimal digits and so on it is now customary to use seven bits.)

For many purposes, however, it is better not to be specific about how the information is coded into bits. More important is the task of describing the kinds of information to be dealt with, the basic operations to be carried out on them and the basic tests to be performed on the information in order to decide what to do next. For bits the basic operations are the logical operations ·, + and − (the last usually placed above a symbol, as in $\bar{A}$), which are read "and," "or" and "not" respectively. Operations are defined by giving all the cases. Thus · is defined by the equations $0 \cdot 0 = 0$, $1 \cdot 0 = 0$, $0 \cdot 1 = 0$, and $1 \cdot 1 = 1$. The basic decision concerning a bit is whether it is 0 or 1. Designers of computers do much of their work at the level of bits [see *illustration on next page*]. They have systematic procedures, as the following article by David C. Evans shows, for translating logical equations into transistor circuits that carry out the functions of these equations.

At the next level above bits come numbers. On numbers the basic operations are addition, subtraction, multiplication and division [see *illustration on page 13*]. The basic tests are whether two numbers are equal and whether a number is greater than zero. Programmers are generally able to work with

numbers because computer designers build the basic operations on numbers out of the logical operations on bits in the design of the circuits in the machine.

Another kind of information is a string of characters, such as A or ABA or ONION. It is well to include also the null string with no characters. A basic operation on characters may be taken to be concatenation, denoted by the symbol *. Thus ABC*ACA = ABCACA. The other basic operations are "first" and "rest." Thus first(ABC) = A and rest(ABC) = BC. The basic tests on strings are whether the string is null and whether two individual characters are equal.

Out of one kind of information, then, more elaborate kinds of information can be built; numbers and characters are built out of bits, and strings are built out of characters. Similarly, the operations and tests for the higher forms of information are built up out of the operations and tests for the lower forms. One can represent a chessboard, for example, as a table of numbers giving for each square the kind of piece, if any, that occupies it. For chess positions a basic operation gives the list of legal moves from that position. A picture may be similarly represented by an array of numbers expressing the gray-scale value of each point in the picture. The *Mariner IV* pictures of Mars were so represented during transmission to the earth, and this representation was used in the memory of the computer by the program that removed noise and enhanced contrast. Christopher Strachey shows in

this issue how programmers put together the basic operations and tests for a given class of information in designing a program to treat such information [see "System Analysis and Programming," by Christopher Strachey, page 70].

What computers can do depends on the state of the art and science of the programming as well as on speed and memory capacity. At present it is straightforward to keep track of the seats available on each plane of an airline, to compute the trajectory of a space vehicle under the gravitational attraction of the sun and planets or to generate a circuit diagram from the specifications of circuit elements. It is difficult to predict the weather or to play a fair game of chess. It is currently not clear how to make a computer play an expert game of chess or discover significant mathematical theorems, although investigators have ideas about how these things might be done [see "Artificial Intelligence," by Marvin L. Minsky, page 123].

Input and output devices also play a significant part in making the capacity of a computer effective. For the engineering computations and the bookkeeping tasks first assigned to computers it seemed sufficient to provide them with punched-card-readers for input and line-printers for output, together with magnetic tapes for storing large quantities of data. To fly an airplane or a missile or to control a steel mill or a chemical plant, however, a computer must receive inputs from such sensory organs

LOGIC

	YES	NO	
	1	0	

NUMERATION

0	0	0	0
1	1	1	1
2	10	2	10
4	100	3	11
8	1000	4	100
16	10000	5	101
32	100000	6	110
64	1000000	7	111
128	10000000	8	1000
256	100000000	9	1001

SEVEN-BIT CODE

COLUMNS

BITS				$b_7 b_6 b_5$	0 0 0	0 0 1	0 1 0	0 1 1	1 0 0	1 0 1	1 1 0	1 1 1
b_4	b_2	b_3	b_1		0	1	2	3	4	5	6	7
0	0	0	0	0	NUL	DLE	SP	0	\`	P	@	p
0	0	0	1	1	SOH	DC1	!	1	A	Q	a	q
0	0	1	0	2	STX	DC2	"	2	B	R	b	r
0	0	1	1	3	ETX	DC3	#	3	C	S	c	s
0	1	0	0	4	EOT	DC4	$	4	D	T	d	t
0	1	0	1	5	ENQ	NAK	%	5	E	U	e	u
0	1	1	0	6	ACK	SYN	&	6	F	V	f	v
0	1	1	1	7	BEL	ETB	'	7	G	W	g	w
1	0	0	0	8	BS	CAN	(	8	H	X	h	x
1	0	0	1	9	HT	EM	)	9	I	Y	i	y
1	0	1	0	10	LF	SS	*	:	J	Z	j	z
1	0	1	1	11	VT	ESC	+	;	K	[	k	{
1	1	0	0	12	FF	FS	,	<	L	~	l	¬
1	1	0	1	13	CR	GS	−	=	M	]	m	}
1	1	1	0	14	SO	RS	.	>	N	∧	n	|
1	1	1	1	15	SI	US	/	?	O	−	o	DEL

ROWS

BINARY NUMBERS serve computers in logic, arithmetic and coding functions. The array of binary numbers at left under "Numeration" shows that the system, which is based on 2, represents each new power of 2 by adding a 0. The same arrangement reappears at right in the binary version of the numbers 1 through 9; it shows, for example, that 111, representing 7, can be read from the left as "one 4, one 2 and one 1." The seven-bit code (*bottom*) is widely used to accomplish the printing done by computers in issuing results and communicating with operators. On receiving pulses representing 1011001, for example, the computer would print Y. Columns 0 and 1 contain control characters; *BS*, for example, means "back space."

as radars, flowmeters and thermometers and must deliver its outputs directly to such effector organs as motors and radio transmitters. Still other input and output devices are demanded by the increasing speed and capacity of the computers themselves. To keep them fully employed they must be allowed to interact simultaneously with large numbers of people, most of them necessarily at remote stations. This requires telephone lines, teletypewriters and cathode-ray-tube devices. For many purposes a picture on the cathode ray tube is more useful than the half-ton of print-out paper that would deliver the underlying numerical information. Simultaneous access to the computer for many users also calls for new sophistication in programming to establish the time-sharing arrangements described in the article by R. M. Fano and F. J. Corbató [see "Time-sharing on Computers," by R. M. Fano and F. J. Corbató, page 79].

It is possible to describe at greater length the perfection and promise of the new technology of information. This discussion must go on to certain pressing questions. To put the questions negatively: Will the computer condemn us to live in an increasingly depersonalized and bureaucratized society? Will the crucial decisions of life turn on a hole punched in Column 17 of a card? Will "automation" put most of us out of work?

Experience with the computerized systems most people have so far encountered in governmental, business and educational institutions has not tended to dispel the anxiety that underlies such questions. One can ascribe the bureaucratic ways of these systems to their computers or to the greed, stupidity and other vices of the people who run them. I would argue three more direct causes: one economic, one technical and one cultural.

In the first place, computers are expensive. When a computer is first installed in an organization, the impulse of the authorities is to use the new machine to cut corners, to do the old job in the old way but more cheaply, to achieve internal economies even at the expense of external relations with citizens, customers and students. Secondly, the external memories that store the data for most large organizations are inherently inflexible. Between runs through a magnetic-tape file, for example, there is no possibility of access to the account that generates today's complaint. Finally, most practitioners in the expanding software professions were beginners; it was all they could do to get the systems going at all.

In my opinion the opportunity to cure these faults is improving steadily. Computers are cheaper, and competition between systems should soon compel more attention to the customers. (The effect is not yet noticeable at my bank.) Secondly, high-speed memory devices such as magnetic-disk files, now used as internal memories, are taking up service in external data-storage. They make access to any record possible at any time. Finally, although there are a lot of young fogies who know how things are done now and expect to see them done that way until they retire in 1996, programmers are acquiring greater confidence and virtuosity.

All of this should encourage the development of systems that serve the customer better without offending either his intelligence or his convenience. In particular, organizations such as schools should not have to ask people questions the answers to which are already on file.

The computer will not make its revolutionary impact, however, by doing the old bookkeeping tasks more efficiently. It is finding its way into new applications that will increase human freedom of action. No stretching of the demonstrated technology is required to envision computer consoles installed in every home and connected to public-utility computers through the telephone system. The console might consist of a typewriter keyboard and a television screen that can display text and pictures. Each subscriber will have his private file space in the computer that he can consult and alter at any time. Given the availability of such equipment, it is impossible to recite more than a small fraction of the uses to which enterprising consumers will put it.

Everyone will have better access to the Library of Congress than the librarian himself now has. Any page will be immediately accessible, although Ben-Ami Lipetz holds that this may come later rather than sooner [see "Information Storage and Retrieval," by Ben-Ami Lipetz, SCIENTIFIC AMERICAN, September, 1966]. Because payment will depend on usage, all levels and kinds of taste can be provided for.

The system will serve as each person's external memory, with his messages in and out kept nicely filed and reminders displayed at designated times.

Full reports on current events, whether baseball scores, the smog index in Los Angeles or the minutes of the 178th

ADDITION

$$\overset{1\ 11}{111}$$
$$11$$
$$\overline{1010}$$

$$7$$
$$+\ 3$$
$$\overline{10}$$

$$\overset{11\quad 1}{110101}$$
$$11001$$
$$\overline{1001110}$$
$${}_{64\ \ 8\,4\,2}$$

$$53$$
$$+\ 25$$
$$\overline{78}$$

SUBTRACTION

$$\overset{11}{1101}$$
$$111$$
$$\overline{110}$$

$$13$$
$$-\ 7$$
$$\overline{6}$$

$$\overset{11}{110101}$$
$$11001$$
$$\overline{11100}$$
$${}_{16\,8\,4}$$

$$53$$
$$-\ 25$$
$$\overline{28}$$

MULTIPLICATION

$$1001$$
$$101$$
$$\overline{1001}$$
$$1001$$
$$\overline{101101}$$
$${}_{32\ \ 8\,4\ \ 1}$$

$$9$$
$$\times\ 5$$

$$45$$

DIVISION

$$11000 \div 110$$

$$24 \div 6$$

$$110\overline{)11000}$$ quotient 100

$$4$$

BINARY ARITHMETIC involves only the manipulation of 0 and 1 and hence is the basis of the extremely rapid calculating done by computers. The superscript colored numerals represent carries; subscript colored numerals show how binary numbers are read decimally.

meeting of the Korean Truce Commission, will be available for the asking.

Income tax returns will be automatically prepared on the basis of continuous, cumulative annual records of income, deductions, contributions and expenses.

With the requisite sensors and effectors installed in the household the public-utility information system will shut the windows when it rains.

The reader can write his own list of assignments. He can do so with the assurance that various entrepreneurs will try to think up new services and will advertise them. In this connection the Antitrust Division of the Department of Justice should see to it that companies set up to operate the computers are kept separate from companies that provide programs. Competition among the programmers will intensify and diversify demand on the public-utility systems. Anyone who has a new program he thinks he can sell should be free to put it in any computer in which he is willing to rent file space and to sell its services to anyone who wants to use it.

As for the conformities currently imposed by mass production, consider how the computer might facilitate the purchase of some piece of household equipment. In the first place, the computer could be asked to search the catalogues and list the alternatives available, together with appraisals from such

institutions as Consumers Union. If the consumer knows how to use an automatic design system such as that described by Steven Anson Coons [see "The Uses of Computers in Technology," by Steven Anson Coons, page 231], he might design the desired equipment himself. The system will deliver not only drawings but also the findings of a simulation study that will show how well the equipment works. The consumer could also consult a designer, who will be able to render his service through the computer at less cost, together with firm estimates from prospective suppliers. With more or less elaboration, the procedures sketched here could do the paper work for the building of an entire house.

Apart from the physical construction of the public-utility information system, the full realization of these possibilities will require new advances in programming. No application illustrates the virtues and limitations of present-day programming so well as do efforts to use computers to aid teaching in elementary and secondary schools. In principle, one computer can give simultaneous individual attention to hundreds of students, each at his own console, each at a different place in the course or each concentrating on a different topic. The treatment of the student can be quite individual because the computer can remember the student's performance in every preceding session of instruction. The pace and the range of study can be entirely determined by the student's progress.

The teaching programs that have been written so far, however, put the student in a passive role. They are extremely pedantic. They have no understanding of the student's state of mind; they decide what to do next only in accordance with rather stereotyped sets of rules. As Patrick Suppes concludes, these programs do not compare too unfavorably with the performance of a teacher who has a large class [see "The Uses of Computers in Education," by Patrick Suppes, page 249]. Particularly where practice and repetition are the dominant ways of learning, the computer may even prove superior. The present programs fail in subjects that ought to cultivate the student's capacity for generating new ideas.

For the future it would be well, perhaps, to think of computers as study aids rather than teachers. The aim of the program should be to place the system under the control of the learner. He should be able to select from a list of topics the one he wants to work on; he should decide whether he prefers to read an exposition or to try to solve a problem. Best of all, he should be able to use the computer as a tool for testing his own ideas.

Reflection on the power of computer systems inevitably excites fear for the safety and integrity of the individual. In many minds the computer is the ultimate threat. It makes possible, for instance, a single national information file containing all tax, legal, security, credit, educational, medical and employment information about each and every citizen. Certainly such a file would be the source of great abuses. The files that exist today are abused. Security files, for example, have provided material for politically motivated persecutions. Credit files, to which access is wide open in the business community, have been used for purposes irrelevant to credit decisions. Accordingly it can be expected that more centralized files will facilitate even greater abuses.

On the other hand, citizens could seize the creation of centralized files as the occasion to cure existing abuses and to establish for each individual certain rights with respect to these files. Such a "bill of rights" might specify the following:

No organization, governmental or private, is allowed to maintain files that cover large numbers of people outside of the general system.

The rules governing access to the files are definite and well publicized, and the programs that enforce these rules are open to any interested party, including, for example, the American Civil Liberties Union.

An individual has the right to read his own file, to challenge certain kinds of entries in his file and to impose certain restrictions on access to his file.

Every time someone consults an individual's file this event is recorded, together with the authorization for the access.

If an organization or an individual obtains access to certain information in a file by deceit, this is a crime and a civil wrong. The injured individual may sue for invasion of privacy and be awarded damages.

At present an organization that claims to be considering extending credit to a person can learn a lot about his financial condition. In the new system no such information will be available without authorization from the person concerned. The normal form of authorization will allow no more than a yes-or-no answer to the question of whether he meets a particular definite credit criterion—whether he meets credit condition C1, for example, and can be expected to manage the installment purchase of a television set.

To establish such rights people must revise their ideas about the source and nature of their freedom. Most individual rights now recognized are based on the claim that the individual always had them; the safeguards of the law are said to be designed to prevent their infringement. Technology is advancing too fast, however, to allow such benevolent frauds to work in the future. The right to keep people from keeping files on us must first be invented, then legislated and actively enforced.

It may be supposed that, as happened with television and then color television, the enthusiasts and the well-to-do will be the first to install computer consoles in their homes. Eventually, however, everyone will consider them to be essential household equipment. People will soon become discontented with the "canned" programs available; they will want to write their own. The ability to write a computer program will become as widespread as the ability to drive a car.

Not knowing how to program will be like living in a house full of servants and not speaking their language. Each of the canned programs will be separately useful. It will be up to the individual, however, to coordinate them for his own fullest benefit. People will find, in fact, that console control of a process leads directly to the writing of one's own programs.

At first the computer says in effect: I can do the following things for you, which do you want? You reply. Then it says: In order to do this I need the following information. You respond and the dialogue continues. After you get used to using a particular facility, the computer's questions become annoying. You know in advance what they will be and you want to give the answers without waiting for the questions. Next you want to be able to give the entire sequence of actions a name and bring forth the sequence by typing only the name. As you become bolder you will want to make a later action conditional on the results of earlier actions and to provide for the repetition of actions until a criterion is reached. You are then already programming in full generality, albeit awkwardly.

As a skill, computer programming is probably more difficult than driving a car but probably less difficult than flying an airplane. It is more difficult than arithmetic but less difficult than writing good English. It does not require long study. Many people can write simple programs after an hour or two of instruction. Some success ordinarily comes quickly, and this reward reinforces further effort. Programming is far easier to learn than a foreign language or algebra.

Success in writing a program to do a particular task depends more on understanding the task and less on mastery of programming technique. To program the trajectory of a rocket, for example, requires a few weeks' study of programming and a few years' study of physics.

Writing a program to carry out some activity requires that an individual make explicit what he wants. The public-utility computer will do exactly what it is told to do within limitations imposed to protect other people's interests. A person who has experienced the unexpected and sometimes unpleasant consequences of the faithful execution of his wishes is usually ready to reexamine his preferences and premises. Fortunately programs can be readily changed. As people acquire greater control over their environment by explicit programming they will discover greater self-understanding and self-reliance. Some people will enjoy this experience more than others.

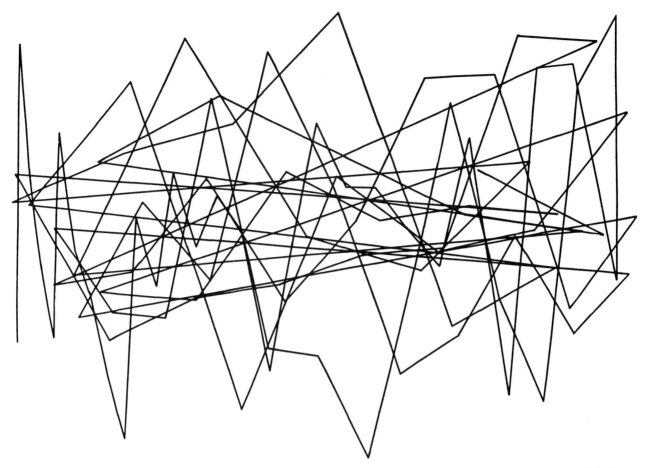

COMPUTER-GENERATED ART includes two works devised by A. Michael Noll of Bell Telephone Laboratories. At top is "Gaussian-Quadratic." The end points of each line have a Gaussian random distribution vertically; the horizontal positions increase quadratically. The pattern begins at left and is "reflected" back from right. At bottom is a portion of "Ninety Parallel Sinusoids with Linearly Increasing Period." The top line was mathematically specified as such a curve; the computer then repeated the line 90 times.

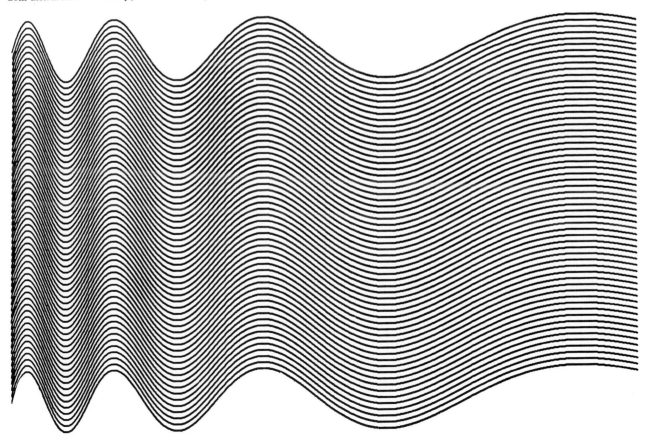

2

COMPUTER LOGIC AND MEMORY

DAVID C. EVANS
September, 1966

Electronic digital computers are made of two basic kinds of components: logic elements (often called switching elements) and memory elements. In virtually all modern computers these elements are binary, that is, the logic elements have two alternative pathways and the memory elements have two states. Accordingly all the information handled by such computers is coded in binary form. In short, the information is represented by binary symbols, stored in sets of binary memory elements and processed by binary switching elements.

To make a digital computer it is necessary to have memory elements and a set of logic elements that is functionally complete. A set of logic elements is functionally complete if a logic circuit capable of performing any arbitrary logical function can be synthesized from elements of the set. Let us examine one such functionally complete set that contains three distinct types of circuit designated *and, or* and *not*. Such circuits can be depicted with input signals at the left and output signals at the right [*see middle illustration on next page*]. Since the logic elements are binary, each input and output is a binary variable that can have the value 0 or 1. In an electrical circuit the logical value 0 corresponds to a particular voltage or

current and the logical value 1 to another voltage or current. For each symbolic circuit one can construct a "truth table," in which are listed all possible input states and the corresponding output states. Each truth table, in turn, can be represented by a Boolean statement (named for the 19th-century logician George Boole) that expresses the output of the circuit as a function of the input. Truth tables and Boolean statements are shown in the illustrations on the next page. In the case of the *and* circuit the output variable C has the value 1 if, and only if, the input variables A and B both have the value 1. In the Boolean statement the operation *and* is designated by the dot; it reads "C is equal to A and B." In the *or* circuit C has the value 1 if at least one of the input variables has the value 1. The Boolean statement is read "C is equal to A or B." The *not* circuit has for its output the logical complement of the input. Its Boolean statement is read "B is equal to *not* A." The *and* and *or* circuits described have only two input variables. Circuits that have a larger number of input variables are normally used.

There are a number of other functionally complete sets of logic elements. Two sets are particularly interesting because each contains only one element, in one case called *nand* (meaning "not

and") and in the other case called *nor* (meaning "not or"). The bottom illustration at the left on the next page shows a symbolic representation of a two-input *nand* circuit with its truth table. Although a practical *nand* circuit is designed as an entity, it is evident that it can be realized by an *and* and a *not* circuit. The reader can easily devise *and, or* and *not* circuits from *nand* circuits to demonstrate to himself that the *nand* circuit is also functionally complete.

With *and* and *not* circuits it is not difficult to construct a decoding circuit that will translate binary digits into decimal digits. The top illustration on page 20 shows such a circuit and its truth table. The decimal digits are each represented by a four-digit binary code (A_0, A_1, A_2, A_3). In the decoding circuit, which yields the first four decimal digits, the input signals A_0, A_1, A_2, A_3 are applied. The signal at each of the numbered outputs is 0 unless the input code is the code for one of the numbered outputs, in which case the signal at that output is 1.

The circuits that store information in a computer can be divided into two classes: registers and memory circuits. Registers are combined with logic circuits to build up the arithmetic, control and other information-processing parts of the computer. The information stored in registers represents the instantaneous state of the processing part of the computing system. The term "memory" is commonly reserved for those parts of a computer that make possible the general storage of information, such as the instructions of a program, the information fed into the program and the results of computations. Memory devices for such storage purposes will be discussed later in this article.

THIN-FILM MEMORY (*opposite page*) consists of an array of rectangular storage elements, only four millionths of an inch thick, deposited on a thin glass sheet. The rectangles are oriented in one of two magnetic states, corresponding to 0 or 1, when electric currents are passed through conductors (*vertical stripes*) printed on the back of the glass. The films can be switched in a few billionths of a second. The states can be made visible if the thin-film surface is illuminated with plane-polarized light and photographed through a suitably adjusted polarizing filter. The magnetic film causes a slight rotation in the plane of polarization of the reflected light. Here the predominantly dark rectangles are in the 1 state; the light rectangles are in the 0 state. The photograph is a 100-diameter enlargement of a thin-film memory developed by the Burroughs Corporation for use in its newest computers.

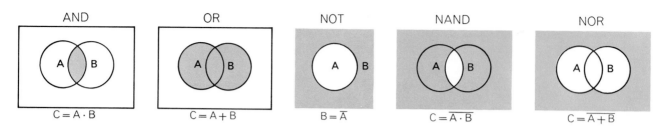

VENN DIAGRAMS use circles to symbolize various logic concepts and relations. Circles represent statements that can be either true or false; they are placed in a universe, or field, that represents all other statements. The logical relation *and* is represented by the shaded area where two circles overlap. This area, C, is "true" only if both circles, A and B, are true; it is "false" if either A or B or both are false. The logical relation *or* (the "inclusive or") is represented by shading the entire area within both circles. This area,

C, is true when either A or B or both are true. *Not* is represented by a circle, A, surrounded by a universe, B, which is not A. The equations below the Venn diagrams are Boolean statements. The dot in the *and* statement stands for "and." The plus sign in the *or* statement stands for "or." The $\overline{A}$ in the *not* statement signifies "not A." *Nand* and *nor* stand respectively for "not and" and "not or," as is made clear in the shading of their Venn diagrams. Such diagrams are named for John Venn, a 19th-century English logician.

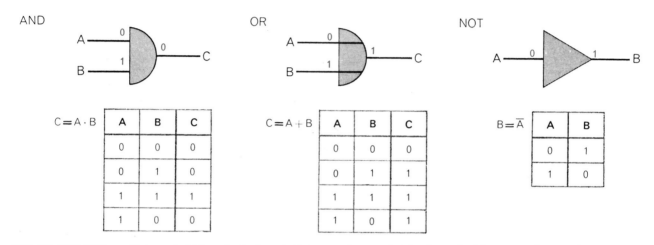

AND, OR AND NOT constitute a set of binary logic elements that is functionally complete. The three symbols represent circuits that can carry out each of these logic functions. Input signals, either 0

or 1, enter the circuits at the left; outputs leave at the right (*colored digits are examples*). Below each circuit is a "truth table" that lists all possible input states and corresponding output states.

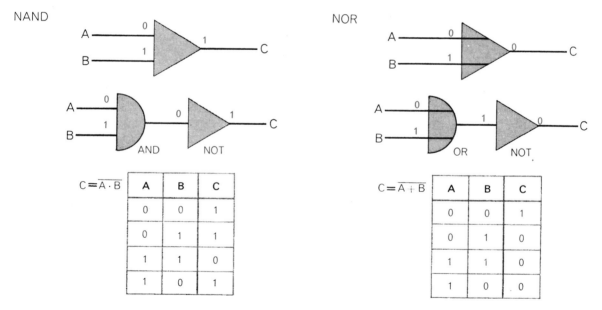

NAND CIRCUIT, which contains only one logic element, is functionally complete; it can do everything that *and*, *or* and *not* circuits can perform collectively. The two-input *nand* circuit symbolized at top is equivalent to the combined *and* and *not* circuit. Outputs of the *nand* truth table are opposite to those of the *and* table.

NOR CIRCUIT is also functionally complete. The two-input *nor* circuit symbolized at top is equivalent to the combined *or* and *not* circuit shown immediately below. The *nor* truth table is the converse of the *or* table. Electronic embodiment of a circuit that can serve as either *nand* or *nor* appears on the opposite page.

Registers are usually made up of one-bit storage circuits called flip-flops. A typical flip-flop circuit, called a set-reset flip-flop, has four terminals [*see bottom illustration on next page*]. It is convenient to refer to such a flip-flop by giving it the name of the variable it happens to store; thus a flip-flop for storing the variable A will be named A. If the inputs to the terminals S and R are 0, the flip-flop will be in one of two states. If A has the value 1, it is in the set state; if it has the value 0, it is in the reset state. It can be switched to the set state by applying a 1 signal to the S terminal and switched to the reset state by applying a 1 to the R terminal. The application of 1's to the S and R terminals at the same time will not yield a predictable result. The flip-flop can therefore be regarded as remembering the most recent input state.

Memories for general storage could be made up of logic circuits and flip-flops, but for practical reasons this is not done. A memory so constructed would be large and expensive and would require much power; moreover, the stored information would be lost if the power were turned off.

We are now ready to consider how logic circuits and registers can be combined to perform elementary arithmetical operations. The upper illustration on page 21 includes a truth table describing one-digit binary addition. The inputs to the adder are the binary digits X and Y, together with the "input carry" C_{i-1}. The outputs are the sum digit S and the "carry out" C_i. Also illustrated is an implementation of the binary adder using *and, or* and *not* logic elements. A logic circuit such as this binary adder, which contains only switching elements and no storage circuits, is called a combinatorial circuit.

In a computer employing binary arithmetic the arithmetic unit may have to process numbers consisting of 60 or more digits in order to produce results with the desired precision. (A computer able to handle 60-digit numbers is said to have 60 bits of precision.) Numbers of such length can be added in two general ways. One way is to use an adder for each digit; the other is to use a single "serial" adder and process the digits sequentially. When an adder is used for each digit, the assembly is called a parallel adder. The lower illustration on page 21 shows a four-digit parallel adder. The inputs for this adder are two four-digit binary numbers: $X_3 X_2 X_1 X_0$ and $Y_3 Y_2 Y_1 Y_0$. The adder

produces the five binary-digit sum $S_4 S_3 S_2 S_1 S_0$. This four-digit adder is also a combinatorial circuit. The X and Y inputs to the parallel adder can be provided by two four-bit registers of four flip-flops each. The inputs are all provided at the same time. The sum can be stored in a five-bit register that has previously had all its stages reset to 0.

For the serial adder we need a means of delivering the digits of the inputs to the adder in sequence and of storing the sum digits in sequence. To implement these requirements special registers that have the ability to shift information from one stage to the next are employed; such a register is called a shift register. Each of the three shift registers of a serial binary adder has an input from the terminal called SHIFT [*see bottom figure on page 22*]. Normal-

NAND

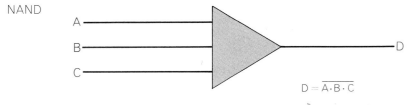

$$D = \overline{A \cdot B \cdot C}$$

NAND CIRCUIT

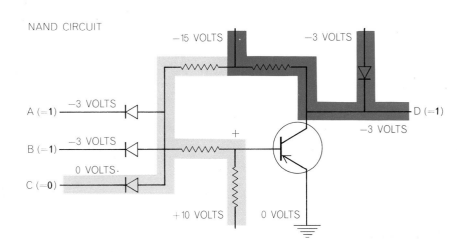

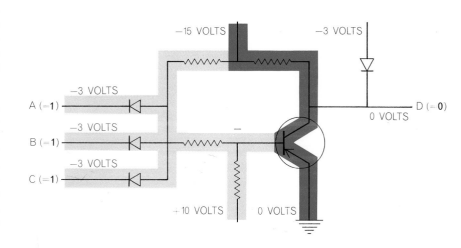

ELECTRONIC EMBODIMENT OF *NAND* CIRCUIT contains four diodes (*triangular shapes*), four resistors (*zigzags*) and one transistor (*inside circle*). The symbol for this three-input *nand* circuit and its Boolean statement appear at the top. In the circuit the dark color represents the flow of large current that is switched to produce the output, 0 or 1, depending on the flow of small current (*light color*), which is controlled by the input voltages. Current flow is shown for two different inputs: 1, 1, 0 and 1, 1, 1. By reversing the choice of voltage the *nand* circuit shown here acts as a *nor* circuit. Such circuits can be designed in many ways.

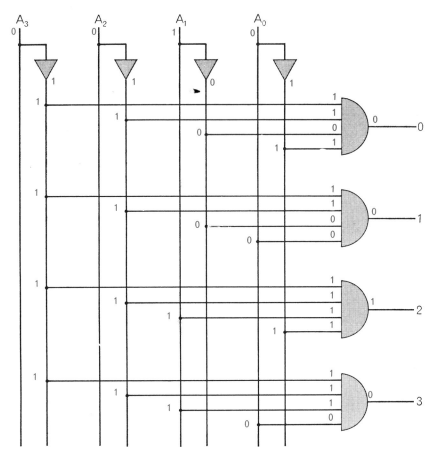

DECIMAL	BINARY			
	A_3	A_2	A_1	A_0
0	0	0	0	0
1	0	0	0	1
2	0	0	1	0
3	0	0	1	1
4	0	1	0	0
5	0	1	0	1
6	0	1	1	0
7	0	1	1	1
8	1	0	0	0
9	1	0	0	1

CONVERSION OF BINARY to decimal digits is accomplished by this circuit, made up of four *not* circuits and four *and* circuits. The truth table at left shows the binary equivalent for the decimal digits from 0 to 9. To show the principle involved in decoding binary digits, the circuit carries the decoding only as far as decimal digit 3. The signal at each of the numbered outputs is 0 unless all the inputs are 1. In the example this is true for the third *and* circuit from the top, labeled 2. Thus the binary digits 0010 are decoded to yield the decimal digit 2.

ly the SHIFT signal has the value 0, but when it is desired to shift the three registers, the SHIFT signal is given the value 1 for a brief period, causing the registers to shift their contents one bit to the right. As in the case of the parallel adder, the serial adder can add one group of binary digits (such as $X_3\ X_2\ X_1\ X_0$) to another group (such as $Y_3\ Y_2\ Y_1\ Y_0$). At the first command to shift, the serial adder stores the sum of the first pair of digits (X_0 and Y_0); at the second command to shift, it stores the sum of the second pair of digits (X_1 and Y_1), and so on. The carry-out (C_i) of each addition is passed along at each command to shift.

Registers are needed for both serial and parallel adders. For the serial adder the registers must be shift registers and only a one-digit binary adder is required. For the parallel adder a binary adder is required for each bit of precision, that is, for each pair of X and Y inputs. The parallel adder is simply a large combinatorial circuit. The serial adder includes the binary adder, a flip-flop (known in this case as the C flip-flop) and associated circuitry. It is not a combinatorial circuit because its output (S) is not merely a function of the immediate inputs (X and Y); it is also a function of the internal state as represented by the value stored in the C flip-flop. Circuits in which the output is not only a function of the immediate inputs but also a function of the circuit's history as represented by its internal state are called sequential circuits. Such circuits are fundamental to the design of computers. Multiplication, for example, is usually implemented by a sequential circuit that repetitively uses an adder circuit.

For most of the period during which computers have evolved, the limiting factor in their design and cost has been memory. The speed of computers has been restricted by the time required to store and retrieve information. The cost of computers has been determined by the information-storage capacity of the memory. As a result much effort has been devoted to the development and improvement of memory devices.

A typical memory, which I have previously described as an array of registers of uniform size, is characterized by word length, storage capacity and access time. Each register in a memory is called a word; its size is expressed in bits and typically is in the range of 12 to 72 bits. The total storage capacity of a memory can be expressed in bits

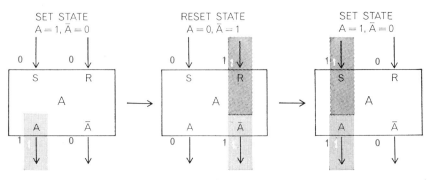

TYPICAL ONE-BIT STORAGE ELEMENT is represented by a "set-reset flip-flop." The one shown here is given the name A because it stores the variable A. A flip-flop "remembers" the most recent input state. If A has the value 1, it is in the set state; if A has the value 0, it is in the reset state. Applying a 1 to the S terminal yields the set state; applying a 1 to the R terminal yields the reset state. Flip-flops provide the transient memory in a computer.

C_{i-1}	X	Y	C_i	S
0	0	0	0	0
0	0	1	0	1
0	1	0	0	1
0	1	1	1	0
1	0	0	0	1
1	0	1	1	0
1	1	0	1	0
1	1	1	1	1

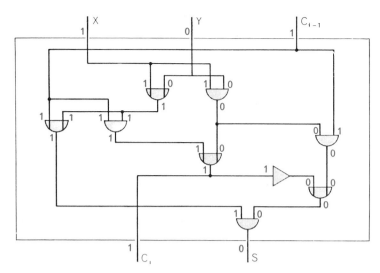

BINARY ADDER CIRCUIT (*right*) can add two one-digit binary numbers. It is made up of *and*, *or* and *not* logic elements. Because the adder will usually be one of several linked in parallel (*see illustration below*) it must also be able to accept a digit known as the input carry (C_{i-1}) produced by an adder immediately to its right. The truth table (*left*) shows the "carry-out" (C_i) and the sum digit (S) for all combinations of three inputs. In the example the inputs are 1, 0 and 1. This is known as a combinatorial circuit.

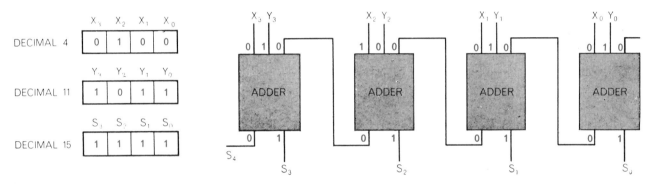

FOUR-DIGIT PARALLEL ADDER consists of four one-digit binary adders like the one shown at the top of the page. In a computer, registers (*not shown*) would be needed to supply the input signals and to store the output signals. In the example illustrated here the binary number 0100 (decimal 4) is being added to 1011 (decimal 11). The sum is the binary number 1111 (decimal 15).

but is more often expressed in words; depending on various factors, which will be examined below, the storage capacity can vary from 100 words to billions of words. The time required to store (write) or retrieve (read) a specified word of information is called the access time; it can range from a fraction of a microsecond to several seconds or minutes.

Access to a particular word in a memory is achieved by means of an addressing scheme. There are two classes of addressing schemes: "structure-addressing" and "content-addressing." In the first, which is the more common, each word is given a number by which it is identified; this number is called its address. Access to a particular word of a memory is achieved by specifying the address as a binary-coded number. In content-addressing, access is determined by the content of the word being sought. For example, each word of a content-addressed memory might contain a person's name and certain information about him (such as his bank balance or his airline reservation); access to that information would be achieved by presenting the person's name to the memory. The internal logic of the memory would locate the word containing the specified name and deliver the name and the associated information as an output. Since most memories are structurally addressed, no further consideration will be given to content-addressing.

Among the various memory designs there is a wide range of compromises among cost, capacity and access time [*see top illustration on page 24*]. Most memories fall into one of three access categories: random, periodic or sequential. In random-access memories the access time is independent of the sequence in which words are entered or extracted. Memories with short random-access times are the most desirable but also the most costly per bit of storage capacity. Magnetic-core devices are the most widely used random-access memories. An example of a memory device that provides periodic access is the magnetic drum, in which information is recorded on the circumference of a cylinder that rotates at a constant rate. Sequentially located words may be read at a high rate as they pass the sensing position. The maximum access time is one revolution of the drum, and the average access time to randomly selected words is half a drum revolution. The most common sequential memories—used when neither random nor periodic access is required—are provided by reels of magnetic tape. To run a typical 2,400-foot reel of tape containing 50 million bits of information past a reading head can take several minutes.

Since magnetic materials, in one form or another, supply the principal

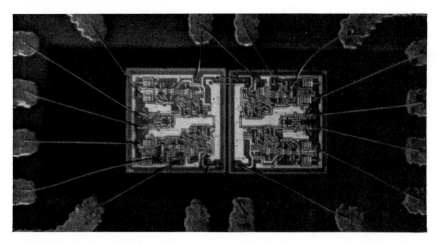

ACTUAL FOUR-DIGIT PARALLEL ADDER can be produced by linking two monolithic integrated circuits; each chip measures only 60 mils (.06 inch) on a side. This adder made by Texas Instruments Incorporated contains the equivalent of 166 discrete components.

storage medium in computers, I shall describe magnetic memories somewhat more fully. The high-speed random-access memory in a typical computer is generally provided by a three-dimensional array of about a million tiny magnetic cores, or rings, each of which can store one bit of information. The cores are threaded on a network of fine wires that provide the means for changing the magnetic polarity of the cores; the polarity determines whether a particular core stores a 1 or a 0. The cores are made of ferrite, a ferromagnetic ceramic. Highly automatic methods have been devised for forming, firing, testing and assembling the cores into memory arrays. In early magnetic-core memories the cores had an outside diameter of about a twelfth of an inch and cost about $1 per bit of storage capacity. The cycle time of these memories (the minimum time from the beginning of one access cycle to the beginning of the next) was in the range of 10 to 20 microseconds.

As the art has developed, the size of the cores has decreased, the cycle time has decreased and the maximum capacity has increased. The cores in most contemporary computers have a diameter of a twentieth of an inch; cycle times are between .75 microsecond and two microseconds. The fastest core memories have cores less than a fiftieth of an inch in diameter and cycle times of less than 500 nanoseconds (half a microsecond).

The essential requirement of a material for a random-access magnetic memory is a particular magnetic characteristic that allows a single element of

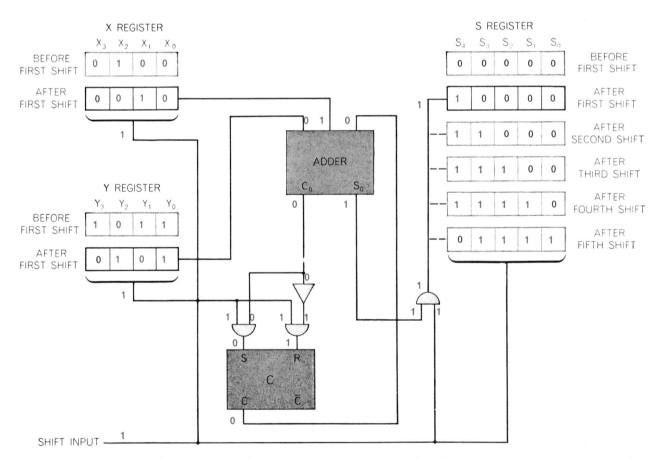

FOUR-DIGIT SERIAL ADDER uses only one adder like the one shown at the top of the preceding page but requires three shift registers and a flip-flop to pass along the carry-out of each addition. Each register has an input from the terminal called SHIFT. At the shift signal each register shifts its contents one bit to the right. Simultaneously the digits shifted out of the X and Y registers enter the adder, together with the input-carry from the C flip-flop. Five shift signals are needed to add two four-digit binary numbers.

a large array of elements of the material to be stably magnetized in either of two directions. Early in the 1950's it was discovered that certain thin metallic films also have this characteristic [see illustration on page 16]. The constant dream of computer designers since this discovery was made has been the development of a practical large-capacity memory that can be constructed directly from bulk materials without fabrication, test or assembly of discrete components for individual bits. Many geometries for thin-film memories, including flat films and films deposited on wires or glass rods, have been devised. Some film memories are in service and many more will be used in the future. It is anticipated that there will be dramatic reductions in the cost of random-access memories over the next few years.

In another widely used memory technology a thin film of magnetic material is deposited on some surface such as a plastic tape or card, or a metallic drum or disk. This magnetic surface is moved with respect to a head that can produce or detect patterns of magnetization in the magnetic film; the patterns are of course coded to represent the binary digits 1 and 0. The film for magnetic recording usually consists of finely ground iron oxides bonded together and to the surface by a small amount of organic binder. For magnetic drums and disks the magnetic medium often consists of a metallic film of a nickel-cobalt alloy.

Magnetic tape about a thousandth of an inch thick, half an inch wide and up to 2,400 feet long per reel has provided the main bulk information store for many years. Tape systems have reached a high state of development: they are able to transport the tape past the head at a rate of more than 100 inches per second and to start or stop the tape in a few milliseconds. Six or eight bits are usually written across the width of the tape; it is common for 800 of these six-bit or eight-bit groups to be written per inch along the tape. A current trend in information-processing systems is toward using tape for dead storage or for transporting data from one location to another. Magnetic recording devices with shorter random-access times are taking over the function of active file storage.

Storage devices with a capacity of a few hundred million words and an access time of a few seconds or less are just beginning to be delivered. These devices employ a number of magnetic

EVOLUTION OF CIRCUITS is reflected in these close-ups showing the central processing units in four generations of computers. UNIVAC I (top), the first large commercial electronic computer, used vacuum-tube logic circuits. The first model was delivered to the Bureau of the Census in 1951. International Business Machines' Model 704 (second from top) was a widely used large-scale vacuum-tube computer with a magnetic-core memory. The first 704 was installed in late 1955. In 1963 IBM delivered the first 7040 (third from top), a typical transistorized computer using discrete components. The Spectra 70/45 (bottom), recently delivered by the Radio Corporation of America, represents the latest generation. It uses monolithic integrated circuits similar to the one shown at the top of the opposite page.

TYPE OF MEMORY	RANDOM ACCESS TIME (MICROSECONDS)	INFORMATION TRANSFER RATE (BITS PER SECOND)	CAPACITY (BITS)	COST (DOLLARS PER BIT)
INTEGRATED CIRCUIT	$10^{-2} - 10^{-1}$	$10^9 - 10^{10}$	$10^3 - 10^4$	10
TYPICAL CORE OR FILM	1	10^8	10^6	10^{-1}
LARGE SLOW CORE	10	10^7	10^7	10^{-2}
MAGNETIC DRUM	10^4	10^7	10^7	10^{-3}
TAPE LOOP OR CARD	10^6	10^6	10^9	10^{-4}
PHOTOGRAPHIC	10^7	10^6	10^{12}	10^{-6}

COMPARISON OF MEMORY SYSTEMS shows a range of roughly a billion to one in access time and capacity and about 10 million to one in cost per bit. The spread in the rate of information transfer is smaller: about 10,000 to one from the fastest memories to the slowest. Integrated circuit memories (similar to logic circuits) and photographic memories (for digital storage) are just appearing.

cards or tape loops handled by various ingenious mechanisms [*see illustration on page 27*].

In memory systems that use magnetic drums and disks rotating at high speed, the heads for reading and writing information are spaced a fraction of a thousandth of an inch from the surface. The surface velocity is about 1,000 or 2,000 inches per second. In early drum systems severe mechanical and thermal problems were encountered in maintaining the spacing between the heads and the recording surface. In recent years a spectacular improvement in performance and reliability has been achieved by the use of flying heads, which maintain their spacing from the magnetic surface by "flying" on the boundary layer of air that rotates with the surface of the drum or disk. One modern drum memory has a capacity of 262,000 words and rotates at 7,200 revolutions per minute; it has a random- access time of about four milliseconds and an information-transfer rate of 11.2 million bits per second.

Magnetic information storage is meeting competition from other memory technologies in two areas: where fairly small stores of information must be accessible in the shortest possible time and where ultralarge stores must be accessible in a matter of seconds. For the first task, which today is usually performed by magnetic cores and thin

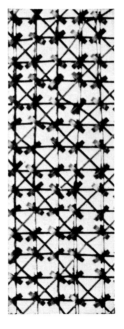
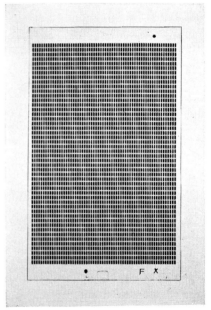

MAGNETIC-CORE MEMORY has been the standard high-speed memory in computers for many years. A typical core memory plane is shown two-thirds actual size at the left; a portion of the plane is enlarged about 10 diameters at the right. This example, made by Fabri-Tek Incorporated, contains 16,384 ferrite cores, each a fiftieth of an inch in diameter.

THIN-FILM MEMORY made by Burroughs, which operates even faster than magnetic-core memories, is shown here actual size. An enlargement in color appears on page 16.

films, one can now obtain memories fabricated by the same techniques used to produce monolithic integrated circuits [see "Microelectronics," by William C. Hittinger and Morgan Sparks; SCIENTIFIC AMERICAN, November, 1965]. Such circuits, resembling flip-flops, can be built up from tiny transistors and resistors; scores of such elements can be packed into an area no more than a tenth of an inch square [see bottom left of illustration on page 27]. A memory of this kind can store about 100 words and have a random-access time of 100 nanoseconds. Although the present cost of such memories is a few dollars per bit, the cost will probably decline to a few cents per bit by 1970. Integrated-circuit memories have the drawback that power is continuously dissipated by each element (unlike magnetic elements) whether it is actively being read (or altered) or not.

For very-high-volume storage and moderately fast access time, magnetic devices are being challenged by high-resolution photography. In these systems bits are recorded as densely packed dots on transparent cards or short strips of photographic film. During the next year or so several such systems will go into service; each will have a capacity of 10^{11} or 10^{12} bits and a maximum access time of a few seconds.

To combine rapid average access time and large storage capacity at a minimum cost to the user, computer designers have recently introduced the concept of the "virtual memory." Such a memory simulates a single large, fast random-access memory by providing a hierarchy of memories with a control mechanism that moves information up and down in the hierarchy, using a strategy designed to minimize average access time.

The logic and main memory of a very large modern computer contains nearly half a million transistors and a somewhat larger number of resistors and other electrical components, in addition to 10 million magnetic cores. In such a machine—or even in a smaller one with a tenth or a hundredth of this number of components—the matters of packaging, interconnection and reliability present very serious design problems.

The active circuit elements in early electronic computers were vacuum tubes. These computers encountered three major problems. First, the rate at which tubes failed was so high that in large computers the ratio of nonproduc-

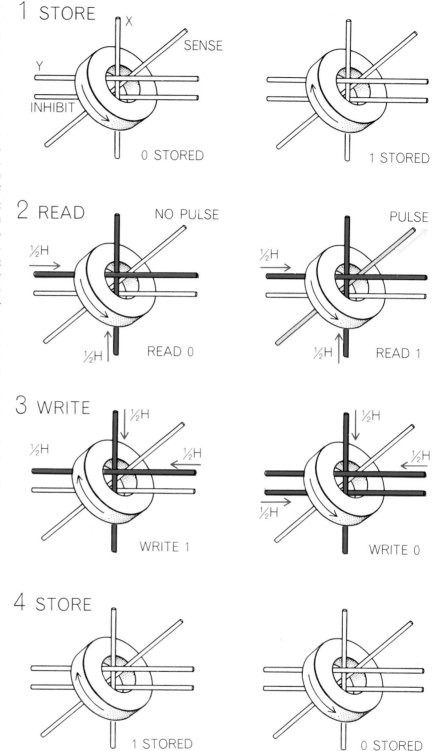

OPERATION OF MAGNETIC-CORE MEMORY involves switching the direction of magnetization, or polarity, of a ferrite core between two positions 180 degrees apart. One position is selected to represent 0, the other to represent 1. "Reading" and "writing" signals are carried on two wires (X and Y), each of which carries only half of the current ($\frac{1}{2}H$) needed to change the core's direction of polarization. During the reading cycle the direction of current flow is selected so that the pulses reverse the polarity of a core that is storing a 1, with the result that a voltage pulse signifying 1 (light color) is created in the "sense" wire. No pulse emanates from a core that is storing a 0. During the writing cycle the flow in the X and Y wires is reversed. This reverses the polarity of the core and writes 1 unless an opposing current is coincidentally passed through an "inhibit" wire, in which case the core polarity remains in the 0 position. A typical memory will contain a million cores.

tive time was nearly prohibitive. Second, power consumed by vacuum tubes was so large that adequate cooling was extremely difficult to achieve. Third, the components were so large that the distances over which signals had to travel would have limited computer speeds to levels that today would be regarded as slow.

In 1948 the point-contact transistor was invented. It was small and used little power, but it was too unstable a device to replace the vacuum tube in large-scale computers. A few years later

the junction transistor was developed, but it was too slow. In 1957 the planar silicon transistor was invented. It provided high-speed transistors that were reliable and made possible the design of the present high-speed computers. Further development of the planar technology led to the monolithic integrated circuit, in which scores of components are created and linked together in a single tiny "chip" of silicon. A variation of this technique is used to create the integrated-circuit memories.

The integrated logic circuit, which is

just beginning to make its way into large-scale use for computers, contributes substantially to the solution of the three problems that beset the vacuum-tube computer and that were only partially solved by discrete transistors. An integrated circuit on one chip of silicon can have the logic capacity of several of the logic circuits described earlier. It occupies far less space and consumes less power than an equivalent transistor circuit. Its small size makes possible systems with higher speeds because the interconnections of the circuits are shorter. Reliability is increased because the interconnections are themselves reliable. Indeed, the reliability of an entire integrated circuit is expected to approach that of an individual transistor. The latest integrated circuits have a signal delay of only a few nanoseconds, and still faster circuits are being developed. However, the physical size of a computer's components, together with their interconnections, remains a fundamental limitation on the complexity of the computer: an electrical signal can travel along a wire at the rate of only about eight inches per nanosecond (two-thirds the speed of light).

Computer technology has a way of confounding those who would predict its future. The thin-film memory, for example, has been "just around the corner" for more than 10 years, but the ferrite core is still the main element of random-access memories. Nevertheless, one can try to make certain predictions based on the situation at present. It now seems clear that integrated-circuit technology will soon produce circuits of great complexity at very low cost. These circuits will include high-speed memory circuits as well as logic circuits. Already one can get commercial delivery of a 100-bit register on a single chip of silicon that is a tenth of an inch in its largest dimension. It is my personal opinion that computer designers will be hard-pressed to develop concepts adequate to exploit the rapid advances in components.

Because computers built with integrated components promise to be much cheaper than present machines, one can expect significant changes in the comparative costs of information processing and information transmission. This in turn will influence the rate of growth of data-transmission facilities. Low-cost computers will also change the cost factors that help in deciding whether it is cheaper to do a job with human labor or to turn it over to a machine.

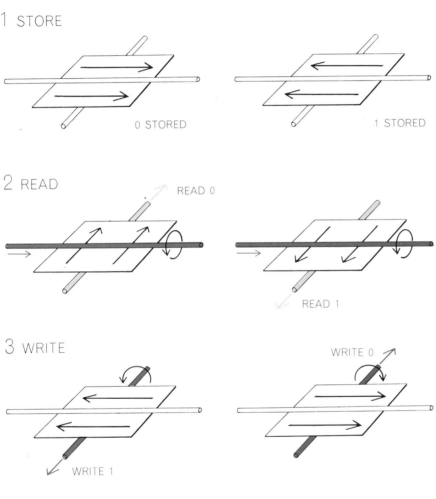

OPERATION OF THIN-FILM MEMORY differs from that of a magnetic-core memory, illustrated on the preceding page. One difference is that the read-out for a 0 or 1 is determined by the polarity of the voltage pulse in the sense wire rather than by the presence or absence of a voltage. Also, in the thin-film memory reading and writing are performed by passing current through different wires. Finally, the change in direction of magnetization that induces a read-out pulse involves a rotation of only 90 degrees rather than 180 degrees.

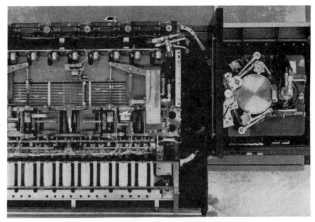

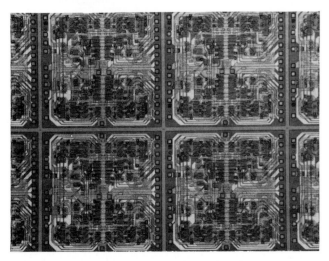

VARIETY OF MEMORY SYSTEMS are based on magnetism, electronic circuitry and photography. Magnetic-drum memory (*top left*), built by Univac Division of Sperry Rand Corporation, provides access in 17 milliseconds to any one of 786,432 36-bit words or some 4.7 million alphanumeric characters. "Random Access Computer Equipment" (*top right*), built by RCA, stores information on 2,048 flexible plastic cards. The basic unit holds 340 million alphanumeric characters; the average access time is 385 milliseconds. Magnetic-disk memory (*middle left*), made by Control Data Corporation, provides access in 34 to 110 milliseconds to any one of 131.9 million six-bit characters. "Data cell" system (*middle right*), offered by IBM, stores data on 2,000 narrow strips of magnetic film. It provides random access in 175 to 600 milliseconds to 800 million bits of information. Integrated-circuit memory (*bottom left*) provides access to 16 bits of information in about .01 microsecond. This example is made by Motorola Semiconductor Products Inc. A new photo-digital memory (*bottom right*) has been devised by IBM to provide rapid access to memory files containing a trillion bits. A single film chip, 1⅜ by 2¾ inches, can store several million bits of information; IBM is not yet ready to disclose the exact number.

3

INTEGRATED COMPUTER MEMORIES

JAN A. RAJCHMAN
July, 1967

The computer has pervaded most fields of human activity and may well be the most important innovation of our age. Born out of the technology of communication, it is capable of handling enormous amounts of information at tremendous speeds. What makes it so potent and pervasive is the fact that a single mechanism, given the proper program, can perform any information-processing task capable of being specified. The same mechanism can calculate taxes and other items on thousands of paychecks, solve complex equations, control industrial processes, write music, form and compose characters for printing, guide space vehicles or help to teach children. This diversity of tasks —which often surprises even the designers of the machines—is made possible by the simple idea of the stored program.

The trick is to control electronically the nature and sequence of arithmetical and logical processes that are themselves electronic. In other words, what determines whether an addition, a multiplication, a simple juxtaposition or some other operation is executed, what determines the inputs of the operation and what determines the disposition of the result are not built into the machine but are part of the electronic process itself. A program is the enumeration of these determining commands; it specifies the method used for the solution of a problem in detail. It is a demonstrable fact that any determinate information-processing task can be performed by a sufficient number of minute steps, and therefore with a sufficiently fast computer can be solved in a reasonable time. When the machine is in operation, both the commands and the numbers or symbols being processed are constantly being taken out of and put into a depository of information known as a memory. This anthropomorphic name was coined by early computer workers; more restrained people, particularly in Britain, use the term "store."

The commands, numbers or symbols needed in a processing task—known collectively as words—are stored in the memory, each with a certain "address." The address identifies the stored word and determines a definite physical location within the memory device. The power and universality of programming arises from the capacity to address the memory selectively, that is, to direct a word into any address and to retrieve it in a very short time, regardless of how the address was previously used. Such selective access is described as "random" to emphasize the programmer's total freedom to dispose of any information under any desired label and to retrieve it at any time, in contrast with "serial" memories, in which information was stored in queues and had to be retrieved in definite sequences. This made it necessary to wait for the desired information while irrelevant material was flowing by, and in general to wait longer with longer queues of information.

Perhaps the most important attribute of random access to a memory is the ease with which it is possible to choose one or another command according to the process being executed, thus allowing branching into one of two or more possible programming sequences. For example, a summation of terms is made by executing whatever operations are prescribed in each term, adding the term to the growing partial sum, and then comparing the number of terms to the total number of terms prescribed. If the prescribed limit is not reached, a new calculation loop proceeds and another term is added. If the number of terms has reached the limit, a new procedure is started: the sum can be printed out, stored for future use or become itself the input of a new process. Such "conditional transfer" and looping are the cornerstones of universal programming and are easy to execute with a random-access memory, since the number of steps in the loop can be readily programmed and conditional transfer merely amounts to the indication of another address to be selected. Clearly a high-speed random-access memory is the essential component that makes possible a modern electronic computer. Let us consider how such a memory can be implemented.

The reader will recall that digital information in a computer is expressed in "bits," each bit being the statement of a single alternative: yes or no, 0 or 1. A group of n bits can code 2^n alternatives, which can express 2^n binary numbers. Accordingly all combinations of four 0's or 1's (0000 to 1111) can express 2^4, or 16, numbers, for example the numbers from 0 to 15. A sequence of bits can equally well represent a collection of arbitrary symbols, English words or artificial words.

Most computers handle a fixed number of bits as a word. The function of a random-access memory is to store the m bits of a word on being supplied with an address specified in n bits. Subsequently the memory will furnish on demand, usually in less than a microsecond, the stored m bits on being supplied with the same n address bits. Such a memory has a storage capacity of 2^n words, corresponding to all possible addresses. Since each word is m bits long, the total capacity of the memory is $m2^n$ bits. In a typical "16 K" word memory n equals 14, so that the actual word capacity is 2^{14}, or 16,384 words; if m equals 40 bits, the total capacity is 655,360 bits.

Since the early 1950's the standard random-access memory has been provided by an array of tiny ring-shaped

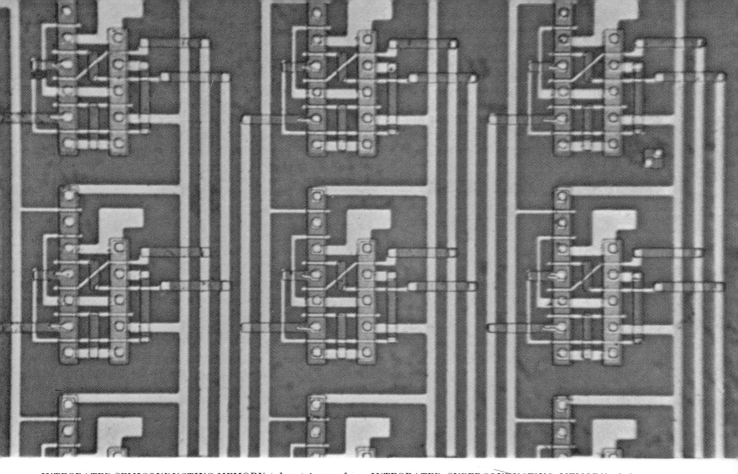

INTEGRATED SEMICONDUCTING MEMORY (*above*) is one of several new types of information-storage elements that are expected to supplant standard magnetic-core memories for certain purposes. The particular network shown here consists of nine one-bit cells, each of which contains 12 metal-oxide-semiconductor (MOS) field-effect transistors (*rows of squares*). Each cell is .015 inch on a side.

INTEGRATED SUPERCONDUCTING MEMORY (*below*) contains more than 13,000 memory cells per square inch. This enlargement shows a small section of a larger experimental memory plane. The circuit patterns were etched photographically in thin films of superconductive metals. Superconducting memories are particularly promising for large capacity, high reliability and great speed.

MONOLITHIC FERRITE MEMORY consists of three sheets of ferrite, an easily magnetized ceramic material. Two of the sheets contain conducting lines set at right angles to each other; these are separated by a third sheet of ferrite to form a sandwich. The intersections of the two sets of lines constitute the memory elements. This type of integrated magnetic memory is a contender by virtue of its high speed, compactness and low cost. The two dark squares at the center contain the memory elements; the fanlike arrays are connections to the digit lines; the staggered arrays are connections to the word lines. The entire structure is about four inches across.

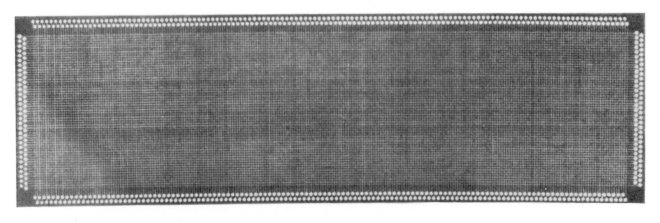

X-RAY PHOTOGRAPH of an experimental monolithic ferrite laminate reveals the 256 digit lines and 64 word lines that give this structure a total of 16,384 intersections, or individual memory elements. The laminate plane is 2.6 inches long and .84 inch wide.

cores made of a ferrite, an easily magnetized material. In its simplest form the array of cores is threaded by 2^n "word" conductors in one direction and by m "digit" conductors in the other [*see bottom illustration at right*]. Each core can hold one bit of information, which is stored in terms of the direction of imposed magnetization; in other words, the core "remembers" the direction of the effective magnetizing current sent through it last.

When the memory is in operation, there is a cycle of two steps: "read" and "write." In the read step a current in a given direction is sent through the selected word line and brings all the cores on it to the same state of magnetization. The magnetic flux of the cores that were in the opposite state is reversed, and this reversal induces voltages on the corresponding digit lines, which in this way sense "destructively" the word information. In a succeeding write step the current in the word line is reversed and also reduced, and simultaneously pulses of current are sent through certain digit lines. The amplitude of the word and digit currents is adjusted to be insufficient to switch a core by themselves but sufficient to switch it when they act together. As a result only the cores on the selected word threaded by energized digit lines will switch; all others will remain unaffected. In the write step the read information can be rewritten, thereby conserving the information within the memory system in spite of the destructive read-out. Until the information is rewritten it is momentarily in the circuits rather than in the cores. Alternatively, new information can be entered in the selected word address that was "cleared" in the read step.

Each of the word lines has to be energized by an active device such as a vacuum tube, a transistor or a diode. Hence a typical 16-K memory would require 16,384 devices, one for each address in the memory. In addition, circuits are needed to decipher the address code, whose function is to select one of the devices for every combination of n input bits. These circuits usually double the required number of devices. In the early days of the computer, when the only suitable devices were vacuum tubes, such a large number of devices would have made core memories impractical if they had had to be organized in the manner I have just described. For that reason this simple organization, called "word-organized," or "2D," was not the first one used.

The concept of coincident addressing,

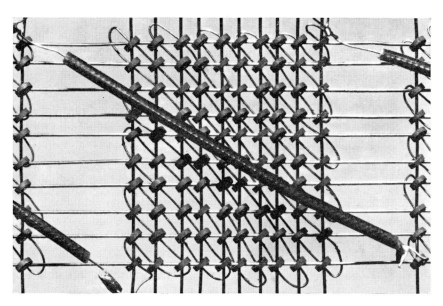

MAGNETIC-CORE MEMORY has been the standard random-access memory in computers since the early 1950's. The memory plane consists of an array of tiny ring-shaped ferrite cores, each of which can store one "bit" of information. The cores are threaded on a network of fine wires that provide the means for changing the magnetic polarity of the cores. This photograph shows one of the first core memories, made by the author in 1950.

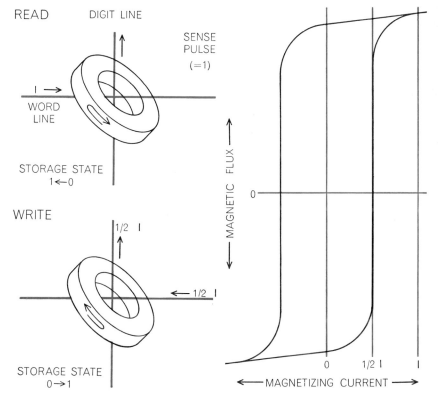

SIMPLEST TYPE of magnetic-core memory (*left*) is threaded by "word" conductors in one direction and by "digit" conductors in the other direction. In the "read" step a current (I) in a given direction is sent through the selected word line and brings all the cores on it to the same state of magnetization. The magnetic flux of a core that was in the opposite state is reversed, and this reversal induces a voltage on the corresponding digit line, which in this way senses "destructively" the word information. In a succeeding "write" step the current in the word line is reversed and also reduced (to $\frac{1}{2}I$), and simultaneously a pulse of current (also $\frac{1}{2}I$) is sent through the digit line. The amplitude of the word and digit currents is adjusted to be insufficient to switch a core by themselves but sufficient to switch it when they act together. A memory organized in this way is said to be "word-organized," or "2D." A typical rectangular hysteresis loop for a magnetic-core memory (*right*) relates the magnetic flux around the core to the magnetizing current that is passed through it.

or "3D," made it possible to have a much smaller number of addressing circuits. In the most widely used form of coincident addressing the cores belonging to the bits of the word are distributed among as many square two-dimensional arrays as there are bits in a word. Thus a memory containing 40-bit words requires 40 arrays. A 16-K memory then calls for 16,384 cores (128×128) per array. Four wires are threaded through each core: a digit (X) wire and a word (Y) wire are connected in series through all the planes; two more wires, one to "sense" and one to "inhibit," are separately threaded through all cores in each plane [*see top illustration on opposite page*].

In the read step, pulses of equal strength are sent simultaneously through selected X and Y lines. Here again the amplitude of any one pulse is insufficient to switch any core by itself but sufficient to do so when acting in coincidence with another pulse. As a result,

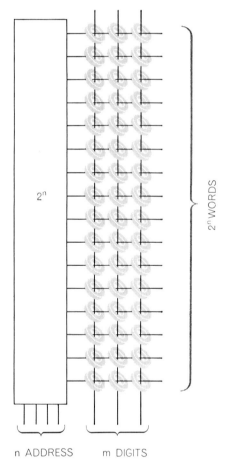

2^n

2^n WORDS

n ADDRESS   m DIGITS

WORD-ORGANIZED MEMORY stores m bits of a word on being supplied with an address specified in n bits. Such a memory has a word-storage capacity of 2^n words and, since each word is m bits long, a total capacity of $m2^n$ bits. In this example n equals four, so that the actual word capacity is 2^4, or 16 words; m equals three, so that the total storage capacity is 48 bits.

in each plane the core at the intersection of an X line and a Y line will switch or not, depending on its magnetic state; no other core will be affected. The voltages induced by the switching of the selected cores appear simultaneously on the corresponding sense lines. In the write step, X and Y currents of the same amplitude but reverse direction are applied, and they tend to switch all 40 selected cores to the opposite direction. This tendency is canceled on selected planes by simultaneous application of inhibit currents of the same amplitude but opposite direction, which travel through the inhibit wire. As before, the write step is used to rewrite information. Addressing in a coincident memory requires two sets of $2^{n/2}$ driving devices. In our example, where $n = 14$, $2^{n/2} = 2^7$, or 128, driving devices per set; this is far less than one set of 2^{14}, or 16,384, driving devices. The gain results from the participation in the decoding function of the core itself, which responds to two signals but not to one, and thus acts as an "and" gate. (In the binary logic of computers an "and" gate is a circuit whose output is 1 if, and only if, all input variables to the circuit have the value 1.)

Coincident addressing is best achieved if all cores have identical magnetic characteristics known as rectangular hysteresis loops [*see bottom illustration on preceding page*]. It is then possible to choose a magnetizing current that will bring the cores on the selected lines just below the "knee" of the loop without causing any switching whatsoever, and yet that will cause complete switching of the selected core on which they act in coincidence.

In practice it is fairly easy to approach these ideal characteristics, so that the cores will not "forget" their magnetic state even when they are subjected to millions of half-selecting pulses that tend to change that state. This is the only requirement in a 2D word-organized memory. In a 3D memory it is necessary to prevent small voltages induced in the sense winding of half-selected cores from "masking" the voltage of the selected cores. These numerous voltages (2×127, or 254, in our example) can usually be made to cancel each other by proper threading of the sense winding, but because the cores are not perfectly uniform and the hysteresis loop has not only a slope but a curvature, the cancellation is not perfect. This is one of the factors limiting the size of such current-coincident memory planes.

In addition to having a rectangular hysteresis loop the core should be capa-

ble of fast switching. Cores of nickel-iron alloy in the form of ultrathin ribbon, made during World War II for high-frequency magnetic amplifiers, had the adequate properties and made it possible to demonstrate the operation of the first memories. Such cores were delicate and expensive. Fortunately ferrites—fast switching magnetic materials made of oxides of iron, manganese, magnesium, zinc or lithium—had been developed during the 1920's and had been perfected for transformers and the electron-beam-guiding yokes of television picture tubes. Minimum hysteresis was sought for these applications. The maximum-hysteresis square loop needed for memories was achieved by ingenious modifications of composition and processing, and today many excellent core materials are available.

Fine powders of these materials, suspended in a binder as a slurry, are pressed into the shape of cores on automatic machines and baked. The cores are then tested and sorted automatically. The result is a low-cost, high-quality, ceramic-like element with a uniformity not surpassed by any other electronic component. The smaller the core, the less driving current it requires, the faster it switches for a given current, the tighter it can be packed to minimize delays along windings and the more difficult it is to handle and thread. As the art has progressed over the years, standard core sizes have gradually decreased from .080 inch outside diameter and .050 inch inside diameter, known in the trade as an 80/50 core, to 50/30, 30/18, 20/12 and recently even to 12/7. Typical arrays of 20/12 cores contain 16,384 of them in a square plane that measures only 6.4 inches on a side.

The cores are wired into arrays by painstaking handwork with only rudimentary mechanical aids. The operation is delicate and expensive, but mechanizing it is economical only for larger cores used in very large quantities. Much of the industry finds it more advantageous to use artisan labor, and some seek it at low wages in Hong Kong, Taiwan and Mexico. The situation is somewhat ironic: the heart of the computer, which itself is the symbol of mechanization, is made by the age-old kind of labor that produced brocades and carpets. The objective of this labor is not to turn out a few exquisite art objects but rather to mass-produce uniform core arrays. The annual production of core arrays in the U.S. alone involves the threading of an estimated 25 billion cores.

Made as they are, the core arrays have

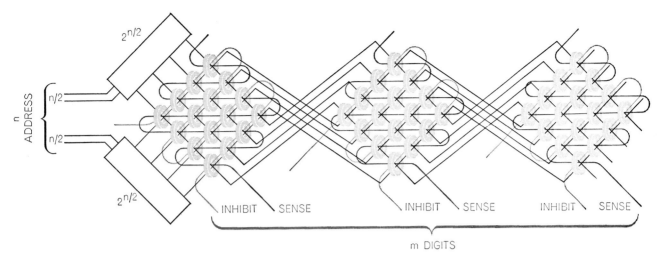

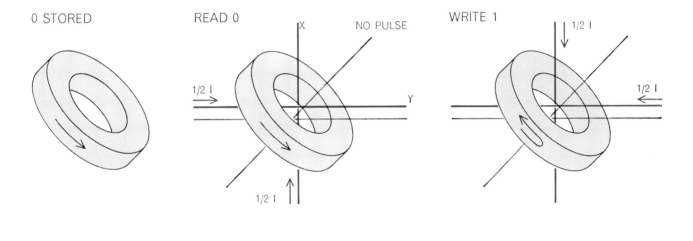

COINCIDENT ADDRESSING, a feature of "3D" magnetic-core memories, has made it possible to have a much smaller number of addressing circuits by distributing the cores belonging to the bits of the word along as many square two-dimensional arrays as there are bits in a word. Four wires are threaded through each core: an X wire and a Y wire (*black*) are connected in series through all the planes; two other wires, one to "sense" and one to "inhibit" (*gray*), are separately threaded through all the cores in each plane.

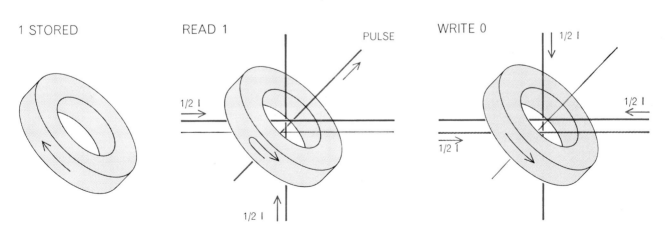

READING AND WRITING in a 3D core memory are carried out in the following way. In the read step, pulses of equal strength ($\frac{1}{2}I$) are sent simultaneously through selected X and Y lines. Here again the amplitude of any one pulse is insufficient to switch any core by itself but sufficient to do so if acting in coincidence with another pulse. As a result the core at the intersection of an X line and a Y line will switch or not, depending on its magnetic state. The voltages induced by the switching of the selected cores appear simultaneously on the corresponding sense lines. In the write step X and Y currents of the same amplitude but reverse direction are applied, and they tend to switch the selected cores to the opposite direction of magnetization. This tendency is canceled on selected planes by simultaneous application of currents of the same amplitude ($\frac{1}{2}I$) but opposite direction through the inhibit wires.

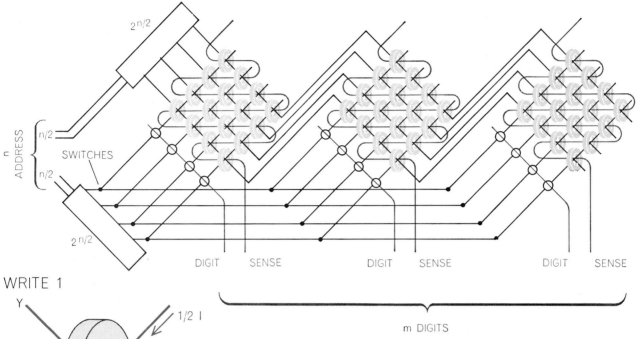

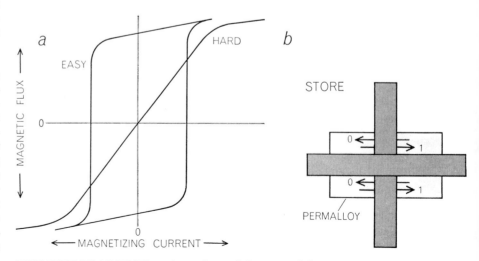

WRITE 1

2½D CORE MEMORY, an organization intermediate between 2D and 3D, drastically reduces the write noise and makes the core technology faster and even more competitive with integrated technologies. The read step is the same as it is in 3D, but for the write step an inhibit winding is replaced by one set of selecting lines, in this case the Y line. The selected Y line in each plane is either energized or not according to the digit to be written in each plane. In the enlargement at left a 1 is written by simultaneously sending a signal through the X and Y lines; to write a 0 the signal would simply be omitted from the Y line.

provided reliable, fast random-access memories for practically all computers in use today. At the same time the possibility of avoiding both the manufacture of cores and the threading of them by hand has fascinated many inventors from the beginning. The stimulus has been not only to lower costs but also to increase speed of operation. The principal goal has been to produce "integrated" memories—memories in which the active elements and their connections are mechanically fabricated in a unitary process.

The problems have turned out to be difficult, and for years the constantly improving core technology has prevailed. It was found nearly impossible to obtain any magnetic element in integrated form that had a sufficiently square hysteresis loop or a switching threshold sharp enough and uniform enough from element to element to allow current-coincident operation. For the large decoder required in word-organized memories, nonintegrated arrays of cores were first used and were found rather expensive and inefficient. Today comparatively inexpensive semiconductor diodes permit a matrix arrangement of word lines for the first

level of decoding, which makes a combination of cores and diodes equivalent to a coincident-addressed core array and about as economical. It was found that integrated technologies are subtle and not necessarily inexpensive. Nevertheless, a great deal of progress was made; some integrated memories have been introduced commercially, and the

initial hopes are still valid, particularly for high speed. There are three significant contenders: the monolithic ferrite, the flat film and the plated wire.

The monolithic ferrite memory is made from the same type of material as the cores. The slurry is spread by a blade onto sheets. During this operation conducting parallel lines of a refractory

THIN PERMALLOY FILMS can be made to exhibit strong differences in magnetic properties along different directions of magnetization. In a "hard" direction there is practically no hysteresis but in an "easy" direction at right angles to it there is an almost perfect hysteresis loop (a). This property leads to two possible approaches to integrated mem-

metal are also formed within the sheets. Two such sheets, with their conducting lines at right angles, face each other and are separated by a third sheet of ferrite to form a sandwich. The sandwich is then heated, pressed and sintered to produce a monolithic structure [*see illustrations on page 30*]. The conducting lines define the memory elements at their crossings. One set of lines are word windings, the other digit windings. Because the lines are at right angles to each other, a current applied to a selected word conductor switches magnetic flux along a path that does not link the digit conductor. If coincident digit pulses are applied, however, there will be flux common to the word lines and the digit lines at the corresponding crossings. The application of a word pulse in the opposite direction switches the mutual flux and induces sense voltages in the digit lines.

The monolithic integrated structure not only is easy to fabricate but also makes it possible to have very small elements. Experimental laminates about .005 inch thick have elements with an effective diameter of .003 inch. The close spacing of the lines (100 to the inch) corresponds to what can be achieved with an integrated row of diodes; indeed, fully integrated combinations of laminated ferrite and diodes have been made. One of these had a capacity of 65,416 bits and operated on a cycle of 400 nanoseconds. (A nanosecond is a billionth of a second.) The most delicate step in the construction is the actual connection between the laminate and the diodes.

The other two approaches to integrated memories involve the use of nickel-iron alloys called permalloys rather than ferrites. One difficulty with metals is that eddy currents develop and slow down the switching speed. If the thickness of permalloy sheets is held to about .00025 inch, the slowing is negligible. If the thickness is further reduced until it is comparable to the wavelength of ultraviolet radiation—say less than 3,000 angstrom units—entirely new properties appear. Switching can then be achieved by the rotation of magnetization, which is inherently a much faster process than the one that takes place in magnetic cores. In cores switching involves a movement of the walls of magnetic "domains." Thin permalloy films can be made to exhibit strong differences in magnetic properties along different directions of magnetization. In a "hard" direction there is practically no hysteresis but in an "easy" direction at right angles to it there is an almost perfect hysteresis loop. Furthermore, thin films are readily deposited by evaporation or electroplating, which lend themselves nicely to integrated fabrication. These advantages became apparent in the middle 1950's and spurred much activity.

In one approach permalloy is evaporated in a vacuum onto glass or metal to a thickness of between 1,000 and 2,000 angstroms in the presence of a direct-current magnetic field, which produces the desired direction of magnetization. Separate spots of permalloy are obtained either by doing the evaporation through a mask or by etching a continuous film. Mylar sheets with photographically formed copper lines are laid on the film and provide the word and digit lines [*see upper illustration on next page*]. The word lines run in the easy direction of magnetization. When a spot is storing a pulse, it is in one or another of the easy states of magnetization. In the read cycle a current pulse is applied to the selected word line; the corresponding spots are forcibly magnetized in the hard direction and thereby induce sense voltages on the digit lines in a direction corresponding to their state. In the write cycle or in rewrite currents are applied to the digit lines while the word current is still on; the combined currents tilt the magnetization one way or another from the hard direction and thereby establish the easy direction at the termination of the pulses.

This arrangement is attractive in that a small digit current suffices to trigger the spot into the desired state. In practice the directions of magnetization are not perfectly aligned and vary from element to element, so that a larger digit current is required to flip the flux in the desired direction in spite of irregularities haphazardly favoring one direction or another. When these imperfections are severe, the minimum digit current can be so large that it can cause elements of unselected word lines to "creep" from one magnetic state to the other. This state of affairs is particularly troublesome in lines near the selected one, which are subjected to its stray word field. The field strays because lines of magnetic flux can extend between storage elements through the air adjacent to the sheet. Still a worse result of having the elements open in this way is a stray field that can demagnetize the elements altogether. In order to keep such fields from diluting the desired sharp magnetic characteristics too much, it is necessary that the length of the storage

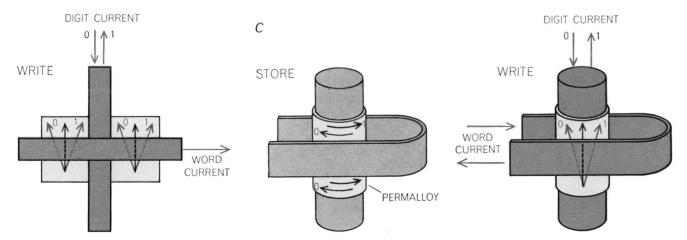

ories: flat-film memories (*b*) and plated-wire memories (*c*). In the storing condition the permalloy element is magnetized in one or the other of the easy directions, which are parallel to the long dimension of the flat film and around the circumference of the plated film. In the writing step the word current brings the direction of magnetization nearly to the hard direction (*black arrows*). The digit current tilts this direction one way or the other and thereby establishes the easy direction at the end of the pulses.

element in the easy direction be about 10,000 times its thickness, that is, more than a millimeter, and this sets a limit on compactness. The elements can be smaller, however, in the hard direction. To minimize creep and demagnetization some memories have a flat ferrite "keeper" plate on top of the sheet of storage elements.

Such inherent obstacles to thin-film integrated memories were at first something of a surprise, but they have been largely overcome. Typical flat thin-film memories have capacities of from 2,500 to 200,000 bits and cycle times as brief as from 100 to 500 nanoseconds. They began appearing in commercial computers early in 1966.

The third kind of integrated memory is the plated wire. A beryllium-copper wire is electroplated with permalloy. Straight parallel lengths of this wire are digit lines; conductive ribbons strapped on at right angles are word lines [*see lower illustration below*]. Storage is accomplished by magnetization around the circumference of the plated film, which is in the easy direction. That direction is established during plating by passing a direct current through the wire. The word current flips the fields toward the axis of the wire, which is the hard direction. This induces sense voltages in the digit lines, and small digit currents flip the fields to the selected easy directions as they do in the flat-film memory.

The plated-wire memory represents several fortunate compromises. Plating can be regarded as a one-dimensional integration. It is amenable to a continuous process, which should be more economical than the hand-threading of individual cores, and it is simpler to control than the lamination of ferrites or the deposition of flat films. Moreover, the plated-wire storage element has magnetic flux lines that are closed within the magnetic material in one direction, again a compromise between cores and flat films. The resulting reduction of demagnetizing effects makes it possible for the film to be comparatively thick: from 15,000 to 20,000 angstroms. This thickness of permalloy provides just the right amount of flux—more flux than the necessarily thin flat films and less flux than the difficult-to-miniaturize ferrite cores.

In spite of these attractions, it took years to develop plating techniques that avoided unfavorable magnetic effects. In addition, the wire on which the permalloy is plated is susceptible to strains that tend to distort the magnetic characteristics of the films. Such effects can be minimized by careful choice of materials, and today plated-wire memories are a technical success. Prototypes with a capacity of some 80,000 bits have operated on a cycle time of 150 nanoseconds. A memory system operating at 600 nanoseconds was announced for a line of commercial computers in 1966. The economy of such systems is still an open question.

All magnetic memories have common characteristics. Access to an element in an array is achieved not by some kind of sharply selective pointer but by the somewhat imperfect means of coincident pulses on electrical lines. I have described the kind of imperfections one encounters in the storage elements; there are also unfavorable interactions between the driving lines and the sense lines. Because the driving currents are a considerable fraction of an ampere, spurious signals can be induced in the sense lines that can easily exceed the desired values (measured in millivolts) of sense signals. Such masking is not difficult to minimize in the read cycle of current-coincident memories. In the write cycle of 2D and 3D types, however, a large voltage can be induced in the sense line, since that line is itself the digit drive line or couples with it in every element of the digit plane. The induced voltage paralyzes the sense amplifier for a period that is often the most significant part of the memory's cycle time.

To minimize write noise in word-organized 2D memories, the two halves of the digit lines are often driven so as

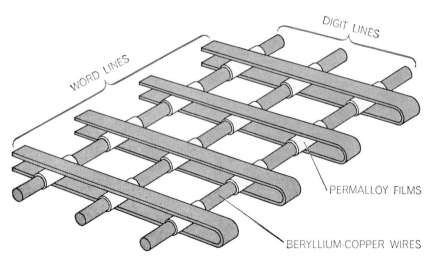

FLAT-FILM MEMORY is fabricated by evaporating permalloy in a vacuum onto glass or metal to a thickness of between 1,000 and 2,000 angstrom units in the presence of a direct-current magnetic field, which produces the desired direction of magnetization. Mylar sheets with photographically formed copper lines provide the word and digit lines.

PLATED-WIRE MEMORY is fabricated by electroplating a beryllium-copper wire with permalloy. Straight parallel lengths of this wire are digit lines; conductive ribbons strapped on at right angles are word lines. The direction of magnetization around the plated film is established during the plating by passing a direct current through the wire.

to induce opposing voltages in the sense amplifier and yet not attenuate the sense voltage. Such a circuit also serves to cancel the coupling by capacitance. In current-coincident 3D memories the inhibit and sense lines are wound in different patterns designed to minimize magnetic and capacitative coupling, but this cannot be done perfectly for both. Recently an organization intermediate between 2D and 3D, called 2½D, has become popular [see top illustration on page 34]. It drastically reduces the write noise and makes the core technology faster and even more competitive with technologies based on integrated laminates or films. The read step is the same as it is in 3D, but for the write step an inhibit winding is replaced by one set of selecting lines, say the X lines. The selected X line in each plane is either energized or not according to the digit to be written in the plane. Clearly write noise is greatly reduced, since the noise now originates from one line rather than from the entire plane. The price for this advantage is more circuitry.

Noise-cancellation techniques and 2½D are examples of stratagems to minimize the imperfections inherent in coincident-line addressing of arrays of magnetic elements. These stratagems can help only up to a point. In general the faster one wishes to operate the memory system, the smaller is the number of elements permissible in the sense and drive lines. This is so not only because of write noise but also because of the time it takes signals to travel through the system and the power required by long drive lines. When detailed designs are worked out for memories of various capacities and speeds based on cores, laminates, flat film and plated wire, it rather surprisingly turns out that about the same speed, within a factor less than two, is obtained for a given ratio of storage elements to switching elements (transistors or diodes) required in the memory system.

For fast systems with a cycle time of from 100 to 200 nanoseconds this bits-to-switches ratio may be as low as 30 to one; for the widely used 3D core systems operating at about one microsecond the ratio is about 300 to one, and for very large, slow systems it may be as high as 700 to one. Although the bits-to-switches ratio is not a complete criterion for choosing between various memory technologies, it determines the relative cost of the associated electronic circuitry. The ratio is most significant, however, in considering whether any magnetic technology can be extended to very high speeds or very large storage capacities.

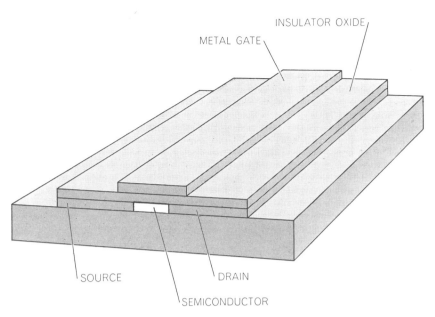

MOS FIELD-EFFECT TRANSISTOR is an almost perfect switch. The conduction between the "source" and "drain" electrodes is controlled by the potential of an insulated metal gate. There are two types of MOS (metal-oxide-semiconductor) transistor: the n type, which conducts by means of electrons, and the p type, which conducts by electron "holes."

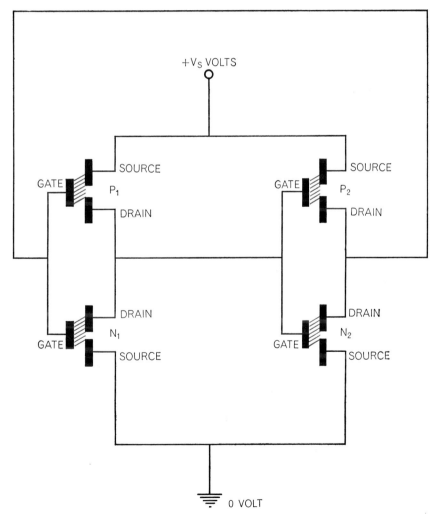

"FLIP-FLOP" CIRCUIT is formed when two pairs of n- and p-type MOS transistors are connected in series and symmetrically cross-connected. Large arrays of such circuits are the basis of a particularly promising class of integrated semiconductor memory systems.

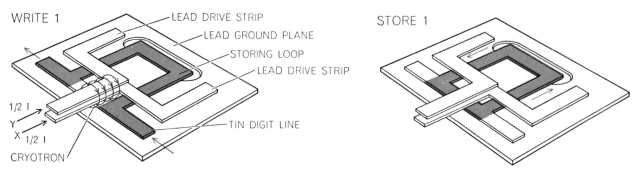

WRITE 1
LEAD DRIVE STRIP
LEAD GROUND PLANE
STORING LOOP
LEAD DRIVE STRIP
1/2 I
Y
X 1/2 I
CRYOTRON
TIN DIGIT LINE

STORE 1

SUPERCONDUCTING MEMORY ELEMENT contains a cryotron switch, which operates by creating a local magnetic field that destroys superconductivity in part of a loop of superconducting tin.

The memory depends on the principle of current coincidence in the selecting X and Y lines, which carry currents that are insufficient to activate the switch singly but are sufficient when they

These questions should be considered separately.

In a computer the time required to put commands and numbers into the memory and to retrieve them should be comparable to the time required to perform logic operations on them before they are again returned to the memory. Electronic logic has become far faster as technology has progressed from vacuum tubes to transistors and integrated circuits. Progress in memories was difficult, and a comparable evolution could be obtained only in memories of small capacity. Accordingly computer designers resorted to a hierarchy of memories: a small, fast "scratch pad" memory and a slower large main memory. In magnetic memories the cycle time—read followed by write—consists of (1) address-decoding time, (2) the time required for signals to travel along lines, (3) the time needed to switch elements twice, (4) delay in amplifiers and (5) delays due to write-in noise and timing imperfections. The fastest magnetic scratch pads use fast decoders, short lines, fast film memory elements and are cleverly designed to minimize delays. They call for much electronic circuitry, and at cycle times less than 100 nanoseconds the bits-to-switches ratio becomes very small. With the advent of integrated circuits the question arises of whether magnetic storage should be eliminated altogether. The economy in circuits achieved by the use of magnetic elements is no longer significant, and the necessity of amplifying the weak magnetic sense signals wastes cycle time.

As a matter of fact nonmagnetic memories have been used for years in all computers. Semiconductor registers, which consist of a row of "flip-flops" each storing one bit, can be regarded as one-word memories. A genuine memory calls for selection among many words. Such selection does not differ from the type of function carried out in the computer by organs responsible for logic control and arithmetic. This type of function is accomplished by "and," "or" and "nor" gates. (The output of an "or" gate is 1 if at least one of the inputs is 1. "Nor" stands for "not or.") For each bit a flip-flop and selecting gates are needed, so that a complete circuit calls for perhaps 10 transistors. Together with peripheral circuitry this yields a bit-to-switches ratio of only about one to 10. Furthermore, direct-current power is continuously required to hold the state of the flip-flops. With the transistors available a few years ago, the high component count and holding power made all-transistor memories impractical. The situation is changed today by the large strides that have been made in integrated circuits and by the advent of the metal-oxide-semiconductor (MOS) field-effect transistor.

The MOS field-effect transistor is an almost perfect switch [*see top illustration on preceding page*]. The conduction between the "source" and "drain" electrodes of the transistor is controlled by the potential of a perfectly insulated metal gate. There are two types of MOS transistor: the *n*-type, which conducts by means of electrons, and the *p*-type, which conducts by means of "holes," or regions deficient in electrons. It is possible to fabricate *n*- and *p*-type transistors that have practically no conduction between the source and the drain when the gate is at the same potential as the source. However, when the gate potential is a few volts positive with respect to the source of an *n*-type MOS transistor, or a few volts negative with respect to the source of a *p*-type MOS transistor, there is good conduction between the source and the drain. Accordingly these devices behave somewhat like relays, and logic networks consisting of MOS transistors resemble relay networks.

When two pairs of *n*- and *p*-type MOS transistors are connected in series and symmetrically cross-connected, they form an almost perfect flip-flop circuit [*see bottom illustration on preceding page*]. Both states of the flip-flop are stable, and practically no current flows through either branch of the circuit except for small currents due to slight leaks in MOS transistors. To make it possible to set the flip-flop in one state to another, six more transistors are ordinarily added. Many words can be connected to the same digit line, and sensing is extremely fast (a few nanoseconds).

The switching speed is limited by the degree to which the transistor can amplify and by the capacitance of the electrodes and windings. Almost no holding power is required (.10 microwatt per cell). The total switching power of the entire memory, no matter how large, can be much less than one watt. There is no write noise and no sense-amplifier delay, since the sense signal is quite strong. The system is nearly ideal, but is any system that contains thousands of transistors practical?

The electronics industry is investing large sums on the assumption that the answer will be yes. The industry bases its hopes on the phenomenal success of integrated circuits for other purposes. This success is due to a mastery of silicon technology: the ability to produce silicon crystals of high purity, to "dope" them precisely with impurities and to create thin insulating layers. Of equal importance is the development of photographic techniques to form conductive, insulating or specifically doped semiconductor areas on a microscopic scale. Over the years the performance of transistors improved, and it became practical to integrate two, four and then eight transistors with all their connections and coupling elements. "Chips" consisting of 20 to 30 transistors have been commercially available for the past year or two. Today the large-scale integration of hundreds or even thousands of transistors is the object of an industry-wide effort.

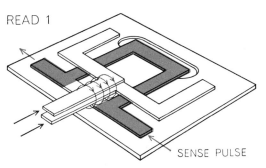

READ 1

SENSE PULSE

act together. The current path in the super-conducting tin digit strip for the write, store and read operations is indicated in color.

Last year MOS memory arrays of *p*-type elements were made that had a capacity of 256 bits. The future belongs, however, to MOS arrays of both *n*- and *p*-type elements. With such elements one can put a one-bit cell, complete with a flip-flop and logic gates, on an area .015 inch square. A memory with a capacity of hundreds of bits can then be made on a chip 1/4 inch on a side. An access time of 30 nanoseconds or less is expected.

Integrated semiconductor memories are inherently more promising than any magnetic memory. After all, the comparison is between an active electronic logic circuit with explicitly designed performance and a passive magnetic element of the same size that depends more or less on the properties of materials provided by nature. The question comes down to one of practicality: Can these intricate microelectronic elements be made in large arrays with adequate perfection and economy? The answer is definitely yes for small, ultrahigh-speed scratch-pad memories with a capacity of a few thousand bits. Concerning larger memories the prophets differ. Some think it is only a matter of time; others believe magnetic memories will retain their position because their associated circuits can also be made faster, cheaper and more reliable by the new microelectronic technology.

What of memories with very large capacities? Over the years the demand for larger computer memories has grown steadily as more ambitious problems with longer programs and more data were attacked, and as higher computer languages called for longer programs. Core memories were too expensive to provide the 100 million to one billion bits required for many uses, and this led to the development of memories based on spinning magnetic drums and disks. These electromechanical devices operate with a cycle time measured not in nanoseconds or microseconds but in milliseconds. When a computer is specially programmed, they seem to the user to be a simple extension of the core memory. This is a tolerable but undesirable state of affairs. Much effort is required to produce such programs (which also consume memory space), and much computer time is lost because of slow access time and the necessity of exchanging information between the cores and the drum or disk. Furthermore, the reliability of drum and disk memories leaves much to be desired.

The challenge is to produce electronic random-access memories with a capacity of billions of bits. Clearly integration on a grand scale is the only solution. Magnetic-integration techniques have yet to achieve anything like such a capacity, and even if they could millions of transistors would be needed. A more promising approach lies in the realm of superconductivity.

Superconductive materials, when cooled below a certain critical temperature, lose all electrical resistance. If current is started in a loop of such material, it will flow forever and therefore "remember" that it was started. The loop is in effect a one-bit memory register. Furthermore, superconductivity is destroyed by a sufficiently strong magnetic field. This effect is the basis of the cryotron switch. In the "on" state the switch has no resistance; an "off" state of finite resistance is created by passage of a current in a nearby controlling conductor that places the switch in a magnetic field. Tin, which is a "soft" superconductor, is a good material for the switch itself, because it can be changed from the superconductive to the resistant state by a weak magnetic field. A "harder" superconductor, which resists the weak field, can be used for circuit wiring. Most experimental cryotrons employ films several thousand angstroms thick. They can be switched in nanoseconds and are amenable to integrated fabrication techniques.

In a recently announced superconducting memory, storage loops made of tin are connected in series along a digit conductor and are on top of a lead sheet from which they are separated by a thin insulating film [*see illustration at left*]. The lead sheet has holes at locations corresponding to one side of each loop. The selecting *X* and *Y* conductors, made of lead and properly insulated, lie atop the other side of each loop and thus form a doubly controlled switch. The switch operates by creating a local magnetic field that destroys superconductivity in part of the loop.

The memory system operates by current coincidence in the following manner. The selecting *X* and *Y* currents are

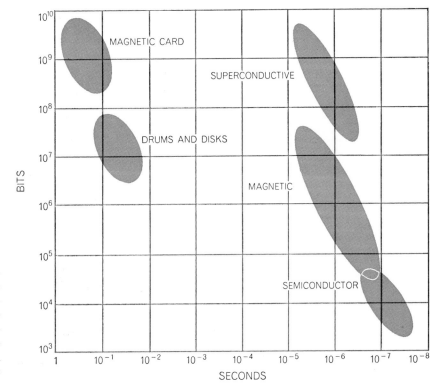

PERFORMANCE CHART shows the storage capacities and access times for various memories. Magnetic techniques include cores, monolithic ferrites, flat films and plated wires.

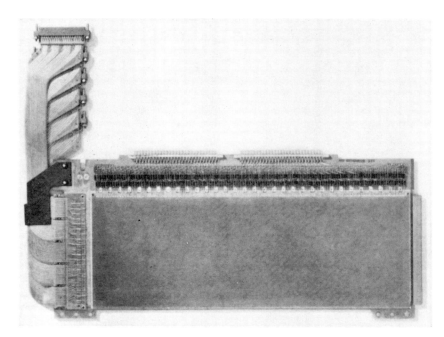

PLATED-WIRE MEMORY ARRAY was built by the Univac Division of Sperry Rand Corporation. Each side of the array holds 40,960 bits, representing the intersections of 256 word straps and 160 plated wires. The wires run in the long direction of the piece; the word straps run in the short direction. The entire assembly is approximately 18 inches long. The active area of the array is covered by a protective layer and is not visible in this photograph.

CLOSEUP VIEW of the memory array at the top of the page reveals the word straps (*black*) and the plated wires (*white*). Straps are .04 inch wide, wires .005 inch in diameter.

insufficient to activate the switch singly but are sufficient when acting together. In write-in the selecting currents are applied and then a current is sent through the digit line. The increased resistivity in the loop below the switch steers the current to the side of the loop over the hole in the lead sheet. Next the selecting currents are turned off and the magnetic field disappears, leaving the switchable side of the loop superconductive. Current does not flow through that side, however, until the digit current is turned off. When this happens, the current circulates as a persistent storing current around the complete loop. In the read cycle the selecting currents are applied and again increase the resistivity of the loop below the switch, thereby causing the persistent loop current to dissipate. As the current dissipates, it generates a sense voltage in the tin digit line. This voltage depends on the loop's magnetic flux, which is made as large as possible by allowing it to extend through the hole in the lead sheet.

Several properties of this superconducting memory are outstanding. In the first place, the loop is a more perfect memory element than any magnetic element, integrated or otherwise. There is absolutely no contribution to the sense signal from half-selected elements, there is no creep and the uniformity of the threshold of switching can be closely controlled. The selecting currents can vary from 80 to 120 percent of their standard value. There is, however, some write noise. Fortunately such noise can be eliminated by the cancellation techniques mentioned earlier. The result of these ideal properties of the loop and the low inductance of the connecting lines is that many loops can be driven and sensed by a single circuit. The bits-to-switches ratio can probably be 100,000 to one or more, which is two or three orders of magnitude better than for any magnetic memory. Furthermore, integration on the grand scale is eminently possible. Thin films of superconductive materials and other metals are easily evaporated over large areas. Photographic techniques are well suited for creating the desired patterns. The degree to which these techniques have been perfected is indicated by an experimental memory plane 4½ by five inches in size that contains 262,144 storage cells. This is a density of more than 13,000 cells per square inch [see *illustrations on opposite page*].

The price to be paid for these ideal properties is the necessity of providing low temperatures: for the lead-tin memory 3.5 degrees Kelvin (degrees centigrade above absolute zero). Such temperatures are no longer confined to the cryogenic laboratory; providing them would not add much to the cost of large-capacity superconducting memories. Memories of this kind may therefore offer capacities comparable to those of electromechanical devices at comparable cost, but with three orders of magnitude higher speed and also greater reliability.

To sum up, the memory gives universal powers to the computer. For more than a decade it was based on separate cores and transistors. The arrival of integrated magnetic, semiconductor and superconductive structures may extend speeds and capacities and make computers still more powerful.

It seems that no one technology will sweep all before it. Rather, one can expect that magnetic techniques (cores,

monolithic ferrites, flat films or plated wire) will provide capacities of from 10,000 to 10 million bits at speeds of a fraction of a microsecond. Integrated semiconductor techniques will provide memories of smaller capacity with speeds measured in tens of nanoseconds. Finally, superconductive mass memories with capacities of from 10 million to a billion bits will have speeds of about a microsecond.

This is not the end. Already under study are various ways to avoid the making of physically distinct cells for each bit without losing the essence of digital addressing. One approach uses sound waves traveling in magnetic materials. Other approaches make use of electro-optical devices such as the laser. As long as the demand for better memory systems continues there will be no shortage of ingenious proposals.

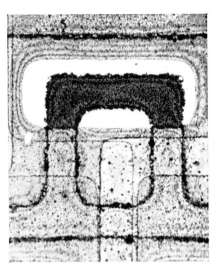

SINGLE STORAGE LOOP, part of the large superconducting memory plane shown in the photograph below, is enlarged approximately 180 diameters in this photomicrograph.

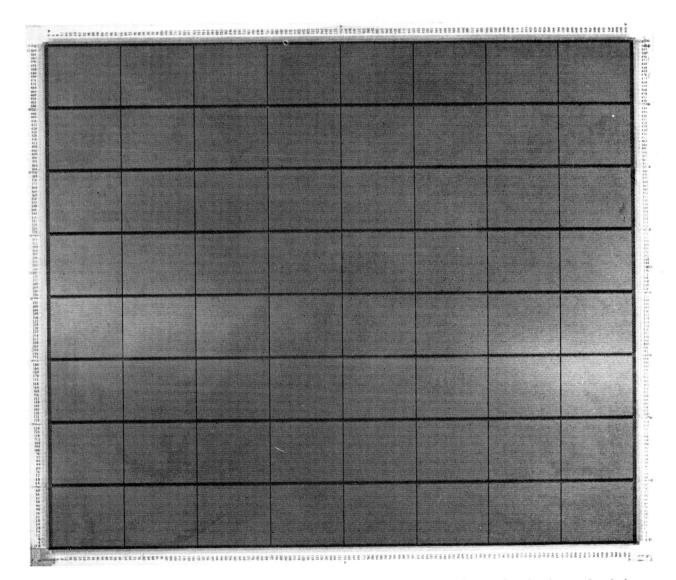

COMPLETE MEMORY PLANE of an experimental superconducting memory built by the Radio Corporation of America measures 4½ by five inches and contains 262,144 individual storage loops. A portion of the plane is shown in the color photograph at the bottom of page 29. Superconducting memories operate at a temperature of 3.5 degrees Kelvin (degrees centigrade above absolute zero).

4

COMPUTER INPUTS AND OUTPUTS

IVAN E. SUTHERLAND

September, 1966

If a computer is to be useful, it must obviously be able to communicate with the outside world. Data and programs have to be put into the machine before it can do any work. The computer must record and store for later reference information it has processed. Answers must come out of the computer in some usable form. The programs, mechanical devices and electronic circuits that perform these essential tasks of communication constitute what is called the input-output system of the computer.

A fact easily lost from view as a computer performs its prodigies of calculation is that a man is the reason for it all. He gives the computer data and programs and uses the results. Hence an input-output system has to cater to human needs as well as those of the computer. The total process from human recognition of a need that can be met by a computer to human use of the computer's answer consists of four parts. First, the data required must be put into a form the computer can use. Second, someone must tell the computer what to do. Third, the computer must read the data, process them and write the answers. Fourth, the computer's answers must be put into a form people can use. Input-output equipment must be designed to make each of these steps as easy as possible.

Improvements in input-output technique can lead to improved performance in all four parts of the computing process. For the input of data it is obvious that new kinds of input equipment make it possible for computers to accept directly a wider variety of information. A case in point is the recent development of stylus devices, such as the "Rand Tablet," that enable the computer to interpret human sketching. These devices make it possible to put diagrams and sketches into the computer without the time-consuming process of reducing them manually to numerical coordinates.

Secondly, and less obviously, the ability of the computer to accept a wider variety of input forms opens new ways of using such forms to specify what the computer is to do. For example, programming languages based on pictures rather than typed instructions may be much more convenient for specifying some processes of calculation to be carried out by the computer. Thirdly, improvements in the speed and organization of input-output systems can reduce computing costs. The "interrupt" systems I shall describe can reduce computing delays by allowing several input and output operations to proceed while computation is being done. Finally, new kinds of output equipment enable computers to produce output in more directly usable forms. A graph is often much more useful than a column of numbers.

Until fairly recently nearly all input-output systems in general use were designed to economize on the computer's time at the expense of some inconvenience to the user. The reason was the costliness of delaying computation, which was considered to be the computer's prime function, just to get data in and out. As a result of many years of work we have learned how to make input-output equipment operate efficiently from the computer's point of view.

Although care is still taken to operate computers efficiently, much more attention is now being paid to human convenience. Recent developments such as time-sharing [see "Time-sharing on Computers," by R. M. Fano and F. J. Corbató, page 79]. and reductions in the cost of computing, console and display devices have given us an unprece-dented freedom in designing input-output equipment. New devices and programs, some of which will be discussed later in this article, are changing computers from hard-to-use consultants into ready tools to aid human thought. For the time being, however, these programs and devices are mainly experimental. First it would be well to consider input-output as it is generally practiced today.

Different computer installations have quite different collections of input-output devices, even though the installations may have the same type of computer. The particular complement of input-output equipment depends on the purpose of the installation and is a strong factor in determining its price. A typical computer installation might have a card-reader, several magnetic-tape units, a typewriter and a high-speed printer. Information prepared on punched cards is entered into the computer through the card-reader. The magnetic-tape units provide the computer with storage for intermediate results. They can also provide for long-term storage of information and, by the transfer of tapes, for communication with other computers. The typewriter can be used for the output of short mes-

CONTROL CONSOLE of a computer representative of the most recent generation of computers is much simpler in appearance than the large panels of some earlier machines. This is the console of a Control Data Corporation 6600 computer at the Courant Institute of Mathematical Sciences at New York University. The keyboard is for input of instructions; the cathode ray tubes display (*left*) data from the computer's core memory and (*right*) the status of the seven problems the computer can handle at once.

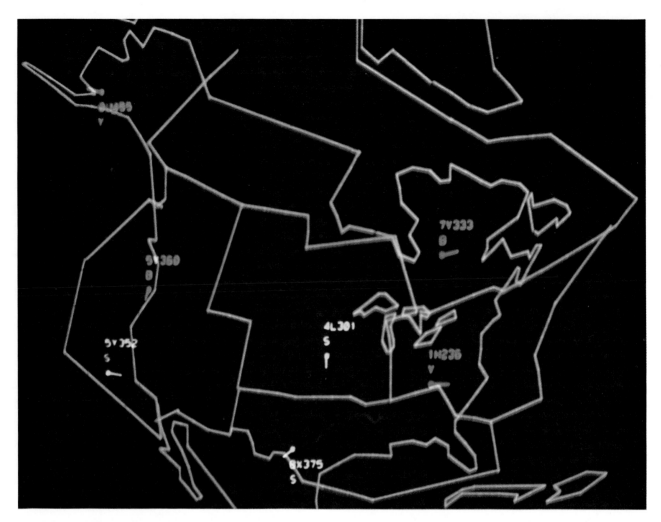

MILITARY DISPLAY at the Combat Operations Center of the North American Air Defense Command (NORAD) can be generated by computer in 10 seconds and projected in seven colors on an area 16 feet by 12 feet. Here blue lines show continent and special subdivisions; other colors designate aircraft positions. The equipment for the display was made by the Burroughs Corporation.

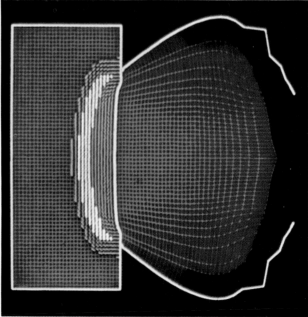

SCIENTIFIC DISPLAYS were produced by computer at the Lawrence Radiation Laboratory of the University of California. Orange contours on meteorological map at left are surface air pressure. White lines at right are explosion shock traveling through a block of metal; orange lines are maximum stress. Computer generated black-and-white diagrams that were used to make a motion picture.

sages, such as one instructing the operator to mount a particular reel of tape. It can also be used by the operator to signal when computations should start, for instance when he has finished mounting the tape. The printer provides for the output of results.

The typical pattern of card-reader, magnetic tapes, typewriter and printer varies when there are special needs. Many installations have card-punches in addition to card-readers. Some low-cost computing systems use punched paper tape instead of cards, substituting tape-readers and tape-punches for card equipment. An array of magnetic disks, usually called a file, is sometimes used with or instead of magnetic tapes.

Switches and lights are often used at the console instead of a typewriter for control by the operator. Some computers drive more than one printer. Others operate entirely without printers, depending on auxiliary computers to print from magnetic-tape output produced by the master computer.

All the input-output devices connected to computers have been designed to run as fast as possible. They seem, when running, to consume or produce information at a prodigious rate. A fast card-reader reads about 1,000 cards per minute; it seems to speed through the pile of cards like a power saw cutting through wood. Similarly, printed pages come out of an output printer much faster than one can read them. Even a computer typewriter, one of the slowest of the input-output devices, types far faster and more accurately than a skilled human typist.

Nonetheless, the speed of such input-output devices is slow compared with that of a modern electronic computer. To see just how slow their operations are from the computer's point of view, let us imagine slowing down an entire computer system a millionfold. Instead of performing a million operations per second, our slowed-down computer will perform at a more human pace: one operation per second. In the slowed-down model a computer typewriter that normally types 10 characters per second would type about one character per day! To put it another way, a computer receiving input from a fast typist is much like a man getting one new character of a telegram each morning.

Most input-output devices are faster than typewriters, but because nearly all of them have mechanical parts they cannot approach the speed of the electronic computer. A computer printer that can print 1,500 lines per minute, each with 132 characters, would accept a new character every five minutes in our millionth-speed model. Magnetic tape that accepts about 100,000 characters per second would accept a new character every 10 seconds. Since it takes about two milliseconds to start or stop a tape in ordinary computer operation, however, it would take the tape unit in the slowed-down model half an hour to deliver its first character. On the other hand, some input-output devices (microsecond clocks, very-high-speed magnetic drums, cathode-ray-tube displays and converters that change data such as voltages into digits) can work as fast as electronic computers. Thus the difficulty of coordinating input-output processes with computing is not only that some input-output devices are extraordinarily slow compared with the speed of computers but also that the range of input-output speeds is very large.

Another difficulty is that the computer must be able to accept information from input devices and deliver information to output devices promptly on demand. Promptness is required because many input-output devices, once they are started, cannot be stopped quickly. For example, once a magnetic tape has started moving, new characters will come from it at regular intervals whether or not the computer accepts them. The inertia of the tape is too great to permit starting and stopping for each character. If the computer fails to accept a character before the next one arrives, information will be lost.

Although the computer must be able to handle each piece of information promptly, it can hardly afford to stand by idly. Modern computers are very costly, and each second they wait for input or output equipment to function corresponds to hundreds of thousands of irretrievably lost computations. Much of the complexity of modern computing systems arises from the desire of the designers to avoid unnecessary waiting for input and output. A well-designed modern computer can operate half a dozen or so input-output devices concurrently and do useful computation in the time left over. This is a juggling act of colossal proportions. Developing the computer hardware and programs to realize it has been a major task.

Most of the early computers lacked the hardware that makes efficient input and output feasible. A typical input-output system consisted of a few special instructions. They enabled a program to select and activate an input-output unit, transfer data to or from it and determine if it was ready for another transfer of data. With only these simple instructions it was easy to write a crude input-output program but nearly impossible to write an efficient one. The input-output programs in common use wasted the time between successive transfers of data in a "waiting loop," a set of instructions in which the computer asked repeatedly if the input-output unit was yet ready for another transfer of data. An efficient input-output program would have provided for useful computation in the time between data transfers.

In the early computers computation between inputs or outputs of information could be done only if the instructions for input-output and those for computation were carefully interwoven. The programmer faced a dilemma. To obtain maximum efficiency he had to provide for as much computation as possible between transfers of data. If he allowed too much computation, however, input-output data would be lost. Writing an efficient program required a detailed knowledge of the timing of both the input-output operations and the computation. Since each new computation program presented its own special timing problems, every program required its own careful interweaving of input-output and computation. It was impossible to write, once and for all, an independent program to accomplish efficient input and output. The only independent input-output programs possible were the crude, time-wasting kind. Programmers either used inefficient input-output routines or faced the long, irksome task of interweaving input-output and computation.

The beauty of today's input-output systems is that they not only enhance efficiency but also provide for a clean separation of input-output programs from computation programs. It is this separation that enables programmers to use the full capacity of the modern computer.

The basic hardware required for efficient use of input-output equipment is the system of devices called the "program-interrupt." This hardware serves the computer as a kind of doorbell that signals the arrival of any important piece of information. When an input-output unit is ready to transfer data, it sends a signal to the interrupt hardware, which causes the computer to suspend whatever it was doing and execute instead a totally independent input-output program located somewhere else in its memory. The input-output

INPUT DEVICE in common use with computers is a card-reader, by means of which the computer "reads" data coded on cards with perforations. A typical card-reader, such as this one made by the Control Data Corporation, can handle about 1,000 cards a minute.

RAND TABLET represents a new generation of input devices that make the use of a computer easier by accepting the direct input of drawings. It has a sheet of Mylar etched with 1,024 copper lines on each side. Each line receives a unique series of electric pulses; they are coupled capacitatively through the stylus to tell the computer where the stylus is.

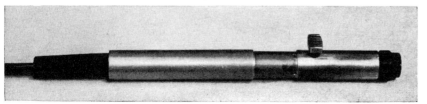

LIGHT PEN is another device that can put drawings into a computer. The pen contains a photocell that responds to spots of light displayed by a computer on a cathode ray tube. The pen has two uses: pointing at parts of a picture and (with a tracking program) drawing.

program transfers the data and then returns the computer to its former activity [see top illustration on page 50].

Program-interrupt hardware provides many advantages. Because it can interrupt a computation at any time, demands for input and output receive the prompt response they require. The input-output program runs efficiently because it is activated only when it is actually needed. Most important of all, efficient handling of input-output transfers no longer requires any complicated interweaving of computation and input-output instructions. Computation programs can now be written without regard for the input-output activities that may be under way simultaneously.

If several input-output units are connected to a computer, many interrupt signals can be generated at once. The priority to be given to these demands for service is usually designed into the interrupt hardware. Faster input-output equipment is generally given a higher priority. Units that operate at irregular intervals may get a lower priority if they can be made to wait; in this way they do not break the pace of synchronous units. Computation itself is given the lowest priority because it can nearly always wait. Computation takes place only when no interrupts are being processed, which usually turns out to be most of the time.

Most input-output interrupts result in the transfer of just one piece of information to or from the memory. Such an operation is described as one memory cycle. Often additional memory cycles are required to control the transfer. Some computers contain special hardware that processes each of the frequent but simple transfers of data in only one memory cycle. Such a unit, called a "data channel" or "memory-snatch" system, takes a single memory cycle away from calculation whenever an input-output device is ready [see bottom illustration on page 50]. A data channel or memory-snatch incorporates a pointer that is changed after each transfer, so that successive data are put into or taken from successive locations in the memory. It also contains a counter, so that only a specified number of transactions can take place automatically. Data channels are useful for very-high-speed tape and disk units that transfer new information every few memory cycles.

Although different types of computers use different kinds of interrupt systems, nearly every computer now being manufactured has some form of program-interrupt. Larger systems with fast input-output equipment usually include at least one data channel. Since it is uneconomical to interrupt the largest computing machines even momentarily for input-output, they are often directly coupled to a smaller computer that does their input and output for them. Since input-output operations rarely require sophisticated arithmetic, this separation of calculation and input-output is becoming more common.

Most computers are delivered with a tape containing a comprehensive program (called an "operating system" or "executive") to do their input-output operations. The operating system should take care of all details of timing, running several input-output programs at the same time and dealing with correctable failure in the input-output equipment. Viewed through a well-designed operating system, input-output equipment is fast, accurate, economical of computer time and easy to use.

In addition to using the program-interrupt hardware to handle input-output operations efficiently, the operating system provides for the scheduling of jobs and the allocation of input-output and memory resources. Without an effective operating system a modern large computer is almost useless. In fact, operating systems are so important that they are usually covered in the specifications for a computer; failure of a manufacturer to deliver a suitable operating system on time usually results in a heavy financial penalty. The task of preparing a good operating system is substantial. Writing a new operating system is roughly equivalent in complexity to designing a new computer.

The operating system enables relatively unskilled programmers to utilize the parts of the computer they need without concern for details of timing, interference from other users or malfunctioning of equipment. For example, a user's program that requires the printing of data can call on a part of the operating system to perform the output. When asked to print, the operating system will accept responsibility for the data to be printed and will return control to the user program. If the printer is free, the operating system may begin to print the data at once. The user's computation program will proceed, interrupted from time to time when the printer actually requires transfers of data. If the printer is not free, the operating system may choose to put the data on magnetic tape for later printing. In this case too the user's computation will proceed, interrupted from time to time for data transfers. The operating system may check the information written on tape for accuracy. Should an error be found, the operating system will rewrite the information correctly.

All the complex activities of the operating system are accomplished by processing interrupts. The user for whom these processes are carried out has no need to be concerned with the details of the processing; indeed, he is quite unaware of them. Needless to say, the highly skilled system programmers who write operating systems must have an intimate knowledge of the input-output equipment and program-interrupt hardware involved.

Although the input-output programs and hardware described here solve the timing problems of using input-output equipment, they do little to assist in specifying the format of the

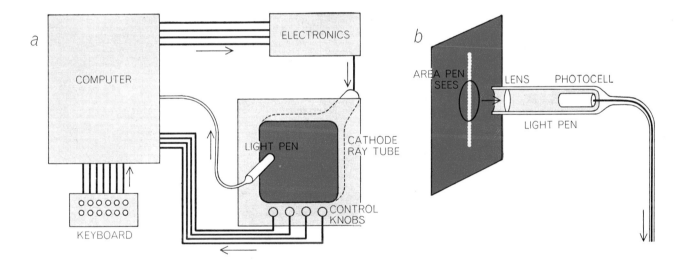

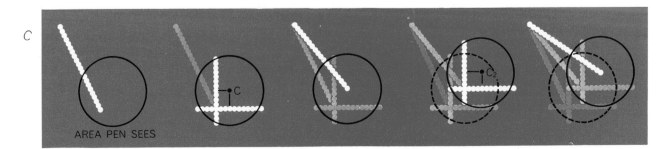

TWO USES of a light pen are pointing and drawing. Pointing ("a" and "b") tells a computer which parts of a drawing to erase or move. Drawing (c) is done with a tracking program. Here, to move the end of a line, the operator points at the end and pushes a "move" button; the computer follows the pen by displaying cross-like arrays of spots 100 times a second. Each time, the computer ascertains the outer vertical and horizontal spots seen by pen, computes position of pen's center and redisplays line to end there.

information transferred. The format in which information appears outside the computer is usually very different from that of the information inside. Humans want to see decimal numbers; computers normally use binary numbers. Humans want dollar signs, decimal points, separately printed units and separately printed exponents; computers just deal with numbers. Specifying the desired format for input-output information is an important part of any programming job. Converting information to and from the specified format is an essential function of the computer.

The specification and conversion of format are well understood for ordinary scientific and business computation. Formats consisting of columns of numbers with headings, convenient spacing and suitable units are easily specified through the "compilers" that most programmers use to help tell the computer what to do. Simple statements enable the programmer to describe each line he wants printed. For example, a format statement such as FORMAT (1H1, 4F10.3,5H FEET) would be interpreted by the computer as follows: 1H1, start a new page; 4F, print four numbers in decimal notation; 10.3, use 10 columns for each number and give three places after the decimal point; 5H, put the

unit designation "feet" at the end of the line. Most compilers make it easy to print numbers as integers, as decimal fractions with a specified number of places before and after the decimal point or in scientific notation, such as 11.73×10^6 (which comes out 11.73 E6 in computers that cannot print superscript). In addition the computer can print comments, units and titles either from internal data or by copying part of the format statement.

Fairly simple formats serve for the large bulk of computer inputs and outputs. They are well matched to the limited capacity of the common output printers. Since most printers can print only capital letters, numbers and a few punctuation symbols, no great complexity of format is required. Most users of computers have become accustomed to receiving columns of numbers as the output from their computations. Research now under way, however, has shown that less common input-output devices and more complicated format-control tools for them can make much more useful forms of input and output possible.

We are beginning to recognize that it is not enough for a computer to calculate and print an answer. The answer

is useful only when it leads to new human understanding. Diagrams, drawings, graphs and sketches are essential tools for human understanding in many scientific and technical fields. All too often users of computers have been forced to convert pictures into numerical coordinates before giving them to a computer and to convert columns of numerical answers back into a picture or graph before understanding the answer. The time it takes a man to do the conversion keeps him from trying many examples; in some cases it may even cause him to lose sight of what it was he wanted. If the computer can accept information in the form most natural for the man and produce answers in the form he can most readily understand, it can be much more useful to him. The difference is readily apparent if one considers that a single straight line flashed on a display tube in one or two milliseconds might require 15 minutes of typed output to give the coordinates of the 1,000 or so points making up the line.

During the past few years several experimental systems have been built that rely on diagrams rather than printed or typed numbers as a medium of communication between a computer and its user. These systems have shown that proper use of graphical input-output equipment can produce a substantial increase in a computer's ability to aid human understanding of complex phenomena. In one such system, developed by Cyrus Levinthal at the Massachusetts Institute of Technology, protein molecules are shown in perspective [see "Molecular Model-building by Computer," by Cyrus Levinthal, page 171]. The effects of various assumptions on the shape of the molecule can be observed directly. In another system, devised by E. E. Zajac of the Bell Telephone Laboratories, the tumbling motion of a simulated satellite was recorded on motion-picture film. Engineers viewing the film were able to decide why the actual satellite's stabilizing system failed to work. Such demonstrations have hastened the development and application of computer systems that can accept and give graphical information.

The basic hardware for graphical output is the cathode-ray-tube display, known around computer installations as the CRT display. Such a display contains a cathode ray tube and some electronic devices that enable a computer to control it. When given a set of coordinates by the computer program, a simple cathode-ray-tube display will flash the

OUTPUT DEVICE in common use is a chain printer, which takes its name from the fact that the type is on a rapidly moving chain. This printer, which is made by the International Business Machines Corporation, produces 1,100 lines of 132 characters each per minute.

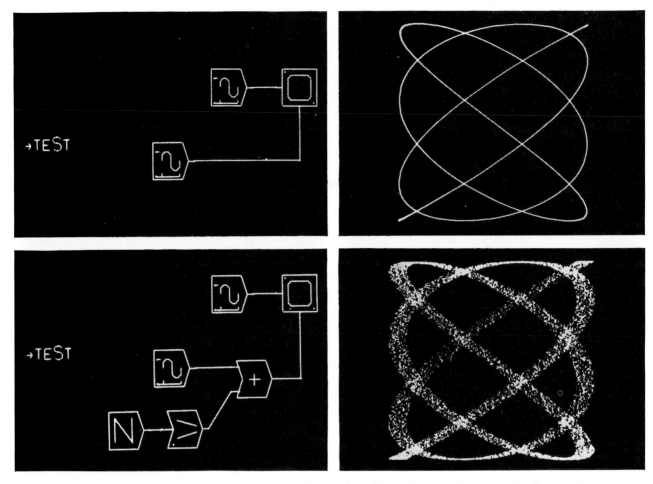

PICTURE INPUT AND OUTPUT on a computer, using a cathode-ray-tube display, are demonstrated with a program written by William R. Sutherland of the Massachusetts Institute of Technology's Lincoln Laboratory. At top left a light pen has been used to position predrawn circuits on the tube and to draw "wires" connecting them. Diagram instructs computer to simulate two sine-wave generators connected to an oscilloscope; the frequency and amplitude of the generators were specified on a typewriter. The resulting output is Lissajous figure at top right. At bottom the addition of a noise generator (*N*) and an attenuator (*slanting bars*) modifies output.

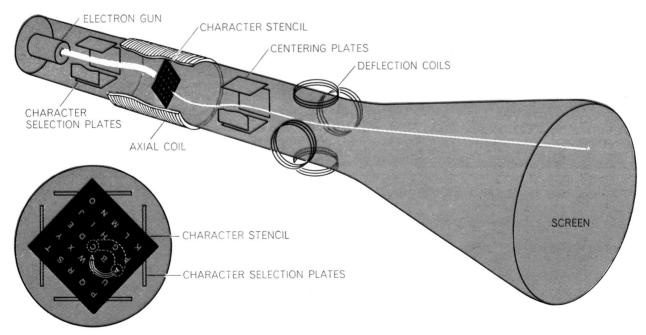

CATHODE RAY TUBE is equipped to print letters and symbols in a computer's output display. A broad beam of electrons emerging from the electron gun passes through electrostatic plates that deflect it toward the desired part of a stencil bearing the characters. In this case the beam is directed through the letter *A*; it is recentered in the tube by the centering plates and then deflected to the desired place on the display tube by the deflection coils. During passage through the tube the beam makes a three-quarter helical turn.

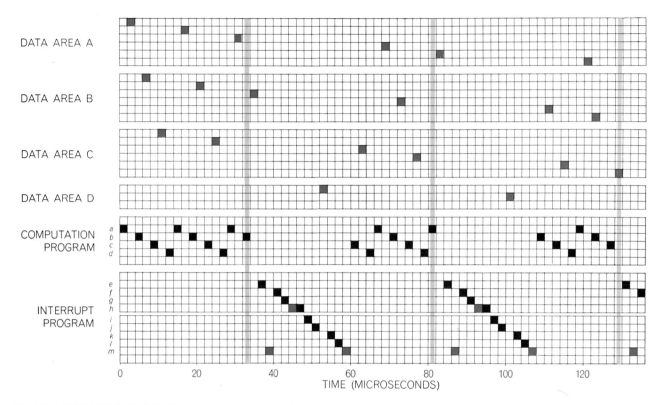

PROGRAM-INTERRUPT SYSTEM stops a computation while a computer deals with the input or output of data. Each square represents a memory cell of the computer; when such a cell is used to instruct the computer it is black, and when a cell is used for the storage or retrieval of data it is in color. In this program the computer is adding pairs of numbers and storing the sums. Periodically (*colored bands*) the computation program receives a signal from an input or output device; computation is then interrupted while the computer goes through the steps (*e–m*) required to deal with the input or output of data. Thereafter the computing is resumed.

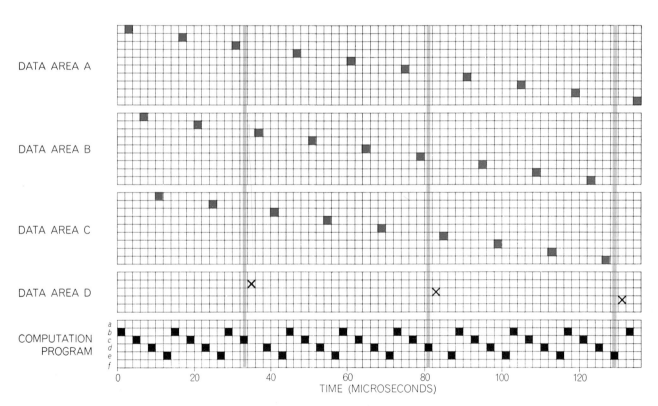

"MEMORY-SNATCH" is similar to a program-interrupt except that each input or output of data takes only one memory cycle (*X*) and so computing is interrupted for shorter periods. In the program-interrupt system control of the computer passes to the interrupt program during the input or output transaction; in the memory-snatch, whenever an input or output unit is ready to transfer data, the single memory cycle immediately after the input-output unit's signal is used to put the datum directly into the computer's memory (*area D*) and computing then proceeds. The computing in these examples has been made simple for illustrative purposes.

corresponding spot on its face. Complete pictures including lines, curves and letters can be made up out of thousands of individual spots. Because the display is entirely electronic, it can work very fast; a single spot may take only a few microseconds to show.

This process has its limitations. The more elaborate the picture, the longer it takes the computer to compute the coordinates of all the thousands of spots in the picture. For this reason some displays have circuits that can paint straight lines on the display face automatically, thus eliminating the need for a program to compute coordinates for all the spots on each line. Since computer output usually contains some letters and numbers, many displays contain character-generating hardware that will cause a letter or number to appear on the display screen automatically. The character is formed either by passing the cathode ray through a letter-shaped mask or by electronically manipulating the beam to paint the letter [see bottom illustration on page 49]. Display hardware for generating various conic sections automatically is now being developed.

Making good use of cathode-ray-tube display equipment often requires quite complex programs. The few installations that now make extensive use of such displays have built up libraries of programs for producing a variety of display formats. Programs for producing bar graphs, contour plots, scatter diagrams and a wide variety of other useful formats are separately available. If the format desired does not fit one of the available forms, careful individual programming of the new format is required. It is fairly easy to program simple formats such as graphs, but it is considerably more difficult to get all the labels, scales and notes in the right places.

Some output formats are quite difficult to achieve. An adequate view of a solid object, for example, must have hidden lines removed [see illustration on next page]. It is easy to write a program that can compute the apparent position of each part of an object from the shape of the object and the desired viewing angle. It is very much harder to write a program that can decide which parts to omit to make the object look solid; moreover, the task of elimination takes much more time than the simple transformation of coordinates. Similarly, it is difficult to program a computer to place the parts of a drawing wisely so that its topology will be clear. For these reasons output plots of family trees, simplified circuit diagrams, organization interaction diagrams and the like are rare.

With suitable attachments a cathode-ray-tube display can also be used as an input device. Since the parts of a picture displayed on a cathode ray tube are "painted" on the tube face one after another, a photocell placed where light from a part of the tube can fall on it will respond when it detects light. The computer can tell what the photocell saw by noting when it responded.

In one arrangement the photocell and cathode ray tube are used as a scanner: the photocell is placed behind an exposed film on which is recorded some data such as the tracks of nuclear particles. The computer can then read the data from the film by noting which displayed points are hidden from the photocell by opaque parts of the intervening film. Scanners of this type are now manufactured commercially for converting data from photographic to digital form, so that the computer can make the desired calculations. These scanners are proving to be a boon to physicists who need to scan hundreds of thousands of frames from a bubble chamber to find a single significant event.

Picture input through scanners requires more complicated programs than picture output. Although a cathode-ray-tube scanner can tell a computer which parts of a photograph are opaque, a complicated program and a good deal of computer time are necessary to convert that information into a simple usable fact. Lawrence G. Roberts of the Lincoln Laboratory of M.I.T. wrote such a program for recognizing solid objects from photographs. Roberts' program demonstrated its ability to recognize simple plane-faced objects by drawing additional views of them. Although the computer required only a few seconds to read prerecorded picture data from tape, it took several minutes (an enormous amount of computing time) for the computer to make sense of the data. Pattern-recognition programs such as Roberts' and those used in analyzing the tracks of nuclear particles must be written on an individual basis. Because of this exacting requirement picture-scanning input is economical only experimentally or where there are large bodies of data to process.

The stylus-photocell arrangement called the light pen can be used to make the cathode-ray-tube display serve for the manual input of sketches and diagrams [see illustration on page 47]. For this purpose the photocell is placed in a small hand-held tube. Since the photocell responds only when light from some part of the cathode-ray-tube drawing falls within its limited field of view, it can tell the computer which part of a drawing its user is pointing at. With an appropriate feedback program a light pen can also be used to enter position information into the computer. Other stylus input devices that detect the position of the stylus through electric and magnetic-field effects can serve a similar function. Some of these, such as the Rand Tablet (developed by Thomas O. Ellis of the Rand Corporation), provide the computer not only with position but also with a "pencil down" indication; that is, the device signifies to the computer not only the position of the stylus but also whether or not the user is pressing it down. The "pressing down" signal can be used to signify lines that are to be retained in the computer.

In a drawing system based on input from a stylus the computer interprets motions of the stylus and instructions given by the operator through push buttons or a typewriter keyboard; from these data the computer constructs a drawing in its memory. The program displays the growing drawing on a cathode-ray-tube display [see top illustration on page 49]. Unlike an ordinary pencil, the stylus itself does not make any direct mark on the display. The computer is placed, in effect, between the "point of the pencil" and the "paper." Because the drawing is built directly in the computer's memory, no complicated pattern-recognition programs are required. A stylus-input device therefore provides a convenient method for getting diagrams, circuits, geometric shapes, chemical symbols and other pictorial data into a computer.

Such a drawing system is very different from ordinary drawing with pencil and paper. Because the computer is placed between the "point of the pencil" and the "paper" it can assist in every step of drawing. For example, the computer can display lines as straight even though they were sketched badly. It can join lines at mathematically precise corners in spite of slight human errors. It will erase without any trace, or temporarily if you prefer, any unwanted line you point to. It can quickly copy any part of the drawing. It can stretch parts of the drawing to make them fit with other parts. It can move lines you have already drawn. It can refuse to draw lines that are meaningless in the context of the work in hand.

Most computer drawing systems use

push buttons as input devices to signal what action is desired. An experimental system at the Rand Corporation, however, uses motions of a stylus as the exclusive control. Since the Rand program is intended for drawing block diagrams, it recognizes crudely sketched blocks and substitutes neat ones for them. It also recognizes lines drawn between boxes as logical connections between them. No matter how you draw the connection, it will appear as a series of straight-line segments. It will have an arrowhead at one end. •The Rand program also recognizes printed characters. It substitutes its own highly precise printing for your letters. It is impossible to leave bad printing on your drawing. You can insert letters by making a caret, whereupon the program will push existing letters aside to make room for your addition. You can erase boxes, lines and letters by making a score-out mark over them. With these facilities you can quickly and easily sketch out or modify a diagram.

The topology of a drawing sketched into a computer with a stylus-input device is available explicitly in the computer's memory. If the drawing represents a circuit, for example, the electrical connections shown in the drawing will be represented in the memory in a form suitable for use in a circuit-simulator. The computer will "know" that two terminals are connected because it will have "watched" while the connecting wire was drawn. There are many computer applications for which specification of topology is important. Stylus input is beginning to be used to state topology for circuit simulation, analysis of communication networks, digital simulation of analogue systems and diagramming the flow of digital-computer programs.

The geometry of shapes is also stated easily with a stylus-input device. The stylus serves to sketch the part. If exact dimensions are important, they can be entered through a keyboard. In one case the parts specified by this technique are cut out by computer-controlled machine tools. In another case the computer does engineering computations on the shapes as an aid to the design of mechanical devices.

Stylus input to computers opens up new vistas for the application of computers. We are just beginning to explore these vistas. The ability to specify topology, for example, will make possible a new generation of computer-programming languages based on pictures rather than on written words. The ability to specify geometry will bring computers into use as aids to mechanical design. The ability to specify graphical-output formats will make possible ever clearer presentations of computed results. Perfection of the techniques for drawing with a stylus will make a stylus and computer easier to use than pencil and paper.

Although the full potential of graphical input and output is still unknown, there is a growing belief that important new insights will be gained through its use. Today graphical capability is unknown at most computer installations, even major scientific ones. Widespread recognition of its potential, however, is a strong motivating force that will bring graphics to the computers in most scientific research programs. It is my conviction that the widespread use of graphical inputs and outputs with computers will bring about a major increase in scientific, engineering and educational productivity.

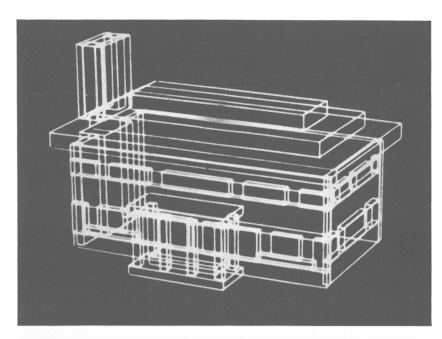

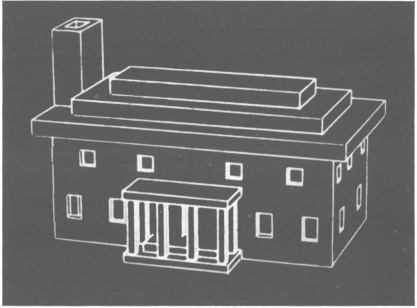

PERSPECTIVE VIEWS of solid objects can be displayed by a computer. It is easy to prepare a program that will cause the computer to display every part of an object (*top*). It is much more difficult to write a program that will achieve the effect shown at bottom by causing the computer to remove certain lines from the display. Even with an appropriate program it takes the computer a relatively long time to carry out the instructions. The program for this display was written by Lawrence G. Roberts of the Lincoln Laboratory.

5

COMPUTER DISPLAYS

IVAN E. SUTHERLAND
June, 1970

Whereas a microscope enables us to examine the structure of a subminiature world and a telescope reveals the structure of the universe at large, a computer display enables us to examine the structure of a man-made mathematical world simulated entirely within an electronic mechanism. I think of a computer display as a window on Alice's Wonderland in which a programmer can depict either objects that obey well-known natural laws or purely imaginary objects that follow laws he has written into his program. Through computer displays I have landed an airplane on the deck of a moving carrier, observed a nuclear particle hit a potential well, flown in a rocket at nearly the speed of light and watched a computer reveal its innermost workings.

My interest for some years has been the programming of computers to draw pictures on the face of a cathode ray tube. Obviously computers can produce pictures in other ways, such as by means of mechanical plotters or by printing arrays of symbols, but because the essential problems in creating pictures by computer can be understood by considering images produced by electron beams I shall ignore these other forms of output. I shall also ignore the kinds of computer-driven picture tubes that present modest amounts of text at high speed in such places as airline terminals and brokerage offices; their operation is straightforward.

Computer displays have become of major importance to two groups of people. One group has a pictorial problem in the workaday world for which it would like computer help. These users, for example, may want to shape a metal part on a computer-controlled machine tool; they begin by describing the part to a general-purpose computer, which draws a picture of the part and verifies that the description is accurate. Other users employ computers to produce the intricate high-resolution photographic masks required for making integrated electronic circuits [*see bottom illustration on next two pages*]. Similar pictorial problems in which computers can help arise in highway planning, automobile and aircraft design, topographical mapping, architecture, the layout of publications and the production of clothing patterns. In these and many more areas, written language is far from adequate.

The other group using computer displays is interested in gaining insight into complex natural or mathematical phenomena. These users simulate physical situations of various kinds in the computer and use display devices to present the results of the simulation. For example, an organic chemist may want to synthesize a particular molecule; he creates a picture of the molecule on a display screen and then initiates a program by which the computer presents a selection of simpler molecules from which the desired substance can be synthesized [*see illustrations on pages 64 and 65*]. An engineer designing a communication circuit asks the computer for a graph showing how circuit response varies with frequency. A physician studying how blood flows through the arteries obtains a plot that reveals high vorticity at exactly the locations where the lesions of atherosclerosis are most common. A physicist programs a computer to illustrate how elementary particles interact with their own electric fields to give his students some feeling for quantum-mechanical behavior. A circuit designer draws a circuit and asks a computer to simulate its operation and to plot its performance in a graph of voltage and current. A feedback theorist describes the location of poles and zeros on a complex plane and watches as the computer plots the root locus. A mathematician enters the equations for conformal mappings and observes the maps produced by each equation. A pilot practices takeoffs and landings on a simulated airfield that can assume any orientation on the display screen as he operates "controls" for engine power and aircraft attitude. All these people, interested in educating themselves or others, use computer displays as one of many tools for gaining deeper understanding of a problem.

Two Kinds of Display

Two broad classes of computer-display system are now in common use: calligraphic displays and raster displays. Calligraphic displays "paint" the parts of a picture on the cathode ray tube in any sequence given by the computer. The electron beam in a calligraphic display is moved from place to place in a pattern that traces out the individual lines and characters that make up the picture. Raster displays make pictures in the same way that television sets do: the image is painted in a fixed sequence, usually from left to right and from top to bottom. The calligraphic display has the advantage that information to be displayed can be stored in computer memory in any order, whereas information for a raster display must first be sorted from top to bottom and from left to right so that it can be put on the screen in the correct sequence. On the other hand, the deflection amplifiers, deflection yokes and other electronic components needed for a raster display are much less costly than those required for a calligraphic display, not only because they need not be so carefully made but also because suitable components are now mass-produced.

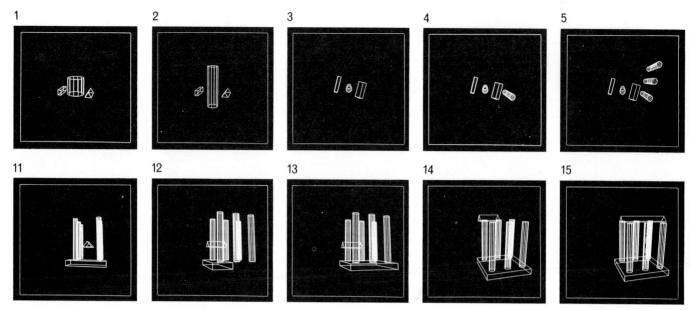

COMPUTER DESIGN OF "GREEK TEMPLE" demonstrates the versatility and speed of present-day graphic displays and computer programs. The sequence was photographed at the International Business Machines Research Laboratory; the computer was an IBM 1130 with a 2250 display unit. The "draftsman" begins by asking the computer to display three geometric solids selected from a library of shapes on file in a disk memory: a hexahedron, a cylinder and a triangular prism (*1*). The remaining operations are carried out by pressing keys on an "interactive" console that can copy, move, rotate or distort anything placed on the screen. The drafts-

The task of sorting information from top to bottom and from left to right for presentation on raster displays has largely precluded their use for anything but presentations of text. In principle, however, a raster display has the potential of producing pictures with a range of light and dark tones, in color if desired, that provide a realism unequaled by the line drawings of a calligraphic display. The potential of this type of presentation can be seen in the pictures on page 67, which were made in our laboratory at the University of Utah by photographing a low-speed simulation of a raster display. I shall describe later some recent algorithms, or mathematical routines, for sorting picture information to eliminate hidden surfaces in making raster displays. I believe such displays will have become a common form of computer output within a very few years.

The information to be projected on the face of a computer display tube is speci-

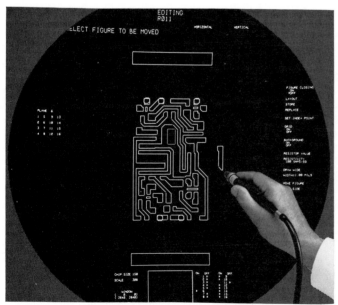

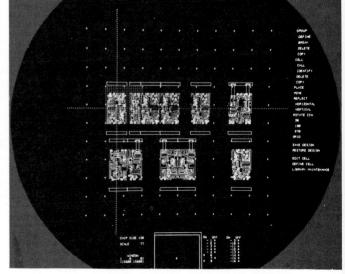

DESIGN OF INTEGRATED CIRCUITS exploits the flexibility and precision now provided by interactive computer displays. This sequence, photographed at Fairchild Semiconductor, was made with a Sanders display unit coupled to an IBM 1130 computer. The goal in this application is to end up with photolithographic masks in which line patterns are located with an accuracy of 50 millionths of an inch. The resolution of the display is defined by a coordinate grid of 1,024 lines and 1,024 columns. The coordinates of the lines drawn on the face of the cathode ray tube are recorded magnetically and then used to control digitally driven machines that cut greatly enlarged versions of the masks. Subsequently the masks are optically reduced in size to the tiny dimensions characteristic of

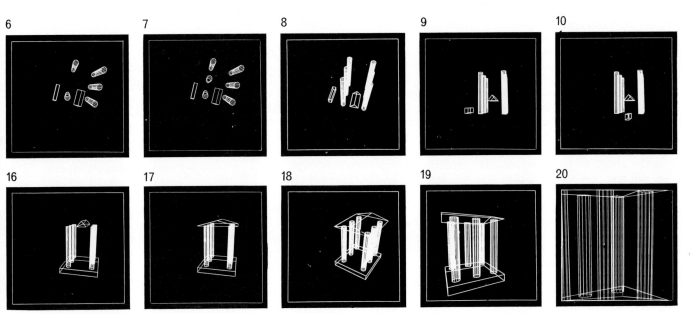

man lengthens the cylinder (2) and rotates the three elements to a plan view (3). He then adds five more columns (4, 5, 6, 7). The display is rotated (8) until the columns are viewed at eye level (9). The hexahedron is then moved to a position below the columns (10) and widened (11). The emerging temple is rotated to a side view (12) and the hexahedron is lengthened until it becomes a floor slab (13). The prism is raised (14) and lengthened (15). Again the temple is rotated (16) and the prism is widened to form a roof (17). The finished temple is displayed from above (18). Back at ground level the viewer walks toward it (19) and enters (20).

fied in terms of a coordinate system that covers the tube face. This coordinate system can be thought of as a grid of points that covers the face of the tube even though the grid is not actually etched on the glass. The resolution of the display system can be specified by saying how many rows and columns of points there are in the coordinate system. Most modern display systems have a minimum resolution of 1,024 rows and 1,024 columns and a few systems have four times as many rows and columns. To specify a point on a 1,024-by-1,024 array requires that each x and y value contain 10 binary digits, or "bits" ($2^{10} = 1,024$); to specify a point in a 4,096-by-4,096 array requires 12 bits for each coordinate. Higher resolution is not generally sought because it is difficult to maintain accuracy at higher resolutions and also because the diameter of the electron beam is so large that having higher deflection resolution improves the appearance of

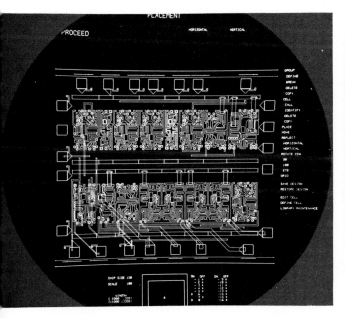

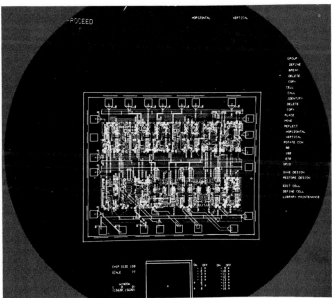

integrated circuits. This circuit will be 150 mils on a side and contain a total of 16 "cells" of seven different types. The pattern in frame 1 is a mask that specifies the location of metal interconnections in a logic cell containing 13 diodes and transistors. In designing the pattern the operator uses a light pen to indicate the two end points of a line segment and the display program automatically completes the line. The pen is also used to move elements around. In this frame the ultimate cell is magnified 308 diameters. In frame 2, at lower magnification (77 diameters), a variety of cells are being summoned up from memory and are being moved into position with the help of grid points. In frame 3 the routing for one level of metal interconnections is being added. In frame 4 the job is done.

the picture only slightly. Recently, however, workers at the Bell Telephone Laboratories have built a device that uses a very fine laser beam to produce computer-controlled film images with a resolution of 32,000 lines and 26,000 columns. The device is being used to make high-resolution circuit masks [see top illustration on pages 58 and 59].

Although modern calligraphic displays have the ability to post dots, straight lines and text, the earliest display systems could post only individual dots on the screen. The computer specified the x and y coordinate for each dot to be posted. The coordinate specifications were converted from digital form to analogue voltages, which were then amplified to drive the deflection system of the cathode ray tube [see top illustration on page 57]. After the transients in the conversion process and the deflection system had subsided, the electron beam was turned on for a microsecond or so to plot the indicated dot. Characters and lines could be built out of individual dots, but of course not very quickly.

To speed up the process of drawing lines and characters, special analogue circuits have been developed that automatically trace outlines on the screen in a continuous process. To post a character the character-generator circuit produces a wave form for the x and y deflection systems and an associated pattern for turning the beam on and off; the two combined cause the character to appear

[see bottom illustration on page 57]. To post a straight line on the screen, the analogue line generator will produce coordinated "ramp" wave forms for the x and y deflection systems so that the electron beam moves smoothly and continuously from one end of the straight line to the other. Modern display systems can produce characters in about five microseconds each and straight lines in three to 40 microseconds, depending on length. Some display systems include analogue equipment for producing simple curves, such as circles, automatically, but such facilities are still rare.

To produce a straight line all the way across a display screen in 40 microseconds is a prodigious feat of electrical engineering. The human eye has a remarkable ability to detect even slight deviations from straightness. Moreover, if two lines are plotted end to plot, any error in their length such as might be produced by overshooting or a failure of the electron beam to be turned on promptly will show up either as an overlap or as a gap in the lines. The lines must be traced not only straight but also at a constant rate because any change in the beam's rate of motion will show up as a change in the brightness of the line. To be sure, one can compensate for changes in the writing rate of the line by changing the electron-beam current, but such a compensation circuit must be accurate or discrepancies will be visible. No display system that I know of is en-

tirely satisfactory in performance, and even the best need periodic tuning to keep operating well. Considering the difficulty of the task, it is amazing that the systems work at all.

The Logic of Displays

In addition to the analogue circuits for generating lines and characters, a computer-display system must incorporate digital logic circuits to connect the display to the computer. Because the logic needed for this purpose often has characteristics in common with the processing unit of a computer, I have come to call these digital circuits the display processor. The display processor fetches information from a memory where the picture to be posted is defined and converts it to the elementary driving signals for the analogue circuits that generate lines and characters.

The display processor interprets different formats of information in the memory to give them meaning in terms of the picture produced. For example, it may interpret sequences of characters to produce rows of text on the screen, or it may distinguish sequences of connected line segments from isolated line segments, in each case producing the individual commands required by the analogue line generator to yield the desired picture. The display processor accounts for more than half of the cost of many display systems and strongly af-

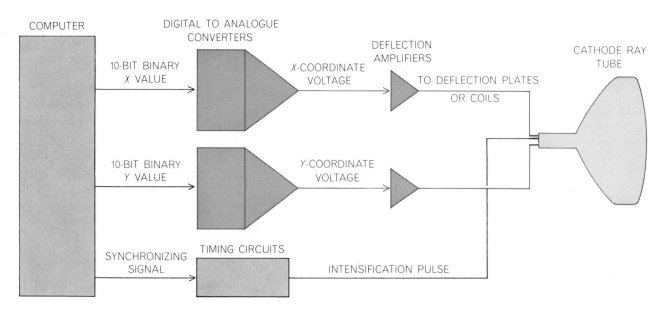

COMPUTER DISPLAY EQUIPMENT consists basically of a digital computer, which specifies the point-by-point coordinates of the desired display, together with circuits that convert the digital output into analogue form for deflecting the electron beam in a cathode ray tube. If the values of x and y are each specified by 10 binary digits (0's and 1's), the electron beam can be directed to any point in an array consisting of 1,024 lines (the y axis) and 1,024 points per line (the x axis). With only the circuits shown here, the image on the screen would have to be built up from discrete points. More modern displays include analogue function generators to sweep the electron beam in a continuous fashion to generate smooth lines, numbers, letters of the alphabet and special symbols.

fects the programming techniques that must be used with the system. Moreover, not much progress has been made in standardizing the design of display processors. For these reasons prospective users must carefully weigh the characteristics of competitive systems.

For the past six or seven years my own professional interest has been in improving the design of display processors. My colleagues and I have designed or influenced the design of a series of display processors of increasing complexity. Although we know that the evolution of display-processor design is far from complete, we have learned much about how the design of a display processor interacts with the programming requirements for the display system. Like computer systems themselves, displays require a great deal of programming to make them useful; enlightened display-processor design simplifies the programming task.

The objective of most computer-graphics programs is easily stated: to represent objects of some kind and to provide a means for manipulating them. For example, if one is designing the mask for an integrated electronic circuit, the objects to be represented are the transistors, resistors, gates, wiring and other elementary components from which the circuit is to be built. In depicting an organic molecule the objects to be represented are the individual atoms of the molecule and the bonds between them. In each application the objects are represented in the memory of the computer in a format suitable to the application. For instance, it may be convenient to list the atoms one after another in a table, giving the type and the three-dimensional coordinates for each atom. It may be convenient to represent the bonds by listing each bond in a table with the index numbers of the two atoms it joins. Such a storage format is convenient not only for display but also for the scientific programs that will manipulate this "data base."

The data base for a computer-display application is utilized in many ways. If the user wants to change the program he is working on, he may give commands that cause the computer to change the data base by replacing, adding or deleting information. Thus the user might add a new atom to his molecule. If he is exploring some line of thought, he may ask that computations be done on the data base. For example, the computer might compute the total weight of the molecule represented, or it might compute new coordinates for the atoms corresponding to some quantum-mechanical law the user is trying to understand. Finally, the user

will want to see some pictorial representation of the data base on his computer-display system. It is important to note that the pictorial representation of the information in the data base is only one of many ways the information is used.

The Data behind the Display

The format of the information in the data base is not usually suitable for direct use by the display processor. The data base represents all the relevant facts about the objects being considered, whereas the display processor needs information about the particular appearance of the objects. For instance, the data base may distinguish among different types of chemical bond, all of which look the same on the display. Or the data base may identify different kinds of atoms according to their atomic number, whereas in the display they are

to be presented with a different code letter, such as C or H or N. The appearance of the objects can be derived from the data base by a suitable program and stored for use by the display processor. The results of this computation form a "display file" [*see bottom illustration on next page*]. The display file is a secondary representation of the objects stored in the data base.

Conversion of the information from the data base to the display file involves geometric computation, selection of the relevant information and expansion of compact notations into individual lines and characters for display. Thus the two-dimensional coordinates required to make a perspective presentation of the molecule from a selected viewpoint might be computed from the three-dimensional coordinates known for each atom. If a magnified view of some portion of the object is desired, it can be

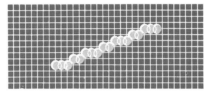 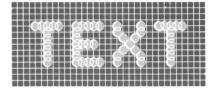

DOT-BY-DOT method of generating lines and characters was originally used in computer graphics. Newer analogue techniques are much faster and create cleaner images (*see below*).

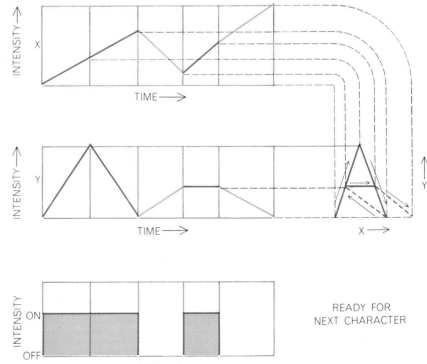

ANALOGUE CHARACTER GENERATOR produces separate wave forms for the *x* and *y* deflections of the electron beam, along with an on-off intensity pattern. Such display systems can write a character in a few microseconds and a page of text in several milliseconds.

HIGH-RESOLUTION LASER BEAM produced this test pattern using a new computer-display technique developed by the Bell Telephone Laboratories. One-third of the 15-by-21-centimeter test pattern is reproduced here actual size. Normally the device is used to make masks for integrated circuits. Modulators and lenses control the fine beam of an argon laser, which is deflected to scan a photographic plate by a 10-sided mirror rotating on air bearings. The laser beam produces an image consisting of 32,000 scan lines with 26,000 image points per line. The accuracy of the beam can be controlled to better than one arc second, equivalent to a deviation of less than a third of an inch in a line a mile long. Not only is the device extraordinarily accurate but also it can produce

provided by geometric scaling as the display file is prepared. Particular items of information in the data base can be selected for display or omitted entirely. For example, it may be desirable to omit from the picture all hydrogen atoms and all bonds connected to them so that the heavier part of the molecule can be seen more clearly. Finally, the compact notations of the data base can be expanded into appropriate symbols on the screen. Each atom might be converted into a circle with a letter in it; each bond might be converted into a pair of lines (in perspective, if that is desired).

It has long been recognized that the dual representation commonly used in display applications—the data base and the display file—leads to a complex program. In many display systems the user can point to an object of interest on the screen by using a light pen, a device that identifies a specific point on the screen by producing a brief pulse when the electron beam sweeps past that point. This tells the computer that some object in the display file is to be changed. The

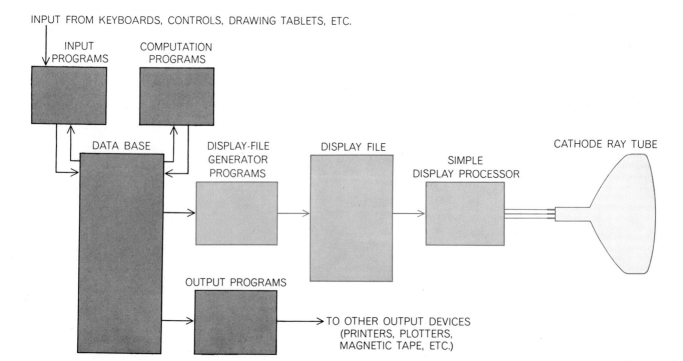

TYPICAL PROGRAM STRUCTURE for computer displays has the form shown here. Information about objects is stored in the data base. Information about the appearance of the objects is stored in the display file. The actual appearance of the objects is specified by programs in the display-file generator. These programs perform geometric operations and expand the definition of objects.

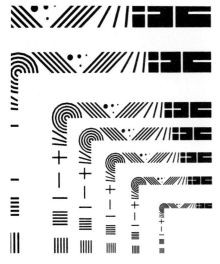

in 12 minutes a circuit mask that formerly took 12 hours of machine time. A portion of the test pattern is enlarged 10 diameters at the right. The effective resolution exceeds 40 lines per millimeter, which is remarkable over a field measuring 15 by 21 centimeters.

computer must somehow be able to relate each item in the display file to the item in the data base that caused it to appear.

If, having identified the item in the data base, the computer is instructed to change it, the computer must then also change the relevant parts of the display file. If the display picture is to be kept up to date so that changes appear promptly after they are initiated, computation of the display file must be done quickly. Unfortunately general-purpose digital computers are not well suited to this kind of geometric computation. For all these reasons designers of display processors have begun to provide more computing capability in the display processor to enable it to interpret the data base directly, thus eliminating the need for a display file altogether [see illustration below]. If the design is successful, changes in the data base will instantly be reflected in the picture and an identification of a part of the picture will instantly identify the corresponding item in the data base. Specialized display processors designed to handle such graphical computations are now beginning to reach the market.

An early innovation in display processors, now almost universal, provided them with the ability to display many symbols from a single symbol definition in memory. With this capability the display file can contain a single definition of a transistor symbol and several references to that symbol's definition. For each reference the display processor fetches the individual lines of the symbol from the single definition and traces the transistor symbol again in a different position on the display screen [see "a" in illustration on page 68]. Obviously all coordinate information in the symbol is stored with respect to the location of the symbol, and the location for the symbol must be established before the symbol definition is called on. This symbol capability in display processors is identical with the subroutine capability found in all general-purpose computers. Like the subroutine capability, it makes possible more compact coding because many symbols can be created from a single definition.

Unfortunately including subroutine capability in the display processor tends to introduce new complexities in the display programming. A display processor capable of handling subroutines must remember during the execution of each subroutine the location of its call; if the display file is changed, such information may be lost. Moreover, the number of parameters that can be provided to display subroutines is generally limited to a simple indication of position. Symbols of different sizes must have different definitions in the display file even though the size of an object may be represented in generalized form in the data base. The display file for a processor equipped for subroutining takes on a structure that may correspond in part, but not entirely, to the structure of the data base, and the display-programming system has to decide when to call on this structure. The subroutining capabilities in the display processor prove most useful when the structure that the display processor can interpret is sufficiently rich to represent everything wanted in the data base. If the symbol parameters available in the subroutining capability cannot handle the variability of the symbols represented in the data base, it is often not worth the effort of using the subroutining capability at all.

The fact that information in display subroutines can be specified with respect to a symbol origin makes it possible to specify a position that is outside the boundary of the display screen. Unfortunately a capacity of only 10 or 12 "bits" of information is usually provided in the memory registers that hold the screen coordinates. Thus if the displacement of an image produces values that lie outside the screen, those values will be truncated to the required 10 or 12 bits by the removal of the most significant parts of the sum.

The "Windowing" Problem

The effect of such truncation is that the coordinate positions immediately beyond the right edge of the screen appear at the left edge of the screen, and

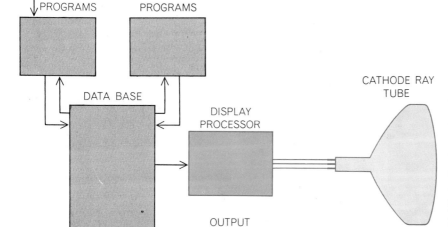

ADVANCED DISPLAY PROCESSOR eliminates the display file and display-file generator by providing more powerful computation and selection functions. This simplifies programming by eliminating elaborate cross-references between the data base and the display file.

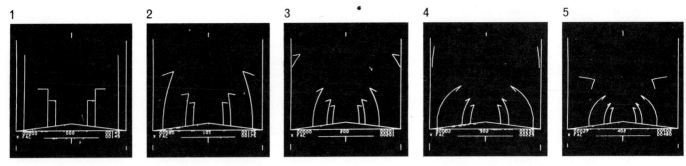

RIDE IN "ROCKET CAR" down a "country road" was programmed by a group under Judah L. Schwartz at the Massachusetts Institute of Technology, which has found computer displays valuable in demonstrating abstruse physical phenomena. The road is lined with telephone poles shaped like inverted *L*'s. The middle number under the picture shows the rocket's velocity as a decimal fraction of the velocity of light (the decimal point before the first digit is omitted). The number at bottom left of the screen is the number of telephone poles passed. The upper number at bottom right is the reading of clocks by the side of the road; the lower number shows the time aboard the rocket. The rocket-borne clock shows a lower cumulative reading than the roadside clocks do.

the coordinate positions just above the top of the screen appear at the bottom of the screen. Symbols that overlap an edge of the screen will reappear at the opposite edge. Consequently if screen coordinates are merely truncated to 10 or 12 bits, the screen will appear to have the topology of a torus. The phenomenon is particularly annoying if one end of a short line moves off the edge of the screen only to reappear at the other edge. The line between such end points will cross the entire screen going in the wrong direction.

The cures for these well-known difficulties all provide the display user with a drawing area much larger than the actual display screen. By one means or another the display tube is made to behave as if it were a window through which this much larger drawing can be seen. The computations involved in providing this illusion are called windowing.

When properly provided, windowing seems to be a natural part of the way the display operates. Objects that move off the screen disappear smoothly at a well-defined edge. Only when windowing is missing from a computer-display system is the absence of this feature immediately evident.

There are two basic methods of windowing. One method is to provide the display system with larger analogue deflection voltages than are needed for covering the screen itself and simply to blank out the beam anytime it is deflected beyond the edge of the screen. This procedure, although it is widely used, has the shortcoming that it places an additional burden of accuracy on the analogue deflection system and that it must of necessity operate slowly, since there is no way to speed up the beam when it is drawing parts of the picture outside the viewing area. The second

method of windowing is to provide a mechanism to precompute digitally the actual coordinates of the part of the picture that should appear in the window. In this method the display tube is provided only with valid data and so does not waste time drawing invisible parts of pictures. This alternative, often called clipping, is widely programmed in software for sophisticated computer-graphics systems.

Windowing is the most important of several kinds of geometric computation needed in preparing information for presentation on a display screen. Unfortunately the programs required for windowing in an ordinary general-purpose digital computer, even a big and fast one, can process only about 1,000 line segments per second. If additional computations are needed, for instance to present a two-dimensional perspective view of a three-dimensional object, the opera-

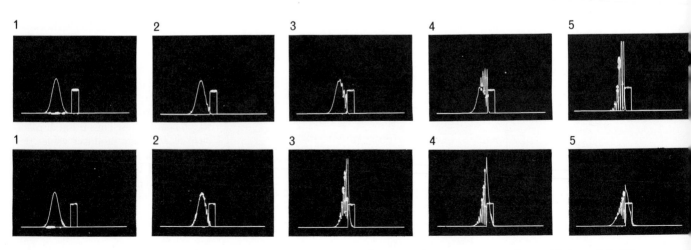

QUANTUM-MECHANICAL SCATTERING, representing what happens when a particle of given energy meets a barrier, is depicted in these M.I.T. computer displays. The particle is represented by a Gaussian curve, or wave packet, which is the probability distribution for finding a particle, such as a proton, in a given region of space. In the upper sequence the particle has only half the energy needed to pass through a square barrier. Nevertheless, at the peak of the collision (*frames 5, 6*) the wave packet penetrates the barrier, thereby indicating a finite probability for finding the particle in a region that should be inaccessible to it according to

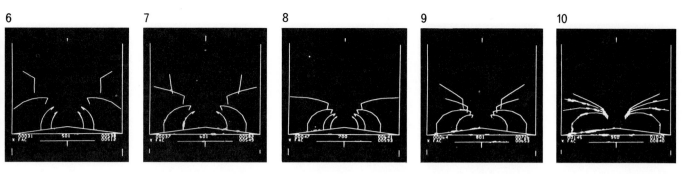

demonstrating the dilation of time experienced by objects (and observers) traveling at a large fraction of the velocity of light. As the rocket car accelerates, the telephone poles appear to bend over the road, as viewed by an observer in the car. Actually they are leaning away from the observer because the tops of the poles are farther away from him than the bottoms of the poles and thus light from the tops takes slightly longer to reach his eye. Therefore he sees the top of each pole at an earlier point in time, hence farther down the road, than the bottom of the pole. The horizontal members atop the poles appear to rotate away from the observer and finally to bend down. This is a more complicated result of the special theory of relativity and was not put into computer program.

tion takes substantially longer. Recently my colleagues and I have spent much time developing special display processors that overcome these delays by transferring the necessary computations to high-speed, special-purpose digital circuits. These processors make it easy to obtain rapid, dynamically changing views of three-dimensional objects [*see top illustration on next two pages*].

I became involved in the development of such high-speed displays through a desire to present an observer with a simulated three-dimensional environment. My idea was very simple: Mount miniature cathode ray tubes on the user's head, one tube in front of each eye, so that the computer can control exactly what he sees. Measure the position of the user's head and compute a perspective picture appropriate to that viewing position. As the user turns his head, the perspective picture should change just as if the object portrayed were really in the room with him. There is no need to measure his eye position because the picture presented on his glasses is not changed by the part of it on which he chooses to focus. Because the three-dimensional objects he sees will appear to remain stationary in space as he moves around them, an illusion that the objects are present in the room with the observer should be created. The equipment illustrated at the bottom of the following page was designed to create this illusion.

The head-mounted display does indeed provide the illusion of seeing three-dimensional objects at identifiable locations in the user's environment. Because the objects presented are transparent and made of glowing lines essentially free of texture, no one is fooled into thinking they are real. On the other hand, even naïve observers are able to identify the size of the objects portrayed and are able to move themselves into an appropriate viewing position to examine a particular feature of the objects portrayed.

Logic of High-Speed Displays

The significant thing about the head-mounted display project is not the operational results but rather that it forced us to think carefully about the problems of presenting a real-time perspective picture. We needed a solution to the windowing problem in three dimensions because as the user turns his head away from objects they move out of the field of view provided by the optical system. If the objects are to move smoothly out of view, the correct end points for the parts still in view must be very rapidly computed, and prompt decisions must be made in order to omit parts that are entirely out of view. Since no general-purpose digital computer is capable of

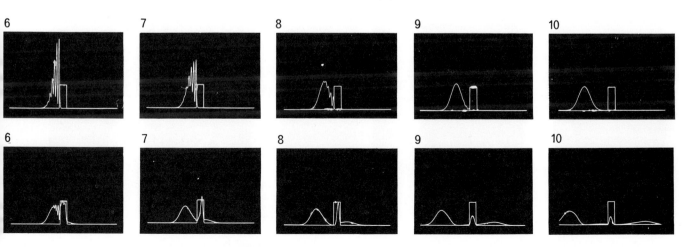

the pre-quantum-mechanical description of nature. Subsequently the packet is reflected and the probability distribution is flattened. In the lower sequence the energy of the wave packet is exactly equal to the barrier height. In classical physics the particle should lose all its energy on entering the barrier and remain there forever. In quantum physics a small probability packet gets temporarily trapped inside the barrier (*frames 7, 8, 9, 10*) while most of the packet is reflected. In addition a small, flat packet is transmitted. This indicates the probability of a particle's "tunneling" through the barrier when the experiment is repeated many times.

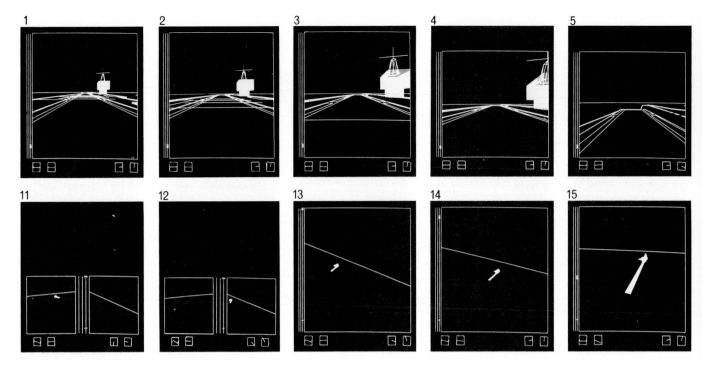

TAKEOFF AND LANDING ON AIRCRAFT CARRIER have been simulated by the Evans & Sutherland Computer Corporation for the Naval Training Device Center. The display system used for this demonstration is installed at Bolt, Beranek and Newman Inc. It follows the design illustrated at the bottom of page 59, in which circuit hardware in the display processor replaces a "software" program for handling information stored in the data base. Only such a system provides the computing speed needed for this kind of real-time simulation in which two complex objects are moving rapidly in three-dimensional space. Frame 1 shows what the "pilot" sees looking down the deck before takeoff. Through a keyboard on the computer he can adjust the engine throttle and the attitude of the aircraft. At the left of the screen is a vertical line with a cross that indicates the aircraft's altitude. The two boxes at the bottom right

doing these computations fast enough to present dynamic views of any but the most trivial objects, we were forced to design and build special-purpose equipment to do rotation, windowing and perspective computation. Having a good solution to the windowing problem in three dimensions quickly led us to a solution in two dimensions for our latest design for a display processor.

Computing a perspective picture of a "wire frame" three-dimensional object is really rather easy. The position of each part of the object on the screen is computed by projecting the object onto the screen in straight lines [*see the illustration on page 65*]. Fortunately straight lines in three-dimensional space project into straight lines on the screen. Thus the rotation and projection computations for each line segment need be done only for

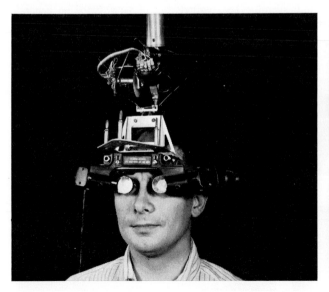

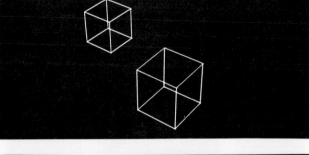

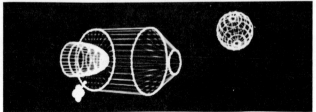

HEAD-MOUNTED DISPLAY at the University of Utah employs a display processor similar to that used for the aircraft carrier sequence. Two miniature cathode ray tubes are built into the goggles. A mechanical linkage tells the computer where the viewer is looking at each instant. The display processor instantaneously supplies the correct image for each head position. The viewer is free to look anywhere in a 360-degree circle and can look up and down through an angle of about 45 degrees. Two samples of what he sees are shown at the right. The objects grow larger or smaller and move with relation to one another as the observer moves around.

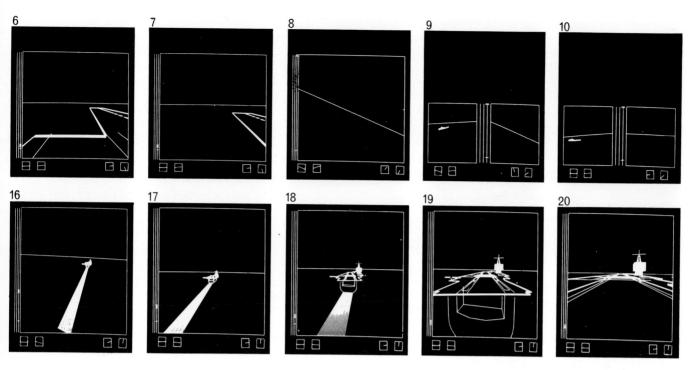

of the screen indicate the aircraft's compass heading (east at take-off) and the direction to the carrier's superstructure. At bottom left are an artificial horizon and a rate-of-climb indicator. Frames 2 through 7 show the aircraft moving down the deck and becoming airborne. The pilot sees the horizon tilt (8) as he banks to the left. In the next four displays (9, 10, 11, 12) the view from the left window of the aircraft is shown on the left half of the screen while the view ahead appears on the right half. Ordinarily the two windows are on separate screens in their normal relation to the pilot. As the pilot continues to bank, the carrier disappears from the left window and reappears in the front window (12, 13). Still flying counterclockwise in a large circle, assisted by being able to see the carrier's wake, the pilot lines up the carrier for his approach (14, 15, 16, 17), and then finally levels off for a perfect landing (18, 19, 20).

the ends of the line; the center parts of the line can be filled in by the two-dimensional analogue line generator. If windowing or clipping in three dimensions is done before projection, the problems of dividing by a zero or a negative depth coordinate are avoided [see the illustration on page 66]. The digital processing equipment we developed for the head-mounted display project is able to accept information in three dimensions, convert it to an appropriate viewpoint and viewing direction and present valid display-screen coordinates to an ordinary line generator for drawing a perspective picture on the screen.

We have found it particularly useful to have a display system in which a three-dimensional computing engine is built into the display processor. In the first place, coordinate information for display can be in three dimensions instead of in two. Symbols can be scaled on the drawing as well as merely being positioned, and three-dimensional symbols can be rotated to any desired angle with respect to other objects in the drawing. Since clipping is done in the display processor, the processor can accept the stored data to a resolution much finer than the actual resolution of the display itself. Such data can be regarded as a drawing on a huge piece of paper (a piece covering a square

mile, say), any part of which, or all of which, can be presented on the display screen. For many applications such capabilities can eliminate the need for a display file altogether and so greatly simplify the programming of the display. Again our hope is to operate the display processor directly on the data base so that changes in the data base are instantly reflected in the display.

To provide for flexibility in the format of the data bases, we have chosen four typical forms in which information commonly appears in applications [see illustration on page 68]. In the first form a sequence of coordinate values is simply connected by a sequence of straight lines. This form is the common one for connecting data points on a graph. In the second form disjoint lines are represented by pairs of pointers that indicate the location of the coordinate data to be used for the end points. This format would be useful for representing the bonds in a molecule. The coordinates can be either two- or three-dimensional. The disjoint-line format is useful in a variety of pictorial representations.

The third form is the simple subroutine, where standard format parameters for position, size and rotation are provided. For all fixed-geometry symbols, such as those used in making circuit

diagrams, this form is adequate. We have also designed the display processor so that it does not execute any subroutine that is entirely outside the viewing area. This provision greatly speeds up the display of magnified views of complex objects. Finally, complete subroutines are available for displaying objects that are similar in a nongeometric way. For example, cross-hatched boxes can be defined by position, size and type of cross-hatching. Such boxes are not geometrically similar because the number of cross-hatch lines must be computed from the size of the box; moreover, the angle of the cross-hatching must be constant regardless of the size or orientation of the box.

The Hidden-Surface Problem

In spite of the advances that have been made in computer graphics in the past decade, most of the objects displayed are still in the form of line drawings. It is difficult to present solid objects with today's computer displays; indeed, only half a dozen research installations even try. The preliminary efforts are nonetheless rewarding. The difficulty is in computing what parts of an object are visible from a given viewing position and what parts are not. If an object repre-

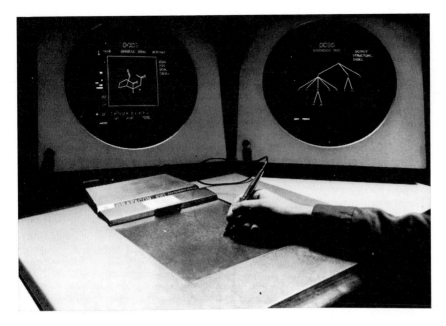

COMPUTER-AIDED CHEMICAL SYNTHESIS program was developed at Harvard University by W. Todd Wipke under the direction of Elias J. Corey. The computer is supplied with a library of chemical compounds and chemical reactions, together with a program for manipulating this information. By interacting with the computer the chemist can select the most efficient way to synthesize a desired compound. The chemist starts his "conversation" with the computer by drawing the structure of the target molecule on a writing tablet. The tablet contains a coordinate grid that relays the position of the pen to the display screen. Here a molecule related to the target molecule appears on the screen at the left, while the screen at right displays a variety of chemical pathways to the target in the form of a "tree." The development of these displays is depicted in the pictures at bottom of these two pages.

sented in three dimensions is to be rendered as being solid, some parts of the object must be able to obscure other parts hidden behind it. Many workers have tackled this "hidden-surface problem," and in the past few years several interesting solutions have been developed.

The effectiveness of a solution to the hidden-surface problem can best be described in terms of the growth of the solution time with the complexity of the situation. Almost any method will work adequately with very simple situations, but because the computation time required by some methods grows with the square of the situation complexity, much computation time may be required for complex situations. Four years ago I showed in *Scientific American* a computer-drawn picture of a solid object produced by Lawrence G. Roberts, which was typical of the best then available [see the article "Computer Inputs and Outputs," by Ivan E. Sutherland, beginning on page 42]. His program took 1.5 minutes to draw a picture containing 40 separate blocks from which hidden lines had been removed; the computing time was roughly proportional to the square of the number of objects examined. Today general-pur-

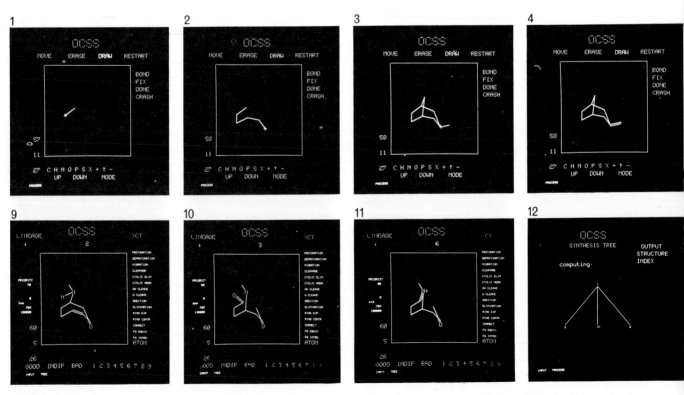

CHEMICAL SYNTHESIS PROBLEM is presented to a venerable PDP-1 computer at Harvard by a chemist who uses a writing tablet to draw a picture of the molecule he wants to make. By frame 3 he has drawn the basic structure of a molecule with eight carbon atoms. He adds a double bond at the extreme right of the molecule (*frame 4*), then bends the bond into the proper stereochemical configuration (5, 6). Addition of an oxygen atom (*O*), a nitrogen atom

(*N*) and another carbon atom (*indicated by the line projecting from the nitrogen*) completes the skeleton structure of the target molecule: longifolene (7). The computer is now asked to search for somewhat simpler compounds that can be converted to longifolene in a single chemical step. The result of the search is shown by the tree in frame 8. Longifolene is designated by the 1 at the top of the tree; three related compounds, designated 2, 3 and 6, are

pose computers of not much greater power can produce pictures such as those shown on page 67 in about a third of the time, and the growth law of these programs appears to be about $N \log N$, where N is the number of objects.

The traditional approach to the hidden-surface problem was to compare each object in the picture with every other object to see which was obscured. This procedure requires $N - 1$ comparisons for the first object, $N - 2$ for the second object, $N - 3$ for the third object, and so on, for a total of $(N^2 - N) \div 2$ comparisons. Moreover, the computations must be executed in three dimensions with high precision because they are done before projection onto the screen. The new methods consider only the task of computing the picture rather than the task of comparing objects. If a picture of the television type is to be produced, there are, after all, only some 250,000 points on the television screen at which intensities can be displayed. Why bother to compute to any better precision than that?

The most elegant, although perhaps not the fastest, algorithm to date is one invented by John Warnock of the University of Utah and somewhat embel-

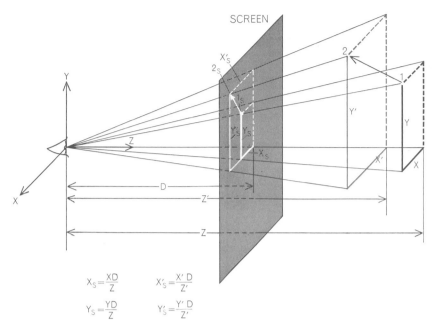

$$X_S = \frac{XD}{Z} \qquad X'_S = \frac{X'D}{Z'}$$

$$Y_S = \frac{YD}{Z} \qquad Y'_S = \frac{Y'D}{Z'}$$

PERSPECTIVE PROJECTION for a computer display is obtained by placing the origin of the coordinate system at the observer's eye. The projection of all points on the screen is then readily computed from the geometry of similar triangles. The diagram shows how the two end points, *1* and *2*, of an arrow are projected to the points 1_s and 2_s. The first equation states that x_s is to x as the distance to the screen, D, is to z. Other dimensions are obtained similarly. Objects extending beyond screen must be "clipped," as shown on page 66.

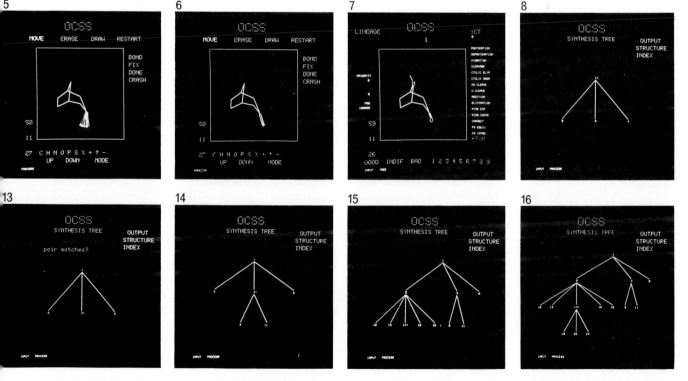

listed at the ends of the branches of the tree. The chemist asks to see the structures of these three molecules and they are presented to him in frames 9, 10 and 11, together with coded information at the left of the screen that describes the chemical reaction that will convert each to longifolene. The computer also evaluates each reaction and assigns a priority, or preference. The computer is then asked to find related compounds that can be converted into com-

pound No. 3. While the search proceeds the computer can be asked what it is "thinking." The words "Computing" (*frame 12*) and "Pair matches?" (*frame 13*) appear on the screen. The last remark indicates the computer is puzzled whether a particular molecular structure is identical with another one. Two routes to compound No. 3 appear in frame 14 and five routes to compound No. 2 appear in frame 15. In the last frame the search is carried still deeper.

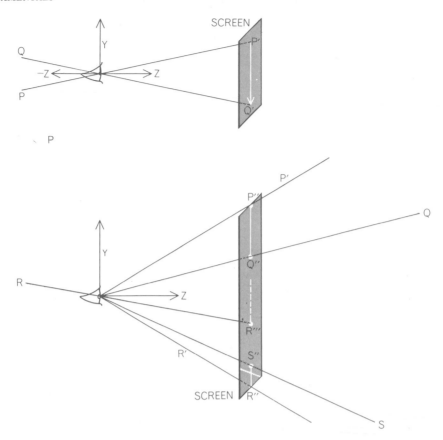

"CLIPPING," OR "WINDOWING," PROBLEM arises when objects in real space extend beyond the limits of the screen or lie behind the observer. In the latter case (*see top part of illustration*) z has a negative value. Although the equations are correct for such points, the result would be to project the object upside down. The problem can be avoided (*see bottom part of illustration*) if all lines are first clipped off at planes defined by the edges of the screen. If one applied the usual equations to the point P, numerical overflow would result. Point R in the line RS would project to point R''', and points close to R would project upward on the screen. By proper windowing, or clipping, the line P'Q appears on the screen correctly as P''Q'' and R'S appears as R''S''.

lished by others (including myself). Warnock's algorithm concentrates on computing shades for parts of the screen, and also on computing shades for as large an area as is possible at one time. I shall describe Warnock's algorithm in some detail not only because it shows much ingenuity in the solution of a difficult problem in computer graphics but also because it utilizes a particularly appealing technique of computation.

Data for Warnock's algorithm are defined in terms of a collection of surfaces that form the objects to be shown. The simplest computations result if these surfaces are planes bounded by straight lines, but the algorithm could be applied to more complex surfaces. Each surface is assigned a color and a shade, and each surface is considered to be opaque. Rotation and translation are used to get the surfaces into the observer's coordinate system, and a perspective division is performed to position the objects on the screen. Depth

information is preserved through the perspective projection.

Warnock's program now breaks the screen up into a few subregions and applies a standard procedure to each one. The standard procedure is to sort all surfaces by x and y position to determine whether they are entirely outside the subregion, surround it or partially intersect it. This sorting is done by first considering gross measures of the surface's position (such as: Is its leftmost point to the right of the subregion?) and then considering, if necessary, the individual edges of the surface. Obviously surfaces that are outside the subregion need not be considered further. The algorithm then considers the surfaces that surround or intersect the region and attempts to prove that certain of them are hidden by others. For example, if a surrounding surface can be shown to be in front of all other surfaces throughout the region, all the other surfaces are eliminated and the program can shade

the entire region according to the shade of that surface. If there is only a single edge in the subregion, perhaps the program can fill in the appropriate pair of shades.

The important thing about Warnock's algorithm is its response to a subregion in which the situation is too complicated to handle. In such cases the algorithm simply subdivides the subregion into smaller regions. The sorting task for a subdivided region is simpler than it was for its predecessor because all surfaces that surrounded the predecessor will surround any of its subdivisions, and all surfaces that were found to lie off to the side of the predecessor will also lie to the side of its subdivisions. Only those surfaces that partially intersected the predecessor region have to be considered in dealing with its successor regions. Thus the number of surfaces to be considered in each subregion becomes quite small as the area of the subregion decreases. If the situation in a subregion of the

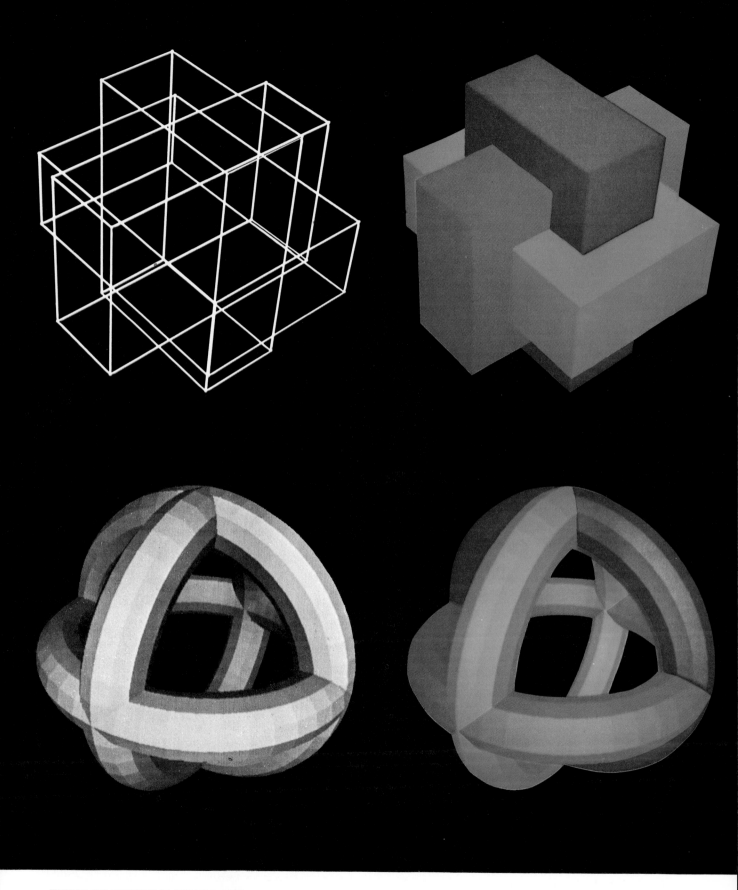

THREE-DIMENSIONAL STRUCTURES were created by a computer using programs developed by Gary Watkins, a graduate student at the University of Utah. The simple "wire frame" version of the interlocking blocks (*top left*) is readily produced because no effort is made to remove hidden lines. By using special programs, however, the hidden lines can be identified and the structure can be displayed as a solid (*top right*). In this case the electron beam in the display tube generates surfaces by a raster technique, point by point and line by line: the entire process takes about a minute per image. To make pictures in color three different black-and-white images are created on the screen, one for each primary color, and then photographed through filters on color film. As the two pictures at the bottom demonstrate, the computer program can also create highlights, as if the pictures were taken with a flashbulb.

smallest possible size is too complex, the algorithm simply picks a shading rule from the nearest adjacent surface, because such a choice affects only a single point on the display screen.

Many varieties of the Warnock algorithm are possible, depending on how complex a situation the algorithm can handle without having to subdivide, and also on the method of subdivision. Warnock's own programs always divided regions into four equal parts and yielded an output only when the entire square was the same shade. The subdivision of such an algorithm is shown in the illustration at top left on page 69. A smarter display program, which avoids subdivision when there is only a single edge in view, will produce the subdivision pattern shown in the adjacent illustration on the same page. This program, of course, requires slightly more time for the computation of each square. Thus there is a trade-off between the complexity of the display program and the number of subareas that need to be considered. We are currently investigating this trade-off statistically in an attempt to discover what kind of algorithm may be the best.

The work of Gary Watkins and Gordon Romney of the University of Utah has developed some interesting statistics about the pictures we are drawing. The most significant and surprising fact is that the sorting task in the hidden-surface problem is not complicated in depth but is quite complicated laterally. The pictures shown in this article, although complicated, are not very deep. That is, if you penetrate the picture with a ray at any particular position, you will hit fewer than 10 surfaces in all but specially contrived cases, and the average number of surfaces struck is more nearly three. We have concluded that the problem in producing hidden-surface pictures of the type shown here is largely the problem of sorting the pictures in the x and y directions to discover those few surfaces for which a depth computation is required.

Once the hidden-surface problem is solved, shading and color are relatively easy to introduce. The hidden-surface computation develops information to tell which surface is visible at each point on the screen. Since each surface in the computer includes a color, as well as other properties, the program can compute precisely what hue, saturation and brightness to display. In the simplest pictures the surface is simply displayed in its appropriate color. It is only slightly more difficult to compute the shade, or brightness level, based on a two-part re-

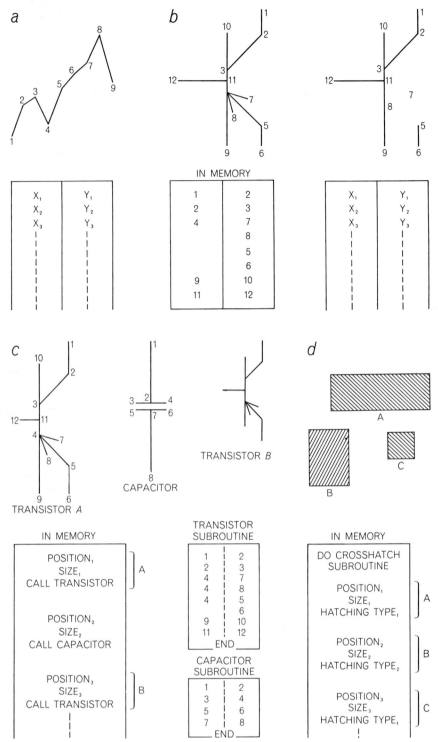

REPRESENTATION OF OBJECTS IN DATA BASE takes four principle forms. Line segments can be represented either as strings of connected coordinates (a) or as sets of disjoint lines, each connecting two coordinates (b). Once such linear displays have been created they can be stored in the memory for recall at any future time. The representation at the upper left in b is the symbol for a transistor. If point No. 4 were shifted downward by changing y_4, all the lines terminating at No. 4 would be shifted simultaneously without, however, destroying the topology. Another common representation (c) stores symbols of fixed geometry, such as elements for designing circuits. These can be called to the screen, placed in any desired location and scaled to any size. The record in the memory will then list "Position," "Size" and a code for calling the subroutine that draws the device. If the device is a transistor, the subroutine might read like the sequence of numbers in b. A capacitor will be called by its own subroutine. Another representation scheme (d) defines a class of objects that are similar in some simple but nongeometric way, such as hatched boxes.

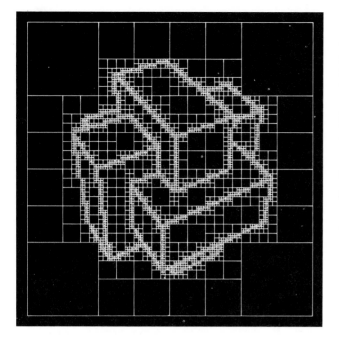

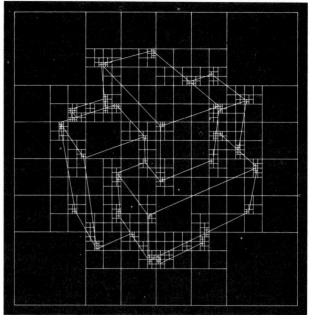

HIDDEN-SURFACE PROBLEM has been solved by special algorithms that answer the question: Which of several surfaces lies in front of all the others? It is no trick, for example, to have a computer draw transparent structures such as that shown at top left on page 67. The computer plots above represent algorithms for analyzing such a structure and removing hidden lines. The approach at the left, invented by John Warnock of the University of Utah, employs an algorithm that systematically divides the screen into subregions (in this case units of four) and applies a standard procedure to each one. All the surfaces that occur in a given subregion are sorted out and the subregion is divided, if necessary, to end up with only a single surface that lies in front of all others. The method is described more fully in the text. A similar algorithm, which often proves faster, is represented at the right. It avoids subdivision when only a single edge appears in any subregion. Improvements on these algorithms led to the "solid" figures on page 67.

flectance property: one part for diffuse reflectance and the other for specular reflectance. The photographic output routines can also compensate for the color sensitivity of the film used in photographing the display, so that the resulting prints come out exactly as desired. As a surface of a given color becomes more nearly perpendicular to the observer's line of sight, its specular reflectance dominates its diffuse reflectance and it becomes whiter as well as brighter. This effect can give objects a shiny appearance if much specular reflection is included, or a dull appearance if only the diffuse reflectance is used.

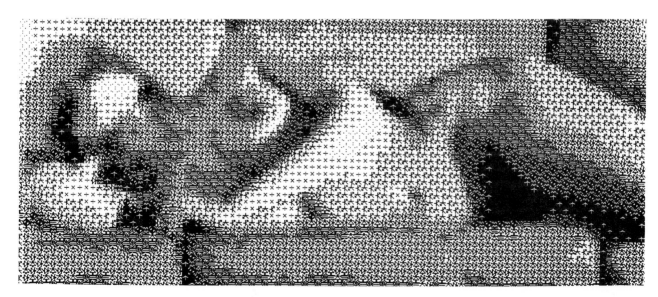

BELL LABORATORIES EXPERIMENT illustrates how a photograph can be analyzed by computer and then redrawn with arbitrary symbols. In this case the Greek letter "alpha" was used as a primary symbol to build up more complex patterns that range from very light to very dense in terms of average density per unit "cell." These cells were then assigned by a computer to match the point-by-point reflectivity of the photograph. Leon D. Harmon and Kenneth C. Knowlton did the experiment as a study in perception.

6

SYSTEM ANALYSIS AND PROGRAMMING

CHRISTOPHER STRACHEY
September, 1966

It is a profoundly erroneous truism, repeated by all copy-books and by eminent people when they are making speeches, that we should cultivate the habit of thinking of what we are doing. The precise opposite is the case. Civilization advances by extending the number of important operations which we can perform without thinking about them. Operations of thought are like cavalry charges in a battle—they are strictly limited in number, they require fresh horses, and must only be made at decisive moments.

—ALFRED NORTH WHITEHEAD

This article is about how to get a computer to do what you want, and why it almost always takes longer than you expect. What follows is not a detailed report on the state of the art of programming but an attempt to show how to set about writing a program. The process of writing a program is primarily intuitive rather than formal; hence we shall be more concerned with the guiding principles that underlie programming than with the particular language in which the program is to be presented to the machine.

We shall start with a specific example of a programming problem that is decidedly nontrivial and yet sufficiently simple to be understood without any previous knowledge of programming. I have chosen an unorthodox approach to the problem, one that will look strange to many professional programmers. This approach enables us to tackle an example that would be much too elaborate to explain otherwise.

Our problem is to program a computer to play checkers. How should we set about it? There are two main aspects to the problem. To equip the computer to deal with the game at all we must find a way to represent the board and positions on it and furnish the computer with a program for identifying legal moves and making them. This is a programming problem. Secondly, we must provide the machine with a method of selecting a suitable move from the ones available. This is mainly a problem in game-playing. Arthur L. Samuel of the International Business Machines Corporation has studied this game-playing aspect extensively and with considerable success [see the article "Artificial Intelligence," by Minsky, beginning on page 123]. Here, however, since we are concerned with programming rather than game-playing, we shall content ourselves with a simple general strategy and leave most of the details unsettled.

The usual approach to writing a program, particularly for a complex problem, divides the process into two stages. The first of these is called system analysis. It involves analyzing the task to decide exactly what needs to be done and adopting an overall plan. Once the general outline of the work to be performed has been decided on, the second stage is to write the required operations in a form suitable for the computer. This involves a large number of more detailed decisions (for example how information is to be represented in the machine and how the representations are to be stored). The detailed form of the program will depend on the particular computer to be used.

Confusion has developed about the naming of these two stages. Some programmers reserve the term "programming" for the second stage; others call the first stage "programming" and the second stage "coding"; still others use the term "programming" for the entire process—stages one and two. My own view is that the distinction between system analysis and programming is not a very useful one. If the system analysis were carried through to a description of the program outline in a slightly more rigorous language than is used at present, it should be possible to relegate the whole of the remaining process of producing a detailed program in machine language to the computer itself.

ORTHODOX APPROACH to the problem of writing a computer program is illustrated on the opposite page. The problem in this example is comparatively simple: to find the function e^x by summing the series $1 + x + x^2/2! + x^3/3! + \ldots$ until the terms become negligible. The process of writing a program to solve such a problem is usually divided into two stages. The first stage, sometimes called system analysis, involves analyzing the task to decide exactly what needs to be done and adopting an overall plan; this stage is represented by the block diagram at left. The second stage, called programming by some programmers and coding by others, involves writing the required operations in a form suitable for the computer. The problem in question is expressed in three different programming languages at right. The diamond-shaped box in the block diagram contains a "decision function"; the straight vertical lines before and after the word "term" signify "absolute value of," and the symbol $\ll$ means that "|term|" is negligible compared with "sum." In CPL (Combined Programming Language) the expression "value of" governs the immediately following statement; "repeat" governs the immediately preceding statement, and the symbols § and $ act as statement brackets. In both CPL and ALGOL the operator ":=" stands for assignment: the quantities on the right of this operator are evaluated and simultaneously assigned to the variables on the left. The symbol * in FORTRAN is a multiplication sign.

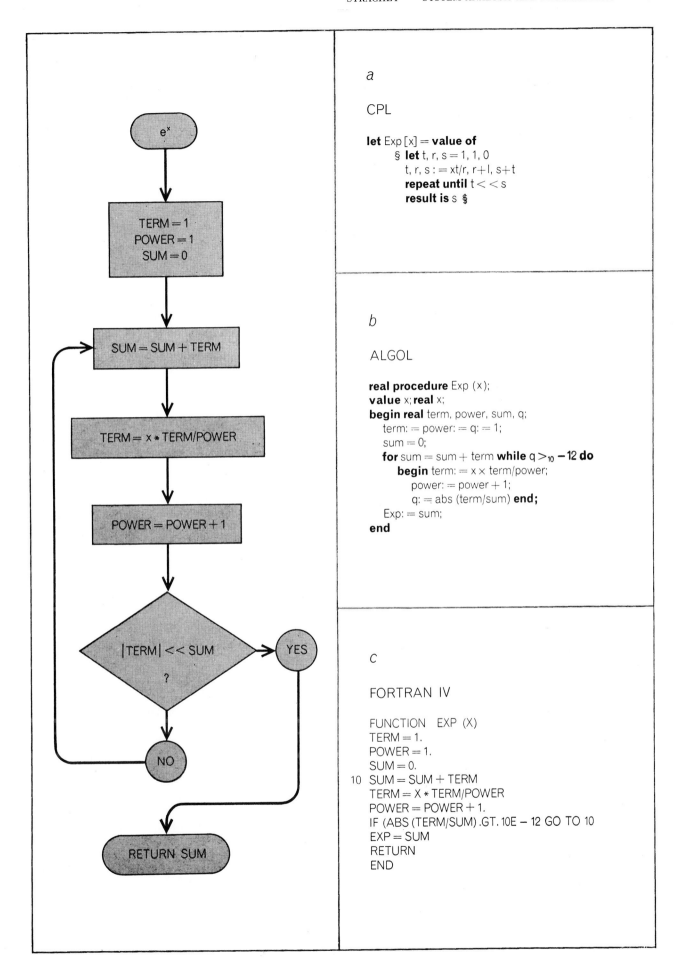

a

CPL

let Exp [x] = **value of**
  § **let** t, r, s = 1, 1, 0
    t, r, s : = xt/r, r+l, s+t
    repeat until t << s
    result is s §

b

ALGOL

real procedure Exp (x);
value x; **real** x;
begin real term, power, sum, q;
  term: = power: = q: = 1;
  sum = 0;
  for sum = sum + term **while** q >₁₀ − 12 **do**
    begin term: = x × term/power;
      power: = power + 1;
      q: = abs (term/sum) **end;**
  Exp: = sum;
end

c

FORTRAN IV

```
      FUNCTION   EXP (X)
      TERM = 1.
      POWER = 1.
      SUM = 0.
   10 SUM = SUM + TERM
      TERM = X * TERM/POWER
      POWER = POWER + 1.
      IF (ABS (TERM/SUM) .GT. 10E − 12 GO TO 10
      EXP = SUM
      RETURN
      END
```

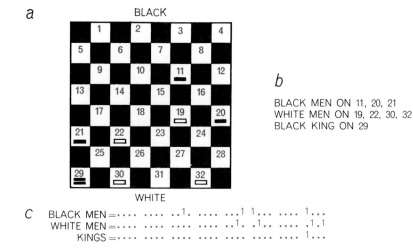

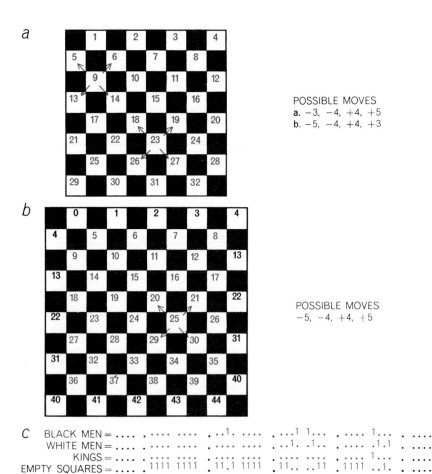

POSITIONS on a checkerboard can be represented in a computer in two different ways. To describe a particular position one has the choice of specifying either what is on each square (*a*) or where the pieces that are still in play are located (*b*). An equivalent alternative to *a* is given in *c*, which uses only binary numbers. Three binary digits, or "bits," are needed to specify each square: one to show the presence of a black man or king, another to show the presence of a white man or king and a third to show the presence of kings of either color.

MOVES on a checkerboard can be represented using the numbering scheme of an ordinary checkerboard (*a*), but this is inconvenient, as there are two kinds of squares (on alternate rows), which need different rules. Arthur L. Samuel of the International Business Machines Corporation devised a neat method of avoiding this difficulty. By extending the board with rows and columns that are not used and renumbering the squares, he produced a scheme in which the possible moves are similar for all squares on that part of the board which is actually used (*b*). The position shown at the top of this page is represented in this new scheme of notation in *c*. Empty squares are indicated by 1's for all the squares on the board proper.

Let us get on to the problem of programming a computer to play checkers against an opponent. How shall we represent the relevant features of the game, and what kind of operations do we want to be able to perform on them? A good working rule is to start with the operations and allow them to determine what it is you need to represent in the machine. In this case we clearly require, to begin with, representations of positions and moves and of the values associated with them.

We can approach the kind of precision the computer requires and still avoid getting bogged down in premature detail by using a functional notation. We let P stand for a position and agree to include in P not only the number and arrangement of the pieces on the board but also various other important facts such as which player is to move. The value of a position can be expressed by a function PositionValue(P). The value of any move (say M) obviously depends on the position from which it is made; therefore we must specify the position in writing the function MoveValue(M,P). Next, in order to be able to look ahead and examine the possible consequences of moves, the computer will need a third function: MakeMove(M,P), with P representing the position from which the move is made. The result of this function is the new position produced by the move. Finally, the program needs a fourth function to find all the legal moves that can be made from a given position: LegalMovesFrom(P). This function has as its result a list of moves.

These four functions, together with the two types of object (P and M), are sufficient to specify the kernel of our checkers program. There are two players in a game of checkers (in our case the machine and its opponent), and a position that is good for one will be bad for the other. We must therefore make our idea of the value of a position more precise by saying that PositionValue(P) gives the value of the position P to the player who has to move from it. We can plausibly assume that the value of the position P to the other player is the negative of this; that is, if the value of a position to one player is v, its value to the other will be $-v$. (This assumption is expressed in the terms of game theory by saying that checkers is a zero-sum game.)

Next we can define the value of a move to the player who makes it as the value *to him* of the resulting position. Suppose the result of making the move

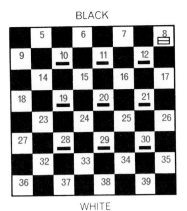

M from the position *P* is the position *P′*. Remembering that it is the opponent who has to make the move from *P′*, we can see that the value of the move *M* to the player who makes it will be −PositionValue(*P′*). Thus in our notation we can define the value of a move as follows: MoveValue(*M,P*) = −PositionValue[MakeMove(*M,P*)]. This formal statement could be paraphrased by saying that to value a move for yourself you make it, find the value of the resulting position to your opponent and change its sign.

How shall we find the value of a position? The basic procedure of the game is to explore all your possible moves and all possible replies by the opponent to some depth and evaluate the resulting positions. Let us call these "terminal" positions and say that their values are produced by the function TerminalValue(*P*). This function makes an immediate assessment of a position (in terms, perhaps, of such factors as the number of pieces still in play, their mobility, the command of the center of the board and so forth) without any further look-ahead. We can now say that if *P* is a terminal position, its value is TerminalValue(*P*), and that if it is not, its value is that of the best legal move that could be made from it. Note that the question of whether a position is terminal or not may depend not only on the position itself but also on what depth (*d*) the look-ahead has reached. This is necessary in order to put some limit on how far the machine looks ahead.

The definitions we have been writing are in fact circular (for example, the definition of PositionValue involves the use of MoveValue and vice versa), and the functions are called recursive, because each is defined in terms of the others. This circularity is no disadvantage; indeed, it makes it possible to start right in the middle of things, to set up a number of functions whose purpose is only intuitively understood at the beginning and to define each of them in terms of the others. This recursive, or hierarchical, approach to programming is by far the simplest method of handling complicated operations, since it allows them to be broken up into smaller units that can be considered separately.

We have now constructed a general game-playing scheme without having decided on either the details of the strategy or the structure of the game itself. We can complete the outline of our program by deciding on the representation of positions and moves and defining four functions. The functions Legal-

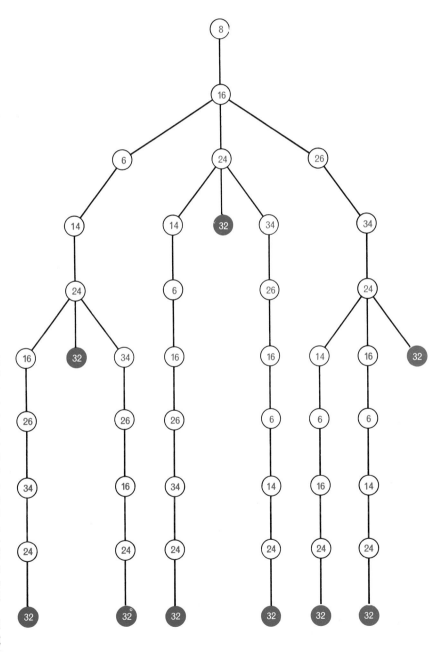

CAPTURE "TREE" depicts all the possible "partial capture moves" for a given piece after the first such move. In checkers a move is not complete until no more captures can be made. A maximum of nine captures in a single move is possible, as shown in this example. Capture-move situation, like that in the main game, can be programmed by using "recursive" functions, that is, functions that are defined in a circular manner in terms of other functions. Program for this situation is incorporated in the complete checkers program on page 75.

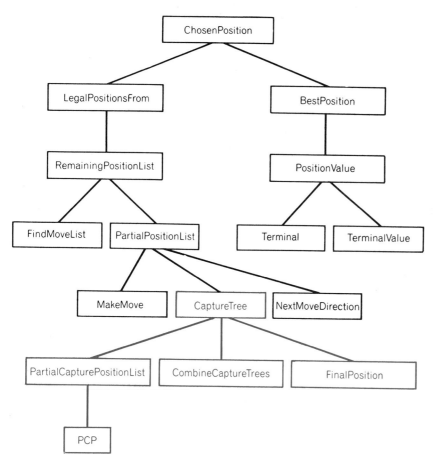

HIERARCHICAL STRUCTURE of the author's checkers program is evident in this diagram. Since there is a limit to the size and complexity of a problem one can keep in mind at one time, it appears that the best way to deal with large and complicated problems is to treat fairly sizable operations as separate units and then combine them hierarchically. The logical function "ChosenPosition" is defined recursively in terms of two other functions: "LegalPositionsFrom" and "BestPosition." The function "LegalPositionsFrom" deals with the problem of finding legal positions on the checkerboard at a given point in the game; all the functions that branch out from "LegalPositionsFrom" treat various aspects of this problem. The part of this major branch that deals with capture moves, for example, is in color. The function "BestPosition" and all the functions that branch out from it deal with the problem of choosing the best position from the list supplied by "LegalPositionsFrom."

When we come to a detailed consideration of the representation of moves, we find that the numbering of squares on the ordinary board is inconvenient because there are two kinds of squares (on alternate rows) that need different rules. Samuel devised a neat method of avoiding this difficulty. By extending the board with rows and columns that are not used and renumbering the squares, he produced a scheme in which the possible moves were similar for all squares on that part of the board which is actually used [*see bottom illustration on page 72*].

All the possible moves (other than those in which pieces are captured) fall into four types, each of which can be represented by a word (consisting of 45 bits, or binary digits) that can specify any move of its type. Within the framework of the scheme of notation we have been using it is also a simple matter to represent capture moves and the promotion of men to kings.

It would go beyond the scope of this article to discuss all the details of a working checkers program. The main outlines of the process of writing such a program should, however, be apparent by now. The first step is to have a vague idea of how to solve the problem. The second step is to specify the operations needed to carry out this initial plan, formalizing it by giving names to the objects on which these operations are to act. The third step is to clarify the definitions of the objects and to settle on a representation for each of them. These representations should be determined primarily by the operations to be performed on the objects. Once the representations have been decided on, the component operations can be defined more precisely in terms of them. One can then go on to refine the program, correcting errors or deficiencies that may show up in the representations and adjusting the operations accordingly.

At this stage the major intellectual

MovesFrom(P) and MakeMove(M,P), together with the form of P and M, will determine the nature of the game, and the functions Terminal(P,d) and TerminalValue(P) between them will determine the strategy.

The selection of ways to represent objects in the computer is an art, and there is little we can do in a systematic fashion to decide the best way. The main requirements are that the representation should be as compact as possible and yet as easy as possible to manipulate.

For representing the various positions on a checkerboard we have two distinct possibilities. To describe a particular position we could either specify whether each of the 32 available squares on the board is or is not occupied, and if it is, by what, or we could merely

give the locations of the pieces still in play. The first of these alternatives is more convenient from the standpoint of finding the legal moves, because it makes it easier to discover which squares are unoccupied [*see top illustration on page 72*].

COMPLETE CHECKERS PROGRAM is given in the left-hand column on the opposite page. The language used in the program is an informal and somewhat extended version of CPL. The names of the logical functions that are specific to this particular program ("ChosenPosition" and so on) were selected to be suggestive of the operations they govern. A list of the primitive, or generalized, functions and the specific data structures used in the program is provided in the right-hand column. The chief omissions from the program are the input and output arrangements and the functions that define the game-playing strategy [Terminal (P,d) and Terminal Value (P)]. The program has not been debugged on a machine and so, in accordance with the views expressed in the article, probably still contains some errors; interested readers may like to look for them. The general notation "Condition → A,B" is a conditional expression whose value is A if the condition is satisfied (that is, if it is true) and B otherwise. The section that deals with capture moves is in color.

ChosenPosition(P) = **value of**
  § **let** L = LegalPositionsFrom(P)
  if Null(L) **then** Resign
  let (p,v) = BestPosition(NIL, − ∝ ,L,0)
  result is p §

BestPosition(P,V,L,d) = Null(L) → (P,V), **value of**
  § **let** (p,l) = Next (L)
  let v = − PositionValue(p,d + 1)
  result is (v > V) → BestPosition(p,v,l,d),
                BestPosition(P,V,l,d) §

PositionValue(P,d) = Terminal(P,d) → TerminalValue(P), **value of**
  § **let** L = LegalPositionsFrom(P)
  let (p,v) = BestPosition(NIL, − ∝ ,L,d)
  result is v §

LegalPositionsFrom(P) = **value of**
  § **let** L = RemainingPositionList(P,Capture,5)
  result is Null(L)→RemainingPosition List(P,NonCapture,5),L §

RemainingPositionList(P,C,s) =
    PartialPositionList(P,C,s,FindMoveList(P,C,s))

PartialPositionList(P,C,s,L) =
    Null(L)→((s = −5)→NIL,
        RemainingPositionList(P,C,NextMoveDirection(s)),
      value of
  § **let** φ = SingleDigitFrom(L)
  let Ip = MakeMove(P,C,s,φ)
  let l = (C = Capture)→CaptureTree(Ip),
              FinalPosition(Ip)
  result is Join (l,PartialPositionList(P,C,s,L − φ))§

NextMoveDirection(s) = (s = 5) → 4, ((s = 4) → − 4, − 5)

FindMoveList(P,C,s) = **value of**
  § **let** (X,Y,K,σ) = P
  let Empty = ∼ X ∧ ∼ Y ∧ Board
  let ψ = (C = Capture) → (Shift(Empty,σs) ∧ Y),Empty
  let φ = Shift(ψ,σs) ∧ X
  result is (s > 0) → φ,φ ∧ K §

MakeMove(P,C,s,φ) = **value of**
  § **let** (X,Y,K,σ) = P
  let ψ = (C = Capture) → Shift(φ, − σs),NIL
  let θ = (C = Capture) → Shift(ψ, − σs),
              Shift(φ, − σs)
  let Xk = Null(φ ∧ K) → (θ ∧ LastRows),(θ − φ)
  result is ((X − φ + θ),(Y − ψ),(K − ψ ∧ K + Xk),σ,θ) §

FinalPosition(Ip) = **value of**
  § **let** (X,Y,K,σ,φ) = Ip
  result is (Y,X,K, − σ) §

CaptureTree(Ip) = **value of**
  § **let** L = PartialCapturePositionList(Ip)
  result is Null(L) → (FinalPosition(Ip)),
              CombineCaptureTrees(L) §

PartialCapturePositionList(Ip) = **value of**
  § **let** (X,Y,K,σ,φ) = Ip
  let P = (X,Y,K,σ)
  result is MinList(PCP(P,φ,5),PCP(P,φ,4),
              PCP(P,φ ∧ K, − 4),PCP(P,φ ∧ K, − 5)) §

PCP(P,φ,s) = **value of**
  § **let** (X,Y,K,σ) = P
  let ψ = Shift(φ, − σs) ∧ Y
  let Empty = ∼ X ∧ ∼ Y ∧ Board
  let θ = Shift(ψ, − σs) ∧ Empty
  let Xk = Null(φ ∧ K) → (θ ∧ LastRows),(θ − φ)
  result is Null(θ) → NIL,
              ((X − φ + θ),(Y − ψ),(K − ψ ∧ K + Xk),σ,θ) §

CombineCaptureTrees(L) = Null(L) → NIL, **value of**
  § **let** (Ip,l) = Next (L)
  result is Join(CaptureTree(Ip),CombineCaptureTrees(l)) §

PRIMITIVE FUNCTIONS

a LIST FUNCTIONS

L   LIST
Null(L)   TRUE IF L IS THE EMPTY
    LIST (NIL), FALSE OTHERWISE
Head(L)   FIRST MEMBER OF L
Tail(L)   WHAT REMAINS OF L AFTER
    Head(L) IS REMOVED
Next(L)   LIST WHOSE MEMBERS
    ARE Head(L) AND Tail(L)
Join(L_1,L_2)   A SINGLE LIST FORMED
    FROM THE MEMBERS
    OF L_1 AND L_2
MinList(L_1,L_2...)   A SINGLE LIST FORMED
    FROM THE MEMBERS OF
    SEVERAL LISTS; ALSO
    LEAVES OUT NULL LISTS
    AND REPETITIONS

b BIT-STRING FUNCTIONS

∼   NOT
∧   AND
∨   INCLUSIVE OR
x + y   SAME AS x ∨ y
x − y   SAME AS x ∧ (∼ y)
SingleDigitFrom(x)   A BIT STRING OF THE
    SAME LENGTH AS x WITH
    A SINGLE 1 IN A
    POSITION CORRESPONDING
    TO ONE OF THE 1'S
    IN BIT-STRING x
Shift(x,n)   THE BIT-STRING x SHIFTED
    n PLACES TO THE RIGHT.
    IF n < 0, THE SHIFT
    WILL BE TO THE LEFT.
    DIGITS THAT ARE
    SHIFTED OFF THE END
    OF THE BOARD ARE LOST.
    DIGITS SHIFTED ONTO
    THE BOARD ARE 0'S.

c STRATEGY FUNCTIONS

Terminal(P,d)   TRUE IF P IS TERMINAL,
    FALSE OTHERWISE
TerminalValue(P)   VALUE OF P (COMPUTED
    WHEN LOOK-AHEAD BEYOND
    P IS UNDESIRABLE)

DATA STRUCTURES

a 45-BIT STRINGS

X   PLAYER'S MEN AND KINGS
Y   OPPONENT'S MEN AND KINGS
K   KINGS ON BOTH SIDES
φ   SQUARE MOVED FROM
ψ   CAPTURED PIECE (IF ANY)
θ   SQUARE MOVED TO
Board   1'S ON BOARD SQUARES,
    0'S ELSEWHERE
LastRows   1'S ON SQUARES
    NUMBERED 5, 6, 7, 8,
    36, 37, 38, 39

b POSITIONS

σ   NEXT PLAY
    σ = +1: BLACK TO PLAY
    σ = −1: WHITE TO PLAY
P,p   ORDINARY POSITIONS WITH
    COMPONENTS X, Y, K, σ
Ip   INTERMEDIATE POSITIONS
    WITH COMPONENTS X, Y,
    K,σ,φ, WHERE φ INDICATES
    THE PIECE THAT CAN MOVE

c MISCELLANEOUS

C   CAPTURE OR NONCAPTURE
s   DIRECTION OF MOVE
    s = 5: FORWARD, LEFT
    s = 4: FORWARD, RIGHT
    s = − 4: BACKWARD, LEFT
    s = − 5: BACKWARD, RIGHT
V,v   POSITION VALUE
d   DEPTH OF LOOK-AHEAD

work of the program seems to be finished. We have specified precisely what we want the computer to do. The rest—converting the program into instructions for the computer—should be merely routine. Unfortunately it does not quite work out that way, and anyone who has not had the experience of using a computer will be unpleasantly surprised by the amount of time and effort that is still needed.

In the first place, the computer is unable to accept directly the rather sophisticated kind of instructions we should like to give it. It is almost certain that we shall have made use of operations that are too much for any computer. To get around the inability of the machine to do directly what we want, we can write our program in a standard programming language and make the machine translate this into its own much simpler code. This seems an excellent use of a computer to do the donkey work for us, but unfortunately it does not get rid of all the labor. We have to do a good deal of apparently irrelevant and *ad hoc* work to force the program into a form suitable for existing programming languages.

There are now a considerable number of these programming languages: FORTRAN, ALGOL and MAD (used primarily for scientific problems); JOVIAL (for military applications); COBOL; SIMSCRIPT; LISP; PL/I; CPL, and others. To give an indication of the varying styles of the languages, three samples are given: a simple program (to find the mathematical function e^x) is written in CPL, in ALGOL and in FORTRAN [*see illustration on page 71*].

The advent of programming languages of this kind some nine years ago vastly enriched the art of programming. Before then a program containing 5,000 instructions was considered quite large, and only the most experienced or foolhardy programmers would attempt one. Today an individual can tackle programs about 10 times larger; a team by cooperative effort may produce a program still larger by a factor of five to 10.

By far the most important of the new programming languages was FORTRAN; until recently, it has been estimated, more than 90 percent of all scientific and engineering programs were written in it. In the past few years it has gradually become clear that current programming languages are by no means perfect and that the great success of FORTRAN was due to its relative merits rather than its absolute ones. Other programming languages such as ALGOL and LISP have shown that

there are easier ways to do at least some things on computers.

To get back to our checkers program: I have written the complete program (except for certain details, including the input and output arrangements) in an informal and somewhat extended version of CPL (which stands for "Combined Programming Language"). The program in symbolic form, together with a list of the terms used and their definitions, is shown on the preceding page. The program is not by any means in final form; it has not been run on a machine and therefore, in accordance with the views expressed below, probably still contains some errors. Interested readers may like to look for them.

In the early days of computer programming—say 15 years ago—mathematicians used to think that by taking sufficient care they would be able to write programs that were correct. Greatly to their surprise and chagrin, they found that this was not the case and that with rare exceptions the programs as written contained numerous errors. The process of discovering, locating and correcting these errors proved to be one of major difficulty, often taking considerably longer than writing the program in the first place and using a great deal of machine time.

Although programming techniques have improved immensely since the early days, the process of finding and correcting errors in programs—known, graphically if inelegantly, as "debugging"—still remains a most difficult, confused and unsatisfactory operation. The chief impact of this state of affairs is psychological. Although we are all happy to pay lip service to the adage that to err is human, most of us like to make a small private reservation about our own performance on special occasions when we really try. It is somewhat deflating to be shown publicly and incontrovertibly by a machine that even when we do try, we in fact make just as many mistakes as other people. If your pride cannot recover from this blow, you will never make a programmer.

It is not, in fact, in the nature of human beings to be perfectly accurate, and it is unrealistic to believe they ever will be. The only reasonable way to get a program right is to assume that it will at first contain errors and take steps to discover these and correct them. This attitude is quite familiar to anyone who has been in contact with the planning of any large-scale operation, but it is completely strange to most people who have not.

The trouble, I think, is that so many educational processes put a high premium on getting the correct answer the first time. If you give the wrong answer to an examination question, you lose your mark and that is the end of the matter. If you make a mistake in writing your program—or, indeed, in many other situations in life outside a classroom—it is by no means a catastrophe; you do, however, have to find your error and put it right. Maybe it would be better if more academic teaching adopted this attitude also.

It is when we first come to grips with a computer and actually try to run a program, either to test it or to obtain some useful results, that we really begin to get frustrated. In spite of the much vaunted speed of the machine itself, it is normally several hours and sometimes several days before one can actually get back the answer to even the shortest program. When this delay is added to the fact that computers and their programming languages and compilers are often most unhelpful, so that the only information you receive at the end of a day's wait may be that your program is still wrong, it is easy to understand why so many people get the impression that using a computer is more a matter of fighting the machine and the system than it is one of cooperation.

The reason for this curious situation is the desire to keep the computer, which is a very expensive machine, fully occupied for as much of the time as possible. The organization outside the computer, which frequently employs quite a large human operating staff, accounts for almost all the "turn-around time" and a fair proportion of the frustration. The introduction of time-sharing systems should remove this source of frustration, at the cost of greatly increasing the size and complexity of the operating programs [see "Time-sharing on Computers," by Fano and Corbató, page 79].

A large part of the work involved in actually getting a program running can be done by the computer itself. Operations such as translating the programming language into detailed machine code, allocating storage space inside the computer, keeping records to assist in the diagnosis of program errors, organizing the scheduling and accounting for a sequence of short jobs from various users and the like are precisely the kind of high-grade routine clerical work a computer can handle, and it is therefore only rational to expect the machine to do it.

The programs to make the machine carry out these operations are of the greatest importance. Most users of the computer will have far more contact with them than they do with the computer itself, and for this reason the operating programs are known as the software of the system (as opposed to the computer itself, which is known as the hardware). In actuality the performance of a system is as much dependent on its software as on its hardware, and the planning and writing of software systems is rapidly becoming a major problem for computer manufacturers. The entire set of these programs, known as the software package, can easily cost the machine manufacturer as much to produce and debug as the machine itself. As a result there is strong pressure not to change either the programming language or the operating system, in spite of the fact that in many respects they are seriously inadequate.

Why is the road from the conception of a program to its execution by the machine so long and tiresome? Why are the operating systems today—the software—so costly and unsatisfactory? Are we perhaps reaching the limit of human ability to write complicated programs, and is the present software crisis really the result of attempting the humanly impossible? Anyone who deals with the large computer systems today knows how close the whole thing is to collapsing under the weight of its own complexity.

There is no doubt that with the current techniques we have nearly reached our limit in programming. Could we not, however, improve the techniques? The checkers example we have considered in this article gives a strong hint that a simplified approach and improvement of the programming language would make things a great deal easier. If a suitable programming language existed, it should clearly be possible to write the entire checkers program in the way outlined above and leave nearly all the remaining stages to be performed by the computer. As a matter of fact, that can almost be done now, and it would probably not be too difficult to construct a language in which it was possible.

The only reasonable way to set up a large and complicated program is to use a hierarchical method. Since there is a limit to the size and complexity of a problem we can hold in our head at one time, it appears that the best way to extend our capability is to treat relatively large and complex operations as single units and combine these units hierarchically. The present programming languages all pay at least lip service to this idea, but many do not allow for a genuine and unlimited hierarchy—only for two or three levels of operation (such as "local" and "global") the programmer has to consider simultaneously. Those languages that do allow a truly hierarchical treatment of a problem have only a limited ability to deal with representations.

The present-day computer is itself a stumbling block to the use of programs that are written hierarchically (or recursively). Because the computers are unsuitable for this kind of organization, the running of such a program is much slower than it is for a program written and coded in the conventional way. I am convinced, however, that the advantages of this kind of programming will far outweigh any increase of machine time that may be required. The advantages are so great that I believe the hierarchical method will eventually be adopted universally. After all, the chief purpose of any machine is to save human beings trouble; therefore we should not be unduly alarmed about giving the computer more of man's work. In addition, there is good reason to expect that it will be possible to design computers that will deal much more naturally and efficiently with deeply hierarchical programs. These machines will probably be slightly more complex than present ones, but the difference in cost will be well worthwhile.

I have left to the end what seems to me to be the most difficult, but also the most interesting and potentially rewarding, problem concerning programming languages. This is to lay a firm mathematical foundation for the construction of hierarchical systems of programs and to develop a calculus for manipulating them.

The difficulty arises basically from the fact that programming presents us with certain new questions that are not present, or at least not important, in any other branch of mathematics. The mathematical problem has two aspects. The first is how to deal explicitly and in a detailed way with complicated structures (involving representations of data) when not only the structure as a whole but also its component parts must be given names and have values assigned to them. The second aspect of the difficulty is that the use of imperatives (or commands) in programming introduces variables, and mathematics in general does not recognize the existence of variables in this sense, that is, values varying over a period of time. In its traditional branches mathematics deals only with static situations. Even the calculus, which is concerned with the approaches of objects to a limit, deals with the subject in terms of a series of fixed values. In general the things mathematicians call variables are either constants whose values are not yet known or nonexistent quantities (such as "nobody") that are introduced for purposes of logical syntax. In programming, on the other hand, we deal with time-varying variables by the very nature of the process; a program is essentially a schedule of changes.

An experienced programmer reading this article will have been struck by the fact that in the formulation of the checkers program I have used no commands, and in particular by the fact that the program contains no assignment statements (statements assigning values to names or objects). The reason for this is that we know how to combine recursively defined functions into hierarchical structures only in the absence of assignment statements. There is still no satisfactory way of doing the same thing if they are included.

Investigation of the mathematical problems I have discussed has now begun. It is clear at the start that the field to be explored is almost entirely new, without established guidelines such as exist in most other areas of mathematical research. It is also evident that the first and most difficult task is to clarify what we mean, in a programming context, by terms such as "name" and "value." The chief trouble is that the introduction of assignments (changes of value with changes in circumstances) makes the meaning of the terms ambiguous from the standpoint of the way they are ordinarily used in mathematics, so that it seems probable we shall need to generate new concepts in order to get a firm grasp of the situation.

Much of the theoretical work now being done in the field of programming languages is concerned with language syntax. In essence this means the research is concerned not with *what* the language says but with *how* it says it. This approach seems to put almost insuperable barriers in the way of forming new concepts—at least as far as language *meaning* is concerned. I believe the way to progress for programmers lies along the path of research on meaning rather than syntax. It is primarily through the study of meaning that we shall develop the concepts required to build up hierarchical structures.

7

TIME-SHARING ON COMPUTERS

R. M. FANO AND F. J. CORBATÓ

September, 1966

The history of the modern computer has been characterized by a series of quantum leaps in our view of the machine's possibilities. To mention only two of the crucial advances, the application of electronics, vastly increasing the computer's speed of operation, and later the invention of special languages, facilitating communication with the machine, each in its turn opened new vistas on the computer's potentialities. Within the past few years the technique called time-sharing has again stimulated the imagination. It has created an unexpected new order of uses for the computer.

At first thought time-sharing seems simply a convenience: a means of allowing fuller use of the machine by more people and of saving time for the users. In practice, however, experiments with the technique have demonstrated a wide range of more interesting possibilities. It enables the user to conduct a continuous dialogue with the machine and in effect makes the computer his intellectual assistant. Further, the system makes it possible for the users to carry on a discourse with one another through the machine, drawing on its large store of knowledge and its computing speed as they do so. The time-sharing computer system can unite a group of investigators in a cooperative search for the solution to a common problem, or it can serve as a community pool of knowledge and skill on which anyone can draw according to his needs. Projecting the concept on a large scale, one can conceive of such a facility as an extraordinarily powerful library serving an entire community—in short, an intellectual public utility.

It was Christopher Strachey, the author of the article on system analysis and programming in this book, who first proposed (in 1959) a time-sharing system. The large, expensive computing machines had become far removed from their users, both in time and in distance. An applicant in effect had to deliver his problem or program to a receptionist and then wait hours or sometimes days for an answer that might take the machine only seconds or even less time to produce. The computer, working on one program at a time, kept a queue of users waiting for their turn. If, as commonly happens, a submitted program contained a minor error that invalidated the results, the user often had to wait several hours for resubmission of his corrected program. Strachey suggested that the rapidity of a computer's operations made all this waiting unnecessary. By segregating the central processing operations from the time-consuming interactions with the human programmers, the computer could in effect work on a number of programs simultaneously. Giving only a few seconds or often less than a second at a time to each program or task, the machine could deal with many users at once, as if each had the machine to himself. The execution of various programs would be interspersed without their interfering with one another and without detectable delays in the responses to the individual users.

The Computation Center at the Massachusetts Institute of Technology quickly took up Strachey's suggestion. By November, 1961, the center had implemented and demonstrated a first model of the Compatible Time-Sharing System, using an International Business Machines Corporation 709 computer. Two years later an improved version of this system was operating on two IBM 7094 computers, one at the Computation Center and another at M.I.T.'s Project MAC (an acronym that has been variously translated as standing for multiple-access computer, machine-aided cognition or man and computer). By that time three other time-sharing systems had been developed: at Bolt, Beranek and Newman, Inc., at M.I.T.'s Research Laboratory of Electronics and at the System Development Corporation, and several more have since been developed at other research institutions.

Inherent in the time-sharing concept is a system of multiple direct connections to the computer from many points, near and far. At M.I.T. there are now 160 such stations, each with a teletypewriter that enables the user to enter his message directly in the computer's input and to receive its replies. These stations are installed in various offices and laboratories on the M.I.T. campus and in

PROJECT MAC time-sharing system at the Massachusetts Institute of Technology has 160 terminals on the M.I.T. campus and nearby and is also available from distant terminals. As many as 30 terminals can be connected at one time, with each user carrying on a direct and in effect uninterrupted dialogue with the computer. The terminals, 30 of which are shown on the opposite page, are for the most part simple teletypewriters such as the IBM 1050 (6) and Teletype models 33 (19), 35 (5) or 37 (10). Some are in offices, some in large "pool" rooms, some in laboratories and a few in private homes (1). In addition to students and staff members doing their own research, the users shown here include secretaries preparing papers for publication (13), authors Fano (8) and Corbató (24) and a psychiatrist at the Massachusetts General Hospital (18). More elaborate terminals are shown on the next page.

SPECIALIZED TERMINAL of Project MAC has a small computer, the Digital Equipment Corporation's PDP-8, operating a braille printer (*foreground*) for a blind staff member.

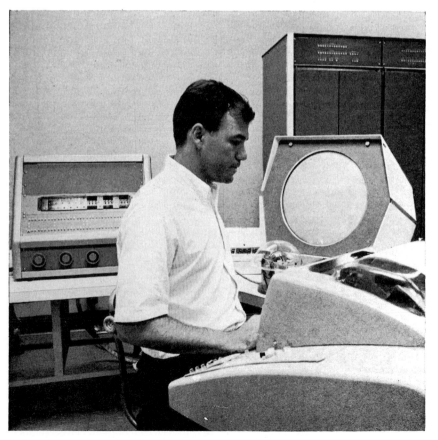

ANOTHER TERMINAL is the "Kluge" display system developed by M.I.T.'s Electronic Systems Laboratory. It has a control unit, display screen, light pen and other equipment.

the homes of some of the research staff and faculty members. Through a private branch exchange each station can by dialing reach either the Project MAC computer or the one in the Computation Center. Moreover, the Project MAC installation is connected to the teletype networks of the Bell System and Western Union, so that access to the computer can be had from thousands of terminals in the U.S. and abroad. Thus the two computer systems at M.I.T. are being used daily by a large and varied community, with each of them providing prompt response for up to 30 simultaneous users. The systems constitute an operating model of the information utility that John McCarthy, the author of the introduction to this issue, described in 1961 in an address picturing computer services of the future.

For professional programmers the time-sharing system has come to mean a great deal more than mere ease of access to the computer. Provided with the opportunity to run a program in continuous dialogue with the machine, editing, "debugging" and modifying the program as they proceed, they have gained immeasurably in the ability to experiment. They can readily investigate new programming techniques and new approaches to problems. The bolder exercise of the imagination encouraged by the new system has resulted not only in more flexibility in attacks on problems but also in the undertaking of important new researches in a variety of areas.

Let us now examine the operation of a time-sharing system. Taking the M.I.T. Compatible Time-Sharing System (CTSS) as our model, we shall first present a sample of what it can do, using a program dialogue for illustration, and then describe the anatomy and machinery of the system in schematic terms.

To begin with, the system contains a large store of information—supervisory and utility programs, language-translating facilities, a library of subroutines and so on—adding up to nearly a million computer words, which is equivalent to about 2,000 book pages crowded with nonredundant symbols. The basic content of the system is a set of some 100 programs, each of which is called into play by a specific command issued through a teletypewriter. They have to do with the ordinary operations of the system and involve communication, control of its various processes, the use and translation of computer languages and so forth. In addition to these 100 basic programs the system contains a great variety of special programs that are also available for general use. To all this "public" information there is added a large amount of material consisting of individual users' private files of programs and information.

Consider, then, an illustrative dialogue between a user and the computer [*see illustrations on page 82 through 84*]. The user introduces himself by giving the command "login" and stating the project he wants to work on and his name. The machine responds by printing the time of day (to the hour, minute and tenth of a minute), and the user is

now called on to give his password. This has been found to be a highly important requirement: it is necessary to guard the privacy of each personal set of files and protect the information and programs from accidental or malicious alteration by someone else. (Experience has shown that some people are unable to resist the temptation to commit mischievous vandalism of that kind.) The printer is disconnected while the password is being typed so that no record of it appears on the print-out.

If the given password does not check with the person's name and problem number, or if he has exhausted his

monthly allowance of time on the computer, or if the machine is already being used to capacity (the maximum number of people who can use the computer at one time in our present system is 30), the machine prints a message stating that access is not available. If access can be granted, the user is allowed to proceed with further commands. Before beginning his work he may ask for an accounting of the amount of time and storage space he has used up from his allotted quotas (as one illustration shows). After this housekeeping query the user goes to work on his problem. Here, in our simple illustration, he

COMPUTER ROOM at M.I.T. houses the IBM 7094 central processing unit, memories and other central units of the Project MAC system. Disk and drum files are visible in left background, central processor in right background, tape-storage units at right.

```
login t193 fano
W 2237.7
Password
  T0193  2859 LOGGED IN  05/27/66     2237.8 FROM 20000N

  CTSS BEING USED IS      MAC5A4
  LAST LOGOUT WAS  05/27/66    2237.0
R 2.833+.900


ttpeek
W 2238.2

5/27  2238.2 TUSED =   .1

SHIFT       MINUTES
        ALLOTTED    USED
   1       60        3.8
   2       20        1.0
   3        5        0.
   4       30         .3

        STORAGE
DEVICE  QUOTA   USED
DISK     100     4

R 1.950+.350


ed mad
W 2238.8
INPUT:
start read and print data
      an"mean = (x+y)/2.
      gmean = (x?  gmean = sqrt.(x*y)
      print results g"amean, gmen
      transfer to start
      end of program

EDIT:
top
print 10

START      READ AND PRINT DATA
           AMEAN = (X+Y)/2.
           GMEAN = SQRT.(X*Y)
           PRINT RESULTS AMEAN, GMEN
           TRANSFER TO START
           END OF PROGRAM
END OF FILE REACHED BY:
PRINT 10
file demo
R 3.983+2.550


mad demo
W 2242.9
  THE FOLLOWING NAMES HAVE OCCURRED ONLY ONCE IN THIS PROGRAM.
  COMPILATION WILL CONTINUE.
        GMEAN
        GMEN
LENGTH 00066.  TV SIZE 00005.  ENTRY 00017
R 1.750+.650

ed demo mad
W 2243.3
EDIT:
locate gmen
change /gmen/gmean/
print
            PRINT RESULTS AMEAN, GMEAN
top
change /amean/armean/ 10
END OF FILE REACHED BY:
CHANGE /AMEAN/ARMEAN/ 10
file
R 3.800+1.300

mad demo
W 2244.7
LENGTH 00063.  TV SIZE 00005.  ENTRY 00016
R 1.466+.416

loadgo demo
W 2245.0
EXECUTION.
x = 123.456, y = 234.567 *
X = 123.456, Y = 234.567 *

        ARMEAN =     179.011499,       GMEAN =    170.172569
  QUIT,
R 5.483+1.283

save demo
W 2245.9
R .866+.283
```

RUNNING DIALOGUE between man and machine is demonstrated by a computer print-out. The user (*lowercase letters*) announces himself; the computer (*uppercase*) gives the time. The user gives his password (which, to preserve privacy, is not printed) and the machine logs him in and reports the number of seconds used by the central processor in the exchange. In response to the command "ttpeek" the machine summarizes Fano's time and memory-space account. With "ed mad" Fano writes and edits a program in MAD language for computing the arithmetic and geometric means of any two numbers. (The symbols " and ? erase the preceding character or all the preceding characters in the line respectively.) The program is filed under the name "demo." The machine queries a typing error ("GMEN" for "GMEAN"), which is corrected, and "AMEAN" is changed to "ARMEAN." The program is translated and executed. After a test computation the execution is interrupted. The computer acknowledges the interruption ("QUIT") and is instructed to "save" the program.

writes, translates and executes a program to compute the arithmetic mean and the geometric mean of two given numbers. A command signified by "ed" (for "editing") brings into play a subsystem in the computer that accepts various editing instructions, so that the user can call on it to write his program in a particular language (here it is the language called Michigan Algorithmic Decoder, or MAD) and make alterations, corrections or other manipulations of the program text as directed. Typing errors have been introduced deliberately in our example to illustrate some of these editing functions. The corrections are carried out through a dialogue between the user and the computer. Finally the program is translated and tested on a pair of numbers. The user presses an "interrupt" button at that point to end the computation and the computer prints out "QUIT" in acknowledgment. The user then gives the command "save demo," which instructs the machine to file the program in what becomes a new private file named "demo saved." This file is stored permanently in the system's mass memory.

The owner can command the system to print out the list of files in his file directory by giving the instruction "listf." He may also give a command authorizing the system to allow other named users access to one of his files, and conversely may gain access to other private or public files he is permitted to use. Although a person given access to someone else's file is not usually allowed to change that file, he can copy its contents, file the information separately under his own name and then modify the data or program for his own use. This technique is employed by a second person to use the program for computing the arithmetic and geometric means of a pair of numbers [*see bottom illustration on opposite page*]. Another convenient feature of the time-sharing system that is illustrated allows the depositing of messages from one user to another in the computer. On logging into the computer a user may be informed by the machine that there is a message in his "mail box," and the computer will then print the message on command.

To illustrate the editing capabilities of the system we have added a sample print-out of a paper delivered at a conference, together with the commands that enabled the computer to present it in the desired typographical form. The system includes a special facility for editing English text, and this facility has been used in the preparation of technical reports and other publications.

Not the least useful feature of the Compatible Time-Sharing System is the fact that it carries its own set of instructions to its users. Stored in its mass memory is the manual describing the system; this is indexed by a table of contents listing the various services and sections in the reverse chronological order of their addition to the system; that is, the latest are listed first. Thus a user can readily check at any time to see whether or not his copy of the manual is up to date and can then obtain a print-out of any new or modified sections.

To explain the workings of the system we have focused on the dialogue carried on between the user and the computer through the medium of printed commands and responses. The Project MAC system also includes two display stations with facilities for light-pen drawing on a cathode ray tube and for viewing the projection of continuously rotating three-dimensional objects. This equipment has been used by Cyrus Levinthal for studying the structure of biological molecules [see the article "Molecular Model-building by Computer," by Cyrus Levinthal, page 171].

Of the anatomy and internal operations of the M.I.T. time-sharing system we can only give a schematic outline. It employs a very large and complex installation, built around an IBM 7094 computer and containing in addition a number of special units [see illustration on page 85].

The heart of the system is a complex of programs called "the supervisor." It coordinates the operation of the various units, allocates the time and services of the computer to users and controls their access to the system. The allocation function includes scheduling of users' requests, transferring control of the central processor from one user to another, moving programs in and out of the core memory and managing the users' private files. Obviously the time allowance for each program-run must be closely regulated. If a program runs too long without interruption, other users will be kept waiting unduly; on the other hand, if the execution of a program is interrupted many times, the repeated movement of the program in and out of the core memory will entail a waste of time. We have adopted a time-allowance scheme based on task priorities that in

```
listf
W 2246.0

     6 FILES    24 RECORDS
NAME1  NAME2 MOD NOREC    USED
 DEMO   SAVED 000       18 05/27/66
(MOVIE TABLE) 001        1
 DEMO    BSS 000         1
 DEMO    MAD 000         1
PERMIT  FILE 120         1
 FJCC (MEMO) 000         3 05/19/66

    28 LINKS
NAME1  NAME2 MOD PROBN. PROGN. LNAME1 LNAME2
BASIS   SAVED 104  T0173     44
CIRKIT  SAVED 000  T0113 CMFL04
CONVOL  SAVED 104  T0173     44
CONVT    BSS 104
 DATA   SAVED 104
DATTOC (MEMO) 104  T0254   3212
DOCTOR  SAVED 144  T0109   2531
 GETF   SAVED 104  T0173     44
GRPS1    DGET 144  T0263     32
- QUIT,
R 1.666+.300



permit demo saved 4 t100 385
W 2248.4
R .816+.266

edl permit mills
W 2248.9
 FILE PERMIT MILLS NOT FOUND.
Input
t 19?t193 2859 per "mits file demo saved to t100 385 mills

Edit
top

print 2

T193 2859 PERMITS FILE DEMO SAVED TO T100 385 MILLS
file
R 4.400+1.500

mail permit mills t100 385
W 2254.7
R 1.366+.433
```

DIRECTORY of Fano's personal files is printed out in response to the command "listf." It includes three files associated with the new "DEMO" program as well as "LINKS" to public and private files that Fano may use. Fano goes on to give permission for another user named Mills to use the new means-computing program and sends a message to Mills telling him so.

```
login t100 mills
W 2255.4
Password
YOU HAVE    MAIL  BOX
T0100    385 LOGGED IN 05/27/66    2255.7 FROM 20000A

CTSS BEING USED IS   MAC5A4
LAST LOGOUT WAS 05/27/66    1555.3
R 2.766+.716

print mail box
W 2256.2

    MAIL    BOX    05/27 2256.3

FROM   T0193 2859 05/27 2254.7
T193 2859 PERMITS FILE DEMO SAVED TO T100 385 MILLS
R .683+.516

link demo saved t193 2859
W 2257.9
R 1.266+.433

resume demo
W 2258.0
x = 345.678, y = 456.789 *
X = 345.678, Y = 456.789 *

        ARMEAN =    401.233498,    GMEAN =    397.368725
QUIT,
R .133+1.450

logout
W 2259.2
T0100    385 LOGGED OUT 05/27/66    2259.3 FROM 20000A
TOTAL TIME USED=    .1 MIN.
```

USER MILLS, logging in, is told that there is a message in his "MAIL BOX." After reading the message he asks that a link be established to the "demo saved" program that has been permitted to him. When this has been done, he asks the computer to "resume" the program, applying it to two new numbers he provides. The machine does so and prints the answers.

```
resume who
W 2300.6

MAC5A4 STARTED AT 1451.1 05/27

  BACKGROUND USED 142.6.    PERCENTAGE =    0
17 USERS AT  2300.9 05/27

LINE  USER    NAME  GRP UNIT  TUSED TIMEON
 1 C0056 99995 FIBMON  0 (FIB)    .1 2217.9
 2 C0056 99999 DAEMON  0 DAEMON 37.6 1451.2
 4 T0269  8048 ENNING  3 200007  2.0 2115.9
 5 T0143   799   LIU   1 20000+  7.8 1923.7
 6 T0281  3712 MAURER  1 20000+  8.8 1805.0
 7 T0113  4619 WYLIE  -1 600040   .8 2250.0
 8 T0193  2859  FANO   2 20000N   .7 2237.8
 9 T0269  8031 SSANNA  3 20000.  3.6 2044.0
10 T0234  1122 GARMAN  1 700168  1.4 2211.7
11 T0186  4288 INTOSH 15 20000+  5.9 2128.2
12 T0109  2531 ENBAUM  1 20000W  4.5 2125.9
13 T0145  3667 HITMAN  1 600038  1.8 2218.7
14 T0312  3047 NICHEL  1 20000Y  1.9 2222.5
15 T0335  4655 ULIANO -1 20000+   .1 2258.2
16 T0113  3556 EPHUIS  1 200000  3.3 2139.8
17 T0186  3187 MORRIS -1 100035   .4 2223.9
19 T0234  3308 WIDRIG  1 100001  1.4 2227.8

R 1.850+2.133
```

THROUGH A LINK to the system's public file, Fano asks for and receives a print-out of the system's current users, the time they logged in and the amount of time they have used.

```
typset fjcc
W 2303.3
Edit
top
print 20

.page
.header SOCIAL IMPLICATIONS OF ACCESSIBLE COMPUTING
.center
SOME THOUGHTS ABOUT THE SOCIAL
.center
IMPLICATIONS OF ACCESSIBLE COMPUTING
.space
.center
by
.space
.center
E. E. David, Jr.
.center
Bell Telephone Laboratories
.space
.center
R. M. Fano
.center
Massachusetts Institute of Technology
file
R 5.733+.916



runoff fjcc
W 2305.8
Load paper, hit return




            SOME THOUGHTS ABOUT THE SOCIAL
          IMPLICATIONS OF ACCESSIBLE COMPUTING

                         by

                  E. E. David, Jr.
              Bell Telephone Laboratories

                    R. M. Fano
          Massachusetts Institute of Technology


                    ABSTRACT


  The pattern of our business and private lives has been
shaped by many important technological developments such as
automobiles, electric power and telephones.   The influence
of these products of technology was felt  when  they  became
available to a large segment of the population.  We are now
at that stage with computers.

  As  with  previous  products  of  technology,  accessible
computing will undoubtedly benefit  society  but  will  also
face us with  new  problems  and  new  frustrations.    The
underlying issues are very complex and they  deserve  prompt
and thoughtful consideration on the part of all of us.


  logout
  W 2307.9
   T0193  2859 LOGGED OUT 05/27/66    2308.0 FROM 20000N
  TOTAL TIME USED=    .9 MIN.
```

EDITING CAPABILITY of the system is illustrated by the machine's reproduction of the beginning of an article. The command "typset" calls up the program for editing and printing the text. Commands prefaced by a period, such as "center" and "space," are instructions on format. The command "runoff" produces a print-out in the specified format. Logging out, Fano learns that demonstration, which lasted 30.3 minutes, used .9 minute of computer time.

turn are determined initially by the amount of information that must be transferred into the core memory. The smaller the amount of information, the higher the initial priority the task is given. The time allowance is at least two seconds and doubles with each level of decreasing priority. If a task is not completed in its allotted time—or if a higher-priority task is waiting—it is interrupted and enough of the program moved out to a storage drum to make room in the core memory for the next task awaiting the processor's services. If the allotted time has been exhausted, the task's priority is lowered and a correspondingly doubled allocation of time is made. The interrupted task is then continued when its turn comes up again.

The user need not remain in communication with the system while his program is being run. He may write a program in collaboration with the machine, test it and, after he is satisfied that it is correct, instruct the internal supervisor to run the program for him and store the results in a file from which he can retrieve them later at his convenience. This arrangement, called FIB (for "Fore-ground-initiated Background"), is designed particularly for programs involving lengthy computations that do not require human intervention. The present system also allows, in effect, for the concurrent running of programs on a "batch" basis (that is, not time-sharing), but this facility is now largely superseded by FIB.

This, then, in sketchy outline, is the compatible time-sharing system we have been working with so far at M.I.T. It is only a precursor, of course, of systems that will be developed in the future. What improvements or advances are needed to create an installation that will serve a large community as a general public utility?

One obvious necessity is that the system provide continuous and reliable service. A public utility must be available to the community 24 hours a day and seven days a week without interruption. It should not shut down for accidents, repairs, maintenance, modifications or additions to the system. This implies, among other things, that the system should not depend completely on any one unit. It suggests that every part of the system should consist of a pool of functionally identical units (memories, processors and so on) that can operate independently and can be used interchangeably or simultaneously at all times [*see upper illustration on page*

87]. In such a system any unit could be taken out of service for repair or maintenance during a period when the system load was low, and the supervisor would distribute the load among the remaining units. It would also be a simple matter to add units, without interrupting service, as the use of the system grew. Moreover, the availability of duplicate units would simplify the problem of queuing and the allocation of time and space to users.

A second need is more efficient use of the computer's time. In the Compatible Time-Sharing System, as in most conventional batch-processing systems, the central processor is idle for about 40 percent of the time because it must wait while programs and data are being transferred in and out of the core memory and while necessary information is being fetched from or written into the users' files. One way to reduce the processor's idle time would be to have at all times in the core memory several executable programs (instead of only one),

so that as soon as the processor finishes a task or transmission of more data is required, it would find another task available. The computer art now presents a technique for producing this desirable situation without having to waste too much core memory to store entire programs waiting to be executed. A program can be divided into pages, each containing, say, only 1,024 words, and the core memory can be divided into logical blocks of the same size. Pages are transferred into core memory only when needed, if at all, so that tasks can be initiated with minimal use of precious memory space.

Another new technique, called program segmentation, has been advocated by Jack B. Dennis of M.I.T. to increase the ease and flexibility with which subprograms may be linked to form large programs. The process followed by a computer in executing a large program is similar to that followed by the reader of an article that refers to a section of another article that in turn refers to a

chapter of a book, and so on. The traditional technique for linking subprograms is equivalent to having a clerk in the library make copies of all articles and books to be read, assemble them into a single volume, and translate all references into references to specific page numbers of the volume. This technique has the disadvantage that popular subprograms have to be copied and stored many times as parts of different programs. Moreover, programs, unlike articles and books, are often changed and new subprograms have to be incorporated. This is particularly true in a time-sharing system. With the technique of program segmentation the segments, or subprograms, retain their individual identity at all times. They are retrieved from mass storage only when the computer finds a reference to them during the execution of some other segment. Speed of retrieval, and particularly speed of access to individual words of a segment after the segment has been retrieved, is essential. For this purpose

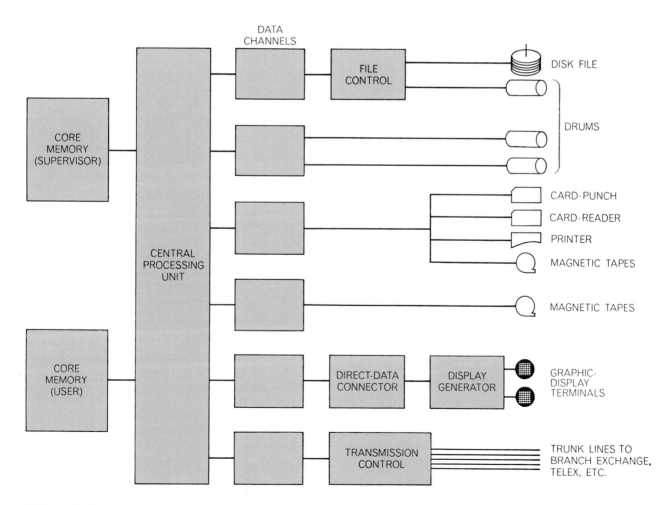

PRINCIPAL ELEMENTS of the M.I.T. time-sharing computer installation are shown in a simplified schematic diagram. One of the two core memories is occupied by the supervisor program, which runs the system; the other is available to users. Files are moved into the core memory as needed from the disk and drum memories. The transmission control is actually a special-purpose computer.

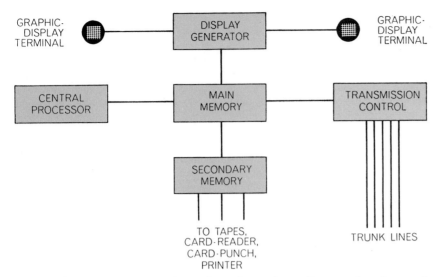

GRAPHIC-DISPLAY TERMINAL

DISPLAY GENERATOR

GRAPHIC-DISPLAY TERMINAL

CENTRAL PROCESSOR

MAIN MEMORY

TRANSMISSION CONTROL

SECONDARY MEMORY

TO TAPES, CARD-READER, CARD-PUNCH, PRINTER

TRUNK LINES

SUPERVISOR has the effect of reducing the equipment layout diagrammed on the preceding page to the functional arrangement illustrated here. The main (core) memory, rather than the central processing unit, is in effect the central unit with which other units communicate; the various mass storage devices are in effect a single secondary memory.

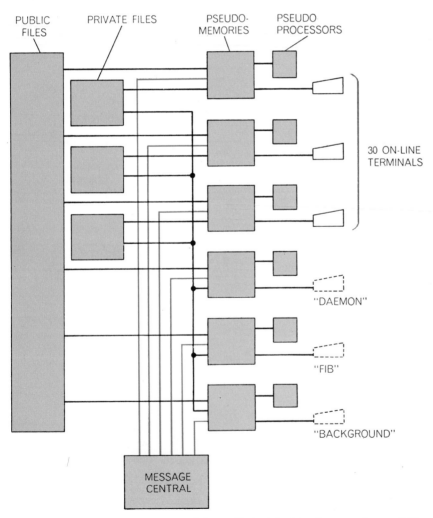

PUBLIC FILES

PRIVATE FILES

PSEUDO-MEMORIES

PSEUDO-PROCESSORS

30 ON-LINE TERMINALS

"DAEMON"

"FIB"

"BACKGROUND"

MESSAGE CENTRAL

"USER'S VIEW" of the system is quite different. Each of the 30 on-line users has available, for all practical purposes, his own processor and memory. Each memory has in effect a capacity of 32,768 words and has access to public files as well as the user's own files. Messages can be exchanged through the message central. Three special pseudo-processors are available to the supervisor. "Daemon" copies files on tape. "FIB" takes over and executes programs for users who do not need to wait for lengthy answers. "Background" operates as a conventional computer, batch-processing large tasks fed into the central computer.

the computer must include special equipment features, and appropriate directories of all segments must be maintained. The position of the computer is then analogous to that of a user of an ideal automatic library who finds in his reading a reference to some article or book. He gives the name or names identifying the article or book and the page or line number in which he is interested, and the desired text is quickly displayed for him so that his reading can continue without appreciable interruption. The technique of program segmentation appears to have many other advantages beyond those suggested here, and these are currently being explored in a number of research laboratories. Segmentation makes it possible for several central processors to combine in working on a program involving much computation and improves intercommunication within the system [see lower illustration on page 87]. Two new commercial computers, the General Electric Company's 645 and the IBM 360/67, include the special features needed for paging and for program segmentation.

Finally, in this catalogue of improvements needed to develop time-sharing computers into general intellectual utilities we must mention a bottleneck for which a practicable solution is not yet in sight. The output devices still leave a great deal to be desired. The teletypewriter is a frustratingly slow means of communication—and it cannot draw a picture. The graphical display devices that are currently available are expensive and require elaborate communication facilities. Inasmuch as, from the standpoint of convenience and of economics, efficient communication between the time-sharing system and its users will become at least as important as the operation of the system itself, this problem presents a crucial challenge to designers.

Three years of experience with the Compatible Time-Sharing System at M.I.T. have been a revelation in many ways. In a sense the system and its users have developed like a growing organism. Most striking is the way the users have built on one another's work and become dependent on the machine. More than half of the commands now written into the system were developed by the users rather than by the professionals charged with programming and developing the system. The users have very generally chosen to link up with one another's private files and the public files. Whereas in conventional computer installations one hardly ever makes use of a program developed by another user, because of the difficulty of exchanging programs and data, here the ease of exchange has encouraged investigators to design their programs with an eye to possible use by other people. They have acted essentially as if they were writing papers to be published in technical journals. Indeed, the analogy is not far-fetched: an editorial board representing the community of users acts as a referee to pass on all new commands that are to be introduced into the system and on all information that is to be stored in the public files.

All in all, the mass memories of our machines are becoming more and more like a community library. The users are beginning to complain about the difficulty of finding out just what the library contains and locating the items that may be of interest to them. The facility actually goes beyond a library's usual services. It already has a rudimentary mechanism whereby one person can communicate with another through a program in real time, that is, while both are using the same program at the same time. There have been cases in which a member of the faculty, sitting at a teletypewriter at home, has worked with a student stationed at a terminal on the campus. It is easy now to envision the use of the system for education or for real-time collaboration between the members of a research team. And it does not take a long stretch of the imagination to envision an entire business organization making and executing all its major decisions with the aid of a time-shared computing system. In such a system the mass memory at all times would contain an up-to-date description of the state of the business.

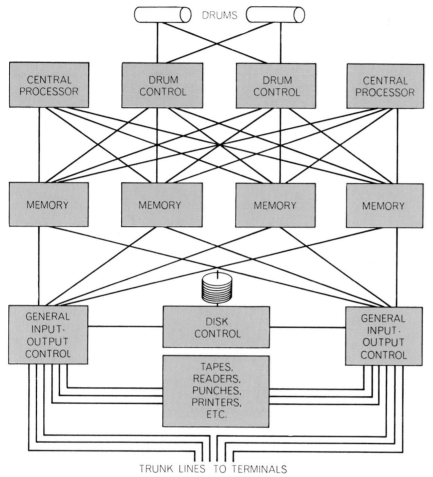

PROPOSED DESIGN for a time-sharing computer would provide more dependability and flexibility than present systems. There would be several elements of each kind, so that no one unit would be critical. The main memories would be central physically as well as functionally. And the supervisor would assign each task to available units as required.

Looking into the future, we can foresee that computer utilities are likely to play an increasingly large part in human affairs. Communities will design systems to perform various functions—intellectual, economic and social—and the systems in turn undoubtedly will have profound effects in shaping the patterns of human life. The coupling between such a utility and the community it serves is so strong that the community is actually a part of the system itself. Together the computer systems and the human users will create new services, new institutions, a new environment and new problems. It is already apparent that, because such a system binds the members of a community more closely together, many of the problems will be ethical ones. The current problem of wiretapping suggests the seriousness with which one must consider the security of a system that may hold in its mass memory detailed information on individuals and organizations. How will access to the utility be controlled? Who will regulate its use? To what ends will the system be devoted, and what safeguards can be devised to prevent its misuse? It is easy to see that the progress of this new technique will raise many social questions as well as technical ones.

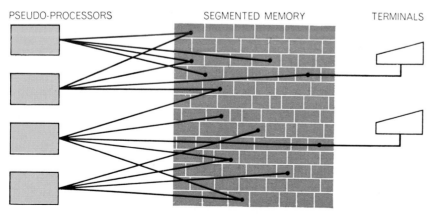

SEGMENTATION OF PROGRAMS adds to the flexibility of a time-sharing system. Each public and private file becomes an independent segment stored in the main memory, each with its own list of authorized users. There are no pseudo-memories, since each pseudo-processor can communicate with a number of segments, some shared with other processors.

II

GAMES, MUSIC, AND ARTIFICIAL INTELLIGENCE

II

GAMES, MUSIC, AND ARTIFICIAL INTELLIGENCE

INTRODUCTION

When a man has been hit on the head, and we want to assure ourselves that his brain has not been damaged, we do not ask him to add. Even *machines* can add. We ask him, as best we can, to demonstrate the highest human intellectual faculties. We ask him to describe the weather, or what country he's in, or how he expects to get home.

Answering such questions is at the border of the capability of today's computers. Addition is well within that border, which is—as might be expected—extended yearly. The fringe area is the area of computer science known as Artificial Intelligence (AI), which is the subject of this section.

Some of the concerns of Artificial Intelligence are hard, at first, to take seriously. Many human activities appear to require no intelligence whatever, and it is dismaying to find that current computer systems can scarcely begin to pursue some of them. Picking out familiar faces in a crowd, for example, is a trivial human task, but no computer today can make any reasonable progress at it.

Other problems under attack by AI workers are more clearly difficult. Everyone knows that it is hard to play a good game of chess. Playing chess with any skill at all requires attention to rules, decisions, plans, and strategies, in increasing order of abstractness. In literary contexts, game-playing has often been used as a metaphor for general intellectual activity; the metaphor is apt, and much AI work has accordingly concentrated in this area.

The position of Artificial Intelligence at the fringe of computer science is a hazardous one. It is similar, in some respects, to the position of philosophy at the fringe of all human knowledge. That is, just as most empirical sciences were once subsumed under "natural philosophy," so many techniques first used only for AI work are now in the computer-science mainstream. And just as philosophy is rarely given credit for initiating the study of (for example) physics, so AI is rarely given credit for its various offspring.

The work of Selfridge and Neisser, as described in "Pattern Recognition by Machines," was once a landmark of Artificial Intelligence. Selfridge and Neisser constructed systems to transcribe hand-sent Morse code, and to recognize hand-printed characters. These tasks, as Selfridge and Neisser explain in their article, are much harder than one might at first assume.

Today, the problems that Selfridge and Neisser attacked are solved routinely in many different applications. Character recognition, for example, is wired into the hardware of a few special-purpose machines; more generally, there exist several editing programs that display text on a screen and allow the user to make his corrections by overwriting new characters.

In the meantime, work in pattern recognition has gone far beyond the Selfridge-Neisser procedure. Selfridge and Neisser used several independent "levels" of analysis in each of their programs. For example, one level of the character-recognition program eliminated isolated image points, which might presumably be due to imperfections in the paper, etc. This elimination was carried out in the absence of any hypothesis about what the character under scan might be; such hypotheses were formed only at a higher level. Today, the interlevel communication that Selfridge and Neisser merely hint at is thought to be essential. In another context, that of understanding natural language (e.g., English), it is easy to see why this should be so.

Computer processing of natural language has always been an attractive goal. Translating and abstracting, for example, seem at first to be mechanical tasks. Certainly they are tedious and costly activities that we would happily turn over to machines.

The most elegant attack on natural language once seemed to be a Selfridge-Neisser-like scheme whose two "levels" were:

(1) Syntactic analysis (parsing);
(2) Semantic analysis (extraction of meaning).

This plan was followed in various projects up to about 1963. None was successful. English "grammars" written for these projects typically contained thousands of rules involving scores of "parts of speech." The basic design remained elegant and natural only to those who could ignore the epicycles being elaborated to make it all work.

In the middle 1960's, work by Bobrow (Minsky, 1963), Raphael (Minsky, 1963), Thompson (1966), and Weizenbaum (1967) showed that, in restricted contexts, English can easily be "understood" if the syntactic analysis is closely guided by concurrent semantic guesswork.

Similarly, picture-processing workers in the period since that of L. G. Roberts (see Minsky, "Artificial Intelligence" p. 123) have come to realize that "low-level" operations (e.g., defining edges) are made much easier if they are based on tentative "high-level" hypotheses (e.g., that a picture portrays a parallelipiped). Procedures that lack the rigid interlevel borders of Selfridge and Neisser are, of course, much harder to understand, and work of this sort (except for language processing) is just beginning.

Two other matters raised by Selfridge and Neisser deserve comment. First, the "random nets" that they speculate on have now been exhaustively analyzed by Minsky and Papert (1969). The analysis is deep and technical, and it does not bear summary here. What *is* worth mentioning is just that the analysis is deep and technical. The possible power of a class of machines can rarely be assessed by uninformed speculation (as in Dreyfus, 1971).

Selfridge and Neisser's enthusiasm for parallel processing has not caught on. Most of the advantages that they claim for parallel processing can be achieved by cleverly organized sequential schemes, and most workers now believe that complex information-processing is generally sequential in man or machine.

As we mentioned, human beings playing formal games use all the identifiable techniques of ordinary intelligence (e.g., setting goals and subgoals, using trial and error, making plans). For this reason, and for others given by Shannon in "A Chess-Playing Machine" and by

Bernstein and Roberts in "Computer vs. Chess-Player," competition in formal games has been a natural application of Artificial Intelligence techniques.

Shannon's classic paper develops most of the important notions of formal game-playing. Shannon points out that complete look-ahead for chess is out of the question, even at electronic speeds. Given that look-ahead must be restricted, Shannon observes the advisability of "selecting" plausible lines of play, in order to apply the restriction both horizontally (alternate moves) and vertically (depth of look-ahead). Finally, Shannon considers (with some skepticism) the possibility of a game-playing program that learns from its mistakes.

The report by Bernstein and Roberts is very much in the spirit of Shannon's speculation. The Bernstein-Roberts program always restricts its look-ahead vertically to four plies, and horizontally to seven choices of move. Presumably because they did not anticipate look-ahead whose restrictions were variable (e.g., look at only one move if it happens to appear very promising, but then look six plies ahead to guard against traps), Bernstein and Roberts are pessimistic about improvements other than development of a machine that is able to learn. Their program was skillful for its time, but hopelessly slow and stupid by human tournament standards (those who do not play chess may not be aware that tournament play is rigidly time-constrained).

A game-playing machine that can learn was implemented with great success by A. L. Samuel of IBM (now at Stanford University). Samuel's checkers-player (1959, 1967) was built along the lines suggested by Shannon, with the ability to reweight the terms entering its position-evaluator. Samuel, himself a mediocre checkers-player, "educated" his program with thousands of recorded master games. The program has defeated state champions, and, although true checkers masters still find Samuel's program no serious match, it certainly plays far above ordinary amateur levels.

Several chess programs have been constructed with similar designs. None has been particularly successful—skill in chess appears to be the sort of highly adapted structure that designless evolution produces only rarely. Psychological studies seem to show differences between chess masters and checkers masters; perhaps it is not surprising that our current chess and checkers programs are different.

In any event, the current champion among chess programs is MACHACK-6, a nonlearning (but continually developed) program by R. Greenblatt of M.I.T. (Greenblatt *et al.*, 1967). By 1968, MACHACK-6 had attained a high "C" rating (out of A, B, C, D) in tournament play with human opponents in the American Chess Federation. MACHACK-6 is constructed along the lines set down by Shannon; its primary distinguishing marks are the subtlety of its (variable) restrictions on look-ahead and its vast knowledge of important special cases.

Comparatively few human beings can play chess at the level of MACHACK-6. Nevertheless, some observers would call MACHACK-6 "intelligent" only if it became a Grand Master. Similarly, these observers claim to be unimpressed by the computer-composed music described by Hiller in "Computer Music." Once again, a linguistic parallel may be illuminating—here, for understanding Hiller's method. Many of us have played the party game in which a sentence is constructed a word at a time, with each participant adding his word knowing only the immediately preceding two or three. This is a Markoff approximation to English composition. Choice of each additional word (like Hiller's choice of each additional note) is contingent on the acceptibility of that word's (that note's) occurrence following the known last few words (notes). The party game is amusing exactly because this approximation to sensible English is so bad.

Any good approximation to English must take account of the *theme* and *hierarchical structure* that underlie any ordinary passage. Words of joint import and common concern form phrases; phrases form sentences; and so on. Most music is similar, and some computer work more recent than Hiller's has focused on this structure (Mathews and Rosler, 1969). Still, the fact is that some listeners enjoy the *Illiac Suite*. Indeed, it is not obvious that Hiller is any less popular, or at least any less popularizable, than many other modern composers of recognized standing.

The final article in this section is the overview, "Artificial Intelligence," by Marvin Minsky. Minsky's general discussion is still pertinent; since 1966, there have been various specific studies within the framework he describes.

Picture-processing continues to be important, and much work has gone into systems that accept television input and analyze the observed scene into objects and space. Current work includes efforts to use textural information and physical knowledge (e.g., solid objects always rest on something) in forming hypotheses about the observed scene.

Generally in conjunction with picture-processing, *physical manipulation* is being studied. Using handlike devices or simple wheeled vehicles, experimenters are attempting to find or make paths through cluttered environments, and to assemble blocks and other simple objects into larger structures.

Some attempt is being made to develop systems with limited supplies of *general knowledge*. For example, one project is attempting to give a program enough general knowledge (e.g., the fact that people wear coats when it is rainy or cold) so that it can read and answer questions about children's stories.

Several different programs of *specialized expertise* are being developed. For example, the MACSYMA system (Martin and Fateman, 1971) provides facilities for formal mathematical manipulation (e.g., indefinite integration) at the level of a college-trained assistant. The DENDRAL system (Duffield *et al.*, 1969) analyzes mass-spectograph output with the skill of a graduate chemist. As we mentioned, however, such systems are widely considered to fall within the area of Artificial Intelligence only until they are in routine operation. So it goes.

8

PATTERN RECOGNITION BY MACHINE

OLIVER G. SELFRIDGE AND ULRIC NEISSER
August, 1960

Can a machine think? The answer to this old chestnut is certainly yes: Computers have been made to play chess and checkers, to prove theorems, to solve intricate problems of strategy. Yet the intelligence implied by such activities has an elusive, unnatural quality. It is not based on any orderly development of cognitive skills. In particular, the machines are not well equipped to select from their environment the things, or the relations, they are going to think about.

In this they are sharply distinguished from intelligent living organisms. Every child learns to analyze speech into meaningful patterns long before he can prove any propositions. Computers can find proofs, but they cannot understand the simplest spoken instructions. Even the earliest computers could do arithmetic superbly, but only very recently have they begun to read the written digits that a child recognizes before he learns to add them. Understanding speech and reading print are examples of a basic intellectual skill that can variously be called cognition, abstraction or perception; perhaps the best general term for it is pattern recognition.

Except for their inability to recognize patterns, machines (or, more accurately, the programs that tell machines what to do) have now met most of the classic criteria of intelligence that skeptics have proposed. They *can* outperform their designers: The checker-playing program devised by Arthur L. Samuel of International Business Machines Corporation usually beats him. They *are* original: The "logic theorist," a creation of a group from the Carnegie Institute of Technology and the Rand Corporation (Allen Newell, Herbert Simon and J. C. Shaw) has found proofs for many of the theorems in *Principia Mathematica*, the monumental work in mathematical logic by A. N. Whitehead and Bertrand Russell. At least one proof is more elegant than the Whitehead-Russell version.

Sensible as they are, the machines are not perceptive. The information they receive must be fed to them one "bit" (a contraction of "binary digit," denoting a unit of information) at a time, up to perhaps millions of bits. Computers do not organize or classify the material in any very subtle or generally applicable way. They perform only highly specialized operations on carefully prepared inputs.

In contrast, a man is continuously exposed to a welter of data from his senses, and abstracts from it the patterns relevant to his activity at the moment. His ability to solve problems, prove theorems and generally run his life depends on this type of perception. We suspect that until programs to perceive patterns can be developed, achievements in mechanical problem-solving will remain isolated technical triumphs.

Developing pattern-recognition programs has proved rather difficult. One reason for the difficulty lies in the nature of the task. A man who abstracts a pattern from a complex of stimuli has essentially classified the possible inputs. But very often the basis of classification is unknown, even to himself; it is too complex to be specified explicitly. Asked to define a pattern, the man does so by example; as a logician might say, ostensively. This letter is A, that person is mother, these speech sounds are a request to pass the salt. The important patterns are defined by experience. Every human being acquires his pattern classes by adapting to a social or environmental consensus—in short, by learning.

In company with workers at various institutions our group at the Lincoln Laboratory of the Massachusetts Institute of Technology has been working on mechanical recognition of patterns. Thus far only a few simple cases have been tackled. We shall discuss two examples. The first one is MAUDE (for Morse Automatic Decoder), a program for translating, or rather transliterating, hand-sent Morse code. This program was developed at the Lincoln Laboratory by a group of workers under the direction of Bernard Gold.

If telegraphers sent ideal Morse, recognition would be easy. The keyings, or "marks," for dashes would be exactly three times as long as the marks for dots; spaces separating the marks within a letter or other character (mark spaces) would be as long as dots; spaces between characters (character spaces), three times as long; spaces separating words (word spaces), seven times as long. Unfortunately human operators do not transmit these ideal intervals. A machine that processed a signal on the assumption that they do would perform very poorly indeed. In an actual message the distinction between dots and dashes is far from clear. There is a great deal of variation among the dots and dashes, and also among the three kinds of space. In fact, when a long message sent by a single operator is analyzed, it frequently turns out that some dots are longer than some dashes, and that some mark spaces are longer than some character spaces.

With a little practice in receiving code, the average person has no trouble with these irregularities. The patterns of the letters are defined for him in terms of the continuing consensus of experience, and he adapts to them as he listens. Soon he does not hear dots and dashes at all, but perceives the characters as wholes. Exactly how he does so is still obscure, and the mechanism probably varies widely from one operator to another. In any event transliteration is impossible if each mark and space is considered individually. MAUDE therefore uses contextual information, but far less than is available to a trained operator. The machine program knows all the standard Morse characters and a few compound ones, but no syllables or words. A trained operator, on the other hand, hears the characters themselves embedded in a meaningful context.

Empirically it is easier to distinguish between the two kinds of mark than among the three kinds of space. The main problem for any mechanical Morse translator is to segment the message into its characters by identifying the character spaces. MAUDE begins by assuming that the longest of each six consecutive spaces is a character space (since no Morse character is more than six marks long), and the shortest is a mark space. It is important to note that although the former rule follows logically from the structure of the ideal code, and that the latter seems quite plausible, their effec-

tiveness can be demonstrated only by experiment. In fact the rules fail less than once in 10,000 times.

The decoding process proceeds as follows [see illustration on page 102]. The marks and spaces, received by the machine in the form of electrical pulses, are converted into a sequence of numbers measuring their duration. (For technical reasons these numbers are then converted into their logarithms.) The sequence of durations representing spaces

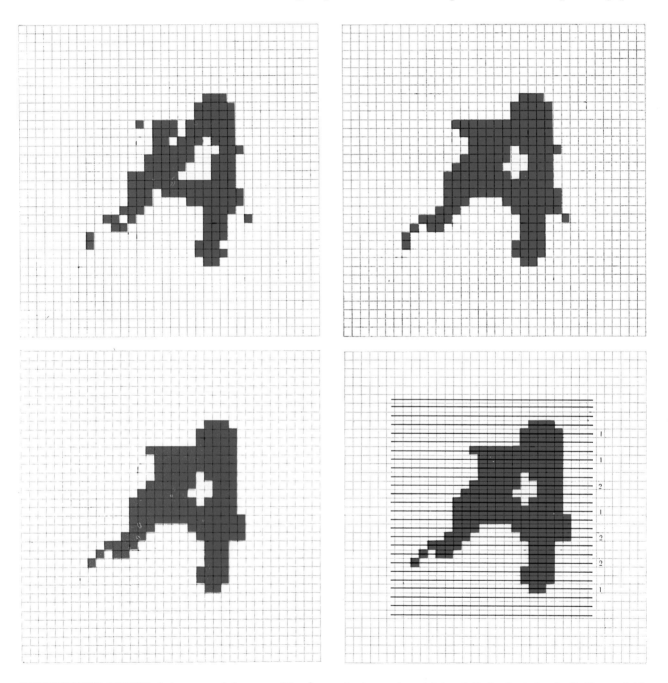

HAND-PRINTED LETTER A is processed for recognition by computer. Original sample is placed on grid and converted to a cellular pattern by completely filling in all squares through which lines pass (*top left*). The computer then cleans up the sample, fill-ing in gaps (*top right*) and eliminating isolated cells (*bottom left*). The program tests the pattern for a variety of features. The test illustrated here (*bottom right*) is for the maximum number of in-tersections of the sample with all horizontal lines across the grid.

is processed first. The machine examines each group of six (spaces one through six, two through seven, three through eight and so on), recording in each the longest and shortest durations. When this process is complete, about 75 per cent of the character spaces and about 50 per cent of the mark spaces will have been identified.

To classify the remaining spaces a threshold is computed. It is set at the most plausible dividing line between the range of durations in which mark spaces have been found and the range of the identified character spaces. Every unclassified number larger than the threshold is then identified as a character space; every one smaller than the threshold, as a mark space.

Now, by a similar process, the numbers representing marks are identified as dots and dashes. Combining the classified marks and spaces gives a string of tentative segments, separated by character spaces. These are inspected and compared to a set of proper Morse characters stored in the machine. (There are about 50 of these, out of the total of 127 possible sequences of six or fewer marks.) Experience has shown that when one of the tentative segments is not acceptable, it is most likely that one of the supposed mark spaces within the segment should be a character space instead. The program reclassifies the longest space in the segment as a character space and examines the two new characters thus formed. The procedure continues until every segment is an acceptable character, whereupon the message is printed out.

In the course of transmitting a long message, operators usually change speed from time to time. MAUDE adapts to these changes. The computed thresholds are local, moving averages that shift with the general lengthening or shortening of marks and spaces. Thus a mark of a certain duration could be classified as a dot in one part of the message and a dash in another.

MAUDE's error rate is only slightly higher than that of a skilled human operator. Thus it is at least possible for a machine to recognize patterns even where the basis of classification is variable and not fully specified in advance. Moreover, the program illustrates an important general point. Its success depends on the rules by which the continuous message is divided into appropriate segments. Segmentation seems likely to be a primary problem in all mechanical pattern-recognition, particularly in the recognition of speech, since the natural pauses in spoken language do not generally come between words. MAUDE handles the segmentation problems in terms of context, and this will often be appropriate. In other respects MAUDE does not provide an adequate basis for generalizing about pattern recognition. The patterns of Morse code are too easy, and the processing is rather specialized.

Our second example deals with a more challenging problem: the recognition of hand-printed letters of the alphabet. The characters that people print in the ordinary course of filling out forms and questionnaires are surprisingly varied. Gaps abound where continuous lines might be expected; curves and sharp angles appear interchangeably; there is almost every imaginable distortion of slant, shape and size. Even human readers cannot always identify such characters; their error rate is about 3 per cent on randomly selected letters and numbers, seen out of context.

The first step in designing a mechanical reader is to provide it with a means of assimilating the visual data. By nature computers consider information in strings of bits: sequences of zeros and ones recorded in on-off devices. The simplest way to encode a character into such a sequence is to convert it into a sort of half-tone by splitting it into a mesh or matrix of squares as fine as may be necessary. Each square is then either black or white—a binary situation that the machine is designed to handle. Making such half-tones presents no problem. For example, an image of the letter could be projected on a bank of photocells, with the output of each cell controlling a binary device in the computer. In the ex-

WORD SPACES

DASHES AND LETTER SPACES

DOTS AND MARK SPACES

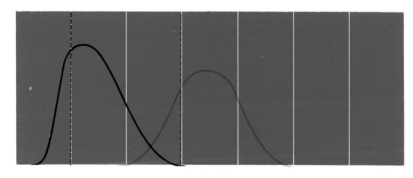

NUMBER OF SYMBOLS

DURATION

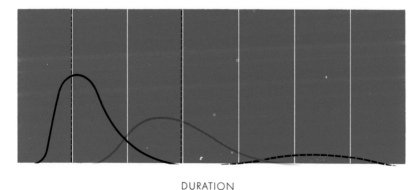

NUMBER OF SPACES

DURATION

VARIABILITY OF MORSE CODE sent by a human operator is illustrated in these curves. Upper graph shows range of durations for dots (*black curve*) and dashes (*gray curve*) in a message. Lower graph gives the same information for spaces between marks within a character (*solid black curve*), spaces between characters (*gray curve*) and between words (*broken curve*). Ideal durations are shown by brackets at top and vertical broken lines.

periments to be described here the appropriate digital information from the matrix was recorded on punch cards and was fed into the computer in this form.

Once this sequence of bits has been put in, how shall the program proceed to identify it? Perhaps the most obvious approach is a simple matching scheme, which would evaluate the similarity of the unknown to a series of ideal templates of all the letters, previously stored in digital form in the machine. The sequence of zeros and ones representing the unknown letter would be compared to each template sequence, and the number of matching digits recorded in each case. The highest number of matches would identify the letter.

In its primitive form the scheme would clearly fail. Even if the unknown were identical to the template, slight changes in position, orientation or size could destroy the match completely [see *top illustration on page 103*]. This difficulty has long been recognized, and in some character-recognition programs it has been met by inserting a level of information-processing ahead of the template-matching procedure. The sample is shifted, rotated and magnified or reduced in order to put it into a standard, or at least a more tractable, form.

Although obviously an improvement over raw matching, such a procedure is still inadequate. What it does is to compare shapes rather successfully. But letters are a good deal more than mere shapes. Even when a sample has been converted to standard size, position and orientation, it may match a wrong template more closely than it matches the right one [see *bottom illustration on page 103.*]

Nevertheless the scheme illustrates what we believe to be an important general principle. The critical change was from a program with a single level of operation to a program with two distinctly different levels. The first level shifts, and the second one matches. Such a hierarchical structure is forced on the recognition system by the nature of the entities to be recognized. The letter A is defined by the set of configurations that people call A, and their selections can be described—or imitated—only by a multilevel program.

We have said that letter patterns cannot be described merely as shapes. It appears that they can be specified only in terms of a preponderance of certain *features*. Thus A tends to be thinner at the top than at the bottom; it is roughly concave at the bottom; it usually has two main strokes more vertical than horizontal, one more horizontal than vertical, and so on. All these features taken together characterize A rather more closely than they characterize any other letter. Singly none of them is sufficient. For example, W is also roughly concave

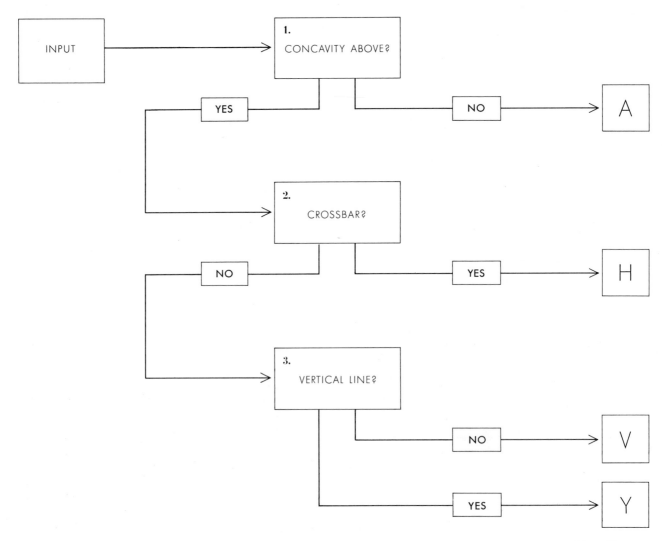

SEQUENTIAL-PROCESSING program for distinguishing four letters, A, H, V and Y employs three test features: presence or absence of a concavity above, a crossbar and a vertical line. The tests are applied in order, with each outcome determining the next step.

at the bottom, and H has a pattern of horizontal and vertical strokes similar to that described for A. Each letter has its own set of probable features, and a successful character recognizer will determine which set is the best fit to an unknown sample.

So far nothing has been said about how the features are to be determined and how the program will use them. The template-matching scheme represents one approach. Its "features," in a sense, are the individual cells of the matrix representing the unknown sample, and its procedure is to match them with corresponding cells in the template. Both features and procedure are determined by the designer. We have seen that this scheme will not succeed. In fact, any system must fail if it tries to specify every detail of a procedure for identifying patterns that are themselves defined only ostensively. A pattern-recognition system must learn. But how much?

At one extreme there have been attempts to make it learn, or generate, everything: the features, the processing, the decision procedure. The initial state of such a system is called a "random net." A large number of on-off computer elements are multiply interconnected in a random way. Each is thus fed by several others. The thresholds of the elements (the number of signals that must be received before the element fires) are then adjusted on the basis of performance. In other words, the system learns by reinforcing some pathways through the net and weakening others.

How far a random net can evolve is controversial. Probably a net can come to act as though it used templates. However, none has yet been shown capable of generating features more sophisticated than those based, like templates, on single matrix-cells. Indeed, we do not believe that this is possible.

At present the only way the machine

can get an adequate set of features is from a human programmer. The effectiveness of any particular set can be demonstrated only by experiment. In general there is probably safety in numbers. The designer will do well to include all the features he can think of that might plausibly be useful.

A program that does not develop its own features may nevertheless be capable of modifying some subsequent level of the decision procedure, as we shall see. First however, let us consider that procedure itself. There are two fundamentally different possibilities: sequential and parallel processing. In sequential processing the features are inspected in a predetermined order, the outcome of each test determining the next step. Each letter is represented by a unique sequence of binary decisions. To take a simple example, a program to distinguish the letters A, H, V and Y

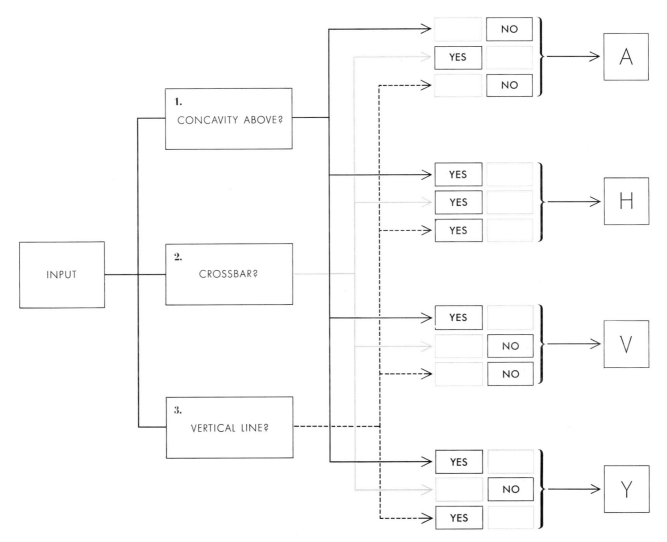

PARALLEL-PROCESSING program uses the same test features as the sequential program on opposite page, but applies all tests simultaneously and makes decision on the basis of the combined outcomes. The input is a sample of one of the letters A, H, V and Y.

LETTER	SAMPLES	OUTCOME			
		1	2	3	4
A	39		33	6	
E	46	6	35	5	
I	25	25			
L	24	7	17		
M	24			18	6
N	28		2	25	1
O	34		27	7	
R	33		28	4	1
S	38	8	30		
T	39	10	22	7	
TOTAL	330	56	194	72	8

"CENSUS" represents information learned by letter-recognition program during training period. This table summarizes the outcomes of the test for maximum number of intersections with a horizontal line, applied to a total of 330 identified samples in the learning process.

might decide among them on the basis of the presence or absence of three features: a concavity at the top, a crossbar and a vertical line. The sequential process would ask first: "Is there a concavity at the top?" If the answer is no, the sample is A. If the answer is yes, the program asks: "Is there a crossbar?" If yes, the letter is H; if no, then: "Is there a vertical line?" If yes, the letter is Y; if no, V [see illustration on page 98].

In parallel processing all the questions would be asked at once, and all the answers presented simultaneously to the decision-maker [see illustration on preceding page]. Different combinations identify the different letters. One might think of the various features as being inspected by little demons, all of whom then shout the answers in concert to a decision-making demon. From this conceit comes the name "Pandemonium" for parallel processing.

Of the two systems the sequential type is the more natural for a machine. Computer programs are sequences of instructions, in which choices or alternatives are usually introduced as "conditional transfers": Follow one set of instructions if a certain number is negative (say) and another set of instructions if it is not. Programs of this kind can be highly efficient, especially in cases where any given decision is almost certain to be right.

But in "noisy" situations sequential programs require elaborate checking and back-tracking procedures to compensate for erroneous decisions. Parallel processing, on the other hand, need make no special allowance for error and uncertainty.

Furthermore, some features are simply not subject to a reasonable dichotomy. An A very surely has a crossbar, an O very surely has not. But what about B? The most we can say is that it has more of a crossbar than O, and less than A. A Pandemonium program can handle the situation by having the demons shout more or less loudly. In other words, the information flowing through the system need not be binary; it can represent the quantitative preponderance of the various features.

Still another advantage of parallel processing lies in the possibility of making small changes in a network for experimental purposes. In typical sequential programs the only possible changes involve replacing a zero with a one, or vice versa. In parallel ones, on the other hand, the weight given to crossbarness in deciding if the unknown is actually B may be changed by as small an amount as desired. Experimental changes of this kind need not be made by the programmer alone. A program can be designed to alter internal weights as a result of

experience and to profit from its mistakes. Such learning is much easier to incorporate into a Pandemonium than into a sequential system, where a change at any point has grave consequences for large parts of the system.

Parallel processing seems to be the human way of handling pattern recognition as well. Speech can be understood if all acoustic frequencies above 2,000 cycles per second are eliminated, but it can also be understood if those below 2,000 are eliminated instead. Depth perception is excellent if both eyes are open and the head is held still; it is also excellent if one eye is open and the head is allowed to move.

A Pandemonium system that learns from experience has been tested by Worthie Doyle of the Lincoln Laboratory. At present it is programmed to identify 10 hand-printed characters, and has been tested on samples of A, E, I, L, M, N, O, R, S and T. The program has six levels: (1) input, (2) clean-up, (3) inspection of features, (4) comparison with learned-feature distribution, (5) computation of probabilities and (6) decision. The input is a 1,024-cell matrix, 32 on a side. At the second level the sample character is smoothed by filling in isolated gaps and eliminating isolated patches [see illustration on page 96].

Recognition is based on such features as the relative length of different edges and the maximum number of intersections of the sample with a horizontal line. (The computer "draws" the lines by inspecting every horizontal row in the matrix, and recognizes "intersections" as sequences of ones separated by sequences of zeros.) No single feature is essential to recognition, and various numbers of them have been tried. The particular program shown here [see illustration on opposite page] uses 28.

Every letter fed into the machine is tested for each of the features. During the learning phase a number of samples

RECOGNITION PROGRAM for hand-printed letters applies the 28 feature tests listed by code name at left. Names represent such features as maximum intersections with horizontal line (HOMSXC), concavity facing south (SOUCAV) and so on. Figures in right-hand section of table are relative probabilities of all letters for each test outcome. The program decides on the letter with the largest total of all probabilities. In the example shown here the decision is for the letter A, with a probability total of 4.579.

TYPE OF TEST AND DESIGNATION		OUTCOME	A	E	I	L	M	N	O	R	S	T
HORIZONTAL AND VERTICAL CROSS-SECTIONS	HOMSXC	3	.083	.070			.250	.347	.097	.056		.097
	VEMSXC	3	.073	.339			.040		.008	.194	.258	.089
	HORUNS	2111111		.500						.500		
	VERUNS	2111111					1.000					
STROKES	HORSTR	1	.182	.006	.125	.125	.125	.146	.016	.057	.016	.203
	VERSTR	2	.178	.007			.170	.207	.229	.207		
EDGE LENGTHS AND RATIOS	SEDGE	1	.267	.007		.014	.158	.115	.007	.165		.266
	WEDGE	1	.083	.071	.024	.024	.035	.012		.047	.318	.389
	NEDGE	2	.259	.024	.153	.024	.106	.106	.071	.059	.189	.012
	EEDGE	4	.232		.161		.214	.286	.107			
	NO:SOU	4	.513				.205	.077		.128		.077
	EA:WES	1	.055	.400		.309	.018	.036		.163		.018
PROFILES	SOUCAV	3	.150				.800	.050				
	WESCAV	2	.047	.094	.023	.012	.023	.035	.035	.059	.412	.259
	NORCAV	1	.133	.177	.100	.092	.004		.133	.108	.116	.137
	EASCAV	1	.155	.005	.115	.095	.105	.130	.170	.010	.050	.165
	SOUBOT	220	.268	.106		.068	.159	.167	.008	.220	.008	
	WESBOT	221	.030	.030	.061						.364	.515
	NORBOT	121	.290	.145					.354	.042	.042	.125
	EASBOT	121	.326				.020	.102	.266	.020	.245	.020
INTERNAL STRUCTURE	SBOTSG	2	.250	.008		.016	.125	.141	.219	.203	.039	
	WBOTSG	1	.161	.076	.090	.099	.108	.121	.063	.081	.045	.157
	NBOTSG	1	.119	.190	.111	.102	.013	.018	.089	.040	.159	.159
	EBOTSG	1	.147	.058	.098	.103	.103	.121	.062	.071	.076	.061
	SOUBEN	20					.333	.167				.500
	WESBEN	10	.198	.143	.011	.022	.121	.132	.011	.099	.022	.241
	NORBEN	10	.169	.180		.135	.079			.146	.247	.045
	EASBEN	10	.211	.012	.012	.118	.176	.106		.176		.188
TOTAL SCORE			4.579	2.648	1.084	1.358	3.490	3.622	1.945	2.851	2.606	3.823

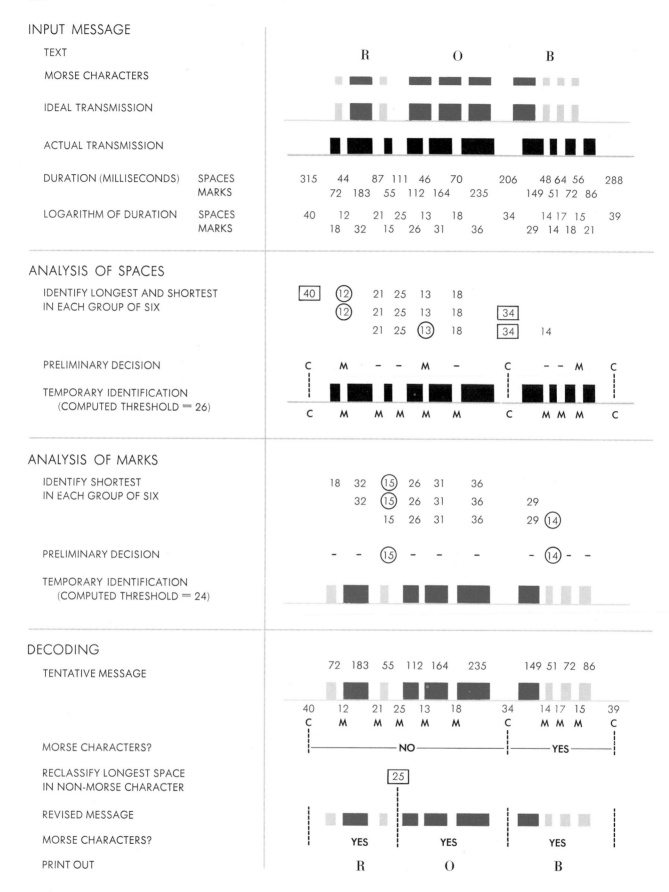

"MAUDE" PROGRAM, described in text, translates Morse code. Marks identified as dots are shown in light color; marks identified as dashes, in dark color. Unidentified marks are in black. Character spaces are denoted by C; mark spaces, by M. A circle around a number indicates that it is the smallest in a group; a rectangle means it is the largest. Analysis of spaces and marks proceeds by an examination of successive groups of six throughout the message. The table shows only the first three such groups in each case.

of each of the 10 letters is presented and identified. For every feature the program compiles a table or "census." It tests each sample and enters the outcome under the appropriate letter. When the learning period is finished, the table shows how many times each outcome occurred for each of the 10 letters. The table on page 100, which refers to maximum intersections with a horizontal line, represents the experience gained from a total of 330 training samples. It shows, for example, that the outcome (three intersections) occurred 72 times distributed among six A's, five E's, 18 M's, 25 N's, seven O's, four R's, seven T's and no other letters. The other possible outcomes are similarly recorded.

Next the 28 censuses are converted to tables of estimated probabilities, by dividing each entry by the appropriate total. Thus the outcome—three intersections—comes from an A with a probability of .083 (6/72); an E, with a probability of .070 (5/72), and so on.

Now the system is ready to consider an unknown sample. It carries out the 28 tests and "looks up" each outcome in the corresponding feature census, entering the estimated probabilities in a table. Then the total probabilities are computed for each letter. The final decision is made by choosing the letter with the highest probability.

This program makes only about 10 per cent fewer correct identifications than human readers make—a respectable performance, to be sure. At the same time, the things it cannot do point to the difficulties that still lie ahead. We would emphasize three general problems: segmentation, hierarchical learning and feature generation.

Characters must be fed in one at a time. The program is unable to segment continuous written material. The problem will doubtless be relatively easy to solve for text consisting of separate printed characters, but will be more formidable in the case of cursive script.

The program learns on one level only. The relation between feature presence and character probability is determined by experience; everything else is fixed by the designer. It would certainly be desirable for a character recognizer to use experience for more general improvements: to change its clean-up procedures, alter the way probabilities are combined and refine its decision process. Eventually we look to recognition of words; at that point the program will have to learn a vocabulary so that it can use context in identifying dubious letters. At the moment, however, neither we nor any other designers have any experience with the interaction of several levels of learning.

The most important learning process of all is still untouched: No current program can generate test features of its own. The effectiveness of all of them is forever restricted by the ingenuity or arbitrariness of their programmers. We can barely guess how this restriction might be overcome. Until it is, "artificial intelligence" will remain tainted with artifice.

TEMPLATE MATCHING cannot succeed when the unknown letter (*color*) has the wrong size, orientation or position. The program must begin by adjusting sample to standard form.

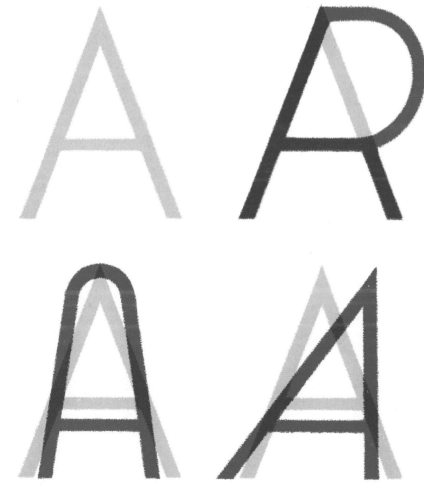

INCORRECT MATCH may result even when sample (*color*) has been converted to standard form. Here R matches A template more closely than do samples of the correct letter.

9

A CHESS-PLAYING MACHINE

CLAUDE E. SHANNON
February, 1950

FOR CENTURIES philosophers and scientists have speculated about whether or not the human brain is essentially a machine. Could a machine be designed that would be capable of "thinking"? During the past decade several large-scale electronic computing machines have been constructed which are capable of something very close to the reasoning process. These new computers were designed primarily to carry out purely numerical calculations. They perform automatically a long sequence of additions, multiplications and other arithmetic operations at a rate of thousands per second. The basic design of these machines is so general and flexible, however, that they can be adapted to work symbolically with elements representing words, propositions or other conceptual entities.

One such possibility, which is already being investigated in several quarters, is that of translating from one language to another by means of a computer. The immediate goal is not a finished literary rendition, but only a word-by-word translation that would convey enough of the meaning to be understandable. Computing machines could also be employed for many other tasks of a semi-rote, semi-thinking character, such as designing electrical filters and relay circuits, helping to regulate airplane traffic at busy airports, and routing long-distance telephone calls most efficiently over a limited number of trunks.

Some of the possibilities in this direction can be illustrated by setting up a computer in such a way that it will play a fair game of chess. This problem, of course, is of no importance in itself, but it was undertaken with a serious purpose in mind. The investigation of the chess-playing problem is intended to develop techniques that can be used for more practical applications.

The chess machine is an ideal one to start with for several reasons. The problem is sharply defined, both in the allowed operations (the moves of chess) and in the ultimate goal (checkmate). It is neither so simple as to be trivial nor too difficult for satisfactory solution. And such a machine could be pitted against a human opponent, giving a clear measure of the machine's ability in this type of reasoning.

There is already a considerable literature on the subject of chess-playing machines. During the late 18th and early 19th centuries a Hungarian inventor named Wolfgang von Kempelen astounded Europe with a device known as the Maelzel Chess Automaton, which toured the Continent to large audiences. A number of papers purporting to explain its operation, including an analytical essay by Edgar Allan Poe, soon appeared. Most of the analysts concluded, quite correctly, that the automaton was operated by a human chess master concealed inside. Some years later the exact manner of operation was exposed.

A more honest attempt to design a chess-playing machine was made in 1914 by a Spanish inventor named L. Torres y Quevedo, who constructed a device that played an end game of king and rook against king. The machine, playing the side with king and rook, would force checkmate in a few moves however its human opponent played. Since an explicit set of rules can be given for making satisfactory moves in such an end game, the problem is relatively simple, but the idea was quite advanced for that period.

AN electronic computer can be set up to play a complete game. In order to explain the actual setup of a chess machine, it may be best to start with a general picture of a computer and its operation.

A general-purpose electronic computer is an extremely complicated device containing several thousand vacuum tubes, relays and other elements. The basic principles involved, however, are quite simple. The machine has four main parts: 1) an "arithmetic organ," 2) a control element, 3) a numerical memory and 4) a program memory. (In some designs the two memory functions are carried out in the same physical apparatus.) The manner of operation is exactly analogous to a human computer carrying out a series of numerical calculations with an ordinary desk computing machine. The arithmetic organ corresponds to the desk computing machine, the control element to the human operator, the numerical memory to the work sheet on which intermediate and final results are recorded, and the program memory to the computing routine describing the series of operations to be performed.

In an electronic computing machine, the numerical memory consists of a large number of "boxes," each capable of holding a number. To set up a problem on the computer, it is necessary to assign box numbers to all numerical quantities involved, and then to construct a program telling the machine what arithmetical operations must be performed on the numbers and where the results should go. The program consists of a sequence of "orders," each describing an elementary calculation. For example, a typical order may read A 372, 451, 133. This means: add the number stored in box 372 to that in box 451, and put the sum in box 133. Another type of order requires the machine to make a decision. For example, the order C 291, 118, 345 tells the machine to compare the contents of boxes 291 and 118; if the number in box 291 is larger, the machine goes on to the next order in the program; if not, it takes its next order from box 345. This type of order enables the machine to choose from alternative procedures, depending on the results of previous calculations. The "vocabulary" of an electronic computer may include as many as 30 different types of orders.

After the machine is provided with a program, the initial numbers required for the calculation are placed in the numerical memory and the machine then automatically carries out the computation. Of course such a machine is most useful in problems involving an enormous number of individual calculations, which would be too laborious to carry out by hand.

THE problem of setting up a computer for playing chess can be divided into three parts: first, a code must be chosen so that chess positions and the chess pieces can be represented as numbers; second, a strategy must be found for choosing the moves to be made; and third, this strategy must be translated into a sequence of elementary computer orders, or a program.

A suitable code for the chessboard and the chess pieces is shown in the diagram to the left at the bottom of this page. Each square on the board has a number consisting of two digits, the first digit corresponding to the "rank" or horizontal row, the second to the "file" or vertical row. Each different chess piece also is designated by a number: a pawn is numbered 1, a knight 2, a bishop 3, a rook 4 and so on. White pieces are represented by positive numbers and black pieces by negative ones. The positions of all the pieces on the board can be shown by a sequence of 64 numbers, with zeros to indicate the empty squares. Thus any chess position can be recorded as a series of numbers and stored in the numerical memory of a computing machine.

A chess move is specified by giving the number of the square on which the piece stands and of the one to which it is moved. Ordinarily two numbers would be sufficient to describe a move, but to take care of the special case of the promotion of a pawn to a higher piece a third number is necessary. This number indicates the piece to which the pawn is converted. In all other moves the third number is zero. Thus a knight move from square 01 to 22 is encoded into 01, 22, 0. The move of a pawn from 62 to 72, and its promotion to a queen, is represented by 62, 72, 5.

The second main problem is that of deciding on a strategy of play. A straightforward process must be found for cal-

culating a reasonably good move for any given chess position. This is the most difficult part of the problem. The program designer can employ here the principles of correct play that have been evolved by expert chess players. These empirical principles are a means of bringing some order to the maze of possible variations of a chess game. Even the high speeds available in electronic computers are hopelessly inadequate to play perfect chess by calculating all possible variations to the end of the game. In a typical chess position there will be about 32 possible moves with 32 possible replies—already this creates 1,024 possibilities. Most chess games last 40 moves or more for each side. So the total number of possible variations in an average game is about 10^{120}. A machine calculating one variation each millionth of a second would require over 10^{95} years to decide on its first move!

Other methods of attempting to play perfect chess seem equally impracticable; we resign ourselves, therefore, to having the machine play a reasonably skillful game, admitting occasional moves that may not be the best. This, of course, is precisely what human players do: no one plays a perfect game.

In setting up a strategy on the machine one must establish a method of numerical evaluation for any given chess position. A chess player looking at a position can form an estimate as to which side, White or Black, has the advantage. Furthermore, his evaluation is roughly quantitative. He may say, "White has a rook for a bishop, an advantage of about two pawns"; or "Black has sufficient mo-

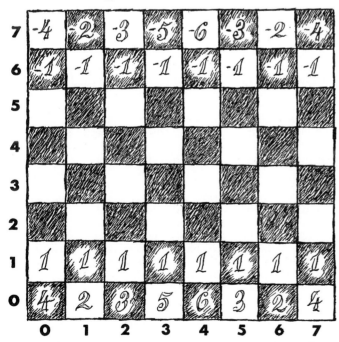

CODE for a chess-playing machine is plotted on a chessboard. Each square can be designated by two digits, one representing the horizontal row and the other the vertical. Pieces also are coded in numbers (*see text*).

PROBLEM that the machine could solve brilliantly might begin with this chess position. The machine would sacrifice a rook and a queen, the most powerful piece on the board, and then win in only one more move.

bility to compensate for a sacrificed pawn." These judgments are based on long experience and are summarized in the principles of chess expounded in chess literature. For example, it has been found that a queen is worth nine pawns, a rook is worth five, and a bishop or a knight is worth about three. As a first rough approximation, a position can be evaluated by merely adding up the total forces for each side, measured in terms of the pawn unit. There are, however, numerous other features which must be taken into account: the mobility and placement of pieces, the weakness of king protection, the nature of the pawn formation, and so on. These too can be given numerical weights and combined in the evaluation, and it is here that the knowledge and experience of chess masters must be enlisted.

ASSUMING that a suitable method of position evaluation has been decided upon, how should a move be selected? The simplest process is to consider all the possible moves in the given position and choose the one that gives the best immediate evaluation. Since, however, chess players generally look more than one move ahead, one must take account of the opponent's various possible responses to each projected move. Assuming that the opponent's reply will be the one giving the best evaluation from his point of view, we would choose the move that would leave us as well off as possible after his best reply. Unfortunately, with the computer speeds at present available, the machine could not explore all the possibilities for more than two moves ahead for each side, so a strategy of this type would play a poor game by human standards. Good chess players frequently play combinations four or five moves deep, and occasionally world champions have seen as many as 20 moves ahead. This is possible only because the variations they consider are highly selected. They do not investigate all lines of play, but only the important ones.

The amount of selection exercised by chess masters in examining possible variations has been studied experimentally by the Dutch chess master and psychologist A. D. De Groot. He showed various typical positions to chess masters and asked them to decide on the best move, describing aloud their analyses of the positions as they thought them through. By this procedure the number and depth of the variations examined could be determined. In one typical case a chess master examined 16 variations, ranging in depth from one Black move to five Black and four White moves. The total number of positions considered was 44.

Clearly it would be highly desirable to improve the strategy for the machine by including such a selection process in it. Of course one could go too far in this direction. Investigating one particular line of play for 40 moves would be as bad as investigating all lines for just two moves. A suitable compromise would be to examine only the important possible variations—that is, forcing moves, captures and main threats—and carry out the investigation of the possible moves far enough to make the consequences of each fairly clear. It is possible to set up some rough criteria for selecting important variations, not as efficiently as a chess master, but sufficiently well to reduce the number of variations appreciably and thereby permit a deeper investigation of the moves actually considered.

The final problem is that of reducing the strategy to a sequence of orders, translated into the machine's language. This is a relatively straightforward but tedious process, and we shall only indicate some of the general features. The complete program is made up of nine sub-programs and a master program that calls the sub-programs into operation as needed. Six of the sub-programs deal with the movements of the various kinds of pieces. In effect they tell the machine the allowed moves for these pieces. Another sub-program enables the machine to make a move "mentally" without actually carrying it out: that is, with a given position stored in its memory it can construct the position that would result if the move were made. The seventh sub-program enables the computer to make a list of all possible moves in a given position, and the last sub-program evaluates any given position. The master program correlates and supervises the application of the sub-programs. It starts the seventh sub-program making a list of possible moves, which in turn calls in previous sub-programs to determine where the various pieces could move. The master program then evaluates the resulting positions by means of the eighth sub-program and compares the results according to the process described above. After comparison of all the investigated variations, the one that gives the best evaluation according to the machine's calculations is selected. This move is translated into standard chess notation and typed out by the machine.

It is believed that an electronic computer programmed in this manner would play a fairly strong game at speeds comparable to human speeds. A machine has several obvious advantages over a human player: 1) it can make individual calculations with much greater speed; 2) its play is free of errors other than those due to deficiencies of the program, whereas human players often make very simple and obvious blunders; 3) it is free from laziness, or the temptation to make an instinctive move without proper analysis of the position; 4) it is free from "nerves," so it will make no blunders due to overconfidence or defeatism. Against these advantages, however, must be weighed the flexibility, imagination and learning capacity of the human mind.

Under some circumstances the machine might well defeat the program designer. In one sense, the designer can surely outplay his machine; knowing the strategy used by the machine, he can apply the same tactics at a deeper level. But he would require several weeks' to calculate a move, while the machine uses only a few minutes. On an equal time basis, the speed, patience and deadly accuracy of the machine would be telling against human fallibility. Sufficiently nettled, however, the designer could easily weaken the playing skill of the machine by changing the program in such a way as to reduce the depth of investigation (*see drawing on opposite page*). This idea was expressed by a cartoon in *The Saturday Evening Post* a while ago.

AS described so far, the machine would always make the same move in the same position. If the opponent made the same moves, this would always lead to the same game. Once the opponent won a game, he could win every time thereafter by playing the same strategy, taking advantage of some particular position in which the machine chooses a weak move. One way to vary the machine's play would be to introduce a statistical element. Whenever it was confronted with two or more possible moves that were about equally good according to the machine's calculations, it would choose from them at random. Thus if it arrived at the same position a second time it might choose a different move.

Another place where statistical variation could be introduced is in the opening game. It would be desirable to have a number of standard openings, perhaps a few hundred, stored in the memory of the machine. For the first few moves, until the opponent deviated from the standard responses or the machine reached the end of the stored sequence of moves, the machine would play by memory. This could hardly be considered cheating, since that is the way chess masters play the opening.

We may note that within its limits a machine of this type will play a brilliant game. It will readily make spectacular sacrifices of important pieces in order to gain a later advantage or to give checkmate, provided the completion of the combination occurs within its computing limits. For example, in the position illustrated at the lower right on page 49 the machine would quickly discover the sacrificial mate in three moves:

White	Black
1. R-K8 Ch	R X R
2. Q-Kt4 Ch	Q X Q
3. Kt-B6 Mate	

Winning combinations of this type are frequently overlooked in amateur play.

The chief weakness of the machine is

that it will not learn by its mistakes. The only way to improve its play is by improving the program. Some thought has been given to designing a program that would develop its own improvements in strategy with increasing experience in play. Although it appears to be theoretically possible, the methods thought of so far do not seem to be very practical. One possibility is to devise a program that would change the terms and coefficients involved in the evaluation function on the basis of the results of games the machine had already played. Small variations might be introduced in these terms, and the values would be selected to give the greatest percentage of wins.

THE GORDIAN question, more easily raised than answered, is: Does a chess-playing machine of this type "think"? The answer depends entirely on how we define thinking. Since there is no general agreement as to the precise connotation of this word, the question has no definite answer. From a behavioristic point of view, the machine acts as though it were thinking. It has always been considered that skillful chess play requires the reasoning faculty. If we regard thinking as a property of external actions rather than internal method the machine is surely thinking.

The thinking process is considered by some psychologists to be essentially characterized by the following steps: various possible solutions of a problem are tried out mentally or symbolically without actually being carried out physically; the best solution is selected by a mental evaluation of the results of these trials; and the solution found in this way is then acted upon. It will be seen that this is almost an exact description of how a chess-playing computer operates, provided we substitute "within the machine" for "mentally."

On the other hand, the machine does only what it has been told to do. It works by trial and error, but the trials are trials that the program designer ordered the machine to make, and the errors are called errors because the evaluation function gives these variations low ratings. The machine makes decisions, but the decisions were envisaged and provided for at the time of design. In short, the machine does not, in any real sense, go beyond what was built into it. The situation was nicely summarized by Torres y Quevedo, who, in connection with his end-game machine, remarked: "The limits within which thought is really necessary need to be better defined . . . the automaton can do many things that are popularly classed as thought."

INEVITABLE ADVANTAGE of man over the machine is illustrated in this drawing. At top human player loses to machine. In center nettled human player revises machine's instructions. At bottom human player wins.

10

COMPUTER v. CHESS-PLAYER

ALEX BERNSTEIN AND M. de V. ROBERTS
June, 1958

Chess is not only one of the most engaging but also one of the most sophisticated of human activities. The game is so old that we cannot say when or where it was invented; millions of games have been played and thousands of books have been written about it; yet the play is still fresh and forever new. Simple arithmetic tells why. On the average, each move in chess offers a choice of about 30 possibilities, and the average length of a full game is about 40 moves. By this reckoning there are at least 10^{120} possible games. To get some idea of what that number means, let us suppose that we had a superfast computing machine which could play a million games a second (a ridiculous supposition). It would take the machine about 10^{108} years to play all the possible games!

So no conceivable machine could play a perfect game of chess, examining all possible moves. This is what makes the problem of programming a computer to play chess so intriguing. A present-day computing machine, with all its speed of calculation, is about as limited as a human being, on any reasonable time scale, in exploring the likely consequences of a chess move. Since it cannot study all the possibilities, the machine must play the game in human

OPPONENTS IN CHESS GAME depicted here are Alex Bernstein, co-author of this article, and an IBM 704 computer. The game is played on an ordinary chessboard, but information about each move is fed into the machine by controls above the board.

terms—that is, it must detect the strategy and anticipate the judgments of its human opponent. In other words, lacking the omniscience that would enable it to win no matter what its opponent does, it must try to outwit the opponent.

Needless to say, devising a program which would give a machine this property—what amounts to the capacity to think—has proved a very difficult job. The late A. M. Turing, the ingenious British theoretician on thinking machines, was one of the first to try his hand at designing a chess-playing program for a computer, but his machine (MADAM) played a very weak game, made stupid blunders and usually had to resign after a few moves. The problem has interested a number of computer experts in the U. S. [see the article "A Chess-Playing Machine," by Claude E. Shannon beginning on page 104], and several groups are currently working on chess programs. We want to report here what we believe is the first satisfactory program—one with which the machine plays a game sophisticated enough so that its opponent has to be something more than a novice to beat it. The program was written by four collaborators—the authors of this article, who work for the International Business Machines Corporation, and Timothy Arbuckle and M. A. Belsky of the Service Bureau Corporation. It is designed for the IBM 704, the very rapid digital computer which has performed as many as one billion calculations in a single day in computing the orbit of an artificial satellite.

The program is a set of explicit instructions to the computer on how it must act in each of the specific situations with which it may be confronted. The instructions are given to the machine on a reel of magnetic tape. The operation of the computer is itself fascinating to watch. You sit at the console of the machine with a chessboard in front of you and press the start button. Within four seconds a panel light labeled "Program Stop" lights up on the console, and you now make your choice of black or white: to choose black you flip a switch on the console; if you want white, you simply leave the switch as it is. Suppose you have picked black. To begin the game you press the start button again. The machine now "thinks" about its first move. There is nothing spectacular about this. Some lights flash on the console, but the computer is working so swiftly that it is impossible to say just what these flashes mean. After about eight minutes, the computer

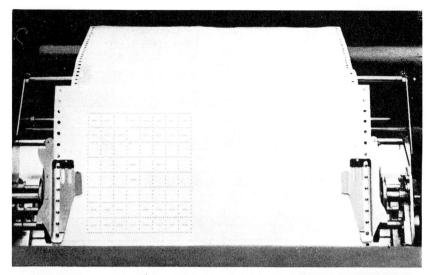

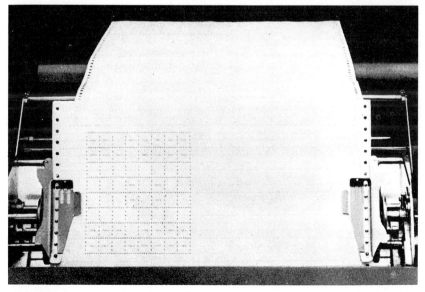

MACHINE TYPES OUT A MOVE in the form of a diagram of the chessboard (*top*). Bernstein makes the move on the board, then makes his own move and communicates it to the machine (*middle*). The machine types this move (*bottom*) before it makes its own.

prints out its move on a sheet of paper.

Let us say the machine's (White's) first move is king's pawn to the king's fourth square. The print-out then is W1 P-K4. The machine proceeds to print the chessboard with the positions of the pieces, designating its own by the letter M and its opponent's by the letter O [*see illustration below*].

Now the "Program Stop" light goes on again and the computer waits for its opponent to reply. You punch your replying move on an IBM card and put this card in a section of the machine which reads it. To signal that it is the machine's turn you press the start button again. The machine prints your move and the new board position and then goes on to calculate its second move. If you have made an illegal move, the computer will refuse to accept it, printing out "PLEASE CHECK LAST MOVE." So the game proceeds. At the end of the game, after a mating move or a resignation, the machine prints the score of the game, and to its opponent. "THANK YOU FOR AN INTERESTING GAME."

In explaining the program of instructions to the machine it will be helpful if we start by contrasting it with an ordinary job performed by a computer—say calculating John Doe's pay check. The machine in the latter case simply takes the data—so many dollars for a 44-hour week, so much for overtime at a certain rate, so much deducted for social security and income tax—and quickly computes what the check has to be. There is one, and only one, correct answer. But in a chess game there are only two questions to which absolutely definite and unavoidable answers can be given: "Is this move legal?" and "Is the game over?" To all other questions there are various possible answers, though some may be more acceptable than others. The problem is to equip the machine with a system of evaluating the merits of the alternatives. This, as

MACHINE

```
* * * * * * * * * * * * * * * * * * * * * * * * * * * * * * * * *
*       *       *       *       *       *       *       *       *
* MRK   * MNT   * MBS   * MKG   * MQN   * MBS   * MNT   * MRK   *
*       *       *       *       *       *       *       *       *
* * * * * * * * * * * * * * * * * * * * * * * * * * * * * * * * *
*       *       *       *       *       *       *       *       *
* MPN   * MPN   * MPN   *       * MPN   * MPN   * MPN   * MPN   *
*       *       *       *       *       *       *       *       *
* * * * * * * * * * * * * * * * * * * * * * * * * * * * * * * * *
*       *       *       *       *       *       *       *       *
*       *       *       *       *       *       *       *       *
*       *       *       *       *       *       *       *       *
* * * * * * * * * * * * * * * * * * * * * * * * * * * * * * * * *
*       *       *       *       *       *       *       *       *
*       *       *       * MPN   *       *       *       *       *
*       *       *       *       *       *       *       *       *
* * * * * * * * * * * * * * * * * * * * * * * * * * * * * * * * *
*       *       *       *       *       *       *       *       *
*       *       *       *       *       *       *       *       *
*       *       *       *       *       *       *       *       *
* * * * * * * * * * * * * * * * * * * * * * * * * * * * * * * * *
*       *       *       *       *       *       *       *       *
*       *       *       *       *       *       *       *       *
*       *       *       *       *       *       *       *       *
* * * * * * * * * * * * * * * * * * * * * * * * * * * * * * * * *
*       *       *       *       *       *       *       *       *
* OPN   * OPN   * OPN   * OPN   * OPN   * OPN   * OPN   * OPN   *
*       *       *       *       *       *       *       *       *
* * * * * * * * * * * * * * * * * * * * * * * * * * * * * * * * *
*       *       *       *       *       *       *       *       *
* ORK   * ONT   * OBS   * OKG   * OQN   * OBS   * ONT   * ORK   *
*       *       *       *       *       *       *       *       *
* * * * * * * * * * * * * * * * * * * * * * * * * * * * * * * * *
```

OPPONENT

CHESSBOARD TYPED OUT BY MACHINE represents the machine's pieces by M and the opponent's pieces by O. The second and third letters in each of the small squares represent rook (RK), knight (NT), bishop (BS), king (KG), queen (QN) and pawn (PN). In chess terminology the move shown here is P-K4 (pawn to king's column, fourth row).

	MACHINE (WHITE)	OPPONENT (BLACK)
1.	P — K4	P — K4
2.	B — B4	P — QN3
3.	P — Q3	N — KB3
4.	B — KN5	B — N2

Black is preparing for a direct attack on the center, via P — Q4.

5.	B × N	Q × B
6.	N — KB3	P — B3
7.	O — O	P — Q4
8.	P × P	P × P
9.	B — N5 ch	N — B3
10.	P — B4?	P × P

White 10 N × P is better because if black replies Q × N, then R — K1. Since the pawn is defended by the queen, N × P seemingly loses material, and the move is discarded.

11.	B × N ch	Q × B
12.	P × P?	P — K5

White 12 is bad, R — K1 is better.

13.	N — N5	Q — N3
14.	N — KR3	P — K6
15.	P — B3	B — B4
16.	R — K1	O — O
17.	N — B3	

Fiddling while Rome burns.

		P — K7 dis ch
18.	N — B2	B × P
19.	P — KN3	P × Q = Q
20.	N(QB3) × Q	Q — B7
21.	P — N3	R (QR1) — Q1
22.	P — KR4	R × N
23.	Resigns	

ACTUAL GAME between computer and human opponent is described in conventional chess terminology. The comments of the human opponent have been interpolated.

we have remarked, is what makes the task interesting. If cut-and-dried answers to all possible situations could be worked out by a computer, chess would immediately lose its fascination.

Obviously the machine's first job is to size up the board. The instructions therefore direct it to start by examining the state of the squares. The computer painstakingly and single-mindedly considers square by square, giving the same minute attention to squares of little interest as to those of key importance. It asks about each square whether it is occupied, by whose man, whether it is attacked, whether it is defended, whether it can be occupied. The information is summed up in tables compiled by the machine. All this takes about one tenth of a second, which is a long time by computer standards. The computer then proceeds to consider its best move.

Here we reach the most difficult and controversial part of the program, for to find a workable basis for the machine's decisions we must make some hypotheses about how a human being plays chess. To begin with, we have to decide on what basis a human player (or the machine) will select the moves that are to be given serious consideration (full consideration of all possible moves being out of the question). There are two distinct philosophies about this. One is that the player concentrates on the moves

that look most plausible in the immediate situation. The other is that the player's approach to the selection is dictated by a grand strategy, and as far as he can he looks for moves which will further his plan. We built our program on the second hypothesis.

Of the various possible moves it might make (usually about 30) the machine selects seven for detailed analysis. It picks these on the basis of eight questions, which it asks in the following order:

1. Am I in check, and if so, can I capture the checking piece, interpose a piece or move away?

2. Are any exchanges possible, and if so, can I gain material by entering upon the exchange, or should I move my man away?

3. If I have not castled, can I do so now?

4. Can I develop a minor piece?

5. Can I occupy an open file?

6. Do I have any men that I can put on the critical squares created by pawn chains?

7. Can I make a pawn move?

8. Can I make a piece move?

Let us take the opening move for illustration. Examining the initial setup of the board, the machine finds that questions 1, 2 and 3 must be answered "No." The answer to question 4 is "Yes"; the machine notes that it can move either

knight and has four possible knight moves (N-KR3, N-QR3, N-KB3, N-QB3). To questions 5 and 6 the answer is "No." It is "Yes" to question 7. Any of the eight pawns may be moved, but the instructions tell the machine to give priority to P-K4, P-K3 and P-Q4. These three pawn moves, with the four knight moves, provide the machine with seven moves for study.

It now proceeds to test each of the seven in turn through four moves ahead, considering its opponent's possible replies and its own possible counter-responses in each case. The machine starts with one of the seven moves and asks itself what it might reply were it the opponent. It generates seven possible replies, on the basis of the questions listed above, and now it takes the first of these and considers its own possible responses. After generating seven plausible responses, it again takes the first of these and in turn generates seven plausible replies by the opponent to this move.

The machine has reached the fourth level: initial move, reply, counter-reply and now the opponent's seven potential responses to its counter-reply [see diagram below]. It goes on to examine each of these seven moves to see which one would net the highest value for its opponent. The value, or score, is measured by four considerations: (1) gain of material (a pawn counting as one unit,

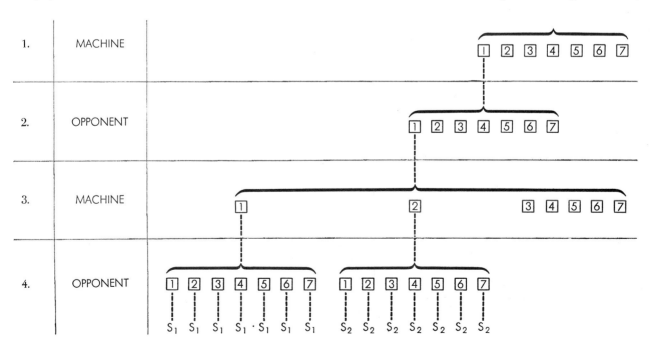

MACHINE MAKES A MOVE by the procedure suggested in this diagram. First, the machine selects, on the basis of eight questions, its seven most logical moves (*row 1*). Second, the machine selects its opponent's seven most logical responses to the first of these seven moves (*row 2*). Third, the machine selects its seven most logical counter-responses to the first of its opponent's responses (*row 3*). Fourth, the machine selects its opponent's seven most logical responses to the first of its seven counter-responses (*row 4*). Fifth, the machine scores its opponent's seven responses to the first of its seven counter-responses (S_1). Sixth, the machine selects its opponent's seven most logical responses to the second of its seven counter-responses. Seventh, the machine scores its opponent's responses to the second of its seven counter-responses (S_2). The machine continues in this manner until it has examined all moves.

a knight or bishop three, a rook five and the queen nine); (2) defense of the king; (3) mobility of the pieces; (4) control of important squares. After the machine has determined the score for the opponent's best move in level 4, it carries this back as the score for its own move 1 in level 3.

In this manner the machine investigates all the possible sequences of plays, taking each of the seven moves at every level of the "tree," and arrives at scores for all the outcomes at the fourth level. In all, it examines 2,800 possible positions. After this examination, the machine then chooses as its first move the one that will lead to the highest score both for itself and for its opponent. It acts, in other words, as if its opponent will make his best possible moves within the limits it is programmed to explore.

These limits—four half-moves ahead with seven choices at each step—are dictated by the time factor. It takes the machine close to eight minutes to decide on each move in most cases. If it had to weigh eight plausible moves instead of seven at each level, it would take about 15 minutes for a move. If it carried the examination through to one more level ahead, a single move would take some six and a half hours. So the present program is considered about the limit for a machine operating at the speed of the IBM 704.

H ow does the machine make out with this program? In the first place, the machine is never absent-minded. It makes no blatant blunders such as letting a piece be caught *en prise*, as every chess master has done at some time or other. When its opponent is careless enough to expose a piece, the machine takes instant advantage of the opportunity to capture it. Secondly, in its choice of individual moves the machine often plays like a master, making what an expert would consider the only satisfactory move [*see example on this page*]. Thirdly, the machine is certainly not in the master class in the play of a complete game.

A typical game played by the machine against a skillful opponent is shown at the right on page 110. We have deliberately chosen a game which the machine lost, because we want to emphasize the point that a machine is not infallible and also because it is more instructive to watch the computer lose than to watch it win. The machine's opening moves in this game are quite acceptable. But by middle game the machine betrays its chief weakness: namely, a heavy bias toward moving attacked pieces rather than defending them (a weakness which could

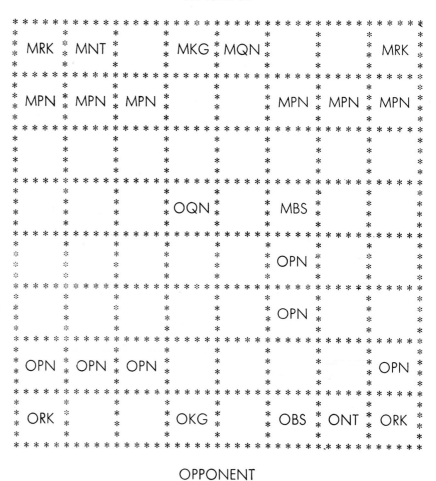

MACHINE

OPPONENT

MASTERLY MOVE was made out of this position by the machine. The move was Q-K2 (queen to king's column, row 2). Experts would consider this the only satisfactory move.

be corrected only by increasing the time for considering moves). At the tenth move White (the machine) makes a weak move which puts Black in a strong position; by the thirteenth move White's position is clearly hopeless, and 10 moves later, seeing the inevitability of a forced mate, the machine resigns.

Our contests with the machine show that anyone good enough to construct a three-move trap can beat it. Knowing how it selects its moves for consideration, you can often think of moves which you can be confident the machine will not consider. The machine will invariably accept a "sacrifice" (but then, so did the grand master José Capablanca). It will offer a sacrifice only to avoid being mated or if it can see an almost immediate mate of its opponent.

Yet notwithstanding its weaknesses, the IBM 704 plays a respectable and not-too-obvious game of chess—a game about which one can ask such questions as "Why did it make that move?" and "What does it have in mind?" We can

even say frequently that "It made an excellent move at this point," or "At this stage it had a good position."

U ndoubtedly our chess player is only a prototype for far more skillful players to be built in the future. Probably they will not go much farther in depth of planning: even with much faster computers than any now in existence it will be impracticable to consider more than about six half-moves ahead, investigating eight possible moves at each stage. A more promising line of attack is to program the computer to learn from experience. As things stand now, after losing a game the machine quite happily makes the same moves again and loses again in exactly the same way. But there are some glimmerings of ideas about how to program a machine to avoid repeating its mistakes, and some day—not overnight—we may have machines which will improve their game as they gain experience in play against their human opponents.

11

COMPUTER MUSIC

LEJAREN A. HILLER

December, 1959

Can a computer be used to compose a symphony? As one who has been engaged in programming a large digital computer to produce original musical compositions, I can testify that the very idea excites incredulity and indignation in many quarters. Such response in part reflects the extreme view of the 19th-century romantic tradition that regards music as direct communication of emotion from composer to listener—"from heart to heart," as Wagner said. In deference to this view it must be conceded that we do not yet understand the subjective aspect of musical communication well enough to study it in precise terms. The appreciation of music involves not only psychological needs and responses but meanings imported into the musical experience by reference to its cultural context. On the

"ILLIAC" DIGITAL COMPUTER at the University of Illinois was used for the experiments in composition described in this article. It has "composed" hundreds of simple melodies as well as more complicated musical structures. At right is the author.

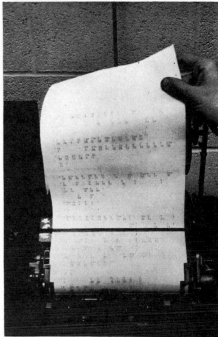

COMPUTER'S MUSICAL OUTPUT is punched into paper tape shown at left, which is then run through a teletype machine to produce sheets of letter-number combinations (*center*). These are then decoded by hand into conventional musical notation (*right*).

other hand, music does have its objective side. This can be defined as existing in the score as such, quite apart from the composer and the listener. The information encoded there relates to such quantitative entities as pitch and time, and is therefore accessible to rational and ultimately mathematical analysis.

In recent years the "physics of music" has disclosed much that is mathematical in music. It reveals how sound waves are formed and propagated, how strings, membranes and air columns vibrate and how timbre depends upon complex wave-structure; it has provided universal standards of frequency and intensity, and clarified the rationale of musical scales. In its most compact form, acoustics reduces the definition of musical sound to a plot of wave-form amplitude versus time. The groove of a phonograph record, for example, contains only this information and yet yields a believable reconstruction of an original musical sound.

Acoustics, however, deals primarily with isolated elements of music and has thus far said relatively little about how these elements may be combined in a musical composition. Musicians have devised various nonmathematical systems for analyzing the structure of compositions. More recently they have begun to draw upon a new branch of applied mathematics known as information theory as a means of clarifying this aspect of musical communication.

Information theory relates the "information content" of a sequence of symbols (be they letters of the alphabet or musical notes) to the number of possible choices among the symbols. Information content thus resembles entropy or the degree of disorder in a physical system. The most random sequence has the highest information content; the least random (or most redundant) has the lowest. The apparent paradox in this statement derives from the definition given the term "information" in the theory. As Warren Weaver has observed, the term "relates not so much to what you *do* say as to what you *could* say" [see "The Mathematics of Communication," by Warren Weaver; SCIENTIFIC AMERICAN, July, 1949]. Information in this sense is not the same thing as meaning, and information theory is concerned more with the reliability of communication systems than it is with problems of meaning. Thus, it can be seen, the general inquiry into communication is confronted with the same dualistic question of form and meaning that faces the study of musical communication. Weaver encourages us to believe, however, that information theory has cleared the way toward "a real theory of meaning."

M usic, sometimes defined as a compromise between chaos and monotony, appears to the information theorist as an ordered disorder lying somewhere between complete randomness and com-

plete redundancy. This viewpoint accords well with much of traditional musical esthetics. As early as the fourth century B. C. the Greek writer Aristoxenus noted that "the voice . . . does not place the [musical] intervals at random, . . . for it is not every collocation but only certain collocations . . . that distinguish the melodious from the unmelodious." The composer, employing what Stravinsky has called "the great technique of selection," introduces redundancy into his relatively random materials in order to organize them into a "meaningful" pattern.

To be sure, meaning is as difficult to define in music as it is in every other kind of communication. But musical sounds are not, as words are, primarily symbols of something else; the meaning of music is peculiarly dependent upon its own structures as such. The study of musical structures by information theory should open the way to a deeper understanding of the esthetic basis of composition. We may be able to respond to Stravinsky's injunction and cease "tormenting [the composer] with the *why* instead of seeking for itself the *how* and thus establish the reasons for his failure or success."

From the analytical standpoint, the esthetic content of music can be treated in terms of fluctuations between the two extremes of total randomness and total redundancy. The significant fluctuations manifest themselves not only between one composition and another but also among elements or sections of the same

Future experiments may develop a method for automatic decoding and printing. Music publishers, who now use much expensive hand labor, would welcome such a technique.

in which the composer sets forth the themes, is fairly redundant (that is, predictable); the "recapitulation," in which he restates them, is even more so. The intervening "development," in which the themes are broken up, recombined and shifted through a number of keys, is far less redundant than either. As a final example, the stylistic device of modulation (key-shift) shows a fairly steady decrease in redundancy over the past 200 years. Mozart employed a limited number of rather standardized modulations. In Chopin and Brahms the modulations are more extreme and occur more frequently and less predictably. Wagner and Debussy modulate so freely that the listener often loses any immediate and unequivocal sense of key. Many modern composers have abandoned the concepts of key and modulation altogether and in this dimension approach complete randomness.

By standards such as these it is possible, at least in theory, to construct tables of probabilities describing a musical style, such as Baroque, Classical or Romantic, and perhaps even the style of an individual composer. Given such tables, one could then reverse the process and compose music in a given style. The task of composition would start from the random condition with choices among musical elements all equally probable. The introduction of redundancy in accord-

composition. To take a very simple example, the "dominant 7th" chord GBDF is highly redundant under the rules of conventional harmony, because it will most frequently be followed by the chord CEG. The "diminished 7th" chord G#BDF, by contrast, is far less redundant, for it can be followed with equal probability by any one of a dozen-odd chords. Or consider the "sonata form" of organization which classical composers typically employed for the first movements of their longer compositions. In this musical structure the "exposition,"

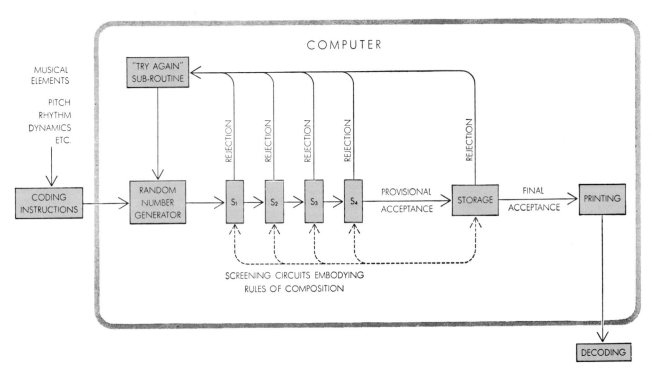

COMPUTER "COMPOSES" by a process of which the general features are here shown schematically. The machine generates random integers which are then screened by computational circuits that are arithmetical analogues of rules of composition. If circuits reject an integer, the "try again" circuit automatically produces a new one. Integers accepted by the screening circuits are stored in the memory until the composition is complete; memory and screening circuits are joined by feedback linkages symbolized by broken arrows. If the machine cannot complete a sequence without breaking the rules, it clears its memory and begins anew.

ance with a particular scheme of probabilities would extract order from chaos. It is not to be thought, however, that order is the sole criterion of beauty; as the musicologist Leonard B. Meyer has observed, "Some of the greatest music is great precisely because the composer has not feared to let his music tremble on the brink of chaos."

A few years ago Richard C. Pinkerton of the University of Florida employed this method to produce a simple "tune maker." He derived his probability tables by averaging the probabilities in a collection of nursery tunes [see "Information Theory and Melody," by Richard C. Pinkerton; SCIENTIFIC AMERICAN, February, 1956]. As he noted, however, this method produces only banal tunes. If more interesting music is desired, criteria other than simple averages must determine the probabilities.

A number of composers, both classical and contemporary, have produced more sophisticated musical structures embodying mathematical or quasi-mathematical "programs" that reflect an explicit concern with order and disorder. Especially illuminating are the extreme types of such structures: random music and totally organized music.

In its literal sense, pure random music is equivalent to "white noise"—the undifferentiated hissing sound made up of all possible audible frequencies occurring at random time intervals. It can be "composed" on any good high-fidelity set simply by turning the volume control high and thereby amplifying the random motions of electrons and ions in the tubes. At the opposite pole, the unvarying dial tone of a telephone provides a good example of totally organized music. Obviously neither extreme has much to offer the listener. To obtain sufficient variation in texture the composer must move away at least a little from total randomness or total redundancy.

Perhaps the simplest method of composing "almost random" music is to spatter ink from a brush on a page of blank music paper. By adding stems to the spots and then selecting the meters of successive measures by picking cards from a deck, one obtains random music that is sometimes playable if not harmonious [see illustration on opposite page]. A second and rather well-known example of chance music is Mozart's "A Musical Dice Game." This piece, one of many similar "compositions" produced as parlor games in the late 18th century, consists essentially of several dozen assorted measures of music, the order of which is determined by rolling dice. A more modern random work, "Imaginary Landscape" by the American composer John Cage, is "scored" for 12 radios and thus derives a strong element of randomness from regional and temporal variations in radio programs. Moreover, the score itself, which specifies the tuning of each radio and changes in volume, is based on chance numbers derived from an ancient Chinese book of oracles. Cage composes by several other chance methods, including "the observations of imperfections in the paper on which I happen to be writing" and the random shuffling of score pages just before performance.

John R. Pierce of Bell Telephone Laboratories, an authority on information theory, has demonstrated other approaches to the composition of simple "probability music." In one, a sequence of chords is chosen by means of dice rolls and a table of random numbers; in another, a series of volunteers each contributes a measure. A number of European composers have produced more elaborate random music electronically by causing random sequences of electrical signals to trigger sequences of tones.

Like random music, highly organized music does not lack historical precedent. A notable example is the "isorrhythmic" music of the 14th and 15th centuries, which was based on abstract formulations that took precedence over conventional rules of harmony. Among contemporary composers, Cage has produced what is probably the most perfect example of the genre in his composition "4:44," which consists of four minutes

"FIRST SPECIES COUNTERPOINT" composed by ILLIAC (top) is compared with a portion of the motet "Adoramus Te Christe," composed in the same style by Palestrina (bottom). The computer produced monotonous rhythms here because its program contained no provision for varying rhythms until later experiments. The computer music is taken from "Illiac Suite for String Quartet," by Lejaren A. Hiller, Jr., and L. M. Isaacson. Copyright 1957 by New Music Editions; assigned to Theodore Presser Company, 1959.

RANDOM MUSIC can be "composed" by spattering ink from a brush onto blank music paper (*top*). When the spots are tran-scribed (*bottom*), the horizontal distance between them defines their time value. Meters are obtained by drawing cards from a deck.

and 44 seconds of silence. Other contemporary composers have produced less totally organized but more audible pieces by composing according to invariant sequences of numbers. Each number is associated with musical elements such as pitch, rhythm, dynamics and orchestration. This method of composing evolved out of Arnold Schönberg's 12-tone technique. Once belabored as rigid and ultra-mathematical, Schönberg's works seem hardly "programmed" at all when compared with those of his "descendants." Karlheinz Stockhausen's "Zeitmasse" is an example of recent programmed music available on phonograph records. Its elaborately organized structure is not readily discernible by ear alone, so that it does not sound very different from the general run of modern compositions.

The concept of mathematically programmed music easily leads to the notion of composition by computer. In 1955 Leonard M. Isaacson and I began a series of experiments in composition with ILLIAC, the high-speed digital computer at the University of Illinois. In due course we completed four groups of experiments, the results of which we have sampled in the "Illiac Suite for String Quartet."

As our first step we set the computer to composing simple melodies. To this end we programmed the machine to generate random integers by a technique borrowed from the "Monte Carlo" method, which physicists have devised to solve certain problems involving multiple probabilities. Random integers from 0 to 14 represented the tones ("white notes" only; no sharps or flats) in a two-octave range of the C-major scale. To introduce redundancy we screened the integers by feeding in additional programming instructions; these embodied arithmetical analogues of rules of composition governing "permissible" sequences of notes. We selected the rules from the elaborate injunctions for "strict first-species counterpoint," a formalized musical idiom based on the methods of such 16th-century composers as Palestrina.

Integers that passed the screening procedure were stored in the computer's "memory" until the machine had completed a melody by returning to C, the note with which it had begun. The complete melody was then printed on perforated tape, from which it could be transcribed into conventional musical notation [*see illustrations at top of pages 114 and 115*]. Rejection of an integer automatically triggered a "try again" program that generated a new integer. The machine continued "trying" until it produced a satisfactory note or until it "concluded" (after 50 unsuccessful trials) that no such note existed, that is, it had "written itself into a corner," as human composers sometimes do. In the latter case it cleared the incomplete melody from its memory and began afresh from C.

In the course of an hour's operation the machine produced several hundred melodies from three to 12 notes long. It was then programmed to produce two-voice counterpoint—two melodies at once—incorporating for this purpose four more instructions that screened out dissonances between the voices. The addition of still other instructions enabled the machine to produce four-voice counterpoint. The more elaborate programs produced more trials and "erasures," but the machine still composed copiously.

For our second experiment we devised additional screening instructions embodying the entire set of 14 rules of strict first-species counterpoint. The machine was first set to turning out random "white-note" music in four voices; randomness was then made to yield to redundancy in small increments by feeding in the screening instructions one by one. The complete set of instructions yielded counterpoint of fair quality, strongly reminiscent, if one ignores a certain monotony in rhythm, of passages from Palestrina.

In Experiment III we sought to find ways of producing the rhythmic and dynamic variety that the earlier compositions lacked. A simple method gave us a considerable variety of rhythm. With 4/8 time as the meter and the eighth-note as the smallest rhythmic unit, all the rhythmic patterns possible under these restrictions were coded in binary digits (that is, numbers expressed by 1 and 0, representing the "on" and "off" positions of a relay). Thus 1111 represented four eighth-notes; 1110, two eighth-notes followed by a quarter-note; 1010, two quarter-notes, and so on. The resulting series of permutations formed a sequence of binary numbers equivalent to the decimal numbers 0 to 15 [see illustration on this page]. Since rhythms in music do not normally shift with every measure, rhythmic redundancy was introduced by a second series of random numbers that programmed the machine to repeat a particular rhythm up to 12 times. To this "horizontal" redundancy in the melodic line of the individual voices another binary code added "vertical" redundancy among the four voices. Here 0000 indicated that all four voices would be rhythmically independent, 1111 called for the same rhythm in all voices, and so on. Similar methods introduced patterns of dynamics (forte, crescendo, and so on) and variations in playing instructions (legato, tremolo, pizzicato, and so on).

Since the object was to produce a type of music less imitative than strict counterpoint, the machine was first permitted to write entirely random chromatic music (including all sharps and flats). The result was music of the highest possible entropy content in terms of note selection on the chromatic scale, and thus it was strongly dissonant. With the minimal redundancy imposed by feeding in only four of the 14 screening instructions, the character of the composition changed drastically. While the wholly random sections resembled the more extreme efforts of avant garde modern composers, the later, more redundant portions recalled passages from, say, a Bartok string quartet [see illustration on opposite page]. The experiment concluded with some exploratory studies in Schönberg's 12-tone technique and similar compositional devices.

Experiments II and III thus developed the contrasts between two widely different styles, that of the 17th and that of the 20th century. One style is highly restrictive and highly consonant but sounds quite simple; the other sounds dissonant, much more complex and difficult to decipher. The contrast underlines an important musical moral: Simplicity of style and hence accessibility

CLOSED RHYTHMS	OPEN RHYTHMS	BINARY NUMBER	DECIMAL NUMBER
		0000	0
		0001	1
		0010	2
		0011	3
		0100	4
		0101	5
		0110	6
		0111	7
		1000	8
		1001	9
		1010	10
		1011	11
		1100	12
		1101	13
		1110	14
		1111	15

RHYTHMIC CODING for the computer is based on 4/8 meter (chosen arbitrarily) with the eighth-note as the smallest rhythmic unit. All rhythms possible under these restrictions can be expressed as binary numbers equivalent to the decimal numbers from 0 to 15. Random choice determines the order of rhythmic patterns and selects "closed" or "open" form.

RANDOM CHROMATIC MUSIC produced by the computer (*top*) resembles the compositions of some extreme modern composers. The introduction of redundancy in melody, rhythm and playing instructions produces a more ordered texture (*middle*) that suggests passages from Bartok. Samples of computer music from "Illiac Suite," Copyright 1957, New Music Editions; assigned to Theodore Presser Company, 1959. Shown below is a passage from the first movement of Bartok's "First String Quartet." Copyright 1929 by Universal Editions; renewed 1956. Copyright and renewal assigned to Boosey and Hawkes Inc. Reproduced by permission.

"MARKOFF CHAIN" MUSIC is composed by selecting intervals between successive notes according to a shifting table of probabilities. During the first two bars, the probability of unison (the "zero" interval) is 1; that of all other intervals, 0. The music necessarily remains on the same note. After each two bars the probabilities shift according to the scheme shown on page 121. From Experiment IV of "Illiac Suite for String Quartet," copyright 1957, New Music Editions; assigned to Theodore Presser Company, 1959.

bear an inverse relationship to freedom of choice. The simpler the style, the more severe the restrictions and the higher the degree of redundancy. By the same token, music that sounds simple may well be more difficult to write. In the freer style the difficulty involved in making the best choices among the larger number of alternatives is offset by the fact that more of the available alternatives are permissible. Each choice, in other words, is less significant to the total effect.

In Experiment IV the objective was the synthesis of music from purely mathematical rules—a style of composition peculiarly appropriate to a computer. To this end the computer was programmed to select the intervals between successive notes according to a table of probabilities instead of at random. Moreover, the probabilities themselves were made to shift in accordance with so-called Markoff probability chains. For example, in the first specimen of this music the "zero" interval (unison) had an initial "weight" of one while all the other intervals had a weight of zero. All voices perforce remained on the same note. After two bars the octave interval was given the weight of one and the weight of unison increased to two (unison was thus twice as probable as the octave). The fifth was the next interval added, and the respective weights of the three intervals, in order of appearance, became three, two and one. Two bars later the fourth interval was added with weights of four, three, two and one now assigned, and so on until all possible intervals had been added [see illustrations on opposite page and on this page].

When the computer had composed under the instruction of a number of similar Markoff programs, the probabilities were programmed to depend partly upon the last choices made. Thus if the last interval was a fifth, the probability of that interval would drop sharply and the probabilities of the others would rise. Another rearrangement linked the choice of interval to the opening note of the sequence. This latter relationship is of particular interest because it bears on the problem of tonality, the factor in conventional music by which the notes of the scale acquire individual significance because of their relationship to the keynote. The suppression of tonality, even to the point of abandoning it completely (atonalism), constitutes perhaps the most characteristic trend in "serious" music during the past 50 years.

We discovered with interest that the sound of "tonal" Markoff music closely resembled that of the "atonal"

INTERVALS	a		b		c		d		e		f		g		h		i	
	W	P	W	P	W	P	W	P	W	P	W	P	W	P	W	P	W	P
UNISON	1	1.00	2	.67	3	.50	4	.40	5	.33	6	.29	7	.25	8	.22	9	.20
OCTAVE	0	.00	1	.33	2	.33	3	.30	4	.27	5	.24	6	.21	7	.19	8	.18
FIFTH	0	.00	0	.00	1	.17	2	.20	3	.20	4	.19	5	.18	6	.17	7	.16
FOURTH	0	.00	0	.00	0	.00	1	.10	2	.13	3	.14	4	.14	5	.14	6	.13
MAJOR 3RD	0	.00	0	.00	0	.00	0	.00	1	.07	2	.09	3	.11	4	.11	5	.11
MINOR 6TH	0	.00	0	.00	0	.00	0	.00	0	.00	1	.05	2	.07	3	.08	4	.09
MINOR 3RD	0	.00	0	.00	0	.00	0	.00	0	.00	0	.00	1	.04	2	.06	3	.07
MAJOR 6TH	0	.00	0	.00	0	.00	0	.00	0	.00	0	.00	0	.00	1	.03	2	.04
MAJOR 2ND	0	.00	0	.00	0	.00	0	.00	0	.00	0	.00	0	.00	0	.00	1	.02
MINOR 7TH	0	.00	0	.00	0	.00	0	.00	0	.00	0	.00	0	.00	0	.00	0	.00
MINOR 2ND	0	.00	0	.00	0	.00	0	.00	0	.00	0	.00	0	.00	0	.00	0	.00
MAJOR 7TH	0	.00	0	.00	0	.00	0	.00	0	.00	0	.00	0	.00	0	.00	0	.00
TRITONE	0	.00	0	.00	0	.00	0	.00	0	.00	0	.00	0	.00	0	.00	0	.00

SHIFTING PROBABILITIES governing one species of Markoff chain music are shown in part here; colored letters key the columns of the table to sections of the music shown on page 120. The probabilities (P) of the intervals are defined by their "weights" (W), which shift according to a simple arithmetical formula. Markoff music has been composed by several similar schemes.

species, though its mathematical basis was quite different. Indeed, large sections of Experiment IV, though based on wholly abstract formulae, sounded much the same as Experiment III, which was generated under relatively unrestricted conditions. These correspondences suggest that if the structure of a composition exceeds a certain degree of complexity, it may overstep the perceptual capacities of the human ear and mind.

Since completing the "Illiac Suite," our efforts have been devoted to more complicated problems of musical structure, the solutions to which may yield a "Second Illiac Suite." As against the rather fragmentary music thus far obtained, the objective is to produce compositions in relatively lengthy conventional forms, such as theme and variation and four-part fugue. The computer will also be put to work on "totally organized" music as well as more complex Markoff chains. These and similar experiments involving a precisely specified degree and type of uncertainty should provide some quantitative criteria for judging the effect of order-disorder fluctuations in music.

A far more elaborate project is suggested by the question that began this discussion: Can a computer be used to compose a symphony? In principle, there seems to be no reason why it cannot. The computer program would have to be far more elaborate than any we have yet devised. Whether the results would justify the necessary labor is another story. With a program of reasonable length, the machine could be made to produce, say, a 42nd Mozart symphony, which would prove to be a representative but almost certainly undistinguished work. So long as the human programmer collaborates in the undertaking, the computer cannot be regarded as a truly independent composer. On the other hand, so long as the input to the computer includes some variant of the Monte Carlo method, the programmer cannot precisely specify the output of the machine. Thus the machine may be said to "compose," or at least to "improvise" within the limits set by its program.

The computer can also be used to make an original contribution to our understanding of the structure that underlies the esthetic qualities of music. As I remarked earlier, these qualities are perceived largely through the articulation of musical forms and can therefore be most fruitfully explored via the investigation of the technical problems of composition. The computer has already proved its value in this line of investigation, and in future studies we plan to explore more deeply its application to problems of musical analysis.

12

ARTIFICIAL INTELLIGENCE

MARVIN L. MINSKY
September, 1966

At first the idea of an intelligent machine seems implausible. Can a computer really be intelligent? In this article I shall describe some programs that enable a computer to behave in ways that probably everyone would agree seem to show intelligence.

The machine achievements discussed here are remarkable in themselves, but even more interesting and significant than what the programs do accomplish are the methods they involve. They set up goals, make plans, consider hypotheses, recognize analogies and carry out various other intellectual activities. As I shall show by example, a profound change has taken place with the discovery that descriptions of thought processes can be turned into prescriptions for the design of machines or, what is the same thing, the design of programs.

The turning point came sharply in 1943 with the publication of three theoretical papers on what is now called cybernetics. Norbert Wiener, Arturo Rosenblueth and Julian H. Bigelow of the Massachusetts Institute of Technology suggested ways to build goals and purposes into machines; Warren S. McCulloch of the University of Illinois College of Medicine and Walter H. Pitts of M.I.T. showed how machines might use concepts of logic and abstraction, and K. J. W. Craik of the University of Cambridge proposed that machines could use models and analogies to solve problems. With these new foundations the use of psychological language for describing machines became a constructive and powerful tool. Such ideas remained in the realm of theoretical speculation, however, until the mid-1950's. By that time computers had reached a level of capacity and flexibility to permit the programming of processes with the required complexity.

In the summer of 1956 a group of investigators met at Dartmouth College to discuss the possibility of constructing genuinely intelligent machines. Among others, the group included Arthur L. Samuel of the International Business Machines Corporation, who had already written a program that played a good game of checkers and incorporated several techniques to improve its own play. Allen Newell, Clifford Shaw and Herbert A. Simon of the Rand Corporation had constructed a theorem-proving program and were well along in work on a "General Problem Solver," a program that administers a hierarchy of goal-seeking subprograms.

John McCarthy was working on a system to do "commonsense reasoning" and I was working on plans for a program to prove theorems in plane geometry. (I was hoping eventually to have the computer use analogical reasoning on diagrams.) After the conference the workers continued in a number of independent investigations. Newell and Simon built up a research group at the Carnegie Institute of Technology with the goal of developing models of human behavior. McCarthy and I built up a group at M.I.T. to make machines intelligent without particular concern with human behavior. (McCarthy is now at Stanford University.) Although the approaches of the various groups were different, it is significant that their studies have resulted in closely parallel results.

Work in this field of intelligent machines and the number of investigators increased rapidly; by 1963 the bibliography of relevant publications had grown to some 900 papers and books. I shall try to give the reader an impression of the state of the field by presenting some examples of what has been happening recently.

The general approach to creating a program that can solve difficult problems will first be illustrated by considering the game of checkers. This game exemplifies the fact that many problems can in principle be solved by trying all possibilities—in this case exploring all possible moves, all the opponent's possible replies, all the player's possible replies to the opponent's replies and so on. If this could be done, the player could see which move has the best chance of winning. In practice, however, this approach is out of the question, even for a computer; the tracking down of every possible line of play would involve some 10^{40} different board positions. (A similar analysis for the game of chess would call for some 10^{120} positions.) Most interesting problems present far too many possibilities for complete trial-and-error analysis. Hence one must discover rules that will

ABSTRACT REASONING is required to complete a figure on the basis of partial information. A program developed by Lawrence G. Roberts in a doctoral thesis at the Massachusetts Institute of Technology allows a computer to interpret a two-dimensional image and reconstruct the three-dimensional object. As shown on page 128, the computer scans a photograph of the object (*1*), displays its local features (*2*) and combines line segments (*3*) to prepare a complete line drawing (*4*). It accounts for the drawing as a compound of three-dimensional shapes (*5-7*) and draws in all the interior lines (*8*). Then it can display the structure from any point of view on request, suppressing lines that would be hidden (*9*).

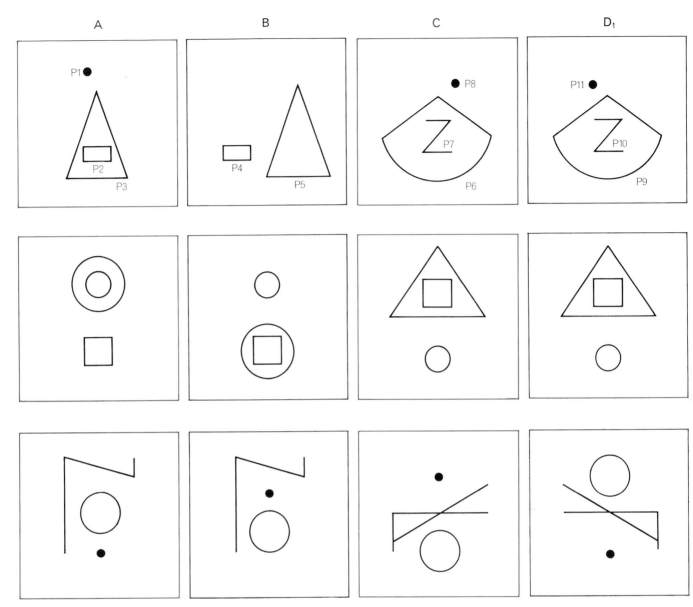

ANALOGICAL REASONING is exhibited in a program developed by Thomas Evans in an M.I.T. doctoral thesis for answering a class of problems frequently included in intelligence tests: "*A* is to *B* as *C* is to (D_1, D_2, D_3, D_4 or D_5?)." Three such problems are illustrated

try the most likely routes to a solution as early as possible.

Samuel's checker-playing program explores thousands of board positions but not millions. Instead of tracking down every possible line of play the program uses a partial analysis (a "static evaluation") of a relatively small number of carefully selected features of a board position—how many men there are on each side, how advanced they are and certain other simple relations. This incomplete analysis is not in itself adequate for choosing the best move for a player in a current position. By combining the partial analysis with a limited search for some of the consequences of the possible moves from the current position, however, the program selects its move as if on the basis of a

much deeper analysis. The program contains a collection of rules for deciding when to continue the search and when to stop. When it stops, it assesses the merits of the "terminal" position in terms of the static evaluation. If the computer finds by this search that a given move leads to an advantage for the player in all the likely positions that may occur a few moves later, whatever the opponent does, it can select this move with confidence.

What is interesting and significant about such a program is not simply that it can use trial and error to solve problems. What makes for intelligent behavior is the collection of methods and techniques that select what is to be tried next, that size up the situation and choose a plausible (if not always good)

move and use information gained in previous attempts to steer subsequent analysis in better directions. To be sure, the programs described below do use search, but in the examples we present the solutions were found among the first few attempts rather than after millions of attempts.

A program that makes such judgments about what is best to try next is termed heuristic. Our examples of heuristic programs demonstrate some capabilities similar in principle to those of the checkers program, and others that may be even more clearly recognized as ways of "thinking."

In developing a heuristic program one usually begins by programming some methods and techniques that can solve comparatively uncomplicated

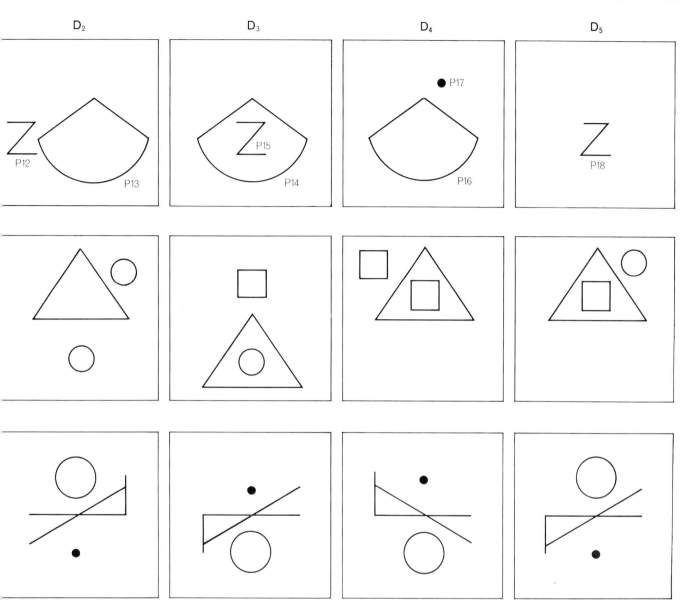

here. A computer selected the "best" answer to the top example and the middle one but missed on the bottom one because the program is weak in assessing relations among more than two objects. A typical solution is demonstrated in the illustrations that follow.

problems. To solve harder problems one might work directly to improve these basic methods, but it is much more profitable to try to extend the problem solver's general ability to bring a harder problem within reach by breaking it down into subproblems. The machine is provided with a program for a three-step process: (1) break down the problems into subproblems, keeping a record of the relations between these parts as part of the total problem, (2) solve the subproblems and (3) combine the results to form a solution to the problem as a whole. If a subproblem is still too hard, apply the procedure again. It has been found that the key to success in such a procedure often lies in finding a form of description for the problem situation (a descriptive "language") that makes it easy to break the problem down in a useful way.

Our next example of a heuristic program illustrates how descriptive languages can be used to enable a computer to employ analogical reasoning. The program was developed by Thomas Evans, a graduate student at M.I.T., as the basis for his doctoral thesis, and is the best example so far both of the use of descriptions and of how to handle analogies in a computer program.

The problem selected was the recognition of analogies between geometric figures. It was taken from a well-known test widely used for college-admission examinations because its level of difficulty is considered to require considerable intelligence. The general format is familiar: Given two figures bearing a certain relation to each other, find a similar relation between a third figure and one of five choices offered. The problem is usually written: "A is to B as C is to (D_1, D_2, D_3, D_4 or D_5?)." The particularly attractive feature of this kind of problem as a test of machine intelligence is that it has no uniquely "correct" answer. Indeed, performance on such tests is not graded by any known rule but is judged on the basis of the selections of highly intelligent people on whom the test is tried.

Now, there is a common superstition that "a computer can solve a problem only when every step in the solution is clearly specified by the programmer." In a superficial sense the statement is true, but it is dangerously misleading if

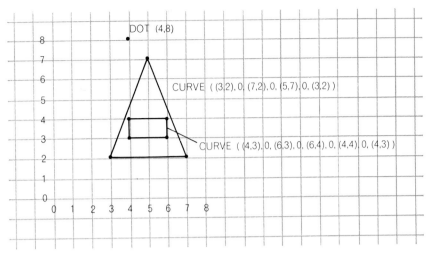

FIRST STEP of the program describes the parts of each figure in terms of a coordinate system, as shown for A in the top problem on the preceding two pages. The triangle and rectangle are "curves" whose apexes are connected by lines of zero curvature, indicated by 0.

	RELATIONS WITHIN
(INSIDE (P_2,P_3), ABOVE (P_1,P_3), ABOVE (P_1,P_2))	A
(LEFT (P_4,P_5))	B
(INSIDE (P_7,P_6), ABOVE (P_8,P_6), ABOVE (P_8,P_7))	C
(INSIDE (P_{10},P_9), ABOVE (P_{11},P_9), ABOVE (P_{11},P_{10}))	D_1
(LEFT (P_{12},P_{13}))	D_2
(INSIDE (P_{15},P_{14}))	D_3
(ABOVE (P_{17},P_{16}))	D_4
(NONE)	D_5

	SIMILARITIES BETWEEN
SIM $(P_2,P_4,0°)$ $(P_2,P_4,180°)$ $(P_3,P_5,0°)$	A AND B
SIM $(P_1,P_8,0°)$	A AND C
NIL	B AND C
SIM $(P_6,P_9,0°)$ $(P_7,P_{10},0°)$ $(P_7,P_{10},180°)$ $(P_8,P_{11},0°)$	C AND D_1
SIM $(P_6,P_{13},0°)$ $(P_7,P_{12},0°)$ $(P_7,P_{12},180°)$	C AND D_2
SIM $(P_6,P_{14},0°)$ $(P_7,P_{15},0°)$ $(P_7,P_{15},180°)$	C AND D_3
SIM $(P_6,P_{16},0°)$ $(P_8,P_{17},0°)$	C AND D_4
SIM $(P_7,P_{18},0°)$ $(P_7,P_{18},180°)$	C AND D_5
SIM $(P_1,P_{11},0°)$ $(P_1,P_{17},0°)$	A AND D_1, A AND D_4

RELATIONS AND SIMILARITIES are discovered by the program. It notes, for example, that the rectangle (P_2) is inside the triangle (P_3), the dot (P_1) above both the triangle and the rectangle, and so on. Then it lists similarities between such elements in different figures and also notes whether or not the similarity persists if an element is rotated 180 degrees.

it is taken literally. Here we understood the basic concepts Evans wrote into the program, but until the program was completed and tested we had no idea of how the machine's level of performance would compare to the test scores of human subjects.

Evans began his work on the problem of comparing geometric figures by proposing a theory of the steps or processes the human brain might use in dealing with such a situation. His theory suggested a program of four steps that can be described in psychological terms. First, in comparing the features of the figures A and B one must select from various possibilities some way in which a description of A can be transformed into a description of B. This transformation defines certain relations between A and B. (For example, in the top series of drawings in the illustration on the preceding two pages a small rectangle is inside the triangle in the figure A and outside the triangle in the figure B.) There may be several such explanations "plausible" enough to be considered. Second, one looks for items or parts in C that correspond to parts in A. There may be several such "matches" worthy of consideration. Third, in each of the five figures offering answer choices one searches for features that may relate the figure to C in a way similar to the way in which the corresponding features in B are related to those in A. Wherever the correspondence, if any, is not perfect, one can make it more so by "weakening" the relation, which means accepting a modified, less detailed version of the relation. Fourth and last, one can select as the best answer the figure that required the least modification of relations in order to relate it to C as B is related to A.

This set of hypotheses became the framework of Evans' program. (I feel sure that rules or procedures of the same general character are involved in any kind of analogical reasoning.) His next problem was to translate this rather complex sketch of mental processes into a detailed program for the computer. To do so he had to develop what is certainly one of the most complex programs ever written. The technical device that made the translation possible was the LISP ("list-processor") programming language McCarthy had developed on the basis of earlier work by Newell, Simon and Shaw. This system provides many automatic services for manipulating expressions and complicated data structures. In particular it is a most convenient method of handling descriptions consisting of lists of items. And it makes it easy to write interlocked programs that can, for example, use one another as subprograms.

The input for a specific problem in Evans' program is in the form of lists of vertices, lines and curves describing the geometric figures. A subprogram analyzes this information, identifies the separate parts of the figure and reconstructs them in terms of points on a graph and the connecting lines. The steps and processes in the solution of a problem are given in some detail in the illustrations on these two pages. Briefly, the program takes the following course: After receiving the descriptions of the figures (*A*, *B*, *C* and the five answer choices) it searches out topological and geometric relations between the parts in each picture (such as that one object is inside or to the left of or above another). It then identifies and lists similarities between pairs of pictures (*A* and *B*, *A* and *C*, *C* and *D*₁ and so on). The program proceeds to discover all the ways in which the parts of *A* and *B* can be matched up, and on the basis of this examination it develops a hypothesis about the relation of *A* to *B* (what was removed, added, moved or otherwise changed to transform one picture into the other). Next it considers correspondences between the parts of *A* and the parts of *C*. It goes on to look for matchings of the *A*-to-*B* kind between the parts in *C* and each of the *D* figures (the answer choices). When it finds something approaching a match that is consistent with its hypothesis of the relation between *A* and *B*, it proceeds to measure the degree of divergence of the *C*-to-*D* relation from the *A*-to-*B* relation by stripping away the details of the *A*-to-*B* transformation one by one until both relations (*A*-to-*B* and *C*-to-*D*) are essentially alike. In this way it eventually identifies the *D* figure that seems to come closest to a relation to *C* analogous to the *A* and *B* relation.

Evans' program is capable of solving problems considerably more complex or subtle than the one we have considered step by step. Among other things, in making decisions about the details of a picture it can take into account deductions from the situation as a whole [*see bottom illustration on this page*]. No one has taken the trouble to make a detailed comparison of the machine's performance with that of human subjects on the same problems, but Evans' evidence suggests that the present program can score at about the 10th-grade

```
      (REMOVE A1 ((ABOVE A1 A3) (ABOVE
        A1 A2) (SIM OB3 A1 (((1.0 . 0.0) .
        (N.N))))))

      (MATCH A2 (((INSIDE A2 A3) (ABOVE
        A1 A2) (SIM OB2 A2 (((1.0 . 0.0) .
        (N.N)))) . ((LEFT A2 A3) (SIM
        OB2 A2 (((1.0 . 0.0) . (N.N)) ((1.0 .
        3.14) . (N.N)))) (SIMTRAN (((1.0 .
        0.0) . (N.N)) ((1.0 . 3.14) . (N.N)
        ))))))

      (MATCH A3 (((INSIDE A2 A3) (ABOVE
        A1 A3) (SIM OB1 A3 (((1.0 . 0.0) .
        (N.N)))) . ((LEFT A2 A3) (SIM
        OB1  A3 (((1.0 . 0.0) . (N.N))))
        (SIMTRAN (((1.0 . 0.0) . (N.N)
        ))))))
```

HYPOTHESIS about how *A* is related to *B* is constructed by the program, which finds ways in which parts of the two figures can be matched up. It lists each element removed, added or matched and also the properties, relations and similarities associated with the element.

```
      (REMOVE A1 ((ABOVE A1 A3) (ABOVE
        A1 A2) (SIM OB3 A1 (((1.0 . 0.0) .
        (N.N))))))

      (MATCH A2 (((INSIDE A2 A3) (ABOVE
        A1 A2)) . ((LEFT A2 A3) (SIMTRAN
        (((1.0 . 0.0) . (N.N)) ((1.0 . 3.14)
        (N.N))))))))

      (MATCH A3 (((INSIDE A2 A3) (ABOVE
        A1 A3)) . ((LEFT A2 A3) (SIMTRAN
        (((1.0 . 0.0) . (N.N)))))))
```

PROGRAM CONCLUDES, after trying matchings between *C* and each of the five *D* figures, that *D*₂ is the best answer. It does so by considering *C*-*D* matchings that are consistent with the *A*-*B* hypothesis. By removing details from the *A*-*B* expression until it fits the *C*-*D* matching, the program selects the *C*-*D* match that is least different from the *A*-*B* hypothesis.

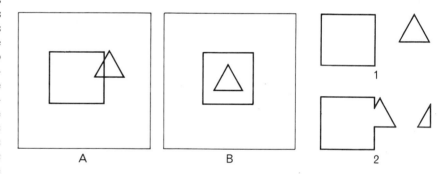

REASONING POWER of the program is illustrated in a different example by its ability to resolve the overlapping objects in *A* into a rectangle and triangle (*1*) rather than the other pieces (*2*). It makes the distinction by observing that the objects at *1* occur in figure *B* whereas the others do not. That is, program can recognize a "global" aspect of the situation.

level, and with certain improvements of the program that have already been proposed it should do even better. Evans' work on his program had to stop when he reached the limitations of the computer machinery available to him. His program could no longer fit in one piece into the core memory of the computer, and mainly for this reason it took several minutes to run each problem in the machine. With the very large memory just installed at M.I.T.'s Project MAC the program could be run in a few seconds. The new capacity will make possible further research on more sophisticated versions of such programs.

The Evans program is of course a single-minded affair: it can deal only with problems in geometrical analogy.

Although its ability in this respect compares favorably with the ability of humans, in no other respect can it pretend to approach the scope or versatility of human intelligence. Yet in its limited way it does display qualities we usually think of as requiring "intuition," "taste" or other subjective operations of the mind. With his analysis of such operations and his clarification of their components in terms precise enough to express them symbolically and make them available for use by a machine, Evans laid a foundation for the further development (with less effort) of programs employing analogical reasoning.

Moreover, it is becoming clear that analogical reasoning itself can be an important tool for expanding artificial

1

2

3

4

5

6

7

8

9

```
(THE PROBLEM TO BE SOLVED IS)
(MARY IS TWICE AS OLD AS ANN WAS WHEN MARY WAS AS OLD AS ANN
IS NOW . IF MARY IS 24 YEARS OLD , HOW OLD IS ANN Q.)

(WITH MANDATORY SUBSTITUTIONS THE PROBLEM IS)
(MARY IS 2 TIMES AS OLD AS ANN WAS WHEN MARY WAS AS OLD AS
ANN IS NOW . IF MARY IS 24 YEARS OLD , WHAT IS ANN Q.)

(WITH WORDS TAGGED BY FUNCTION THE PROBLEM IS)
((MARY / PERSON) IS 2 (TIMES / OP 1) AS OLD AS (ANN / PERSON)
WAS WHEN (MARY / PERSON) WAS AS OLD AS (ANN / PERSON) IS NOW
(PERIOD / DLM) IF (MARY / PERSON) IS 24 YEARS OLD , (WHAT /
QWORD) IS (ANN / PERSON) (QMARK / DLM))

(THE SIMPLE SENTENCES ARE)

((MARY / PERSON) S AGE IS 2 (TIMES / OP 1) (ANN / PERSON) S
AGE G02521 YEARS AGO (PERIOD / DLM))

(G02521 YEARS AGO (MARY / PERSON) S AGE IS (ANN / PERSON) S
AGE NOW (PERIOD / DLM))

((MARY / PERSON) S AGE IS 24 (PERIOD / DLM))

((WHAT / QWORD) IS (ANN / PERSON) S AGE (QMARK / DLM))


(THE EQUATIONS TO BE SOLVED ARE)

(EQUAL G02522 ((ANN / PERSON) S AGE))

(EQUAL ((MARY / PERSON) S AGE) 24)

(EQUAL (PLUS ((MARY / PERSON) S AGE) (MINUS (G02521))) ((ANN
/ PERSON) S AGE))

(EQUAL ((MARY / PERSON) S AGE) (TIMES 2 (PLUS ((ANN / PERSON)
S AGE) (MINUS (G02521)))))


(ANN S AGE IS  18)
```

"STUDENT," an English-reading program created by Daniel Bobrow, solves algebra problems. As shown here, Student restates a problem, then analyzes the words in terms of its library of definitions and relations, sets up the proper equations and gives the solution. The machine has invented the symbol *G02521* to represent the *X* used in text of the article.

intelligence. I believe it will eventually be possible for programs, by resorting to analogical reasoning, to apply the experience they have gained from solving one kind of problem to the solution of quite different problems. Consider a situation in which a machine is presented with a problem that is too complicated for solution by any method it knows. Ordinarily to cope with such contingencies the computer would be programmed to split the problem into subproblems or subgoals, so that by solving these it can arrive at a solution to the main problem. In a difficult case, however, the machine may be unable to break the problem down or may become lost in a growing maze of irrelevant subgoals. If a machine is to be able to deal, then, with very hard problems, it must have some kind of planning ability—an ability to find a suitable strategy.

What does the rather imprecise word "planning" mean in this context? We can think of a definition in terms of machine operations that might be useful: (1) Replace the given problem by a similar but simpler one; (2) solve this analogous problem and remember the steps in its solution; (3) try to adapt the steps of the solution to solve the original problem. Newell and Simon have actually completed an experiment embodying a simple version of such a program. It seems to me that this area is one of the most important for research on making machine intelligence more versatile.

I should now like to give a third example of a program exhibiting intelligence. This program has to do with the handling of information written in the English language.

Since the beginnings of the evolution of modern computers it has been obvious that a computer could be a superb file clerk that would provide instant access to any of its information—provided that the files were totally and neatly organized and that the kinds of questions the computer was called on to answer could be completely programmed. But what if, as in real life, the information is scattered through the files and is expressed in various forms of human discourse? It is widely supposed that the handling of information of this informal character is beyond the capability of any machine.

Daniel Bobrow, for his doctoral research at M.I.T., attacked this problem directly: How could a computer be programmed to understand a limited range of ordinary English? For subject matter he chose statements of problems in high school algebra. The purely mathematical solution of these problems would be child's play for the computer, but Bobrow's main concern was to provide the computer with the ability to read the informal verbal statement of a problem and derive from that language the equations required to solve the problem. (This, and not solution of the equations, is what is hard for students too.)

The basic strategy of the program (which is named "Student") is this: The machine "reads in" the statement of the problem and tries to rewrite it as a number of simple sentences. Then it tries to convert each simple sentence into an equation. Finally it tries to solve the set of equations and present the required answer (converted back to a simple English sentence). Each of these steps in interpreting the meaning is done with the help of a library (stored in the core memory) that includes a dictionary, a variety of factual statements and several special-purpose programs for solving particular kinds of problems. To write the program for the machine Bobrow used the LISP programming language with some new extensions of his own and incorporated techniques that had been developed by Victor H. Yngve in earlier work on language at M.I.T.

The problems the machine has to face in interpreting the English statements are sometimes quite difficult. It may have to figure out the antecedent of a pronoun, recognize that two different phrases have the same meaning or discover that a necessary piece of information is missing. Bobrow's program is a model of informality. Its filing system is so loosely organized (although it is readily accessible) that new information can be added to the dictionary by dumping it in anywhere. Perhaps the program's most interesting technical aspect is the way it cuts across the linguist's formal distinction between syntax and semantics, thus avoiding problems that, it seems to me, have more hindered than helped most studies of language.

The illustrations on page 130 and on this page show three problems as they were solved by Student. The remarkable thing about Student is not so much that it understands English as that it shows a basic capacity for understanding anything at all. When it runs into difficulty, it asks usually pertinent questions. Sometimes it has to ask the person operating the computer, but often it resolves the difficulty by referring to the knowledge in its files. When, for instance, it meets a statement such as "Mary is twice as old as Ann was when Mary was as old as Ann is now," the program knows how to make the meaning of "was when" more precise by rewriting the statement as two simple sentences: "Mary is twice as old as Ann was X years ago. X years ago Mary was as old as Ann is now."

Bobrow's program can handle only a small part of the grammar of the English language, and its semantic dictionaries are quite limited. Yet even though it can make many kinds of mistakes within its linguistic limitations, it probably surpasses the average person in its ability to handle algebra problems stated verbally. Bobrow believes that, given a larger computer memory, he could make Student understand most of the problems that are presented in high school first-algebra textbooks.

As an example of another kind of intelligence programmed into a machine, a program developed by Lawrence G. Roberts as a doctoral thesis at M.I.T. endows a computer with some ability to analyze three-dimensional objects [*see illustration on page 128*]. In a single two-dimensional photograph of a solid object the program detects a number of the object's geometrical features. It uses these to form a description in terms of lines and then tries to analyze the figure as a composite of simpler building blocks (rectangular forms and prisms). Once the program has performed this analysis it can reconstruct the figure from any requested point of view, drawing in lines that were originally hidden and suppressing lines that should not appear in the new picture. The program employs some rather abstract symbolic reasoning.

The exploration of machine intelligence has hardly begun. There have been about 30 experiments at the general level of those described here. Each investigator has had time to try out a few ideas; each program works only in a narrow problem area. How can we make the programs more versatile? It cannot be done simply by putting together a collection of old programs; they differ so much in their representation of objects and concepts that there could be no effective communication among them.

If we ask, "Why are the programs not more intelligent than they are?" a simple answer is that until recently resources—in people, time and computer capacity—have been quite limited. A number of the more careful and serious attempts have come close to their goal (usually after two or three years of work); others have been limited by core-memory capacity; still others encountered programming difficulties. A

few projects have not progressed nearly as much as was hoped, notably projects in language translation and mathematical theorem-proving. Both cases, I think, represent premature attempts to handle complex formalisms without also somehow representing their meaning.

The problem of combining programs is more serious. Partly because of the very brief history of the field there is a shortage of well-developed ideas about systems for the communication of partial results between different programs, and for modifying programs already written to meet new conditions. Until this situation is improved it will remain hard to combine the results of separate research projects. Warren Teitelman of

our laboratory has recently developed a programming system that may help in this regard; he has demonstrated it by re-creating in a matter of hours the results of some earlier programs that took weeks to write.

The questions people most often ask are: Can the programs learn through experience and thus improve themselves? Is this not the obvious path to making them intelligent? The answer to each is both yes and no. Even at this early stage the programs use many kinds of processes that might be called learning; they remember and use the methods that solved other problems; they adjust some of their internal characteristics for the best performance; they

```
O    (THE PROBLEM TO BE SOLVED IS)
     (THE GAS CONSUMPTION OF MY CAR IS 15 MILES PER GALLON . THE
O    DISTANCE BETWEEN BOSTON AND NEW YORK IS 250 MILES . WHAT IS
     THE NUMBER OF GALLONS OF GAS USED ON A TRIP BETWEEN NEW YORK
     AND BOSTON Q.)

O    (THE EQUATIONS TO BE SOLVED ARE)

O    (EQUAL G02556 (NUMBER OF GALLONS OF GAS USED ON TRIP BETWEEN
     NEW YORK AND BOSTON))

O    (EQUAL (DISTANCE BETWEEN BOSTON AND NEW YORK) (TIMES 250 (MILES)))

     (EQUAL (GAS CONSUMPTION OF MY CAR) (QUOTIENT (TIMES 15 (MILES))
O    (TIMES 1 (GALLONS))))

O    THE EQUATIONS WERE INSUFFICIENT TO FIND A SOLUTION

     (USING THE FOLLOWING KNOWN RELATIONSHIPS)
O    ((EQUAL (DISTANCE) (TIMES (SPEED) (TIME))) (EQUAL (DISTANCE)
     (TIMES (GAS CONSUMPTION) (NUMBER OF GALLONS OF GAS USED))))

O    (ASSUMING THAT)
     ((DISTANCE) IS EQUAL TO (DISTANCE BETWEEN BOSTON AND NEW YORK))

O    (ASSUMING THAT)
     ((GAS CONSUMPTION) IS EQUAL TO (GAS CONSUMPTION OF MY CAR))

O    (ASSUMING THAT)
     ((NUMBER OF GALLONS OF GAS USED) IS EQUAL TO (NUMBER OF GALLONS
     OF GAS USED ON TRIP BETWEEN NEW YORK AND BOSTON))

O

O    (THE NUMBER OF GALLONS OF GAS USED ON A TRIP BETWEEN NEW YORK
     AND BOSTON IS  16.66 GALLONS)
```

MOMENTARILY STUMPED at finding unknowns for which it has no equations, Student makes a guess that two phrases describe the same thing and goes on to solve the problem.

```
O    (THE PROBLEM TO BE SOLVED IS)
     (THE GROSS WEIGHT OF A SHIP IS 20000 TONS . IF ITS NET WEIGHT
O    IS 15000 TONS , WHAT IS THE WEIGHT OF THE SHIPS CARGO Q.)

     THE EQUATIONS WERE INSUFFICIENT TO FIND A SOLUTION

O    TRYING POSSIBLE IDIOMS

O    (DO YOU KNOW ANY MORE RELATIONSHIPS AMONG THESE VARIABLES)

O    (GROSS WEIGHT OF SHIP)

O    (TONS)

O    (ITS NET WEIGHT)

O    (WEIGHT OF SHIPS CARGO)

     yes
O    TELL ME

O    (the weight of a ships cargo is the difference between
     the gross weight and the net weight)

O    THE EQUATIONS WERE INSUFFICIENT TO FIND A SOLUTION

O    (ASSUMING THAT)
     ((NET WEIGHT) IS EQUAL TO (ITS NET WEIGHT))

O    (ASSUMING THAT)
     ((GROSS WEIGHT) IS EQUAL TO (GROSS WEIGHT OF SHIP))

O    (THE WEIGHT OF THE SHIPS CARGO IS 5000 TONS)
```

LACKING INFORMATION with which to solve a problem, Student asks for help. The operator (typing in lowercase letters) provides the necessary relations but does not use the same words as the problem used, forcing literal-minded Student to make some assumptions.

```
((STUDENT    ($)   (/ (*S ORGPRB 1))                            *)
(*      ($)    (1 (FN TERPRI) (FN TERPRI) (FN TERPRI))  *)
(*      ((*P THE PROBLEM TO BE SOLVED IS))               *)
(IDIOMS ($)                                              *)
(*      (HOW OLD)   (WHAT)                       IDIOMS)
(*      (IS EQUAL TO) (IS)                       IDIOMS)
(*      (YEARS YOUNGER THAN)   (LESS THAN)       IDIOMS)
(*      (YEARS OLDER THAN)   (PLUS)              IDIOMS)
(*      (PERCENT LESS THAN)   (PERLESS)          IDIOMS)
(*      (LESS THAN)   (LESSTHAN)                 IDIOMS)
(*      (THESE)   (THE)                          IDIOMS)
(*      (MORE THAN)   (PLUS)                     IDIOMS)
(*      (FIRST TWO NUMBERS)   (THE FIRST NUMBER AND THE
            SECOND NUMBER)                       IDIOMS)
(*      (THREE NUMBERS)   (THE FIRST NUMBER AND THE SECOND
            NUMBER AND THE THIRD NUMBER)         IDIOMS)
(*      (ONE HALF)   ( .5000)                    IDIOMS)
(*      (TWICE)   (2 TIMES)                      IDIOMS)
(*      (TWO NUMBERS)                            SIM)
(*      ((* DOLLAR) $1)   (2 DOLLARS)            IDIOMS)
(*      (CONSECUTIVE TO)   ((QUOTE 1) PLUS)      IDIOMS)
(*      (LARGER THAN)   (PLUS)                   IDIOMS)
(*      (PER CENT)   (PERCENT)                   IDIOMS)
(*      (HOW MANY)   (HOWM)                      IDIOMS)
(*      (SQUARE OF)   (SQUARE)                   IDIOMS)
(*      (($.1S) MULTIPLIED BY)   (TIMES)         IDIOMS)
(*      (($.1S) DIVIDED BY)   (DIVBY)            IDIOMS)
(*      (THE SUM OF)   (SUM)                     IDIOMS)
(*      ($)   (/ (*S NONID 1))                   *)
(WORDS  ($1)    0   (/ (*Q SHELF (FN GETDCT 1 DICT)))
            WORDS)
(*      ($)   ((*A SHELF))                       *)
(THE    (THE THE)   (1)                          THE)
(*      ($)   (/ (*S MARKWD 1))                  THE)
(*      (AS OLD AS)                              AGEPROB)
(*      (AGE)                                    AGEPROB)
(*      (YEARS OLD)                              AGEPROB)
(*      ($)   (/ (*D RETURN SENTENCE))           BRACKET)
(SENTENCE   ($)   ((*N PROBLEM))                 *)
(*      ($1)    0   (/ (*S FIND (*E-1)) (*D RETURN SENTENCE
            ))                                   OPFORM)
(QUIET  ($)                                      *)
(SUBSTITUTIONS   ($)   ((FN TERPRI) (*A NONID))  *)
(*      ((*P WITH MANDATORY SUBSTITUTIONS THE PROBLEM IS))
            *)
(TAGGING    ($)   ((FN TERPRI) (*A MARKWD))      *)
(*      ((*P WITH WORDS TAGGED BY FUNCTION THE PROBLEM IS)
            )                                    *)
```

BOBROW'S PROGRAM is written in a language, METEOR, that he developed from the established programming language LISP. A small part of the program is illustrated here.

```
REMEMBER((
(PEOPLE IS THE PLURAL OF PERSON)
(FEET IS THE PLURAL OF FOOT)
(YARDS IS THE PLURAL OF YARD)
(FATHOMS IS THE PLURAL OF FATHOM)
(INCHES IS THE PLURAL OF INCH)
(SPANS IS THE PLURAL OF SPAN)
(ONE HALF ALWAYS MEANS  0.5  )
(THREE NUMBERS ALWAYS MEANS THE FIRST NUMBER AND THE SECOND
NUMBER AND THE THIRD NUMBER)
(FIRST TWO NUMBERS ALWAYS MEANS
THE FIRST NUMBER AND THE SECOND NUMBER)
(MORE THAN ALWAYS MEANS PLUS)
(THESE ALWAYS MEANS THE)
(TWO NUMBERS SOMETIMES MEANS ONE NUMBER AND THE
OTHER NUMBER)
(TWO NUMBERS SOMETIMES MEANS ONE OF THE
NUMBERS AND THE OTHER NUMBER)
(HAS IS A VERB)
(GETS IS A VERB)
(HAVE IS A VERB)
(LESS THAN ALWAYS MEANS LESSTHAN)
(LESSTHAN IS AN OPERATOR OF LEVEL 2)
(PERCENT IS AN OPERATOR OF LEVEL 2)
(PERCENT LESS THAN ALWAYS MEANS PERLESS)
(PERLESS IS AN OPERATOR OF LEVEL 2)
(PLUS IS AN OPERATOR OF LEVEL  2)
(SUM IS AN OPERATOR)
(TIMES IS AN OPERATOR OF LEVEL 1)
(SQUARE IS AN OPERATOR OF LEVEL 1)
(DIVBY IS AN OPERATOR OF LEVEL 1)
(OF IS AN OPERATOR)
(DIFFERENCE IS AN OPERATOR)
(SQUARED IS AN OPERATOR)
(MINUS IS AN OPERATOR OF LEVEL 2)
(PER IS AN OPERATOR)
(SQUARED IS AN OPERATOR)
(YEARS OLDER THAN ALWAYS MEANS PLUS)
(YEARS YOUNGER THAN ALWAYS MEANS LESS THAN)
(IS EQUAL TO ALWAYS MEANS IS)
(PLUSS IS AN OPERATOR)
(MINUSS IS AN OPERATOR)
(HOW OLD ALWAYS MEANS WHAT)
(THE PERIMETER OF $1 RECTANGLE SOMETIMES MEANS
TWICE THE SUM OF THE LENGTH AND  WIDTH OF THE RECTANGLE)
(GALLONS IS THE PLURAL OF GALLON)
(HOURS IS THE PLURAL OF HOUR)
(MARY IS A PERSON)
(ANN IS A PERSON)
(BILL IS A PERSON)
(A FATHER IS A PERSON)
(AN UNCLE IS A PERSON)
(POUNDS IS THE PLURAL OF POUND)
(WEIGHS IS A VERB)
))
REMEMBER ((
(DISTANCE EQUALS SPEED TIMES TIME)
(DISTANCE EQUALS GAS CONSUMPTION TIMES
NUMBER OF GALLONS OF GAS USED)
(1 FOOT EQUALS 12 INCHES)
(1 YARD EQUALS 3 FEET)
))
```

FILING SYSTEM for Student is loosely organized, with different kinds of information listed in an unordered dictionary. This makes it easy to add new information as needed.

"associate" symbols that have been correlated in the past. No program today, however, can work any genuinely important change in its own basic structure. (A number of early experiments on "self-organizing" programs failed because of excessive reliance on random trial and error. A somewhat later attempt by the Carnegie Institute group to get their General Problem Solver to improve its descriptive ability was based on much sounder ideas; this project was left unfinished when it encountered difficulties in communication between programs, but it probably could be completed with the programming tools now available.)

In order for a program to improve itself substantially it would have to have at least a rudimentary understanding of its own problem-solving process and some ability to recognize an improvement when it found one. There is no inherent reason why this should be impossible for a machine. Given a model of its own workings, it could use its problem-solving power to work on the problem of self-improvement. The present programs are not quite smart enough for this purpose; they can only deal with the improvement of programs much simpler than themselves.

Once we have devised programs with a genuine capacity for self-improvement a rapid evolutionary process will begin. As the machine improves both itself and its model of itself, we shall begin to see all the phenomena associated with the terms "consciousness," "intuition" and "intelligence" itself. It is hard to say how close we are to this threshold, but once it is crossed the world will not be the same.

It is reasonable, I suppose, to be unconvinced by our examples and to be skeptical about whether machines will ever be. intelligent. It is unreasonable, however, to think machines could become *nearly* as intelligent as we are and then stop, or to suppose we will always be able to compete with them in wit or wisdom. Whether or not we could retain some sort of control of the machines, assuming that we would want to, the nature of our activities and aspirations would be changed utterly by the presence on earth of intellectually superior beings.

III

MATHEMATICS OF, BY, AND FOR COMPUTERS

III

MATHEMATICS OF, BY, AND FOR COMPUTERS

INTRODUCTION

Computation has always been viewed as a service to problem solving. The architectural monuments of the ancients and their extensive sea voyages testify to the successes of even the earliest reckoners. But in ancient times, even as today, computation raised problems at least as deep and as difficult as those it hoped to solve. Euclid's geometry served the builders of his time in many practical ways, but for Euclid himself it mainly raised problems of axiomatization and theorem proving. The earliest automatic computers — Babbage's analytic engine and the ENIAC (Ulam, "Computers") — were designed to help compute astronomical and ballistic tables, respectively. But man cannot merely own tools, intellectual or otherwise, without soon seeing them as objects for study just like any other objects in his environment. Computers are, on the one hand, mathematical machines; on the other, they are machines capable of doing mathematics. It cannot be surprising, then, that they have stimulated mathematicians to think of both mathematics *of* and mathematics *for* computers.

Mathematics *of* the computer concerns itself mainly with the nature of the computer and hence, perforce, with that of computation itself. Long before the appearance of electronic computers, Alan Turing showed that a very simple machine can serve as a model for all computers (see Kemeny, "Man Viewed As a Machine," p. 206). Much of modern mathematical logic has concerned itself with the border between what computers — as modeled by Turing — can and cannot do. The article by Hao Wang, "Games, Logic, and Computers," is of this genre. Wang shows that all questions about the power of computers can be engaged in an unlikely guise that resembles a game of dominoes.

Quite recently, logicians have turned their attention to the fine structure of that domain of problems that computers *can* solve. Computers can, for example, add and multiply pairs of integers. It seems intuitively obvious that multiplication is "harder" than addition. Shmuel Winograd ("How Fast Can Computers Add?") refines the expression of this intuition. He shows, incidentally, that intuition can be a poor guide; much of the work of Winograd and his colleagues has not so much added to a stable body of knowledge as it has discredited various baseless mathematical old wives' tales.

The article by Ulam ("Computers") comprises a list of mathematical jobs that computers are actually doing. The list would undoubtedly have surprised Babbage, for Ulam concerns himself not with the astronomical calculations foreseen a hundred years ago (and carried out, to be sure, on computers today), but rather with the somewhat isolated branch of mathematics known as number theory. Ulam's use of the computer, especially of visual displays, is highly imaginative. It anticipates the progress described by Sutherland ("Computer Displays") and Fano and Corbató ("Time-Sharing on Computers") in articles published years later.

Ulam also very briefly mentions the Monte Carlo technique he invented; it is covered in more detail in McCracken's article, "The Monte Carlo Method." As both authors point out, computers are sometimes asked to model processes that involve random events. It was once thought that computers could be made subject to random stimuli by giving them input signals from naturally random signal sources, such as Geiger counters. But an inherent advantage of most computational models is that their behavior is repeatable. There is usually strong reason to consider computers as deterministic machines. How can one reconcile the wish for determinacy with the occasional need for randomness? That is the question Ulam touches on, and to which McCracken gives one possible answer.

Neither Ulam nor McCracken deals with the question of defining randomness, nor do they discuss where the random numbers that a Monte Carlo process must use come from. In earlier days, tables of random numbers were *stored* in the computer's memory. Nowadays, random numbers are *generated* by algorithmic processes. Much work has been done on the twin questions of defining randomness and of the generation of random numbers since these articles were written (Knuth, 1969).

A truly rigorous definition of randomness has proved to be remarkably elusive. One deceptively simple idea of what it means for a sequence of numbers—one might as well say of digits—to be random is that it is impossible to devise a successful strategy for gambling against it. Imagine two players, A and B; A has an allegedly random sequence of digits written on a piece of paper. He reveals one digit at a time to B. Each time he does so, B may place a bet on a prediction of the next digit. If B can detect a pattern in the sequence of digits being revealed to him, then he can eventually begin to win. Since sequences of random numbers in modern computer applications are generated by algorithmic processes, they clearly attain systematic patterns. Their generating algorithms are, in a sense, pattern descriptions, and no such sequences are truly random. Nevertheless, they may have degrees of randomness in the sense that they can be shown to win against powerful gambling strategies, i.e., strong, tight statistical criteria.

Current work in the theory of random-number generation concerns itself with ways to rapidly generate pseudorandom sequences that defy very strong gambling strategies, and with the design of gambling strategies, i.e., statistical tests, that provide ever stronger tests of randomness.

13

GAMES, LOGIC AND COMPUTERS

HAO WANG
November, 1965

Today much of the work once done by human muscles and brains is being delegated to machines, and people in all walks of life are asking: What human abilities are irreplaceable? What can machines not do? It may surprise the reader to learn that, whereas the first question has no definite answer, the second has a straightforward mathematical solution.

Even before the first modern computing machine was built the late British logician Alan Turing asked the question: What can computers not do? In his attempt to create a theory of what can be computed and what cannot, Turing devised a slow and simple imaginary computer that he proved to be theoretically capable of performing all the operations of *any* computer. He used his machine to demonstrate the close kinship of computer theory and logic, branches of mathematics that are both concerned with mathematical proof and with notations that can present our thoughts in exact form. This article will undertake to illustrate some fundamental concepts in the area of overlap between computer theory and logic by means of games.

The human mind can grasp only relatively small numbers and quantities. The discipline of mathematics, on the other hand, is primarily concerned with infinity. Finite mathematical operations and infinite mathematical entities present a significant and fascinating contrast. The smooth transition from intuitively comprehensible individual cases to unrestricted general situations is a remarkable achievement of the human intellect. Abstract considerations concerning games can introduce us to this phenomenon quite naturally.

Finding the sequence of moves most likely to lead to victory in a game such as ticktacktoe presents a logical problem precisely analogous to finding the series of steps that will yield a solution to any mathematical problem of a given class. In certain games there is no optimum strategy that will guarantee victory; in certain classes of problems there is no algorithm—no general method of supplying a series of steps leading to a solution. Since a computer program is simply an algorithm designed for execution by machine, this means that there are classes of problems that computers cannot solve. Before considering the difficulties of constructing algorithms for solving problems (also of devising programs for arriving at solutions and of working out optimum strategies for winning games), let us examine why it is that their construction not only is useful but also represents an ultimate goal of mathematics.

Obviously it would take infinite time and energy to memorize the multiplication table if, instead of just including the products of all single-digit numbers taken two at a time, the table included the products of all multidigit numbers taken in this way. Man has made this infinite multiplication table unnecessary by memorizing, along with the multiplication table for single-digit

numbers, a list of steps involving "carrying" and the addition of partial products that will yield the product of any two multidigit numbers.

We know that the operations of elementary arithmetic involve formal rules, and most of us recall that certain other operations, such as the extraction of a square root, can be done according to a fixed list of sequential steps. As we get to problems of greater complexity it becomes less clear that they can be solved by algorithm. Consider the following problem: "Given the two positive integers 6 and 9, find their largest common divisor." The reader will immediately see the answer: 3. If the two numbers were 68 and 153, readers who are inclined to try various possibilities might still find the answer (17). If it could be shown, however, that the general problem "Given two positive integers *a* and *b*, find their greatest common divisor" can be solved by algorithm, then anyone or any machine capable of performing the specified operations could solve it for any *a* and *b*. Such an algorithm exists; it was devised by Euclid [*see illustrations at top of page 138*].

The usefulness of algorithms is equal-

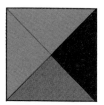

DOMINO PROBLEM involves assembling three colored tiles called domino types to form a block that can be infinitely extended with colors matching on all adjacent edges (*opposite page*). It is assumed that the player has an infinite quantity of each domino type and that no domino can be rotated in two dimensions. The problem is solved by finding a rectangular block in which the color sequence on the top edge is the same as that on the bottom edge and the sequence on the left edge is the same as that on the right. Such a unit (*heavy outline on opposite page*) can be repeated in all directions to fill an infinite plane.

```
      :R
  GCD :R        THIS ROUTINE COMPUTES THE GREATEST COMMON
      :R        DIVISOR OF TWO INTEGERS A AND B.
      : R
      EXTERNAL FUNCTION (A,B)
      NORMAL MODE IS INTEGER
      ENTRY TO GCD.
 LOOP REMAIN = B - A*(B/A)
      WHENEVER REMAIN.E.O,FUNCTION RETURN .ABS.(A)
      B = A
      A = REMAIN
      TRANSFER TO LOOP
      END OF FUNCTION


      TYPE INPUT              TYPE INPUT
      A=8,B=12*               A=12345678,B=87654321*
      THE GCD OF A AND B IS   THE GCD OF A AND B IS
            4                       9
```

1. Consider two positive integers, a and b. Proceed to next instruction.

2. Compare the two numbers under consideration (determine if they are equal, and if not, which is larger). Proceed to next instruction.

3. If the numbers are equal, each is the answer; stop. If not, proceed to next instruction.

4. Subtract the smaller number from the larger one and replace the two numbers under consideration by the subtrahend and the remainder. Proceed to instruction 2.

ALGORITHM IN COMPUTER LANGUAGE provides a series of steps by which the largest common divisor of any two numbers can be found. At bottom are computed solutions for two pairs of numbers. Procedure is in the language called MAD (for Michigan algorithm decoder). Letter O is printed with a line through it to distinguish it from zero.

SAME ALGORITHM is stated in ordinary language. The process of division is rendered as repeated subtraction. The series of steps is known as the Euclidean algorithm.

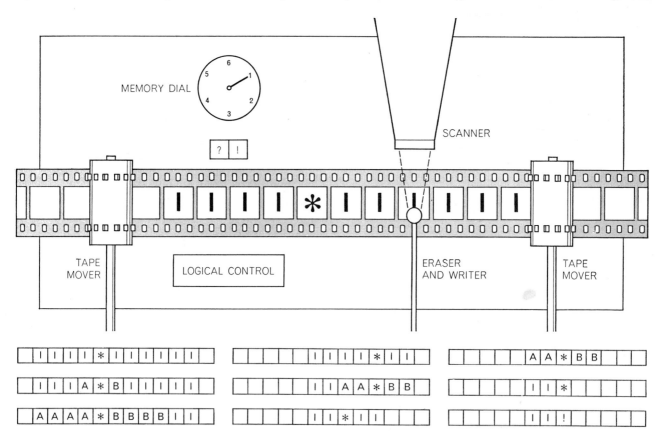

TURING MACHINE designed to perform steps of the Euclidean algorithm displays the numbers 4 and 6 on its tape in this schematic illustration. (Each digit is represented by a stroke; asterisk signals separation of numbers.) The logical control of the machine consists of instructions determined by a mark on the square of tape being scanned and the position of the memory dial. Steps of the Euclidean algorithm lead to changes on the tape illustrated in sequence at bottom. The machine first determines which number is larger by a "comparison loop" in which it replaces strokes to right and left of asterisk with symbols ("A" at left and "B" at right).

When one set of strokes is exhausted, the machine begins a "subtraction loop," erasing the symbols of the smaller number and converting the symbols of the larger number back into strokes. These are separated from the two strokes representing the remainder of the subtraction by an asterisk. The process of comparison and subtraction is repeated with 4 and 2 on tape, and then with 2 and 2; finally, 2 and 0 appear on tape. As comparison loop begins, blank tape on one side of asterisk evokes a halt signal (!) from logical control, and the machine stops with the answer (2) on its tape. Machine is idealized because its tape is potentially infinite.

ly apparent in the realm of games, where they provide instructions for the most advantageous moves. The mathematician, of course, is less interested in winning a game than in understanding the abstract structure of that class of games. By considering the existence or nonexistence of a winning strategy, he gains insight into the abstract structure of the game and those of the same kind.

Take, for example, the game known as nim. Any number of objects, say six matches, are arranged in three piles. Two players, A and B, draw in turn, each taking any number of matches from any one pile. Whoever takes the last match is the winner. Since the finite quantity of matches will in the end be exhausted, it is obvious that the game allows no draw. It is significant that only one of the two players has a winning strategy, depending on the size of the initial three piles and who moves first. In the particular game defined by piles of one, two and three matches the winning strategy belongs to B, the player who moves second. This can be proved by means of a schematic tree with the node of each set of branches representing a situation at a stage of the game, and the branches from each node the possible moves a player can make in that situation [see top illustration at right].

Suppose we are to play this game with three piles containing 10 million, 234 and 2,729 matches. It is theoretically feasible to tabulate all the possible sequences of moves with these three piles and then to tell by inspection whether A or B has a winning strategy. No one, however, would be willing or able to undertake such a tabulation. The mathematician would undertake a systematic search for shortcuts to make the operations easier and to achieve economy of thought. A search of this kind has in fact been made for the game of nim, and a simple recipe has been worked out for determining which player has the winning strategy. The recipe states that A can always win if, when the numbers of objects in the three piles are expressed in binary notation, they add up to a figure that contains an odd number. Such a recipe can represent a dazzling but unimportant stunt or a way of achieving significant mathematical insight, depending on the nature of the game and the directness of its relation to major mathematical and logical problems.

A game such as nim is said to be "unfair," because one player always has a winning strategy. A game such as

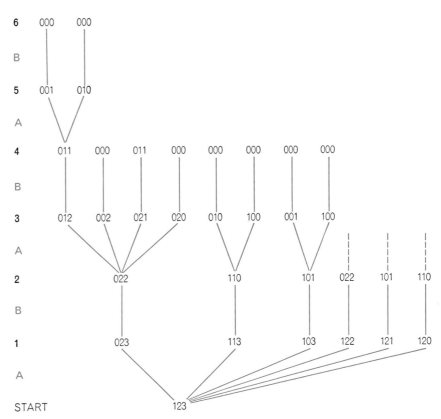

TREE FOR GAME OF NIM indicates that the player who moves second, B, has a winning strategy. At beginning of game (*bottom*) there are piles of one, two and three matches (*digits at each node of tree give number of matches remaining in piles*). Players remove one or more matches from a single pile until someone wins by removing the last match. Branches show all the possible moves for A and the unanswerable response of B to each of them.

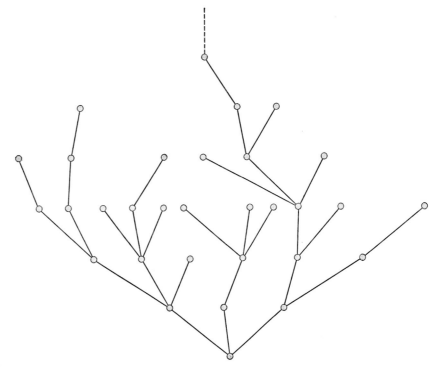

INFINITY LEMMA is suggested by a tree that continues at top. The lemma is a proposition to the effect that if there are infinitely many connected branches in a tree, and only finitely many branches from each of its nodes, then there must be one node at every level from which branches extend indefinitely upward; these, taken together, form an infinite path through the tree. The lemma can be paraphrased: "If the human species never disappears, there exists today someone who will at any future time have a living descendant."

ticktacktoe is said to be "futile," because each player has a nonlosing strategy that eliminates the possibility of a winner. These characterizations can be restated as a theorem: Every game is either futile or unfair if there is a fixed, finite upper boundary to the length of each path on its tree and only finitely many branches come directly from each node. The theorem holds because if there are no endless games and only finitely many legal moves at each stage,

then the total number of possible sequences of moves is finite. If we represent all the permissible plays by a tree, we see that if neither player has a winning strategy, then each player has a nonlosing strategy.

The theorem does not apply directly to the game of chess, because there are no precise rules to prevent endless matches. Let us assume, however, that we could introduce rules to exclude endless chess matches, without

imposing a limit on the absolute number of moves allowed in a complete match. We would then be able to apply to chess a proposition known as the infinity lemma, which states that if there are infinitely many connected branches in the tree of a game and only finitely many branches from each node, then there is an infinite path.

Given the infinity lemma and the assumption that new rules have excluded endless matches, it follows that the

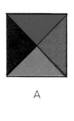

A   B   C

⌣ = NOT
v = OR
∧ = AND
x′ = x + 1

1

(Axy ∧ Bx′y) v (Bxy ∧ Cx′y) v (Cxy ∧ Ax′y)

   OR      OR

2

(Ayx ∧ Byx′) v (Byx ∧ Cyx′) v (Cyx ∧ Ayx′)

4

Axx

   OR   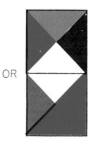   OR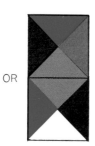

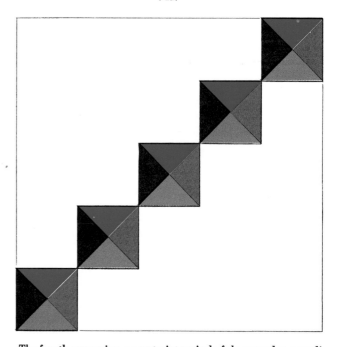

3

⌣ (Axy ∧ Bxy) v ⌣ (Bxy ∧ Cxy) v ⌣ (Cxy ∧ Axy)

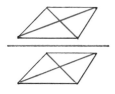

RULES FOR DOMINO PROBLEMS are set forth in the formal shorthand used by students of mathematical logic (*glossary is at top right*). At top center is a set of dominoes: *A, B* and *C*. The first expression states that colors must match on left and right edges, second that colors must match on top and bottom edges. The third rule is that dominoes must not be placed one atop another.

The fourth expression, a constraint typical of those used to complicate games in approximating difficult problems of computation, states that only *A* can lie on the main diagonal of the plane. The positions on the plane are described by Cartesian coordinates. In designation such as "*Ayx*" domino's position on horizontal axis is given by the first variable, *y*, and vertical position by the second.

tree representing the game of chess has only finitely many branches. Otherwise, in view of the fact that there are only finitely many branches from each node, there would be an infinite path (an endless game). Hence there are only finitely many possible sequences of moves and, as we showed earlier, chess is either unfair or futile.

The proof of the infinity lemma is fairly straightforward. Take the node at the very bottom of the tree. Since we are assuming infinitely many branches but only finitely many branches directly from any one node, at least one of the nodes on the next level must be the bottom of a subtree with infinitely many branches. Let us call this node X. Our hypothesis states, however, that there are only finitely many branches directly from X. Therefore one of the nodes on the next level above X must be the root of an infinite subtree. By repeating this argument we see that on every level there is at least one node that is the root of an infinite subtree and that these roots together determine an infinite path through the tree. An anthropomorphic way of applying the infinity lemma would be to state that if the human species never disappears, there exists today someone who will at any future time have a living descendant.

One chooses to examine a game, of course, according to the importance of the mathematical questions it raises. In 1960, while I was studying certain problems in logic at the Bell Telephone Laboratories, I devised a new game of solitaire played with "dominoes" that are actually colored tiles. More recently my colleagues and I at the Harvard Computation Laboratory have found some surprising and significant applications of this game. Several problems that arise in the domino game are exact analogues of problems that Turing machines are designed to solve. The conditions under which a domino game is played can be made to correspond to the computations of Turing machines, so that working with dominoes grants us another view—sometimes a particularly revealing one—of certain mathematical problems.

In a domino game we are given a finite set of square tiles (the dominoes); the tiles are all the same size but each edge of a tile has a stipulated color and the colors are combined in several specified ways. We assume that we have infinitely many copies of each type of domino, and that we are not permitted to rotate a domino in two dimensions. The object of the game is to cover

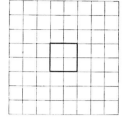

Cover a section of the Cartesian plane with black and white tiles so that no block (of the size outlined at right or larger) has edges at left and right and top and bottom that match. Is there a method of filling an infinite plane in this way?

FOUR PROBLEMS are presented by the author to the resolute reader. Only this problem and the problem at bottom have known solutions. Solution to this problem is on next page.

We can make a string of 0's and 1's yield "progeny" by these rules:
1. If the string has fewer than three symbols, stop.
2. If the string begins with 0, delete the first three symbols and append 00 to the end.
3. If the string begins with 1, delete the first three symbols and append 1101 to the end.

Is there an algorithm to determine whether one of two given strings is a progeny of the other?

011010001001	101110110011
01000100100	1101100111101
0010010000	11001111011101
001000000	011110111011101
00000000	11011101110100
0000000	111011101001101
000000	0111010011011101
00000	101001101110100
0000	0011011101001101
000	10110100110100
00	1101001101001101
(stop)	(progeny continue)

SECOND PROBLEM is to find an algorithm that shows whether two strings of 0's and 1's are related. The problem is complicated by the fact that certain strings may give rise to infinite progeny. An alternative solution would be to prove that no such algorithm can exist.

Is there an algorithm to decide if a polynomial equation with integral coefficients has roots that are integers?

Equations of this type include

$$x^2 - 4x + 3 = 0$$

and

$$a^2 + b^2 - c^2 = 0 .$$

The first equation has only one unknown, x. It thus has the form

$$a_n x^n + a_{n-1} x^{n-1} + ... + a_1 x + a_0 = 0$$

and for such equations the desired algorithm is known:
1. Find all the divisors of a_0.
2. Substitute each for x and calculate the resulting values for the left side of the equation.
3. If any yields the value 0, it is a root. If none do, the equation has no roots that are integers.

The problem is to devise such an algorithm for equations, such as the second, that contain more than one unknown.

THIRD PROBLEM has been known as "Hilbert's 10th problem" since the German mathematician David Hilbert listed it in 1900 as an outstanding problem confronting mathematics.

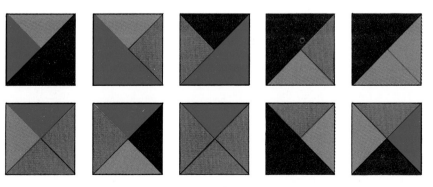

TEN-DOMINO PROBLEM calls for arranging these tiles in a block in which the color scheme is the same for top and bottom and left and right edges. Solution is on page 143.

a

a b

a b b a

a b b a b a a b

a b b a b a a b b a a b a b b a ...

SOLUTION TO FIRST PROBLEM on preceding page is illustrated. To repeat its construction, let *a* represent a black tile, *b* a white one (*left*). Write *a* and replace it with *ab*. Replace *b* with *ba* and continue to replace *a* and *b* in this way. Transcribe this sequence onto top row of plane and copy each symbol along diagonal from top right toward bottom left.

an infinite plane with dominoes in such a way that adjoining edges have the same color. If the plane can be covered with a given set of dominoes, the set is said to be solvable.

Consider the set of three dominoes in the illustration on page 136. The set is solvable because it can be assembled into a nine-domino block that satisfies the rule with respect to edges and can be repeated in every direction. Given a solution for the whole plane, we can obviously chop off three quadrants, or quarters, to get a solution over one quadrant. The converse is less obvious, but it can be established with the help of the infinity lemma. Since there exists a solution over an infinite quadrant, there exist partial solutions of *its* quadrants—solutions of any area *n* by *n*. We can make an infinite tree out of such partial solutions and show by the infinity lemma that there is an infinite path in the tree that yields a solution over the whole plane. Thus if it is possible to fill a quadrant of the infinite plane, it is possible to fill the whole plane.

We can use dominoes to simulate various Turing machines and to create an equivalent of Turing's important "halting problem." This is more easily done if we specify what domino goes at the origin of the plane—what domino we put down first. With greater effort we can accomplish the same thing either by specifying that certain dominoes occur on the main diagonal or by omitting any restriction other than those mentioned earlier. Let us consider this equivalence between the halting problem and the domino game in greater detail.

Turing devised his simple computer to emulate a human calculator. A man solving a mathematical problem is likely to use pencil and paper for writing and erasing numbers; he may also have a collection of mathematical facts in the form of a book of tables and, contained in his mind or in the book, a set of instructions for performing the proper steps in the proper sequence. The imaginary Turing machine also has a marking device and an eraser for writing numbers according to instructions from a logical control unit that follows a prepared table of commands. The numbers are written in the form of single strokes on square cells of an infinitely long tape serving as the memory unit. (Since no actual machine can have an infinite memory, the Turing machine is idealized.)

One square of the tape at a time is considered by a scanner that relays the symbol on the square to the control [*see bottom illustration on page 138*]. The control then consults its internal instructions by means of a dial that points to a location designated "Current instruction." Depending on the symbol at hand, the instruction specifies one of four commands: (1) Print a mark on the square, erasing it if necessary, (2) Move the tape one square to the right, (3) Move the tape one square to the left, (4) Halt! Then the instruction indicates the next instruction location. A Turing machine can be endowed with the requisite number of instruction locations and commands, as well as a tape with infinitely many squares, to solve any specified mathematical problem (if that problem is in a class solvable by algorithm).

Turing devised the halting problem

to exemplify a problem for which no program could yield all the correct solutions. He surpassed the power of any possible single machine by formulating a question about all Turing machines. He was able to show that although each machine, depending on its tape, would either halt or continue operating indefinitely, there is no general algorithm to determine this behavior, no recipe equivalent to the one for determining the invariable winner of a given game of nim. Now, it is possible to find for each Turing machine a set of dominoes such that the machine will eventually halt if and only if the set of dominoes does not have a solution. It is then a direct consequence that the domino problem is unsolvable. If we could solve the domino problem, we could solve the halting problem; we cannot solve the halting problem and so we cannot solve the domino problem. In other words, there is no general method for deciding if any given set of dominoes has a solution.

The domino problem is an example of an infinite decision problem of the kind that frequently turns up in logic, in computer theory and in mathematics in general. It is an infinite problem in the following sense. Any solution to the domino problem must be a single method that provides the correct yes or no answer to an infinite number of questions in the form: "Does a certain set of dominoes cover the plane?" Whereas any specified set of domino types is finite, there is of course an infinite set of such sets, and therefore an infinite number of questions.

We have thus reduced problems about sets of dominoes to problems about machines, and we have established results about dominoes by appealing to known results about machines. The next step is to reduce the question of interpreting a formula in logic to the problem of solving a set of dominoes. Since the condition that a set of dominoes has a solution can be expressed by a simple formula in logic, this reduction yields an answer to a long-outstanding decision problem in logic.

If we wish to express the condition that a set of three domino types has a solution in the first quadrant of our infinite plane, we think of the familiar Cartesian coordinates for the positions of dominoes in the quadrant and represent each domino by a predicate: *Axy*, for example, indicates that domino *A* occurs at position (x,y). If we use x' for $x + 1$, the required condition can be

given by a number of clauses that require very few quantifiers (constructions with "for all" and "there is"). We are generous only with such finite operations of formal logic as "not," "and" and "or" [*see illustration on page 140*]. We can conclude that for any given set of dominoes we can find a corresponding "*AEA* formula" (a sentence beginning "For all x there is a y such that for all z...," followed by a logical combination of predicates without quantifiers) such that the set has a solution if and only if the formula is not self-contradictory. In other words, we can translate a domino question into a logical formula by specifying certain constraints and then determine if the domino set is solvable by seeing if the formula is or is not self-contradictory. Therefore, since the general domino problem is unsolvable, there is no general method for deciding if an arbitrary *AEA* formula is self-contradictory.

The result is useful because the complexity of formulas in logic is to a large extent measured by the number and order of quantifiers, and the formulas of logic are often put into different classes according to the structure of quantifiers. It is surprising that as simple a class as that of *AEA* formulas (with three quantifiers only) is undecidable. In fact, with this result the decision problems for all quantifier classes are answered. Given any string of quantifiers we can now tell if the class of formulas determined by it is decidable.

The decision problem of logic is significant because all mathematical theories can be formulated in the framework of elementary logic. The question of whether or not a formula (F) can be derived from a set of axioms (A) is reduced to deciding if the logical formula "A but not F" is not self-contradictory. In this sense all mathematics is reducible to logic. Indeed, one measure of the complexity of a mathematical problem is given by the structure of its corresponding formula in logic. It is therefore an important enterprise to determine the complexity of various classes of logical formulas.

We can justifiably say that all mathematics can be reduced, by means of Turing machines, to a game of solitaire with dominoes. In most instances the reduction does not make a mathematical problem any easier to handle. Nevertheless, proving certain problems to be unsolvable by computer can be facilitated by reducing them to domino problems.

SOLUTION TO 10-DOMINO PROBLEM is a rectangular block of 36 dominoes, two of which are separated by heavy black line through center of illustration. The solution is not unique, that is, other configurations of the 10 dominoes are possible and equally acceptable.

14

HOW FAST CAN COMPUTERS ADD?

SHMUEL WINOGRAD

October, 1968

The first large digital computers of the late 1930's could add two numbers at the rate of about three pairs of digits per second. This performance has been improved by more than six orders of magnitude: today's computers can carry out 10 million additions in a second. Multiplication by computers has advanced even further. Its speed has increased from one calculation every three seconds to more than three million per second. It is these phenomenal gains in the rate of computation that have transformed the role of the computer, for example making possible the processing of data in "real time," that is, as events are actually taking place.

An increase in the speed of computation by an additional order of magnitude is forecast for the next few years. Looking to the future, the designers of computers and mathematicians concerned with computer theory are confronted by fundamental questions. How fast can computers be expected to operate? Is there any limit to their speed and, if so, what is it? These questions involve two different considerations. One has to do with the performance of tomorrow's computer components, the "hardware" of the future. Whatever ultimate limits there may be to the operating speed of components, they will be determined by the laws of physics and lie beyond the scope of this article. Here I shall take up a second consideration. What improvements are possible in the ways computer components are organized to do their work?

For some years I have been interested in finding out what limitations there may be on the speed of computers in terms of their organization. The number of possible computer designs is of course limitless. It is only by mathematical reasoning, and not by experimentation, that

one can determine the least possible time it would take the computer to add or multiply two numbers. At this point it will be useful to briefly review computer circuitry and computer arithmetic and to give some examples of how unorthodox computer organization can achieve gains in speed.

The basic elements in the arithmetic section of a computer are its switching circuits. A switching circuit has one or more input leads, through which incoming signals are received, and an output lead to carry away whatever output signal is predetermined by the design of the switch. Usually input and output leads carry only one of two possible signals: either a high voltage or a low voltage, a large amount of current or a small amount. It is this "either-or" characteristic of switching circuits that is responsi-

ble for the fact that the notation of computer arithmetic is customarily binary notation. The two binary digits, 0 and 1, can represent any number, and they are admirably suited to a high-voltage, low-voltage switching system. A high-voltage signal is read as a 1 and a low-voltage signal as a 0.

The signal on the output lead of a switching circuit depends on the input signals. Let us consider four switching circuits that can be combined to form a standard adder. The first is a two-input circuit called an "and" switch: a high-voltage 1 appears on its output lead only when the signals on both its input leads are high-voltage 1's. A second two-input circuit is called an "exclusive or" switch; here the outgoing signal is a 1 only if one or the other, but not both, of the incoming signals is a 1 [*see top illustration on next page*].

BASE 10	BASE 2	BASE 10	BASE 2	BASE 10	BASE 2	BASE 10	BASE 2
0	0						
1	1	9	1001	17	10001	25	11001
2	10	10	1010	18	10010	26	11010
3	11	11	1011	19	10011	27	11011
4	100	12	1100	20	10100	28	11100
5	101	13	1101	21	10101	29	11101
6	110	14	1110	22	10110	30	11110
7	111	15	1111	23	10111	31	11111
8	1000	16	10000	24	11000	32	100000

BINARY NOTATION needs only a sequence of two digits, 0 and 1, to represent numbers of any size (the numbers from 0 to 32 are shown in base-10 and base-2 representation). Such an "either-or" system is ideally suited to computers with switching circuits that respond either to high-voltage signals (which can be read as 1's) or to low-voltage signals (which can be read as 0's). Binary notation can be used for many representations other than base-2.

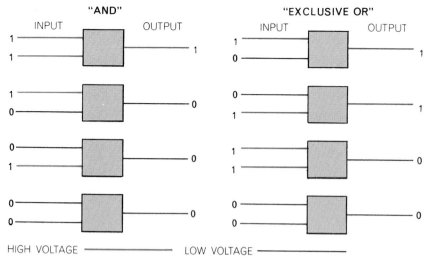

"AND"   "EXCLUSIVE OR"

HIGH VOLTAGE ———— LOW VOLTAGE ————

TWO COMPUTER SWITCHES, each with two input leads and one output lead, are designed to respond in different ways. The "and" switch (*left*) has a high-voltage output (readable as the binary digit 1) when both input signals are high-voltage, but not otherwise. The "exclusive or" switch (*right*) has a high-voltage output (readable as 1) when either input signal is high-voltage but not when both are high-voltage or low-voltage.

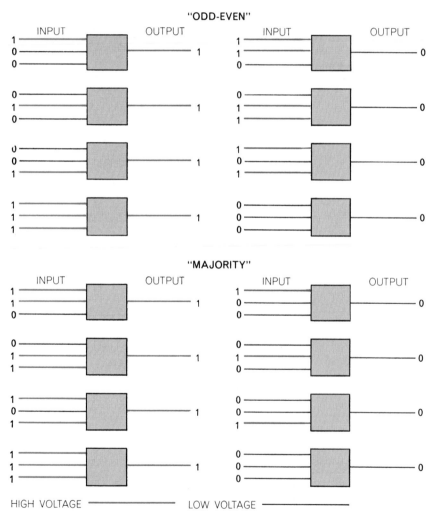

"ODD-EVEN"

"MAJORITY"

HIGH VOLTAGE ———— LOW VOLTAGE ————

SWITCHES WITH THREE INPUTS are more complex; they can receive eight possible signals compared with only four possible with two-input switches. The "odd-even" switch (*top*) has a high-voltage output, readable as 1, in the four instances when the number of high-voltage input signals is odd. The "majority" switch (*bottom*) has a high-voltage output when two or more input signals are high-voltage. These two switches and the two in the top illustration, combined, form an adding circuit (*see illustration on opposite page*).

The other two switching circuits have three input leads. The output signal of one, the "odd-even" switching circuit, is a 1 only when the number of 1 signals on the input side is odd. Thus when any one, but only one, of the three odd-even input leads carries a high-voltage signal, the output signal will be high-voltage, and the same is true when all three of its input leads carry a high-voltage signal. The second three-input switching circuit, the "majority" circuit, has an output signal of 1 when, and only when, at least two of the input signals are 1's. Therefore in one instance the odd-even and majority switches have the same output: when all three of their input leads carry high-voltage signals [*see bottom illustration at left*].

No switching circuit acts instantaneously; there is a brief delay between the instant incoming signals appear on the input leads and the instant an outgoing signal appears on the output lead. In the days of vacuum-tube circuitry the delay was about 10 microseconds (millionths of a second). Some of today's solid-state circuits have a switching delay no greater than one nanosecond (a billionth of a second). This represents a gain in speed of four orders of magnitude in about a decade. Large or small, switching delay is a factor that affects the speed of computation. Called delay time, it is represented by the expression Δt.

Another factor that must be considered in relation to computation speed is the physical limit on the number of input leads a switching circuit can have. Typically the number of input leads varies from three to five. If a circuit could have many more than five input leads, it could process more information simultaneously, and its increased capacity would greatly increase computation speeds. Regardless of whether the circuit has two input leads or 20, however, the number of leads is a factor that sets a limit on its performance. The number of input leads is called the "fan-in," and it is represented by the letter r. In any formula that expresses the least possible time it takes a computer to add or multiply, both Δt and r must appear. The numbers they stand for will depend on the characteristics of the particular components involved.

Let us take the switching circuits described above and make an adder that can combine any two numbers between 0 and 31. I set this limit for the sake of simplicity; in the "base-2" representation only five digits are needed to write numbers of this magnitude. Base-2 means that the value of each digit from

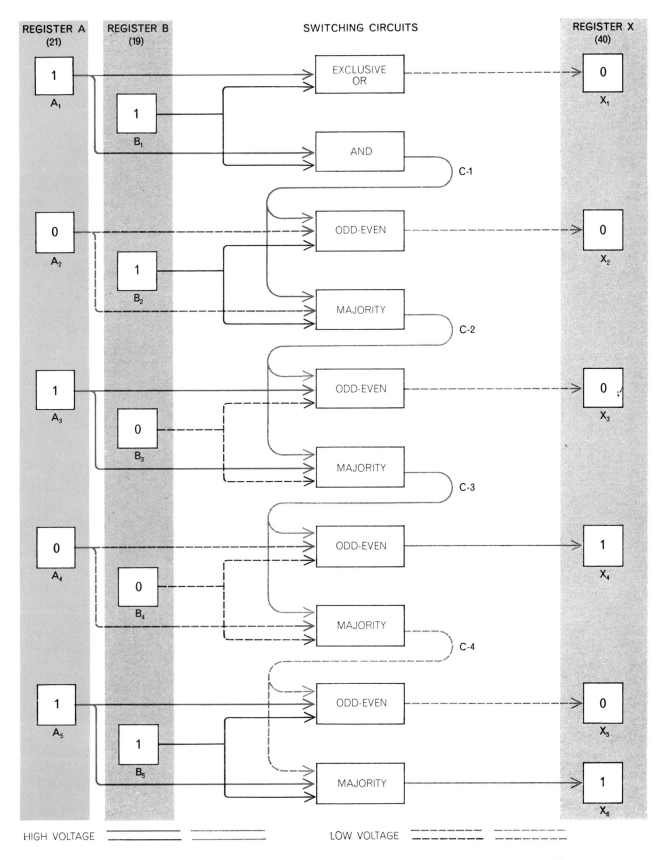

| REGISTER A (21) | REGISTER B (19) | SWITCHING CIRCUITS | REGISTER X (40) |

FIVE-DIGIT ADDER contains 10 switches grouped in five pairs (*vertical row, center*): an "exclusive or" and "and" pair to start, followed by four sets of paired odd-even and majority switches. The registers *A* and *B* (*left*) contain the numbers to be added, 21 and 19, in base-2 representation. The input leads of each pair of switches receive signals from matching sections of the registers. All 1's in the registers are received as high-voltage signals (*solid lines*) and all 0's as low-voltage signals (*broken lines*). The consequent output signal is a 1 or a 0, depending on switch design (*see illustrations on opposite page*). The output of the first switch in each pair appears as a 1 or a 0 in register *X* (*right*), which stores the result of each addition. Simultaneously the second switch of the pair sends a "carry" of 1 or 0 to the next pair of switches. Because five consecutive steps are involved in the process, five delays are required.

right to left is twice the preceding power of two. Thus the digit at right represents 2^0, or one; the next to the left, 2^1, or two; the next, 2^2, or four; the next, 2^3, or eight, and the last, 2^4, or 16.

The task we shall set our adder is to combine the number 21 (10101 in base-2 representation, 21 equaling one 16 plus no 8 plus one 4 plus no 2 plus one 1) and the number 19 (10011, 19 equaling one 16 plus no 8 plus no 4 plus one 2 plus one 1). Because each of the two numbers is smaller than 31, the largest number that can be written in five binary digits, each of the input registers of the adder, in which the numbers are stored, will have only five positions. The sum of 21 plus 19, however, is greater than 31; for this reason the output register, in which the product of the addition appears, will need to have six positions (the number needed to display binary numbers from 32 to 63).

The way our adder works is similar to the way binary addition is taught in school. Starting at the right side of the two numbers, as if one were working with pencil and paper, the first addition is 1 plus 1. This, of course, is 2, written as 10 in base-2 representation, so one puts down 0 and carries 1 to the next place to the left. Here one adds the 1 plus the 0 plus the "carry" of 1; again the total is 2. Again one puts down 0 and carries the 1 to the next place to the left. When the two digits plus the carry add up to less than 2 (which happens, for example, in the fourth position from the right), the adder—human or mechanical—sets down the number 1; otherwise 0 is set down and the 1 is carried to the next place to the left. Our final result is 101000, the base-2 representation of the number 40.

Substituting switching circuits for pencil and paper, we find that after five consecutive switching operations have taken place the same six-digit representation of the product, 40, appears in the output register. (It is possible to obtain a six-digit number in only five steps because the final carry, which produces the sixth digit in the output register, takes place at the same time as the switching action that combines the fifth digits of the input registers.) Assuming that each switching circuit has a delay time of 10 nanoseconds, our adder needs 50 nanoseconds to complete the operation.

The length of time taken by the adder to complete its task was dictated by three implicit decisions we had made at the start. First, we decided that the adder would handle only the numbers from 0 to 31. Second, we decided that we would use base-2 representation. The fact that our switching circuits are binary does *not* dictate this choice; for example, in Morse code all numbers are written in binary symbols (a dot and a dash), but the number representation in Morse code is not base-2. Third, we decided on a way to carry out the addition process, choosing a method much like the schoolroom one. If we change any one of these three decisions, we find that the addition time also changes.

In the world of real computers the de-

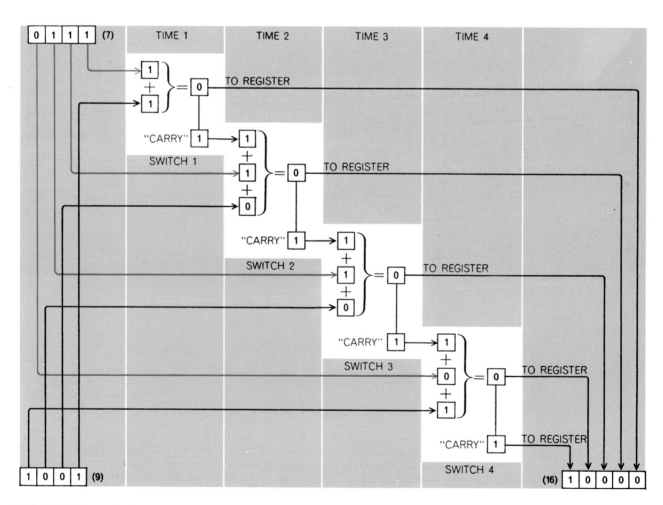

DELAY TIME involved in conventional computer addition is shown schematically; the numbers 7 and 9 are being added. Because 9 is represented by four binary digits, four switching circuits must be activated consecutively, producing four delays. Unorthodox arithmetic procedures and methods of representing numbers can reduce the number of steps required, thus minimizing delay.

signer is faced with the same choices. His first choice is to pick a size for his output register, that is, to establish the largest number that can be represented without "overflow." In our five-position adder, for example, the largest number that can be represented is 31, because the binary representation of 32 (2^5) will overflow into a sixth position. Real adder circuits, of course, handle numbers many thousands of times larger than 2^5. One common adder handles numbers with magnitudes on the order of 2^{36}, which is roughly 100 billion. Another goes up to 2^{48}, which means that numbers in excess of 100 trillion can be added without overflowing the output register. Our five-position adder could easily be extended to handle such enormous numbers, and could accomplish the addition of any two numbers between 0 and $2^n - 1$ in n times the delay time ($n \times \Delta t$).

Having set his maximum number, the designer has two more choices to make. First he must decide how to represent the numbers of the real world. His customary choice is the base-2 representation, but he can elect any other method he wishes. His second choice is the means by which his arithmetic operation will be carried out. He is certainly not required to use the orthodox arithmetic organization used in our model five-position adder. Increases in the speed of computation can be achieved both by performing arithmetic in unorthodox ways and by choosing novel means of number representation. Because these two tactics are unfamiliar to most people outside the computer field I shall give an example of each.

The first example is a method known as conditional-sum addition. This method uses the base-2 representation of numbers but handles the numbers in an unusual manner. To allow comparison with the orthodox arithmetic of our model adder I shall again combine the numbers 21 and 19. This time, however, we shall break up the five binary digits representing each number into groups. First we set aside the three lower digits of each number (a grouping I shall call "addition problem A"). We then write down the two higher digits of each number twice (groupings I shall call "addition problems B and C"). We add a carry of 1 to the digit at the right in addition problem B but leave addition problem C as it is. We now add A, B and C simultaneously. If A propagates a carry when it is added, then B will be the correct sum of the higher numbers; if it does not, then C will be correct. Since all three adding operations go on at the

NUMBER	REPRESENTATION	NUMBER	REPRESENTATION
0	0,0	8	3,2
1	1,1	9	4,0
2	2,2	10	0,1
3	3,0	11	1,2
4	4,1	12	2,0
5	0,2	13	3,1
6	1,0	14	4,2
7	2,1		

UNORTHODOX NUMBER REPRESENTATION uses the modulus method to obtain unique two-digit representations of the numbers from 0 to 14. Representations of this kind can be used for "remainder addition," the familiar method by which, for example, time is told. The table is in modulo-15, 15 being 5 times 3. The left digit in each digit-pair is the remainder after the number it represents is divided by 5; the right, after its division by 3.

same time, they are all completed in the time required by the longest one. This is the addition of the three lower digits, A, which requires three delay times. (B and C are completed in only two delay times.) When the addition of A is completed, it is evident that a carry has been propagated. This means that B is the correct sum to be recombined with A. The recombination costs us a fourth delay time and we arrive at the final number: 101000. Assuming that a machine working with conditional-sum addition contains switching circuits like those of our orthodox model adder, our use of the unorthodox arithmetic method will save us 10 nanoseconds per addition. The reason for the saving is that we are doing several operations simultaneously rather than consecutively.

My example of unorthodox number representation is the "modulus" technique, which is used in the arithmetic method called remainder addition. Daily experience has made us all familiar with remainder addition, indeed so familiar that we are seldom conscious of using it. When a train leaves on a four-hour trip at 10:00 A.M., we know that we should reach our destination at 2:00 P.M. because we have done a sum in modulo-12 addition. Ten plus 4, modulo-12, equals 2 because 14 (the sum of 10 plus 4) divided by 12 yields a quotient of 1 (which is ignored) and a remainder of 2. We deal with the days of the week in modulo-7, with the months of the year in modulo-12 and, three years out of four, with the days of the year in modulo-365. Indeed, when the computer designer selects the largest number his machine is to handle, he is preparing for addition

modulo-N, the value of N being the maximum number he chooses.

To see how remainder addition can save computation time, let us try adding modulo-15. I choose modulo-15 because of its simplicity. The number 15 is equal to 5 times 3; this property allows us to obtain an unorthodox, two-digit representation of every number from 0 through 14 in the following manner. The digit at the left in each two-digit pair will be the remainder after dividing the chosen number by 5; in the case of 0, for example, the digit at the left will be 0. The digit at the right will be the remainder after dividing the number by 3; in the case of 0, again 0. Thus the representation of 0, modulo-15, is 0,0. In the same manner the number 7 is represented by 2,1 because 7 divided by 5 yields a quotient of 1 (which is ignored) and a remainder of 2, whereas 7 divided by 3 yields a quotient of 2 (also ignored) and a remainder of 1. Following this method number by number, we find that every number from 0 to 14 is represented by a unique pair of digits, modulo-15 [see table in illustration above]. In writing the table I have used familiar decimal notation; only five digits, 0 through 4, are needed to write all 15 numbers. In actual practice, of course, the digit pairs would have to be translated into binary notation before they could be handled by a computer's switching circuits.

To do modulo-15 addition we set down the digit pairs representative of the numbers to be added and proceed by adding the two right-hand digits modulo-3 and the two left-hand digits modulo-5. As an example we shall add 4 and 12. The digit pair, modulo-15, for

a	b	c	d	e

```
        a              1              b          1 1             c        1 1 1           d    0 1 1 1            e   0 1 1 1
    1 0 0 1 1                  1 0 0 1 1                1 0 0 1 1              1 0 0 1 1              1 0 0 1 1
    1 0 1 0 1                  1 0 1 0 1                1 0 1 0 1              1 0 1 0 1              1 0 1 0 1
   [      |   |   |   | 0]     [   |   |   | 0 | 0]    [   |   | 0 | 0 | 0]  [   | 1 | 0 | 0 | 0] [1 | 0 | 1 | 0 | 0 | 0]
```

CONVENTIONAL ADDITION requires as many sequential steps as there are digits in the numbers. Adding 19 (10011 in base-2 representation) and 21 (10101 in base-2) requires the five steps illustrated (numerals in color are "carries"). The addition problem is the same as the one handled by the adder illustrated on page 95, where a pair of switches was activated for each step shown here.

4 is 4,1; the pair for 12 is 2,0. Starting at the right and adding 1 and 0, we obtain 1 (which, since it does not overflow modulo-3, stands as 1 in the sum). Adding 4 and 2, we obtain 6. This sum overflows modulo-5 by 1, so that we set down 1. Thus our final result is 1,1. Reference to the table of modulo-15 representations shows that 1,1 is the representation for the number 1. This is the correct answer: 4 plus 12 is 16 and 16 overflows modulo-15 by 1.

Done with pencil and paper, remainder addition is tedious and seems a very hard way to achieve a simple result. As with conditional-sum addition, however, the method has great potential advantages for computers because the two digits in each pair can be added simultaneously rather than consecutively, thereby accelerating the computation. Furthermore, remainder numbers are obviously not peculiar to modulo-15. If any number N is a product of two numbers N_1 and N_2 such that no number except 1 divides both N_1 and N_2, then we can represent every number between 0 and $N - 1$ by a unique pair of numbers. The first number will represent the remainder after dividing by N_1 and the second the remainder after dividing by N_2. Modulo-N addition is then performed exactly as modulo-15 addition was; the first numbers are added modulo-N_1 and the second modulo-N_2. The only numbers, N, that are not the product of two such numbers, N_1 and N_2, are those that are the powers of a single prime number. This means that remain-

der addition cannot be used to add modulo-2^n, because 2 is a prime number, divisible only by itself and 1.

The two examples I have given are representative of the two principal tactics available to the computer designer: a free choice of representation and operation methods. From a theoretical point of view the dilemma is that no imaginable system of number representation or way of performing arithmetic can be declared advantageous or worthless without a trial, yet to try each and every one of an essentially unlimited number of tactics would be impossible.

Four years ago M. O. Rabin of the Hebrew University of Jerusalem visited us at the IBM Watson Research Center, and he and I were discussing such matters. Among other things we wondered how base-2 representation had become such a *sine qua non* in computer arithmetic. Why not some other base? For that matter, why any base representation at all? The result of our discussion was that I set out to seek the minimum time for addition that would hold true regardless of the hardware involved, of the way the numbers were represented (except that each must comprise a unique combination of 0's and 1's) or of the method of doing the addition. Unless a sound theoretical basis for calculating the least possible time of computation was available, the designers of computers could never be certain if their intuitive schemes were the most efficient ones possible.

As a starting point, let us compute the

time required for addition with both conditional-sum adding and remainder arithmetic. One first breaks down N, the number selected as the modulus, into its constituent powers of prime numbers. The largest of these constituents is our bottleneck; its size is a key factor in determining the length of the computation process. We denote this number, the largest power of a single prime that divides N, as the alpha of N, $\alpha(N)$.

To suit the computer's switching circuits the various parts of the remainder-arithmetic representation have to be translated into binary notation. Because we want to use the conditional-sum method of addition, we choose a base-2 representation. The number of binary digits necessary to represent the integers 0 through $\alpha(N) - 1$ is $\lceil \log_2 \alpha(N) \rceil$. I use $\lceil \log_a b \rceil$ to denote the smallest integer, x, such that $a^x \geq b$. The reader can easily verify for himself that, by repeated application of conditional-sum addition, it takes $\lceil \log_2 2n \rceil \Delta t$ to add two n-digit numbers. Conditional-sum addition can, however, be generalized by breaking the numbers into r parts, rather than just the two parts shown in our example. Under these circumstances $\lceil \log_r 2n \rceil \Delta t$ is required to add two n-digit numbers. Combining the two formulas, we find that the delay time for performing addition with remainder arithmetic and conditional-sum addition is expressed by the formula $\lceil \log_r 2 \lceil \log_2 \alpha(N) \rceil \rceil \Delta t$.

I was surprised to discover that no way exists to improve this method of performing addition. This is to say that

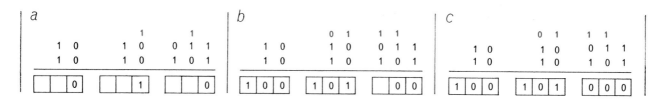

UNORTHODOX ADDITION, using the conditional-sum method, sets apart the three lower digits of the same two binary numbers and then enters their two higher digits twice, once with a carry (*color*) and once without it. Next, all three groups are added simul-

taneously. The largest group comprises three digits; all addition is therefore complete after three delays. If addition of the lower digits propagates a carry (as in this example), the product of the higher digits that included the conditional carry is the correct one. A

no matter what representation is used or what method of operation is selected, the process of addition has to take *at least* the delay time shown by the formula.

Let us now use the formula to find the least time for modulo-2^{48} addition. We start by assuming a computer component technology in which r, the input-lead fan-in, is equal to three, and Δt, the delay time, is a hundred-millionth of a second (10^{-8} second). To find the least time we must first determine the alpha of 2^{48}, the largest number that is a power of a prime number and by which 2^{48} is divisible. Since 2^{48} is a power of a prime number, the alpha of N proves to be 2^{48} itself. We next find the logarithm to the base-2 of 2^{48}; it is 48. Entering all these values in the formula, we learn that the least time is $\lceil \log_3 2 \times 48 \rceil 10^{-8}$, or five hundred-millionths of a second (5×10^{-8} second).

How close to the absolute maximum speed of addition are contemporary computers getting? By using the formula we can move for the first time from an area of intuition to the realm of hard fact. For example, one high-performance computer has an input-lead fan-in of four, a delay time of one nanosecond (10^{-9} second) and an N of 2^{32} (equal to 4,294,967,296). Using these values, we learn that the computer cannot possibly add two numbers faster than $\lceil \log_4 64 \rceil 10^{-9}$, or three nanoseconds ($3 \times 10^{-9}$ second). In point of fact, the machine takes five nanoseconds to add. The formula enables us to show that five-nanosecond addition is within 40 percent of the maximum speed possible. The establishment of absolute maximums gives designers a much clearer measure of the amount of room for improvement that may exist in any computer.

Let us give N an even larger value— 13,762,686,640—and find the speed with which addition at that modulus value is possible. The number is more than three times the size of 2^{32}; intuition would sug-

0	0,0,6	16	0,0,4	32	0,0,5	48	0,1,4
1	0,0,0	17	12,0,0	33	8,0,0	49	4,0,0
2	0,0,1	18	6,0,1	34	4,0,1	50	2,0,1
3	3,1,0	19	7,1,0	35	11,1,0	51	15,1,0
4	0,0,2	20	1,0,2	36	2,0,2	52	3,0,2
5	1,0,0	21	13,0,0	37	9,0,0	53	5,0,0
6	3,1,1	22	5,1,1	38	7,1,1	54	1,1,1
7	10,1,0	23	14,1,0	39	2,1,0	55	6,1,0
8	0,0,3	24	1,1,3	40	1,0,3	56	0,1,3
9	6,0,0	25	2,0,0	41	14,0,0	57	10,0,0
10	1,0,1	26	7,0,1	42	5,0,1	58	3,0,1
11	5,1,0	27	9,1,0	43	13,1,0	59	1,1,0
12	3,1,2	28	2,1,2	44	1,1,2	60	0,1,2
13	15,0,0	29	11,0,0	45	7,0,0	61	3,0,0
14	10,1,1	30	4,1,1	46	6,1,1	62	0,1,1
15	4,1,0	31	8,1,0	47	12,1,0	63	0,1,0

MODULUS MULTIPLICATION offers advantages similar to those of remainder addition because the system of number representation allows the computer to process several groups of digits simultaneously. The table shows the unique triplets representing the numbers from 0 to 63 that are used in multiplication modulo-64. The method is as fast as adding modulo-16.

gest that addition with so much larger a modulus would be more time-consuming. The number I have selected, however, is a special one: it is the product of nine numbers—$5 \times 7 \times 9 \times 11 \times 13 \times 16 \times 17 \times 19 \times 23$—that are mutually divisible only by 1. The largest of the numbers, the alpha of this N, is 23 and $\lceil \log_2 23 \rceil$ is 5. With a fan-in of four and a delay time of one nanosecond, the time of addition using this modulus proves to be only two nanoseconds. Thus even though N is substantially larger, adding with this modulus is faster than modulo-2^{32} addition.

Why have computer designers left such phenomena unexploited and continued to use moduli that are powers of 2? Because modulo-N addition involves a companion process that cannot be speeded up. Modulo-N addition and conventional addition give the same answers only as long as the product does not overflow the modulus. In every modulo-N addition it is necessary to know if an overflow occurs (in which case some correction is necessary) or if it does not (in which case the final result is correct). This companion process, called "overflow indication," cannot be speeded up using remainder arithmetic. I have proved that no representation of num-

bers can increase the speed of overflow indication beyond what can be achieved by base-2 representation. As long as both the addition operation and the overflow indication must be completed in order to accomplish the entire operation of addition there can be no speed gained by substituting remainder addition for base-2 representation.

A surprisingly different picture emerges with regard to multiplication. Primary school pencil-and-paper multiplication, which is the method used in most computers, is simply consecutive addition in which one of the two numbers is added to itself over and over again. Since the operation is consecutive it has been assumed that multiplication has to be more time-consuming than addition. Surprisingly this is not the case. Consider the most common computer situation, in which binary representation is used and N is therefore a power of 2. Denoting N as 2^n, we discover that in multiplication modulo-2^n the formula is $t \geq \lceil \log_r 2(n-2) \rceil \Delta t$.

Comparing this with the result for addition modulo-2^n, one finds that the multiplication process is not necessarily slower than addition and may even be faster. Once again the key to this ap-

d SELECT CORRECT CARRY AND COMBINE

```
              0  1 <———> 1   1
     1  0    1  0    0  1  1
     1  0          1  0  1
   ┌──┬──┬──┬──┐ ┌──┬──┬──┬──┬──┬──┐
   │  │  │  │  │ │ 1│ 0│ 1│ 0│ 0│ 0│
   └──┴──┴──┴──┘ └──┴──┴──┴──┴──┴──┘
```

fourth switching delay combines that product with the three lower digits. With only four delays, conditional-sum addition proves 20 percent faster than conventional addition.

parent contradiction of intuition lies in how the numbers are represented. The familiar "base" method of representation, including base-2 and base-10, is quite efficient insofar as addition is concerned. For fast multiplication, however, another unorthodox representation is necessary. I shall describe it with another example: modulo-64 multiplication.

As in modulo-15 addition, in modulo-64 multiplication each number from 0 upward is represented by a special combination of digits. Each combination in our example is a triplet; the digit at the right ranges from 0 to 6, the center digit is either 0 or 1, and the number at the left ranges from 0 to 15 [*see illustration on preceding page*]. As in modulo-15 addition, each modulo-64 triplet is a unique representation of one of a series of numbers, in this instance the series running from 0 to 63.

An instance of modulo-64 multiplication, performed according to its own special rules, is the following: Let us multiply 23 (represented by the triplet 14,1,0) by 43 (the triplet 13,1,0). We begin by adding the pair of digits at the right, both of which are 0; this yields a total of 0 to set down. (According to the rules, if the total of the digits at the right is more than 6—as would be the case if we multiplied 48 by 8—the total is set back to 6.) Next the center digits are added, modulo-2. In this case 1 plus 1 equals 2, and 2, modulo-2, is 0. Therefore we set a second 0 to the left of the first one. We now add the pair of digits at the left, 14 plus 13, for a total of 27. The rule governing the addition of this pair of numbers says it is to be done modulo-2^{4-k}, where k is the result of the addition of the pair of digits at the right. Here k equals 0, and the modulus for the

addition of the digits at the left is therefore 16. The result is 11 (the remainder when 27 is divided by 16) and the final triplet, showing our result, is 11,0,0. Reference to the table shows that 11,0,0 is the representation for 29. This checks: 23 times 43 is 989; 989, modulo-64, is 29 because 989 divided by 64 yields a quotient of 15, which is ignored, and a remainder of 29.

The rules for modulo-64 multiplication are exacting and seem even more complicated than those for modulo-15 addition insofar as paper-and-pencil computation is concerned. The reader will note, however, that the modulo-64 system consists of three groups of digits that the computer can process simultaneously. Indeed, the most time-consuming part of the operation is the addition of the digits at the left, which, as the example shows, is done according to a variety of moduli depending on the value of k. The "worst case," that is, the most complex possible modulus for this pair, is modulo-16; thus modulo-64 multiplication is essentially no more time-consuming than modulo-16 addition.

The method of multiplication described here is about as fast as any possible method. I should mention that the same qualitative comparison between addition and multiplication holds not just for powers of 2 but for any number N. Accordingly it is clear that the intuitive feeling that multiplication is a more time-consuming operation than addition arises mainly from the nature of the base representation that is usually adopted. It is not an inherent property of these operations.

The logical deductions I have outlined provide the computer designer with

a means of evaluating various designs. Knowing the capabilities of the available hardware, he can determine how fast his computer will compare with an ideally fast one. Let us assume that the designer's objective is to add modulo-2^{48} in 20 nanoseconds. As long as his components' input fan-in is three and their delay time is 10 nanoseconds, the shortest time the operation could take proves to be 50 nanoseconds. Thus in order to attain his goal the designer will need either components with an input fan-in that has been raised to 10 or components with a delay time that has been shaved to four nanoseconds. The formula does not and cannot decide which approach the designer should take; what it does provide is a quantitative measure of the effect on the speed of arithmetic operations that any imaginable change in hardware can produce.

Finding the absolute speed limits for addition and multiplication has been only one in a series of continuing investigations of the effort required to compute functions. For example, we should like to know what is the minimum number of arithmetic operations necessary to compute an nth-degree polynomial and the minimum number of operations necessary for matrix multiplication. Just as the widespread use of the steam engine in the 19th century greatly increased theoretical interest in thermodynamics, the increasing use of computers today is a driving force behind the study of computational complexity. It is safe to assume that as work on these questions continues mathematicians will gain a better insight into the whole realm of computation.

15

COMPUTERS

STANISLAW M. ULAM

September, 1964

Although to many people the electronic computer has come to symbolize the importance of mathematics in the modern world, few professional mathematicians are closely acquainted with the machine. Some, in fact, seem even to fear that individual scientific efforts will be pushed into the background or replaced by less imaginative, purely mechanical habits of research. I believe such fears to be quite groundless. It is preferable to regard the computer as a handy device for manipulating and displaying symbols. Even the most abstract thinkers agree that the simple act of writing down a few symbols on a piece of paper facilitates concentration. In this respect alone—and it is not a trivial one—the new electronic machines enlarge our effective memory and provide a marvelous extension of the means for experimenting with symbols in science. In this article I shall try to indicate how the computer can be useful in mathematical research.

The idea of using mechanical or semiautomatic means to perform arithmetical calculations is very old. The origin of the abacus is lost in antiquity, and computers of some kind were evidently built by the ancient Greeks. Blaise Pascal in the 17th century constructed a working mechanism to perform arithmetical operations. Gottfried Wilhelm von Leibniz, one of the creators of mathematical logic as well as the coinventor of the infinitesimal calculus, outlined a program for what would now be called automatized thinking. The man who clearly visualized a general-purpose computer, complete with a flexible programming scheme and memory units, was Charles Babbage of England. He described a machine he called the analytical engine in 1833 and spent the rest of his life and much of his fortune trying to build it.

Among the leading contributors to modern computer technology were an electrical engineer, J. Presper Eckert, Jr., a physicist, John W. Mauchly, and one of the leading mathematicians of this century, John von Neumann. In 1944 Eckert and Mauchly were deep in the development of a machine known as ENIAC, which stands for Electronic Numerical Integrator and Computer. Designed to compute artillery firing tables for the Army Ordnance Department, ENIAC was finally completed late in 1945. It was wired to perform a specific sequence of calculations; if a different sequence was needed, it had to be extensively rewired. On hearing of the ENIAC project during a visit to the Aberdeen Proving Ground in the summer of 1944, von Neumann became fascinated by the idea and began developing the logical design of a computer capable of using a flexible stored program: a program that could be changed at will without revising the computer's circuits.

A major stimulus for von Neumann's enthusiasm was the task he faced as consultant to the theoretical group at Los Alamos, which was charged with solving computational problems connected with the atomic-bomb project. After a discussion in which we reviewed one of these problems von Neumann turned to me and said: "Probably in its solution we shall have to perform more elementary arithmetical steps than the total in all the computations performed by the human race heretofore." I reminded him that there were millions of schoolchildren in the world and that the total number of additions, multiplications and divisions they were obliged to perform every day over a period of a few years would certainly exceed that needed in our problem. Unfortunately we could not harness this great reservoir of talent for our purposes, nor could we in 1944 command the services of an electronic computer. The atomic-bomb calculations had to be simplified to the point where they could be solved with paper and pencil and the help of old-fashioned desk calculators.

Down the hall from my present office at the Los Alamos Scientific Laboratory is an electronic computer known as MANIAC II (Mathematical Analyzer, Numerical Integrator and Computer), an advanced version of MANIAC I, which von Neumann and his associates completed at the Institute for Advanced Study in 1952. MANIAC II, which was put in operation in 1957, can add two numbers consisting of 13 decimal digits (43 binary digits) in about six microseconds (six millionths of a second). In a separate building nearby is a still newer computer called STRETCH, built by the International Business Machines Corporation, which can manipulate numbers containing 48 binary digits with about 10 times the overall speed of MANIAC II.

MANIAC II and STRETCH are examples of dozens of custom-designed computers built throughout the world in the past 20 years. The first of the big commercially built computers, UNIVAC I, was delivered to the Bureau of the Census in 1951; three years later the General Electric Company became the first industrial user of a UNIVAC I. In the 13 years since the first UNIVAC more than 16,000 computer systems of various makes and sizes have been put to work by the U.S. Government, industry and universities. Of these about 250 are of the largest type, with speed and power roughly comparable to MANIAC II.

Together with increases in arithmetical speed have come increases in memory capacity and in speed of access to stored numbers and instructions. In the biggest electronic machines the memory capacity is now up to about

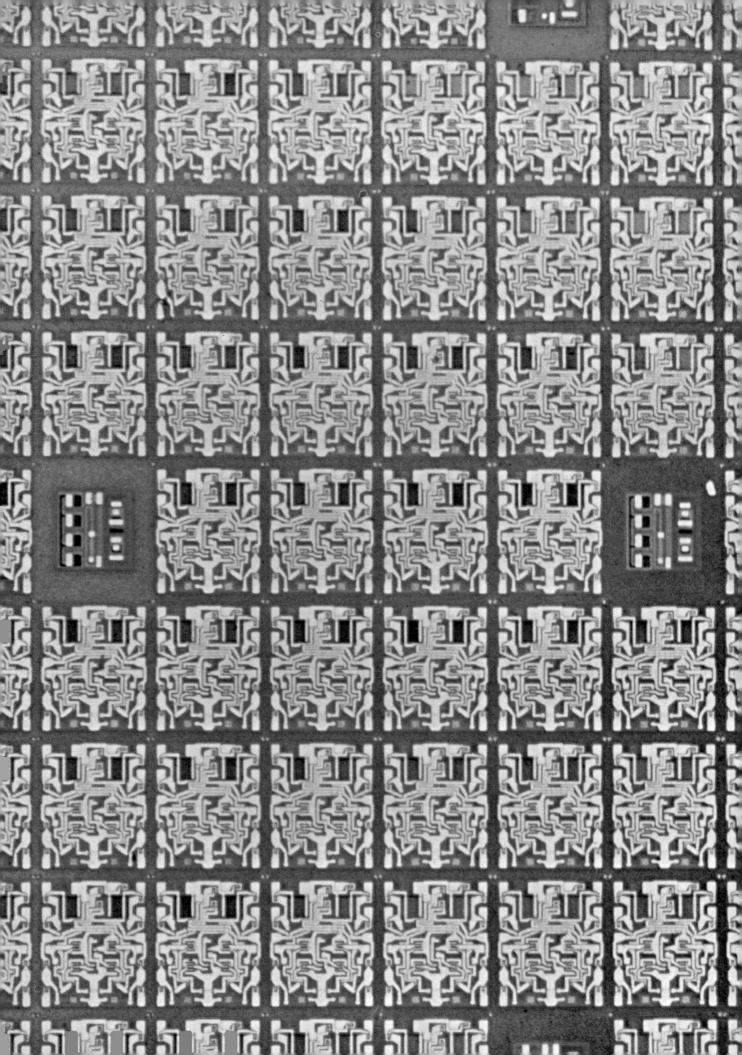

100,000 "words," or several million individual binary digits. I am referring here to the "fast" memory, to which the access time can be as short as a microsecond. This time is steadily being reduced; a hundredfold increase in speed seems possible in the near future. A "slow" memory, used as an adjunct to the fast one, normally consists of digits stored on magnetic tape and can be of almost unlimited capacity. The size of memory devices and basic electronic circuits has been steadily reduced, until now even the most elaborate computers can fit into a small room. The next generation of computers, employing microelectronic circuits, will be smaller by a factor of 100 to 1,000.

It is apparent that many problems are so difficult that they would tax the capacity of any machine one can imagine being built in the next decade. For example, the hydrodynamics of compressible fluids can be studied reasonably well on existing machines if the investigation is limited to problems in two dimensions, but it cannot be studied very satisfactorily in three dimensions. In a two-dimensional study one can imagine that the fluid is confined in a "box" that has been divided into, say, 10,000 cells; the cells are expressed in terms of two coordinates, each of which is divided into 100 parts. In each cell are stored several values, such as those for density and velocity, and a new set of values must be computed for each successive chosen unit of time. It is obvious that if this same problem is simply extended to include a third dimension, storage must be provided for a million cells, which exceeds the capacity of present machines. One of the

COMPUTER CIRCUITS have become almost microscopic. Although each of the Westinghouse binary integrated circuits (*square units*) on the opposite page is smaller than the head of a pin, it contains six transistors, 12 diodes, 11 resistors and two capacitors. The tiny units are now employed primarily in special computers for military and space applications. More than 100 of them are made at one time on a thin silicon wafer the size of a half-dollar. The four patterns that do not match the others are used for alignment and testing during fabrication. In commercial computers such circuits are expected to provide greater speed and reliability at lower cost than the larger circuits in common use today.

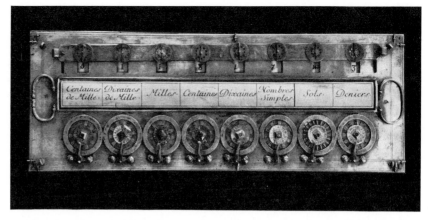

FIRST MECHANICAL COMPUTER was probably this adding machine, designed in 1642 by the French philosopher and mathematician Blaise Pascal. The machine adds when the wheels are turned with a stylus. Gears inside automatically "carry" numbers from one wheel to the next. Similar but somewhat simpler devices, made of plastic, are widely sold.

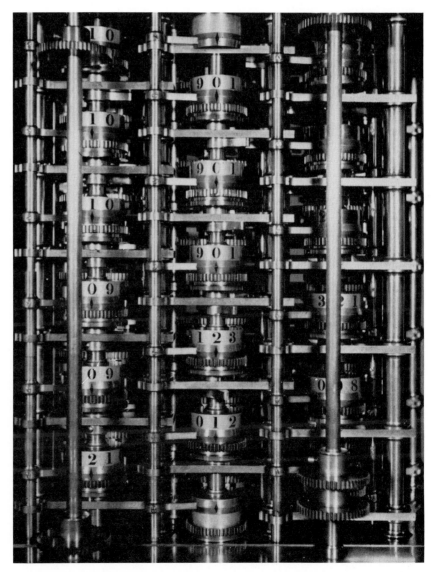

"DIFFERENCE ENGINE," often called the first modern mathematical machine, was conceived in 1820 by the English mathematician Charles Babbage. He built a small version of it but the larger engine he envisioned was never completed. Parts of it, such as this unit, are now in South Kensington Science Museum. Babbage spent many years trying unsuccessfully to create an "analytical engine" that would do almost everything the modern computer does.

studies that is limited in this way is the effort to forecast the weather, for which it would be desirable to use a many-celled three-dimensional model of the atmosphere.

Sometimes when a problem is too complex to be solved in full detail by computer, it is possible to obtain a representative collection of specific solutions by the "Monte Carlo" method. Many years ago I happened to consider ways of calculating what fraction of all games of solitaire could be completed satisfactorily to the last card. When I could not devise a general solution, it occurred to me that the problem could be examined heuristically, that is, in such a way that the examination would at least give an idea of the solution. This would involve actually playing out a number of games, say 100 or 200, and simply recording the results. It was an ideal task for a computer and was at the origin of the Monte Carlo method.

This method is commonly applied to problems of mathematical physics such as those presented by the design of nuclear reactors. In a reactor neutrons are released; they collide, scatter, multiply and are absorbed or escape with various probabilities, depending on the geometry and the composition of the fuel elements and other components. In a complicated geometry no way is known to compute directly the number of neutrons in any given range of energy, direction and velocity. Instead one resorts to a sampling procedure in which the computer traces out a large number of possible histories of individual particles. The computer does not consider all the possible things that might happen to the particle, which would form a very complicated tree of branching eventualities, but selects at each branching point just one of the eventualities with a suitable probability (which is known to the physicist) and examines a large class of such possible chains of events. By gathering statistics on many such chains one can get an idea of the behavior of the system. The class of chains may have to be quite large but it is small compared with the much larger class of all possible branchings. Such sampling procedures, which would be impracticable without the computer, have been applied to many diverse problems.

The variety of work in mathematical physics that has been made possible in recent years through the use of computers is impressive indeed. Astronomy journals, for instance, contain an increasing number of computer results bearing on such matters as the history of stars, the motions of stars in clusters, the complex behavior of stellar atmospheres and the testing of cosmological theories. It has long been recognized that it is mathematically difficult to obtain particular solutions to problems involving the general theory of relativity so that the predictions of alternative formulations can be tested by observation or experiment. The computer is

FIRST ELECTRONIC DIGITAL COMPUTER, the Electronic Numerical Integrator and Computer (ENIAC), was built at the University of Pennsylvania for the Army Ordnance Department. Completed in the fall of 1945, it had 19,000 vacuum tubes, 1,500 relays and hundreds of thousands of resistors, capacitors and inductors. It consumed almost 200 kilowatts of electric power. Power and tube failures and other difficulties plagued its first few years of operation. To change its program it was necessary to rewire thousands of circuits. With constant improvements ENIAC was kept in service at the Ballistic Research Center, Aberdeen, Md., until late 1955.

now making it possible to obtain such predictions in many cases. A similar situation exists in nuclear physics with regard to alternative field theories.

I should now like to discuss some particular examples of how the computer can perform work that is both interesting and useful to a mathematician. The first examples are problems in number theory. This subject deals with properties of ordinary integers and particularly with those properties that concern the two most fundamental operations on them: addition and multiplication.

As in so much of "pure" mathematics the objective is to discover and then prove a theorem containing some general truth about numbers. It is often easy to see a relation that holds true in special cases; the task is to show that it holds true in general.

Karl Friedrich Gauss, called "the prince of mathematicians" by his contemporaries, greatly favored experiments on special cases and diligent work with examples to obtain his inspirations for finding general truths in number theory. Asked how he divined some of the remarkable regularities of numbers, he replied, *"Durch planmässiges tattonieren"* —through systematic trying. Srinivasa Ramanujan, the phenomenal Indian number theorist, was equally addicted to experimentation with examples. One can imagine that in the hands of such men the computer would have stimu-

lated many more discoveries in number theory.

A fascinating area of number theory is that dealing with primes, the class of integers that are divisible only by themselves and by one. The Greeks proved that the number of primes is infinite, but even after centuries of work some of the most elementary questions about primes remain unanswered.

For example, can every even number be represented as the sum of two primes? This is the famous Goldbach conjecture. Thus $100 = 53 + 47$ and $200 = 103 + 97$. It has been shown that all even numbers smaller than 2,000,000 can be represented as the sum of two primes, but there is no proof that this holds true for *all* even integers.

MANIAC II (Mathematical Analyzer, Numerical Integrator and Computer) was built at the Los Alamos Scientific Laboratory in 1957. STRETCH, built by the International Business Machines Corporation and installed at Los Alamos four years later, is about 10 times faster than MANIAC II. Both have been used extensively by the author and his colleagues for experimentation in mathematics.

It is an interesting fact that there are many pairs of primes differing by two, for instance 11 and 13, 17 and 19, 311 and 313. Although it might seem simple to show that there are infinitely many such pairs of "twin primes," no one has been able to do it. These two unsolved problems demonstrate that the inquiring human mind can almost immediately find mathematical statements of great simplicity whose truth or falsehood are inordinately difficult to decide. Such statements present a continual challenge to mathematicians.

The existence of a proof does not always appease the mathematician. Although it is easily proved that there is an infinite number of primes, one would like to have a formula for writing down an arbitrarily large prime. No such formula has been found. No mathematician can now write on demand a prime with, say, 10 million digits, although one surely exists.

One of the largest known primes was found not long ago with the help of an electronic computer in Sweden. It is $2^{3217} - 1$, a number containing 967 digits. A number of this form, $2^n - 1$, is called a Mersenne number. There may be an infinite number of primes of this form. No one knows.

Other special numbers that may or may not yield many primes are Fermat numbers, which have the form $2^{2^n} + 1$. For n's of 0, 1, 2 and 3 the corresponding Fermat numbers are 3, 5, 17 and 257. Even for moderate values of n Fermat numbers become extremely large. It is not known, for instance, if the Fermat number with an n of 13 is a prime (the number is $2^{2^{13}} + 1$, or $2^{8192} + 1$).

It is convenient for computer experimentation that both Mersenne and Fermat numbers have a particularly simple appearance when they are written in binary notation [see top illustration on next page]. Fermat numbers start with a 1, are followed by 0's and end with a 1. Mersenne numbers in binary notation consist exclusively of 1's. With computers it is an easy matter to study empirically the appearance of primes written in binary form.

The following statement is most likely true: There exists a number n such that an infinite number of primes can be written in a binary sequence that contains exactly n 1's. (The number of 0's interspersed among the 1's, of course, would be unlimited.) Although this statement cannot be proved with the present means of number theory, I sus-

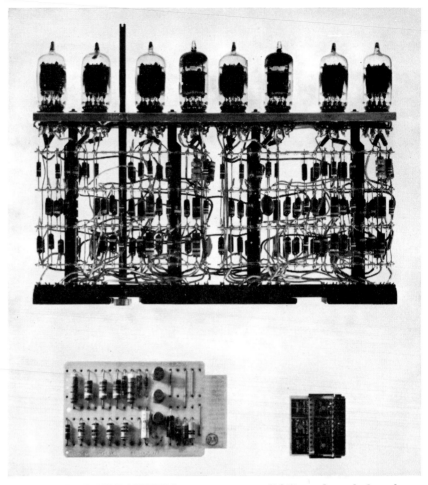

SHRINKAGE OF COMPONENTS has meant greater reliability and speed plus substantial savings in construction and operation of computer systems. The vacuum-tube assembly at top was used in first generation of computers built by International Business Machines Corporation, starting in 1946. First transistorized computers, built in 1955, used circuits such as that at lower left. At lower right is a card of six microminiaturized circuits, each containing several transistors and diodes, which is going into the newest IBM computers.

pect that experimental work with a computer might provide some insight into the behavior of binary sequences containing various numbers of 1's. The following experience may help to explain this feeling.

A few years ago my colleague Mark B. Wells and I planned a computer program to study some combinatorial properties of the distribution of 0's and 1's in prime numbers when expressed in binary form. One day Wells remarked: "Of course, one cannot expect the primes to have, asymptotically, the same number of ones and zeros in their development, since the numbers divisible by three have an even number of ones." This statement was based on the following argument: One would expect a priori that in a large sample of integers expressed in binary form the number of 1's and 0's ought to be randomly distributed and that this should also be the case for a large sample of primes. On

the other hand, if it were true that all numbers divisible by three contain an even number of 1's, then the distribution of 1's and 0's in a large sample of primes should not be random.

Returning to my office, I tried to prove Wells's statement about numbers divisible by three but was unsuccessful. After a while I noticed that the statement is not even true. The first number to disprove it is 21, which has three 1's in its binary representation [see middle illustration on next page].

Nevertheless, a great majority of the integers divisible by three seem to have an even number of 1's. Beginning with this observation, Wells managed to prove a general theorem: Among all the integers divisible by three from 1 to 2^n, those that have an even number of 1's always predominate, and the difference between their number and the number of those with an odd number of 1's can be computed exactly: it is

MERSENNE NUMBER $(2^n - 1)$			FERMAT NUMBER $(2^{2^n} + 1)$		
n	DECIMAL	BINARY	n	DECIMAL	BINARY
1	1	1	0	3	11
2	3	11	1	5	101
3	7	111	2	17	10001
4	15	1111	3	257	100000001
5	31	11111	4	65,537	10000000000000001

MERSENNE AND FERMAT NUMBERS have a simple appearance when written in binary notation. Although many Mersenne numbers are not primes (for example 15), there may be an infinite number of primes of this form. There may also be an infinite number of Fermat primes, but even the Fermat number for an n as small as 13 has not yet been tested.

3	11	27	11011
6	110	30	11110
9	1001	33	100001
12	1100	36	100100
15	1111	39	100111
18	10010	42	101010
21	10101	45	101101
24	11000	48	110000

INTEGERS DIVISIBLE BY THREE usually contain an even number of 1's when written in binary form. This observation led to the proof of a general theorem, described in the text.

$3^{(n-1)/2}$. Wells developed corresponding proofs for statements on integers divisible by five, seven and certain other numbers, although he found these theorems increasingly harder to prove.

By now quite a few problems in number theory have been studied experi-mentally on computers. Not all of this work is restricted to tables, special examples and sundry curiosities. D. H. Lehmer of the University of California at Berkeley has made unusually effective use of the computer in number theory. With its help he has recently

obtained several general theorems. Essentially what he has done is to reduce general statements to the examination of a large number of special cases. The number of cases was so large that it would have been impracticable, if not impossible, to go through them by hand computation. With the help of the computer, however, Lehmer and his associates were able to determine all exceptions explicitly and thereby discover the theorem that was valid for all other cases. Unfortunately Lehmer's interesting work is at a difficult mathematical level and to describe it would take us far afield.

It must be emphasized that Lehmer's theorems were not proved entirely by machine. The machine was instrumental in enabling him to obtain the proof. This is quite different from having a program that can guide a computer to produce a complete formal proof of a mathematical statement. Such a program, however, is not beyond the realm of possibility. The computer can operate not only with numbers but also with the symbols needed to perform logical operations. Thus it can execute simple orders corresponding to the basic "Boolean" operations. These are essentially the Aristotelian expressions of "and," "or" and "not." Under a set of instructions the computer can follow such orders in a prescribed sequence and explore a labyrinth of possibilities, choosing among the possible alternatives the ones that satisfy, at any moment, the result of previous computations.

With such techniques it has been possible to program a computer to find proofs of elementary theorems in Euclid's geometry. Some of these efforts, particularly those pursued at the International Business Machines Research Center, have been quite successful. Other programs have enabled the computer to find proofs of simple facts of

1,2	1,3	1,4	1,5	1,6	1,7
	2,3	2,4	2,5	2,6	2,7
		3,4	3,5	3,6	3,7
			4,5	4,6	4,7
				5,6	5,7
					6,7

1,2,3	1,3	1,4,5	1,5	1,6,7	1,7
	2,3	2,4,6	2,5,7	2,6	2,7
		3,4,7	3,5,6	3,6	3,7
			4,5	4,6	4,7
				5,6	5,7
					6,7

STEINER PROBLEM poses this question: Given n objects, can they be arranged in a set of triplets so that every pair of objects appears once and only once in every triplet? The problem can be solved only when $n = 6k + 1$ or $6k + 3$, in which k can be any in-teger. One solution for $k = 1$, in which case $n = 7$, is shown here. The table at left lists all possible pairs of seven objects. The table at right shows seven triplets that contain all pairs only once. The 21 digits in these triplets can be regrouped into other triplets.

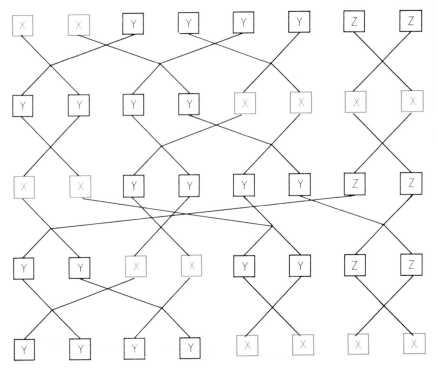

GENEALOGICAL "TREES" raise many interesting combinatorial questions. In the simple case shown here individuals of three different colors mate in pairs. Strictly, x, y and z specify the fraction of each color in each generation, but here they also identify color type. Each mating produces a pair of offspring and the color of the offspring is uniquely determined by the colors of the parents according to a fixed rule. (For example, 2 y's or 2 z's produce 2 x's.) Assuming an initial population containing hundreds of members, one might ask such questions as these: Given an individual in the fifth generation, how many different ancestors does he have in, say, the first generation? What are the proportions of x's, y's and z's among the ancestors of a given individual in the nth generation?

projective geometry. I have no doubt that these efforts mark only the beginnings; the future role of computers in dealing with the "effective" parts of mathematics will be much larger.

I shall now turn from the study of integers to combinatorial analysis and discuss some of the uses of the computer in this field. Very briefly, combinatorial analysis deals with the properties of arrangements and patterns defined by means of a finite class of "points." Familiar examples are the problems on permutations and combinations studied in high school algebra. In a typical case one starts with a finite set of n points and assumes certain given, or prescribed, relations between any two of them or more generally, among any k of them. One may then wish to enumerate the number of all possible structures that are related in the prescribed way, or one may want to know the number of equivalent structures. In some cases one may consider the finite set of given objects to be transformations of a set on itself. In the broadest sense one could say that combinatorial analysis deals with relations and patterns, their

classification and morphology. In this field too electronic computers have proved to be extremely useful. Here are some examples.

Consider the well-known problem of placing eight queens on a chessboard in such a way that no one of them attacks another. For an ordinary 8 × 8 chessboard there are only 12 fundamentally different solutions. The mathematician would like to know in how many different ways the problem can be solved for n queens on an $n \times n$ board. Such enumeration problems are in general difficult but computer studies can assist in their solution.

The following problem was first proposed in the 19th century by the Swiss mathematician Jakob Steiner: Given n objects, can one arrange them in a set of triplets in such a way that every pair of objects appears once and only once in a triplet? If n is five, for example, there are 10 possible pairs of five objects, but a little experimentation will show that there is no way to put them all in triplets without repeating some of the pairs. The problem can be solved only when $n = 6k + 1$ or $6k + 3$, in which k is any integer. The solution for

$k = 1$ (in which case n = 7) is shown in the illustration at the bottom of page 157. The number of triplets in the solution is seven. In how many ways can the problem be solved? Again, the computer is very useful when k is a large number.

The shortest-route problem, often called the traveling-salesman problem, is another familiar one in combinatories. Given are the positions of n points, either in a plane or in space. The problem is to connect all the points so that the total route between them is as short as possible. Another version of this problem to find the route through a network of points (without necessarily touching all the points) that would take the minimum time to traverse. These problems differ from the two preceding ones in that they necessitate finding a method, or recipe, for constructing the minimum route. Strictly speaking, therefore, they are problems in "meta-combinatorics." This term signifies that a precise formulation of the problem requires a definition of what one means by a recipe for construction. Such a definition is possible, and precise formulations can be made. When the n points are distributed in a multidimensional space, the problem can hardly be tackled without a computer.

A final example of combinatorics can be expressed as a problem in genealogy. Assume, for the sake of simplicity, that a population consists of many individuals who combine at random, and that each pair produces, after a certain time, another pair. Let the process continue through many generations and assume that the production of offspring takes place at the same time for all parents in each generation. Many interesting questions of combinatorial character arise immediately.

For instance, given an individual in the 15th generation of this process, how many different ancestors does he have in, say, the ninth generation? Since this is six generations back it is obvious that the maximum number of different ancestors is 2^6, but this assumes no kinship between any of the ancestors. As in human genealogy there is a certain probability that kinship exists and that the actual number is smaller than 2^6. What is the probability of finding various smaller numbers?

Suppose the original population consists of two classes (that is, each individual has one or the other of two characteristics); how are these classes mixed in the course of many generations? In other words, considering any individual in the *n*th generation, one would like to know the proportion of the two characteristics among all his ancestors.

Let us now make a slightly more realistic assumption. Consider the process as before but with the restriction removed that all offspring appear at the same time from parents of the same age. Assume instead that the production of the new generation is spread over a finite period of time according to a specific probability distribution. After this process has continued for some time the individuals of the most recent generation will be, so to speak, of different generations. A process of this kind actually occurs in human populations because mothers tend to be younger, on the average, than fathers. Therefore going back, say, 10 generations through the chain of mothers yields a smaller number of total years than going back through the chain of 10 fathers. It becomes a complex combinatorial problem to calculate the average number of generations represented in the genealogical history of each individual after many years have elapsed from time zero. This and many similar questions are difficult to treat analytically. By imitating the process on a computer, however, it is easy to obtain data that throw some light on the matter.

The last mathematical area I should like to discuss in connection with computers is the rather broad but little-explored one of nonlinearity. A linear function of one variable has the form $x' = ax + b$, where a and b are constants. Functions and transformations of this form are the simplest ones mathematically, and they occur extensively in the natural sciences and in technology. For example, quantum theory employs linear mathematics, although there are now indications that future understanding of nuclear and subnuclear phenomena will require nonlinear theories. In many physical theories, such as hydrodynamics, the equations are nonlinear from the outset.

The simplest nonlinear functions are quadratic; for one variable such functions have the form $y = ax^2 + bx + c$, where a, b and c are constants. It may surprise nonmathematical readers how little is known about the properties of such nonlinear functions and transformations. Some of the simplest questions concerning their properties remain unanswered.

As an example, mathematicians would like to learn more about the behavior of nonlinear functions when subjected

to the process known as iteration. This simply means repeated application of the function (or transformation) to some starting value. For instance, if the point described by a function is the square root of x, the iteration would be the square root of the square root of x; each succeeding iteration would consist of again taking the square root.

A transformation given by two functions containing two variables each de-

fines a point on a plane; its iteration gives rise to successive points, or "images" [see illustration below]. Finding the properties of the sequence of iterated images of a single point, when described by a nonlinear function, is in general difficult. Present techniques of analysis are inadequate to unravel the behavior of these quite simply defined transformations.

Here again empirical work with the

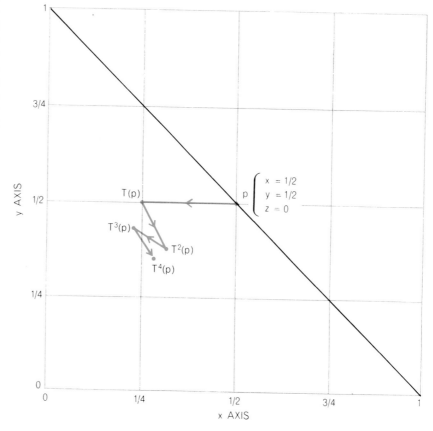

$$x' = y^2 - z^2 \qquad y' = 2xy - 2xz \qquad z = x^2 + 2yz$$

INITIAL POINT p	FIRST ITERATION T(p)	SECOND ITERATION $T^2(p)$	THIRD ITERATION $T^3(p)$	FOURTH ITERATION $T^4(p)$
x = 1/2	x' = 1/4	x'' = 5/16	x''' = 61/256 = .238	x'''' = .295
y = 1/2	y' = 2/4	y'' = 6/16	y''' = 110/256 = .430	y'''' = .363
z = 0	z' = 1/4	z'' = 5/16	z''' = 85/256 = .332	z'''' = .342
SUM 1	1	1	1 = 1.000	1.000

PROCESS OF ITERATION involves repeated application of a function (or transformation) to an initial value or a point. Here three equations containing three variables define a point in a plane. Iteration gives rise to successive points, or "images." Because the three variables always add up to 1, only two variables (say x and y) need be plotted. The first iteration, T(p), is obtained by inserting the initial values of x, y and z (½, ½, 0) in the three equations. The new values, x', y', z' (¼, ½, ¼), are then inserted to produce the second iteration, $T^2(p)$, and so on. Computers can quickly compute and display thousands of iterations of a point so that their behavior can be studied (see examples on next page).

computer can be of great help, particularly if the computer is equipped to display visually the location of many iterated points on the face of an oscilloscope. MANIAC II at Los Alamos has been equipped in this way and enables us to see at a glance the results of hundreds of iterations.

In examining such displays the mathematician is curious to learn whether or not the succession of iterated images converge to a single location, or "fixed point." Frequently the images do not converge but jump around in what appears to be a haphazard fashion—when they are viewed one by one. But if hundreds of images are examined, it may be seen that they converge to

curves that are often most unexpected and peculiar, as illustrated in the four oscilloscope traces below. Such empirical work has led my associates and me to some general conjectures and to the finding of some new properties of nonlinear transformations.

What are the obvious desiderata that would make the electronic computer an even more valuable tool than it is today? One important need is the ability to handle a broader range of logical operations. As I have noted, the simplest operations of logic, the Boolean operations, have been incorporated in electronic computers from the outset. In order to encompass more of con-

temporary mathematics the computer needs a "universal quantifier" and an "existential quantifier." The universal quantifier is required to express the statement one sees so frequently in mathematical papers: "For all x such and such holds." The existential quantifier is needed to express another common statement: "There exists an x so that such and such is true." If one could add these two quantifiers to the Boolean operations, one could formulate for computer examination most of traditional and much of modern mathematics. Unfortunately there is no good computer program that will manipulate the concepts "for all" and "there exists."

One can take for granted that there will be continued increases in processing speed and in memory capacity. There will be more fundamental developments too. Present computers operate in a linear sequence: they do one thing at a time. It is a challenge to design a machine more on the model of the animal nervous system, which can carry out many operations simultaneously. Indeed, plans exist for machines in which arithmetical operations would proceed simultaneously in different locations.

A multitrack machine would be of great value in the Monte Carlo method. The task of the machine is to compute individual histories of fictitious particles, and in many problems the fates of the particles are independent of one another. This means that they could be computed in parallel rather than in series. Moreover, it is not necessary that the computations be carried out to the many decimal places provided by present high-speed machines; an accuracy of four or five digits would often be enough. Thus it would be valuable to have a machine that could compute hundreds of histories simultaneously with only moderate accuracy. There are many other cases where a machine of such design would be efficient.

Further development is also desirable in facilitating the ease of transaction between the computer and its operator. At present it is difficult to change the course of a calculation as partial results become available. If access to the machine were more flexible and if the problem could be studied visually during the course of its development, many mathematicians would find experimentation on the computer more congenial than they do today.

One can imagine new methods of calculation specifically adapted to the automatic computer. Thanks to the speed of the machine one will be able to explore,

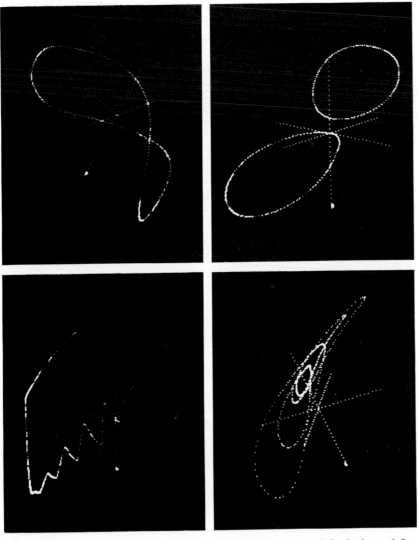

ITERATIONS OF NONLINEAR TRANSFORMATIONS performed by high-speed Los Alamos computers are displayed on the face of an oscilloscope. The objective of this study by P. R. Stein and the author was to examine the asymptotic properties, or "limit sets," of iterates of certain nonlinear transformations of relatively simple form. These iterations are for sets of four functions containing four variables and therefore must be plotted in three dimensions; the straight dotted lines indicate the coordinate axes (*see two-dimensional plotting on preceding page*). The figure at top left is a twisted space curve. That at top right consists of two plane curves. The two bottom figures are more complicated.

almost palpably, so to say, geometrical configurations in spaces of more than three dimensions and one will be able to obtain, through practice, new intuitions. These will stimulate the mathematician working in topology and in the combinatorics of new mathematical objects. These objects may be ordinary integers, but integers far exceeding in size and number any now used for experimentation. One should also be able to develop mathematical expressions with many more existential quantifiers than are now employed in formal mathematical definitions. New games will be played on future machines; new objects and their motions will be considered in spaces now hard to visualize with our present experience, which is essentially limited to three dimensions.

The old philosophical question remains: Is mathematics largely a free creation of the human brain, or has the choice of definitions, axioms and problems been suggested largely by the external physical world? (I would include as part of the physical world the anatomy of the brain itself.) It is likely that work with electronic machines, in the course of the next decade or so, will shed some light on this question. Further insight may come from the study of similarities between the workings of the human nervous system and the organization of computers. There will be novel applications of mathematics in the biological sciences, and new problems in mathematics will be suggested by the study of living matter.

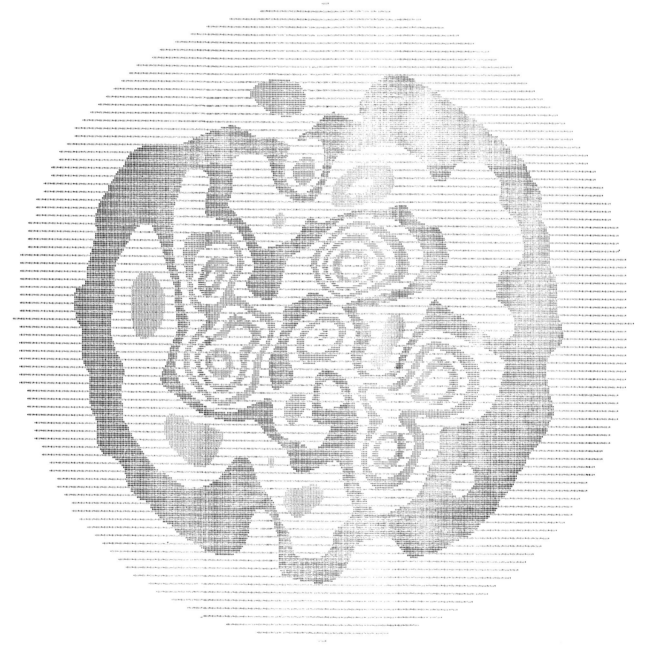

SIMULATED WEATHER PATTERN for the entire Northern Hemisphere was produced by the STRETCH computer at the General Circulation Research Laboratory of the U.S. Weather Bureau. In an effort to develop and test new theories of atmospheric behavior, investigators program the computer with equations that attempt to account for atmospheric phenomena. Data from real observations are then fed in, from which the computer produces changing model weather patterns for days and weeks. These are compared with actual observations over the period. The shaded "contours" on this map show simulated sea-level atmospheric pressure during one of these studies. The pattern is built up entirely of densely packed numbers and letters printed out directly by the computer itself.

16

THE MONTE CARLO METHOD

DANIEL D. McCRACKEN
May, 1955

During World War II physicists at the Los Alamos Scientific Laboratory came to a knotty problem on the behavior of neutrons. How far would neutrons travel through various materials? The question had a vital bearing on shielding and other practical considerations. But it was an extremely complicated one to answer. To explore it by experimental trial and error would have been expensive, time-consuming and hazardous. On the other hand, the problem seemed beyond the reach of theoretical calculations. The physicists had most of the necessary basic data: they knew the average distance a neutron of a given speed would travel in a given substance before it collided with an atomic nucleus, what the probabilities were that the neutron would bounce off

instead of being absorbed by the nucleus, how much energy the neutron was likely to lose after a given collision, and so on. However, to sum all this up in a practicable formula for predicting the outcome of a whole sequence of such events was impossible.

At this crisis the mathematicians John von Neumann and Stanislaw Ulam cut the Gordian knot with a remarkably simple stroke. They suggested a solution which in effect amounts to submitting the problem to a roulette wheel. Step by step the probabilities of the separate events are merged into a composite picture which gives an approximate but workable answer to the problem.

The mathematical technique von Neumann and Ulam applied had been known for many years. When it was re-

vived for the secret work at Los Alamos, von Neumann gave it the code name "Monte Carlo." The Monte Carlo method was so successful on neutron diffusion problems that its popularity later spread. It is now being used in various fields, notably in operations research.

To illustrate the method let us start with the simple, classic Buffon needle problem. You get a short needle, draw on a sheet of paper several parallel lines spaced precisely twice the length of the needle apart, and then toss the needle onto the paper again and again in a random fashion. How often will the needle land on a line? The mathematicians say that the ratio of hits to trials should be 1 to 3.1416. That is, dividing the number of hits into the number of throws, you should come out with the number 3.1416 (pi) if you continue the trials long enough (and throw the needle truly at random, without trying either to hit or to miss the lines).

I tried the experiment, with the following results. In the first 10 throws, the needle landed on a line four times. In the language of the statistician, there were four "successes" in 10 trials. The quotient is 2.5, which one must admit is not very close to 3.1416. In 100 trials there were 28 hits for an estimate of 3.57, also not good, but better. After 1,000 trials there were 333 hits for an estimate of 3, and my arm was tired.

This was hardly good enough to quit on, but the improvement with increasing numbers was not rapid, so it did not seem practicable to go on by hand. The fact is that the accuracy of a Monte Carlo approximation improves only as the square of the number of trials: to double the expected accuracy of the an-

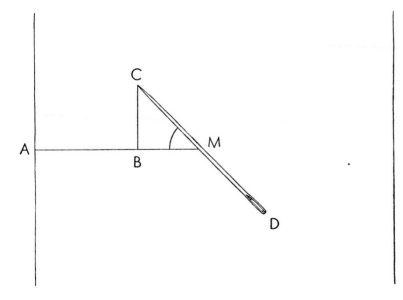

NEEDLE PROBLEM is illustrated by a needle lying on a piece of paper ruled with parallel lines. The length of the needle is two inches; the distance between the lines, four inches. If the needle is thrown on the paper at random, how often will it land on one of the lines?

swer, you must quadruple the number of trials. I decided to make a calculating machine do the work, and I translated the problem to a medium-sized electronic calculator.

It is no difficult matter to make a calculating machine carry out operations which simulate the results of dropping a needle on ruled paper. Consider the diagram on the preceding page. To describe the situation to the machine we must decide on a way of specifying the position of the needle relative to the nearest line. It does not matter on which side of this line the needle lies; nothing is changed if we turn the paper around. We can see that the distance from the midpoint of the needle to the nearest line (MA) is specified by a number between zero and two inches. The only other information needed to specify the position of the needle completely is the angle it makes with the perpendicular (MA) to the line. The angle is somewhere between zero and 90 degrees (not 180 degrees, because we are concerned only with the closer end of the needle). Given these two quantities, the machine can easily decide whether the needle touches a line; all it needs to do is to compute the distance MB (the cosine of the angle) and note whether it is less or greater than the distance MA—in the machine's terms, whether the difference is positive or negative.

Now to find out by experiment in what proportion of the trials a needle dropped at random would touch the line, we would like to test all possible positions in which the needle might land. To do this we would have to consider all possible combinations of distances and angles—essentially the method of the integral calculus. Obviously we are not going to tackle this infinite task. But in place of attempting a systematic exploration of all positions, we can take a random sample of them, and this should give us a reasonably accurate approximation of the correct answer, as a sampling poll may do.

How shall we select the random sample? This is where the Monte Carlo method comes in. Suppose we built a roulette wheel with 20 compartments, representing 20 different distances from the line (up to two inches) for the needle midpoint. A spin of the wheel would select the distance for us in a random manner, and over many trials each of the 20 distances would be selected about the same number of times. With a similar wheel we would pick the angle each time in the same random fashion. Then

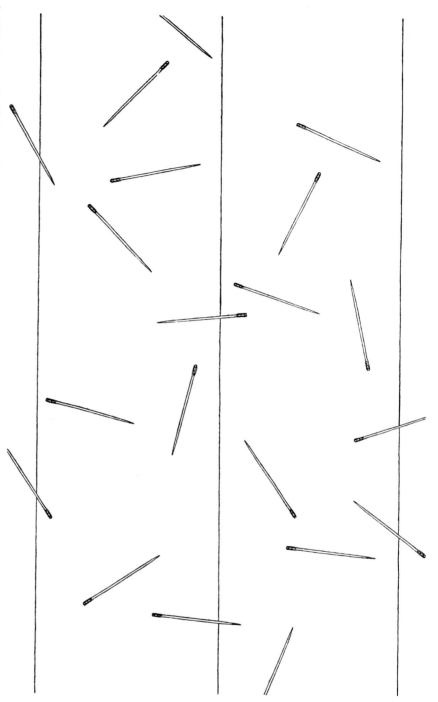

ACTUAL EXPERIMENT on the needle problem was tried by artist Eric Mose. Each needle represents a toss and shows the position in which the needle landed with respect to the lines. In a sufficiently large number of trials, the ratio of hits to trials will be 1 to 3.1416 or pi.

a series of spins of the two wheels would give us a random set of positions, just as if we had actually dropped a needle at random on ruled paper.

Of course the wheel-spinning method would be more cumbersome than dropping the needle, but there are ways of doing about the same thing with numbers and a calculating machine. First we get up two lists of numbers: one for

distances in the range between zero and two inches, the other for angles in the range between zero and 90 degrees. The numbers are chosen at random to cover the whole range in each case without favoring any part of the range; we can take them from some list of numbers already checked for randomness or we can make our own list from, say, a table of logarithms, taking the numbers' last three digits. Then we put the calculator to work computing whether various combinations of the distance and angle numbers place the needle on a line or not (*i.e.*, whether the difference between MB and MA is positive or negative). Repeating the operation many, many times, we can get as close to precision as we like; statistical principles tell us the degree of precision we can expect from a given number of trials.

The moderately fast computer I had available when I made the experiment was able to perform 100 "trials" per minute. In about an hour the machine ran through 6,000 trials, and there were 1,925 "hits." In other words, the estimate of pi was 3.12, which is as good as can be expected for 6,000 trials.

Even this simple case required a rapid computer. Most applications of the Monte Carlo method of course are much more complex. However, the present high-speed computers make them feasible: there are machines which can perform 5,000 trials per minute on the Buffon needle problem.

Let us see now how the method works on a simple problem in neutron diffusion. Suppose we want to know what percentage of the neutrons in a given beam would get through a tank of water of a given size without being absorbed or losing most of their speed. No formula could describe precisely the fate of all the neutrons. The Monte Carlo approach consists in pretending to trace the "life histories" of a large sample of neutrons in the beam. We imagine the neutrons wandering about in the water and colliding occasionally with a hydrogen or oxygen nucleus—remember that to a neutron water looks like vast open spaces dotted here and there with tiny nuclei. We shall follow our neutrons one by one through their adventures.

We know how far a neutron travels, on the average, before it encounters a nucleus, the relative probability that this encounter will be with oxygen or with hydrogen, the relative chances that the neutron will be absorbed by the nucleus or bounce off, and certain other necessary information. Let us, then, take a specific neutron and follow its life history. It is a slow-moving neutron, and its first incident is a collision with a hydrogen nucleus. We know (from experiments) that the chances are 100 to one the neutron will bounce off from such a collision. To decide what it will do in this instance, we figuratively spin a roulette wheel with 100 equal compartments marked "bounced off" and one marked "absorbed." If the wheel says "absorbed," that is the end of the neutron's history. If it says "bounced off," we perhaps spin another appropriately marked wheel to decide what the neutron's new direction is and how much energy it lost. Then we must spin another wheel to decide how far it travels to the next collision and whether that collision is with oxygen or hydrogen. Thus we follow the neutron until it is absorbed, loses so much energy that it is no longer of interest or gets out of the tank. We go on to accumulate a large number of such histories and obtain a more or less precise figure for the percentage of neutrons that would escape from the tank. The degree of precision depends on the number of trials.

In practice, of course, we do not use roulette wheels but random numbers, as in the previous example. I have omitted much of the detail of the calculation for the sake of simplicity and clarity. In one very simple problem on which I assisted, an electronic calculator labored for three hours to trace the life histories of 10,000 neutrons through 1.5 million collisions. I would have had to sit at a desk calculator for some years to accomplish the same results.

As a third illustration of the Monte Carlo method, let us take a simple problem in operations research. Imagine a woodworking shop consisting of a lathe, a drill press and a saw, with three men to operate the machines. The shop makes one model of chair and one model of table. The question is: How should the work of the shop be scheduled to yield the greatest production, considering a number of variable conditions affecting output?

Certain basic information must be gathered before any calculation can begin. How long does it take on each machine to do the necessary work on each piece of wood? How much does the time needed for each job fluctuate because of fatigue, boredom or other personal factors? How frequently do the machines break down? After the data are gathered, a way is devised to make the computer simulate the operation of the shop under specified conditions of scheduling. We will not go into the details here; perhaps enough has been presented in the other examples to give an indication of what has to be done. The computation is properly classified as Monte Carlo

ROULETTE WHEEL especially designed for the needle problem depicted on the preceding two pages illustrates a basic feature of the Monte Carlo method. Each compartment of the wheel represents one of 20 distances between zero and two inches, the length of the needle.

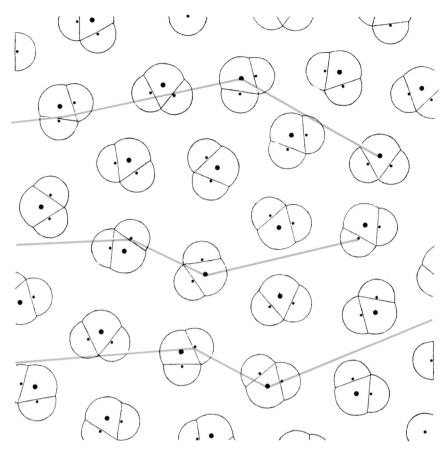

NEUTRONS wander through water in a series of events, each with a known probability. Here the microscopic structure of water is depicted in highly idealized form as consisting of simple molecules of H_2O. The larger sphere in each molecule is oxygen; the two smaller spheres are hydrogen. The neutrons (*colored lines*) may be absorbed by either an oxygen or a hydrogen nucleus or may bounce off from the collision. Some may escape from the water.

because it is necessary to spin a roulette wheel, or the equivalent, to pick samples from the known distributions. For example, we may know that a certain job may take anywhere from 12 to 16 minutes, and we have noted the percentages of the cases in which it is performed in 12, 13, 14, 15 and 16 minutes respectively. Which time shall we use for a particular case as we follow the course of a day's work in the shop? The question must be decided by random sampling of the type I have described.

With the Monte Carlo method high-speed computers can answer such questions as these: How should the schedule be changed to accommodate a market change demanding twice as many chairs as tables? How much could the shop produce, and at what cost, if one man should be absent for two days? How much would the total output be increased if one man should increase his work rate 20 per cent? Under a given schedule of work flow, what percentage of the time are the men idle because the work is piled up behind a bottleneck machine? If money values can be assigned to idle time, loss of orders due to

low production and so on, dollars-and-cents answers can be given to problems of this kind in business operation.

The Monte Carlo method, in general, is used to solve problems which depend in some important way upon probability—problems where physical experimentation is impracticable and the creation of an exact formula is impossible. Often the process we wish to study consists of a long sequence of steps, each of which involves probability, as for instance the travels of the neutron through matter. We can write mathematical formulas for the probabilities at each collision, but we are often not able to write anything useful for the probabilities for the entire sequence.

Essentially the Monte Carlo method goes back to probability theory, which was developed from studies of gambling games. But it takes the opposite approach. The mathematicians who originated the probability theory derived their equations from theoretical questions based on the phenomenon of chance; the Monte Carlo method tries

to use probability to find an answer to a physical question often having no relation to probability.

In the neutron problem, for example, the investigator's thinking might have been along these lines: "I have a physical situation which I wish to study. I don't think I'll even try to find an equation representing the entire problem. Even if I could find one, which is very doubtful, I probably wouldn't be able to get much useful information out of it. I'll just see if I can't find a game of chance which will give an answer to my questions, without ever going through the step of deriving an equation." In some other situations the investigator would reason: "The physical situation I am interested in has resulted in an equation which is very difficult to solve. I cannot possibly solve it in any reasonable length of time by usual methods. I wonder if I could devise some statistical method which would approximate the answer to my problem."

Much work remains to be done on the method. One is always faced with the unhappy choice of either inaccurate results or very large amounts of calculation. A problem which demands 100 million trials of some "experiment" is still impracticable, even on the fastest present computers. Another difficulty is that it is seldom possible to extend the results of a Monte Carlo calculation to another set of conditions. For instance, after we have solved the problem of the passage of neutrons through ordinary water, we have to start all over again to find out how they will behave in heavy water. Nevertheless, in spite of its various limitations the Monte Carlo method is able to give at least approximate answers to many questions where other mathematical techniques fail.

Many mathematicians are working to improve the method, especially to reduce the computation required and to determine exactly how much reliability can be attributed to its results in various types of problems. Up to now the technique has been used mainly on problems of nuclear physics, such as the diffusion of neutrons, the absorption of gamma rays, atomic pile shielding and the like. In the author's opinion, one of the most promising applications of the method is in operations research. It could be useful not only on production problems such as the one described here but also in telephone operation, traffic control, department-store inventory control and so on. Some of these possibilities are already being investigated. It is safe to say that we shall hear more from Monte Carlo in the next few years.

IV

COMPUTER MODELS OF THE REAL WORLD

IV

COMPUTER MODELS
OF THE
REAL WORLD

INTRODUCTION

We often wish to study a domain of facts, even though we cannot or do not wish to deal with that domain directly. We then study another set of facts that shares essential characteristics with the original domain. In such circumstances, the second set is a model of the first. Whatever theory we develop about the second set, to the extent that the theory deals exclusively with "essential characteristics" that the two sets have in common, it is also a theory of the first set. More formally, the system A is a model of the system B if some theory $T(A)$ is also a theory of B. The theory of the modeled system need not be in any sense complete. Indeed, model building is most often used and useful when no complete theory of the modeled system is known. What is important is that the model A behave exactly like the modeled system B in all its essentials. The purpose of the modeling effort dictates what is and what is not essential.

Perhaps the most important contribution the modern art of computation has made to both engineering and science is that it has provided an environment in which domains of facts (models) may be created at will. By judicious programming, a specific domain of facts can be manufactured to share "all the essential characteristics" of another (real-world) domain. The study of an artificial computer model can therefore shed light on the behavior of real-world systems.

There are, of course, building blocks other than computer programs out of which models can be built. The power of the computer as a host for models lies in its universality. Kemeny ("Man Viewed as a Machine") points out that "the secret of the universal machine is that it can imitate." Kemeny follows Turing in demonstrating that computers are "universal" in a nontrivial sense. He also fills out the word "imitate" by speaking of machines "performing" tasks. The difference between a mathematical model and a computer model is precisely that the latter is capable of *behavior* that itself has all the essential characteristics of the behavior of the modeled system. A mathematical model is, on the other hand, static; it does not in and of itself *behave*. A model M of the system S will almost always behave differently from S in some ways. The difference may be that there are aspects of the behavior of S that are of no relevance to an emerging theory of S. On the other hand, M may have characteristics (for example, size) not shared by S.

Sometimes small inessential characteristics of M inhibit the modeling process. Levinthal, for example, ("Molecular Model-building by Computer") points out that three-dimensional tinkertoy models of molecular structures often simply collapse mechanically. The mechanical properties of tinkertoys are largely irrelevant, one way or the other, to biological theories. They nevertheless interfere with model building. A computer model, on the other hand, is ultimately a formal system that can, in a formal sense, be constructed to reflect any property of the modeled domain. The modeler need understand only the properties he wishes his model to have. The computer itself is, at least in principle, not the ultimate limiting factor.

The papers presented in this section, except for the ones by Kemeny and Slotnick, may all be thought of as tutorials in computer modeling. Each author explains what his reason was for not dealing directly with the original domain of facts. Levinthal needed feedback from his model so that he could interfere with its behavior on the basis of his own human judgment, and he needed to observe the actual *behavior* of his model in order to make his judgments. Neither actual molecules nor mechanical models could be made to yield the desired information. It was exactly Levinthal's not having a complete theory of his domain of interest that led him to construct a computer model that at least satisfied the fragmentary theory he did have.

Hamilton and Nance ("Systems Analysis of Urban Transportation") also did not have a complete theory of their domain, that of urban transportation systems. But their primary reason for appealing to computer modeling was that they wished to experiment with transportation systems in a way that reality simply does not permit. For example, they wished to improve and extend old subway lines and build new ones, and they introduced entirely new types of transportation systems into their model. Their article is an impressive account of the power of computer models to stimulate the thinker's imagination by rewarding him with concrete evidence of the consequences of his ideas.

Harlow and Fromm ("Computer Experiments in Fluid Dynamics") describe the use of the computer as both a theoretical and an experimental tool. There is, in fact, a reasonably complete theory of fluid dynamics, but the mathematics to allow its full exploitation has not yet been worked out. The computer may help to provide the insights necessary to develop the appropriate mathematical formalisms. Apart from that, the authors vividly demonstrate a number of reasons that led them to computer modeling. They could, for example, study phenomena that are inaccessible to wind-tunnel experiments, and they could choose to include or exclude certain effects in ways that are physically not realizable at all.

Modeling of hydrodynamic systems begins, as Harlow and Fromm point out, with a conceptual division of the fluid body into many small elements of fluid, each independently obeying the simple laws of mechanics. Similar conceptual division into more-or-less independent elements is appropriate in many other situations, some of which are described by Slotnick.

In nature, of course, the several parts of an observed system usually operate all at once. It is quite plausible, then, that an appropriate vehicle for models should be a system in which some simple "laws" are simultaneously obeyed by an array of "elements."

Unfortunately, many processes that are generally parallel do contain a crucial sequential component. Calculation of a payroll distribution, for example, is — as Slotnick suggests — substantially parallel. But if checks are being computer-printed, then their total value must be computed. Indeed, a constructively known balance may be required just before and just after each check is printed. Worries like these —

about other problems than payrolls—have led to some skepticism about the breadth of applicability of ILLIAC IV. At worst, however, ILLIAC IV will almost surely become our standard tool for large systems of fluid thermodynamics. It will succeed here exactly because its hardware is so good a *model* of thermodynamic reality.

The Ledley and Ruddle article ("Chromosome Analysis By Computer") is somewhat different from the rest in that its model (of the chromosome) is incidental to the overall purpose, i.e., the analysis or classification of the chromosome. Ledley and Ruddle went to a computer to eliminate the human labor of constructing and analyzing idiograms of chromosomes. But the difference between their work and that reported in the other papers is, in terms of computer modeling, more apparent than real. The authors chose to describe and emphasize the way their computer program constructs and analyzes idiograms. They pass over the fact that their program is an explicit model of a specific theory of the structure of such idiograms.

Finally, Kemeny's paper attempts to describe the computer itself as a model of thinking man. His is a very early contribution to the debate about whether machines can think or not—a debate that will undoubtedly continue to rage for many more years. The question again is whether the model (in this case, the computer) shares essential characteristics with what it is intended to model (in this case, thinking man). The answer depends, as usual, on what it is that one considers essential. The section on artificial intelligence offers evidence that machines can indeed perform in ways that are usually called intelligent. Kemeny presents Turing's argument that machines can reproduce themselves. The assertion that man *is* a machine, in any important sense, will probably never be accepted by very many people. But the view that, for certain purposes, a machine may be viewed as a model of man has already proved useful in explicating certain theories of thinking. Indeed, some such theories were themselves unthinkable before the development of information-processing machines.

17

MOLECULAR MODEL-BUILDING BY COMPUTER

CYRUS LEVINTHAL
June, 1966

Many problems of modern biology are concerned with the detailed relation between biological function and molecular structure. Some of the questions currently being asked will be completely answered only when one has an understanding of the structure of all the molecular components of a biological system and a knowledge of how they interact. There are, of course,

a large number of problems in biology into which biologists have some insight but concerning which they cannot yet ask suitable questions in terms of molecular structure. As they see such problems more clearly, however, they invariably find an increasing need for structural information. In our laboratory at the Massachusetts Institute of Technology we have recently started using a

computer to help gain such information about the structure of large biological molecules.

For the first half of this century the metabolic and structural relations among the small molecules of the living cell were the principal concern of biochemists. The chemical reactions these molecules undergo have been studied intensively. Such reactions are specifically catalyzed by the large protein molecules called enzymes, many of which have now been purified and also studied. It is only within the past few years, however, that X-ray-diffraction techniques have made it possible to determine the molecular structure of such protein molecules. These giant molecules, which contain from a thousand to tens of thousands of atoms, constitute more than half of the dry weight of cells. Protein molecules not only act as enzymes but also provide many of the cell's structural components. Another class of giant molecules, the nucleic acids, determine what kind of protein the cell can produce, but most of the physiological behavior of a cell is determined by the properties of its proteins.

The X-ray-diffraction methods for investigating the three-dimensional structure of protein molecules are difficult and time-consuming. So far the structures of only three proteins have been worked out: myoglobin, hemoglobin and lysozyme [see "The Three-dimensional Structure of a Protein Molecule," by John C. Kendrew, SCIENTIFIC AMERICAN Offprint 121, and "The Hemoglobin Molecule," by M. F. Perutz Offprint 196]. In their studies of the hemoglobin molecule M. F. Perutz and his associates at the Laboratory of Molecular Biology in Cambridge, England, have observed that the structure of the molecule changes slightly when

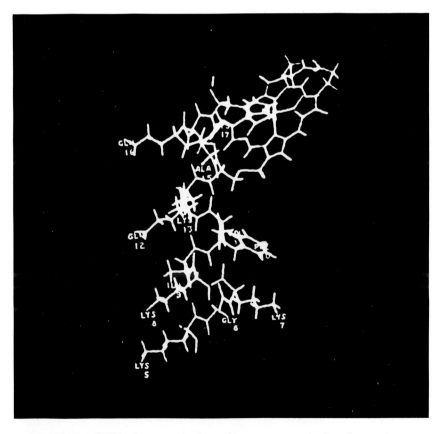

MOLECULAR MODEL of a segment of cytochrome *c*, a protein that plays an important role in cell respiration, is shown as it is displayed on an oscilloscope screen. The protein has 104 amino acid subunits; this segment consists of units 5 through 18 (designated here by their abbreviated names). The heme group, which acts as a carrier of electrons, is known to be attached to amino acids 14 and 17. In the hypothetical structure shown here this stretch of the molecule is assumed to be in the characteristic "alpha helix" configuration.

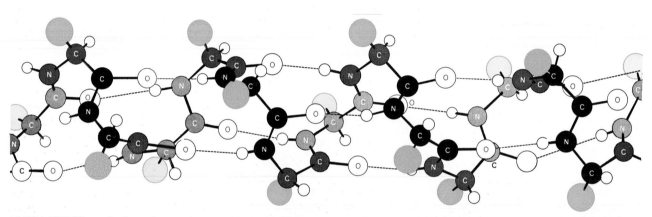

GLYCINE LEUCINE LEUCINE SERINE PHENYLALANINE

HISTIDINE LYSINE THREONINE ISOLEUCINE LEUCINE LYSINE

PROTEIN BACKBONE is a chain of peptide groups (six atoms: carbon, carbon, oxygen, nitrogen, hydrogen, carbon). Each amino acid in a chain contributes a group to the backbone and also has a distinguishing side group (*color tint*). The amino acid sequence of a number of proteins is known. What is shown here is a short segment of the protein myoglobin, which stores oxygen in muscle.

ALPHA HELIX results from the arrangement of planar peptide groups (CCONHC) pivoted about the carbons to which side groups (*color*) are attached. Shade of atoms indicates nearness to viewer. The entire helix is held rigid by hydrogen bonds (*broken lines*).

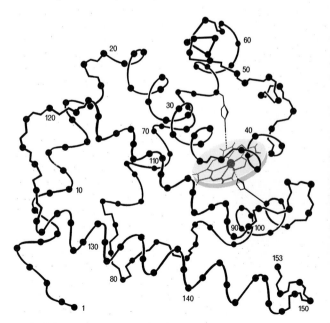

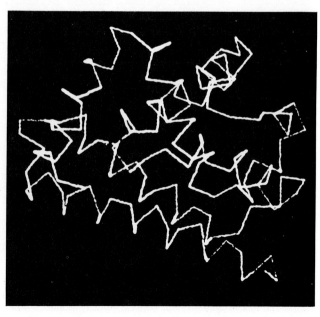

MYOGLOBIN MOLECULE is a folded, partly helical chain, as shown in drawing (*left*) of its form as determined through X-ray analysis by John C. Kendrew of the Laboratory of Molecular Biology in Cambridge, England. The chain enfolds an oxygen-carrying heme group (*colored disk*). Every 10th amino acid is numbered. The computer model of myoglobin is shown at right.

oxygen is attached to it or removed from it. The hemoglobin molecule is the only one for which this kind of study has as yet been carried out. It is known, however, that many proteins change their shape as they perform their functions and that their shape is further modified by the action of the small molecules that activate or inhibit them. The large number of enzyme systems involved in regulating the complex metabolic pathways of the living cell have been studied so far only at the level of the overall shape of the enzyme molecule; practically nothing is known of the specific structural changes that may be important for enzyme function and control.

Another problem currently being investigated by many workers concerns the way in which proteins achieve their final three-dimensional configuration when they are synthesized. During the past few years many of the processes involved in protein synthesis have become rather well understood. As a result one knows, at least in general terms, how the cell determines the sequence of amino acids from which protein molecules are assembled and how this sequence establishes the way in which the atoms of a protein are connected [see top illustration on opposite page]. It is not, however, the chemical sequence, or connectedness, that establishes the functional properties of a protein. These properties are a consequence of the exact three-dimensional arrangement of the molecule's atoms in space.

As a result of work in the past 15 years, there is now a considerable body of evidence showing that the three-dimensional configuration of a protein molecule is determined uniquely by its amino acid sequence. The number of possible sequences is immense because the cell has at its disposal 20 kinds of amino acid building block. The configuration assumed by any particular sequence reflects the fact that the molecule arranges itself so as to minimize its total free energy. In other words, each protein has the shape it has because outside energy would be needed to give it any other shape. The experimental evidence for this conclusion comes from results obtained with many different proteins.

The first really critical experiments in this regard were carried out by Christian B. Anfinsen and his collaborators at the National Institutes of Health with the enzyme ribonuclease, a protein consisting of 153 amino acids

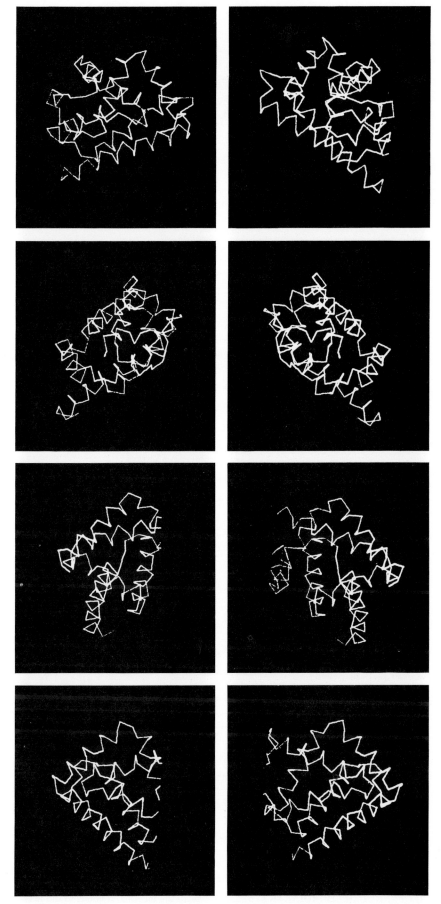

COMPUTER MODEL of myoglobin, which was based on coordinates supplied by Kendrew, is rotated on the screen in this sequence (*top to bottom, left to right*). This display omits the heme group. The pictures are selected frames from a 16-millimeter motion-picture film.

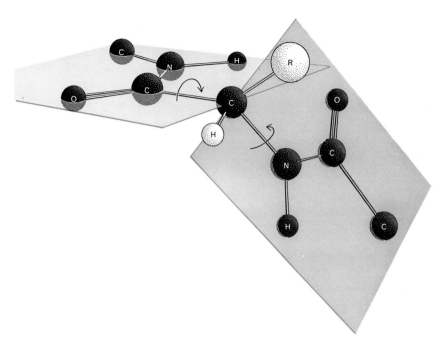

ROTATION ANGLES determine the relation of two successive peptide groups in a chain. Two such groups are shown here. The six atoms (CCONHC) of each group lie in a plane. Two adjacent planes have one atom—the carbon to which a hydrogen and a side group (R) are bonded—in common. Two rotation angles (arrows) give the relation of the two planes.

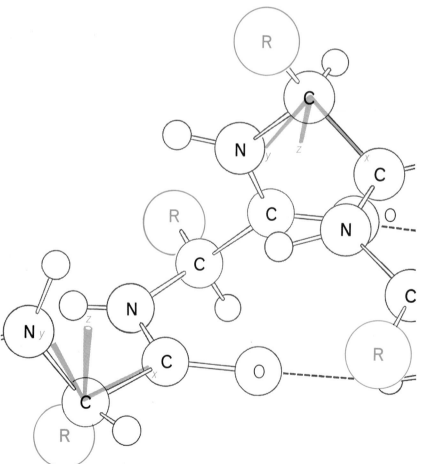

RECTANGULAR COORDINATE SYSTEMS establish the location of atoms in the model. One (left), at the amino end of the peptide chain, is the frame of reference for the entire chain. Others (right) are local systems defining positions of atoms in side groups. The computer calculates the transformation that refers local systems back to the original system.

in a single chain. In our laboratory we have studied the enzyme alkaline phosphatase, which consists of about 800 amino acids arranged in two chains. Both proteins can be treated so that they lose their well-defined three-dimensional configuration without breaking any of the chemical bonds that establish the connectedness of the molecule. In this "denatured" state the proteins are no longer enzymatically active. But if the denaturing agent is removed and the proteins are put in a solution containing certain salts and the correct acidity, the activity can be reestablished.

The alkaline phosphatase molecule has two identical subunits that are inactive by themselves. They can be separated from each other by increasing the acidity of the solution, and they reassemble to form the active "doublet" when the solution is made neutral once again. In addition the subunits themselves can be denatured, with the result that they become random, or structureless, coils. Under the proper conditions it takes only a few minutes to reestablish the enzymatic activity from this disrupted state, along with what appears to be the original three-dimensional configuration of the doublet molecule. An enzymatically active hybrid molecule can even be formed out of subunits from two different organisms. The individual subunits from the two organisms have different amino acid sequences, but they fold into a shape such that the subunits are still able to recognize each other and form an active molecule. These renaturation processes can take place in a solution containing no protein other than the denatured one, and without the intervention of other cellular components.

Apart from the renaturation experiments, the mechanism of synthesis has suggested an additional factor that may be relevant in establishing the correct three-dimensional form of the protein. It is known that the synthetic process always begins at a particular end of the protein molecule—the end carrying an amino group (NH_2)—and proceeds to the end carrying a carboxyl group (COOH). It is plausible to imagine that proteins fold as they are formed in such a way that the configuration of the amino end is sufficiently stable to prevent its alteration while the rest of the molecule is being synthesized. Although this hypothetical mechanism seems to be contradicted by the renaturation experiments just described, it may represent the way some proteins are folded. Because the mechanism would place certain constraints on the folding of a protein molecule, it implies that the active protein is not in a state in which free energy is at a minimum but rather is in a metastable, or temporarily stable, state of somewhat higher energy.

A molecular biologist's understanding of a molecular structure is usually reflected in his ability to construct a three-dimensional model of it. If the molecule is large, however, model-building can be frustrating for purely mechanical reasons; for example, the model collapses. In any event, the building of models is too time-consuming if one wishes to examine many different configurations, which is the case when one is attempting to predict an unknown structure. When one is dealing with the largest molecules, even a model is not much help in the task of enumerating and evaluating all the small interactions that contribute to the molecule's stability. For this task the help of a computer is indispensable.

Any molecular model is based on the nature of the bonds that hold particular kinds of atoms together. From the viewpoint of the model-builder the important fact is that these bonds are the same no matter where in a large molecule the atom is found. For instance, if a carbon atom has four other atoms bonded to it, they will be arranged as if they were located at the corners of a tetrahedron, so that any two bonds form an angle of approximately 109.5 degrees. The lengths of bonds are even more constant than their angles; bonds that are only one to two angstrom units long are frequently known to be constant in length with an accuracy of a few percent. In general the details of atomic spacing are known from the X-ray analysis of small molecules; this knowledge simplifies the task of building models of large molecules.

An example of the value of such knowledge was the discovery by Linus Pauling and Robert B. Corey at the California Institute of Technology that the fundamental repeating bond in protein structures—the peptide bond that joins the CO of one amino acid to the NH of the next—forms an arrangement of six atoms that lie in a plane. This knowledge enabled them to predict that the amino acid units in a protein chain would tend to become arranged in a particular helical form: the alpha helix. It was subsequently found that such helixes provide a significant portion of the structure of many protein molecules. Thus in advance of any crystallographic information about the structure of a particular protein molecule, one knows

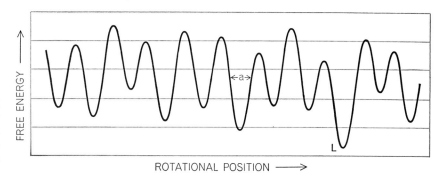

TOTAL ENERGY of a configuration varies with distance between atoms, which depends on all the rotation angles. It is easy to distinguish lowest-energy point L from local valleys, or metastable states, by visual inspection, but a computer must calculate each point in the curve, repeating the operation often enough not to miss a valley. It must calculate the energy at angles separated by no more than a small fraction of the interval indicated as a.

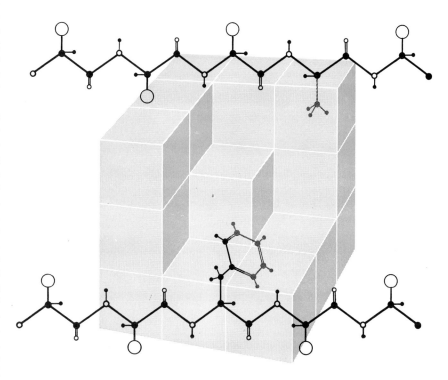

CUBING PROCEDURE eliminates unnecessary computation by identifying atoms that are sufficiently near each other to affect the molecule's energy. The computer searches the area around an atom residing in the center cube and reports if there are any atoms in the 26 adjacent cubes. This also helps to reveal a molecule's edges and holes inside it.

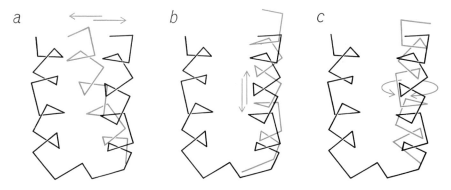

MANIPULATION of the computer-built model is accomplished by three different routines. The routine called "close" in effect puts a spring between any pair of points indicated by the investigator (a). The routine "glide" causes a single helical region to be pulled along its own axis (b). "Revolve" imposes a torque that rotates a region about its axis (c).

the spatial arrangement of atoms within the peptide bonds, as well as the detailed geometry of its alpha-helical regions.

The planar configuration of the peptide bond allows an enormous reduction in the number of variables necessary for a complete description of a protein molecule. Instead of three-dimensional coordinates for each atom, all one needs in order to establish the path of the central chain of the molecule are the two rotation angles where two peptide bonds come together [see top illustration on page 174]. The complete description requires, in addition to this information, the specification of the rotation angles of the side chains in those amino acids whose side chains are not completely fixed.

A further reduction in the number of variables would be possible if one could predict from the amino acid sequence which parts of the molecule are in the form of alpha helixes. The few proteins whose structures have been completely determined provide some indication of which amino acids are likely to be found in helical regions, but not enough is yet known to make such predictions with any assurance.

Because protein chains are formed by linking molecules that belong to a single class (the amino acids), the linkage process can be expressed mathematically in a form that is particularly suited for a high-speed digital computer. We have written computer programs that calculate the coordinates of each atom of the protein, using as input variables only those angles in which rotational changes can occur; all other angles and bond lengths are entered as rigid constraints in the program. The method of calculation involves the use of a local coordinate system for the atoms in each amino acid unit and a fixed overall coordinate system into which all local coordinates are transformed.

The transformation that relates the local coordinate systems to the fixed coordinate system is recalculated by the computer program each time a new atom is added to the linear peptide backbone. Each chemical bond is treated as a translation and a rotation of this transformation. The process requires a substantial amount of calculation, but each time the backbone reaches the central atom of a new amino acid the relative positions of the side-group atoms can be taken from the computer memory where this information is stored for each of the 20 varieties of amino acid. It is then a simple matter to translate and rotate the side-group

atoms from their local coordinate system into the fixed-coordinate system of the entire molecule.

The new value of the transformation at each step along the backbone is determined by the fixed rotation angles and translation distances that are built into the computer program and by the variable angles that must somehow be determined during the running of the program. The principal problem, therefore, is precisely how to provide correct values for the variable angles. A number of investigators are working on this problem in different ways. Before discussing any of these approaches I should emphasize the magnitude of the problem that remains even after one has gone as far as possible in using chemical constraints to reduce the number of variables from several thousand to a few hundred. Because each bond angle must be specified with an accuracy of a few degrees, the number of possible configurations that can result when each angle is varied by a small amount becomes astronomical even for a small protein. Moreover, these small rotations can produce a large effect on the total energy of the structure [see top illustration on preceding page].

One way to understand the difficulty

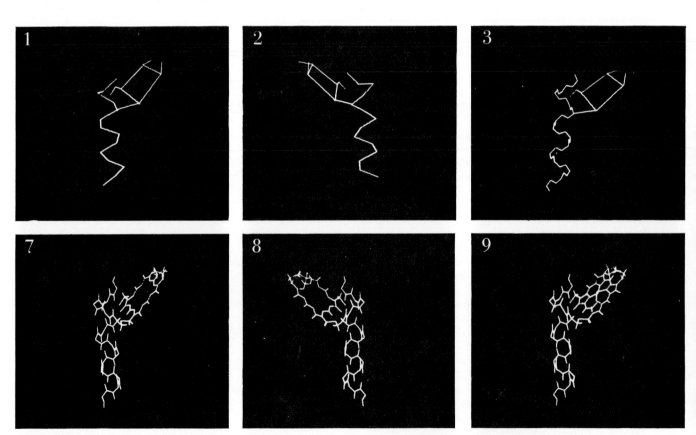

CYTOCHROME C segment seen in the two opening illustrations is shown on this page and the opposite page in the various degrees of detail of which the system is capable. At first only the carbon atoms to which the side groups are attached are displayed, along with the

of finding a configuration of minimum energy is to imagine the problem facing a man lost in a mountainous wilderness in a dense fog. He may know that within a few miles there is an inhabited river valley leading into a calm lake. He may also know that the lake is at the lowest point in the area, but let us assume that he can only determine his own elevation and the slope of the ground in his immediate vicinity. He can walk down whatever hill he is standing on, but this would probably trap him at the bottom of a small valley far from the lake he seeks. In finding a configuration of minimum energy the comparable situation would be getting trapped in a metastable state far from a real energy minimum. Our lost man has only two dimensions to worry about, north-south and east-west; the corresponding problem in a molecule involves several hundred dimensions.

Our approach to this problem has assumed that even sophisticated techniques for energy minimization will not, at least at present, be sufficient to determine the structure of a protein from its amino acid sequence in a fully automatic fashion. We therefore decided to develop programs that would make use of a man-computer combination to do a

kind of model-building that neither a man nor a computer could accomplish alone. This approach implies that one must be able to obtain information from the computer and introduce changes in the way the program is running in a span of time that is appropriate to human operation. This in turn suggests that the output of the computer must be presented not in numbers but in visual form.

I first became aware of the possibilities of using visual output from a computer in a conversation with Robert M. Fano, the director of Project MAC at the Massachusetts Institute of Technology. (MAC stands for multiple-access computer.) It soon became clear that the new types of visual display that had been developed would permit direct interaction of the investigator and a molecular model that was being constructed by the computer. All our subsequent work on this problem has made use of the large computer of Project MAC, which operates on the basis of "time-sharing," or access by many users. The system, developed by Fernando J. Corbató, allows as many as 30 people to have programs running on the computer at the same time. For all practical purposes it seems to each of them that he is alone on the system. A user can have

any of his data in the high-speed memory printed out on his own typewriter, and he can make whatever changes he wants in this stored data. What is more important from our point of view is the ability to make changes in the commands that control the sequential flow of the program itself.

It is true, of course, that one of 30 users has access to a computer that, when it is fully occupied, has only a thirtieth of the speed of the normal machine, but for many problems this is enough to keep the man side of the man-machine combination quite well occupied. The program that acts to supervise the time-sharing system is organized in such a way that no user can interfere with the system or with any other user, and the computer is not allowed to stand idle if the man takes time out to think.

In working with molecular models we are interested in being able to obtain data quickly in order to evaluate the effect of changing the input variables of the program. For any particular molecular configuration the computer can readily supply the positions (in the three-dimensional coordinates x, y and z) of all the atoms. The important question is: What can be done with 5,000 to 10,000 numbers corresponding to the

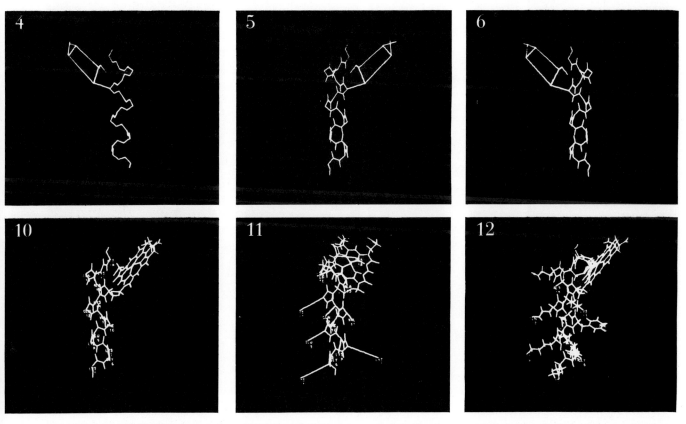

square outline of the heme group connected to this segment (1, 2). The other atoms of the backbone are added (3, 4), then the oxygen and hydrogen atoms (5, 6). The heme group is shown in more detail (7–9), and side groups are named (10) and displayed (11, 12).

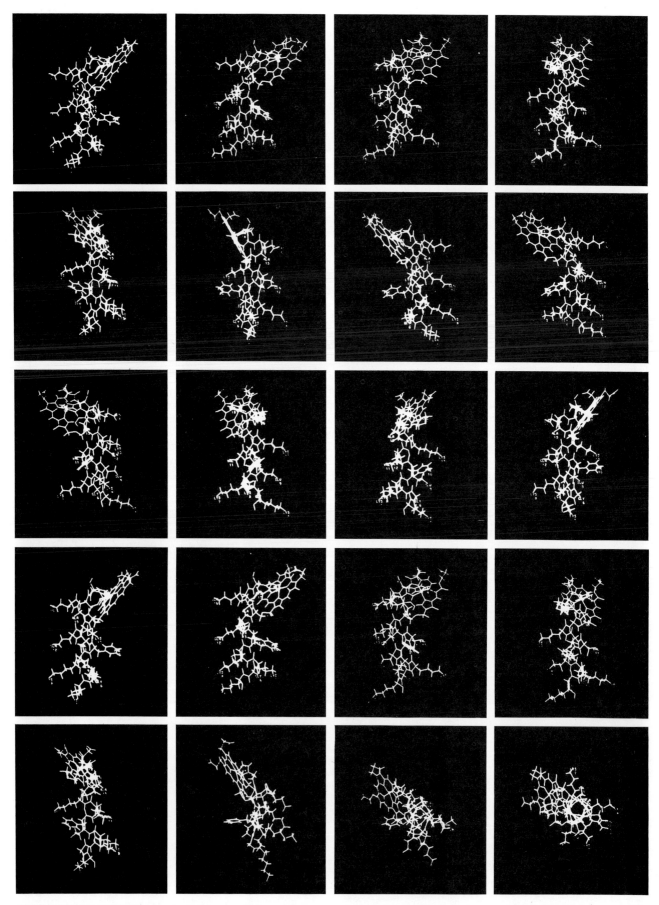

CYTOCHROME HELIX is rotated on the screen (*left to right, top to bottom*), a procedure that makes it possible for the investigator to perceive the three-dimensional arrangement of the atoms. A set of three-dimensional vectors connecting the atoms of the molecule is stored in the computer's high-speed memory. The computer calculates the projection of those vectors on a plane and draws the projected vectors on the screen. The operator controls the rotation of the plane, thus apparently turning the model.

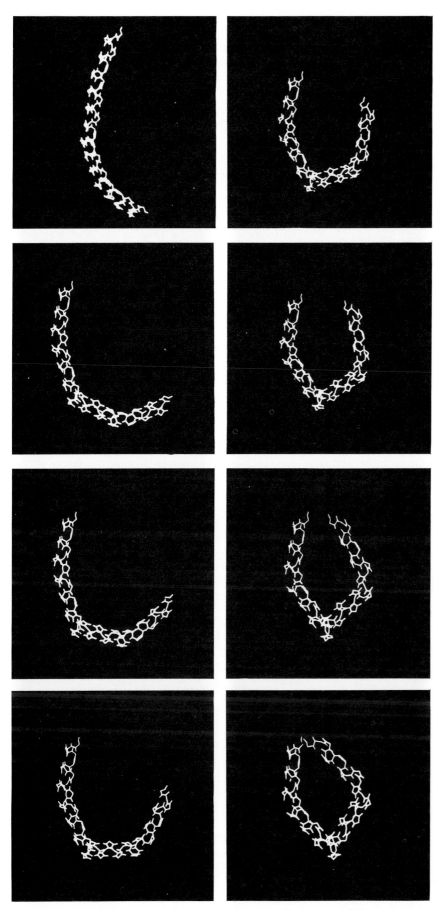

"CLOSING" ROUTINE is applied to a hypothetical peptide chain assumed to consist of several helical sections. The individual sections do not bend, but the rotation angles between sections are changed (*top to bottom, left to right*) to close the chain into a circle.

position of every atom in even a small protein? Obviously if we could formulate specific questions concerning energy, bond angles and lengths, overall shape, density and so on, the computer could calculate the answer and there would be no need for a man ever to look at the numerical values of the co-ordinates. We realized that our best hope of gaining insight into unexpected structural relations—relations that had not been anticipated—lay in getting the computer to present a three-dimensional picture of the molecule.

Although computer-controlled oscilloscopes have been available for about 10 years, they have been used mainly to display numbers and letters. It is only recently that they have been used to produce the output of computer programs in graphical form. The oscilloscope tube can of course present only a two-dimensional image. It is no great trick, however, to have the computer rotate the coordinates of the molecule before plotting their projection. If this is done, the brain of the human viewer readily constructs a three-dimensional image from the sequential display of two-dimensional images. Such sequential projections seem to be just as useful to the brain as simultaneous stereoscopic projections viewed by two eyes. The effect of rotation obtained from the continuously changing projection nonetheless has an inherent ambiguity. An observer cannot determine the direction of rotation from observation of the changing picture alone. In the Project MAC display system, designed by John Ward and Robert Stotz, the rate of rotation of the picture is controlled by the position of a globe on which the observer rests his hand; with a little practice the coupling between hand and brain becomes so familiar that any ambiguity in the picture can easily be resolved.

In evaluating the energy of a particular configuration of a protein molecule one must add up all the small interactions of atomic groups that contribute to this energy. These must include interactions not only between the different parts of the protein molecule but also between the parts of the protein molecule and the surrounding water molecules. If we are interested in altering the configuration in the direction of lower energy, we must be able to calculate the derivative of each of the energy terms—that is, the direction in which the energy curves slope—as changes are made in each of the rotation angles. Accordingly we must calculate a very large number of interatomic distances and the derivative of these distances with respect to the allowed rotation angle.

The derivatives can be calculated, however, without going through the extended transformation calculations needed to generate the coordinates themselves. The rotation around any chemical bond will cause one part of the molecule to revolve with respect to another. If both members of a pair of atoms are on the same side of the bond being altered, the rotation will not give rise to a change in their distance. If the two atoms are on opposite sides of the rotating bond, one of the atoms will move in a circle around the axis of rotation while the other remains stationary. By analyzing the geometry of this motion we can simplify the derivative calculations to the point where they require very little computation.

Even though each of these derivative calculations can be done in a few hundred microseconds of computer time, there would still be an excessive amount of calculation if it were done for all possible pairs of atoms within the molecule. Fortunately the interactions with which we are concerned are short-range ones, and most of the pairs of atoms are too far apart to contribute appre-

ciably to the overall energy. In order to select out all pairs of atoms that are close to each other, we have developed a procedure called cube-testing. All the space in the region of the molecule is divided into cubes of some predetermined size, let us say five angstroms on an edge (two or three times the typical bond length) and each atom is assigned to a cube. To consider the interactions involving any given atom one need only determine the distance between this atom and all others in the same cube and in the 26 surrounding ones [*see middle illustration on page 175*]. Although the procedure is still time-consuming, it is much faster than having to do calculations for all possible pairs of atoms in the molecule.

In addition to enabling us to screen the data for close pairs, the cubing procedure provides information about which groups in the protein molecule can interact with the surrounding water molecules. In order to enumerate such interactions, we first define the "insideness" and "outsideness" of the molecule, outsideness meaning that a particular atom or group of atoms is accessible to the surrounding water and insideness that it is not. If we examine the cubing pattern for a particular molecule, an atom on the outside would be in a cube

that is surrounded on one side by filled cubes and on the other by empty ones. In a similar way we can detect holes in the midst of the structure by looking for empty cubes that are surrounded on all sides by filled ones.

By suitable use of derivative calculation and cubing we can alter any configuration of the molecule in the direction of lower energy. This procedure, however, would almost certainly lead to a structure that is trapped in one of the local minima—one of the higher valleys of our wilderness analogy—and may not even be close to the true minimum-energy configuration we are looking for. For a real molecule floating in solution, the local minima would not represent traps because the normal thermal vibration of the molecule and its parts supplies enough energy to move the structure out of any valley that is not a true minimum.

Although there are various ways in which one can use random elements in a computer calculation to simulate thermal vibration, it is our experience that an investigator who is looking at the molecule can frequently understand the reason for the local minimum and by making a small alteration in the structure can return the program to its

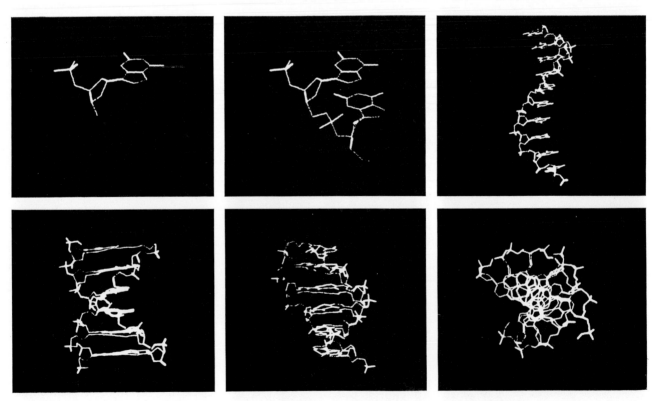

DEOXYRIBONUCLEIC ACID (DNA) is modeled by a program devised by Robert Langridge and Andrew A. MacEwan of the Children's Cancer Research Foundation and Harvard Medical School. This DNA sequence (*left to right, top to bottom*) begins with a single nucleotide: a pentagonal sugar plus a phosphate group and a base. A second nucleotide is added, and then more to make a helical chain that joins with a second chain to form the characteristic double helix. Then the helix is rotated in space.

DISPLAY UNIT designed by John Ward and Robert Stotz has access to the large time-shared central computer at the Massachusetts Institute of Technology. The investigator communicates with the computer by typing commands or punching preset buttons on a keyboard or by pointing with the light pen. He regulates the direction and the speed of rotation of the model by moving the gimbaled control on which his right hand rests.

downhill path. Such alterations can be accomplished in the computer by changing the program in such a way as to introduce pseudo-energy terms that have the effect of pulling on parts of the structure. A few simple subprograms that introduce the appropriate pseudo-energies enable us to do the same kind of pulling and pushing in the computer that we can do with our hands while building actual models.

Pulling a structure by means of these pseudo-energy terms is also useful for building a model that observes all the chemical constraints and at the same time has its atoms as close as possible to the positions indicated by X-ray diffraction studies. In this case the pseudo-energies can be regarded as springs pulling designated atoms to their experimentally determined positions. Such calculations have been carried out by Martin Zwick, a graduate student at M.I.T., in order to make a model of myoglobin fit the configuration determined from X-ray data by John C. Kendrew and Herman Watson at the Laboratory of Molecular Biology in Cambridge. For this type of problem a helpful procedure has been developed by William Davidon of Haverford College. In his program one starts by "walking" in the direction of the steepest slope, but with each successive step one builds up information as to how the slope of the hillside changes.

Once we had produced a computer model of myoglobin, we could ask questions concerning the relative importance of short-range forces acting between various parts of the molecule. There are, for example, Van der Waals forces: electrostatic attractions due to the electric dipoles that all atoms induce in one another when they are close together. There are also electrostatic interactions that arise from the permanent electric dipoles associated with the peptide bonds. The permanent dipole attractions turned out to be larger than we had expected. It is thus possible that the electrostatic interaction between different regions of a protein may play a substantial role in stabilizing its structure. This results in part from the fact that the electric dipoles in an alpha helix are added to one another along the direction of the axis. For this reason two helixes that wind in the same direction will repel each other and two that wind in opposite directions will attract each other. In myoglobin the overall effect is a substantial attractive force. This calculation requires some form of model-building, because the electrically charged regions are associated with the C–O and N–H groups along the backbone, and the hydrogen atom is not detected in the X-ray analysis.

Although the electrostatic interaction energy is of the same order of magnitude as that required to denature a protein, it is probably not the dominant energy for the folding of a protein molecule. The primary source of energy for this purpose probably comes from the interaction of the amino acid side chains and the surrounding water; the electrostatic interactions may do no more than modify the basic structure.

We still have much to learn about the magnitude of the various energy terms involved in holding a protein molecule together. Meanwhile we have been trying to develop our computer technique, using the knowledge we have. Is this knowledge enough to enable us to find the lowest energy state of a protein molecule and to predict its structure in advance of its determination by X-ray analysis?

The answer to this question probably depends on how well we understand what really happens when a protein molecule in a cell folds itself up. Our work has been based on the hypothesis that the folding starts independently in several regions of the protein and that the first structural development is the formation of a number of segments of alpha helix. Our assumption is that these segments then interact with one another to form the final molecular structure. In this method of analyzing the problem the units that have to be handled independently are the helical regions rather than the individual amino acids. Thus the number of independent variables is greatly reduced. The success of the procedure depends, however, on the assumption that we can deduce from the amino acid sequence alone which regions are likely to be helical. It is not necessary, however, that we guess the helical regions correctly the first time; we can see what happens when helical regions are placed in many different parts of the molecule. Several other groups working on this problem are following the hypothesis that the folding proceeds only from the amino end of the protein. Until one of these approaches succeeds in predicting the structure of a protein and having the prediction confirmed by X-ray analysis, we can only consider the different hypotheses as more or less plausible working guides in studying the problem.

It is still too early to evaluate the usefulness of the man-computer combination in solving real problems of molecular biology. It does seem likely, however, that only with this combination can the investigator use his "chemical insight" in an effective way. We already know that we can use the computer to build and display models of large molecules and that this procedure can be very useful in helping us to understand how such molecules function. But it may still be a few years before we have learned just how useful it is for the investigator to be able to interact with the computer while the molecular model is being constructed.

18

SYSTEMS ANALYSIS OF URBAN TRANSPORTATION

WILLIAM F. HAMILTON AND DANA K. NANCE
July, 1969

There is a growing recognition that many of the ills of U.S. cities stem from the problem of transportation within the metropolis. Although the automobile has endowed the American people with unprecedented mobility, the long-range trend toward movement by private automobile rather than by public transit has created a new complex of difficulties for urban living. The price being paid for the privacy and convenience provided by the automobile is enormous. It includes the engulfing of the city by vehicles and expressways, congestion, a high rate of accidents and air pollution. The automobile has brought another consequence that tends to be overlooked but is no less serious: by fostering "urban sprawl" it has in effect isolated much of the population. In the widely dispersed metropolis, much of which is not served by public transit, those who cannot afford a car or who cannot drive are denied the mobility needed for full access to the city's opportunities for employment and its cultural and social amenities.

These "transportation poor" constitute a far larger proportion of the population than is generally realized. Half of all the U.S. families with incomes of less than $4,000, half of all Negro households and half of all households headed by persons over 65 own no automobile. Even in families that do own one it is often unavailable to the wife and children because the wage earner must drive it to work. The young, the old, the physically handicapped—all those who for one reason or another cannot drive must be counted among the transportation poor in the increasingly automobile-oriented city. The generalization concerning the mobility made possible by the private automobile must be qualified by the observation that 100 million Americans, half of the total population, do not have a driver's license, and the proportion of nondrivers in the big cities is higher than in the country at large.

The gravity of the urban transportation problem prompted Congress three years ago to direct the Department of Housing and Urban Development (HUD) to look into the entire problem. HUD awarded 17 study contracts to a wide variety of groups: transportation experts, university laboratories, research institutes and industrial research organizations. Our group, the General Research Corporation of Santa Barbara, Calif., which is experienced in the discipline known as systems analysis, was assigned to apply such analysis to the transportation problem, considering the entire complex of transportation facilities for a city as an integrated system. In analytic method our study resembled a number of earlier ones devoted to this subject. It is nonetheless unique in that it weighed not only existing systems of transportation but also future systems. Furthermore, it carried cost-benefit accounting to a new breadth and depth of coverage.

We set out to build a mathematical model of urban transportation and to test with the aid of a large computer the effectiveness and the costs of various possible networks. Systems analysis is a general approach that consists in examining a complex system by exploring the interactions of its many parts. One "wiggles" each part in order to see what will happen to the whole when all the parts are taken into account. When the system does not exist and would be too expensive or too risky to build for testing by direct experimentation, the analyst tries to construct a model representing it and does the experiments on the model. Most often the model turns out to be a set of equations that can be solved together. For a system of any complexity the model usually is so complicated that the experiments can only be performed with a high-speed computer.

Our goal was to model all the significant modes, actual and potential, of transporting people in an urban area. We were not trying to design a particular optimal system; rather, we undertook to examine various combinations of the possible modes to see how the system as a whole would work.

To make our model as realistic as possible it was plainly desirable to use data from actual cities rather than from a hypothetical average city. We therefore decided on a case-study approach, selecting four representative cities as models. On the basis of an elaborate factor

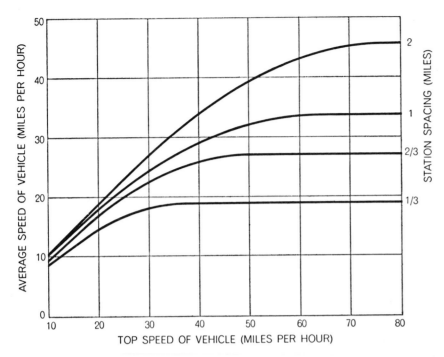

AVERAGE SPEED OF SUBWAY IS LIMITED by the spacing of stations and the acceleration that passengers can tolerate. It is assumed that the maximum tolerable acceleration is three miles per hour per second and that stops are 20 seconds long. Thus regardless of what the top speed of the train is, it can only average (if stations are a mile apart) 33 miles per hour. Improved equipment cannot overcome this limitation of conventional transit.

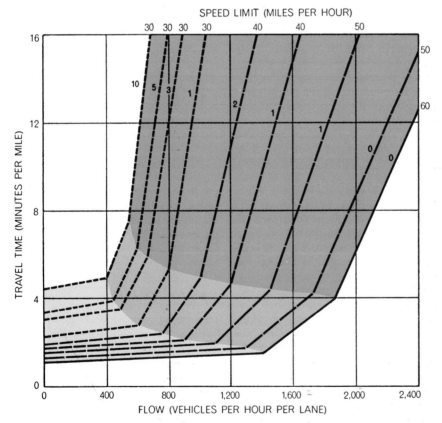

STREET CAPACITIES were represented in mathematical models of a city's transportation by the equations of these lines. At low traffic flow (*light color*) the speed and number of signal-marked intersections per mile (*numbers within grid*) are governing factors. The region above (*medium color*) is mainly governed by car density. Where flow exceeds street capacity (*dark color*) the slope was calculated from queuing theory. Data for particular streets are from city maps. The number of signal-marked intersections is an approximation.

analysis of census data we chose Boston as a typical example of a large city that was strongly oriented to public transit, Houston as a large city oriented to the private automobile and New Haven and Tucson as corresponding representatives of smaller cities (between 200,000 and 400,000 in population). These four cities offered the valuable advantage that detailed studies of their traffic flows had recently been made in each of them, so that they provided data not only for building our model but also for validating the results of experiments with the model.

The formulation of the model for each city started off with a description of present transportation facilities and considered the travel needs of its people both now and in the future. We described for the computer the streets, freeways, bus service and rail service (if any). For evaluation of the present system and of possible future improvements the model had to take into account a great deal of demographic and technical detail: the population density and the average family income in each area of the city, the location of residential and business areas, the traffic flows over the transportation routes at typical peak and off-peak hours, how the speed of flow over each route would be affected by the number of vehicles using it, the amount of air pollution that would be generated by each type of vehicle and a great many other factors that must enter into the measurement of the costs and benefits of a transportation system.

Starting with computer runs that evaluated how well the existing system performed, we went on to model progressively more advanced systems and compare their performance. All together we tested some 200 models, each loaded with a tremendous amount of detail and each taking about an hour for the runthrough in our computer. The project occupied a large team of specialists: engineers, city planners, mathematicians, sociologists, economists and computer programmers. A measure of the amount of work entailed is the fact that our final report, written by 17 authors, ran to 500,000 words—and we tried hard to be brief!

As our study proceeded, the results of the experiments showed that the possible strategies for the improvement of urban transportation fell into two sharply different categories from the standpoint of effectiveness. One of these was an approach we called "gradualism." It consisted in building improvements into the existing methods of transporta-

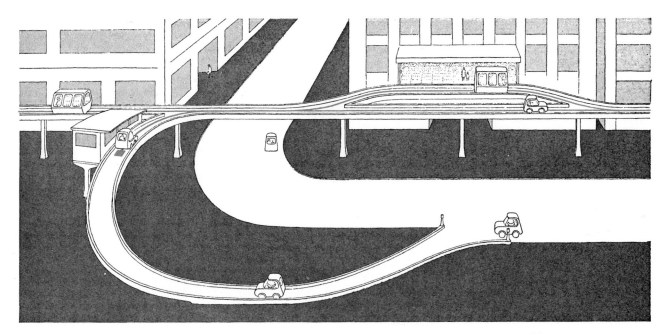

HYPOTHETICAL PERSONAL-TRANSIT SYSTEM would combine the speed and privacy of the automobile with the advantages of rail transit. A passenger entering the automated guideway network at a station would be carried by a small vehicle nonstop to his destination at speeds of up to 60 miles per hour. Specially equipped automobiles could enter the guideway by ramp, affording the driver swift, safe and effortless transport. Such dual use would make it feasible to extend the system to urban fringe areas.

tion. These, for example, included modernizing and extending old subway lines and building new ones, redesigning buses to make them quieter and easier to enter and speeding up their movement, equipping automobiles with devices to minimize air pollution, and so forth. The other approach, which we labeled "new technology," consisted in a jump to entirely new modes of transport, involving the creation of new kinds of vehicles and interconnections. Our tests of models indicated, as we shall show, that the gradualistic approach could not meet the future transportation needs of the cities, whereas innovations already in sight promise to do so.

Let us briefly examine some of the most promising of these new concepts. Engineers have described a system called "personal transit" that will operate like a railroad but will transport individual passengers or small groups nonstop to stations of their own selection. Its cars will be small, electrically propelled vehicles, with a capacity of two to four passengers, running on an automated network of tracks called "guideways." All stations will be on sidetracks shunted off the through line [see illustration above]. A passenger will enter a waiting car at a station, punch his destination on a keyboard and then be carried to the designated station with no further action on his part—no transfers, no station stops, no waiting, no driving. It appears that such a system could take the pas-

senger from starting point to destination at an average speed of 60 miles per hour, as against the present average speed of 20 miles per hour counting station stops in U.S. subways.

The guideways could be designed to carry private automobiles as well as the public-transit cars, so that a driver coming into the city could mount the guideway at a station and ride swiftly to a downtown destination. Transport of the automobile by the guideway could be arranged either by providing flatbed vehicles that carried ordinary automobiles "piggyback" or by building into automobiles special equipment that enabled them to be conveyed by the guideway itself. The dual-mode use of guideways—by automobiles as well as by passengers in the small public vehicles—could make it financially feasible to extend the guideway system to outlying districts of a metropolitan area.

In some of our models of transportation systems incorporating new technology we also postulated entirely new automobiles designed from scratch for maximum safety and minimum air pollution. Such steam-engine automobiles are a feasible alternative to vehicles that could be combined with a personal-transit system. In contrast to gradualistic improvements, such as the padded dashboard or the smog-control device added to an internal-combustion engine, all-new automobiles would dramatically reduce accident casualties and fatalities and essentially eliminate air pollution. On the

other hand, these cars would not help to defray the cost of personal-transit facilities nor would they automate any part of the burdensome task of driving.

For the suburbs, to transport people between their homes and local guideway stations or ordinary railroad stations, a promising possibility is a system known as "Dial-A-Bus." It would employ small buses (for eight to 20 passengers) and provide door-to-door service at a cost substantially less than that for a taxi. A commuter preparing to go into town would simply dial the bus service and be picked up at his front door in a few minutes to be taken to the nearest rapid-transit station. As calls for the bus service came in, a computer would continuously optimize the routes of the buses in transit for speedy responses to the developing demand. The computer technology to make such a system work is already developed, and the system could be tried out on a large scale immediately in connection with present suburban railroads. The Dial-A-Bus system would be most effective, however, in conjunction with a guideway network for personal transit.

For short-distance travel in the dense central areas of cities something is needed that would be faster than buses and cheaper than taxis. One classic proposal is the moving sidewalk. Unless someone can think of a better way of getting on and off than any yet proposed, however, the moving-sidewalk idea would work only for those who are content to travel at about two miles per hour or for people with a certain amount of athletic agility. A small-scale version of the personal-transit guideway looks like a more practical solution to the problem. The tracks for this system would stand above street level, to avoid interference with other traffic. The passenger would enter a personal "capsule" (which might hold one or two people) at a siding, dial his destination and travel to it at a speed of about 15 miles per hour. Such a system could be very compact and quiet.

Engineers generally agree that these innovations, specifically the personal-transit and personal-capsule systems, are already within the realm of feasibility. There are problems of safety and reliability to be solved, and decisions have to be made as to the best methods for propulsion, suspension and control. There is little doubt, however, that a system based on the innovations here described could be operating within a few years.

The big question is not whether such a system *could* be built but whether it *should*. The new system would take several years to develop, and there can be no guaranty that it would live up to its promise when it was completed. Meanwhile cities are hard-pressed for immediate relief from their transportation crisis. Would it not be wiser to adopt the gradualistic approach, to invest in improved buses, in better scheduling and perhaps in rapid-transit networks, than to invest millions of dollars in an untried system that in any case could not bring any help to our cities until years hence? This was the major question our computer tests of the various alternatives sought to answer. Our systems analysis attempted to compare the alternatives as fairly as possible in terms of the measurable costs and benefits—social as well as financial.

The heart of our model was a network representing a city's transportation. Network-flow analysis is an outgrowth of the mathematical theory of graphs. In the abstract, the question it deals with is this: Given a set of "nodes" (points) connected by a set of "arcs" (lines), with a specified cost associated with each arc, how can each shipment from node to node be routed at minimum cost, taking into account all other shipments? In our network each node represented a district, or "zone," in the city under study (for precision the node was defined as the center of population in the district) and each arc represented the capacity of the collection of streets that carried traffic from one node to the next. Besides the city streets we added separate arcs to

represent expressways, rail lines, bus routes and walking and waiting for a conveyance, all of which had to be taken into account in order to calculate the minimum cost of travel from one node to another. Our basic measure of "cost" was the time required to traverse an arc, which depends not only on the length of the arc but also on how many other users are on the arc at the same time. We assumed, as could reasonably be done, that people usually take the fastest route (not necessarily the shortest in distance) between points.

A city's transportation system involves thousands of places to go, dozens of ways to get there and thousands of possible choices by an individual. As powerful as a large computer is, it can handle only so many calculations an hour. For our program the computer was limited to dealing with a maximum of 200 zones, 1,500 nodes and 5,000 arcs. Hence we had to divide each of our model cities into no more than 200 zones. We varied the zones in size from just a few blocks in the dense central city to substantially larger sections in areas away from the center. The criterion for zone size was that travel within a zone

be negligible compared with travel among zones. We also had to make certain other simplifications.

The most crucial simplification had to do with the expected behavior of individuals in choosing their routes and means of travel. For a precise prediction of the traffic flows from zone to zone in the network we would have needed answers to a number of specific questions. Would a given resident going downtown take the bus, drive his car or have his wife drive him to the subway? How far would a $5,000-a-year male worker living in Zone 27 in Boston walk on an average winter day to save a 25-cent fare? How heavy would the traffic have to get before a person contemplating a nonessential trip decided not to go at all? If we had had detailed information such as this, we could have computed who went how by routing each person in the way that cost him the least in time, money and trouble—or, as economists say, "minimized the disutility to him."

Lacking sufficiently detailed data on such questions, we developed a general basis for predicting behavior that turned out to be reasonably reliable. First, we applied a simple formula, which had

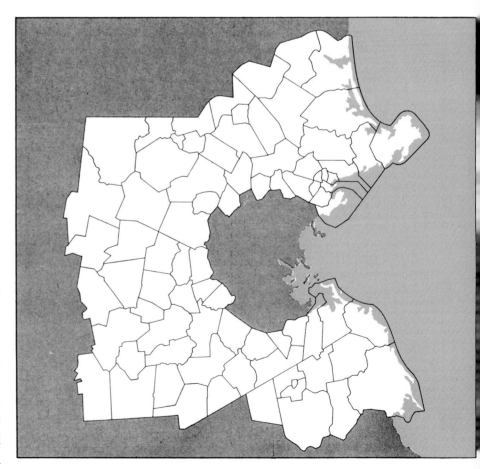

TRAFFIC-ZONE BREAKDOWN of the Boston area formed the basic of a model (*see illustration on page 188*). **Boston represents a typical example of a large city strongly oriented to**

been developed by the Traffic Research Corporation and had been found valid in traffic studies in several cities, to determine what proportion of the people in any given home zone would choose public over private transportation. (The formula computes this "modal split" on the basis of the average family income in the home zone, the relative amounts of time needed to reach a target zone by the two transportation methods and the relative "nuisance time" spent in walking and waiting.) Second, we assumed that within either of the two modes, public or private, each traveler will simply choose the route that minimizes his total travel time.

After thus working out a program for computing the expected zone-to-zone traffic flows in a city network under given conditions, we fed our data for each city into the computer to calculate the flow in the network with given demand for travel. The procedure was "iterative," employing a series of trials to arrive at the final allocation of flows. The program first calculated what the travel time for each arc would be if there were no congestion. Then it considered the

destination zones one at a time and calculated the quickest route to each destination from all the other zones. Next it introduced, for each route, the complicating factor of the relative numbers of travelers who would use the public mode and the private mode respectively. When this had been done for all the arcs, the program went back to the beginning and recomputed the travel times on the basis of the traffic flows indicated by the foregoing trials. It took about five such iterations to produce a stable picture of traffic flow that did not change in further trials.

For a quantitative assessment of what benefits could be brought about by improvements of the system, we modeled not only the existing modes of transportation but also various possible future systems with entirely different flow characteristics. The program included a number of subroutines that measured the costs and benefits of each system, in social terms as well as in terms of travel speed and money. Among the factors we introduced into the calculation were air pollution, the intrusion of automobiles into the city, the accessibility of key areas and the mobility of ghetto resi-

dents. Thus the transportation system judged to be "best" was not necessarily the one that was simply the cheapest or the fastest.

Obviously no model or program is worth much if it overlooks crucial factors or if its key assumptions are wrong. How much confidence could we place in the general model we finally developed? Fortunately it passed every validation test we could apply.

In the first place, as the work proceeded we took a skeptical view of the model's basic assumptions, trying out different assumptions to see how they would affect the results and encouraging each expert to criticize the others' work. We had some lively conferences and threw away a lot of computer printouts before we settled on a model we felt we could trust.

As it happened, the representation of traffic flow that we developed on the basis of our experience in studying quite different systems turned out to be very similar to flow models that had been devised by transportation engineers for use in traffic planning. Since we had had no prior knowledge of the traffic engineers' ideas, the fact that we had arrived

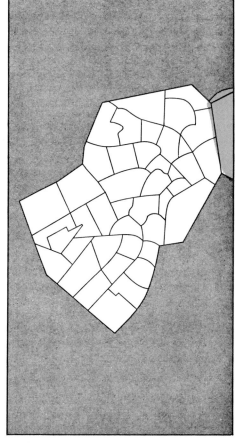

public transit. The size of a zone varies with population density and relative contribution to total traffic. In the dense core of the city (*right*) a zone often comprises only a few blocks. The total number of zones (200) represent an area of 2,300 square miles.

at much the same method of predicting traffic flow gave us considerable confidence that we were on the right track. Furthermore, we found that our network-flow program reproduced a faithful picture of the known flow in specific situations. As we have mentioned, each of the four cities we modeled had recently undergone a detailed traffic survey. These studies had recorded the average speed of traffic movement on the major streets, the numbers of people using public-transit facilities, the times for various trips in the city and so forth. To test the prediction ability of our network-flow program, we fed into the program the characteristics of the city's population and transportation network as of the time of the survey and let the program route the flow according to its own rules. In each case the results in the computer print-out corresponded so closely to the actual flow pattern as the direct, on-the-spot survey had described

it that we were satisfied our model could do a realistic job of representing a city's traffic flows.

Further validation of the general usefulness of our model emerged when we came to testing the alternative approaches for dealing with the urban transportation problem. In all four of our model cities the results of the analysis pointed to the same major conclusion: the best hope of meeting the cities' future needs lies in developing new transportation systems rather than in merely improving or adding to present systems.

A summary of our tests of various systems in Boston will serve to illustrate our findings. The story begins with the situation in 1963 [see illustration on page 190]. In that year the average door-to-door speed of public-transit travelers in the peak hours was nine miles per hour; the average automobile traveler's speed in the city was 16.4 miles per

hour; 32 percent of the people used public transit at peak hours, and the downtown streets were heavily burdened with automobile traffic. We next projected what the situation would be by 1975 if there were no change in the transportation facilities and traffic reached the level predicted by the Boston Regional Planning Project. Our calculations showed that public-transit travel would slow to 7.8 miles per hour and automobile travel to 15.7 miles per hour; the use of public transit would fall to 23 percent, and the intrusive concentration of automobile traffic downtown would rise by more than 15 percent. (One disastrous day in 1963 automobile traffic in downtown Boston reached a level of congestion that stopped all movement for several hours.)

We then proceeded to consider the effects of improvements in the transportation network. Addition of the costly freeways and extensions of rapid transit

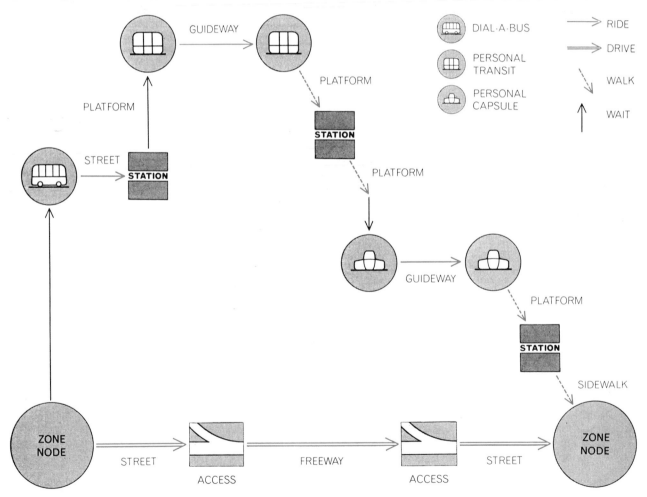

NETWORK simulates a city's transportation in terms of nodes (points) and arcs (lines). A zone node represents the center of population of a traffic zone and the point at which any trip begins or ends. Other nodes represent transfer points. Here two trips are represented in diagrammatic form, both beginning at the zone node at left and ending at the zone node at right. One trip utilizes transport by "Dial-A-Bus" (a hypothetical door-to-door system where the bus is routed by telephone calls of prospective passengers), personal transit and personal capsule, a version of the personal-transit guideway that could serve a central urban area, traveling at a speed of about 15 miles per hour. The second trip is by automobile. The parking and walking time at the end of this trip are not indicated. The relative lengths of the lines are not significant. Boston's transportation was modeled in terms of network flow.

that metropolitan Boston planned to build by 1975, it turned out, would bring about some improvement in speed over 1963 (to 10 miles per hour for public transit and 20.7 miles per hour for private automobiles) and somewhat reduce the crush of automobile traffic in the downtown streets. Replacement of buses by personal capsules for short-distance travel downtown would produce modest additional improvements, at a small net reduction in transit cost. In order to see what effects might result if public transit were considerably speeded up by improvements in the conventional system, we fed into the program an arbitrary assumption of a 50 percent rise in speed (disregarding the cost). On this assumption (which represents the maximum speedup that is likely to be attained on the basis of any current proposal) we found that automobile travel also would speed up substantially, because more people would be drawn to public trans-

portation and congestion on the freeways and in the streets would be relieved. The percentage increase in the use of public transit was only moderate, however, which suggests that an investment in speeding up conventional public facilities will not pay for itself unless it can be done very cheaply.

When we came to testing systems incorporating a network of personal transit by means of guideways, we saw really striking improvements in service. Speeds took a jump, particularly in the public mode, and more riders were attracted to public transportation. Had our calculations taken into account the comfort and privacy that personal transit offers in relation to conventional transit, the fraction of public-mode travelers would doubtless have been considerably higher. Furthermore, the introduction of a guideway network reduced the intrusion of vehicles and congestion in the downtown streets to less than half the 1963

level. Installation of a 400-mile network for personal transit in the Boston area would speed up travel to an average of 24.6 miles per hour in public facilities and 25.7 miles per hour in private automobiles, and 38 percent of the city's travelers (in 1975) would use public transit. If the network were extended to 600 miles and provided for the transport of automobiles as well as transit cars on the guideways, the average speeds of travel and the use of public transit would increase still further.

More important than these gains is the great improvement a personal-transit system would provide in mobility for the transportation poor or disadvantaged populations in the city. The 400-mile network we postulated for 1975 would make some 204,000 jobs in outlying areas of the metropolis accessible within half an hour's travel to people living in the city center; at present these

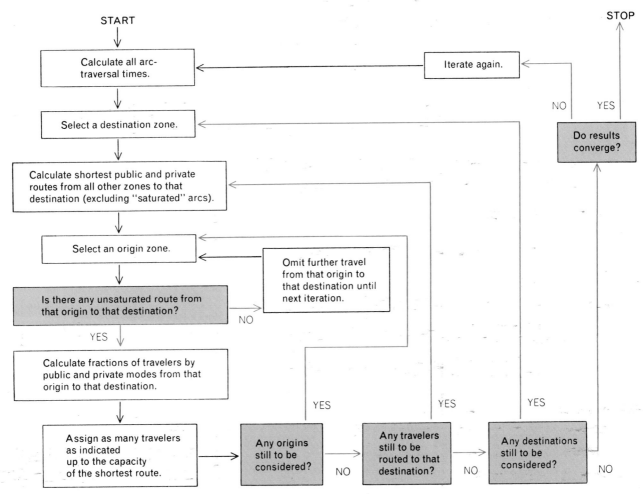

CALCULATION OF NETWORK PERFORMANCE utilized a computer program that employs a series of trials, or iterations, to compute the flow in the network. The program first calculates what the travel time for each arc would be if there were no traffic congestion. After the quickest route to each zone from all the others is calculated, the program introduces, for each route, the complicating factor of "modal split," namely the proportion of people traveling by public mode. If these numbers cannot be handled within the capacities of the shortest routes, the program goes back and computes the next-shortest routes. After the first iteration the program computes travel times as they are influenced by the flow assigned on earlier iterations. The exclusion of "saturated" arcs is an artifice to keep all the flow from following a few routes on early iterations. It speeds the convergence of the iteration process.

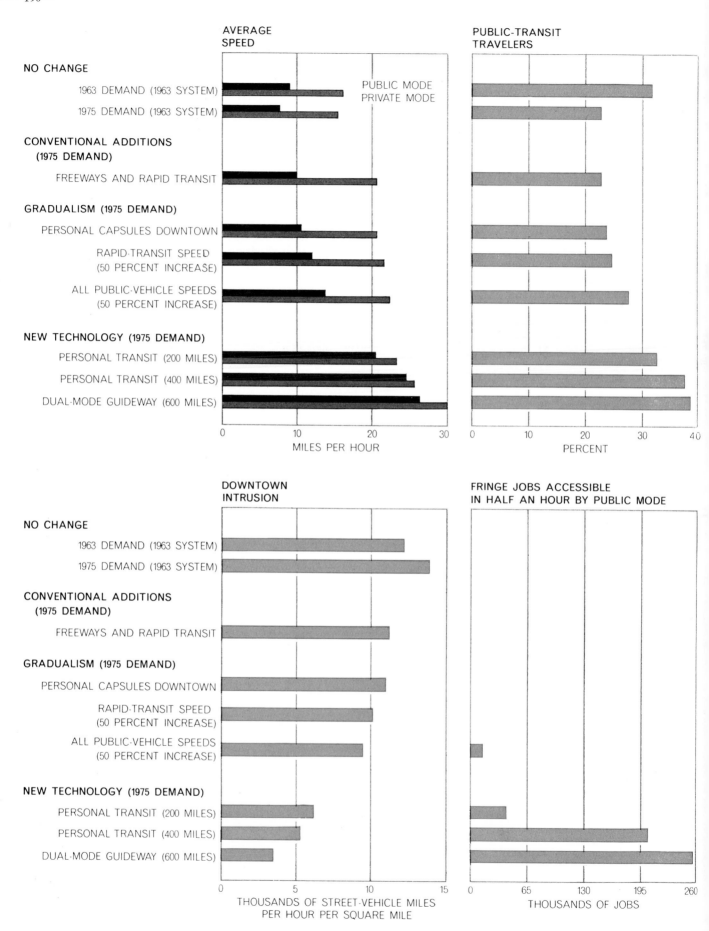

AVERAGE
SPEED

PUBLIC-TRANSIT
TRAVELERS

NO CHANGE

1963 DEMAND (1963 SYSTEM)

PUBLIC MODE
PRIVATE MODE

1975 DEMAND (1963 SYSTEM)

CONVENTIONAL ADDITIONS
(1975 DEMAND)

FREEWAYS AND RAPID TRANSIT

GRADUALISM (1975 DEMAND)

PERSONAL CAPSULES DOWNTOWN

RAPID-TRANSIT SPEED
(50 PERCENT INCREASE)

ALL PUBLIC-VEHICLE SPEEDS
(50 PERCENT INCREASE)

NEW TECHNOLOGY (1975 DEMAND)

PERSONAL TRANSIT (200 MILES)

PERSONAL TRANSIT (400 MILES)

DUAL-MODE GUIDEWAY (600 MILES)

0   10   20   30
MILES PER HOUR

0   10   20   30   40
PERCENT

DOWNTOWN
INTRUSION

FRINGE JOBS ACCESSIBLE
IN HALF AN HOUR BY PUBLIC MODE

NO CHANGE

1963 DEMAND (1963 SYSTEM)

1975 DEMAND (1963 SYSTEM)

CONVENTIONAL ADDITIONS
(1975 DEMAND)

FREEWAYS AND RAPID TRANSIT

GRADUALISM (1975 DEMAND)

PERSONAL CAPSULES DOWNTOWN

RAPID-TRANSIT SPEED
(50 PERCENT INCREASE)

ALL PUBLIC-VEHICLE SPEEDS
(50 PERCENT INCREASE)

NEW TECHNOLOGY (1975 DEMAND)

PERSONAL TRANSIT (200 MILES)

PERSONAL TRANSIT (400 MILES)

DUAL-MODE GUIDEWAY (600 MILES)

0   5   10   15
THOUSANDS OF STREET-VEHICLE MILES
PER HOUR PER SQUARE MILE

0   65   130   195   260
THOUSANDS OF JOBS

PERFORMANCE MEASURES from the authors' cost-benefit summary show how different transportation systems behaved in the case of the Boston model. All figures except public-mode cost refer to travel at a peak hour. In the full cost-benefit summary there

PUBLIC-MODE
COST

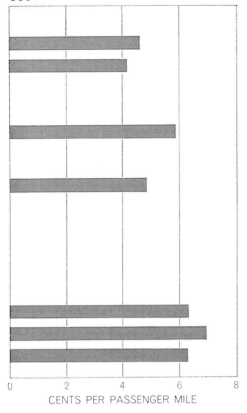

0   2   4   6   8
CENTS PER PASSENGER MILE

DOWNTOWN ACCESS
IN HALF AN HOUR BY PUBLIC MODE

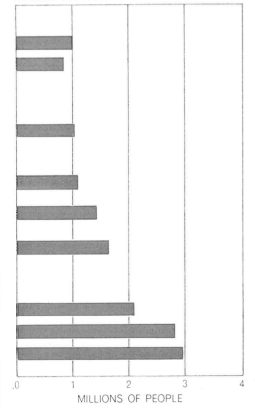

.0   1   2   3   4
MILLIONS OF PEOPLE

were 229 performance measures. The term
"downtown intrusion" refers to automobiles.

job areas are beyond that range of accessibility. The system would also make the downtown area, the airport, universities and hospitals quickly accessible even in peak hours to millions of people in the suburbs. Our full "cost-benefit" survey of the system indicated other benefits such as reductions of traffic accidents and air pollution.

In general, the results of our analysis made clear that, even with the most optimistic view of what might be achieved through improvement of the existing methods of transportation, such improvement could not satisfy the real needs of our cities in terms of service. Automobiles, even if totally redesigned for safety and smog-free steam propulsion, have the irremediable drawbacks that they must be driven by the user and are unavailable to a substantial percentage of the population. Buses and trains, however fast, comfortable and well scheduled, are unavoidably limited in average speed by the necessity of making frequent stops along the line to let riders on or off. All in all, our study suggested strongly that the course of gradualism is not enough: at best it is merely an expensive palliative for the transportation ailments of the cities.

On the other hand, our tests of the new-technology approach, particularly the personal-transit type of system, showed that it could provide really dramatic improvements in service. The personal-transit system would offer city dwellers a degree of convenience that is not now available even to those who drive their own cars. The city and its suburbs could be linked together in a way that would bring new freedoms and amenities to urban living—for the ghetto dweller now trapped in the city's deteriorating core as well as for the automobile-enslaved suburban housewife.

One must take account of the probability that drastic alteration of a city's transportation will bring about changes in the structural pattern of the city itself. We tested certain structural variations, such as concentration of the city population in a few dense nuclei, and found that the personal-transit system still offered striking advantages.

How would a personal-transit system compare with improvement of the existing system in the matter of financial cost? In Boston the cost of building and operating a personal-transit system would be somewhat more expensive per passenger-mile than a conventional rapid transit even if the city built an entirely new subway system from scratch. Remember, however, that we are talking about a personal-transit network of 400 miles, whereas Boston's rail system with its planned extensions by 1975 will consist of only 62 route-miles. Nevertheless, Boston and other cities that already have rather extensive rail rapid-transit systems may well think twice before scrapping the existing system to replace it with personal transit, even though personal transit offers benefits that rail rapid transit cannot approach.

For most of our large cities, now lacking rapid transit, personal transit looks like a much better bet than a subway. In automobile-oriented Houston, for example, personal transit in our calculations came out far cheaper than rail rapid transit, as well as far more effective. In such a city personal transit is clearly a best buy.

For smaller cities such as Tucson or New Haven personal transit looks less attractive. Because of their limited extent and lower density of population (and consequently smaller use of the system) the cost of personal transit per passenger-mile would be about three times the cost for a large city. It appears that a personal-transit system (as well as rail rapid transit, for that matter) would be too costly for cities with a population of less than half a million. Such cities, however, do not have to contend with the congestion that is overwhelming large cities.

To sum up, the installation of a personal-transit system, perhaps serviced by Dial-A Bus feeders (the performance of such vehicles is not yet predictable), and designed from the start for eventual expansion to dual-mode service, seems well worth considering for the immediate future of many U.S. cities. We estimate that a personal-transit system could be developed and tested on a fairly large scale within five years at a cost of about $100 million. Compared with the cost of any sizable subway this development cost is insignificant. (A rail rapid-transit system recently proposed for Los Angeles, and rejected by the voters, would have cost about $2.5 billion.)

On the basis of the reports HUD has received from the groups it commissioned to study the urban transportation problem the department has submitted a number of recommendations to Congress, giving prominence to the proposed systems for personal transit, dual-mode transit and Dial-A-Bus. If the funds for development of these systems were made available immediately, the systems could be ready for installation in cities five years hence. Our study has convinced us that no time should be lost in proceeding with these developments.

19

COMPUTER EXPERIMENTS IN FLUID DYNAMICS

F. H. HARLOW AND J. E. FROMM
March, 1965

The natural philosophers of ancient Greece liked to do experiments in their heads. Centuries later Galileo developed the "thought" experiment into a fruitful method of inquiry and in our own time the method appealed strongly to such men as Albert Einstein and Enrico Fermi. Now the arrival of the modern electronic computer has made the method immensely more powerful and versatile. The computer makes it possible to simulate nature with numerical models and to investigate it in ways that have never been practicable before. Physical processes of enormous complexity are being examined minutely and with considerable realism. New hypotheses are being proved true or false. In physics, engineering, economics and even anthropology the computer has become a revolutionary tool.

One of the great attractions of experiment by computer is that it can avoid some of the uncertainties of measurement. Moreover, it provides a technique that can be classed as both theoretical and experimental. It is theoretical because it deals with abstract (that is, mathematical) statements of how things relate to one another. It is experimental because the computer is given only data specifying the initial state of a system and a set of rules for calculating its state at some time in the future. The computer worker has no more idea how this future state will unfold than has the traditional worker who conducts a comparable experiment in an actual laboratory. To demonstrate the power of computer experiments we have chosen a single example involving the dynamic behavior of fluids. The particular experiment is a study of the flow of air past a rectangular rod.

At first thought the use of a computer for calculating this flow may seem to be a needlessly roundabout procedure.

Would it not be simpler and more enlightening to put the rod in a wind tunnel and observe how air containing filaments of smoke flows around it? Actually it would not. For many of the questions to be investigated the physical experiment would be more complicated and costly, and it would not provide as much information as the experiment by computer.

For an example one can point to the problem of redesigning the Tacoma Narrows Bridge after it had been shaken to pieces by wind-induced vibrations soon after it was built. For the rebuilding of the bridge many elaborate models

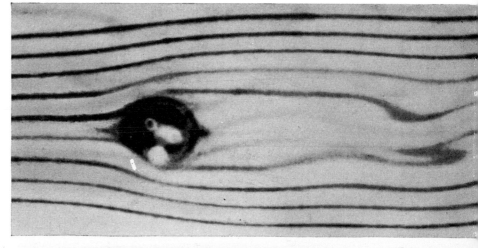

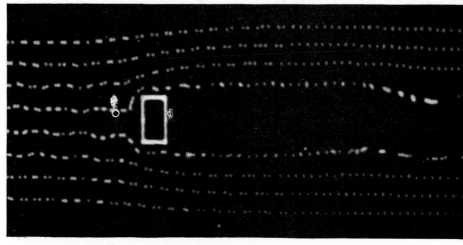

VORTEX EXPERIMENT with a fluid is compared with a similar computer experiment using a mathematical model. In a tank dark lines of dye within a moving body of water (*top*) flow past a cylindrical obstacle; the water's velocity is great enough to disrupt lami-

were made and tested again and again before a safe design was finally developed. Without doubt much of the cost and time spent on the problem could have been saved by computer calculations if the computers and appropriate numerical techniques had then been available. Experiments with numerical models can show the interaction of winds and a bridge in detail and produce answers in far less time than it takes to prepare a physical experiment. The Soviet physicist A. A. Dorodnitsyn has remarked about such problems that computer calculation "can give a solution that is not only more rapid and cheaper but also more accurate" than the physical experiment itself.

Experimentation by computer also allows the investigation of many phenomena that are either inaccessible to direct study or involve factors that cannot be measured accurately. In the flow problem that we shall discuss, for example, it is difficult to measure directly in a wind tunnel the temperature distribution in the complicated downstream wake. Computer experiments, however, can yield a reliable description of the temperature distribution.

Another benefit of a computer experiment is that it usually affords far better control of the experimental conditions than is possible in a physical experiment. In wind tunnel studies, for instance, the experimenter must modify his interpretations to include the consideration of such effects as those due to the compressibility of the working fluid, variations in fluid viscosity and uncertainties in flow velocity. In a computer experiment such properties often can be excluded or included at will. Moreover, the computer program can isolate crucial features for examination, can eliminate irrelevant factors and can often assess the experimental uncertainties.

Finally, and most importantly, experiments by computer provide a test of the applicability of theory to the complicated phenomena under investigation. Do the equations of fluid dynamics really represent the correct theoretical description when applied to phenomena as complicated, say, as the oscillatory flow that develops in the wake of a rectangular rod? For such problems the mathematician would like to obtain what he calls an analytical solution—the kind of exact solution that can be obtained by the processes of mathematical analysis. For problems in fluid dynamics, however, the necessary mathematical techniques for obtaining the complete solution have not yet been developed. The detailed results provided by a computer can actually help in the development of analytical solutions to the basic equations of fluid dynamics. Usually in the mathematical model of a complex problem some of the factors can only be approximated, and obtaining a realistic solution depends on finding out which features are crucial for a reasonable representation. With the help of computer experiments one tries to discover workable approximations that will simplify the mathematics needed to solve complicated problems—in this case a problem in oscillatory fluid flow.

The reader will find the "computer

nar flow and generate a characteristic double row of vortices. In the computer experiment (*bottom*) comparable marker lines are simulated and their motions are recorded on microfilm; although the obstacle is a rectangle rather than a cylinder, the real and model patterns show close agreement. The dye-line experiment was performed by Alexander Thom of the University of Oxford.

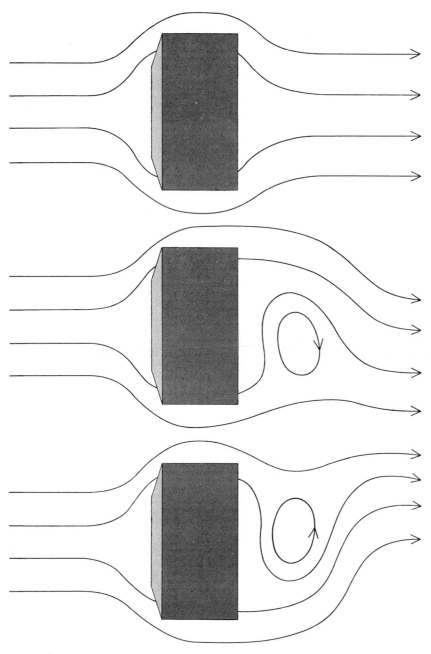

CLASSIC PROBLEM in fluid dynamics is to predict the progression from orderly laminar flow past an obstacle at slow speed (*top illustration*) to total turbulence at high speed. A crucial midpoint in this progression is reached when vortices form alternately at opposite edges of the obstacle (*middle and bottom illustrations*) and then are shed downstream.

rapidly through the air and for the whine of a ship's rigging in the wind. It was resonant vibration produced by the wind that caused the Tacoma Narrows Bridge to break and fall into the bay. As the air speed increases, the vortices in the vortex street become more and more ragged and eventually break up into tiny eddies whose motion is almost entirely random. At this stage fully developed turbulence has been reached.

The known patterns of air motion past an object, then, give us certain definite phenomena to look for in the computer experiments. If the computer reproduces a vortex street and, at a later stage, turbulence, it will show that the theoretical understanding of fluid dynamics is accurate and therefore can be relied on to predict what will happen when a fluid flows past objects of various shapes and at various speeds.

To set up the calculational experiment we must first translate the physical situation into the language of numbers for the computer. For bookkeeping purposes the experimental area in the computer wind tunnel is divided into many square cells, which form the basic computing mesh. A typical mesh requires at least 49 cells in the direction of horizontal flow and 24 cells in the vertical dimension, for a total of 1,176 cells. Each cell must contain two numbers representing the components of average air velocity in two directions, together with other numbers representing such variable quantities as "vorticity," "stream function" and, if heat flow is desired, temperature as well. Finally, the computer must be supplied with a set of operating instructions, or "code," that spells out in detail exactly how the computer must manipulate every number in every cell in order to calculate how the flow configuration will change from instant to instant. It can require billions of mathematical operations and anywhere from a few minutes to a few hours of computing time to carry out the calculations needed to represent the flow of air for a time interval of several minutes. In our studies we have used either an IBM 7090 computer or the somewhat faster machine, also built by the International Business Machines Corporation, known as Stretch.

The actual development of a successful code is a time-consuming process and is carried out in three steps. The first involves the testing of detailed numerical methods and is strewn with pitfalls. It is no trick, for example, to invent methods that develop numerical instability: the computer results rapidly

wind tunnel" experiment easier to follow if we consider briefly how a fluid behaves when it flows around a fixed object such as a rectangular rod. At low speed the airflow is smooth and steady, a condition described as laminar flow. At a certain critical speed, which depends on the size of the rod, the laminar flow breaks down. For a rod one inch in height the critical speed in air is about one inch per second; the smaller the rod, the higher the speed at which turbulence begins. If the fluid is more viscous than air, laminar flow is more easily maintained and the critical

speed for turbulence becomes higher.

Above the critical speed the airstream breaks up into vortices that are similar to the small whirlpools seen when a cup of coffee is stirred. These vortices are shed alternately from the top and bottom of the object placed in the airstream. This oscillating wake was first extensively studied by the aerodynamicist Theodor von Kármán and is known as a "von Kármán vortex street." The oscillating wake sends out pulses that react back on the object itself. The vibration so produced is responsible for the sound made by a golf club swung

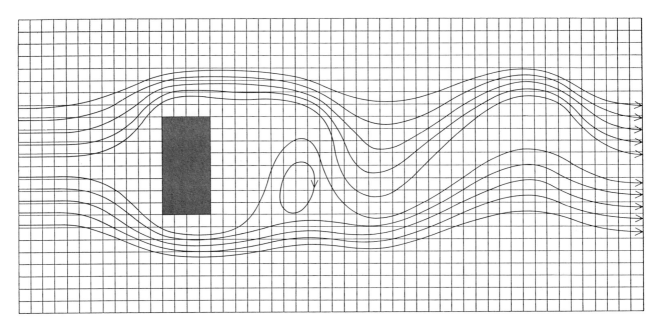

BASIC COMPUTING MESH for a mathematical wind tunnel is a grid of 1,176 individual cells, arrayed in rows 49 cells long and 24 cells wide. The obstacle, twice as high as it is deep, is located 12 cells away from the input flow at the left margin of the mesh. At the start of an experiment each cell is programmed with a minimum of two numbers, which represent the horizontal and vertical components of the average air velocity at that point in space. The cells can also be programmed to contain numerical notations for additional variables such as heat flow, vorticity and stream function. During the run of a calculation the computer must carry out billions of mathematical operations in order to determine how the flow configuration varies. In this example the flow of air past the obstacle has reached the critical speed at which alternating vortices are formed (see *illustration on opposite page*).

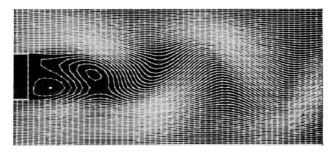

SIMULATED MOTION OF AIR past an obstacle (*extreme left*) that is stationary with respect to the observer produces a plot of swirling streamlines. The course of each line parallels the direction of the adjacent air current's flow; the narrower the spacing between lines, the higher the speed. This is one of four plots that show different data from the same instant in a single experiment.

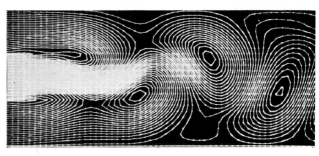

SIMULATED MOTION OF OBSTACLE through a body of still air, although mathematically identical with the situation illustrated at the left, produces a quite different streamline plot. In this instance the air mass rather than the obstacle is stationary with respect to the observer; the pattern of vortices traced by the streamlines resembles the turbulence in the wake of a passing ship.

STREAK-LINE PLOT is a third kind of configuration possible in computer experiments. In this case, indicator numbers that do not play any part in the flow calculations have been inserted in four cells of the computer mesh at the rear of the obstacle. These numbers become "computational particles" that trace out the downwind eddies in streaks, as do smoke filaments in a wind tunnel.

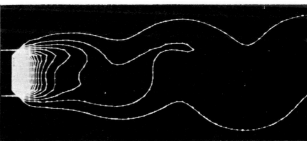

ISOTHERM PLOT provides a fourth example of the data that can be obtained by means of computer experiments. A set of temperature values simulating a heated body has been inserted in the eight cells along the rear of the obstacle. As the flow of air passes downwind the computer calculates the rate at which the heat is conducted; the lines connect points of equal reduction in temperature.

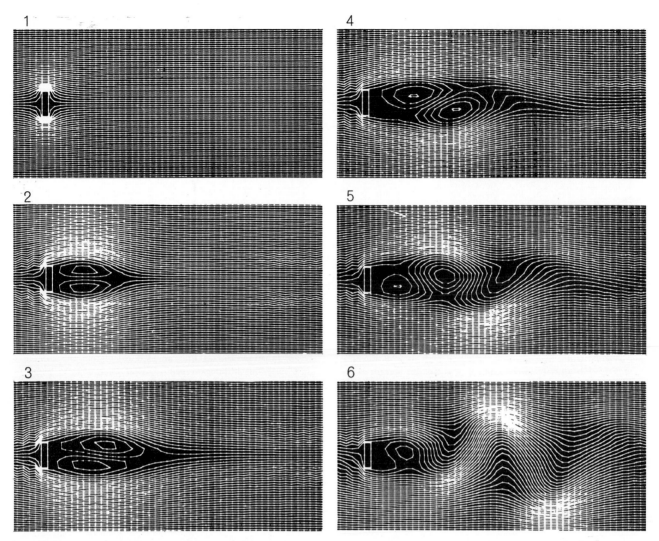

DEVELOPMENT OF A VORTEX STREET is documented in six consecutive streamline plots (*left and center illustrations, top to bottom*). The laminar flow at the outset (*1*) quickly changes to a stable pair of eddies behind the obstacle (*2*). The stability ends when one or another of the eddies begins to grow. The larger eddy shifts position both downstream and toward the center line, thus pushing the smaller, upstream eddy out of its normal position (*3 and 4*). The upstream eddy is now exposed to acceleration both by

run askew and lead to complete nonsense. Like physical experiments, computer experiments are also subject to interference by gremlins. Just as the vibration of a motor may produce extraneous turbulence in a wind tunnel, so the numerical approximations fed into a computer may lead to equally unwanted "truncation turbulence."

The second step is to prepare a full-scale code. For our problem in fluid dynamics this required many months, most of them consumed by "debugging," or ferreting out errors in, the step-by-step instructions. Such a code is written with sufficient generality so that it can be used to solve a wide variety of roughly similar problems. Thus

a good code can be used for years and will often be a source of inspiration for workers in other laboratories.

The third step is to formulate the code in terms of a specific problem. In our oscillating-wake study an important part of the formulation was to determine the "initial" and "boundary" conditions. The initial condition describes the state

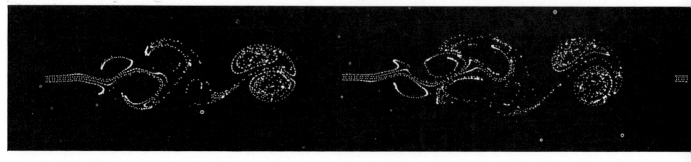

SEQUENCE OF STREAK LINES traces the transformation of a jet of air as turbulence progressively increases (*four steps from left to right*). In this experiment computational particles are introduced through a single cell (*horizontal streaks*), as though squirting

a

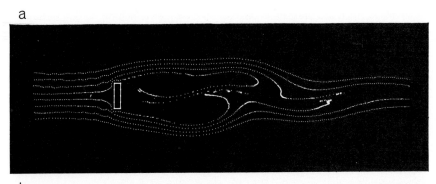

b

c

the main stream and by the reverse currents of the downstream eddy (4) and begins to grow in its turn. Soon the growing upstream eddy pinches off the downstream one, which is then shed as a vortex while a new eddy forms behind the obstacle (5 and 6). The streak-line plots ("a," "b" and "c" at right) outline the formation of the vortices during stages 4, 5 and 6.

into the computing region in a way that created a minimum of mathematical disturbance.

The computing process itself can be compared to the making of a motion picture. Starting with the initial conditions prescribed for each of the 1,176 cells in "frame" No. 1, the computer follows the coded instructions to determine the conditions in each cell a brief instant of time later, thereby producing frame No. 2 of the film. Each successive frame is similarly generated on the basis of numerical data computed for the preceding frame. The fastest computer available to us, Stretch, can generate about 10 frames a minute. When the calculation has proceeded far enough, the results are gathered up for study.

The computer's results can be presented in any of several different forms. One form of print-out consists of all the numbers describing the flow in each frame. Usually this form of print-out is restricted to samplings taken at selected intervals, because the complete data for every one of the hundreds or thousands of cycles in an experiment would be far too much for an analyst to digest, to say nothing of storing the reams of paper. Sometimes the computer is programmed to print certain calculations that supply particular points of information, such as the amount of air drag caused by the obstacle at specific wind speeds. The most useful and popular type of print-out, however, is the actual plotting of the flow in pictorial form.

The computer itself can generate plots of the flow configurations and put them on film by means of a microfilm recorder. Several selected frames from such recordings, exactly as they came from the computer, are among the illustrations on this page and preceding pages of this article. The sequence of all the frames of an experiment, combined in a film strip and run through a motion-

of the air at the start of the computation. We could have assumed, for example, that the air was at rest, corresponding to the condition in a real wind tunnel before the fan is turned on. We found that it was simpler, however, to start with the fluid behaving as if it were flowing past the rod in a simple laminar manner without viscosity.

The boundary conditions refer to what is happening at the edges of the computational mesh. Our decision was to have the top and bottom edges represent the walls of the wind tunnel and to have the left edge represent an air input of uniform flow. The right edge gave us more trouble, but we finally arranged for the fluid to flow out and back

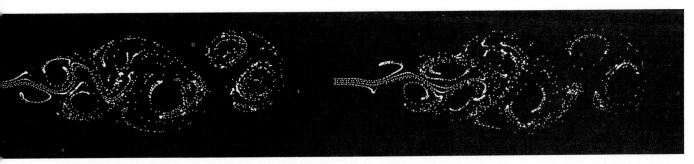

colored water into a clear tank. The jet of air is unstable and soon breaks into expanding, irregular vortices like those exhibited by a

plume of smoke. Similar but far more complex experiments can be used to test theories about aircraft jet engine noise suppression.

picture projector, gives a very vivid picture of the development of vortices and other features as a fluid flows around an obstacle.

From the numbers describing the flow in each cell of the computing mesh, the computer generates streamlines that show both the direction and the speed of flow throughout the space. The speed is indicated by the spacing between the streamlines: where the lines are close together the flow is fast; where they are farther apart the flow is slower. The computer can show the streamline patterns in either of two ways: as if a camera were photographing a stream of air flowing past it or as if the camera were moving along with the stream. The latter view shows the pattern of vortices in clear detail.

The computer can even simulate the motion of markers often used to make flow visible, such as filaments of smoke in air or of dye in water. In the computer the markers consist of "computational particles." At certain desired points in the computation these particles are thrown in (the magic of the computer allows their creation anywhere at will) and thereafter they are carried along wherever the flow of air goes. Their paths of motion produce lines called streak lines. The streak lines generated by the computer give a remarkably faithful impression of the behavior of smoke or dye filaments. Perhaps the most striking of these computer constructions is the configuration of streak lines emerging from a jet: it looks like a filament of cigarette smoke.

Usually the computer is programmed to furnish several different configuration plots, showing features of the flow from various points of view. These are by no means merely an interesting album of pictures. They show the qualitative features of the development of the flow and provide precise quantitative information about the flow at every point. In many cases the computer reveals important details that would be extremely difficult to obtain from physical experiments.

The example we have described of a computer technique for investigating fluid flow is only one of many successful efforts that have been made to carry out complex experiments by computer. Other workers have used computers to tell in detail what is going on inside a nuclear reactor and to assess in an instant the progress of a rocket soaring into space. Tomorrow the computer may give accurate forecasts of the weather, of the future of the economy and of the state of man's health.

20

CHROMOSOME ANALYSIS BY COMPUTER

R. S. LEDLEY AND F. H. RUDDLE
April, 1966

In recent years a number of human disorders have been found to be related to abnormalities in the chromosomes, the bodies in the living cell that contain the genetic material. Accordingly many medical institutions have undertaken programs of examining in the microscope the chromosomes of samples of tissue taken from numerous patients. Such programs have been limited by the fact that the examination of chromosomes takes time and calls for individuals who have been trained in recognizing chromosomal abnormalities. An obvious way to circumvent this limitation is to devise some kind of machine that can examine the chromosomes automatically, although of course it is less obvious how the machine would work. Such a machine, the central component of which is an electronic computer, has now been assembled and successfully operated.

Human somatic cells (as distinguished from sperm or egg cells) normally contain 46 chromosomes. The chromosomes can most conveniently be examined in the white cells of the blood, which are readily available in a blood sample. (Mature red blood cells contain no chromosomes.) After the white cells have been segregated, however, they must be kept alive in tissue culture and induced to undergo mitosis, or to divide; it is only during mitosis that chromosomes and their abnormalities are clearly visible. Treating the cells with the drug colchicine halts mitosis exactly at metaphase—the stage of somatic-cell division in which each chromosome has divided into two mirror-image halves lying side by side and connected at one point called the centromere. The cell preparation is now treated with a dilute salt solution, which causes the cells to swell and the chromosomes to move apart.

Finally the cells are fixed and stained, so that the chromosomes can be observed and photographed through the microscope [*see upper illustration on page 200*].

For purposes of analysis a photomicrograph must be made and enlarged; then the chromosome images are cut out and arranged on a white card in what is called an idiogram. The chromosomes are matched into 22 pairs of homologous, or related, chromosomes, plus the two sex chromosomes. (One member of each pair and one sex chromosome is descended from each parent at the fertilization of the egg.) The pairs are arranged in a standardized order based on size, shape and the ratio of the length of the "arms" on each side of the centromere [*see lower illustration on page 200*]. Only when the cells are thus arranged can abnormalities be readily identified. Even when the abnormality is as gross as the presence of extra chromosomes the idiogram is needed to detect with which normal pair the extra chromosome is associated. Some of the disorders that have been linked with chromosomal abnormalities are Down's syndrome (mongolism), chronic myeloid leukemia, Klinefelter's syndrome (a congenital disorder of males involving infertility) and Turner's syndrome (a congenital disorder of females involving infertility). Also detectable by such analysis is chromosome damage caused by certain substances or by ionizing radiation; accordingly chromosome analysis can play an important role in the screening of foods and drugs and in the evaluation of radiation hazards.

The construction and examination of the idiogram—both of which are time-consuming and somewhat subjective procedures—are eliminated by the automatic regime we shall describe. This means of analysis still requires the collection of blood samples, of course, and the preparation of cells for photomicrography, but the photomicrographs need not be enlarged and the manual analysis need not be made. Instead a series of photomicrographs on a roll of film are "read" directly into the memory unit of a computer by a scanning device called FIDAC (Film Input to Digital Automatic Computer). The computer is programmed to recognize and classify the objects under consideration by doing the same things an investigator would: counting the total number of chromosomes and measuring their lengths, areas and other morphological features. The FIDAC procedure reduces the time required to study the human complement of 46 chromosomes to about 20 seconds; this is some 500 times faster than analysis by visual means.

When a roll of photographic film is ready for examination, it is placed in the film-transport unit of the FIDAC instrument and the "Start" button of the computer is pushed. The computer system—FIDACSYS, a combination of several basic programs for recognizing and analyzing patterns—signals FIDAC to consider the first frame. The instrument scans the photomicrograph and within .3 second transmits a digital image of it into the magnetic-core memory unit of the computer. In this digitalized image the photomicrograph is represented by a rectangular grid of numbers that correspond to the densities of points in a similar grid on the photomicrograph. The numbers on this "gray scale" run from 0 to 6; the number 7 is reserved to denote boundaries during processing. If at this stage the contents of the memory are printed out, they form a rudimentary image of the objects in the photomicrograph [*see illustration on preceding page*].

No significant information is lost in translating the pictorial data into numerical data. The resolution of a good optical microscope at a magnification of 1,000 is .2 micron, that is, .2 micron is the narrowest spacing that can be distinguished between two lines. The FIDAC instrument can sample three picture points within a span of .2 micron on the specimen; in other words, its resolution is comparable to that of the microscope. The instrument has another feature worth mentioning: because it transmits directly ("on line") into the computer's memory, information that would ordinarily be rerecorded onto intermediate magnetic storage tapes can remain instead on the original roll of photomicrographic film for reprocessing whenever it is desired. A 100-foot roll of this 16-millimeter film, containing 4,000 photomicrographs, can fit into a can smaller than four inches in diameter. Recording that much information on magnetic tapes would require more than 50 reels, making a stack more than four feet high.

When the processing of a frame has been completed, the computer program signals FIDAC to advance the film and consider the next frame. If any frame is blank—that is, either 98 percent black or 98 percent white—the program signals FIDAC to move to the next frame. In this way blank frames or leader can be skipped automatically. If the frame is not blank, the computer program establishes a value on the gray scale as a cutoff level between those values that represent points inside the chromosomes and those that represent the background. The task of recognizing patterns in the frames as chromosomes is accomplished by first sweeping a programmable "bug," or detecting pointer, in a horizontal raster pattern to find points with a gray value greater than the cutoff level. The bug then traces around the boundary of each object, and every number in the original digital representation of the boundary that has a value just above the cutoff level is replaced by 7. The silhouette that is formed is now automatically examined to determine if it has the most obvious feature of a chromosome: arms originating at a centromere. If the silhouette does not meet this criterion, it is eliminated from further analysis.

When all the chromosomes in a frame have been silhouetted, the bug will have reached the lower right-hand corner of the frame. At this point the machine evaluates the contents of the frame. The chromosomes are counted and their total length is computed, so that the length of individual chromosomes can be considered as a fraction of the total

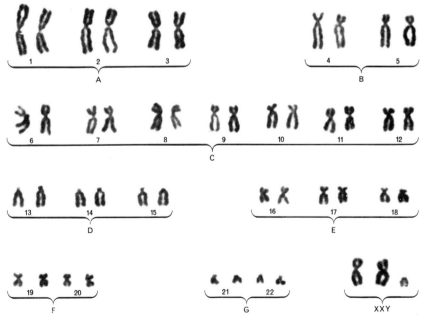

PHOTOMICROGRAPH OF CHROMOSOMES from the white blood cell of a man reveals an abnormal total of 47 (one too many). It is impossible to determine which one is in excess until the chromosomes are reassembled into a standard classification called an idiogram.

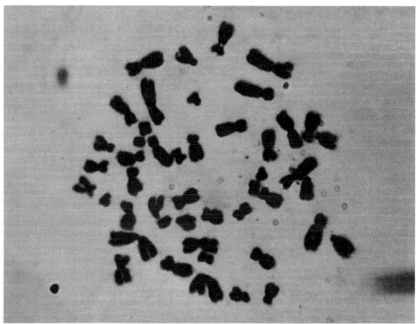

IDIOGRAM of a complement of human chromosomes reveals an abnormality. Chromosomes matched according to size, area and ratio of the lengths of the "arms" on each side of the centromere were put into sequence by Herbert A. Lubs, Jr., of Yale University. The three sex chromosomes at right of bottom row (normal men have one X and one Y sex chromosome) provide evidence of Klinefelter's syndrome, a disorder of males involving infertility.

IMAGES OF CHROMOSOMES appear as grid of numerals in computer print-out that provides a rudimentary picture of a photomicrograph. Details of the micrograph were conveyed to memory unit of the computer by a scanning device called FIDAC. Numerals from 0 to 6 on a gray scale describe the darkness of corresponding points on micrograph, made during phase of cell division at which a chromosome consists of two strands (chromatids) connected in one area (the centromere). Dots correspond to the background.

length of the chromosomes in the frame. Homologous chromosomes are matched according to area, length and arm-length ratio, and the pairs are classified according to the standardized sequence of the idiogram. When the analysis of a frame is finished, the FIDAC instrument is instructed to move to the next frame and the process is repeated. After a predetermined number of frames have been processed the statistics of all the photomicrographs on the roll of film are automatically collated and analyzed.

Let us consider more closely the essential step in this procedure: the recognition and analysis of individual chromosomes. The location of anything encountered by the bug—the boundary of an object, for example—can be given in a Cartesian-coordinate system mapping the entire frame. Thus when the bug first meets an object, its point of contact can be located on a grid in terms of horizontal and vertical positions denoted by X and Y coordinates. The bug now proceeds along the boundary of the object in a clockwise direction, and points on the boundary are delineated in the same notation. When a certain number of boundary points have been traversed, they are said to constitute a segment. The bug continues to mark boundary points and segments until it returns to the original point of contact; it is now ready to search for a "next object."

The computer program characterizes the individual segments in terms of their direction and curvature. This involves several measurements. First the center point of a segment is ascertained. The arc of the segment reached by moving clockwise from the center point is called the leading half; the arc reached by moving counterclockwise, the trailing half. A vector arrow is drawn in each half; the length of the segment is chosen as a distance short enough so that the angle between the leading and the trailing vector will be an approximation of the segment's curvature. The arrow that is the vector sum of the leading and trailing vectors is approximately the tangent to the segment at its center point and so provides a measure of the direction of the segment.

In determining the curvature of the segments the FIDAC system uses a small vocabulary of 13 terms to describe degrees of curvature. For purposes of explanation let us consider a vocabulary of four terms: a fairly straight segment is called Type O; a clockwise curve, Type E; a slight counterclockwise curve, Type

COMPUTER AND SCANNING DEVICE used by the authors are located at the Goddard Space Flight Center outside Washington, D.C. The IBM 7094 computer (*foreground*) receives descriptions of photomicrographs of chromosomes from the FIDAC scanner (*background*), on the basis of which it counts, analyzes and collates data on the chromosomes.

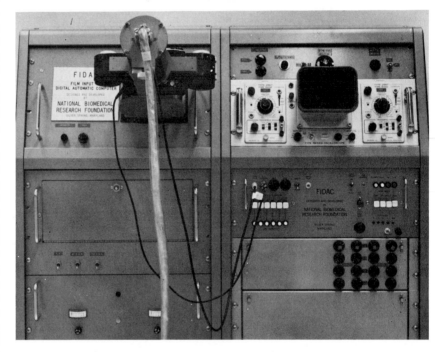

FIDAC INSTRUMENT is named for its function: "Film Input to Digital Automatic Computer." A roll of film containing a great many photomicrographs of chromosomes is put into the film transport unit at top left (*behind the cylindrical photomultiplier*). A detailed description of each micrograph is transmitted by FIDAC to the memory unit of the computer. A video amplifier displays the micrograph being scanned on the small screen at top right.

V, and a pronounced counterclockwise curve, Type Y. By combining such terms the complete outline of a chromosome can be described.

The program by which the computer "builds up" the shape of a chromosome from combinations of curve types is relatively simple in conception. One arm of a chromosome, for example, might have Type O curves on its sides and a Type E curve at its end; between this arm and another on the same chromosome there would be a Type Y curve. The programmer's role is to set forth,

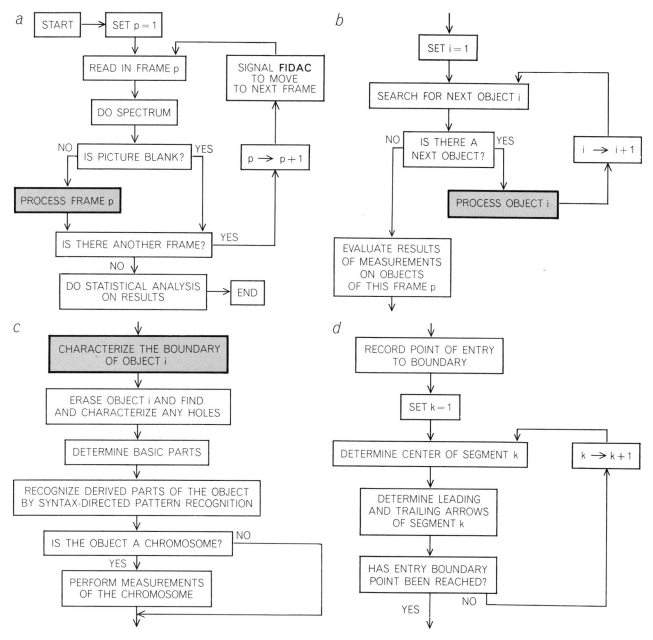

STEPS PERFORMED BY COMPUTER in examining photomicrographs of chromosomes are presented on four levels of detail. The overall procedure (a) entails advancing the roll of photomicrographic film, instructing FIDAC to "read" the image of a frame into the computer's memory unit, computing the spectrum of the image, processing the frame if it is not blank, again advancing the film and finally, when the roll is finished, collating data pertaining to all the photomicrographs that have been inspected. The key step

in the sequence is the processing of a frame (b), which involves a search for individual objects. The boundary of each object is considered (c) in terms of the segments that comprise it. The curvature and directionality of each segment are analyzed (d) and the segments are defined as "curve types." Certain sequences of curve types are recognized by the program as arms or other parts of chromosomes. (This is called "syntax-directed pattern recognition.") An object composed of such parts is thus identified as a chromosome.

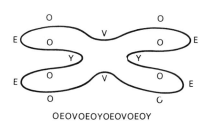

OEOVOEOYOEOVOEOY

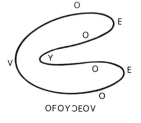

OFOYƆEOV

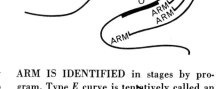

SEGMENTS on boundary of a chromosome are defined as types of curve. O is a fairly straight segment; E, a clockwise curve; V, a slight counterclockwise curve; Y, a sharp counterclockwise curve. Different sequences of curve types represent a four-armed submedian chromosome (left) and a teleocentric chromosome (right) in the computer program.

ARM IS IDENTIFIED in stages by program. Type E curve is tentatively called an arm (notation outside brackets). Scan showing it between O types confirms this fact.

in the notation of symbolic logic, a recursive definition (one that can be used repetitively in the program) by which a "derived part" such as an arm can be recognized from its component curves [*see bottom illustrations on preceding page*]. The process is then taken up by an element of FIDACSYS called the mobilizer, which is analogous to the translator program for a computer language. The mobilizer operates on a list of terms describing the parts of a particular object; by using a general syntactical description of various kinds of chromosome it determines whether or not an object is a chromosome and, if so, what type of chromosome it is. This technique, called syntax-directed pattern recognition, was developed by one of the authors (Ledley) at the National Biomedical Research Foundation in Silver Spring, Md.

The results of each step in the analytic process can be printed out by the computer. First come data describing the coordinates of the chromosome's center of gravity, its area and its perimeter. The lengths of the arms are given and the arm-length ratio is computed by comparing the average length of the two long arms to the overall length of the chromosome [*see illustration at right*]. Next come the coordinates locating the centers of the boundary segments and designations describing the curvature of these "basic parts." FIDACSYS then prints out the derived parts, giving coordinates for the positions of the arms and the centromere. In the print-outs the code letter *E* is placed at points representing the ends of the arms, and the letter *C* at the points marking the centromere. On the basis of all these data an automatic plotting device makes a tracing of all the chromosomes in the original photomicrograph. The plotter also numbers the chromosomes and draws a line to indicate their centromeres [*see illustration on next page*].

There is still another way in which a computer programmed by FIDACSYS translates numerical data back into graphic form: the final print-out consists of a schematic idiogram of the complement of chromosomes under inspection. To evaluate the accuracy of chromosome analysis by computer we must ask: How does the automatic idiogram compare with one based on visual observation and measurement? Assessments made by the authors indicate that the figures for areas and arm lengths worked out by computer are sufficiently precise. There is reason to

```
FOUR-ARMED CHROMOSOME FOUND WITH CENTER OF GRAVITY AT X = 404, Y = 116.

          AREA = 289.0, PERIMETER =  89.2.

          LENGTHS OF FIRST ARM PAIR IDENTIFIED ARE  17.5 AND 16.3.
          LENGTHS OF SECOND ARM PAIR IDENTIFIED ARE  9.6 AND 10.0.

          ARM-LENGTH RATIO = 0.645

          OVERALL LENGTH =  26.2

ARM-END COORDINATES,

                    1ST ARM, X = 396, Y = 106
                    2ND ARM, X = 408, Y = 105
                    3RD ARM, X = 412, Y = 126
                    4TH ARM, X = 399, Y = 129

THE CENTROMERES ARE LOCATED AT X = 407, Y = 120, AND AT X = 403, Y = 122

BASIC PARTS LIST
  OU   OC   CY   OB   OB   OB   OV   OO   OF   OC   OY   OA   OA   OD   OE   OU   CA   OC   OB

DERIVED PARTS LIST
  95   93   95   90   72   93   95   90   72   93   95   93   93   90   72   95   93   90   72
```

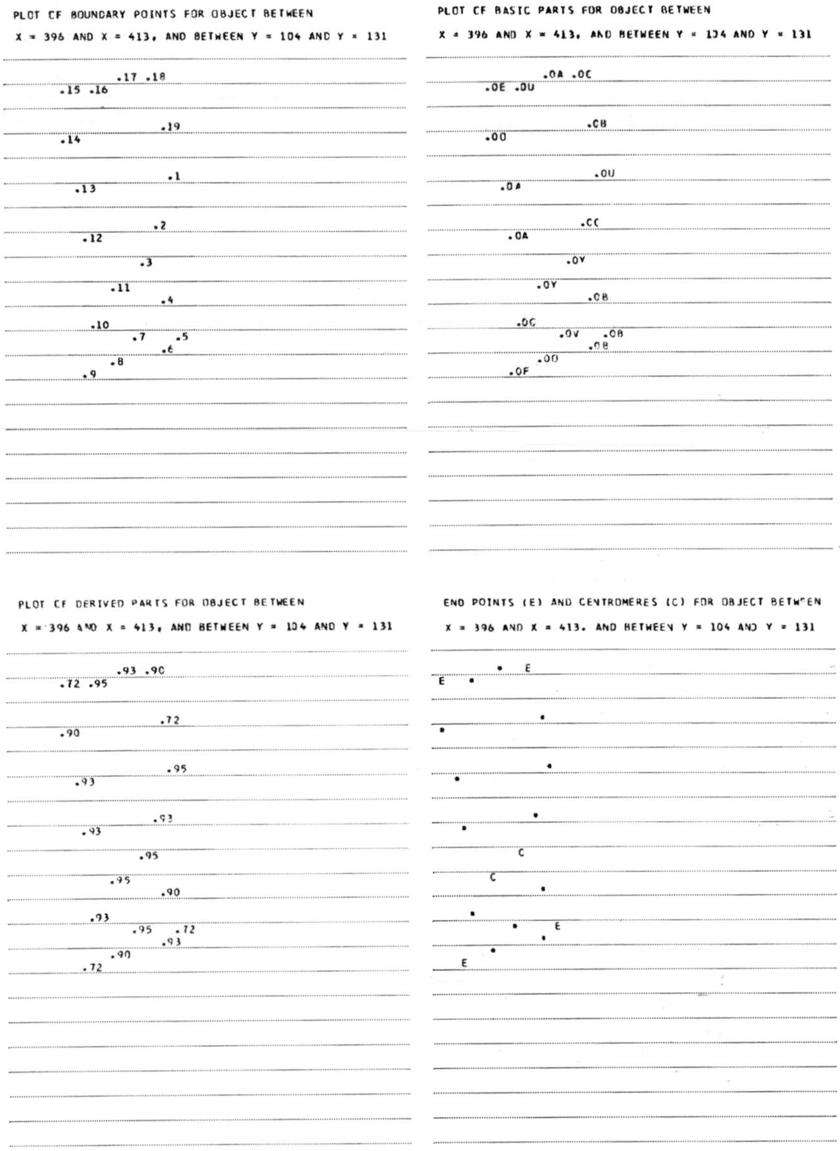

INTERMEDIATE PRINT-OUTS from computer examining chromosomes by syntax-directed pattern recognition are assembled. At top are data giving location and size of chromosome and its arm-length ratio; in middle, plots of boundary points and segments ("Basic parts"); at bottom, plots with labels for ends of arms and centromere ("Derived parts").

| CHROMOSOME ANALYSIS SUMMARY | | | | | | | | | | | | |
FR NO	CH NO	T	CENTER GRAVITY	PERI METER	OVRALL LENGTH	2 LONG LENGTHS	2 SHORT LENGTHS	LENGTH RATIO	AREA	LONG AREA	SHORT AREA	AREA RATIO
1	1	C	328, 37	100.3	34.7	26.2,26.5	7.9, 8.6	.761	499.	390.	105.	.788
1	2	A	321, 70	183.6	73.3	38.5,37.9	34.9,35.2	.522	1013.	512.	489.	.512
1	3	C	245, 69	89.5	28.8	19.2,19.5	8.6,10.3	.673	434.	303.	128.	.703
1	4	D	416, 87	59.7	18.9	8.4,10.9	8.1,10.3	.511	219.	110.	110.	.501
1	5	C	259, 90	81.2	29.0	24.9,24.7	3.8, 4.5	.856	378.	357.	35.	.910
1	6	C	288,113	68.5	24.4	19.5,19.0	5.3, 5.0	.788	295.	235.	56.	.808
1	7	D	338,134	53.5	16.1	8.6, 8.6	7.3, 7.8	.533	171.	93.	76.	.549
1	8	B	220,156	112.3	40.5	24.7,23.8	16.4,16.1	.598	572.	324.	242.	.572
1	9	D	248,146	64.5	20.1	12.0,10.8	8.9, 8.5	.568	240.	143.	100.	.589
1	10	C	441,151	80.7	28.2	21.0,19.4	8.2, 7.8	.716	397.	293.	97.	.750
1	11	A	427,183	199.7	78.7	42.3,40.9	37.5,36.7	.529	1114.	591.	499.	.542
1	12	D	208,184	49.5	15.6	8.7, 7.5	7.6, 7.4	.520	153.	79.	72.	.521
1	13	B	304,190	117.6	41.0	25.2,21.5	20.0,15.3	.570	531.	295.	237.	.555
1	14	B	356,208	99.2	32.1	18.5,18.7	12.7,14.2	.580	451.	246.	205.	.545
1	15	D	326,215	63.6	19.8	11.9,11.0	9.1, 7.5	.580	219.	128.	87.	.596
1	16	D	265,264	51.7	16.5	8.7, 9.2	7.9, 7.1	.544	154.	81.	69.	.540
1	17	B	214,275	90.9	30.5	19.1,18.7	12.0,11.2	.619	382.	253.	125.	.669
1	18	C	442,274	76.5	24.7	21.0,18.5	5.3, 4.6	.799	351.	277.	64.	.813
1	19	A	250,307	161.0	59.7	32.4,32.0	28.0,26.9	.540	895.	450.	426.	.514
1	20	C	285,305	71.6	23.9	23.2,21.6	1.5, 1.5	.937	301.	297.	7.	.977
1	21	C	366,318	90.9	30.2	22.0,22.4	8.9, 7.1	.735	382.	310.	69.	.818
1	22	A	303,356	203.2	83.0	45.4,46.0	36.5,38.2	.550	1139.	592.	550.	.518
1	23	B	356,394	120.5	39.3	23.5,19.9	20.5,14.7	.552	596.	318.	262.	.548

hope that analysis by computer will eventually uncover small but important chromosomal abnormalities that have not been discerned by eye. It is known, for example, that one of the chromosomes in the cells of individuals with chronic myeloid leukemia lacks only a small portion of one arm; it is quite likely that other small deletions or additions have been overlooked by investigators and will be revealed by means of the computer.

It can be said with some assurance that the procedure we have described will soon be sufficiently refined and tested for clinical use by physicians who want to examine the chromosomes of a significant number of people. The method will also be available for screening new drugs and biologicals (such as vaccines) for possible chromosomal effects. Moreover, it will now be possible to conduct large-scale studies in such matters as the effects of radiation and aging on chromosomes. The main limitations of the procedure—limits on the speed of the scan and on the number of points that are sampled per picture—are imposed not by the FIDAC device or the basic technique of syntax-directed pattern recognition but by the cycle time and capacity of the memory of the International Business Machines 7094 computer we have been using in our investigations. Newer machines, such as the IBM 360-series computers, will have a larger memory and greater speed, allowing an even faster and more accurate procedure.

It is also safe to predict that methods of automatic analysis closely akin to those described in this article will be employed by biologists and research physicians for tasks other than the study of human chromosomes. There are many branches of biology in which pictorial data have been collected in quantities so large that systematic analysis has heretofore seemed impractical. Examples of such material are sequences of pictures made through the microscope that show the myriad dendritic extensions of nerve cells; electron micrographs of muscle fibers or virus particles; autoradiographs showing the uptake of a tracer element, and X-ray pictures of bone revealing the distribution of calcium. Pictures from these and other categories of material, which describe the structural characteristics of cells in terms of lengths, areas, volumes and densities, can be translated into numerical information. Like photomicrographs of chromosomes, they readily lend themselves to study by computer.

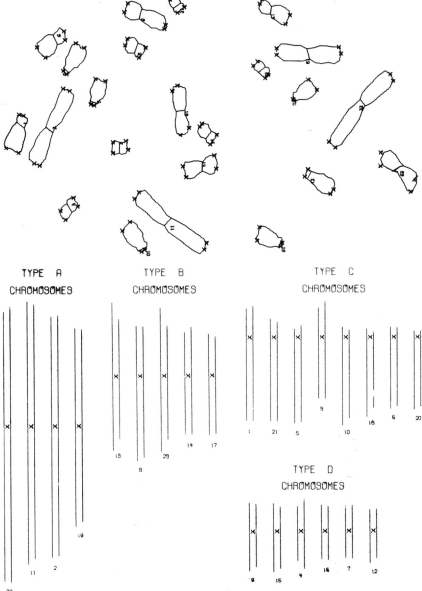

THREE DESCRIPTIONS of the complement of chromosomes of a Chinese hamster were printed by machine. At top are data describing the morphology of each of the animal's 23 chromosomes. In middle is a tracing of the chromosomes, made by an automatic plotting device in which chromosomes are numbered, ends of arms marked and centromeres represented by a line. At bottom is an idiogram of the chromosomes arranged by computer.

21

MAN VIEWED AS A MACHINE

JOHN G. KEMENY
April, 1955

Is man no more than a machine? The question is often debated these days, usually with more vigor than precision. More than most arguments, this one tends to bog down in definition troubles. What is a machine? And what do we mean by "no more than"? If we define "machine" broadly enough, everything is a machine; and if by "more than" we mean that we are human, then machines are clearly less than we are.

In this article we shall frame the question more modestly. Let us ask: What could a machine do as well or better than a man, now or in the future? We shall not concern ourselves with whether a machine could write sonnets or fall in love. Nor shall we waste time laboring the obvious fact that when it comes to muscle, machines are far superior to men. What concerns us here is man as a brain-machine. John von Neumann, the mathematician and designer of computers, not long ago made a detailed comparison of human and mechanical brains in a series of lectures at Princeton University. Much of what follows is based on that discussion.

We are often presented with Utopias in which all the hard work is done by machines and we merely push buttons. This may sound like a lazy dream of heaven, but actually man is even lazier than that. He is no sooner presented with this Utopia than he asks: "Couldn't I build a machine to push the buttons for me?" And indeed he began to invent such machines as early as the 18th century. The flyball governor on a steam engine and the thermostat are elementary brain-machines. They control muscle machines, while spending only negligible amounts of energy themselves. Norbert Wiener compared them to the human nervous system.

Consider the progress of the door. Its earliest form must have been a rock rolled in front of a cave entrance. This may have provided excellent protection, but it must also have made the operation of going in and out of the cave quite difficult. Slowly, as man found better means of defending himself, he made lighter and more manageable doors, until today it is literally child's play to open a door. But even this does not satisfy us. To the delight of millions of railroad passengers, the Pennsylvania Railroad installed electric eyes in its New York terminal. Man need only break the invisible signal connecting the two photoelectric "eyes," and immediately the little brain-machine commands the door to open. This control device needs only a negligible amount of energy, is highly efficient and is vastly faster than any doorman.

The central switchboard in an office is another brain-machine, especially if the office has installed the dial system. Messages are carried swiftly and efficiently to hundreds of terminals, at the expense of only a small quantity of electricity. This is one of those brain-machines without which modern life is supposed to be not worth living.

And, finally, there is the example most of us are likely to think of when brain-machines are mentioned: namely, the high-speed computer. Electric eyes and telephone exchanges only relieve us of physical labor, but the calculators can take the place of several human brains.

The Slow Brain

In economy of energy the human brain certainly is still far ahead of all its mechanical rivals. The entire brain with its many billions of cells functions on less than 100 watts. Even with the most efficient present substitute for a brain cell—the transistor—a machine containing as many cells as the brain would need about 100 million watts. We are ahead by a factor of at least a million. But von Neumann has calculated that in theory cells could be 10 billion times more efficient in the use of energy than the brain cells actually are. Thus there seems to be no technical reason why mechanical brains should not become more efficient energy-users than their human cousins. After all, just recently by inventing the transistor, which requires only about a hundredth of a watt, we have improved the efficiency of our machines by a factor of 100; in view of this the factor of a million should not frighten us.

While we are still ahead in the use of energy, we are certainly far behind in speed. Whereas a nerve cannot be used more than 100 times a second, a vacuum tube can easily be turned on and off a million times a second. It could be made to work even faster, but this would not contribute much to speeding

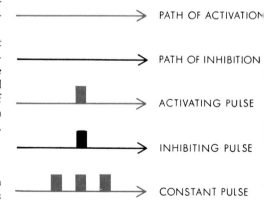

PATH OF ACTIVATION

PATH OF INHIBITION

ACTIVATING PULSE

INHIBITING PULSE

CONSTANT PULSE

SIMPLE CIRCUITS for a brain machine are depicted on the next five pages. The activating and inhibiting pulses are identical but follow different paths.

up the mechanical brain at the moment. No machine is faster than its slowest part, so we must evaluate various components of the machine.

In a calculating machine four different problems confront the designer: the actual computations, the "logical control," the memory and the feeding of information to the machine and getting answers out. Speed of computation, a bottleneck in mechanical computers such as the desk calculator, has been taken care of by the vacuum tube. The next bottleneck was the logical control—the system for telling the machine what to do next after each step. The early IBM punch-card machine took this function out of the hands of a human operator by using a wiring setup on a central board which commanded the sequence of operations. This is perfectly all right as long as the machine has to perform only one type of operation. But if the sequence has to be changed frequently, the wiring of the board becomes very clumsy indeed. To improve speed the machine must be given an internal logical control. Perhaps the greatest step forward on this problem has been accomplished by MANIAC, built at the Institute for Advanced Study in Princeton. This machine can change instructions as quickly as it completes calculations, so that it can operate as fast as its vacuum tubes will allow.

That still leaves the problems of speeding up the memory and the input and output of information. The two problems are closely related. The larger the memory, the less often the operator has to feed the machine information. But the very fact that the machine performs large numbers of computations between instructions clogs its memory and slows it down. This is because an accumulation of rounding errors makes it necessary to carry out all figures in a calculation to a great number of digits. In each computation the machine necessarily rounds off the last digit; in succeeding operations the digit becomes less and less precise. If the computations are continued, the next-to-last digit begins to be affected, and so on. It can be shown that after 100 computations the last digit is worthless; after 10,000 the last two digits; after 1,000,000, the last three. In the large new computers an answer might easily contain four worthless figures. Hence to insure accuracy the machine must carry more digits than are actually significant; it is not uncommon to carry from eight to 12 digits for each number throughout the calculation. When the machine operates on the binary system of numbers, instead of the decimal system, the situation is even worse, for it takes about three times as many digits to express a number in the binary scale.

MANIAC uses up to 40 binary digits to express a number. Due to the necessity for carrying this large number of digits, even MANIAC's celebrated memory can hold no more than about 1,000 numbers. It has an "external memory," in the form of a magnetic tape and magnetic drums, in which it can store more information, but reading from the tape or drums is a much slower operation than doing electrical computations.

In spite of the present limitations, the machines already are ahead of the human brain in speed by a factor of at least 10,000—usually a great deal more than 10,000. They are most impressive on tasks such as arise in astronomy or ballistics. It would be child's play for MANIAC to figure out the position of the planets for the next million years.

Still we are left with the feeling that there are many things we can do that a machine cannot do. The brain has more than 10 billion cells, while a computer has only a few tens of thousands of parts. Even with transistors, which overcome the cost and space problems, the difficulty of construction will hardly allow more than a million parts to a machine. So we can safely say that the human brain for a long time to come will be about 10,000 times more complex than the most complicated machine. And it is well known that an increase of parts by a factor of 10 can bring about differences in kind. For example, if we have a unit that can do addition and multiplication, by combining a few such units with a logical control mechanism we can do subtraction, division, raising to powers, interpolation and many other operations qualitatively different from the original.

The Complex Memory

Part of man's superior complexity is his remarkable memory. How does MANIAC's memory compare with it? For simplicity's sake let us measure the information a memory may hold in "bits" (for binary digits). A vacuum tube can hold one digit of a binary number (the digit is 1 if the tube is on, 0 if it is off). In vacuum-tube language it takes 1,500 bits to express the multiplication table. Now MANIAC's memory holds about 40,000 bits, not in 40,000 separate tubes but as spots on 40 special picture tubes, each of which can hold about 1,000 spots (light or dark). Estimates as to how much the human memory holds vary widely, but we certainly can say conservatively that the brain can remember at least 1,000 items as complex

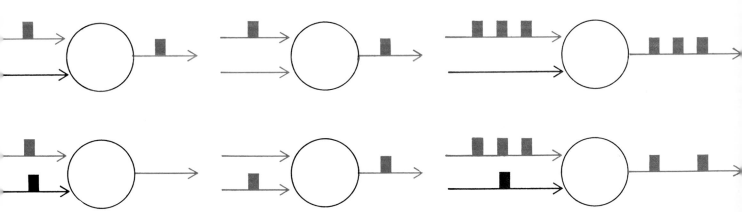

BASIC CELL (*circle*) will fire when it is activated (*top*). It will not fire, however, if it is inhibited at the same time (*bottom*).

"OR" CIRCUIT requires two paths of activation. The cell fires if a pulse arrives on one path (*top*) "or" the other (*bottom*).

"NOT" CIRCUIT incorporates constant activating pulses. The cell can thus fire constantly (*top*). It signals "not" when it is briefly inhibited (*bottom*).

as the multiplication table (1.5 million bits), and a reasonable guess is that its capacity is closer to 100 million bits—which amounts to acquiring one bit per 20 seconds throughout life. So our memory exceeds that of MANIAC by a factor of 1,000 at least.

Is the difference just a matter of complexity? No, the fact is that machines have not yet imitated the human brain's method of storing and recovering information. For instance, if we tried to increase MANIAC's memory by any considerable amount, we would soon find it almost impossible to extract information. We would have to use a complex system of coding to enable the machine to hunt up a given item of information, and this coding would load down the memory further and make the logical control more complex. Only when we acquire a better understanding of the brain's amazing ability to call forth information will we be able to give a machine anything more than a limited memory.

The Logical Machine

Let us now consider the inevitable question: Can a machine "think"? We start with a simple model of the nervous system such as has been constructed by Walter Pitts and Warren S. McCulloch of the Massachusetts Institute of Technology. Its basic unit is the neuron—a cell that can be made to emit pulses of energy. The firing of one neuron may activate the next or it may inhibit it. The neurons are assumed to work in cycles. This corresponds to our knowledge that after firing a neuron must be inactive for a period. To simplify the model it

is assumed that the various neurons' cycles are synchronized, i.e., all the neurons active during a given period fire at the same time. For a given neuron to fire in a given cycle two conditions must be satisfied: in the previous cycle it must have been (1) activated and (2) not inhibited. If, for example, a neuron has two others terminating in it of which one activates and one inhibits, and if the former fires in a given cycle and the latter does not, then the neuron will fire in the following cycle. Otherwise it will be inactive for a cycle.

Out of this basic pattern we can build the most complex logical machine. We can have a combination that will fire if a connected neuron did not fire (representing "not") or one that will fire if at least one of two incoming neurons fired (representing "or") or one that will fire only if both incoming neurons fired (representing "and"). Combining these, we can imitate many logical operations of the brain. The simple arrangement diagrammed on pages 210 and 211 will count up to four, and it is easy to see how to generalize this technique.

We can also construct a very primitive memory: e.g., a system that will "remember" that it has been activated until it is instructed to "forget" it. But if it is to remember anything at all complex, it must have an unthinkably large number of neurons—another illustration of the fact that human memory acts on different principles from a machine.

The Turing Machine

If we were to stop here, we might conclude that practical limitations of memory and complexity must forever re-

strict the cleverness or versatility of any machine. But we have not yet plumbed the full possibilities. The late A. M. Turing of England showed, by a brilliant analysis, that by combining a certain few simple operations in sufficient number a machine could perform feats of amazing complexity. Turing's machines may be clumsy and slow, but they present the clearest picture of what a machine can do.

A Turing machine can be thought of as a mechanical calculator which literally works with pencil and paper. The paper it uses is a long tape divided into successive squares, and it operates on one square at a time. As it confronts a particular square it can do one of six things: (1) write down the letter X; (2) write down the digit 1; (3) erase either of these marks if it is already in the square; (4) move the tape one square to the left; (5) move the tape one square to the right; (6) stop.

Essentially this machine is a number writer. It writes its numbers in the simplest possible form, as a string of units. This is even simpler than the binary system. In the binary system the number 35, for example, is written 100011. In a Turing machine it is a string of 1's in 35 successive squares. The X's are merely punctuation marks to show where each number starts and ends.

The machine has the following parts: a device that writes or erases, a scanner, a motor to move the tape, a numbered dial with a pointer, and a logical control consisting of neuron-like elements, say vacuum tubes. The logical control operates from a prepared table of commands which specifies what the machine is to do in each given state. The

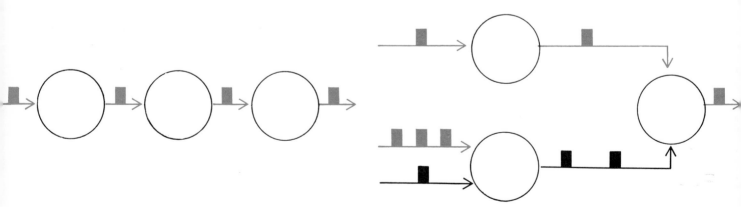

DELAY CIRCUIT is based on the fact that the basic cell receives a pulse in one "cycle" and fires it in the next. In this arrangement of three basic cells the pulse would be delayed three cycles.

"AND" CIRCUIT utilizes three cells. The first (*upper left*) has only an activating input. The second (*lower left*) has a constant activating input and an inhibiting input. The third (*right*) is the conventional basic cell. In the first

state consists of two elements: what the scanner "sees" in the square before it, and where the pointer is on the dial. For example, the table of instructions may say that whenever the square has an X and the pointer is at the number 1 on the dial, the machine is to erase the X, and move the pointer to the number 2 on the dial. As the machine proceeds from step to step, the logical control gives it such commands, the command in each case depending both on the position of the dial and on what the scanner sees in the square confronting it. Observe that the dial functions as a primitive "memory," in the sense that its position at any stage is a consequence of what the scanner saw and where the pointer stood at the step immediately preceding. It carries over the machine's experience from step to step.

Turing's machine thus consists of a tape with X's and 1's in some of its squares, a dial-memory with a certain number of positions, and a logical control which instructs the machine what to do, according to what it sees and what its memory says. The diagram on pages 212 and 213 shows a very simple version of the machine, with a dial having only six positions. Since the scanner may see one of three things in a square—blank, 1 or X—the machine has 18 possible states, and the logical control has a command for each case [see table at right of illustration]. This machine is designed to perform a single task: it can add two numbers—any two numbers. Suppose it is to add 2 and 3. The numbers are written as strings of 1's with X's at the ends. Say we start with the dial at position 1 and the scanner looking at the second digit of the number 3

[see diagram]. The instructions in the table say that when it is in this state the machine is to move the tape one square to the right and keep the dial at position 1. This operation brings the square to the left, containing another digit 1, under the scanner. Again the instructions are the same: "Move the tape one square to the right and keep the dial at position 1." Now the scanner sees an X. The instructions, with the dial at position 1, are: "Erase (the X) and move the dial to position 2." The machine now confronts a blank square. The command becomes: "Move the tape one square to the right and keep the dial at position 2." In this manner the machine will eventually write two digit 1's next to the three at the right and end with the answer 5—a row of five digits enclosed by X's. When it finishes, an exclamation point signifies that it is to stop. The reader is advised to try adding two other numbers in the same fashion.

This surely is a cumbersome method of adding. However, the machine becomes more impressive when it is expanded so that it can solve a problem such as the following: "Multiply the number you are looking at by two and take the cube root of the answer if the fifth number to the left is less than 150." By adding positions to the dial and enlarging the table of instructions we can endow such a machine with the ability to carry out the most complex tasks, though each operational step is very simple. The Turing machine in fact resembles a model of the human nervous system, which can be thought of as having a dial with very many positions and combining many simple acts to accomplish the enormous number

of tasks a human being is capable of.

Turing gave his machines an infinite memory. Of course the dial can have only a finite number of positions, but he allowed the machine a tape infinite in length, endless in both directions. Actually the tape does not have to be infinite—just long enough for the task. We may provide for all emergencies by allowing the machine to ask for more tape if it needs it. The human memory is infinite in the same sense: we can always make more paper to make notes on.

The Universal Machine

If we allow the unlimited tape, the Turing idea astounds us further with a universal machine. Not only can we build a machine for each task, but we can design a single machine that is versatile enough to accomplish all these tasks! We must try to understand how this is done, because it will give us the key to our whole problem.

The secret of the universal machine is that it can imitate. Suppose we build a highly complex machine for a difficult task. If we then supply the universal machine with a description of the task and of our special machine, it will figure out how to perform the task. It proceeds very simply, deducing from what it knows about our machine just what it would do at each step. Of course this slows the universal machine down considerably. Between any two steps it must carry out a long argument to analyze what our machine would do. But we care only about its ability to succeed, not its speed. There is no doubt about it: anything any logical machine can do can be done by this single mechanism.

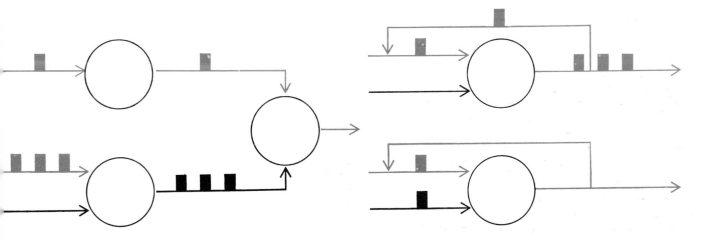

diagram the pulse received by the first cell is not fired by the third. The third cell will fire the pulse only if the activating pulse of the first cell "and" the inhibiting pulse of the second are fired on the same cycle (second diagram).

MEMORY CIRCUIT feeds the output of a cell back into its input. Thus if the cell is activated, it "remembers" by firing constantly (top). If it is inhibited at any time later, it stops firing (bottom).

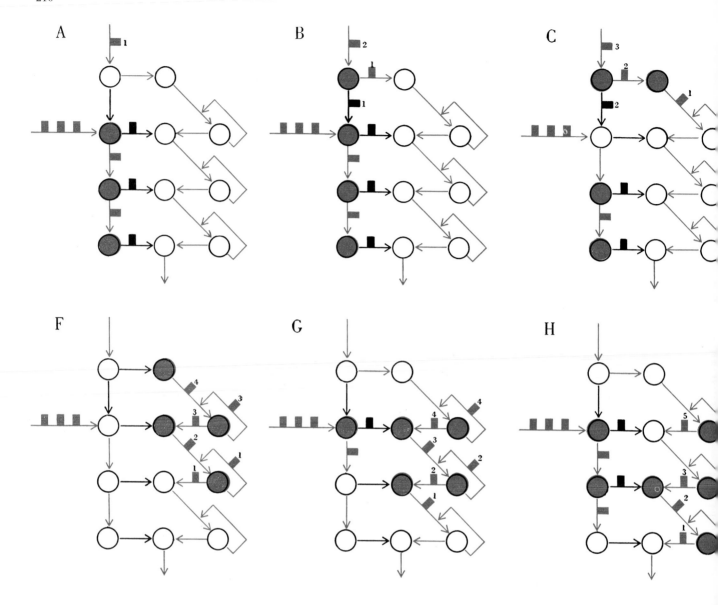

COUNTING CIRCUIT "counts" to four and then fires. The conventions in this series of diagrams are the same as those in the illustrations on the four preceding pages, with two important exceptions. The first is that, where the diagrams on the preceding pages show each circuit during two or more cycles, each of these diagrams shows the circuit during a single cycle. The second exception is that, when a cell fires, it lights up (*red tone*). The input of this circuit is the activating pathway at the top. The output of the circuit is the activating pathway at the bottom. In addition one of the cells has a constant activating input (*left*). The three cells at the right are memory cells (*see diagram at the right on preceding page*). These cells can activate the three cells to the left of them.

The key question is: How do you describe a complex machine in terms that a relatively simple machine can understand? The answer is that you devise a simple code which can describe any machine (or at least any Turing machine), and that you design the universal machine so that it will be able to understand this code. To understand a Turing machine we need only know its table of commands, so it suffices to have a simple code for tables of commands. We will sketch one possible way of representing each conceivable table of commands by an integer. Of course there are infinitely many such tables, but there are also infinitely many integers—that is

why they are so useful in mathematics.

A table of commands consists of P rows. Each row has three commands in it, corresponding to seeing a blank, an X or a 1. The first step is to get rid of the letters in the table [*refer again to page 213*]. This can be done by replacing E, X, D, L, R and S by 1 through 6 respectively. Thus the commands on the first line of the table of our sample machine become 3–6, 1–2, 5–1. Step two: Get rid of the question mark and the exclamation point, say by putting 1 and 2 for them respectively. (Since these occur only in conjunction with an S, there is no danger of confusing them with memory positions 1 and 2.) Thus

the second row of our table becomes 5–2, 1–3, 6–1. Step three: Represent each row by a single integer. There is a famous simple way of doing this; namely by treating the numbers as exponents to primes and obtaining a product which completely specifies the series of numbers. As the final step, we epresent the entire table with a single number obtained by the same trick. Our code number for this table will be $2^{2991509440920}$ times 3 raised to the number of the second row. It is an enormous number, but it does identify our table of commands uniquely. And it is a straightforward mechanical task to design the universal machine so that it can

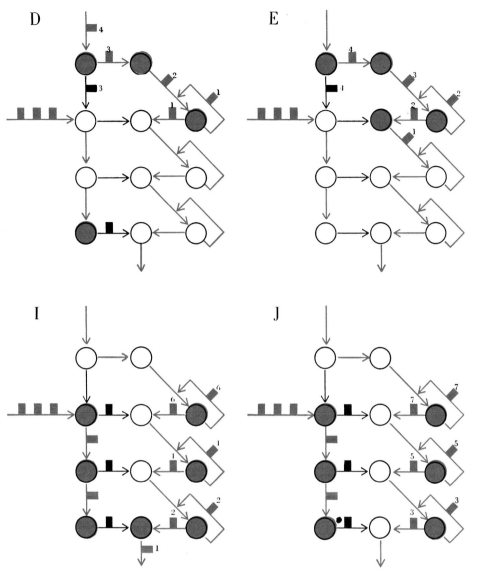

These three cells can in turn be inhibited by the three cells to the left of them. Now in the first four cycles (A, B, C and D) four pulses are put into the circuit. The position of each pulse in succeeding cycles is indicated by small numbers. In the ninth cycle (I) the circuit, having "counted" the four pulses, fires once. In the 10th cycle (J) the circuit returns to its original state with the exception that pulses are still circulating through the memory cells. A practical counting circuit would be fitted with a device to wipe out these memories.

sand entries, it seems to be able to do essentially all the problem-solving tasks that we can. Of course it might take a billion years to do something we can do in an hour. The "outside world" from which it can learn is much more restricted than ours, being limited to Turing machines. But may not all this be just a difference of degree? Are we, as rational beings, basically different from universal Turing machines?

The usual answer is that whatever else machines can do, it still takes a man to build the machine. Who would dare to say that a machine can reproduce itself and make other machines?

Von Neumann would. As a matter of fact, he has blue-printed just such a machine.

The Reproducing Machine

What do we mean by reproduction? If we mean the creation of an object like the original out of nothing, then no machine can reproduce, but neither can a human being. If reproduction is not to violate the conservation of energy principle, building materials must be available. The characteristic feature of the reproduction of life is that the living organism can create a new organism like itself out of inert matter surrounding it.

If we agree that machines are not alive, and if we insist that the creation of life is an essential feature of reproduction, then we have begged the question: A machine cannot reproduce. So we must reformulate the problem in a way that won't make machine reproduction logically impossible. We must omit the word "living." We shall ask that the machine create a new organism like itself out of simple parts contained in the environment.

Human beings find the raw material in the form of food; that is, quite highly organized chemicals. Thus we cannot even say that we produce order out of complete disorder, but rather we transform more simply organized matter into complex matter. We must accordingly assume that the machine is surrounded with pieces of matter, simpler than any part of the machine. The hypothetical parts list would be rolls of tape, pencils, erasers, vacuum tubes, dials, photoelectric cells, motors, shafts, wire, batteries and so on. We must endow the machine with the ability to transform pieces of matter into these parts and to organize them into a new machine.

Von Neumann simplified the problem by making a number of reasonable assumptions. First of all he realized that it is inessential for the machine to be

decode the large number and reproduce the table of commands. With the table of commands written down, the machine then knows what the machine it is copying would do in any given situation.

The universal machine is remarkably human. It starts with very limited abilities, and it learns more and more by imitation and by absorbing information from the outside. We feel that the potentialities of the human brain are inexhaustible. But would this be the case if we were unable to communicate with the world around us? A man robbed of his five senses is comparable to a Turing machine with a fixed tape, but a normal human being is like the universal machine. Given enough time, he can learn to do anything.

But some readers will feel we have given in too soon to Turing's persuasive argument. After all a human being must step in and give the universal machine the code number. If we allow that, why not give the machine the answer in the first place? Turing's reply would have been that the universal machine does not need a man to encode the table; it can be designed to do its own coding, just as it can be designed to decode.

So we grant this amazing machine its universal status. And although its table of logical control has only a few thou-

able to move around. Rather, he has the mechanism sending out impulses which organize the surroundings by remote control. Secondly, he asssumed that space is divided into cubical cells, and that each part of the machine and each piece of raw material occupies just one cell. Thirdly, he assumed that the processes are quantized not only in space but in time; that is, we have cycles during which all action takes place. It is not even necessary to have three dimensions: a two-dimensional lattice will serve as well as the network of cubes.

Our space will be a very large (in principle infinite) sheet, divided into squares. A machine occupies a connected area consisting of a large number of squares. Since each square represents a part of the machine, the number of squares occupied is a measure of the complexity of the machine. The machine is surrounded by inert cells, which it has to organize. To make this possible the machine must be a combination of a brain and a brawn machine, since it not only organizes but also transforms matter. Accordingly the von Neumann machine has three kinds of parts. It has neurons similar to those discussed in the model of the nervous system. These provide the logical control. Then it has transmission cells, which carry messages

from the control centers. They have an opening through which they can receive impulses, and an output through which the impulse is passed on a cycle later. A string of transmission cells, properly adjoined, forms a channel through which messages can be sent. In addition the machine has muscles. These cells can change the surrounding cells, building them up from less highly organized to more complex cells or breaking them down. They bring about changes analogous to those produced by a combination of muscular and chemical action in the human body. Their primary use is, of course, the changing of an inert cell into a machine part.

As in the nervous system, the operation proceeds by steps: the state of every cell is determined by its state and the state of its neighbors a cycle earlier. The neurons and transmission cells are either quiescent or they can send out an impulse if properly stimulated. The muscle cells receive commands from the neurons through the transmission cells, and react either by "killing" some undesired part (i.e., making it inert) or by transforming some inert cell in the environment to a machine part of a specified kind. So far the machine is similar in structure to a higher animal. Its neurons form the central nervous system;

the transmission cells establish contact with various organs; the organs perform their designated tasks upon receiving a command.

The instructions may be very long. Hence they must in a sense be external. Von Neumann's machine has a tail containing the blueprint of what it is to build. This tail is a very long strip containing coded instructions. The basic box performs two types of functions: it follows instructions from its tail, and it is able to copy the tail. Suppose the tail contains a coded description of the basic box. Then the box will, following instructions, build another box like itself. When it is finished, it proceeds to copy its own tail, attaching it to the new box. And so it reproduces itself.

The secret of the machine is that it does not try to copy itself. Von Neumann designed a machine that can build any machine from a description of it, and hence can build one like itself. Then it is an easy matter to copy the large but simple tail containing the instructions and attach it to the offspring. Thereafter the new machine can go on producing more and more machines until all the raw material is used up or until the machines get into conflict with each other—imitating even in this their human designers.

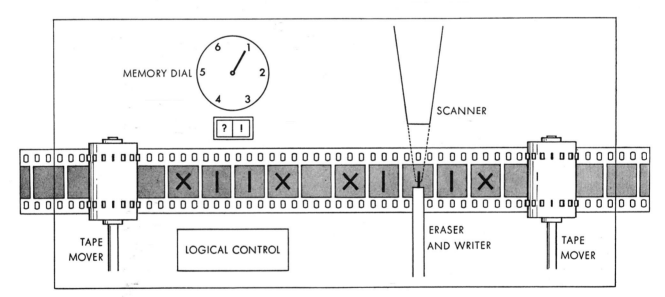

TURING MACHINE designed for simple addition is confronted with the numbers 2 and 3. The numbers are indicated on the tape; each digit is represented by a 1. X is a signal that a number is about to begin or has just ended. The logical control of the machine is depicted in the table on the opposite page. The horizontal rows of the table represent the position of the memory dial (1, 2, 3, 4, 5 or 6). The vertical columns represent the symbol on the tape (blank, X or 1). The symbols at the intersection of the rows and columns are commands to the machine. E means erase the symbol on the tape; X, write an X on the tape; D, write the digit

1 on the tape; R, move the tape one frame to the right; L, move the tape one frame to the left; S, stop; ?, something is wrong; !, the operation is completed; 1, 2, 3, 4, 5 or 6, turn the memory dial to that position. Thus at the upper left in the table the memory dial is in position 1 and the tape is blank; the command is D6, or write the digit 1 on the tape and turn the memory dial to position 6. Then in the beginning position shown above the machine begins to operate as follows. In the first step the memory dial is in position 1 and the tape shows a 1. The command is R1: move the tape one frame to the right and leave the memory dial in position 1. In the second

It is amazing to see how few parts such a machine needs to have. Von Neumann's blueprints call for a basic box of 80 by 400 squares, plus a tail 150,000 squares long. The basic box has the three kinds of parts described—neurons, transmission cells and muscle cells. The three types of cells differ only as to their state of excitation and the way in which they are connected. The tail is even simpler: it has cells, which are either "on" or "off," holding a code. So we have about 200,000 cells, most of which are of the simplest possible kind, and of which only a negligible fraction is even as complex as the logical control neuron. No matter how we measure complexity, this is vastly simpler than a human being, and yet the machine is self-reproducing.

The Genetic Tail

Pressing the analogy between the machine and the human organism, we might compare the tail to the set of chromosomes. Our machine always copies its tail for the new machine, just as each daughter cell in the body copies the chromosomes of its parent. It is most significant that while the chromosomes take up a minute part of the body, the tail is larger than the entire basic box

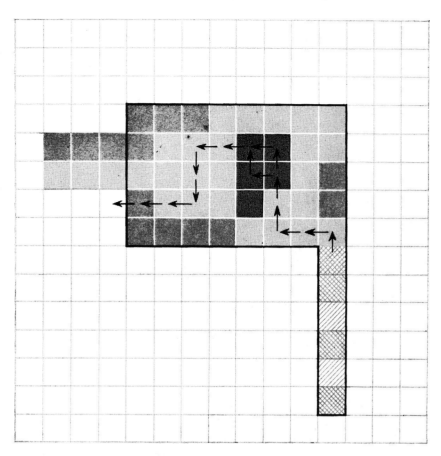

VON NEUMANN MACHINE is theoretically capable of reproducing itself. This is a highly simplified diagram of its conceptual units. The darkest squares are the "nerve cells" of the "brain." The next lightest squares are "muscle cells." The next lightest are transmission cells. The crosshatched squares are the "tail" which bears the instructions of the machine. The double hatching represents an "on" signal; the single hatching, an "off" signal. The empty squares are units of the environment which the machine manipulates. The arrows indicate that instructions are coming from the tail, on the basis of which the brain instructs a muscle cell to act on its surroundings. The machine has sent out a "feeler" to the left.

	▦	✕	▮
1	D6	E2	R1
2	R2	E3	?2
3	R3	E4	E5
4	L4	?4	R6
5	L5	?5	R1
6	X6	!6	R3

step the situation and the response are the same. In the third step the memory dial is in position 1 and the tape shows an X. The command is E2: erase the X and turn the memory dial to position 2. In this way the machine comes up with the answer 5 on its memory dial in 36 steps. On the 37th step the machine stops and signals with a ! that it is finished. If the reader is skeptical and hardy, he is invited to trace the whole process!

in the machine. This indicates that the coding of traits by chromosomes is amazingly efficient and compact. But in all fairness we must point out that the chromosomes serve a lesser role than the tail. The tail contains a complete description of the basic box, while the chromosome description is incomplete: the offspring only resembles the parent; it is not an exact duplicate. It would be most interesting to try to continue von Neumann's pioneer work by designing a machine that could take an incomplete description and build a reasonable likeness of itself.

Could such machines go through an evolutionary process? One might design the tails in such a way that in every cycle a small number of random changes occurred (e.g., changing an "on" to an "off" in the code or vice versa). These would be like mutations; if the machine could still produce offspring, it would pass the changes on. One could further arrange to limit the supply of raw ma-

terial, so that the machines would have to compete for Lebensraum, even to the extent of killing one another.

Of course none of the machines described in this article has actually been built, so far as I know, but they are all buildable. We have considered systematically what man can do, and how much of this a machine can duplicate. We have found that the brain's superiority rests on the greater complexity of the human nervous system and on the greater efficiency of the human memory. But is this an essential difference, or is it only a matter of degree that can be overcome with the progress of technology? This article attempted to show that there is no conclusive evidence for an essential gap between man and a machine. For every human activity we can conceive of a mechanical counterpart.

Naturally we still have not answered the question whether man is more than a machine. The reader will have to answer that question for himself.

22

THE FASTEST COMPUTER

D. L. SLOTNICK
February, 1971

The computer ILLIAC IV, which is now nearing completion, is the fourth generation in a line of advanced machines that have been conceived and developed at the University of Illinois. ILLIAC I, a vacuum-tube machine completed in 1952, could perform 11,000 arithmetical operations per second. ILLIAC II, a transistor-and-diode computer completed in 1963, could perform 500,000 operations per second. ILLIAC III, which became operational in 1966, is a special-purpose computer designed for automatic scanning of large quantities of visual data. Since it processes nonarithmetical data it cannot be compared with the earlier ILLIAC's in terms of operational speed. ILLIAC IV, employing the latest semiconductor technology, is actually a battery of 64 "slave" computers, capable of executing between 100 million and 200 million instructions per second. Even that basic rate, although it is faster than that of any other computer yet built, does not express the true capacity of ILLIAC IV.

Unlike its three predecessors and all computers now on the market, which solve problems by a series of sequential steps, ILLIAC IV is designed to perform as many as 64 computations simultaneously. For such a computing structure to be utilized efficiently the problem must be amenable to parallel, rather than sequential, processing. In actuality problems of this kind constitute a considerable part of the total computational spectrum, ranging from payroll calculations to linear programming to models of the general circulation of the atmosphere for use in weather prediction. For example, a typical linear-programming problem that might occupy a large present-generation computer for six to eight hours should be solvable by ILLIAC IV in less than two minutes—a time reduction of at least 200 to one.

Subsystems for ILLIAC IV are being manufactured in a number of plants and are being shipped to the Burroughs Corporation in Paoli, Pa., for final assembly and testing. When the machine is finished a few months from now, it will be available over high-speed telephone lines to a variety of users, including the Center for Advanced Computation of the University of Illinois.

The ultimate limitation on the operating speed of a computer designed to operate sequentially [*see illustration on page 219*] is the speed with which a signal can be propagated through an electrical conductor. In practice this is somewhat less than the speed of light, which takes one nanosecond (10^{-9} second) to travel about one foot. Although integrated circuits containing transistors packed together with a density ranging from several hundred to several thousand per square inch have helped greatly to reduce the length of interconnections inside computers, designers have been increasingly aware that new kinds of logical organization are needed to penetrate the barrier set by the speed of light.

Over the past 10 years designers have introduced a number of variations on the strictly sequential mode of operation. One stratagem has been to overlap the operation of the central processing unit and the operation of input-output devices (such as magnetic-tape readers and printers). By means of a fine-grained separation of the computer's functional units a high degree of overlapping has been attained. Current efforts in "pipelining" the processing of "operands" will allow a further significant increase in speed.

Overlapping and pipelining, however, are both fundamentally limited in the advances in speed they can provide. The approach taken in ILLIAC IV surmounts fundamental limitations in ultimate computer speed by allowing—at least in principle—an unlimited number of computational events to take place simultaneously. The logical design of ILLIAC IV is patterned after that of the SOLOMON computers, prototypes of which were

COMPUTER ILLIAC IV is nearing completion at the Great Valley Laboratories of the Burroughs Corporation in Paoli, Pa. Unlike conventional computers, which carry out logical and arithmetical operations in

built by the Westinghouse Electric Corporation in the early 1960's. In this design a single master control unit sends instructions to a sizable number of independent processing elements and transmits addresses to individual memory units associated with these processing elements ("processing-element memories"). Thus, while a single sequence of instructions (the program) still does the controlling, it controls a number of processing elements that execute the same instruction simultaneously on data that can be, and usually are, different in the memory of each processing element [*see top illustration on page 220*].

Each of the 64 processing elements of ILLIAC IV is a powerful computing unit in its own right. It can perform a wide range of arithmetical operations on numbers that are 64 binary digits (bits) long, where a digit is either 0 or 1, corresponding to the two "positions" of an electronic device with two stable states. These numbers can be in any one of six

possible formats; the number can be processed as a single number 64 bits long with either a fixed or a "floating" point (corresponding to the decimal point in decimal notation), or the 64 bits can be broken up into smaller numbers of equal length. Each of the memory units has a capacity of 2,048 64-bit numbers. The time required to extract a number from memory (the access time) is 188 nanoseconds, but because additional logical circuitry is needed to resolve conflicts when two or more sections of ILLIAC IV call on memory simultaneously, the minimum time between successive operations of memory is increased to 350 nanoseconds.

Each processing element has more than 100,000 distinct electronic components assembled into some 12,000 switching circuits. A processing element together with its memory unit and associated logic is called a processing unit [*see illustrations on next two pages*]. In a system containing more than six million components one can expect a component

or a connection to fail once every few hours. For this reason much attention has been devoted to testing and diagnostic procedures. Each of the 64 processing units will be subjected regularly to an extensive library of automatic tests. If a unit should fail one of these tests, it can be quickly unplugged and replaced by a spare, with only a brief loss of operating time. When the defective unit has been taken out of service, the precise cause of the failure will be determined by a separate diagnostic computer [*see top illustration on page 220*]. Once the fault has been found and repaired the unit will be returned to the inventory of spares.

ILLIAC IV could not have been designed at all without much help from other computers. Two medium-sized Burroughs B 5500 computers worked almost full time for two years preparing the artwork for the system's printed circuit boards and developing diagnostic and testing programs for the system's logic and hardware. These formidable design, programming and operating efforts

strict sequence, ILLIAC IV will solve complex problems in an all-at-once manner by coordinating the simultaneous operation of 64 "slave" computers, or independent processing units. ILLIAC IV was conceived and developed at the University of Illinois Center for Advanced Computation.

OPEN DOORS OF ILLIAC IV reveal vertical cases holding eight of the big machine's 64 independent but centrally controlled processing units. The 12 drawers at the top of the picture hold the power-supply modules associated with the eight processing units. A group of four processing units lies behind each of the 16 bottom doors in the photograph at the left.

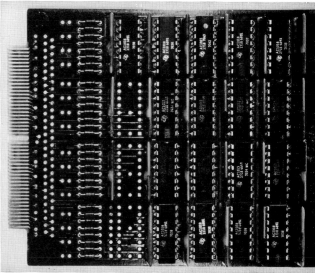

BACK-PLANE ASSEMBLY (*far left*) of one of ILLIAC IV's 64 processing elements contains up to 210 printed circuit boards arranged in six rows of 35 columns. Each circuit board (*second from left*) holds up to 20 "dual-in-line" packages (four rows by five columns) as well as some other electronic components such as resistors. Each dual-in-line package (*third from left*) contains 16 pins, which

were under the direction of Arthur B. Carroll, who during this period was the project's deputy principal investigator.

In the course of a calculation it is frequently necessary to transfer data from one processing element to another; data paths are provided for this purpose [*see bottom illustration on page 221*]. In solving certain problems these data paths can be used to simulate directly the problem's geometric structure.

Although the 64 processing elements are under centralized control, only the simplest problems could be handled if the elements did not have some degree of individual control. Such control is provided by means of a "mode value," which can be set by each processing element and which depends on the different data values unique to each element. The program sets the mode value that identifies

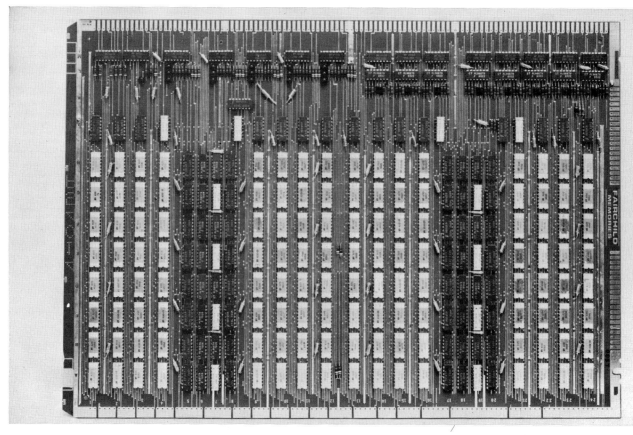

MEMORY ARRAY BOARD (*left*) is one of four that together constitute the high-speed, 131,072-bit memory associated with each of the 64 processing elements in ILLIAC IV. Each board holds up to 128 dual-in-line packages. Each package (*middle*) holds one chip and

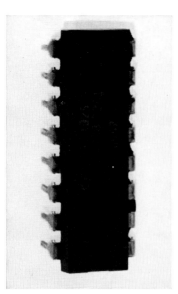

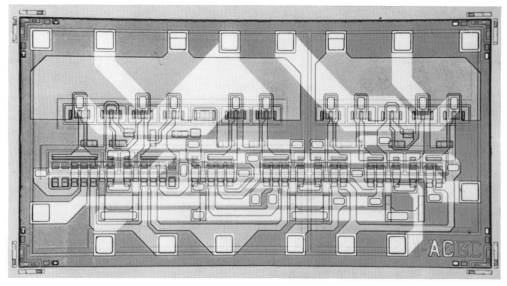

connect to an integrated circuit built up on a single chip of silicon measuring .095 by .05 inch. The integrated circuit, magnified 55 diameters at the far right, contains 34 transistors organized into seven "logic gates." The circuit chips are manufactured by Texas Instruments Incorporated. In all more than a quarter of a million chips will be used in ILLIAC IV's 64 processing elements.

those processing elements whose state (as defined by their mode value) enables them to respond to a given instruction or sequence of instructions. The elements not in this state are turned off. As a simple example, suppose at the start of a problem all mode values are set to 1, or "on." Now the program causes the control unit to "broadcast" to all 64 processing elements: Search your memory for X (some particular value). Each element carries out the search, and any element finding the value X sets its mode value to 0, or "off." The control unit may now issue a sequence of instructions to be performed only by those elements whose mode value is still 1, which allows them to keep operating. Similarly, the contents of two registers within a processing element can be compared, and the mode value can be set on the outcome of the

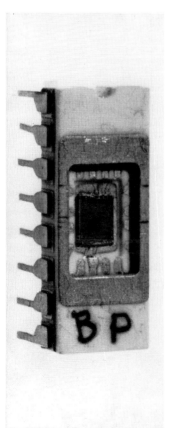

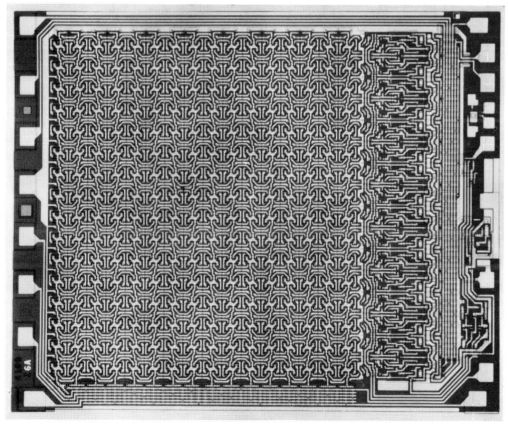

each chip contains integrated semiconductor circuits (*right*) with a storage capacity of 256 bits. The chips, each containing 2,485 transistors, resistors and diodes, were developed by the Semiconductor Division of Fairchild Camera and Instrument Corporation.

DIAGNOSTIC COMPUTERS, called exercisers, are housed in the cabinets at the right in each photograph. When one of ILLIAC IV's processors or memory units fails, it is immediately unplugged and replaced with a spare unit. The exact cause of the failure is then determined by a diagnostic computer. A defective processor has been unplugged and rolled over to the diagnostic computer in the photograph at the left; a defective memory unit is being examined by a different diagnostic computer in the photograph at the right.

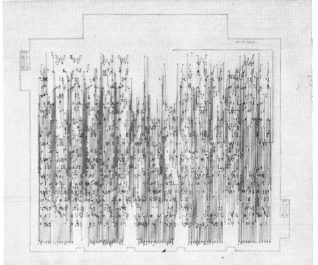

CONTROL-UNIT CARD (top left) is laminated from 12 separate layers that embody the complex wiring pattern for interconnecting several thousand electronic components. Three of the glass photographic positives of wiring patterns and etched copper wiring layers are shown in the other photographs. ILLIAC IV requires 64 control-unit cards, each of which can be removed for test or replacement.

comparison. Mode values are also used to determine when an iterative calculation should be terminated or when quantities have exceeded specified numerical limits. In short, mode values are the principal means for imposing a data-dependent, logical structure on a program.

In addition to the high-speed primary memories associated with each processing element, ILLIAC IV has two memories that are somewhat slower but have capacities that are considerably larger. The total capacity of the 64 primary memories is $64 \times 2,048$, or 131,072, numbers, each 64 bits in length. Thus the total high-speed storage is some 8.4 million bits. Most of the problems suitable for ILLIAC IV will require data capacities far exceeding this primary storage.

The additional data can be held either in a rotating-disk magnetic memory or in a new "archival" memory whose writing mechanism is a laser beam. The rotating-disk memory has a capacity of a billion bits, or about 120 times the capacity of the primary memory. The disk has 128 tracks, each with its own reading and recording head. The access time is determined by the time required for the disk to rotate into the position where the desired datum is under one of the fixed heads. Since the disk revolves once in 40 milliseconds, the average access time is 20 milliseconds, which is about 100,000 times slower than the access time of the primary memory. Once the disk is in position, however, data can be transferred to any of the 64 primary memories at the rate of half a billion bits per second, or roughly 100 times the rate at which data can be transmitted over a standard television channel. The archival memory, which has a capacity of a trillion bits, has a longer access time and a lower data-transfer rate [*see top illustration on page 221*].

These memory subsystems plus the more conventional peripheral equipment (punched cards, disk and tape units, printers, displays and so on) are under the direction of a medium-size general-purpose computer, the Burroughs B 6500 [*see bottom illustration on next page*]. This computer also bears the major responsibility for translating programs from the various programming languages available to the users into the detailed, hardware-determined language of the computer itself.

Let us now examine how ILLIAC IV can be used to solve a simplified problem in mathematical physics. The problem belongs to the very large class of problems whose calculation can be performed in an "all at once" manner, using

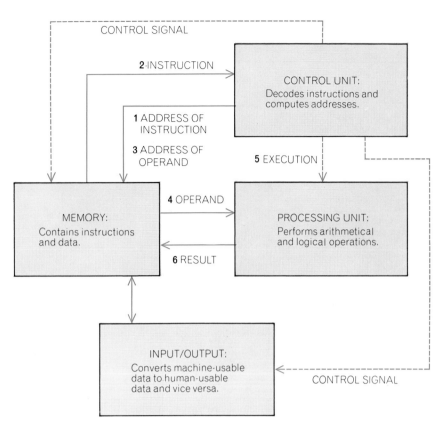

CONVENTIONAL COMPUTER is organized to carry out operations in sequence. A counter in the control unit determines the address of the next instruction in the sequence to be executed and transmits the address to the memory (1). The memory returns the instruction to the control unit (2). The instruction contains the address in the memory of the data (operand) on which an arithmetical or logical operation (also specified) is to be performed. This address is sent to the memory (3). The memory furnishes the selected operand to the processing unit (4). The control unit then transmits to the processor a sequence of electronic signals that contains the fine structure of the arithmetical or logical operation required by the program (5). The calculated result is then stored at a specified location in memory (6) for use in a subsequent operation or for conversion to printed form for the user of the machine. Advanced computers carry out this entire sequence in a few millionths of a second. Billions of repetitions may be needed to solve a complex problem.

either ordinary or partial differential equations. The problem we shall trace requires the solution of Laplace's partial differential equation describing the distribution of temperature on the surface of a slab. Even the reader who is unfamiliar with such equations should be able to follow this example because the method for reaching a solution relies completely on the commonsense notion that the temperature at any point on the slab tends to become the average of the surrounding values.

Laplace's equation for solving the problem is $\delta^2 U / \delta x^2 + \delta^2 U / \delta y^2 = 0$, where U corresponds to the temperature at a given position specified by the coordinates x and y on the surface of the slab. In this example we are asked to imagine that we are dealing with a rectangular slab of some material whose four edges are maintained at different temperatures. Eventually all the points on the surface of the slab will reach a steady-state temperature distribution re-

flecting the way heat flows from hotter edges to the cooler ones. The temperatures at the edges of the slab, which are held constant, are called the boundary conditions. If we use an x-y coordinate system to designate the location of any point on the surface of the slab, we can say that the temperature at any point is a function of x and y. In other words, every point x,y on the slab has associated with it a temperature $U(x,y)$.

When one uses a digital computer to solve this problem, one cannot, of course, obtain the temperature at an infinite number of points. The standard procedure is to digitize the variables x and y so that the slab is covered by a mesh, each square of the mesh being h units on a side. For the sake of simplicity we shall assume that our slab is a square and that it has been digitized into 64 x,y values or mesh points [*see illustration on pages 222 and 223*].

The method of solution can now be stated very simply: The temperature at

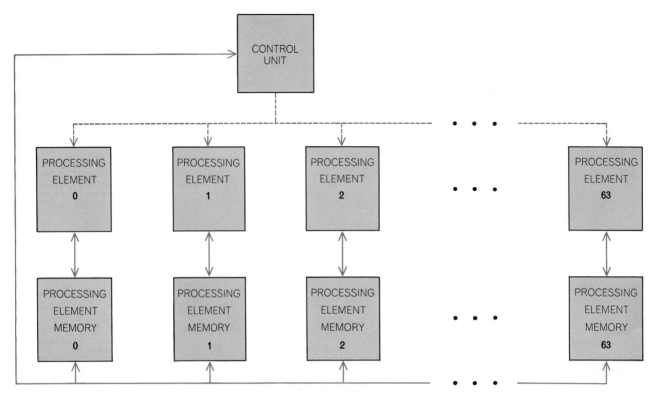

PARALLEL ORGANIZATION OF ILLIAC IV enables the control unit to orchestrate the operation of 64 processing elements, each with its own memory. There is a large class of mathematical problems that can be solved in an all-at-once manner by independent processors operating simultaneously, each about twice as fast as the single processor in an advanced sequential computer.

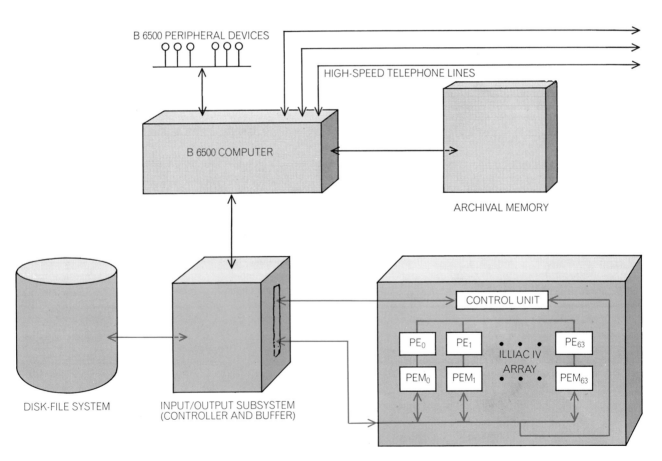

BLOCK DIAGRAM OF ILLIAC IV SYSTEM shows how the ILLIAC's control unit, together with its 64 processors and primary memory units, will be connected to ancillary pieces of equipment. A secondary memory is provided by a disk-file system with a capacity of a billion bits (binary digits). A tertiary memory is provided by a new "archival" memory system, which uses a laser beam for reading and writing. Accessed through a medium-size Burroughs B 6500 computer, it will have storage for a trillion bits.

any interior mesh point is the average of the temperatures of the four closest mesh points. Thus the value of $U(x,y)$ equals the sum of four neighboring values of $U(x,y)$ divided by four. When this equation is made true for all points, there can be only one correct value for each point. This method is called "relaxation."

When the relaxation method is applied with a sequential, or conventional, computer, the usual procedure is to start at the top left of the slab and apply the basic equation at each interior point moving from left to right along each row of points and proceeding downward row by row. Since the 28 boundary points in our example are already specified, the equation would have to be applied 36 times (64 minus 28) to produce one relaxation of the relaxation method. As succeeding relaxations are performed on the set of mesh points the values of the temperatures converge to the exact solution. When values for two successive relaxations are very close to each other (within a specified error tolerance), one stops the process and says that the steady-state solution has been reached.

Let us now consider how this same problem could be solved by parallel processing on ILLIAC IV. If one stored each value of U in a separate processing element, all 36 inner values could be calculated simultaneously. A program could be written to compute new values for $U(x,y)$ not from top left to bottom right but all at once. When the first set of relaxation values for all 36 inner points has been obtained by simultaneous calculation, these values are available for the second relaxation.

Not only are the two algorithms, or mathematical routines, different for sequential and parallel computation but also the way the temperatures converge is different [see illustration on pages 224 and 225]. In the sequential method the temperatures at bottom right converge faster to the exact solution than those at top left. This happens because in sweeping from top left to bottom right the last computations in each relaxation sequence contain more new data than the computations made at the start of the sequence.

When the parallel algorithm is used, the values closest to the edges converge faster than those in the center of the mesh. The reason is that the outer values are closest to the boundary values, and at each iteration they have more new data available than the inner values. The convergence process can be likened to freezing. The sequential algorithm begins freezing at bottom right and proceeds to top left; the parallel algorithm begins

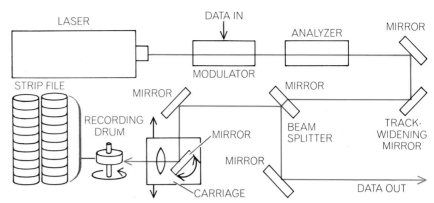

ARCHIVAL MEMORY is a new high-capacity secondary memory, developed by the Precision Instrument Company. The beam from an argon laser records binary data by burning microscopic holes in a thin film of metal coated on a strip of polyester sheet, which is carried by a rotating drum. Each data strip can store some 2.9 billion bits, the equivalent of 625 reels of standard magnetic tape in less than 1 percent of the volume. The "strip file" provides storage for 400 data strips containing more than a trillion bits. The time to locate data stored on any one of the 400 strips is about five seconds. Within the same strip data can be located in 200 milliseconds. The read-and-record rate is four million bits a second.

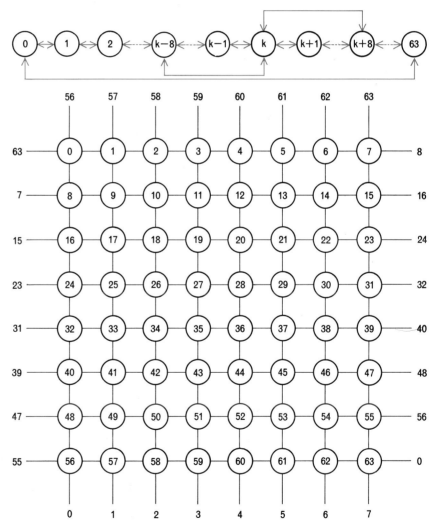

ARRAY OF 64 PROCESSING ELEMENTS in ILLIAC IV is connected in a pattern that can be regarded in either of two ways, which are topologically equivalent. The elements can be viewed as a linear string (top) with each processing element connected to its immediate neighbors and to neighbors spaced eight elements away. Equivalently, one can regard the processing elements as a square array (bottom) with each element connected to its four nearest neighbors. One can imagine the array rolled into a cylinder so that the processing elements in the top row connect directly to those in the bottom row. The last processing element in each row is connected to the first in the next row to produce a linear sequence.

freezing around the edges and proceeds toward the center.

The time saved by using the parallel algorithm rather than the sequential one depends on the number of iterations needed to produce convergence. If both algorithms require the same number of iterations and both compute the same number of interior values, P (or 36 in the case of the example above), the parallel process is faster by a factor of P. Since the parallel process uses less new information for each iteration, however, it will normally take more parallel iterations to produce the same degree of accuracy as a sequential calculation. Inasmuch as ILLIAC IV has 64 "channels" available for processing iterations in parallel, it is up to 64 times faster than a sequential computer of comparable speed. This advantage in overall speed far outweighs the few extra iterations necessary to obtain a solution equal in accuracy to that produced by sequential processing.

The reader may well ask at this point: "To what purpose can a computer of this large size be applied, and, indeed, is it necessary?" Or more pointedly he may ask: "Is it worth $30 million of public funds in these days of so many identified, competing needs?" Each of us must determine the answer for himself after examining the potential value of the machine. Let us, therefore, look at some of the applications.

Among the intended tasks for ILLIAC IV is linear programming, a mathematical technique for allocating the use of limited resources to maximize or minimize a specified objective. The resource limitations (constraints) are expressed as linear inequalities in which the variables are quantities of resources. The objective is specified as a linear function of these variables. Typical linear-programming problems presented to computers involve hundreds or even thousands of variables. Examples include routing deliveries to minimize distance traveled or to maximize deliveries per trip; blending, mixing, cutting or trimming raw materials to minimize waste or to maximize output value; selecting production methods that minimize cost or maximize output; scheduling production facilities to minimize delay or to maximize throughput.

ILLIAC IV will be able to solve in reasonable time much bigger problems than have been attempted in the past. This capability flows from the use of parallel computation and the high data-transfer rate of the ILLIAC IV memory disk. The linear-programming problem mentioned above that ILLIAC IV should be able to solve in less than two minutes (but which would take six to eight hours on a present-generation computer) is one that has 4,000 constraints and 10,000 variables.

A problem of this order of difficulty is now under active study at the University of Illinois under the direction of Ian W. Marceau. It involves optimizing the output of the agricultural sector of the economy, ranging in size from a large region to an entire nation. The desired objectives will reflect national policy, and they will range from production of enough food to nourish a given population to producing export crops so that a developing country can obtain foreign-exchange credits. The resources to be managed include land, labor, machinery, fertilizers, pesticides, herbicides, storage facilities and capital. As Marceau has demonstrated, linear-program-

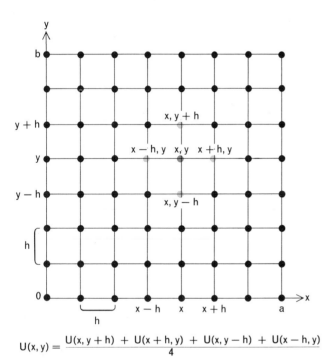

$$U(x, y) = \frac{U(x, y + h) + U(x + h, y) + U(x, y - h) + U(x - h, y)}{4}$$

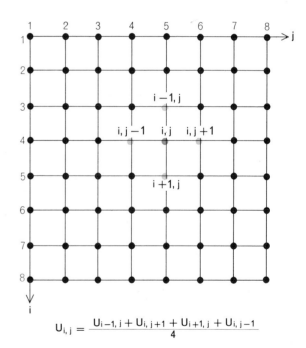

$$U_{i, j} = \frac{U_{i-1, j} + U_{i, j+1} + U_{i+1, j} + U_{i, j-1}}{4}$$

PROBLEM OF FINDING TEMPERATURES ON A SLAB must be prepared for a computer by digitizing the slab into an array of points, with some arbitrary mesh spacing (h). The purpose of this illustration and those on the next three pages is to compare how such a problem would be solved by sequential methods with a standard computer and by parallel methods using ILLIAC IV. In this problem one imagines that the edges of a slab are arbitrarily held at certain fixed temperatures. The computer is asked to calculate the temperature at a network of interior points after the slab has reached equilibrium. Two methods of identifying the points in the network are depicted above. The more familiar method at the left expresses each point in terms of x and y. The temperature U at any point x,y is the average of the temperatures at the four nearest mesh points. The equation specifies these points in terms of x and y and the mesh spacing h. In programming a computer it is more convenient to use the integers i and j as positional indicators, in which case the temperature equation is rewritten as shown at the right. The temperatures at 28 points on the perimeter of the slab are the known quantities supplied to the computer (*see illustration on opposite page*). The temperatures at the 36 interior points are the unknowns. In this example all the points on the bottom of the slab and on the right edge are held at zero degrees. The values along the top and left edge vary according to position. These boundary temperatures do not change during the calculation. The

ming models of a region or nation can also recognize constraints involving social costs, for example the harm done by the intensive application of nitrogenous fertilizers, the use of certain pesticides (such as DDT) or cultivation practices with long-term deleterious effects on the productivity of the land.

It must be pointed out that in order to apply linear programming to an entire economic sector one must incur considerable expense in gathering the data to be used in the model. Here too, however, the computer can help by making experimental trials and estimating the accuracy with which various input data need to be known in order to secure answers with a given level of precision. It is also possible to simulate alternative policies on the computer and estimate their effects on agricultural productivity. To test such

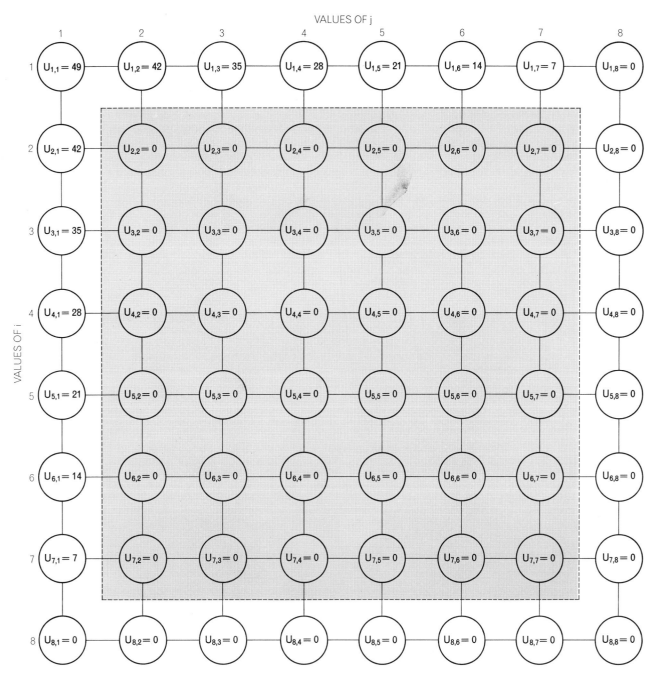

36 interior points are initially set to zero. When the problem is solved sequentially, the computer starts with the top left interior point $U_{2,2}$ and calculates its value using the numbers given above:

$$U_{2,2} = \frac{U_{1,2} + U_{2,3} + U_{3,2} + U_{2,1}}{4} = \frac{42 + 0 + 0 + 42}{4} = 21 .$$

The computer then calculates the value of $U_{2,3}$ using the *new* value of $U_{2,2}$ just obtained, which is 21, instead of the initial value, 0:

$$U_{2,3} = \frac{U_{1,3} + U_{2,4} + U_{3,3} + U_{2,2}}{4} = \frac{35 + 0 + 0 + 21}{4} = 14 .$$

The equation is similarly solved for the remaining 34 interior points, using at each step all the new values previously calculated. This sequence of 36 calculations is one "relaxation" of the relaxation method. If the problem were programmed for ILLIAC IV, on the other hand, each of the 36 interior points could be assigned to a separate processing element and 36 simultaneous solutions of the equation obtained. In this method the first relaxation consists of the 36 simultaneous solutions using *only* the numbers initially given. Thus the first solution of $U_{2,3}$ is $(35 + 0 + 0 + 0) \div 4 = 8.75$ rather than the value of 14 obtained in the sequential method. Succeeding simultaneous relaxations, however, can make use of values obtained previously. The way the two methods converge to yield the final answer is shown in the tables on the next page.

policies directly "in vivo" can be very costly. There is no reason why a computer program should not be the white rat or guinea pig for a proposed cure to a social problem.

Another application contemplated for ILLIAC IV is the establishment of natural-resource inventories to be used by municipal and regional planners. A Natural Resource Information System is now being developed at the University of Illinois in cooperation with the Northeast Illinois Natural Resource Service Center. The Ford Foundation has provided funds for the initial research and development program. The system will contain a wide range of information on the natural resources of a selected area: geology, hydrology, forestry and vegetation, climate, topography, soil characteristics and current land use. Marengo Township of McHenry County in Illinois has been selected for a pilot study.

The system is being designed so that it can easily be used by any decision-maker (including an individual taxpayer) regardless of his technical or administrative training. For example, an individual may want to know whether or not he can have a housing subdivision (or a tennis court or a fishpond) on his land. On the other hand, county administrators may be looking for the best site for a new hospital. The search for a hospital site could be reformulated into a series of commands that could be presented to the computer. For instance, search all tracts that lie between town *A* and town *B* and that are within two miles of route *C;* the area should be no smaller than five acres and no larger than 25 acres with the following characteristics: (1) one acre of soil capable of supporting a five-story hospital, with a gradient of less than 8 percent and not subject to flooding; (2) at least four acres (for a parking lot) that can be covered with asphalt without disturbing the underground water table; (3) trees at least 20 years old. If no tracts satisfied all these requirements, one or more of the less important conditions could be relaxed until a site was located.

The output of the information system is being designed to meet three levels of need. The simplest level will consist of a concise inventory listing. The next level will be an interpretation of the computer's search in prose that should be clear to an educated layman. The third level will be a highly technical description suitable for use by a specialist, such as a geologist or an ecologist. The objective of the information system is to shorten the planning process and to improve the quality of decisions. Although the system will use existing techniques of information retrieval, ILLIAC IV, with its speed and archival memory, will be able to analyze the stored information to a far greater depth than would be possible with any earlier computer.

Our unaugmented intellectual resources have not been capable of producing satisfactory solutions to the types of large-scale planning problems just described. It is in fact evident that we are currently faced with socially debilitating aftermaths of piecemeal planning—and nonplanning—in both of these areas. A rational 20th- (or 21st-) century society will not emerge solely on the basis of universal goodwill.

ONE RELAXATION — SEQUENTIAL METHOD

VALUES OF i \ VALUES OF j	1	2	3	4	5	6	7	8
1	49	42	35	28	21	14	7	0
2	42	21.00	14.00	10.50	7.88	5.47	3.12	0
3	35	14.00	7.00	4.38	3.06	2.13	1.31	0
4	28	10.50	4.38	2.19	1.31	0.86	0.54	0
5	21	7.88	3.06	1.31	0.66	0.38	0.23	0
6	14	5.47	2.13	0.86	0.38	0.19	0.11	0
7	7	3.12	1.31	0.54	0.23	0.11	0.05	0
8	0	0	0	0	0	0	0	0

ONE RELAXATION — PARALLEL METHOD

VALUES OF i \ VALUES OF j	1	2	3	4	5	6	7	8
1	49	42	35	28	21	14	7	0
2	42	21	8.75	7.00	5.25	3.50	1.75	0
3	35	8.75	0	0	0	0	0	0
4	28	7.00	0	0	0	0	0	0
5	21	5.25	0	0	0	0	0	0
6	14	3.50	0	0	0	0	0	0
7	7	1.75	0	0	0	0	0	0
8	0	0	0	0	0	0	0	0

10 RELAXATIONS — SEQUENTIAL METHOD

VALUES OF i \ VALUES OF j	1	2	3	4	5	6	7	8
1	49	42	35	28	21	14	7	0
2	42	35.37	29.01	22.90	17.03	11.31	5.66	0
3	35	29.01	23.41	18.24	13.44	8.88	4.44	0
4	28	22.90	18.24	14.05	10.26	6.75	3.38	0
5	21	17.03	13.44	10.26	7.44	4.88	2.44	0
6	14	11.31	8.88	6.75	4.88	3.19	1.60	0
7	7	5.66	4.44	3.38	2.44	1.60	0.80	0
8	0	0	0	0	0	0	0	0

10 RELAXATIONS — PARALLEL METHOD

VALUES OF i \ VALUES OF j	1	2	3	4	5	6	7	8
1	49	42	35	28	21	14	7	0
2	42	34.27	27.05	20.53	14.81	9.60	4.74	0
3	35	27.05	19.87	14.08	9.48	5.90	2.83	0
4	28	20.53	14.08	9.06	5.62	3.22	1.49	0
5	21	14.81	9.48	5.62	3.09	1.61	0.69	0
6	14	9.60	5.90	3.22	1.61	0.73	0.28	0
7	7	4.74	2.83	1.49	0.69	0.28	0.10	0
8	0	0	0	0	0	0	0	0

50 RELAXATIONS — SEQUENTIAL METHOD

VALUES OF i \ VALUES OF j	1	2	3	4	5	6	7	8
1	49	42	35	28	21	14	7	0
2	42	36.00	30.00	24.00	18.00	12.00	6.00	0
3	35	30.00	25.00	20.00	15.00	10.00	5.00	0
4	28	24.00	20.00	16.00	12.00	8.00	4.00	0
5	21	18.00	15.00	12.00	9.00	6.00	3.00	0
6	14	12.00	10.00	8.00	6.00	4.00	2.00	0
7	7	6.00	5.00	4.00	3.00	2.00	1.00	0
8	0	0	0	0	0	0	0	0

50 RELAXATIONS — PARALLEL METHOD

VALUES OF i \ VALUES OF j	1	2	3	4	5	6	7	8
1	49	42	35	28	21	14	7	0
2	42	35.98	29.96	23.96	17.96	11.96	5.98	0
3	35	29.96	24.94	19.92	14.92	9.94	4.96	0
4	28	23.96	19.92	15.90	11.90	7.92	3.96	0
5	21	17.96	14.92	11.90	8.90	5.92	2.96	0
6	14	11.96	9.94	7.92	5.92	3.94	1.96	0
7	7	5.98	4.96	3.96	2.96	1.96	0.98	0
8	0	0	0	0	0	0	0	0

DIFFERENT STAGES IN RELAXATION PROCESS are compared for sequential relaxations and parallel relaxations. The exact values are given in the array on the opposite page. The two methods for calculating the temperature of each of 36 interior points on a slab are described in the illustration on the preceding two pages. There one sees that a standard computer using sequential methods would obtain a value of 21 for point $U_{2,2}$ and 14 for $U_{2,3}$ in performing one relaxation. Here it is seen that after 10 relaxations by the sequential method the value of $U_{2,2}$ has climbed to 35.37 and the value of $U_{2,3}$ to 29.01. After 50 relaxations $U_{2,2}$ and $U_{2,3}$ have reached their exact values: 36 and 30. Using parallel relaxations ILLIAC IV would converge on the exact solution in a distinctly dif-

A quite different assignment for ILLIAC IV is numerical weather prediction, which early computer theorists such as John von Neumann regarded as one of the important motivations for their work. Numerical techniques developed over the past two decades are now in daily use and yield good results for periods of from 24 to 48 hours. These techniques involve the simulation of complex atmospheric processes by a mathematical model that combines extensive knowledge of the relevant physical processes with sophisticated mathematics and advanced computer technology.

The physical basis for all numerical simulations of the atmosphere is the conservation of mass, momentum and energy. These conservation principles are embodied in sets of differential equations (Laplace's equation is an example of a differential equation describing heat distribution on a slab), which cannot be solved without a computer. The physical scales of atmospheric phenomena that are simulated on the computer range from the microphysical processes of clouds to the continental motions of frontal systems. At the upper end of the physical scale there are general-circulation models that describe the atmosphere as a heat engine driven by the sun.

The complexity of these models is illustrated by the operational model of the atmosphere used by the National Weather Service in its daily forecasts. The atmosphere over the Northern Hemisphere is represented by six horizontal slices ranging from sea level to the stratosphere. Each slice contains 3,000 points at which initial values of wind velocity, temperature and pressure are inserted. The computer then applies the appropriate equations to predict what the velocity, temperature and pressure will be in the future at 10-minute intervals. A 24-hour forecast requires about an hour of computing time on a computer that can execute 300,000 instructions per second, or more than a billion instructions in all.

If the distance between the grid points were to be halved, the number of grid points would be quadrupled and the computer time needed for a 24-hour forecast would be increased eightfold. In other words, a third of a day would be consumed merely in making a 24-hour prediction. If the model yields significantly better short-range predictions than the 3,000-point model now in use, there is a good chance that numerical forecasts can be extended to five days with an accuracy comparable to that of the 48-hour forecasts now being generated.

The actual computer techniques of weather forecasting can be advanced by testing them on ILLIAC IV. Until now investigators have been reluctant to experiment with a new predicting technique when it might involve many computer simulations, each of which could take up to 100 hours of computing time. When ILLIAC IV can reduce the running time from 100 hours to one hour, extensive experimentation will become feasible.

Mathematical models exist today for a large variety of physical systems and are in constant use as the basis for calculation aimed at prediction. Biological and biochemical systems have not been modeled with the same intensity of effort or success. There are a number of reasons for this. One can, for example, write a system of ordinary differential equations that might plausibly seem to describe the growth of a living cell. One can even measure initial concentrations with seemingly sufficient accuracy to do meaningful calculation. The number of equations in the system, however, corresponds to the number of genes in the chromosome, which is just too large a number to be handled in the cases of most interest. On the scale of real ecological systems, on the other hand, population models can be developed but measurements are extremely elusive. (How many alewives are in Lake Michigan?) Calculations would have to be performed with statistical variables to estimate a population range for each species of organism. This consumes computational capacity of a higher order of magnitude than deterministic calculation. Even the methodology of such calculation poses significant theoretical problems.

To summarize, I believe computers on the scale of ILLIAC IV will remove some of the very real barriers of capacity from certain calculations that have a direct bearing on our ability to produce a rational and enduring basis for life. Counterpoised is the computer's potential to play a significant role in the depersonalization and disordering of society. Scientists must not share the neutrality of the computer to the outcome.

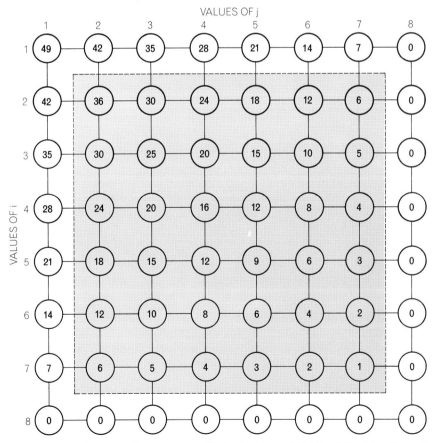

VALUES OF j

VALUES OF i

ferent manner. After 10 relaxations it would obtain values of 34.27 and 27.05 for $U_{2,2}$ and $U_{2,3}$ respectively. The results after 50 relaxations, however, would be virtually the same. For this particular problem the parallel method requires a few more relaxations than the sequential method to achieve comparable results. ILLIAC IV, however, will be able to carry out 36 complete relaxations (and as many as 64 given a suitable problem) in the time that a comparably fast sequential computer would need to carry out one sequential relaxation.

V

FOUR ESSAYS ON THE USES OF THE COMPUTER

V

FOUR ESSAYS
ON THE USES
OF THE COMPUTER

INTRODUCTION

This section consists of four essays on the uses of computers in four fields that are not generally thought to overlap greatly. Nevertheless, there are striking parallels and common areas of concern among these essays.

The article by Coons, "The Uses of Computers in Technology," is the most straightforward of the four. Creative opportunities in engineering practice have always been widely separated by essential detail work; Coons mentions such details as operation of machine tools, solution of simple equations, computation of stresses in structures, and synthesis of smooth curves with given boundary conditions. Details like these, and such even more tedious others as replication of substructure on drawings, have traditionally been the work of engineering apprentices and technicians, not always so-called. Today, computers are replacing these assistants to the practicing engineer.

As Coons points out, the chief consequences of this replacement are not simple economies of mechanization. Because the computer methods are so much faster than the manual ones, the engineer is now free to experiment in ways that, a few years ago, would have entailed prohibitive delays to his project.

The situation in organizations is, perhaps surprisingly, similar to that in technology. In "The Uses of Computers in Organizations" Martin Greenberger lists various examples of man-machine systems used for management. Except perhaps for the outlying case of industrial process-control, these examples never show an *essential* use of computers. Just like Coons' engineers, Greenberger's managers could —and did—get along without today's elaborate information-processing aids. But computers have brought to the manager, as to the engineer, new possibilities for optimization and simultaneously new opportunities for experimentation and innovation.

Greenberger also touches on a cultural flow in the reverse direction, from management to computer science. The notion of programming management is a new one in most circles. Up until the middle 1960's, few computer programs had ever required work by more than a dozen people, and most programs had actually been one-man projects. There had been a few more heavily staffed programs; none of these had been more than marginally successful. Almost all these large programs, however, had been military or proprietary, so that information about them was hard to obtain.

In the last five years or so, many more large and visible programming projects have been undertaken. Of these, even the most successful have typically sustained three years of unanticipated delay. It is now recognized (Buxton and Randell, 1969) that management problems constitute the most serious obstacle to completion of ambitious programming projects.

Patrick Suppes' article "Uses of Computers in Education," is still sound, as far as it goes. Drill and practice has not changed its nature in hundreds of years, and computers are evidently well-suited to supervision of it. Suppes' "tutorial" systems give a new medium to the teacher who might otherwise have lectured or written a book. To such a teacher, the computer is as little and as much a boon as the microphone or the typewriter. The primary problems, as Suppes well points out, are still problems of organizing the curriculum.

The "dialogue" systems described by Suppes are advancing only slowly. Any such system must know and understand its topic. This may be easy with a few subjects, such as Suppes' example of the propositional calculus, but others involve vast webs of interrelated information. The development of dialogue systems in substantive areas of study will be a considerable achievement of artificial intelligence.

Quite recently, a fourth stream of educational uses of computers has developed. This new stream was anticipated by Christopher Strachey, who remarks (p. 76) that error is human and that life and programming—unlike traditional schoolwork—consist largely of correcting, rather than being cursed by, errors once made.

Children are rarely taught this truth. A child who cannot "get" something is usually at a total loss; he perceives no substructure in the skill being taught, so it either must "come to him" or he is stymied. This is cognate to the situation of the novice programmer, who knows no error-correcting techniques, when faced with his first program bug.

To acquaint children with problem-solving *per se* as a set of widely applicable techniques, Seymour Papert and others are exposing elementary-school children to computer programming (Papert, 1970). These efforts will be the first computer application to education that has been more than automation of the most mechanical aspects of human pedagogy.

If Papert succeeds, it will be because computer programming provides a model of the mind. That is, the concepts that encapsulate our understanding of computer software (e.g., "subroutine," "recursion," "interrupt," etc.) are similarly fruitful when applied to the organization of our own thinking. The fact that the computer model allows us to "debug" our thinking tells us that the model is structural (revealing of inner structure) and not merely functional (behavioristic). Of course, as Oettinger remarks in "The Uses of Computers in Science," this excellent *mind*-model is of no value whatever in understanding the *brain*, any more than it is of value in understanding the semiconductor technology of computer hardware.

Oettinger's article is a rich and difficult one. Some of it has unfortunately become dated; for example, his work on English grammar is no longer of interest in computer circles (see the introduction to Section II of this book), although it is still representative of a dominant style in linguistics.

The core of Oettinger's article is his distinction between the computer as an instrument and the computer as a vehicle for theories. In part, of course, Oettinger's "instruments" are no different from the mechanical aids of Coons, Greenberger, and Suppes. One of Oettinger's instruments, for example, simply punches cards to record the output of a photomultiplier tube.

But Oettinger's instruments do more than this. Most significantly, they convert "raw observations" to "intuitively intelligible representations." Perhaps Oettinger's best example is the program by Cyrus Levinthal (see Levinthal, "Molecular Model-building by Computer," p. 171) which computes three-dimensional structural formulas from electron-density examination of crystals. From Oettinger's description (or Levinthal's), it might appear that his instrument is as unbiased and theory-free as a micrometer. In fact, this is not so.

Unlike such older instruments as the telescope, the computer is not limited to a single form for its "intuitively intelligible representations." By choosing a form of output, Levinthal (for example) chose a *language* in which to discuss the nature of protein molecules. And by choosing a language, Levinthal necessarily chose a *theory*, or at least a class of theories, with which to understand these molecules. Ontology, as James Grier Miller has remarked, recapitulates philology, and the simple effect of computers on science is that theory and experimental instrument may be made one.

23

THE USES OF COMPUTERS IN TECHNOLOGY

STEVEN ANSON COONS
September, 1966

The uses of computers in technology fall into two categories. One is traditional (if so new a field can be said to have a tradition), the other quite novel. The first category includes the multifarious applications in which the computer carries out a program of instructions with little or no intervention by human beings. This is a powerful way to use an information-processing machine, and it has dominated the early years of the computer era. The second category embraces a new class of applications in which the computer is an active partner of man. I believe that within the next few years this new way of using computers will bring about deep changes in the large segment of technology that might be called "creative engineering."

As the computer is traditionally applied to a technological task, it acts as it is told to act. This is not to say that a machine so instructed cannot accomplish impressive tasks. Its program can be quite elaborate—so complex that no human being could follow it in a reasonable length of time (even, in some instances, in an unreasonable length of time). In obeying instructions a computer often deals appropriately with changing circumstances and adjusts to variations in its environment, achieving its purpose by a process so subtle as to give the impression of adaptive intelligence. The machine is nonetheless acting as an automaton. Its behavior, although complex, is mechanical and predictable. Man's ingenuity is applied to presenting the problem or setting up the task; thereafter the machine grinds away at the solution or execution.

This is not the case when the computer and man are linked in what J. C. R. Licklider of the International Business Machines Corporation calls a symbiotic relationship, a relationship in which each can perform the kind of activity for which it is best suited. Man is quite good at inventing and organizing ideas, making associations among apparently unrelated notions, recognizing patterns and stripping away irrelevant detail; he is creative, unpredictable, sometimes capricious, sensitive to human values. The computer is almost exactly what man is not. It is capable of paying undivided attention to unlimited detail; it is immune to distraction, precise and reliable; it can carry out the most intricate and lengthy calculation with ease, without a flaw and in much less than a millionth of the time that would be required by its human counterpart. It is emotionless, or so we suppose. It suffers from neither boredom nor fatigue. It needs to be told only once; thereafter it remembers perfectly until it is told to forget, whereupon it forgets instantly and absolutely.

When man and machine work together, the shortcomings of each are compensated by the other, which leaves both partners free to exercise their individual powers in a common enterprise. The potential of such a combination is greater than the sum of its parts.

It was clear when the first electronic computers were being developed that the machines could by their nature deal easily with repetitive calculations. During World War II computers worked out firing tables for artillery. Another early application was the calculation of logarithmic and trigonometric tables to a large number of significant figures. It was startling to find that some of the classic tables that had been calculated "by hand" contained errors that were discovered only after computer calculation. Computers have continued to specialize in bulky calculations, particularly those in which the procedure is either involved and complicated or repetitive.

It soon became apparent, however, that the computer could also maintain quite sophisticated control over its own procedures and could successfully attack problems of a more difficult kind. Specifically, the ability of the computer to compare two numbers and to elect any one of two or three courses of action based on the outcome of the comparison, although simple in principle,

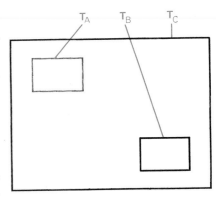

THE COMPUTER-GENERATED display on the following page is a graphical solution of a typical "equilibrium" problem in engineering: to show the heat distribution in a slab. The rectangular slab (*see illustration above*) has two regions whose boundaries are maintained at temperatures (T_A and T_B) that are respectively the same amount higher and lower than the temperature (T_C) at which the boundary of the slab itself is maintained. The curves connecting the three rectangles in the display give the heat distribution, with the temperatures indicated by the z coordinate. The display was generated on a Project MAC terminal at the Massachusetts Institute of Technology; the computer program was Equilibrium Problem-Solver, designed by Coyt Tillman of M.I.T.

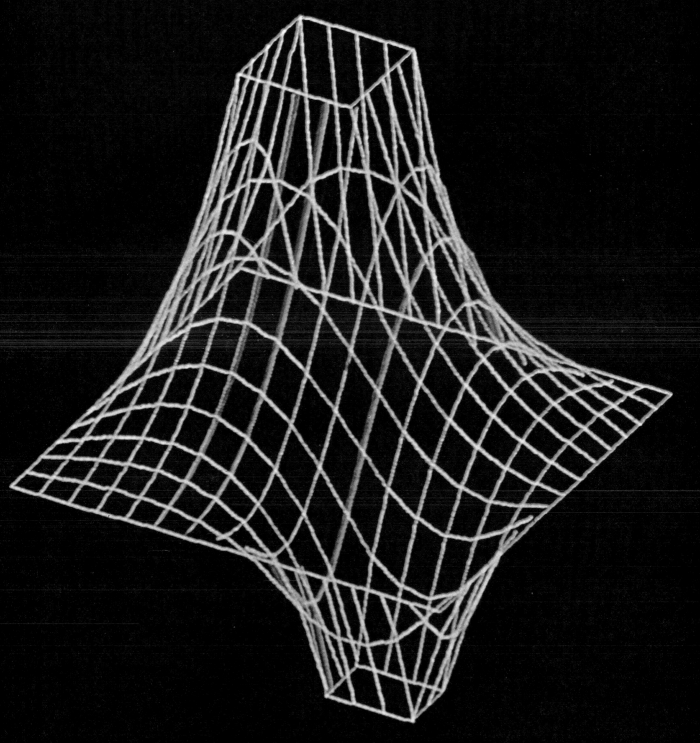

has led to some sophisticated applications. A computer can in fact be relied on to carry out the most intricate processes in the manipulation and transformation of information, provided that these processes are understood well enough by humans to be described in complete detail to the computer.

A computer can, for example, control industrial processes. Not all "automated" industrial plants have computer systems and not all computerized plants are equally automatic. It is possible to construct complex control systems based on continuous monitoring and feedback loops without including computers. Sometimes computers are introduced to make calculations and inform a human operator what needs to be done. Moreover, a computer can on its own control an individual subprocess or regulate an important variable in a production line. In some cases (still largely confined to the petroleum and chemical industries) a computer system actually controls the routine operations of the plant.

The control of chemical plants is a good example of an application in which the computer can deal with a large amount of information, monitoring the many variables involved in such a way as to maintain optimum production and quality of product. The variables in a chemical process—temperature, pressure, flow, valve settings, viscosity, color and many others—are interrelated in complicated ways, and usually the relations are highly nonlinear. If two ingredients must flow into a reaction vessel in a certain ratio, and the flow rate of one ingredient is deficient for some reason, it does no good for the computer system to attempt to rectify the deficiency by opening the supply valve wider if the valve is already fully open; instead the computer should take account of the state of affairs and close the valve on the other supply line until the desired ratio of flows is achieved.

A computer is able to receive information from many measuring stations located at strategic places in the process plant, to perform the necessary calculations and comparisons of these detailed data, to make decisions on how to monitor the control mechanisms and to send commands back to them in such a way as to maintain optimum operation. This capability is highly reliable, and since there is essentially no limit to the complexity of the information with which the computer can deal, industrial engineers can now devise processes so intricate that it would be difficult, if not

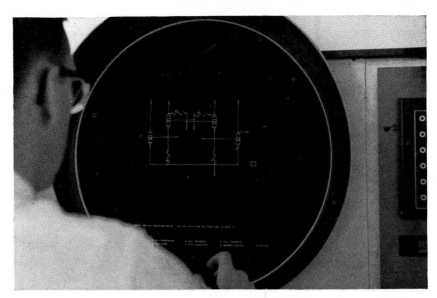

MACHINES MAKE MACHINES in International Business Machines Corporation plants producing System 360 computers. Drawings for circuit modules can be produced with a 1620 computer. The designer draws a schematic circuit diagram (*shown here*) and module layout with a light pen. The computer produces the module design used in manufacturing.

DRILLING MACHINE that produces panels for printed-circuit cards for the System 360 is controlled by a unit (*left*) of a 1710 control system. The 1710, on a time-shared basis, sends instructions to position the 24-spindle drill, which drills 6,000 holes in less than a minute. The computer also controls an electron-beam "hole-tester" that spot-tests diameters.

MICROCIRCUIT ASSEMBLIES for the System 360 move through a computer-controlled final test line. The testing machine, controlled by an IBM 1410 (*left background*), can perform hundreds of different tests for shorts, impedance or logical integrity on each card.

PAPER MACHINE at the Mead Corporation's Kingsport Division in Tennessee has a computer process-control system. The 405-foot-long machine produces rolls of paper up to 16 feet wide at the rate of 2,000 feet per minute. An IBM 1710 control system monitors the process and directly controls one of the important variables, the average "basis weight" of the paper. The remote unit shown here includes a printer (*right*) that brings data to the operator and an input unit through which he communicates with the computer.

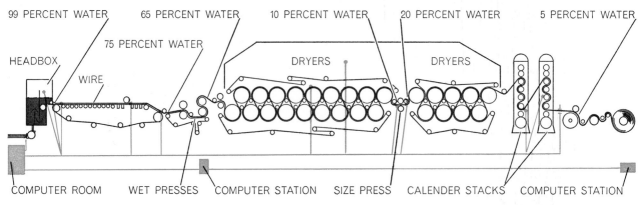

COMPUTER INSTALLATION is shown in color in this simplified schematic diagram with colored dots indicating typical measuring points. A mixture of wood pulp, water and additives emerges from the headbox, is spread on a wire screen and carried through pressing and drying operations. The basis weight is measured by a beta-ray gauge (*right*); the computer reports any variations from the desired standard, warns the operators and computes and initiates corrections in the flow rate of materials at the headbox (*left*).

impossible, to control them with human workers.

Another industrial application of computers lies in the numerical control of machine tools. A great many parts of machines are produced by either milling or routing, processes in which a cutting tool moves so as to cut some contoured shape out of sheet metal or heavier stock. In conventional methods this demands the constant attention of a skilled machine operator, particularly if the contour to be formed is irregularly curved. Under the control of a computer the cutter can be made to move in any desired path, and it is in principle no more difficult to produce "sculptured" shapes bounded by complex curved surfaces than it is to produce objects with flat faces. The numerical control of machine tools has enjoyed an extraordinary success because it guarantees the reliability and reproducibility of even the most elaborate shapes. The spoilage due to human error is reduced to the vanishing point, and many parts are now practicable that would be prohibitively expensive to produce if a human operator had to monitor the settings of the machine.

A striking example is the milling of airplane-wing "skins" from slabs of aluminum alloy. For structural reasons these sheet metal skins need to be thicker near the wing roots, where the bending stress is high, than they do near the wing tips, where it is less. For a long time this has been accomplished by assembling an elaborate laminated structure, with sheets of varying thickness fastened together by hundreds of rivets and stiffened by bulkheads and frames. The assembly of such structures is complicated and time-consuming. Now it has been found that much of the wing structure can literally be cut out of solid slabs—tapered thickness, stiffening members and all—at a cost and in a time substantially less than is needed for conventional assembly methods. Wing skins cut from slabs two inches thick, 10 feet wide and 40 feet long are not at all uncommon.

The increasing capabilities of modern computers suggested that a more direct partnership between the machines and their human operators would be effective, and several developments described in other articles in this issue combined to make this possible. First, the languages by which men communicate with computers have evolved rapidly. Language forms have now begun to appear that are much more "problem-

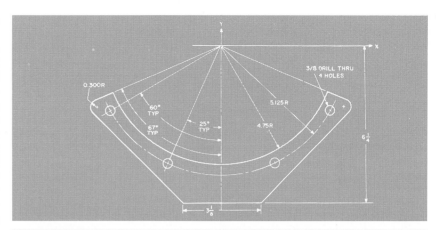

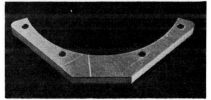

MACHINE TOOLS can be controlled by computers. At the IIT Research Institute the process begins with a conventional engineering drawing of a part to be machined, in this case a small "radius plate" (*top*). From the drawing the part programmer, writing in the APT (Automatic Programming for Tools) language, prepares a set of instructions that describe the part (*second from top*) and also the path to be followed by the tool. A computer calculates the detailed motions required to move the tool along that path, translating the programmer's word-symbols into numerical signals in the form of a punched tape. The tape controls the machine (*third from top*), in this case an "Omnimil" with 60 tools that are automatically interchangeable. A milling tool (*bottom left*) shapes the part (*bottom right*).

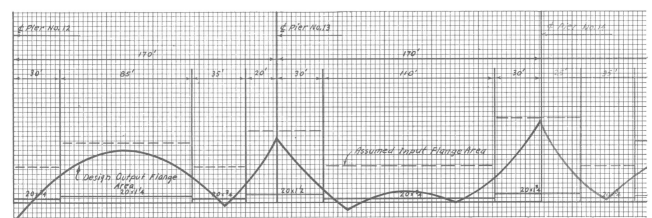

BRIDGE DESIGN can be largely accomplished by a computer. This sequence illustrates the design of two spans of a continuous-plate-girder portion of a bridge designed by Louis Berger & Associates for the New Jersey Turnpike Authority, using the computer system and facilities of Omnidata Services, Inc. On the basis of an assumed design the engineer plots (*broken lines*) estimated cross-sectional areas of the "flanges," or horizontal members of the girder. For example, he assumes 20-by-¾-inch flanges for the first 30-foot segment.

1	5	4	0	1.21	0.	0.
170.	1.373	1250.				
1	170.	78.	78.			
2	30.	20.	.75			
2	115.	20.	1.25			
2	150.	20.	.75			
2	170.	20.	1.50			
3	30.	20.	.75			
3	115.	20.	1.25			
3	150.	20.	.75			
3	170.	20.	1.50			
4	170.	99999.	.5			
170.	1.375	1250.				
1	170.	78.	78.			
2	30.	20.	1.5			
2	140.	20.	.75			
2	170.	20.	1.75			
3	30.	20.	1.5			
3	140.	20.	.75			
3	170.	20.	1.75			
4	170.	99999.	.5			

```
160001000000
NON-COMPOSITE CONTINUOUS BEAM PROGRAM
3 2 20. 27. 0.

      NON-COMPOSITE CONTINUOUS STEEL BEAM DESIGN @ X/10 POINTS

SPANS          STRESS-1          STRESS-2          STRESS-3
  3               20                27                 0

SPAN
 1

X-POINT       FLANGE-AREA       FLANGE-AREA       FLANGE-AREA

  1            9.5910076         5.4189283
  2           21.283315         14.079896
  3           28.591007         19.493002
  4           31.552546         21.686734
  5           30.198700         20.683885
  6           24.575623         16.518643
  7           14.744853          9.2365921
  8            .85254615        -1.0540062
  9           17.044853         10.940295
 10           39.760238         27.766506


SPAN
 2

X-POINT       FLANGE-AREA       FLANGE-AREA       FLANGE-AREA

  1           20.775623         13.703828
  2            7.5294692         3.8918626
  3            1.7294692         -.40443361
  4            7.3987000         3.7949965
  5            9.1679307         5.1055379
  6            6.7063923         3.2821760
  7            4.6140846         1.7323185
  8           13.367930          8.2166490
  9           28.206392         19.208102
 10           48.560238         34.285025
STOP
```

INPUT TO COMPUTER (*left*) includes coded specifications (*top*) and estimated flange areas for segments of the assumed girder. The computer calculates stresses on the girder and gives, for two kinds of steel, exact flange areas at 10 points along each span (*right*).

COMPUTED FLANGE AREAS are then plotted (*color*) on the engineer's work sheet. In this case the computer has confirmed the estimated design of the girders, as can be seen here because the colored line falls within the estimated values for the flange areas.

oriented" or "user-oriented" than the original languages; they are easy to learn because they resemble ordinary English and involve more or less conventional mathematical notation.

Another important development that makes the man-machine combination feasible is time-sharing [see "Time-sharing on Computers," by R. M. Fano and F. J. Corbató, page 79]. Computers can be operated economically only if they are kept constantly busy at productive work. A man working at a computer console cannot keep the machine busy, because the machine can receive a command, interpret and act on it and return a reply or a result in a few microseconds; then it must wait while the human operator digests the reply, thinks about it and decides on his next action. Enough people at individual consoles can provide the time-shared computer with a work load that will keep it gainfully employed.

A third development is the display console, on which the computer can create symbols, graphs and drawings of objects and can maintain the display statically or cause it to move, simulating dynamic behavior. Together with input devices such as the "light pen," the display console becomes a window through which information can be transferred between the man and the machine.

The comfortable and congenial combination of man and machine made possible by these three developments has found some of its first applications in computer-aided design. By "design" I mean the creative engineering process, including the analytical techniques of testing, evaluation and decision-making and then the experimental verification and eventual realization of the result in tangible form. In science and engineering (and perhaps in art as well) the creative process is a process of experimentation with ideas. Concepts form, dissolve and reappear in different contexts; associations occur, are examined and tested for validity on a conscious but qualitative level, and are either accepted tentatively or rejected. Eventually, however, the concepts and conjectures must be put to the precise test of mathematical analysis. When these analytical procedures are established ones (as they are in such disciplines as stress analysis, fluid mechanics and electrical-network analysis), the work to be done is entirely mechanical. It can be formulated and set down in algorithms: rituals of procedure that can be described in minute detail and can be performed by a computer. Indeed, this part of the creative process *should* be done by the computer in order to leave man free to exercise his human powers and apply his human values.

There is much talk of "automated design" nowadays, but usually automated design is only part of the design process, an optimization of a concept already qualitatively formed. There are, for example, computer programs that produce complete descriptions of electrical transformers, wiring diagrams or printed-circuit boards. There are programs that design bridges in the sense that they work out the stresses on each structural member and in effect write its specifications. Such programs are powerful new engineering tools, but they do not depend on an internal capability of creativity; the creativity has already been exercised in generating them.

I can best give some idea of the potentialities of computer-aided design by describing one of the tools that makes it possible. One of the early and epochal instances of man-machine symbiosis was the program called Sketchpad, which was completed late in 1962 by Ivan E. Sutherland of the Massachusetts Institute of Technology [see "Computer Inputs and Outputs," by Ivan E. Sutherland, page 42]. Sutherland used the TX-2 computer, an experimental machine that was built at the Lincoln Laboratory of M.I.T. with the idea of providing direct man-machine interaction at the console long before such a notion had much currency in computer technology and long before the notion of multiple users of a machine was much more than a dream.

When Sutherland began work on Sketchpad, the TX-2 had a cathode-ray-tube screen and a light pen as existing rudimentary pieces of equipment, but little had been done to exploit their possibilities. Sutherland set out to develop a system that would make possible direct conversation between man and machine in geometric, graphical terms. In the course of the development of Sketchpad he would invite people in to try out his system so that he could observe their reactions. On one occasion Claude E. Shannon, Sutherland's adviser on his doctoral thesis, wanted to perform a geometric construction. Rather than work out the construction on

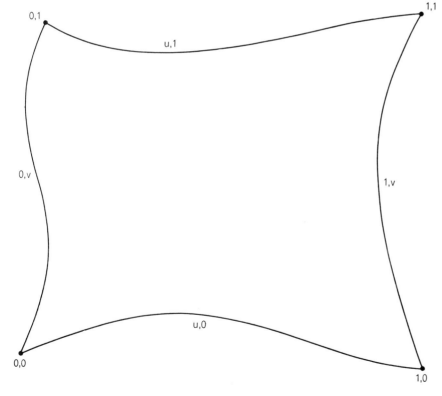

COMPUTER-AIDED DESIGN of complex forms requires a method of describing surfaces mathematically. In the author's method free-form surfaces are built up from a number of surface "patches," each limited and defined by four boundary curves. Any point on the surface of a patch such as this one has three space coordinates, each a function of two independent variables, designated *u* and *v*, the values of which are allowed to range between 0 and 1.

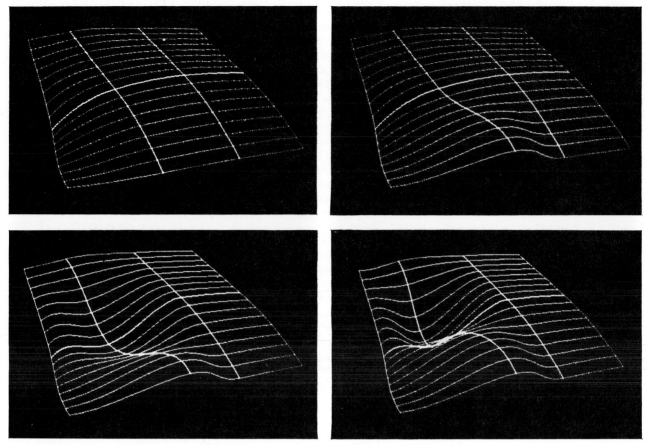

MODIFICATION OF A SURFACE on the display scope of a computer is illustrated in these photographs from the Metal Stamping Division of the Ford Motor Company. The six-patch surface, representing half of a windshield, is shown at the upper left. The coordinates of a corner along one edge are raised (*top right*) and the coordinates of an interior corner are lowered (*bottom left*). Finally a tangent vector, which helps define one edge of a patch, is twisted. A requirement in manipulations of this kind is that the surface behave plastically rather than elastically: the change must be restricted to one site and continuity of slope must be maintained.

the console screen, Shannon automatically turned to paper and pencil to make a preliminary sketch. This came as a disappointment to Sutherland, who intended the system to be so congenial to the user that it would not intrude on his thought processes. He thereupon disassembled his program and rewrote it. It went through several such revisions, and it stands today as a classic of well-considered human engineering.

Learning to use Sketchpad is so easy that it can scarcely be thought of as learning; one simply begins and then becomes more skillful with experience. The program is remarkably versatile. Using Sketchpad, I was able one evening to set up and experiment with the following problems and constructions:

1. Evaluate a cubic polynomial equation. There is a simple geometric construction for polynomials of any degree and for real and complex values of the various terms. By manipulating the x variable with the light pen I could cause y to vanish, thus "solving" the cubic equation.

2. Construct a general conic section, or second-degree curve, using the basic principles of projective geometry.

3. Draw and set in simulated motion a "four-bar" mechanical linkage. Although such linkages are simple in outward form, their analysis is troublesome and is still the subject of investigation.

4. Draw a pin-jointed structure (such as a bridge), displace one of the joints (as if loading the structure) and observe the "relaxation" that is thereupon carried out by the computer to minimize the energy of the system, thereby simulating the actual deflection.

5. Plot the potential field typical of the flow of an ideal fluid within a region of specified shape.

Now, it is clear that these five problems are not much related to one another and that a conventional computer program written to deal with one of them would not be of the slightest use for any of the others. The computer did not contain a set of programs—one for each of the problems. Instead it had a flexible and quite general capability for performing a set of primitive geometric constructions and for applying a set of primitive geometric constraints. The computer played the role of an intelligent but innocent assistant, and together the machine and I set up and solved the problems. The time it took to do so was not more than 10 or 15 minutes in each case, so that something less than two hours was spent in not only achieving solutions but also experimenting with these solutions by changing the input variables. During this time the computer was mostly idle, waiting for me to decide what to do next. It probably spent not much more than five minutes in actual cooperative work.

This experiment in man-machine interaction is described not because the problems are significant or because the solutions were obtained efficiently. On the contrary, the computer was compelled to obtain solutions in an inefficient way compared with what might have happened if special conventional programs had been written for each problem. Five such special programs, however, could well have taken weeks to write and "debug."

Whereas Ivan Sutherland's Sketchpad

is purely geometric, William R. Sutherland, also of M.I.T., has extended his brother's work to include abstractions. With his program one can draw diagrams, attach meanings to them and then cause the computer to take appropriate action based on the diagrams and their associated meanings. One can draw a circuit diagram, for example, stipulate the characteristics and functional behavior of the elements of the diagram and then simulate the actual circuit performance. One can also draw a logical flow diagram of a computational procedure and then "activate" the diagram, so to speak, to obtain numerical results from numerical inputs to the procedural diagram.

The two Sutherlands' systems illustrate the striking possibilities of direct and natural communication with the machine. It is perhaps no mere coincidence that these highly congenial systems are graphical, and that the two-dimensional nature of their communicative form greatly enhances the ease of their use and the "transparency" of the interface they create between man and computer. The line of type from conventional typewriter keyboards has until recently been the only economically

available means of "on line" communication with the computer. This one-dimensional string of symbols has had a somewhat stultifying influence on computer technology, partly because it bears little resemblance to standard and familiar mathematical notation and perhaps partly because its awkward syntactic constructions force some unnatural formulations in programming.

In many fields of engineering the geometric description of objects is a fundamentally important task. Airplane fuselages, ship hulls and automobile bodies are all complex free forms (as opposed to simpler specified forms such as spheres, cones, toruses or ellipsoids) and take many months to design and define by conventional methods. All kinds of smaller objects are also free forms: the hand set of a telephone, the bowl of a tobacco pipe, a differential housing of an automobile. In the design and ultimate detailed description of all such shapes the computer can make an extremely important contribution.

Objects are bounded by surfaces, and once the surfaces are designed and described we know a great deal about the object. The computer has made it pos-

sible, at least in principle, to perform all kinds of geometric operations on surfaces, provided that they can be described in mathematical terms. Unfortunately the traditional mathematical treatment of surfaces says a great deal about the analytical relations of surfaces that already exist and are expressible mathematically but very little about the problem of bringing them into existence. The emphasis has been on analysis, and until recently the study of the synthesis of surfaces has been neglected.

The design of a free-form shape begins with the design of a few salient outlines; once these important design curves are established, the complete and detailed description of the object's surface is to some extent a matter of mechanical extension of the implicit information. For example, an engineer can define a few contour curves for a casting. His drawing goes to a patternmaker in the shop, who creates a pattern in wood. The surface of the pattern is suggested by the design curves but is necessarily more completely specified; the patternmaker extends the original meager information by interpreting the intent of the designer. In the process he has done nothing inherently creative,

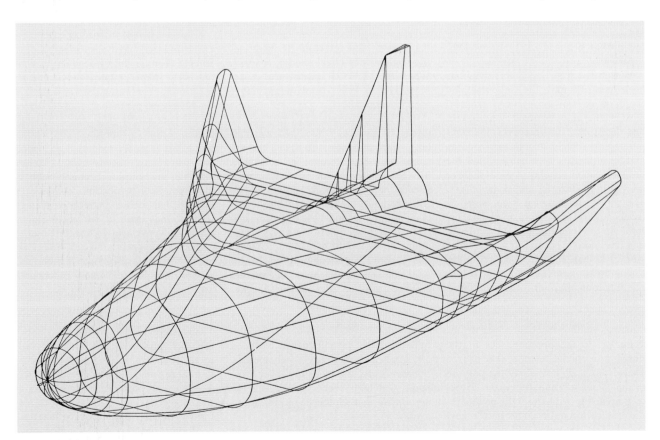

PERSPECTIVE DRAWING of a vehicle designed for reentry from space was produced by a computer-graphics program in the Aerospace Group of the Boeing Company. Orthogonal (head-on, top and side) views are prepared and points from these drawings are stored in the computer numerically. The computer projects the points and a tape from the computer drives a plotting machine.

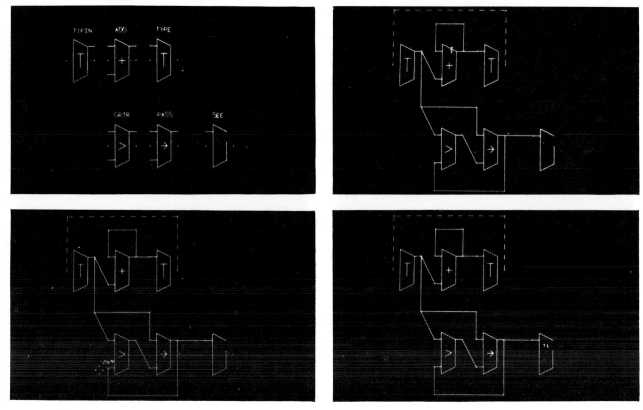

DIAGRAMS can be "activated" by a program devised by William R. Sutherland of M.I.T. Here a computer procedure is developed that will cause the computer to accept a series of numbers, print out the running sum and present in the last box of the display the largest of the input numbers. The individual symbols are displayed (*top left*) and are connected in a way that establishes the procedure (*top right*). One of the numbers to be added is introduced (*bottom left*) and finally the high number is displayed (*bottom right*).

but he has behaved like a benevolent, experienced and skillful machine.

Within the past few years a way has been found to make the computer play the part of the experienced pattern-maker. The designer need only draw a few descriptive design curves; the computer immediately generates a surface that incorporates these curves, and the designer can either accept the surface or modify it by drawing additional curves. The surface so designed is contained in the computer in definite mathematical form and is constructed automatically in a fraction of a second. If the designer wishes, he can command the computer to operate a plotter and draw out a full-size contour map or other graphical representation of the object, or he can require that the computer control a multiaxis milling machine to carve out a model. If the designer sees in the drawing or model features that do not please him or do not satisfy the purpose of the shape, he can either make changes graphically with the light pen or indicate dimensional changes on the keyboard. The computer will immediately and obediently incorporate these modifications in its internal mathematical description of the surface of the object and will display the modified shape on

the screen. The full-scale drawing can then be redrawn or the model recarved. When the shape is satisfactory, it can be machined from metal or any other desired material.

The saving in time and effort can be great. Five grossly modified versions of a ship hull were designed in the space of a few minutes on a Project MAC computer console at M.I.T.; each version was completely described by the computer in about a tenth of a second. A point anywhere on the hull could have been determined with a precision of one part in 10 million—certainly more than adequate precision for most engineering purposes. The mathematical algorithm that makes this possible is extremely simple in concept, and it is designed to be quick and easy for computer implementation. It is also quite general. It will accept virtually any kind of design curve: polynomials, transcendental functions and even freehand sketched curves possessing no descriptive mathematical formula whatever.

Given this power to do what might be called mathematical sculpture, the engineer can use the computer representation of an object as the base for a variety of analytical treatments. He can

perform stress analyses, predict pressures and other fluid forces on airplane and ship shapes, simulate dynamic effects such as vibration, study heat flow or do any of a number of calculations that depend partly on precise knowledge of the shape in question. The surface algorithm is easily extended to hypersurfaces of any dimensionality, making possible the graphical presentation of multidimensional functions. It has been learned that such surfaces, even though they do not exist in our three-dimensional universe, can be exhibited on a cathode-ray-display tube and, when they are observed in dynamic motion, can convey meaning and elicit understanding.

In the near future—perhaps within five and surely within 10 years—a handful of engineer-designers will be able to sit at individual consoles connected to a large computer complex. They will have the full power of the computer at their fingertips and will be able to perform with ease the innovative functions of design and the mathematical processes of analysis, and they will even be able to effect through the computer the manufacture of the product of their efforts. Through their consoles they will be in communication with one another to ensure that the separate elements of the design are compatible. Engineering standards, parts catalogues and other data will be accessible through the display screens of their consoles. Some mechanical parts will be produced directly from the design information generated within the computer, without the necessity of drawings. (When drawings are required to provide information for final assembly or for maintenance manuals, these drawings will be prepared by the computer from the primary design information, and the drawings will even be tailored to match the use. For example, electrical wiring drawings will subordinate actual structure, showing only enough to clarify the task of the electrician.)

It would be difficult to compile even a representative list of the agencies and individuals who are making contributions toward the realization of this new age of the computer. At M.I.T., Douglas Ross and I have been directing efforts toward this goal under Air Force sponsorship for about seven years. In the Electronic Systems Laboratory, Ross is engaged in a formidable effort in the areas of data structures, computer languages and general compilers for engineering design. My group in the department of mechanical engineering has been working on graphical displays and on design tasks such as three-dimensional stress analysis, the solution of equilibrium field problems, kinematics and data storage and retrieval. Almost all universities with computer facilities are engaged in some phase of the problem. Work closely parallel to the work at M.I.T. is being done by Bertram Herzog and his colleagues at the University of Michigan. In industry the Lockheed Aircraft Corporation, the General Motors Corporation and the Ford Motor Company have experimental computer-aided design systems in operation, and these systems are beginning to be used to a limited extent in production engineering. The Boeing Company and the Douglas Aircraft Company are involved in similar activities.

Much energy and talent is being devoted to making computer-aided design and man-machine interaction a convenient everyday reality, and as time goes on more fresh effort is being channeled into this exciting enterprise. One may hope that engineers, economists, psychologists, sociologists and other men can help to provide the appropriate human adjustments to it.

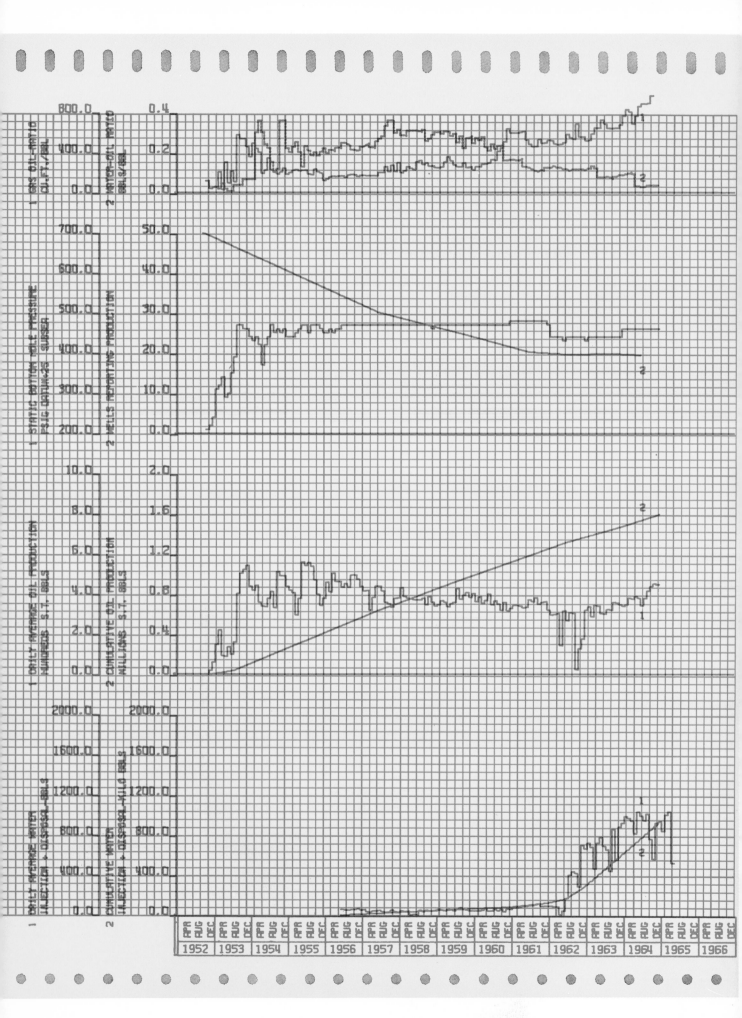

24

THE USES OF COMPUTERS IN ORGANIZATIONS

MARTIN GREENBERGER

September, 1966

The computer systems under development today are beginning to mirror man and his industrial society, both in structure and in the pattern of their evolution. Our industrial civilization is characterized by the division of labor, the specialization and routinization of functions, mechanization, stratification of control and a hierarchical form of organization that integrates the activities of planning, management and operations. Coordination is accomplished by an elaborate system of information-handling and communication. The computer is being brought into the organization primarily to help with information-handling, but in the process it is incorporating in its programs almost all the characteristics of the organization as a whole.

This may come as no surprise, since computer systems and programs are designed by human beings and might therefore be expected to assume aspects of man and his organizations. Indeed, all the machines man has devised possess the characteristics of organizations to some extent. But the computer is not just another machine. It has a versatility, a logical flexibility and an open-endedness—an ability to grow—that is not matched by anything short of the living organism. The computer, a comparatively recent addition to the organization, has within it the potential for

completely remolding the organization. Accordingly it has new and important implications for the future of human society. In this article we shall first consider the past and present uses of the computer in the organizational setting and then explore the computer's possible future in that setting.

The use of the digital computer as a generally available (that is, commercially produced) tool is only 15 years old. Its first applications were in science and engineering. Its early users took a rather restricted view of its capabilities. It was put to work composing lengthy numerical tables and performing other prosaic calculations. Soon, however, its wider potentialities gained the interest of the military authorities, among others, and substantial amounts of money were made available to promote its evolution. The digital computer became a yeast in research and development. Without the computer there might be no nuclear power plants today, no communication satellites, no space program, perhaps no commercial fleets of jet airplanes. In the laboratories of science the computer likewise grew rapidly in power, versatility and esteem [see "The Uses of Computers in Science," by Anthony G. Oettinger, page 261]. By expanding the ability to deal with complex problems, the computer

has stepped up the rate of scientific and technological advance.

The story is much the same for the use of the computer in business and government. Its first employment outside the fields of science and engineering was by the Bureau of the Census in 1951. There and in the business firms that began to use the machine it was assigned exclusively to standard clerical and statistical tasks. Most engineers and business executives foresaw little use for the computer in business except for record-keeping and other mechanical operations. The General Electric appliance division installed a UNIVAC I in 1954 and gave it the job of preparing the payroll, which was successfully achieved only after a certain amount of agony and mishap. A few banks, insurance companies, mass-circulation magazines and public utilities arranged to use digital computers for customer accounting and billing; some manufacturers and distributors applied the computer to inventory control.

It is startling to recall that this was the situation barely a decade ago. Today tens of thousands of digital computers are employed in business and government in the U.S. By virtue of their flexibility and great improvements in their speed, capacity and reliability, they have been able to take on a wide variety of new jobs. The computer has been graduated from a specialist in drudgery to an information processor adept in a broad range of functions. Interestingly enough, this broadening of the computer's capability has been achieved in part by creating a high degree of specialization within the machine. As the art of programming advances, the devices used for the organization of computer programs are coming to resemble those that have proved

PERFORMANCE CURVES, automatically plotted from data stored in a computer's memory, present eight key aspects of operations at an oil field in the Canadian province of Alberta. The two lower pairs of curves on the opposite page plot the daily averages of oil production and water injection against the field's cumulative totals in these categories. These and the production data shown in the two upper pairs of curves provide a continuous performance record of the kind that many industries produce today from computer-stored information as a basis for decision-making. This display was generated in less than four minutes from production records kept by the Triad Oil Company by means of a computer-linked plotting device that is manufactured by California Computer Products, Incorporated.

useful in the organization of human society. The large programs today contain a considerable array of differentiated services and multiple levels of control.

The programmed unit of specialization in a computer system is called a routine. It is a set of instructions for performing a distinguishable task; it can be likened to a human worker doing a specific job or using a particular skill. There are routines that exercise control (managers) and others that execute operations (workers). Subserving the specialized operations are standardized routines, called subroutines, that perform functions of general utility.

Computer routines are the programmer's device for coping with complexity. They not only enable him to break down a complex program into manage-

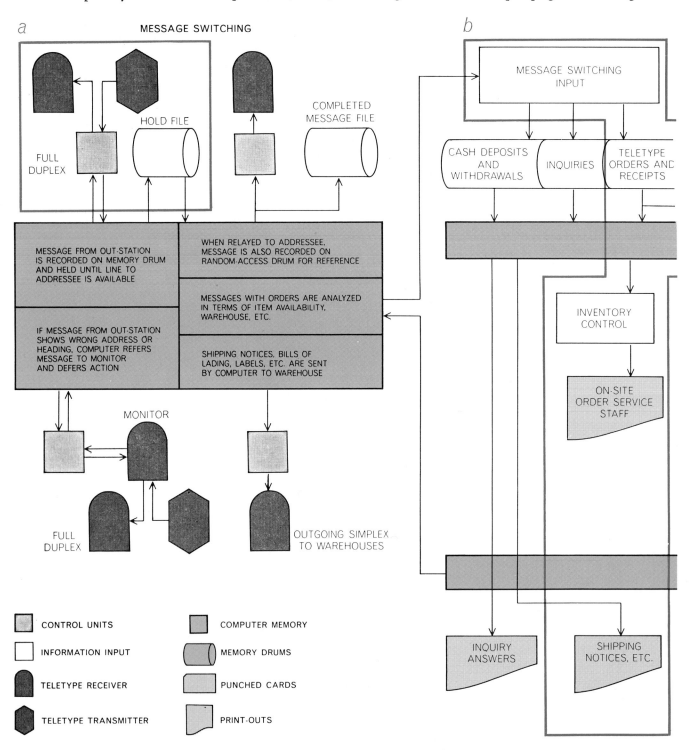

CORPORATION NERVE CENTER has evolved from a computer-assisted message-relay system developed by the Westinghouse Electric Corporation in the early 1960's. The diagram shows the scope of the system's activities in simplified form; some examples of its many functions are outlined in color. The center, located in Pitts-

burgh, was planned as a control point for teletype communications between Westinghouse's more than 300 sales offices, distributors, warehouses, factories and repair centers throughout the U.S. At first the center's computers served such simple purposes as overnight memory storage of a West Coast message to an East Coast

able parts but also confer other important advantages. A program can be organized in modules, or building blocks, consisting of self-contained routines, and this makes it easy to reach in and replace a defective module or to add a new one. Most large computer systems have been built by the modular approach. Those that have not have demonstrated how important it is to allow for change and growth. Modularity facilitates growth. Just as new workers, skills, machines and instruments can be added to an industrial or research establishment to enlarge its scope of operations or deepen its capabilities, so in a modular computer system new routines can be added to improve its operation.

The modular structure is also a great convenience when a team of program-

ORDER PROCESSING AND CASH MANAGEMENT

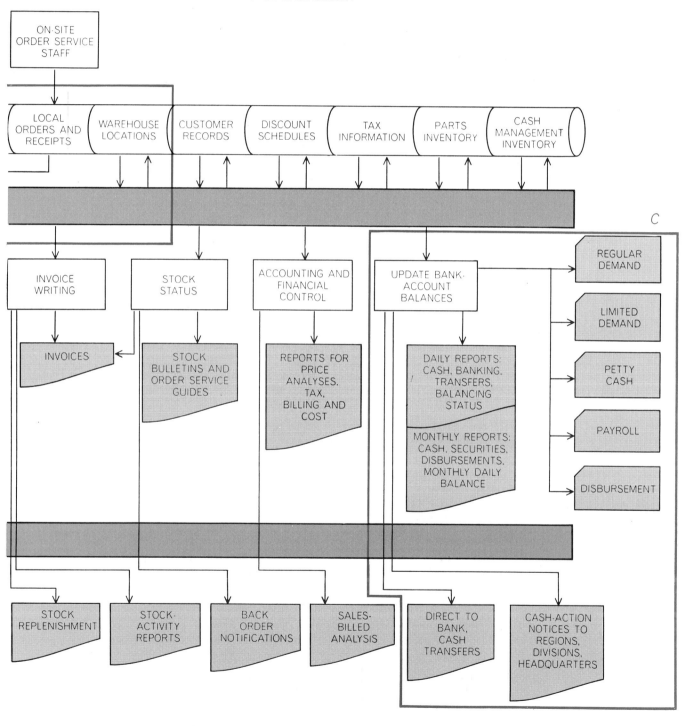

addressee received after close of business and automatic forwarding of the message the following day (*a*). The computers were also programmed to analyze incoming orders and to check them automatically against continuously revised inventory compilations. This program directed the computers to forward orders selectively to the stocked warehouses closest to the originators of the orders (*b*). Computer analysis of sales and purchases soon produced an additional bonus (*c*). A running record of nationwide cash receipts and disbursements has permitted banking practices that substantially reduce cash surpluses and allow investment of these once idle funds.

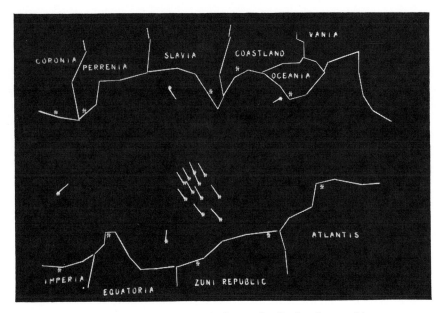

COMMAND PROBLEM appears in a cathode-ray-tube display that combines computer-generated data with a projected background. The 11 comet-like dashes (*center*) represent a navy convoy crossing a sea bordered by a number of imaginary nations. One convoy vessel signals distress; the command problem is to avoid additional disruption of the convoy by requesting help from the nearest friendly port or from independent fleet units. The computer can draw from memory and display such facts as the treaty status and repair facilities of the nearest ports and mission priorities of fleet units in range of the vessel. The display console, designed as a visual aid to command, is produced by the Bunker-Ramo Corporation.

mers undertakes to collaborate on a large project, as a group of us at Harvard University did in 1957 in the course of building a demographic model of the U.S. economy. Each member was assigned to an independent section. We were able to work in relative isolation; responsibilities were clearly established; program checking was simplified, and the project proceeded along several lines simultaneously.

A good illustration of modular design is our system called OPS (for "On-Line Process Synthesis") at the Massachusetts Institute of Technology. It was developed within the time-sharing system of Project MAC, which is itself constructed on the modular plan [see "Time-sharing on Computers," by R. M. Fano and F. J. Corbató, page 79]. OPS is one of numerous user programs filed in the memory of the time-sharing system. This particular program, however, like a division of a large corporation, is a complete operating system in its own right. It has its own retinue of control routines and a wide assortment of subroutines and operational programs known as "operators." There is an operator corresponding to each of the customary statements in an algebraic programming language, such as FORTRAN or ALGOL, and there are also operators for individually tailored and complex compounds of these statements.

One operator solves general linear programming problems. Another does a multiple regression analysis. A third locates the critical path in a network. A fourth performs a general computation involving vectors and matrices. A fifth smooths a time series, providing an economic forecast. A sixth schedules an event during a simulation run. A seventh presents information in tabular format. And so on. The user can add operators that are particularly relevant to his own interests. By its modular structure the OPS system makes room within the physical limitations of the machine for a high degree of growth and variety.

A user of the OPS system addresses each operator by its name, which may be an English word such as SET, PRINT or READ. He can combine operators into a compound operator and give it a name of its own. Since the OPS system runs in a time-sharing environment, the user can program himself into the computer operation and from his on-line terminal perform those aspects of the operation that call for human judgment or are amorphous and undefined. In the same way he can control the operation of the program externally.

Thus time-sharing makes possible the flexible inclusion of people in a computer operation. The potential for human participation is particularly significant in operations conducted in "real

time." This term simply means that the computer interacts with the external environment and carries out appropriate operations as the situation develops. In other words, the computer is linked directly to the work to be done in the real world. A straightforward example is the guidance of a missile or space vehicle to its destination by continual computer adjustments to the changing conditions en route. A more elaborate example is the SAGE computer, which receives information on possible enemy activity from radar stations, aircraft and picket ships spread over a vast area. The computer must rapidly summarize on display screens the information coming in from all these sources, and it must act as adviser and controller for any defensive action that is indicated.

It is with the advent of real-time systems that the organization of programming has begun to resemble human organizations most closely. A real-time system requires considerably more complicated programming than the more conventional batch-processing operation does. Whereas in batch processing jobs typically are fed to the computer continuously and serially from a single tape on which they have previously been accumulated, in a real-time operation they can enter instantly, sporadically and simultaneously from any of many remote terminals connected to the computer. Jobs are processed transaction by transaction rather than batch by batch. Since the execution of the program is interrupted whenever external conditions dictate, a variety of special routines must be provided to handle each of the contingencies. To make the system workable, information within the computer must be arranged in randomly accessible form, and programs are needed to make storage and retrieval of this information convenient. The result may be a complex organization of specialized routines whose coordination and control are a central function of the real-time operation.

The technology for real-time systems is already fairly well advanced, thanks largely to military developments such as SAGE. The available terminal equipment, however, particularly that providing for the input and output of information in graphical form, is still too expensive. Moreover, such "conversational" teleprocessing is costly, because present communication systems are designed for voice signals and continuous transmission of data, not for scattered bursts of data. Nevertheless, in spite of the temporary obstacles of high cost and the relative difficulty of real-time programming, real-time systems are already entrenched in the military sphere and have been making decided progress in business and industry.

The first commercial application of a real-time system on a large scale was the SABRE reservation system of American Airlines. Its computer center is in Briarcliff Manor, N.Y. To this center more than 1,000 reservation clerks at airports and offices throughout the U.S. address their queries and instructions. The clerks type their messages into the computer from their typewriter terminals, using a code SABRE can comprehend. The transactions occur at unpredictable times, placing an uneven load and a wide variety of demands on the system. Yet SABRE is tuned to respond to a request within three seconds.

Several airlines and railroads have followed this lead and installed reservation systems of the same type. Real-time computers soon will also be landing airliners in fog and scheduling railroad freight-yard activities and the movement of boxcars. A computer will control the running and spacing of the high-speed passenger trains of the new rapid-transit line in the San Francisco-Oakland bay area. Real-time systems are being set up to control automobile traffic in large cities, including New York. It is not farfetched to anticipate that someday an integrated information-and-control system will link together not only transportation facilities but also hotels, motels, car rentals and all other agencies of travel.

In the field of finance real-time systems are being put to work by banks, insurance companies and stock markets. Many savings banks have installed on-line systems in which deposits and withdrawals are recorded directly in a computer. Commercial banks are beginning to use random-access computers for handling demand-deposit accounting and recording stock transfers. Insurance companies are planning to make the files of their policyholders available to their agents in field offices through on-line queries to the central office. Several stock-quotation services enable brokers and their clients to obtain the price of a security simply by dialing the computer. The New York and American stock exchanges are embarked on programs that will facilitate the eventual automation of all their floor activities, with the possible exception of the setting of prices. It is perhaps not overly fanciful to foresee a day when most trading and financial transactions will

be carried out not on the floors of exchanges and in the conference rooms of banks but over computer communication networks linking together widely separated offices of the transactors. Such a development might have important implications for the future of our cities, one of whose chief functions at present is to serve as financial centers.

Real-time computers have also entered the fields of retail and wholesale commerce. There are now service companies that make real-time computation available in the manner of public utilities to enterprises of modest size. One such company is the Keydata Corporation in Cambridge, Mass. Some of its subscribers are wholesale distributors. When a sale is made, a clerk types an invoice for the customer on a teletypewriter that is connected to the Keydata computer by a leased telephone line. The clerk identifies the customer simply by a number; the items he has bought are also identified by number, and the only other information supplied is the amount of each item bought. The computer fills in, from information stored in its files, all the rest of the necessary data for the invoice: the date, the invoice number, the name and address of the customer, descriptions of the items sold and their prices. It calculates and prints the total amount of the sale and checks for clerical errors. All in all it types about 80 percent of the information on a typical invoice. The computer retains information concerning the transaction and therefore is equipped to provide the services of inventory control and sales analysis.

In industry one of the pioneers in the development of real-time systems has been the Lockheed Missiles and Space Company. Its computer center at Sunnyvale, Calif., operates an "automatic data-acquisition system" that collects information on work flow from more than 200 factory stations spread over a 300-mile radius from the center. The system records and controls the movement of more than 200,000 separate items manufactured or stored at these locations. Also connected to the computer are 25 stations from which, on inquiry, prompt information can be obtained about the location of shop and purchase orders, inventory levels and labor charges. The system, which has been operating since 1962, has saved the company millions of dollars in its Polaris and Agena programs. It has relieved supervisory personnel of much pressure and confusion and has freed them to devote more time to planning. It has also eliminated hundreds of jobs

in the areas of purchasing, expediting and production scheduling.

The reduction of jobs by the computer and its acquisition of detailed data about the activities of workers produced an eruption of resentment among the workers. This subsided after Lockheed put restrictions on the use of the data by management, instituted training programs and assigned to other jobs employees who had been displaced by the machine.

Probably the most extensive and advanced use of a real-time system in industry today is that at the Westinghouse Electric Corporation. Its telecomputer center in Pittsburgh is becoming the nerve center of the corporation. The center started operating in 1962 as an automatic switchboard for messages in the teletype network that serves all the Westinghouse divisions. Today this system, in continual communication with about 300 plants, field offices, warehouses, distributors and appliance-repair centers, is taking over the functions of inventory control and order processing on a vast scale. It has also begun to take a hand in production control and is steadily moving into new fields.

The improvements in the company's operations have been dramatic. By directing shipments to customers from the nearest warehouse that has the ordered item in stock the system has speeded up deliveries and reduced transportation costs. It provides salesmen with information about the availability of products and about prices within minutes. It updates sales statistics continuously. It automatically requisitions replenishments when inventories fall below a given level. The data captured by the computer from the messages it is continually receiving and transmitting give the management a growing fund of timely information.

One interesting application of the Westinghouse computer system is a "cash-management information program" that keeps a running account of the cash flow. All receipts and disbursements of the various Westinghouse divisions are immediately transmitted by teletype to the telecomputer center and recorded in the appropriate accounts. When the balance in any of the corporation's 250 regional bank accounts falls below a preset level, the computer automatically orders a transfer of cash from the central bank account. When the balance in the central account is higher than necessary, the treasury office invests the excess in marketable securities, notifying the computer as it does so. The net result is that the company's management knows the company's cash position at all times and is able to put formerly idle funds to work earning interest.

A device for the graphical display of financial information has been installed at Westinghouse headquarters and is now being tested and "debugged." It will picture for the Westinghouse executives trends in the company's financial operations and will compare financial forecasts with actual accomplishments. The system has important implications for planning by top management. Other applications of the computer to planning are being made at the General Electric Company, the International Business Machines Corporation, the Standard Oil Company (New Jersey) and many other large corporations.

What has occurred in real-time programming up to now is obviously only a prelude to much more far-reaching developments that are likely to follow in the coming years. Let us speculate a bit on the nature of these developments and their possible broad-scale effects on our business and industrial organizations.

One aspect of the organization that is likely to be affected is the degree to which its control is centralized. Over the past 30 years, as enterprises have grown enormously in size, the trend has been toward decentralization of company operations through the setting up of divisions and profit centers. The giant corporations have found, however, that decentralization can be a mixed blessing. It tends to multiply jobs, duplicate functions and establish local goals that may run orthogonally to the objectives of the organization as a whole. It also places a burden on the company's information system by multiplying the need for information at the same time that it disperses information in a multitude of separate files spread through the organization. It may be days or weeks before new information is processed, summarized, transmitted and made available to the people who need it for operations and decisions.

Clearly the computer can help to correct this situation. Data from the many divisions and hierarchical levels of the organization will flow directly into a central computer memory, in the same way that information about hundreds of thousands of inventory items now feeds into Lockheed's automatic data-acquisition system from hundreds of remote

terminals. The computer programs will promptly sort the information, place each item in an appropriate list or report, link it to related information already stored and make the processed information quickly accessible to those who need it for authorized purposes.

Some investigators in this field believe that systems for integrating the company files will eventually reverse the trend toward decentralization. That is a moot question; the centralization of information need not imply the centralization of control. It will surely streamline operations, however, and save the company money. Most important, it will give the company a new coherence and sense of unity, and it will pave the way to further mechanization of the company's activities.

Much of this mechanization may take place within the computer. The further evolution of computer programs may repeat the history of industrialization: in the first phase, the division of labor into easy-to-execute tasks; in the second phase, the delegation of these tasks to machines. The first phase was demonstrated by Adam Smith two centuries ago in *The Wealth of Nations*. Smith observed how the division of labor speeded the manufacture of pins: "One man draws out the wire, another straightens it, a third cuts it, a fourth points it, a fifth grinds it at the top for receiving the head; to make the head requires two or three distinct operations; to put it on, is a peculiar business, to whiten the pins is another ...and the important business of making a pin is, in this manner, divided into about 18 distinct operations.... I have seen a small manufactory of this kind where...ten persons could make among them upwards of 48,000 pins in a day." Today a single machine, going through much the same process Smith described, turns out several hundred thousand pins per hour.

In the future enactment of this process programs will play the part of machines. Suppose a company has a real-time, time-shared computer that participates as a central instrument of operations. Suppose its body of programming is open-ended, like the OPS system, and is able to grow and assume new functions easily. The routine the computer employs to store away incoming transaction data does the work of a team of file clerks. The routines it has to make this data available on demand to customer representatives and to summarize the data in periodic reports to management are like staff assistants.

The company will be able to expand its work force by hiring employees with the requisite skills, or by extending its real-time computer program, or by a combination of both. Additions and modifications to the program can be kept tentative and flexible until they are judged to perform satisfactorily by human monitors at the consoles. Programs may be refined and made more efficient by a continual policy of replacement and improvement. Over a period of time the computer system will become larger in scope, better in detail and a vital part of the company organization. There will be an intriguing interplay of centripetal and centrifugal forces, tasks for which the computer shows an aptitude being drawn into the body of programming and tasks that are better performed by the human touch or mind drifting outward to the operators at the consoles (and beyond). Ultimately the parallel organizations of people and programs in an enterprise may blend together and appear as one, just as organizations of people and machines have done in the past.

What this means for the future of our economy and society remains to be seen. It appears likely that our organizations and institutions will function more efficiently and smoothly and thus become significantly more productive. As others have remarked, there is no reason to suppose this will result in a glut of goods and services or in massive unemployment, even though job descriptions may change drastically.

Much has been written about the dangers that may lie in wait for a computerized society: the cult of the machine, overdelegation of our activities to the computer, too much faith in its simplifications and quantifications, the invasion of privacy and individual rights by overzealous programs of industry or government, criminal misuses of the computer. These possibilities are real and should not be waved aside. Computer scientists take them seriously and are today in an uncomfortable position somewhat like that of the nuclear physicists after the discovery of uranium fission.

It should be perfectly clear, however, that the dangers arise from the way man may use the computer, not from the machine itself. The computer remains under human control. The programs of the future will have the character man designs into them, and prevention of abuses is an important part of the design problem.

25

THE USES OF COMPUTERS IN EDUCATION

PATRICK SUPPES
September, 1966

As other articles in this issue make abundantly clear, both the processing and the uses of information are undergoing an unprecedented technological revolution. Not only are machines now able to deal with many kinds of information at high speed and in large quantities but also it is possible to manipulate these quantities of information so as to benefit from them in entirely novel ways. This is perhaps nowhere truer than in the field of education. One can predict that in a few more years millions of schoolchildren will have access to what Philip of Macedon's son Alexander enjoyed as a royal prerogative: the personal services of a tutor as well-informed and responsive as Aristotle.

The basis for this seemingly extravagant prediction is not apparent in many examinations of the computer's role in education today. In themselves, however, such examinations provide impressive evidence of the importance of computers on the educational scene. As an example, a recent report of the National Academy of Sciences states that by mid-1965 more than 800 computers were in service on the campuses of various American universities and that these institutions spent $175 million for computers that year. The report goes on to forecast that by 1968 the universities' annual budget for computer operations will reach $300 million and that their total investment in computing facilities will pass $500 million.

A similar example is represented by the fact that most colleges of engineering and even many high schools now use computers to train students in computer programming. Perhaps just as important as the imposition of formal course requirements at the college level is the increasingly widespread attitude among college students that a knowledge of computers is a "must" if their engineering or scientific training is to be up to date. Undergraduates of my generation who majored in engineering, for instance, considered a slide rule the symbol of their developing technical prowess. Today being able to program a computer in a standard language such as FORTRAN or ALGOL is much more likely to be the appropriate symbol.

At the graduate level students in the social sciences and in business administration are already making use of computers in a variety of ways, ranging from the large-scale analysis of data to the simulation of an industry. The time is rapidly approaching when a high percentage of all university graduates will have had some systematic training in the use of computers; a significant percentage of them will have had quite sophisticated training. An indication of the growth of student interest in computers is the increase in student units of computer-science instruction we have had at Stanford University over the past four years. Although total enrollment at Stanford increased only slightly during that period, the number of student units rose from 2,572 in 1962–1963 to 5,642 in 1965–1966.

The fact that time-sharing programs are rapidly becoming operational in many university computation centers justifies the forecast of another increase in the impact of computers on the universities [see "Time-sharing on Computers," by R. M. Fano and F. J. Corbató, page 79]. Under time-sharing regimes a much larger number of students can be given direct "on line" experience, which in itself is psychologically attractive and, from the practical viewpoint, facilitates deeper study of the use of computers. There is still another far from trivial way in which the computer serves the interests of education: The large school system that does not depend on computers for many administrative and service functions is today the exception rather than the rule.

The truly revolutionary function of computers in education, however, lies in the novel area of computer-assisted instruction. This role of the computer is scarcely implemented as yet but, assuming the continuation of the present pace of technological development, it cannot fail to have profound effects in the near future. In this article I shall describe some experiments in computer-assisted instruction that are currently being conducted at levels ranging from the comparatively simple to the quite complex and then examine some unsuspected problems that these experiments have revealed. First, however, the reader deserves an explanation of why computer-assisted instruction is considered desirable at all.

The single most powerful argument

COMPUTER-ASSISTED INSTRUCTION in elementary arithmetic is illustrated in the photographs shown on page 254. A first-grade pupil, receiving "readiness" work preparatory to instruction in addition, is shown two possible answers to a question implicit in the symbols occupying the top line of a cathode-ray-tube display. As he watches (**top photograph**), his earphones carry a verbal message asking him to select from the symbolic statements of union shown in the second and third lines of the display the one that is identical with the equation shown in the top line. The pupil signals his choice (*bottom photograph*) by pointing to the statement he prefers with light pen; the computer records the answer.

for computer-assisted instruction is an old one in education. It concerns the advantages, partly demonstrated and partly conjectured, of individualized instruction. The concept of individualized instruction became the core of an explicit body of doctrine at the end of the 19th century, although in practice it was known some 2,000 years earlier in ancient Greece. For many centuries the education of the aristocracy was primarily tutorial. At the university level individualized tutorial instruction has been one of the glories of Oxford and Cambridge. Modern criticisms of the method are not directed at its intrinsic merit but rather at its economic inefficiency. It is widely agreed that the more an educational curriculum can adapt in a unique fashion to individual learners —each of whom has his own characteristic initial ability, rate and even "style" of learning—the better the chance is of providing the student with a successful learning experience.

The computer makes the individualization of instruction easier because it can be programmed to follow each student's history of learning successes and failures and to use his past performance as a basis for selecting the new problems and new concepts to which he should be exposed next. With modern information-storage devices it is possible to store both a large body of curriculum material and the past histories of many students working in the curriculum. Such storage is well within the capacity of current technology, whether the subject is primary school mathematics, secondary school French or elementary statistics at the college level. In fact, the principal obstacles to computer-assisted instruction are not technological but pedagogical: how to devise ways of individualizing instruction and of designing a curriculum that are suited to individuals instead of groups. Certain obvious steps that take account of different rates of learning can be made with little difficulty; these are the main things that have been done so far. We have still, however, cut only a narrow path into a rich jungle of possibilities. We do

not have any really clear scientific idea of the extent to which instruction can be individualized. It will probably be some time before a discipline of such matters begins to operate at anything like an appropriately deep conceptual level.

A second important aspect of computers in education is closer in character to such familiar administrative functions as routine record-keeping. Before the advent of computers it was extremely difficult to collect systematic data on how children succeed in the process of learning a given subject. Evaluative tests of achievement at the end of learning have (and will undoubtedly continue to have) a place both in the process of classifying students and in the process of comparing different curriculum approaches to the same subject. Nonetheless, such tests remain blunt and insensitive instruments, particularly with respect to detailed problems of instruction and curriculum revision. It is not possible on the basis of poor results in a test of children's mastery of subtraction or of irregular verbs in French to draw clear inferences about ways to improve the curriculum. A computer, on the other hand, can provide daily information about how students are performing on each part of the curriculum as it is presented, making it possible to evaluate not only individual pages but also individual exercises. This use of computers will have important consequences for all students in the immediate future. Even if students are not themselves receiving computer-assisted instruction, the results of such instruction will certainly be used to revise and improve ordinary texts and workbooks.

Let me now take up some of the work in computer-assisted instruction we have been doing at Stanford. It should be emphasized that similar work is in progress at other centers, including the University of Illinois, Pennsylvania State University, the University of Pittsburgh, the University of Michigan, the University of Texas, Florida State University and the University of California at Santa Barbara, and within such companies as the International Business Machines Corporation, the System Development Corporation and Bolt, Beranek and Newman. This list is by no means exhaustive. The work at these various places runs from a primary emphasis on the development of computer hardware to the construction of short courses in subjects ranging from physics to typing. Although all these efforts, including ours at Stanford, are

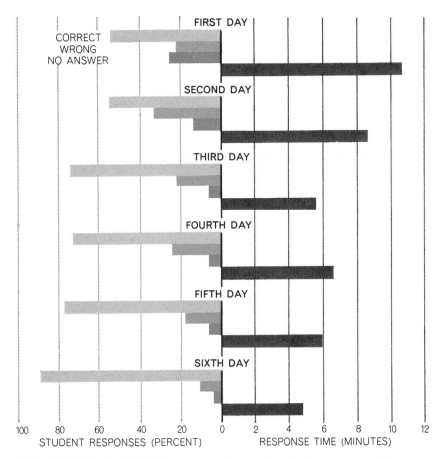

IMPROVEMENT IN LEARNING is one evident result of drill and practice. The graph summarizes the results of a six-day drill on the commutative, associative and distributive laws of arithmetic. The computer program covered 48 concepts; each day's session presented 24 problems. Two days' drill therefore reviewed all 48 concepts, although no identical problems were presented during the six days. By the last day student responses were more than 90 percent correct and the speed of reply was twice what it was at the start.

still in the developmental stage, the instruction of large numbers of students at computer terminals will soon (if academic and industrial soothsayers are right) be one of the most important fields of application for computers.

At Stanford our students are mainly at the elementary school level; the terminals they use, however, are also suitable for secondary school and university students. At each terminal there is a visual device on which the student may view displays brought up from the computer memory as part of the instruction program. A device that is coming into wide use for this purpose is the cathode ray tube; messages can be generated directly by the computer on the face of the tube, which resembles a television screen. Mounted with the cathode ray tube is a typewriter keyboard the student can use to respond to problems shown on the screen. At some additional cost the student can also have a light pen that enables him to respond directly by touching the pen to the screen instead of typing on the keyboard. Such a device is particularly useful for students in the lowest elementary grades, although when only single-digit numerical responses or single-character alphabetical ones are required, the use of a keyboard is quite easy even for kindergarten children to learn.

After the display screen and the keyboard the next most important element at a terminal is the appropriate sound device. Presenting spoken messages to students is desirable at all educational levels, but it is particularly needed for younger children. It would be hard to overemphasize the importance of such spoken messages, programmed to be properly sensitive to points at which the student may encounter difficulty in learning. Such

COMPUTER SUMMARY of drill results makes possible the analysis essential for assessment and revision of various study curriculums. The results of 37 children's replies to 20 questions designed to test elementary arithmetic skills are summarized graphically in this illustration. The most troublesome question proved to be No. 7; not only did it take the most time to answer but also 26 students failed to answer it at all and only two answered it correctly. Although question No. 9 is the exact reverse of question No. 7, it received 13 correct answers. Evidently obtaining an unknown quantity by subtraction is harder than obtaining one by addition, and the students found it harder to multiply 12 by 6 than to multiply 6 by 12.

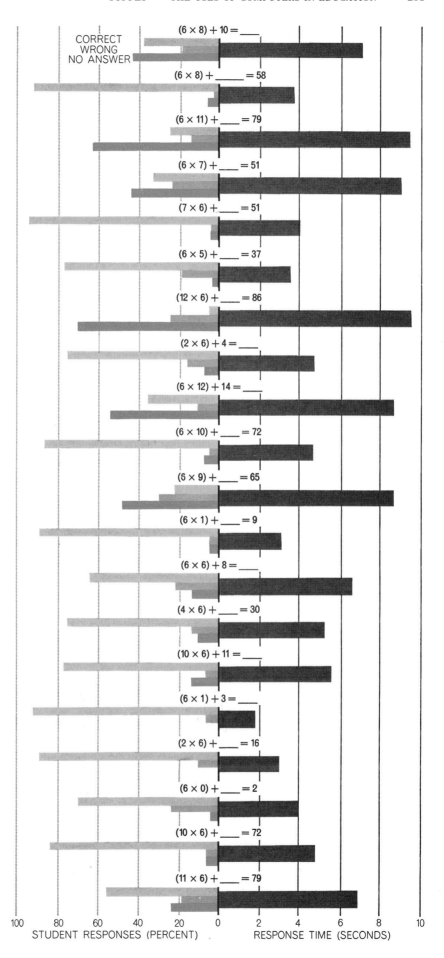

messages are the main help a good tutor gives his pupil; they are the crucial missing element in noncomputerized teaching machines. All of us have observed that children, especially the younger ones, learn at least as much by ear as they do by eye. The effectiveness of the spoken word is probably stronger than any visual stimulus, not only for children but also most of the time for adults. It is particularly significant that elementary school children, whose reading skills are comparatively undeveloped, comprehend rather complicated spoken messages.

A cathode ray tube, a keyboard and a loudspeaker or earphones therefore constitute the essential devices for computer-assisted instruction. Additional visual displays such as motion pictures or line drawings can also be useful at almost all levels of instruction. Ordinary film projectors under computer control can provide such displays.

So far three levels of interaction between the student and the computer program have received experimental attention. At the most superficial level (and accordingly the most economical

GLOSSARY

α MOIST AIR RISES

β MOIST AIR COOLS OR WILL COOL

γ CLOUDS WILL FORM

→ FORMAL IMPLICATION

¬ NOT

RULES OF INFERENCE

TRI TRANSIVITY OF IMPLICATION
(FROM X→Y AND Y→Z, DERIVE X→Z)

IF MODUS PONENS
(FROM X→Y AND X, DERIVE Y)

CP CONTRAPOSITIVE
(FROM X→Y, DERIVE ¬Y→¬X)

DNEG DOUBLE NEGATION
(FROM ¬¬X, DERIVE X)

RED CONTRADICTION OF CONSEQUENT
(FROM Y AND X→¬Y, DERIVE ¬X)

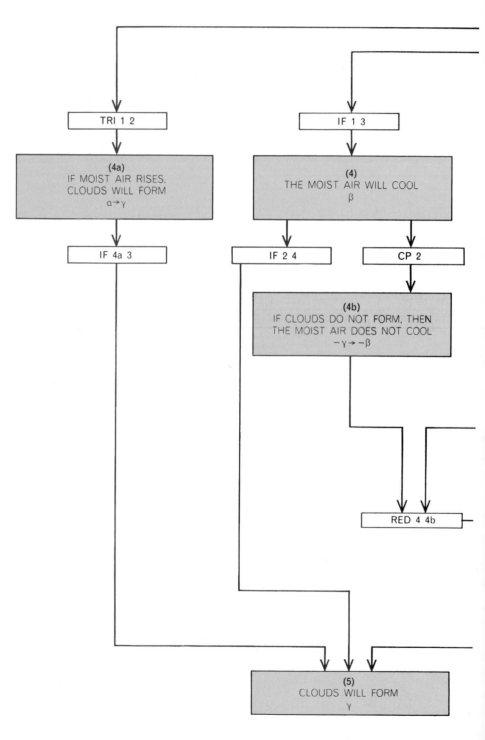

TUTORIAL EXERCISE in mathematical logic is an example of a more complex variety of computer-assisted instruction. The student may proceed from a set of given hypotheses (*top*) to a given conclusion (*bottom*) by any one of several routes. Each of the illustrated downward paths represents a legitimate logical attack on the problem and each constitutes a unique sequence of inferences (*see legend and statements in logical notation below each of the numbered verbal statements*). Ideally a tutorial computer program will show no preference for one path over another but will check the soundness of each step along any path and tell the student if he makes any mistakes in logic.

one) are "drill and practice" systems. Instruction programs that fall under this heading are merely supplements to a regular curriculum taught by a teacher. At Stanford we have experimented a great deal with elementary school mathematics at the drill-and-practice level, and I shall draw on our experience for examples of what can be accomplished with this kind of supplementation of a regular curriculum by computer methods.

Over the past 40 years both pedagogical and psychological studies have provided abundant evidence that students need a great deal of practice in order to master the algorithms, or basic procedures, of arithmetic. Tests have shown that the same situation obtains for students learning the "new math." There seems to be no way to avoid a good deal

of practice in learning to execute the basic algorithms with speed and accuracy. At the elementary level the most important way in which computer-assisted instruction differs from traditional methods of providing practice is that we are in no sense committed to giving each child the same set of problems, as would be the case if textbooks or other written materials were used. Once a number

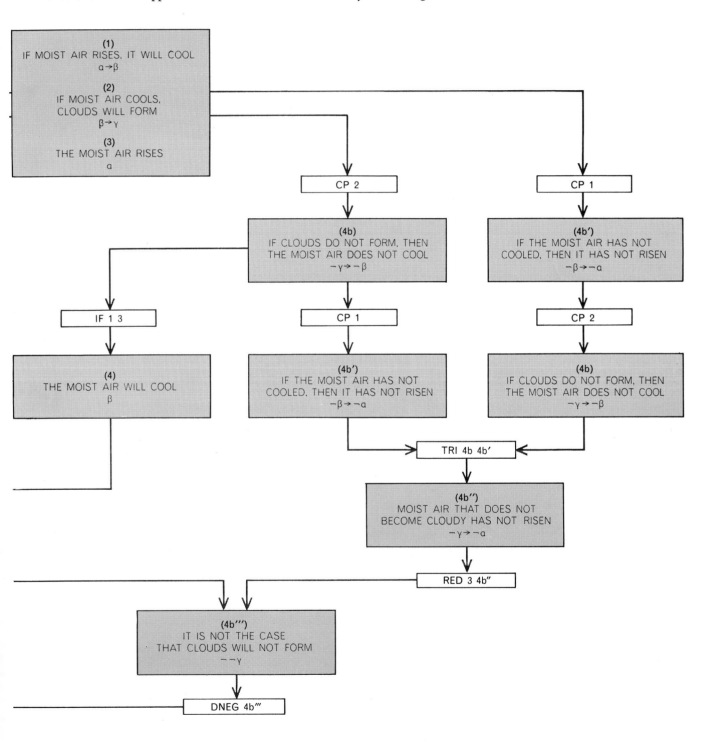

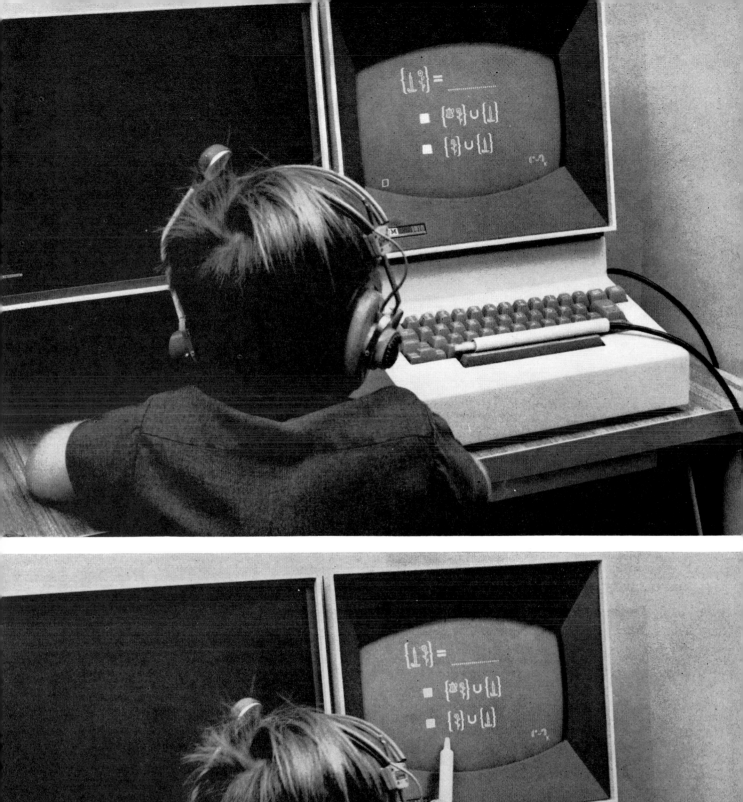

```
PLEASE TYPE YOUR NAME

ROBERT VALENTINE

DRILL NUMBER 604032

L.C.M.  MEANS  LEAST COMMON MULTIPLE

___  IS THE L.C.M. OF  4 AND  9

TIME IS UP

 36  IS THE L.C.M. OF  4 AND  9

 23  IS THE L.C.M. OF 12 AND  8

WRONG

 24  IS THE L.C.M. OF 12 AND  8

  1  IS THE L.C.M. OF 15 AND 10

WRONG

___  IS THE L.C.M. OF 15 AND 10

TIME IS UP, ANSWER IS 30

 30  IS THE L.C.M. OF 15 AND 10

 60  IS THE L.C.M. OF 12 AND 30

 12  IS THE L.C.M. OF  2,  4, AND  6
```

```
 40  IS THE L.C.M. OF  8, 10, AND  5

S. FOR SUMMARY S.

             NUMBER    PERCENT
CORRECT        14        70
WRONG           5        25
TIMEOUT         1         5
70% CORRECT IN BLOCK, 70% OVERALL TO DATE
GOOD BYE, 0 FEARLESS DRILL TESTER.
TEAR OFF ON DOTTED LINE

...........................................
```

DRILL-AND-PRACTICE EXERCISE, shown in abbreviated form, is typical of a simple computer-assisted instruction program that is designed to be responsive to the needs of individual students. The illustrated exercise is one of five that differ in their degree of difficulty; when the student types his name (*color*), the exercise best suited to him on the basis of computer-memory records of his previous performance is selected automatically. The first three questions and answers exemplify the ways in which the computer is programmed to deal with various shortcomings. The student fails to answer the first question within the allotted 10-second time limit; the computer therefore prints TIME IS UP and repeats the question, which the student then answers correctly (*color*). A wrong answer to the next question causes the computer to announce the error and repeat the question automatically; a second chance again elicits a correct answer. A wrong answer to the third question is compounded by failure to respond to the reiterated question within the time limit. Because this question has now drawn two unsatisfactory responses the automatic TIME IS UP statement is followed by a printing of the correct answer. The question is now repeated for a third and last time. Whether or not the student elects to copy the correct answer (he does so in this instance), the computer automatically produces the next question. Only six of the 20 questions that compose the drill are shown in the example. After the student's last answer the computer proceeds to print a summary of the student's score for the drill as well as his combined average for this and earlier drills in the same series. The drill-and-practice exercise then concludes with a cheery farewell to the student and an instruction to tear off the teletype tape.

of study "tracks," representing various levels of difficulty, have been prepared as a curriculum, it is only a matter of computer programming to offer students exercises of varying degrees of difficulty and to select the appropriate level of difficulty for each student according to his past performance.

In the program we ran in elementary grades at schools near Stanford during the academic year 1965–1966 five levels of difficulty were programmed for each grade level. A typical three-day block of problems on the addition of fractions, for example, would vary in the following way. Students at the lowest level (Level 1) received problems involving only fractions that had the same denominator in common. On the first two days levels 2 and 3 also received only problems in which the denominators were the same. On the third day the fraction problems for levels 2 and 3 had denominators that differed by a factor of 2. At Level 4 the problems had denominators that differed by a factor of 2 on the first day. At Level 5 the denominators differed by a factor of 3, 4, 5 or 6 on the first day. Under the program the student moved up and down within the five levels of difficulty on the basis of his performance on the previous day. If more than 80 percent of his exercises were done correctly, he moved up a level. If fewer than 60 percent of the exercises were done correctly, he moved down a level. The selection of five levels and of 80 and 60 percent has no specific theoretical basis; they are founded on practical and pedagogical intuition. As data are accumulated we expect to modify the structure of the curriculum.

Our key effort in drill-and-practice systems is being conducted in an elementary school (grades three through six) a few miles from Stanford. The terminals used there are ordinary teletype machines, each connected to our computer at Stanford by means of individual telephone lines. There are eight teletypes in all, one for each school classroom. The students take turns using the teletype in a fixed order; each student uses the machine once a day for five to 10 minutes. During this period he receives a number of exercises (usually 20), most of which are devoted to a single concept in the elementary school mathematics curriculum. The concept reviewed on any given day can range from ordinary two-digit addition to intuitive logical inference. In every case the teacher has already presented the concept and the pupil has had some classroom practice; the computer-assisted drill-and-practice work therefore supplements the teacher's instruction.

The machine's first instruction—PLEASE TYPE YOUR NAME—is already on the teletype paper when the student begins his drill. The number of characters required to respond to this instruction is by far the longest message the elementary student ever has to type on the keyboard, and it is our experience that every child greatly enjoys learning how to type his own name. When the name has been typed, the pupil's record is looked up in the master file at the computer and the set of exercises he is to receive is determined on the basis of his performance the previous day. The teletype now writes, for example, DRILL 604032. The first digit (6) refers to the grade level, the next two digits (04) to the number of the concept in the sequence of concepts being reviewed during the year, the next two digits (03) to the day in terms of days devoted to that concept (in this case the third day devoted to the fourth concept) and the final digit (2) to the level of difficulty on a scale ranging from one to five.

The real work now begins. The computer types out the first exercise [*see illustration on opposite page*]. The carriage returns to a position at which the pupil should type in his answer. At this point one of three things can happen. If the pupil types the correct answer, the computer immediately types the second exercise. If the pupil types a wrong answer, the computer types WRONG and repeats the exercise without telling the pupil the correct answer. If the pupil does not answer within a fixed time (in most cases 10 seconds), the computer types TIME IS UP and repeats the exercise. This second presentation of the exercise follows the same procedure regardless of whether the pupil was wrong or ran out of time on the first presentation. If his answer is not correct at the second presentation, however, the correct answer is given and the exercise is typed a third time. The pupil is now expected to type the correct answer, but whether he does or not the program goes on to the next exercise. As soon as the exercises are finished the computer prints a summary for the student showing the number of problems correct, the number wrong, the number in which time ran out and the corresponding percentages. The pupil is also shown his cumulative record up to that point, including the amount of time he has spent at the terminal.

A much more extensive summary of student results is available to the teacher. By typing in a simple code the teacher can receive a summary of the work by the class on a given day, of the class's work on a given concept, of the work of any pupil and of a number of other descriptive statistics I shall not specify here. Indeed, there are so many questions about performance that can be asked and that the computer can answer that teachers, administrators and supervisors are in danger of being swamped by more summary information than they can possibly digest. We are only in the process of learning what summaries are most useful from the pedagogical standpoint.

A question that is often asked about drill-and-practice systems is whether we have evidence that learning is improved by this kind of teaching. We do not have all the answers to this complex question, but preliminary analysis of improvement in skills and concepts looks impressive when compared with the records of control classes that have not received computer-assisted instruction. Even though the analysis is still under way, I should like to cite one example that suggests the kind of improvement that can result from continued practice, even when no explicit instructions are given either by the teacher or by the computer program.

During the academic year 1964–1965 we noticed that some fourth-grade pupils seemed to have difficulty changing rapidly from one type of problem format to another within a given set of exercises. We decided to test whether or not this aspect of performance would improve with comparatively prolonged practice. Because we were also dissatisfied with the level of performance on problems involving the fundamental commutative, associative and distributive laws of arithmetic, we selected 48 cases from this domain.

For a six-day period the pupils were cycled through each of these 48 types of exercise every two days, 24 exercises being given each day [*see illustration on page 250*]. No specific problem was repeated; instead the same problem types were encountered every two days on a random basis. The initial performance was poor, with an average probability of success of .53, but over the six-day period the advance in performance was marked. The proportion of correct answers increased and the total time taken to complete the exercises showed much improvement (diminishing from an average of 630 seconds to

279 seconds). Analysis of the individual data showed that every pupil in the class had advanced both in the proportion of correct responses and in the reduction of the time required to respond.

The next level of interaction of the pupil and the computer program is made up of "tutorial" systems, which are more complex than drill-and-practice systems. In tutorial systems the aim is to take over from the classroom teacher the main responsibility for instruction. As an example, many children who enter the first grade cannot properly use the words "top" and "bottom," "first" and "last" and so forth, yet it is highly desirable that the first-grader have a clear understanding of these words so that he can respond in unequivocal fashion to instructions containing them. Here is a typical tutorial sequence we designed to establish these concepts: 1. The child uses his light pen to point to the picture of a familiar object displayed on the cathode-ray-tube screen. 2. The child puts the tip of his light pen in a small square box displayed next to the picture. (This is the first step in preparing the student to make a standard response to a multiple-choice exercise.) 3. The words FIRST and LAST are introduced. (The instruction here is spoken rather than written; FIRST and LAST refer mainly to the order in which elements are introduced on the screen from left to right.) 4. The words TOP and BOTTOM are introduced. (An instruction to familiarize the child with the use of these words might be: PUT YOUR LIGHT PEN ON THE TOY TRUCK SHOWN AT THE TOP.) 5. The two concepts are combined in order to select one of several things. (The instruction might be: PUT YOUR LIGHT PEN ON THE FIRST ANIMAL SHOWN AT THE TOP.)

With such a tutorial system we can individualize instruction for a child entering the first grade. The bright child of middle-class background who has gone to kindergarten and nursery school for three years before entering the first grade and has a large speaking vocabulary could easily finish work on the concepts I have listed in a single 30-minute session. A culturally deprived child who has not attended kindergarten may need as many as four or five sessions to acquire these concepts. It is important to keep the deprived child from developing a sense of failure or defeat at the start of his schooling. Tutorial "branches" must be provided that move downward to very simple presentations, just as a good tutor will use an increasingly simplified approach when he realizes that his pupil is failing to understand what is being said. It is equally important that a tutorial program have enough flexibility to avoid boring a bright child with repetitive exercises he already understands. We have found it best that each pupil progress from one concept in the curriculum to another only after he meets a reasonably stiff criterion of performance. The rate at which the brightest children advance may be five to 10 times faster than that of the slowest children.

In discussing curriculum materials one commonly distinguishes between "multiple-choice responses" and "constructed responses." Multiple-choice exercises usually limit the student to three, four or five choices. A constructed response is one that can be selected by the student from a fairly large set of possibilities. There are two kinds of constructed response: the one that is uniquely determined by the exercise and the one that is not. Although a good part of our first-grade arithmetic program allows constructed responses, almost all the responses are unique. For example, when we ask for the sum of 2 plus 3, we expect 5 as the unique response. We have, however, developed a program in mathematical logic that allows constructed responses that are not unique. The student can make any one of several inferences; the main function of the computer is to evaluate the validity of the inference he makes. Whether or not the approach taken by the student is a wise one is not indicated until he has taken at least one step in an attempt to find a correct derivation of the required conclusion. No two students need find the same proof; the tutorial program is designed to accept any proof that is valid [see illustration on pages 252 and 253]. When the student makes a mistake, the program tells him what is wrong with his response; when he is unable to take another step, the program gives him a hint.

It will be evident from these examples that well-structured subjects such as reading and mathematics can easily be handled by tutorial systems. At present they are the subjects we best understand how to teach, and we should be able to use computer-controlled tutorial systems to carry the main load of teaching such subjects. It should be empha-

ESSENTIAL COMPONENTS that allow interaction of computer and student are grouped at this terminal console. The cathode ray tube (right) replaces the earlier teletypewriter roll as a more flexible means of displaying computer instructions and questions. Earphones or a loudspeaker reproduce spoken words that are particularly important in primary school instruction. Students may respond to instructions by use of the terminal's keyboard or by use of a light pen (extreme right); programs that will enable the computer to receive and respond to the student's spoken words are under study. Supplemental displays are shown on the screen at left.

sized, however, that no tutorial program designed in the near future will be able to handle every kind of problem that arises in student learning. It will remain the teacher's responsibility to attempt the challenging task of helping students who are not proceeding successfully with the tutorial program and who need special attention.

Thus a dual objective may be achieved. Not only will the tutorial program itself be aimed at individualized instruction but also it will free the teacher from many classroom responsibilities so that he will have time to individualize his own instructional efforts. At Stanford we program into our tutorial sessions an instruction to the computer that we have named TEACHER CALL. When a student has run through all branches of a concept and has not yet met the required criterion of performance, the computer sends a teacher call to the proctor station. The teacher at the proctor station then goes to the student and gives him as much individualized instruction as he needs.

At the third and deepest level of student-computer interaction are systems that allow a genuine dialogue between the student and the program. "Dialogue systems" exist only as elementary prototypes; the successful implementation of such systems will require the solving of two central problems. The first may be described as follows: Suppose in a program on economic theory at the college level the student types the question: WHY ARE DEMAND CURVES ALWAYS CONVEX WITH RESPECT TO THE ORIGIN? It is difficult to write programs that will recognize and provide answers to questions that are so broad and complex, yet the situation is not hopeless. In curriculum areas that have been stable for a long time and that deal with a clearly bounded area of subject matter, it is possible to analyze the kinds of questions students ask; on the basis of such an analysis one can make considerable progress toward the recognition of the questions by the computer. Nonetheless, the central intellectual problem cannot be dodged. It is not enough to provide information that will give an answer; what is needed is an ability on the part of the computer program to recognize precisely what question has been asked. This is no less than asking the computer program to understand the meaning of a sentence.

The second problem of the dialogue system is one that is particularly critical with respect to the teaching of elementary school children. Here it is essential that the computer program be able to recognize the child's spoken words. A child in the first grade will probably not be able to type even a simple question, but he can voice quite complex ones. The problem of recognizing speech adds another dimension to the problem of recognizing the meaning of sentences.

In giving an example of the kind of dialogue system we are currently developing at Stanford I must emphasize that the program I am describing (which represents an extension of our work in mathematical logic) is not yet wholly operational. Our objective is to introduce students to simple proofs using the associative and commutative laws and also the definitions of natural numbers as successors of the next smallest number (for example, $2 = 1 + 1$, $3 = 2 + 1$ and $4 = 3 + 1$). Our aim is to enable the student to construct proofs of simple identities; the following would be typical instances: $5 = 2 + 3$ and $8 = (4 + 2) + 2$. We want the student to be able to tell the computer by oral command what steps to take in constructing the proof, using such expressions as REPLACE 2 BY $1 + 1$ or USE THE ASSOCIATIVE LAW ON LINE 3. This program is perfectly practical with our present computer system as long as the commands are transmitted by typing a few characters on the keyboard. A major effort to substitute voice for the keyboard is planned for the coming year; our preliminary work in this direction seems promising.

But these are essentially technological problems. In summarizing some other problems that face us in the task of realizing the rich potential of computer-assisted individual instruction, I should prefer to emphasize the behavioral rather than the technological ones. The central technological problem must be mentioned, however; it has to do with reliability. Computer systems in education must work with a much higher degree of reliability than is expected in computer centers where the users are sophisticated scientists, or even in factory-control systems where the users are experienced engineers. If in the school setting young people are put at computer terminals for sustained periods and the program and machines do not perform as they should, the result is chaos. Reliability is as important in schools as it is in airplanes and space vehicles; when failure occurs, the disasters are of different kinds, but they are equally conclusive.

The primary behavioral problem involves the organization of a curriculum.

For example, in what order should the ideas in elementary mathematics be presented to students? In the elementary teaching of a foreign language, to what extent should pattern drill precede expansion of vocabulary? What mixture of phonics and look-and-say is appropriate for the beginning stages of reading? These are perplexing questions. They inevitably arise in the practical context of preparing curriculum materials; unfortunately we are far from having detailed answers to any of them. Individualized instruction, whether under the supervision of a computer or a human tutor, must for some time proceed on the basis of practical judgment and rough-and-ready pedagogical intuition. The magnitude of the problem of evolving curriculum sequences is difficult to overestimate: the number of possible sequences of concepts and subject matter in elementary school mathematics alone is in excess of 10^{100}, a number larger than even generous estimates of the total number of elementary particles in the universe.

One of the few hopes for emerging from this combinatorial jungle lies in the development of an adequate body of fundamental theory about the learning and retention capacity of students. It is to be hoped that, as systematic bodies of data become available from computer systems of instruction, we shall be able to think about these problems in a more scientific fashion and thereby learn to develop a more adequate fundamental theory than we now possess.

Another problem arises from the fact that it is not yet clear how critical various kinds of responses may be. I have mentioned the problem of interpreting sentences freely presented by the student, either by the written or by the spoken word. How essential complex constructed responses to such questions may be in the process of learning most elementary subjects is not fully known. A problem at least as difficult as this one is how computer programs can be organized to take advantage of unanticipated student responses in an insightful and informative way. For the immediate future perhaps the best we can do with unanticipated responses is to record them and have them available for subsequent analysis by those responsible for improving the curriculum.

The possible types of psychological "reinforcement" also present problems. The evidence is conflicting, for instance, whether students should be immediately informed each time they make a mistake. It is not clear to what extent students should be forced to seek the right answer, and indeed whether this search should take place primarily in what is called either the discovery mode or the inductive mode, as opposed to more traditional methods wherein a rule is given and followed by examples and then by exercises or problems that exemplify the rule. Another central weakness of traditional psychological theories of reinforcement is that too much of the theory has been tested by experiments in which the information transmitted in the reinforcement procedure is essentially very simple; as a result the information content of reinforcement has not been sufficiently emphasized in theoretical discussions. A further question is whether or not different kinds of reinforcement and different reinforcement schedules should be given to children of different basic personality types. As far as I know, variables of this kind have not been built into any large-scale curriculum effort now under way in this country.

Another pressing problem involves the effective use of information about the student's past performance. In standard classroom teaching it is impossible to use such records in a sensitive way; we actually have little experience in the theory or practice of the use of such information. A gifted tutor will store in his own memory many facts about the past performance of his pupil and take advantage of these facts in his tutorial course of study, but scientific studies of how this should be done are in their infancy. Practical decisions about the amount of review work needed by the individual, the time needed for the introduction of new concepts and so forth will be mandatory in order to develop the educational computer systems of the future. Those of us who are faced with making these decisions are aware of the inadequacy of our knowledge. The power of the computer to assemble and provide data as a basis for such decisions will be perhaps the most powerful impetus to the development of education theory yet to appear. It is likely that a different breed of education research worker will be needed to feel at home with these vast masses of data. The millions of observational records that computers now process in the field of nuclear physics will be rivaled in quantity and complexity by the information generated by computers in the field of instruction.

When students are put to work on an individualized basis, the problem of keeping records of their successes and failures is enormous, particularly when those records are intended for use in making decisions about the next stage of instruction. In planning ways to process the records of several thousand students at Stanford each day, we found that one of the most difficult decisions is that of selecting the small amount of total information it is possible to record permanently. It is not at all difficult to have the data output run to 1,000 pages a day when 5,000 students use the terminals. An output of this magnitude is simply more than any human being can digest on a regular basis. The problem is to reduce the data from 1,000 pages to something like 25 or 30. As with the other problems I have mentioned, one difficulty is that we do not yet have the well-defined theoretical ideas that could provide the guidelines for making such a reduction. At present our decisions are based primarily on pedagogical intuition and the traditions of data analysis in the field of experimental psychology. Neither of these guidelines is very effective.

A body of evidence exists that attempts to show that children have different cognitive styles. For example, they may be either impulsive or reflective in their basic approach to learning. The central difficulty in research on cognitive styles, as it bears on the construction of the curriculum, is that the research is primarily at an empirical level. It is not at all clear how evidence for the existence of different cognitive styles can be used to guide the design and organization of individualized curriculum materials adapted to these different styles. Indeed, what we face is a fundamental question of educational philosophy: To what extent does society want to commit itself to accentuating differences in cognitive style by individualized techniques of teaching that cater to these differences? The introduction of computers in education raises this question in a new and pressing way. The present economics of education is such that, whatever we may think about the desirability of having a diverse curriculum for children of different cognitive styles, such diversity is not possible because of the expense. But as computers become widely used to offer instruction in the ways I have described here, it will indeed be possible to offer a highly diversified body of curriculum material. When this occurs, we shall for the first time be faced with the practical problem of deciding how much diversity we want to have. That is the challenge for which we should be prepared.

26

THE USES OF COMPUTERS IN SCIENCE

ANTHONY G. OETTINGER

September, 1966

In its scientific applications the computer has been cast in two quite distinct but complementary roles: as an instrument and as an actor. Part of the success of the computer in both roles can be ascribed to purely economic factors. By lowering the effective cost of calculating compared with experimenting the computer has induced a shift toward calculation in many fields where once only experimentation and comparatively direct measurement were practical.

The computer's role as an instrument is by far the more clear-cut and firmly established of the two. It is in its other role, however, as an active participant in the development of scientific theories, that the computer promises to have its most profound impact on science. A physical theory expressed in the language of mathematics often becomes dynamic when it is rewritten as a computer program; one can explore its inner structure, confront it with experimental data and interpret its implications much more easily than when it is in static form. In disciplines where mathematics is not the prevailing mode of expression the language of computer programs serves increasingly as the language of science. I shall return to the subject of the dynamic expression of theory after considering the more familiar role of the computer as an instrument in experimental investigations.

The advance of science has been marked by a progressive and rapidly accelerating separation of observable phenomena from both common sensory experience and theoretically supported intuition. Anyone can make at least a qualitative comparison of the forces required to break a matchstick and a steel bar. Comparing the force needed to ionize a hydrogen atom with the force that binds the hydrogen nucleus together is much more indirect, because the chain from phenomenon to observation to interpretation is much longer. It is by restoring the immediacy of sensory experience and by sharpening intuition that the computer is reshaping experimental analysis.

The role of the computer as a research instrument can be readily understood by considering the chain from raw observations to intuitively intelligible representations in the field of X-ray crystallography. The determination of the structure of the huge molecules of proteins is one of the most remarkable achievements of contemporary science. The highlights of this work have been reported in a number of articles in *Scientific American*, notably "The Three-dimensional Structure of a Protein Molecule," by John C. Kendrew [Offprint 121], and "The Hemoglobin Molecule," by M. F. Perutz [Offprint 196]. The labor, care and expense lavished on the preparation of visual models of protein molecules tes- tify to a strong need for intuitive aids in this field. The computational power required to analyze crystallographic data is so immense that the need for high-speed computers is beyond doubt.

The scope and boldness of recent experiments in X-ray crystallography have increased in direct proportion to increases in computer power. Although computers seem to be necessary for progress in this area, however, they are by no means sufficient. The success stories in the determination of protein structures have involved an interplay of theoretical insight, experimental technique and computational power.

In work of this kind a rotating protein crystal is bombarded by a beam of X rays; the rays diffracted by the crystal are recorded on a photographic plate, where they produce characteristic patterns of bright spots on the dark background. Measurements of the relative positions and intensities of the spots in the diffraction pattern are the raw material for calculations that have as their result a table of coordinates of the three-dimensional distribution of electrons in the molecule. The electron-density data are then used to draw density-contour maps, which are interpreted as a three-dimensional model of the particular protein molecule under study.

Many of the links in this chain are now automated. The laborious manual measurement of photographs, for example, is no longer necessary. In the laboratory of William N. Lipscomb, Jr., at Harvard University a mounted crystal is rotated automatically through the required sequence of orientations while a photomultiplier tube measures the intensity of the diffracted X rays [*see top illustration on next page*]. Machines convert information about position and intensity into digital form and record it on punched cards for input to a computer.

SYMMETRICAL PATTERN of colored dots on the opposite page was produced by a computer for use in an experiment on visual perception. The pattern has fourfold symmetry around the central point, similar to the pattern produced in a kaleidoscope. In the actual experiment transparent slides containing the pattern are projected in various colors to see how well the perception of symmetry survives the different combinations. In such experiments the colors are adjusted to have equal subjective brightness; this is difficult to do with inks and was not attempted in this reproduction. The experiment is part of a study of texture and visual perception being conducted by Bela Julesz of the Bell Telephone Laboratories.

X-RAY DIFFRACTION APPARATUS in the laboratory of William N. Lipscomb, Jr., at Harvard University makes unnecessary the laborious manual measurement of X-ray diffraction photographs of crystal structures. A beam of X rays (*from housing at center*) is directed at a mounted crystal (for example a protein), which is rotated automatically through a series of orientations while a photomultiplier tube (*top left*) measures the intensity of the diffracted rays. Information about the position and intensity of the diffracted rays is then converted from analogue to digital form and recorded on punched cards for input to a computer.

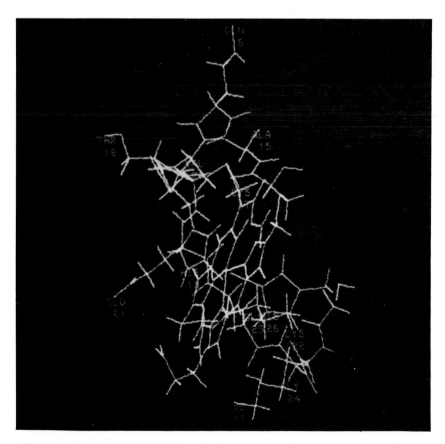

MODEL OF PROTEIN MOLECULE is displayed on an oscilloscope screen in the laboratory of Cyrus Levinthal at the Massachusetts Institute of Technology. The electron density of the molecule was determined by an analysis of X-ray diffraction photographs. A computer program converted the electron-density measurements into an image of a fragment of the molecular structure on the oscilloscope. Once the picture of the molecule has been calculated for a standard orientation the orientation can be changed at will by simple controls.

At the other end of the chain Cyrus Levinthal of the Massachusetts Institute of Technology and Robert Langridge of Harvard have used the time-shared computer and display facilities of M.I.T.'s Project MAC to develop a remarkable set of programs that accept electron densities calculated for a three-dimensional region and turn these into an image of molecular structure on an oscilloscope [*see bottom illustration at left*]. Gone is the time-consuming task of drawing and building the electron-density map. Once the picture of a molecule has been calculated for a standard orientation the orientation can be changed at will by simple controls that actuate special circuits for transforming the coordinates of the picture before displaying it. Slight motions provide excellent depth perception without the expense of stereoscopic image pairs. The molecule can be turned in order to view it from any angle, or it can be sliced by a plane in order to see it in cross section [see "Molecular Model-building by Computer," by Cyrus Levinthal, beginning on page 171].

Joining these two links is the next step. A new coaxial-cable network will soon carry Lipscomb's raw data directly to a computer at the Harvard Computing Center. No technical obstacle bars the further transmission of calculated electron densities to the system at M.I.T., where the molecular display could be prepared and then sent back for direct viewing on a screen at the experimental site. Once the time-shared computer utility emerges from its present experimental stage to spread throughout institutions and regions, such doings will very likely be commonplace [see "Time-sharing on Computers," by Fano and Corbató beginning on page 79]. It is only tame speculation to visualize a graduate student "looking through" a computer at a protein molecule as directly as he now looks at a cell through a microscope.

The metaphor of the transparent computer describes one of the principal aims of contemporary "software" engineering, the branch of information engineering concerned with developing the complex programs (software) required to turn an inert mound of apparatus (hardware) into a powerful instrument as easy to use as pen and paper. As anyone can testify who has waited a day or more for a conventional computing service to return his work only to find that a misplaced comma had kept the work from being done at all, instant transparency for all is not yet here. Nevertheless, the advances described in the accompanying articles toward making computer languages congenial and expressive, toward making it easy to communicate with the machine and toward putting the machine at one's fingertips attest to the vigor of the pursuit of the transparent computer.

A few critics object to the principle of transparency because they fear that the primary consequence will be atrophy of the intellect. It is more likely that once interest in the *process* of determining molecular structure becomes subordinate to interest in the molecule itself, the instrument will simply be accepted and intellectual challenge sought elsewhere. It is no more debasing, unromantic or unscientific in the 1960's to view a protein crystal through the display screen of a computer than it is to watch a paramecium through the eyepiece of a microscope. Few would wish to repeat the work of Christian Huygens each time they need to look at a microscope slide. In any case, computers are basically so flexible that nothing but opaque design or poor engineering can prevent one from breaking into the chain at any point, whenever one thinks human intuition and judgment should guide brute calculation.

It is essential, of course, for anyone to understand his instrument well enough to use it properly, but the computer is just like other commonplace instruments in this regard. Like any good tool, it should be used with respect. Applying "data reduction" techniques to voluminous data collected without adequate experimental design is a folly of the master not to be blamed on the servant. Computer folk have an acronym for it: GIGO, for "garbage in, garbage out."

X-ray crystallography is the most advanced of many instances in which similar instrumentation is being developed.

Four experimental stations at the Cambridge Electron Accelerator, operated jointly by Harvard and M.I.T., are currently being connected to a time-shared computer at the Harvard Computing Center to provide a first link. A small computer at each experimental station converts instrument readings from analogue to digital form, arranges them in a suitable format and transmits them to the remote computer. There most data are stored for later detailed calculation; a few are examined to instruct each of the small local machines to display information telling the experimenter whether or not his experiment is going well. Heretofore delays in conventional batch-processing procedures occasionally led to scrapping a long experiment that became worthless because poor adjustments could not be detected until all calculations were completed and returned.

This type of experiment is described as an "open loop" experiment, since the computer does not directly affect the setting of experimental controls. Closed-loop systems, where the experiment is directly controlled by computer, are currently being developed. Their prototypes can be seen in industrial control systems, where more routine, better-understood devices, ranging from elevators to oil refineries, are controlled automatically.

The problem of "reading" particle-track photographs efficiently has been a persistent concern of high-energy physicists. Here the raw data are not nearly as neat as they are in X-ray diffraction patterns, nor can photography as readily be bypassed. Automating the process of following tracks in bubble-chamber photographs to detect significant events presents very difficult and as yet unsolved problems of pattern recognition, but computers are now used at least to reduce some of the tedium of scanning the photographs [*see illustration on next page*]. Similar forms of man-machine interaction occur also in the study of brain tumors by radioactive-isotope techniques. Where the problem of pattern recognition is simpler, as it is in certain types of chromosome analysis, there is already a greater degree of automation [see "Chromosome Analysis by Computer," by Robert S. Ledley and Frank H. Ruddle, beginning on page 199].

Let us now turn from the computer as instrument to the computer as actor, and to the subject of dynamic expression of theory. To understand clearly words such as "model," "simulation" and others that recur in this context, a digression is essential to distinguish the functional from the structural aspects of a model or a theory.

A robot is a functional model of man. It walks, it talks, but no one should be fooled into thinking that it is a man or that it explains man merely because it acts like him. The statements that "the brain is like a computer" or that "a network of nerve cells is like a network of computer gates, each either on or off," crudely express once popular structural theories, obviously at different levels. Both are now discredited, the first because no one has found structures in the brain that look anything like parts of any man-made computer or even function like them, the second because nerve-cell networks were found to be a good deal more complicated than computer networks.

A functional model is like the electrical engineer's proverbial "black box," where something goes in and something comes out, and what is inside is unknown or relevant only to the extent of somehow relating outputs to inputs. A structural model emphasizes the contents of the box. A curve describing the

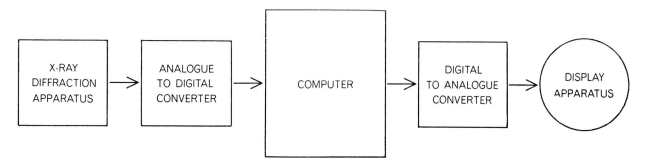

LINKUP of the two facilities represented on the opposite page is the next step toward the goal of a "transparent" computer in the field of X-ray crystallography. A new coaxial-cable network will soon carry Lipscomb's raw data directly to a computer at the Harvard Computing Center. No technical obstacle bars the further transmission of the calculated electron densities to the system at M.I.T., where the molecular display could be prepared and then sent back for direct viewing on a screen at the experimental site. It should then be possible to "look through" a computer at a protein molecule as directly as one now looks at a cell through a microscope.

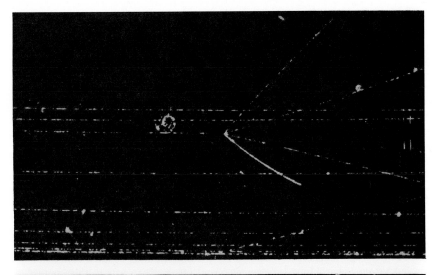

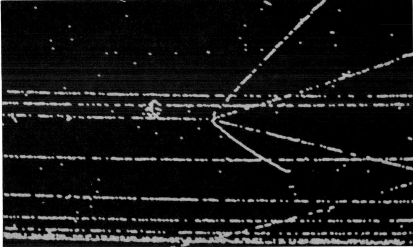

BUBBLE-CHAMBER PHOTOGRAPH (*top*) of a typical particle interaction was made at the Lawrence Radiation Laboratory of the University of California. The negative of the photograph was scanned by a device called the "flying spot digitizer," and the digitized information was sent directly to a computer, which produced a copy of the original photograph (*bottom*). No operator is required in the scanning process. The machine is directed to the location of a significant event by instructions on magnetic tape. Other computer programs further analyze the data to provide a description of the interaction recorded in photograph.

current passing through a semiconductor diode as a function of the voltage applied across its terminals is a functional model of this device that is exceedingly useful to electronic-circuit designers. Most often such curves are obtained by fitting a smooth line to actual currents and voltages measured for a number of devices. A corresponding structural model would account for the characteristic shape of the curve in terms that describe the transport of charge-carriers through semiconductors, the geometry of the contacts and so forth. A good structural model typically has greater predictive power than a functional one. In this case it would predict changes in the voltage-current characteristic when the geometry of the interfaces or the impurities in the semiconductors are varied.

If the black box is opened, inspiration, luck and empirical verification can turn a functional model into a structural one. Physics abounds with instances of this feat. The atom of Lucretius or John Dalton was purely functional. Modern atomic theory is structural, and the atom with its components is observable. The phlogiston theory, although functional enough up to a point, evaporated through lack of correspondence between its components and reality. Although the description of the behavior of matter by thermodynamics is primarily functional and its description by statistical mechanics is primarily structural, the consistency of these two approaches reinforces both.

The modern computer is a very versatile and convenient black box, ready to act out an enormous variety of func-

tional or structural roles. In the physical sciences, where the script usually has been written in mathematics beforehand, the computer merely brings to life, through its program, a role implied by the mathematics. Isaac Newton sketched the script for celestial mechanics in the compact shorthand of differential equations. Urbain Leverrier and John Couch Adams laboriously fleshed out their parts in the script with lengthy and detailed calculations based on a wealth of astronomical observations. Johann Galle and James Challis pointed their telescopes where the calculations said they should and the planet Neptune was discovered. In modern jargon, Leverrier and Adams each ran Neptune simulations based on Newton's model, and belief in the model was strengthened by comparing simulation output with experiment. Computers now routinely play satellite and orbit at Houston, Huntsville and Cape Kennedy. Nevertheless, there is little danger of confusing Leverrier, Adams or a computer with any celestial object or its orbit. As we shall see, such confusion is more common with linguistic and psychological models.

The determination of protein structures provides an excellent example of how computers act out the implications of a theory. Finding a possible structure for a protein molecule covers only part of the road toward understanding. For example, the question arises of why a protein molecule, which is basically just a string of amino acid units, should fold into the tangled three-dimensional pattern observed by Kendrew. The basic physical hypothesis invoked for explanation is that the molecular string will, like water running downhill, fold to reach a lowest energy level. To act out the implications of this hypothesis, given an initial spatial configuration of a protein chain, one might think of calculating the interactions of all pairs of active structures in the chain, minimizing the energy corresponding to these interactions over all possible configurations and then displaying the resultant molecular picture. Unfortunately this cannot be done so easily, since no simple formula describing such interactions is available and, with present techniques, none could be written down and manipulated with any reasonable amount of labor. Sampling more or less cleverly the energies of a finite but very large number of configurations is the only possibility. An unsupervised computer searching through a set of samples for a minimum would, more likely than not, soon find itself blocked at some local minimum—unable, like a man in a hollow at the top of a mountain, to see deeper valleys beyond the ridges that surround him.

The close interaction of man and machine made possible by new "on line" time-sharing systems, graphical display techniques and more convenient programming languages enables Levinthal and his collaborators to use their intuition and theoretical insight to postulate promising trial configurations. It is then easy for the computer to complete the detail work of calculating energy levels for the trial configuration and seeking a minimum in its neighborhood. The human operator, from his intuitive vantage point, thus guides the machine over the hills and into the valley, each partner doing what he is best fitted for.

Even more exciting, once the details of the interactions are known theoretically, the X-ray diffraction pattern of the molecule can be calculated and compared with the original observations to remove whatever doubts about the structure are left by ambiguities encountered when going in the other direction. This closing of the circle verifies not only the calculation of molecular structure but also the theoretical edifice that provided the details of molecular interactions.

In this example the computer clearly mimics the molecule according to a script supplied by underlying physical and chemical theory. The computer represents the molecule with a sufficient degree of structural detail to make plausible a metaphorical identification of the computer with the molecule. The metaphor loses its force as we approach details of atomic structure, and the submodels that account for atomic behavior are in this case merely functional.

The remarkable immediacy and clarity of the confrontation of acted-out theory and experiment shown in the preceding example is by no means an isolated phenomenon. Similar techniques are emerging in chemistry [see "Computer Experiments in Chemistry," by Don L. Bunker; SCIENTIFIC AMERICAN, July, 1964], in hydrodynamics [see "Computer Experiments in Fluid Dynamics," by Francis H. Harlow and Jacob E. Fromm, beginning on page 192 of this book] and in other branches of science. It is noteworthy, as Don L. Bunker has pointed out, that computers used in this way, far from reducing the scientist to a passive bystander, reinforce the need for the creative human element in experimental science, if only because witless calculation is likely to be so voluminous as to be beyond the power of even the fastest computer. Human judgment and intuition must be injected at every stage to guide the computer in its search for a solution. Painstaking routine work will be less and less useful for making a scientific reputation, because such "horse work" can be reduced to a computer program. All that is left for the scientist to contribute is a creative imagination. In this sense scientists are subject to techno-

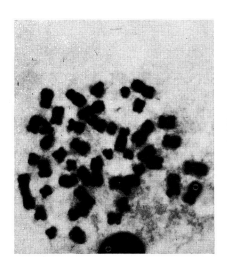

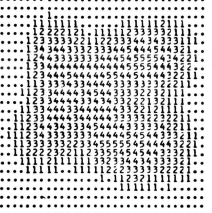

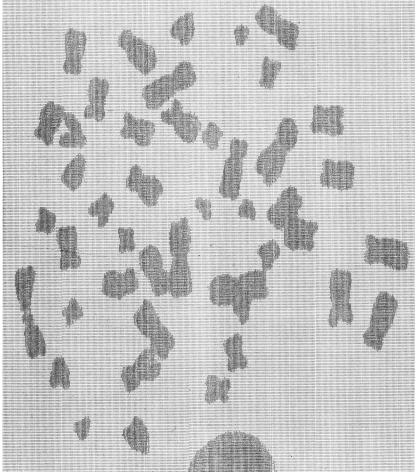

CHROMOSOME ANALYSIS BY COMPUTER makes it possible to examine automatically large numbers of cells for chromosome abnormalities. A photomicrograph of a complement of human chromosomes is shown at top left. An image of the photomicrograph is provided by the grid of numerals in computer print-out at right. Enlargement of a single chromosome appears at bottom left. Printouts were made with a scanning device called FIDAC and an IBM 7094 computer at the National Biomedical Research Foundation.

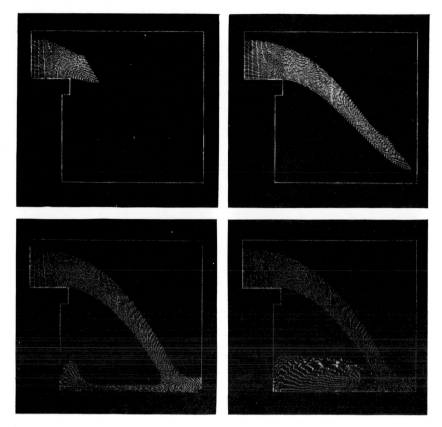

SIMULATED WATERFALL spills over the edge of a cliff and splashes into a pool in this computer experiment performed by John P. Shannon at the Los Alamos Scientific Laboratory as part of a general study of dynamic behavior of fluids with the aid of numerical models.

logical unemployment, just like anyone else.

In the "softer" emerging sciences such as psychology and linguistics the excitement and speculation about the future promise of the computer both as instrument and as actor tend to be even stronger than in the physical sciences, although solid accomplishments still are far fewer.

From the time modern computers were born the myth of the "giant brain" was fed by the obvious fact that they could calculate and also by active speculation about their ability to translate from one language into another, play chess, compose music, prove theorems and so on. That such activities were hitherto seen as peculiar to man and to no other species and certainly to no machine lent particular force to the myth. This myth (as expressed, for example, in *New Yorker* cartoons) is now deeply rooted as the popular image of the computer.

The myth rests in part on gross misinterpretation of the nature of a functional model. In the early 1950's, when speculation about whether or not computers can think was at the height of fashion, the British mathematician A. M. Turing proposed the following ex-

periment as a test. Imagine an experimenter communicating by teletype with each of two rooms (or black boxes), one containing a man, the other a computer. If after exchanging an appropriate series of messages with each room the experimenter is unable to tell which holds the man and which the computer, the computer might be said to be thinking. Since the situation is symmetrical, one could equally well conclude that the man is computing. Whatever the decision, such an experiment demonstrates at most a more or less limited functional similarity between the two black boxes, because it is hardly designed to reveal structural details. With the realization that the analogy is only functional, this approach to the computer as a model, or emulator, of man loses both mystery and appeal; in its most naïve form it is pursued today only by a dwindling lunatic fringe, although it remains in the consciousness of the public.

In a more sophisticated vein attempts continue toward devising computer systems less dependent on detailed prior instructions and better able to approach problem-solving with something akin to human independence and intelligence. Whether or not such systems, if they

are achieved, should have anything like the structure of a human brain is as relevant a question as whether or not flying machines should flap their wings like birds. This problem of artificial intelligence is the subject of speculative research described by Marvin Minsky in article beginning on page 123. Once the cloud of misapplied functional analogy is dispelled the real promise of using the computer as an animated structural model remains.

Mathematics has so far made relatively few inroads in either linguistics or psychology, although there are now some rather beautiful mathematical theories of language. The scope of these theories is generally limited to syntax (the description of the order and formal relations among words in a sentence). Based as they are on logic and algebra, rather than on the now more familiar calculus, these theories do not lend themselves readily to symbolic calculation of the form to which mathematicians and natural scientists have become accustomed. "Calculations" based on such theories must generally be done by computer. Indeed, in their early form some of these theories were expressed only as computer programs; others still are and may remain so. In such cases the language of programs is the language of science; the program is the original and only script, not just a translation from mathematics.

Early claims that computers could translate languages were vastly exaggerated; even today no finished translation can be produced by machine without human intervention, although machine-aided translation is technically possible. Considerable progress has been made, however, in using computers to manipulate languages, both vernaculars and programming languages. Grammars called phrase-structure grammars and transformational grammars supply the theoretical backdrop for this activity. These grammars describe sentences as they are generated from an initial symbol (say S for sentence) by applying rewrite rules followed (if the grammar is transformational) by applying transformation rules. For example, the rewrite rule $S \rightarrow SuPr$, where Su can be thought of as standing for subject and Pr as standing for predicate, yields the string $SuPr$ when it is applied to the initial symbol S. By adding the rules $Su \rightarrow John$ and $Pr \rightarrow sleeps$ one can turn this string into the sentence "John sleeps." Transformations can then be applied in order to turn, for example, the active sentence "John followed the girl" into the passive one "The girl was followed by John."

Under the direction of Susumu Kuno and myself a research group at Harvard has developed, over the past few years, techniques for inverting this generation process in order to go from a sentence as it occurs in a text to a description of its structure or, equivalently, to a description of how it might have been generated by the rules of the grammar. Consider the simple sentence "Time flies like an arrow." To find out which part of this sentence is the subject, which part the predicate and so on, a typical program first looks up each word in a dictionary. The entry for "flies" would show that this word might serve either as a plural noun denoting an annoying domestic insect or as a verb de-

noting locomotion through the air by an agent represented by a subject in the third person singular.

The specific function of a word in a particular context can be found only by checking how the word relates to other words in the sentence, hence the serious problem of determining which of the many combinations of possible functions do in fact fit together as a legitimate sentence structure. This problem has been solved essentially by trying all possibilities and rejecting those that do not fit, although powerful tests suggested by theory and intuition can be applied to eliminate entire classes of possibilities at one fell swoop, thereby bringing the process within the realm of practicality.

A grammar that pretends to describe

English at all accurately must yield a structure for "Time flies like an arrow" in which "time" is the subject of the verb "flies" and "like an arrow" is an adverbial phrase modifying the verb. "Time" can also serve attributively, however, as in "time bomb," and "flies" of course can serve as a noun. Together with "like" interpreted as a verb, this yields a structure that becomes obvious only if one thinks of a kind of flies called "time flies," which happen to like an arrow, perhaps as a meal. Moreover, "time" as an imperative verb with "flies" as a noun also yields a structure that makes sense as an order to someone to take out his stopwatch and time flies with great dispatch, or like an arrow.

A little thought suggests many minor modifications of the grammar sufficient to rule out such fantasies. Unfortunately too much is then lost. A point can be made that the structures are legitimate even if the sentences are meaningless. It is, after all, only an accident of nature, or for that matter merely of nomenclature, that there is no species of flies called "time flies." Worse yet, anything ruling out the nonexistent species of time flies will also rule out the identical but legitimate structure of "Fruit flies like a banana."

Still more confusing, the latter sentence itself is given an anomalous structure, namely that which is quite sensible for "Time flies..." but which is nonsensical here since we know quite well that fruit in general does not fly and that when it does, it flies like maple seeds, not like bananas.

A theory of syntax alone can help no further. Semantics, the all too nebulous notion of what a sentence means, must be invoked to choose among the three structures syntax accepts for "Time flies like an arrow." No techniques now known can deal effectively with semantic problems of this kind. Research in the field is continuing in the hope that some form of man-machine interaction can yield both practical results and further insight into the deepening mystery of natural language. We do not yet know how people understand language, and our machine procedures barely do child's work in an extraordinarily cumbersome way.

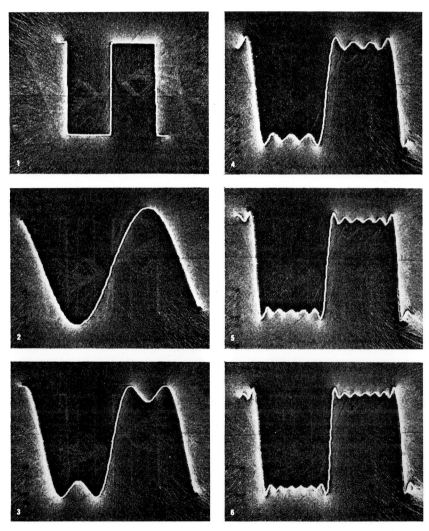

PROBLEM IN MATHEMATICS illustrates the author's experimental use in Harvard classrooms of a keyboard-and-display system developed by Glen Culler of the University of California at Santa Barbara. It is well known that any periodic function (in this example the square wave at top left) can be approximated by the sum of a series of terms that oscillate harmonically, converging on the curve of the function. Culler's apparatus makes possible quick intuitive exploration of the nature of this approximation. The other curves show the effect of increasing the number of terms in the partial sum of the series. The spikes near the corners of the square wave are caused by nonuniform convergence near a discontinuity.

The outlook is brighter for man-made programming languages. Since these can be defined almost at will, it is generally possible to reduce ambiguity and to systematize semantics well enough for practical purposes, although numerous challenging theoretical problems remain. The computer is also growing in power as an instrument of routine language data processing. Concordances, now easily made by machine, supply scholars in the humanities and social sciences with tabular displays of the location and context of key words in both sacred and profane texts.

Psychologists have used programming languages to write scripts for a variety of structural models of human behavior. These are no more mysterious than scripts for the orbit of Neptune or the structure of hemoglobin. The psychological models differ from the physical ones only in their subject and their original language. Convincing empirical corroboration of the validity of these models is still lacking, and the field has suffered from exaggerated early claims and recurrent confusion between the functional and the structural aspects of theory. Psychology and the study of artificial intelligence are both concerned with intelligent behavior, but otherwise they are not necessarily related except to the extent that metaphors borrowed

from one discipline may be stimulating to the other.

In actuality it is the languages, not the scripts, that are today the really valuable products of the attempts at computer modeling of human behavior. Several languages, notably John McCarthy's LISP, have proved invaluable as tools for general research on symbol manipulation. Research on natural-language data processing, theorem-proving, algebraic manipulation and graphical display draws heavily on such languages. Nevertheless, the computer as instrument is rapidly making a useful place for itself in the psychology laboratory. Bread-and-butter applications include the administration, monitoring and evaluation of tests of human or animal subjects in studies of perception and learning.

The business of science, both in principle and in practice, is inextricably involved in the business of education, particularly on the university level. The

paradigm of the computer as instrument and as actor, although described in terms of research, seems to apply to instruction as well. Because on-line, time-shared systems are still experimental and expensive, especially with graphical display facilities, their use for instruction lags somewhat behind their use for research.

Hopes for computers in education at the elementary or secondary level are described in the article by Patrick Suppes beginning on page 249. My own current exploration of the potential value of technological aids to creative thought focuses rather on the undergraduate or graduate student and in the transition from learning in the classroom to learning when practicing a profession.

The desire to keep labor within reasonable bounds generally leads to oversimplified and superficial experiments in student laboratories. Where the observation and intelligent interpretation of a variety of significant phenomena

```
***** ANALYSIS NUMBER   1       SENTENCE NUMBER   000001              CORPUS NUMBER

ENGLISH   SENTENCE STRUCTURE    SWC    SWC MNEMONIC     SYNTACTIC ROLE              RL NUM PREDICTION POOL
                                                                                          SE
TIME      1S                    NOUS   NOUN 1           SUBJECT OF PREDICATE VERB   SENNNO
                                                                                          PD VSA
FLIES     1V                    VI1S   COMPLETE VI      PREDICATE VERB              VXVI10
                                                                                          PD
LIKE      1VPR                  PRE    PREPOSITION      PREPOSITION                 PDPREO
                                                                                          PD NQG
AN        1VPOA                 ART    PRO-ADJECTIVE    OBJECT OF PREPOSITION       NQAAAO
                                                                                          PD N5G
ARROW     1VPO                  NOUS   NOUN 1           OBJECT OF PREPOSITION       N5MMMO
                                                                                          PD
.         1.                    PRD    PERIOD           END OF SENTENCE             PDPRDO

-----------------------------------------------------------------------------------------

***** ANALYSIS NUMBER   2       SENTENCE NUMBER   000001              CORPUS NUMBER

ENGLISH   SENTENCE STRUCTURE    SWC    SWC MNEMONIC     SYNTACTIC ROLE              RL NUM PREDICTION POOL
                                                                                          SE
TIME      1SA                   NOUS   NOUN 1           SUBJECT OF PREDICATE VERB   SENOUO
                                                                                          PD VZA7ZA
FLIES     1S                    NOUP   NOUN 1           SUBJECT OF PREDICATE VERB   7XMMMO
                                                                                          PD VPA
LIKE      1V                    VT1P   NOUN-OBJECT VT   PREDICATE VERB              VXVT11
                                                                                          PD N2A
AN        10A                   ART    PRO-ADJECTIVE    OBJECT OF PREDICATE VERB    N2AAAO
                                                                                          PD N5A
ARROW     10                    NOUS   NOUN 1           OBJECT OF PREDICATE VERB    N5MMMO
                                                                                          PD
.         1.                    PRD    PERIOD           END OF SENTENCE             PDPRDO

-----------------------------------------------------------------------------------------

***** ANALYSIS NUMBER   3       SENTENCE NUMBER   000001              CORPUS NUMBER

ENGLISH   SENTENCE STRUCTURE    SWC    SWC MNEMONIC     SYNTACTIC ROLE            RL NUM PREDICTION POOL
                                                                                          SE
TIME      3V                    IT1    INFINITE VT1     IMPERATIVE VERB           SEIT10
                                                                                          PD N2B
FLIES     30                    NOUP   NOUN 1           OBJECT OF IMPERATIVE VERB N2NNNO
                                                                                          PD
LIKE      30PR                  PRE    PREPOSITION      PREPOSITION               PDPREO
                                                                                          PD NQG
AN        30POA                 ART    PRO-ADJECTIVE    OBJECT OF PREPOSITION     NQAAAO
                                                                                          PD N5G
ARROW     30PO                  NOUS   NOUN 1           OBJECT OF PREPOSITION     N5MMMO
                                                                                          PD
.         3.                    PRD    PERIOD           END OF SENTENCE           PDPRDO

-----------------------------------------------------------------------------------------
```

SYNTACTIC ANALYSIS BY COMPUTER of the sentence "Time flies like an arrow" yields three different structural interpretations, which are represented here by computer print-out (*left*) and by conventional sentence-structure diagrams (*right*). The first structure is one in which "time" is the subject of the verb "flies" and "like an arrow" is an adverbial phrase modifying the verb (*Analysis Number 1*). "Time" can also serve attributively, however, as in "time bomb," and "flies" of course can serve as a noun. Together with "like" interpreted as a verb, this yields a structure that becomes obvious only if one thinks of a kind of domestic insect called "time flies," which happen to like an arrow, perhaps as a meal (*2*). Moreover, "time" as an imperative verb with "flies" as a noun also yields a

are the primary objectives of a laboratory exercise, using a transparent computer should reduce unnecessary drudgery to the point where judgment and interpretation, even of realistic experiments, can prevail.

The transparent computer also promises to be effective as a kind of animated blackboard. This hardly implies the disappearance of chalk, films or books. The computer merely adds another powerful and versatile tool to the teacher's kit. In fact, where repetition or polish is necessary, the computer itself can serve to make films or equivalent visual recordings. We have found that whereas films cannot be interrupted or altered, a recorded computer sequence can easily be stopped in response to a student's question; the lecturer can then explore alternatives by returning either to the informal direct use of the computer or to the conventional blackboard. The prerecorded sequence can then be resumed.

Best of all, there need be no distinc-

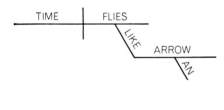

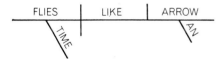

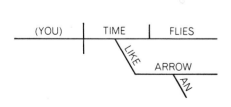

structure that makes sense as an order to someone to take out his stopwatch and time flies with great dispatch, or like an arrow (3). No computer techniques now known can deal effectively with semantic problems of this kind, but research in the field is continuing.

tion between the classroom tool and that available to students for homework assignments, laboratory calculations or individual research projects. The transition from classroom to life therefore promises to be made smoother. Since computers are not yet either as transparent or as cheap as one might wish, many problems of technique and finance remain to be faced. In any case, no panacea has been found for education's ills, only a richer range of choices to be made.

An example based on our experimental use in Harvard classrooms of a keyboard-and-display system developed by Glen Culler at the University of California at Santa Barbara will illustrate both the promise and the problems. Since the static printed page cannot adequately portray the effect of dynamic display, the problems may be more evident than the promise. The topic chosen is mathematical in nature, since such problems are best suited for the equipment currently available. The objective is to develop a natural and perspicuous presentation of topics traditionally reserved for more advanced treatment, to develop others in greater depth than conventional methods allow and to stimulate the student's intuition and his resourcefulness in solving problems. The objective is not to eliminate theory and rigor in favor of witless calculation, but rather to restore the close link between theory and calculation that characterized mathematics before the advent of rigor late in the 19th century led to the aberrant but currently fashionable split between pure and applied mathematics.

It is well known that any periodic function can be approximated by the sum of a series of terms that oscillate harmonically, converging on the curve of the function. Culler's apparatus makes possible quick intuitive exploration of the nature of this approximation. Consider, for example, the square wave shown at top left in the illustration on page 267. The accompanying computer-generated curves show the effect of increasing the number of terms in the partial sum of the series. The spikes near the corners of the square wave are caused by nonuniform convergence near a discontinuity. For the pure mathematician this demonstration can motivate a more formal treatment of nonuniform convergence. For the engineer the phenomenon can be clarified by displaying the components of the approximation in such a way as to make it obvious intuitively why the spikes occur. In prin-

ciple the instructor, or an interested student on his own, could follow up such a demonstration by modeling the effect of a linear circuit element, say a resistor or a simple amplifier, on a square wave, on its individual components and on their sum.

At present any concurrent formal algebraic manipulations require pencil or chalk. Current progress toward machine-aided algebraic manipulation raises the exciting possibility that machines will eventually help with both symbolic and numerical manipulation and with easy transitions between these two modes of expression. Working in both modes simultaneously or in whatever combination rigor and intuition demand would profoundly affect the thought of pure and applied mathematicians alike.

Other types of teaching experiment can be conducted by building an appropriate structural model into the computer. One might assume the structure and examine its behavior, as is frequently done in management games, or one might treat only the behavior as observable, leaving the model to be determined as an exercise in theory-building. As paradigms are developed by research in some area, these paradigms could then be applied as well to teaching in that area. It will be interesting, for example, to experiment with the teaching of a foreign language for which a transformational grammar of the type I described earlier has been implemented on a computer.

It is also interesting to speculate on the use of on-line computers as tools for the investigation of the psychology of learning and problem-solving. Experiments in this area have been difficult, contrived and unrealistic. When the interactive computer serves as a problem-solving tool, it is also easily adapted to record information about problem-solving behavior. Here again the problem will not be the collection of data but rather devising appropriate experimental designs, since an hour's problem-solving session at a computer console can accumulate an enormous amount of data.

In short, computers are capable of profoundly affecting science by stretching human reason and intuition, much as telescopes or microscopes extend human vision. I suspect that the ultimate effects of this stretching will be as far-reaching as the effects of the invention of writing. Whether the product is truth or nonsense, however, will depend more on the user than on the tool.

BIOGRAPHICAL NOTES AND BIBLIOGRAPHIES

I FUNDAMENTALS

1. Information

The Author

JOHN MCCARTHY is Professor of Computer Science and Director of the Artificial Intelligence Laboratory at Stanford University. A graduate of the California Institute of Technology in 1948, he received a Ph.D. in mathematics at Princeton in 1951. Thereafter he taught at Princeton, Stanford, Dartmouth, and the Massachusetts Institute of Technology before taking up his present work. McCarthy's special interest are computer programming languages, the theory of computation, and artificial intelligence.

Bibliography

Greenberger, Martin, edited by. 1962. *Computers and the World of the Future.* The M.I.T. Press.

Weiner, Norbert. 1961. *Cybernetics: Or Control and Communication in the Animal and the Machine.* The M.I.T. Press.

Gruenberger, Fred. 1969. *Computing: An Introduction.* Harcourt, Brace, & Jovanovich.

Hull, T. E. 1966. *Introduction to Computing.* Prentice-Hall.

Leeds, Herbert D., and Gerald M. Weinberg. 1961. *Computer Programming Fundamentals.* McGraw-Hill.

2. Computer Logic and Memory

The Author

DAVID C. EVANS is Director of Computer Science at the University of Utah and President of the Evans-Sutherland Computer Corporation in Salt Lake City; the firm manufactures computer display equipment. He was graduated from Utah in 1949, and obtained a Ph.D. in physics there four years later. From 1953 to 1962, he was director of engineering in the Bendix Corporation's computer division. He then spent three years as Professor and Associate Director of the computing system at the University of California at Berkeley before going to the University of Utah.

Bibliography

Bartee, Thomas C., Irwin L. Lebow, and Irving S. Reed. 1962. *Theory and Design of Digital Machines.* McGraw-Hill.

Caldwell, S. H. 1958. *Switching Circuits and Logical Design.* John Wiley & Sons.

Phister, Montgomery. 1958. *Logical Design of Digital Computers.* John Wiley & Sons.

Pressman, Abraham I. 1959. *Design of Transistorized Circuits for Digital Computers.* John F. Rider.

Quartly, C. J. 1962. *Square-Loop Ferrite Circuitry: Storage and Logic Techniques.* Prentice-Hall.

3. Integrated Computer Memories

The Author

JAN A. RAJCHMAN is Staff Vice President, Information Sciences, RCA Laboratories, David Sarnoff Research Center, Princeton, N.J. He has been with RCA since 1935, when he began work as a student engineer, and has been at the Princeton Laboratories since 1942. There he developed the magnetic-core memory system that is standard equipment in modern computers. Rajchman has obtained more than 100 U.S. patents. He holds degrees, including a doctorate in technical sciences, from the Federal Institute of Technology in Zurich. His first work was in the development of electron photomultipliers; during World War II he was one of the first to apply electronics to computers. Work that he did later on the betatron won for him the Levy Medal of the Franklin Institute. At RCA he is in charge of advanced research in electronic digital computers.

Bibliography

Burns, J. R., J. J. Gibson, A. Harel, K. C. Hu, and R. A. Powlus. 1966. "Integrated Memories Using Complementary Field-Effect Transistors." *International Solid State Circuit Conference Digest of Technical Papers,* **9** (February 1966), 118–119.

Fedde, George A. 1967. "Plated-Wire Memories; Univac's Bet to Replace Toroidal Ferrite Cores." *Electronics*, **40**. no. 10 (May 15, 1967), 109.

Gilligan, T. J. 1966. "2–1 2D High-Speed Memory Systems—Past, Present, and Future." *IEEE Transactions on Electronic Computers*, **EC-15**, no. 4 (August 1966), 475–485.

Rajchman, J. A. 1952. "Static Magnetic Matrix Memory and Switching Circuits." *RCA Review*, **13**, no. 2 (June 1952), 183–201.

Sass, A. R., E. M. Nagle, and L. L. Burns. 1966. "Three-Wire Cryolectric Memory Systems." *IEEE Transactions on Magnetics*, **MAG-2**, no. 3 (September 1966), 398–402.

Shahbender, R., C. Wentworth, K. Li, S. E. Hotchkiss, and J. A. Rajchman. 1963. "Laminated Ferrite Memory." *Proceedings of the AFIPS Fall Joint Computer Conferences*, **24** (Fall 1963), 77–90. Spartan Books and Cleaver-Hume Press.

4. Computer Inputs and Outputs

The Author

IVAN E. SUTHERLAND is Vice President, Research and Development, of the Evans-Sutherland Computer Corporation in Salt Lake City; the firm manufactures computer-display equipment. Before joining the firm Sutherland was Associate Professor of Electrical Engineering at Harvard University. He is continuing his research on computer graphics on a part-time basis at the University of Utah, where he is Associate Professor of Electrical Engineering. Sutherland writes: "I have found the transition from university professor to corporate executive a very educational one. I had not accurately predicted how much effort goes into management and how little into engineering. I look forward to the day when I can concentrate again, as I did at Harvard, on technical activities and leave the management to someone else." Sutherland received a bachelor's degree in electrical engineering at the Carnegie Institute of Technology in 1959, a master's degree at the California Institute of Technology in 1960, and a Ph.D. from the Massachusetts Institute of Technology in 1963.

Bibliography

Roberts, L. G. 1963. *Machine Perception of Three-Dimensional Solids. Lincoln Laboratory Technical Report*, no. 315. Massachusetts Institute of Technology.

Sutherland, I. E. 1963. *Sketchpad, A Man-Machine Graphical Communication System. Lincoln Laboratory Technical Report*, no. 296. Massachusetts Institute of Technology.

Sutherland, W. R. 1966. *The On-Line Graphical Specification of Computer Procedures. Lincoln Laboratory Technical Report*, no. 405. Massachusetts Institute of Technology.

5. Computer Displays

The Author

For information on IVAN E. SUTHERLAND, see the biographical note under Article 4, "Computer Inputs and Outputs."

Bibliography

Myer, T. H., and I. E. Sutherland, M. K. Vosbury, and R. W. Watson. 1969. "A Display Professor Design." *Proceedings of the AFIPS Fall Joint Computer Conference*, **35** (Fall 1969), 209–217. AFIPS Press.

Sutherland, I. E. 1963. "Sketchpad, A Man-Machine Graphical Communication System." *Proceedings of the AFIPS Spring Computer Conference*, **23** (Spring 1963), 329–346. Spartan Books and Cleaver-Hume Press.

Sproull, Robert F., and Ivan E. Sutherland. 1968. "A Clipping Divider." *Proceedings of the AFIPS Fall Joint Computer Conference*, **33**, part I (Fall 1968), 765–776. Thompson.

6. System Analysis and Programming

The Author

CHRISTOPHER STRACHEY is Reader in Computation at the University of Oxford. He was graduated from the University of Cambridge in 1939, and spent the war years as a physicist working on the design of radar tubes. From 1944 to 1951, he taught in preparatory schools; since then he has been working with computers. "My chief interest," he writes, "is to develop the mathematical foundations of programming and, if possible, to simplify programming (particularly that of large "software" systems) and to make the design of machines more rational."

Bibliography

Barron, D. W. 1968. *Recursive Techniques in Programming*. American Elsevier.

Baumann, R., M. Feliciano, F. L. Bauer, and K. Samelson. 1964. *Introduction to Algol*. Prentice-Hall.

Fox, L., ed. 1966. *Advances in Programming and Non-numerical Computation*. Pergamon Press.

McCracken, Daniel D. 1961. *A Guide to Fortran Programming*. John Wiley & Sons.

Samuel, Arthur L. 1960. "Programming Computers to Play Games." In Franz L. Alt, ed., *Advances in Computers*, vol. 1. Academic Press.

Samuel, Arthur L. 1969. "Some Studies in Machine Learning Using the Game of Checkers: Recent Progress." *Annual Review of Automatic Programming*, **6**, 1–36. Pergamon Press.

7. Time-Sharing on Computers

The Authors

R. M. FANO and F. J. CORBATÓ are both at the Massachusetts Institute of Technology. Fano is Professor of Engineering; he organized Project MAC, an M.I.T.

research effort on multiple-access computer systems, and was its director until September 1968. He was born in Italy, came to the U.S. in 1939, and since 1941 has been at M.I.T., where he obtained a doctorate in electrical engineering in 1947. He is the author of *Transmission of Information*, and coauthor of two textbooks on electromagnetic theory. Corbató is Professor of Electrical Engineering, and heads the systems research and development group of Project MAC. He received a bachelor's degree from the California Institute of Technology in 1950 and a doctorate in physics at M.I.T. in 1956, and is widely recognized for his work on the design and development of multiple-access computer systems. Among his publications, one book that Corbató coauthored, which describes the use of the M.I.T. time-sharing system, is *The Compatible Time-Sharing System: A Programmer's Guide*. The work reported in the article by Fano and Corbató was supported by Project MAC, which is sponsored by the Advanced Research Projects Agency of the Department of Defense under a contract from the Office of Naval Research. The work reported in the articles by Martin Greenberger and Marvin Minsky had the same sponsorship.

Bibliography

Corbató, F. J., V. A. Vyssotsky, and R. M. Graham. 1965. "Structure of the Multics Supervisor." *Proceedings of the AFIPS Fall Joint Computer Conference*, **27**, part 1 (Fall 1969), 203–212. Spartan Books.

Crisman, P. A., ed. 1965. *The Compatible Time-Sharing System: A Programmer's Guide*. The M.I.T. Press.

Dennis, Jack B. 1965. "Segmentation and the Design of Multiprogrammed Computer Systems." *Journal of the Association for Computing Machinery*, **12**, no. 4 (October 1965), 589–602.

Licklider, J. C. R. 1960. "Man-Computer Symbiosis." *IRE Transactions on Human Factors in Electronics*, **HFE-1**, no. 1 (March 1960), 4–11.

Samuel, Arthur L. 1965. "Time-Sharing on a Computer." *New Scientist*, **26**, no. 445 (May 27, 1965), 583–587.

Editors' Note: The following letter was published in the January 1967 issue of *Scientific American*, and is reprinted here at the request of its authors.

Sirs:

It has been brought to our attention that our article entitled "Time-sharing on Computers" in the September 1966 issue of *Scientific American* gave the incorrect impression that the work at the M.I.T. Computation Center had its sole root in the paper presented by Christopher Strachey at the 1959 UNESCO Congress. In fact, the idea of time-sharing a large computer grew simultaneously and independently at the M.I.T. Computation Center. The implementation of a time-sharing system was proposed in an internal memorandum by Professor John McCarthy, dated January 1, 1959, entitled "A Time-sharing Operator Program for Our Projected IBM 709." Strachey's paper is, to our knowledge, the first formal publication that proposed and discussed in substantial detail the design of a general-purpose time-sharing system. Of course, computers already had been time-shared for special purposes, as in the SAGE air defense system in the early 1950's. General-purpose systems, however, did present a host of new, difficult problems. Thus there is no question that Strachey's paper had a very significant effect on the development of general-purpose time-sharing systems at M.I.T. as well as elsewhere.

R. M. FANO
F. J. CORBATÓ

Massachusetts Institute
of Technology
Cambridge, Mass.

II GAMES, MUSIC, AND ARTIFICIAL INTELLIGENCE

Introduction

Bibliography

Dreyfus, Hubert. 1971. *What Computers Can't Do: A Critique of Artificial Reason*. Harper & Row.

Duffield, A. M., *et al.* 1969. "Applications of Artificial Intelligence for Chemical Inference, II: Interpretation of Low-Resolution Mass Spectra of Ketones." *Journal of the American Chemical Society*, **91**, no. 11 (May 1969), 2977–2981.

Greenblatt, Richard D., Donald E. Eastlake, III, and Stephen D. Crocker. 1967. "The Greenblatt Chess Program." *Proceedings of the AFIPS Fall Joint Computer Conference*, **31** (Fall 1967), 801–810. Thompson (Academic Press).

Martin, W. A., and R. J. Fateman. 1971. "The MACSYMA System." *Proceedings of SIGSAM Conference (1971)*, 59–75. Association for Computing Machinery.

Mathews, M. V., and L. Rosler. 1969. "Graphical Language for the Scores of Computer-Generated Sounds." In Heinz van Foerster and James W. Beauchamp, eds., *Music by Computers*. John Wiley & Sons.

Minsky, Marvin, ed. 1968. *Semantic Information Processing*. The M.I.T. Press.

Minsky, Marvin, and Seymour Papert. 1969. *Perceptrons: An Introduction to Computational Geometry*. The M.I.T. Press.

Thompson, Fred B. 1966. "English for the Computer." *Proceedings of the AFIPS Fall Joint Computer Conference,* **29** (Fall 1966), 349–356. Spartan Books.

Samuel, Arthur L. 1959. "Some Studies in Machine Learning Using the Game of Checkers, Part I." *IBM Journal of Research and Development,* **3**, no. 3 (1959), 210–229.

Samuel, Arthur L. 1967. "Some Studies in Machine Learning Using the Game of Checkers, Part II." *IBM Journal of Research and Development,* **11**, no. 4 (1967), 601–618.

Weizenbaum, Joseph. 1967. "Contextual Understanding by Computers." *Communications of the Association for Computing Machinery,* **10**, no. 8 (August 1967), 474–480.

8. Pattern Recognition by Machine

OLIVER G. SELFRIDGE and ULRIC NEISSER are, respectively, a member of the staff at the Lincoln Laboratory of the Massachusetts Institute of Technology, and Professor of Psychology at Cornell University. Selfridge was born in London in 1926, and acquired his bachelor's degree in mathematics at M.I.T. in 1945. He pursued graduate work in mathematics there from 1947 to 1950, studied electronic countermeasures at Fort Monmouth in New Jersey for two years, and then joined Lincoln Laboratory, where, he says, "my interests in communications techniques and information theory were soon supplemented by an interest in pattern recognition and other aspects of artificial intelligence." Neisser, born in Germany in 1928, took his B.A. in psychology at Harvard University in 1950, his M.A. at Swarthmore College in 1952, and his Ph.D. at Harvard in 1956. He held a post-doctoral fellowship from the National Science Foundation from 1955 to 1957, and then joined the faculty of Brandeis. He was a member of the summer research staff at Lincoln Laboratory in 1958 and 1959. He is the author of the recent book, *Cognitive Psychology.*

Bibliography

Bledsoe, W. W., J. S. Bomba, I. Browning, R. J. Evey, R. A. Kirsch, R. L. Mattson, M. Minsky, U. Neisser, and O. G. Selfridge. 1959. "Discussion of Problems in Pattern Recognition." *Proceedings of the Eastern Joint Computer Conference,* **16** (1959), 223–237. National Joint Computer Committee.

Gold, Bernard. 1959. "Machine Recognition of Hand-Sent Morse Code." *IRE Transactions of the Professional Group on Information Theory,* **IT-5**, no. 1 (March 1959), 17–24.

Hebb, D. O. 1949. *The Organization of Behavior.* John Wiley & Sons.

Pitts, Walter, and Warren S. McCulloch. 1947. "How We Know Universals: The Perception of Auditory and Visual Forms." *The Bulletin of Mathematical Biophysics,* **9**, no. 3 (1947), 127–147.

9. A Chess-Playing Machine

The Author

CLAUDE E. SHANNON is Donner Professor of Science at the Massachusetts Institute of Technology, where he is a member of both the Department of Mathematics and the Department of Electrical Engineering. He was born in Michigan and did his undergraduate work at the University of Michigan before coming to M.I.T., where he took simultaneously an S.M. in electrical engineering and a Ph.D. in mathematics. After a year at the Institute for Advanced Study in Princeton, N.J., he began a long association with the Bell Telephone Laboratories in Murray Hill, N.J., that lasted until he returned to M.I.T. in 1956. While at Murray Hill, he published his "Mathematical Theory of Communication" in the Bell System Technical Journal, 1947–48; this paper established the theoretical foundations for communications engineering—a kind of "thermodynamics of communications"—which, until that time, had been missing. Dr. Shannon is the author of numerous papers and two books, has received several honorary degrees, and, in 1967, received the National Medal of Science from President Lyndon B. Johnson.

Bibliography

Shannon, C. E. 1948. "A Mathematical Theory of Communication." *Bell System Technical Journal,* **27**: (July 1948), 379–423; (October 1948), 623–656.

Shannon, C. E., and W. Weaver. 1949. *The Mathematical Theory of Communication.* University of Illinois Press.

10. Computer v. Chess-Player

The Authors

ALEX BERNSTEIN and MICHAEL de V. ROBERTS were, respectively, a mathematician and a computer-programming expert in the International Business Machines Corporation when their article was written. Bernstein was born in Italy, graduated from the City College of the City of New York, and studied medieval literature and industrial engineering at Columbia University. Roberts was born in England, graduated from the University of Manchester, and acquired a doctorate in chemistry from the University of Cambridge. While at C.C.N.Y., Bernstein was U.S. intercollegiate chess champion.

Bibliography

Kister, J., P. Stein, S. Ulam, W. Walden, and M. Wells. 1957. "Experiments in Chess." *Journal of the Association for Computing Machinery,* **4**, No. 2 (April 1957), 174–177.

Newell, Allen. 1955. "The Chess Machine: An Example of Dealing with a Complex Task by Adaptation." *Proceedings of the Western Joint Computer Conference (1955),* pp. 101–111. Institute of Radio Engineers.

Shannon, Claude E. 1950. "A Chess-Playing Machine." *Scientific American*, **182**, no. 2 (February 1950), 48–51.

11. Computer Music

The Author

LEJAREN HILLER was once a chemist, but is now a composer who holds the position of Slee Professor of Music at the State University of New York at Buffalo. He was born in New York City in 1924, and studied at Princeton University, where he received his Ph.D. in chemistry in 1947. While there, he also studied electrical engineering, and took courses in composition with Milton Babbitt and Roger Sessions. He was research chemist for E. I. duPont de Nemours at Waynesboro, Va., until 1952, when he joined the chemistry faculty at the University of Illinois. While there, he employed the ILLIAC computer and, since he had never stopped composing music, he began to think that a computer could be used to study musical problems. By 1958, he had acquired an M.A. in music, and switched to the School of Music at the institution, where he became Professor of Music and Director of its Experimental Music Studio. In 1968, he moved to his present position where he continues research in electronic music and musical acoustics, as well as composition and direction of a group for new music.

Bibliography

Hiller, Lejaren A., Jr., and Leonard M. Isaacson. 1959. *Experimental Music*. McGraw-Hill.

Hiller, Lejaren. 1964. *Informations theorie und Computer Musik. Darmstadter Beitrage zur Neue Musik*, vol. 8. Mainz, Deutschland: B. Schottes Sohne.

Hiller, Lejaren. 1970. "Music Composed with Computers: A Historical Survey." In Harry B. Lincoln, ed., *The Computer and Music*. Cornell University Press. (Contains a complete bibliography of articles written on this topic through 1968.)

12. Artificial Intelligence

The Author

MARVIN L. MINSKY is Professor of Electrical Engineering at the Massachusetts Institute of Technology. He is also director of the Artificial Intelligence group there. Minsky was graduated from Harvard College in 1950, and received a doctorate in mathematics at Princeton University in 1954. For the next three years he was a member of the Society of Fellows at Harvard, working on neural theories of learning and on optical microscopy. He joined the mathematics department at M.I.T. in 1958, and transferred to the electrical engineering department in 1962.

Bibliography

Feigenbaum, Edward A., and Julian Feldman, eds. 1963. *Computers and Thought*. McGraw-Hill.

Minsky, Marvin L. 1968. "Matter, Mind, and Models." In Marvin L. Minsky, ed., *Semantic Information Processing*. The M.I.T. Press.

Minsky, M. L., and Seymour Papert. 1969. *Perceptrons: An Introduction to Computational Geometry*. The M.I.T. Press.

Samuel, A. L. 1959. "Some Studies in Machine Learning Using the Game of Checkers, Part I." *IBM Journal of Research and Development*, 3, no. 3 (July 1959), 210–229.

III MATHEMATICS OF, BY, AND FOR COMPUTERS

Introduction

Bibliography

Knuth, D. E. 1969. *Seminumerical Algorithms*. Addison-Wesley.

13. Games, Logic and Computers

The Author

HAO WANG is Professor of Mathematics and Philosophy at The Rockefeller University. Wang was born in China, and received a bachelor's degree in mathematics and a master's degree in philosophy in Kunming. He came to the U.S. in 1946 and obtained a Ph.D. in logic at Harvard, remaining there as research fellow and assistant professor for several years. After a year of work on computers in industry, he went to England in 1954. He was John Locke Lecturer in philosophy at the University of Oxford in 1955, and Reader in the Philosophy of Mathematics from 1956 to 1961, when he returned to Harvard as Gordon MacKay Professor of Mathematical Logic and Applied Mathematics. He took up his present position in 1966. Wang is a fellow of the American Academy of Arts and Sciences, and a foreign fellow of the British Academy. He is the author of *A Survey of Mathematical Logic* (first published in 1962, reissued by Chelsea in 1970 under the title *Logic, Computers, and Sets*).

Bibliography

Berger, Robert. 1966. "The Undecidability of the Domino Problem." *Memoirs of the American Mathematical Society*, no. 66.

Davis, Martin, ed. 1965. *The Undecidable: Basic Papers on Undecidable Propositions, Unsolvable*

Problems, and Computable Functions. Raven Press.

Hilbert, D., and W. Ackermann. 1950. *Principles of Mathematical Logic.* Chelsea.

Rogers, Hartley, Jr. 1967. *Theory of Recursive Functions and Effective Computability.* McGraw-Hill.

Wang, Hao. 1963. "Dominoes and the AEA Case of the Decision Problem." *Proceedings of the Symposium on Mathematical Theory of Automata: MRI Symposia Series,* vol. 12. Polytechnic Press of the Polytechnic Institute of Brooklyn.

14. How Fast Can Computers Add?

The Author

SHMUEL WINOGRAD is a member of the staff of the Thomas J. Watson Research Center of the International Business Machines Corporation. His early training was in electrical engineering; he received his bachelor's and master's degrees in that subject at the Massachusetts Institute of Technology. In 1968 he obtained his Ph.D. in mathematics from New York University. He joined IBM in 1961, and has worked in the mathematical sciences department of the Watson Research Center. Concerning his work there Winograd writes: "Was interested in construction of reliable automata from less reliable components, and in particular in the connection between information theory and redundancy techniques. Currently trying to determine the minimum number of arithmetic operations required to compute various functions."

Bibliography

Brent, Richard P. 1970. "On the Addition of Binary Numbers." *Institute of Electrical and Electronics Engineers Transactions on Computers,* **C-19,** no. 8 (August 1970), 758–759.

Flores, Ivan. 1963. *The Logic of Computer Arithmetic.* Prentice-Hall.

Spira, P. M. 1969. "The Time Required for Group Multiplication." *Journal of the Association for Computing Machinery,* **16,** no. 2 (April 1969), 235–243.

Winograd, S. 1965. "On the Time Required to Perform Addition." *Journal of the Association for Computing Machinery,* **12,** no. 2 (April 1965), 277–285.

Winograd, S. 1967. "On the Time Required to Perform Multiplication." *Journal of the Association for Computing Machinery,* **14,** no. 4 (October 1967), 793–802.

15. Computers

The Author

STANISLAW ULAM is a research adviser at the Los Alamos Scientific Laboratory of the University of California. A native of Lwow, Poland, Ulam received an M.A. and a D.Sc. in mathematics from the Polytechnic Institute at Lwow in 1932 and 1933, respectively. He lectured at various institutions in Poland, England, and France before coming to the U.S. in 1936 as a visiting member of the Institute for Advanced Study in Princeton, N.J. Shortly thereafter he joined the Harvard University Society of Fellows. He left Harvard in 1940 to join the faculty of the University of Wisconsin. Since going to Los Alamos in 1943 to work on the atomic bomb as a member of the Manhattan Engineer District, Ulam has taught for short terms at the University of Southern California, Harvard, the Massachusetts Institute of Technology, the University of Colorado, and the University of California at San Diego. At Los Alamos, Ulam collaborated with Edward Teller on the development of the hydrogen bomb. He also invented the so-called Monte Carlo method, a procedure for finding solutions to mathematical and physical problems by random sampling. This technique, made practical by the development of high-speed computers, permits the solution of problems not amenable to more orthodox methods of analysis. Ulam is the author of *Problems in Modern Mathematics,* published in 1964.

Bibliography

Lehmer, D. H. 1960. "Teaching Combinatorial Tricks to a Computer." *Combinatorial Analysis: Proceedings of Symposia in Applied Mathematics,* vol. 10 (1960). American Mathematical Society.

Ulam, Stanislaw. 1960. *A Collection of Mathematical Problems.* John Wiley & Sons.

Von Neumann, John. 1958. *The Computer and the Brain.* Yale University Press.

Wilkes, M. V. 1956. *Automatic Digital Computers.* John Wiley & Sons.

Yovits, Marshall C., and Scott Cameron, eds. 1960. *Self-Organizing Systems: Proceedings of an Interdisciplinary Conference.* Pergamon Press.

16. The Monte Carlo Method

The Author

DANIEL D. MCCRACKEN is President of McCracken Associates in Ossining, New York. He has degrees in mathematics and chemistry from Central Washington State College, and is a graduate of the Union Theological Seminary in New York, where he received the Bachelor of Divinity degree. Before becoming a consultant specializing in writing on computer programming and programmer education, he worked for the General Electric Company for seven years, and briefly in 1958 with the Atomic Energy Commission Computing Center at New York University. He is the author of ten textbooks on computer programming, and is a student of the social problems caused by misuse of computer technology.

Bibliography

Householder, Alston S. 1953. *Principles of Numerical Analysis.* McGraw-Hill.

Kahn, Herman. 1950. "Random Sampling (Monte Carlo) Techniques in Neutron Attenuation Problems." *Nucleonics:* **6**, no. 5 (May 1950), 27–33, 37, **6**, no. 6 (June 1950), 60–65.

Milne, William Edmund. 1953. *Numerical Solution of Differential Equations.* John Wiley & Sons.

17. Molecular Model-Building by Computer

The Author

CYRUS LEVINTHAL is Professor of Biology at Columbia University. He had previously been at M.I.T. until 1968, when he left to serve as chairman of the biology department at Columbia. His original bent was toward physics; he took a Ph.D. in nuclear physics at the University of California at Berkeley in 1950, and spent seven years in the physics department of the University of Michigan, starting as instructor and leaving as associate professor. In 1957 he began work in the biology department of M.I.T. Levinthal did his undergraduate work at Swarthmore College, from which he received a bachelor's degree in 1943.

Bibliography

Anfinsen, C. B., E. Haber, M. Sela, and F. H. White, Jr. 1961. "The Kinetics of Formation of Native Ribonuclease During Oxidation of the Reduced Polypeptide Chain." *Proceedings of the National Academy of Sciences,* **47**, no. 9 (September 15, 1961), 1309–1334.

Levinthal, Cyrus, Ethan R. Signer, and Kathleen Fetherolf. 1962. "Reactivation and Hybridization of Reduced Alkaline Phosphatase." *Proceedings of the National Academy of Sciences,* **48**, no. 7 (July 1962), 1230–1237.

Pauling, Linus. 1960. *The Nature of the Chemical Bond and the Structure of Molecules and Crystals: An Introduction to Modern Structural Chemistry.* Cornell University Press.

Ramachandran, G. N., C. Ramakrishnan, and V. Sasisekharan. 1963. "Stereochemistry of Polypeptide Chain Configurations." *Journal of Molecular Biology,* **7**, no. 1 (July 1963), 95–99.

18. Systems Analysis of Urban Transportation

The Authors

WILLIAM F. HAMILTON II and DANA K. NANCE are with the General Research Corporation in Santa Barbara, Calif.; Hamilton is director of the civil systems department and Nance is editorial director. Hamilton took his bachelor's degree in physics at Yale University and his master's degree in applied physics at Harvard University. After two years at the Instrumentation Laboratory of the Massachusetts Institute of Technology, he moved to Santa Barbara, where he was with the General Electric Company until he joined his present firm in 1962. Nance was graduated from Vanderbilt University with a degree in English. He writes: "After an exposure to the fascination of electronic gadgetry during service in the Air Force I changed fields and studied physics and mathematics at Purdue University. For seven years I was a research engineer with General Motors, finally combining my two loves—words and gadgets—as a technical editor."

Bibliography

General Research Corporation. 1968. *Systems Analysis of Urban Transportation.* U.S. Department of Housing and Urban Development.

Meyer, J. R., J. F. Kain, and M. Wohl. 1965. *The Urban Transportation Problem.* Harvard University Press.

Office of Metropolitan Development. 1968. *Tomorrow's Transportation: New Systems for Urban Future.* U.S. Department of Housing and Urban Development.

19. Computer Experiments in Fluid Dynamics

The Authors

FRANCIS H. HARLOW and JACOB E. FROMM were investigators at the Los Alamos Scientific Laboratory when their article appeared. Harlow, who remains there, was born in Seattle, and received his entire university education at the University of Washington, where he obtained a Ph.D. in 1953. That same year he went to Los Alamos, where he is currently involved with theoretical work on numerical methods for fluid dynamics studies. Fromm, who is from Colorado, did undergraduate work at the University of Colorado and graduate work at the University of California at Los Angeles. He was at Los Alamos from 1956 to 1966, and is now with the Large Scale Scientific Computation Group of the IBM Research Laboratory at San Jose, California. Currently he is working on extensions of the numerical methods for computation of laminar-turbulent transition.

Bibliography

Fromm, Jacob. 1964. "The Time-Dependent Flow of an Incompressible Viscous Fluid." In B. Alder, S. Fernbach, and M. Rotenberg, eds., *Computational Physics: Advances in Research and Applications,* vol. III: *Fundamental Methods in Hydrodynamics.* Academic Press.

Fromm, Jacob E. To be published. "A Numerical Method for Computing the Nonlinear, Time-Dependent, Buoyant Circulation of Air in Rooms." *IBM Journal of Research and Development.*

Fromm, Jacob E., and Francis H. Harlow. 1963. "Numerical Solution of the Problem of Vortex Street Development." *The Physics of Fluids,* **6**, no. 7 (July 1963), 975–982.

Harlow, F. H., and A. A. Amsden. 1970. *Fluid Dynamics: An Introductory Text. Los Alamos Scientific Laboratory Report,* no. LA-4370.

20. Chromosome Analysis by Computer

The Authors

ROBERT S. LEDLEY and FRANK H. RUDDLE are, respectively, President of the National Biomedical Research Foundation and Assistant Professor of Biology at Yale University. Ledley arrived at his position by an unusual route. At Columbia University he specialized in physics and mathematics, but since "in those days a mathematician or a physicist could not make too much of a living, my parents decided to make a dentist of me." As a dentist Ledley was sent by the Army to do dental research at the National Bureau of Standards. There he had occasion to use a computer, and since he was "not happy using an instrument without knowing how it worked," he became a digital-computer engineer and served for a time as Associate Professor of Electrical Engineering at George Washington University. In 1960 he organized the National Biomedical Research Foundation to "apply computers in biomedical research on a full-time basis." Ruddle, who met Ledley during a seminar at Yale, received bachelor's and master's degrees at Wayne State University and a Ph.D. at the University of California at Berkeley.

Bibliography

Ledley, Robert Steven. 1965. *Use of Computers in Biology and Medicine.* McGraw-Hill.

Patau, Klaus. 1960. "The Identification of Individual Chromosomes, Especially in Man." *The American Journal of Human Genetics*, **12**, no. 3 (September 1960), 250–276.

21. Man Viewed as a Machine

The Author

JOHN G. KEMENY was inaugurated President of Dartmouth College in March 1970, after serving as Professor of Mathematics there for 16 years, including 12 years as chairman of the department. Born in Budapest, Hungary, he came to the U.S. at the age of 13 and attended George Washington High School in New York City, graduating first in his class. He then entered Princeton University, but was interrupted by the U.S. Army, which put him to work on calculating machines at Los Alamos. He returned to Princeton, graduated first in his class, and went to take a Ph.D. in mathematics. He spent his last year of graduate study as Albert Einstein's assistant at the Institute for Advanced Study. His own research has been in symbolic logic and probability theory. At Dartmouth he was instrumental in the creation of the Kiewit Computation Center and the Dartmouth Time-Sharing System, and coauthored the computer language BASIC.

Bibliography

Turing, A. M. 1954. "Solvable and Unsolvable Problems." *Science News*, no. 31 (1954), pp. 7–23. Penguin Books.

Von Neumann, John. 1966. *Theory of Self-Reproducing Automata.* University of Illinois Press.

22. The Fastest Computer

The Author

D. L. SLOTNICK is Professor of Computer Science and Director of the Center for Advanced Computation at the University of Illinois. He received his bachelor's and master's degrees in mathematics from Columbia University in 1951 and 1952, respectively, and then worked for two years at the Institute for Advanced Study. In 1956 he obtained his Ph.D. in applied mathematics (celestial mechanics) at New York University. He spent the next ten years in industry in various engineering activities, going to the University of Illinois in 1965. Slotnick writes: "I have written far too many articles and book chapters and hold a number of patents, including the basic patent on parallel computers. I live on a small farm where I raise horses, ride them, and pick my two little girls and occasionally my wife up out of the sawdust. I have a compulsion to plant trees; I have indulged it some 9,000 times on my 40 acres. I read too much and listen to and occasionally play music."

Bibliography

Denenberg, S. A. 1970. "An Introductory Description of the ILLIAC IV System." *ILLIAC IV Research Document*, no. 225 (July 15, 1970). Available from C. Corbin, ILLIAC IV Project, 153A Engineering Research Laboratory, University of Illinois at Urbana-Champaign, Urbana, Ill. 61801.

Roberts, Lawrence G., and Barry D. Wessler. 1970. "Computer Network Development to Achieve Resource Sharing." *Proceedings of the AFIPS Spring Joint Computer Conference,* **36** (Spring 1970), 543–549. AFIPS Press.

Slotnick, D. L., W. C. Borck, and R. C. McReynolds. 1962. "The Solomon Computer." *Proceedings of the AFIPS Fall Joint Computer Conference,* **22** (Fall 1962), 97–107. Spartan Books.

V FOUR ESSAYS ON THE USES OF THE COMPUTER

Introduction

Bibliography

Buxton, J. N., and B. Randell, eds. 1969. *Software Engineering Techniques.* Brussels: NATO (Scientific Affairs Division).

Papert, Seymour. 1964. "Teaching Children Thinking." *Proceedings of the IFIP World Conference on Computer Education.*

23. The Uses of Computers in Technology

The Author

STEVEN ANSON COONS has been Professor of Systems and Information Science at Syracuse University since July 1969. He was formerly with the mechanical engineering department at M.I.T., where he was in charge of the computer-aided design group of the design division of that department; he was simultaneously a research associate at Harvard. For eight years before that he was a design engineer with the Chance-Vought Division of the United Aircraft Corporation, where he devised mathematical methods for describing the shape of airplane fuselages by computer. He is the author of numerous papers on design and the geometry and description of shapes, and is coauthor of a textbook on graphics.

Bibliography

Coons, Steven A. 1964. "Surfaces for Computer-Aided Design of Space Figures." *Project MAC Technical Memorandum.* Massachusetts Institute of Technology.

Englebart, Douglas C. 1962. *Augmenting Human Intellect: A Conceptual Framework.* Stanford Research Institute.

General Motors Corporation. 1964. "The GM DAC-1 System, Design Augmented by Computers." GMR-430 Computer Technology Department, General Motors Corporation Research Laboratories, Warren, Michigan (October 28, 1964).

Hamilton, M. L., and A. D. Weiss. 1965. "An Approach to Computer-Aided Preliminary Ship Design." *Technical Memorandum,* no. 228. Electronic Systems Laboratory, Massachusetts Institute of Technology (January 1965).

24. The Uses of Computers in Organizations

The Author

MARTIN GREENBERGER is Professor and Chairman of Computer Science and Director of Information Processing at the John Hopkins University. He describes himself as "an applied mathematician by training, with interests in economics and psychology" and says that his work with computers "sometimes enables me to bring these different affinities together." Greenberger received his bachelor's, master's, and doctor's degrees in applied mathematics at Harvard University, and served nine years on the M.I.T. faculty. He is editor of a new book (1971) on *Computers, Communications, and the Public Interest.*

Bibliography

Greenberger, Martin, et al. 1962. *On-Line Computation and Simulation: The OPS-3 System.* The M.I.T. Press.

Greenberger, Martin, ed. 1971. *Computers, Communications, and the Public Interest.* The Johns Hopkins Press.

Simon, Herbert A. 1965. *The Shape of Automation for Men and Management.* Harper & Row.

25. The Uses of Computers in Education

The Author

PATRICK SUPPES is Professor of Philosophy and of Statistics at Stanford University and also Chairman of the Department of Philosophy and Director of the Institute for Mathematical Studies in the Social Sciences at the university. Suppes went to Stanford as an instructor in 1950, the year he obtained a Ph.D. at Columbia University. He did his undergraduate work at the University of Chicago, from which he was graduated in 1943. His extensive writings include two books, *Introduction to Logic* and *Axiomatic Set Theory,* three other books of which he is a coauthor, and several mathematics books for use in elementary schools. His special interests are mathematical methods in the social sciences and the philosophy of science.

Bibliography

Bushnell, Donald D., and Dwight W. Allen, eds. In press. *The Computer in American Education.* John Wiley & Sons.

Coulson, John E., ed. 1962. *Programmed Learning and Computer-Based Instruction.* John Wiley & Sons.

Goodman, E., ed. 1965. *Automated Education Handbook.* Automated Education Center.

26. The Uses of Computers in Science

The Author

ANTHONY G. OETTINGER is Professor of Linguistics, Gordon McKay Professor of Applied Mathematics, and

Research Associate to the Program on Technology and Society at Harvard University. Except for the academic year 1951–1952, when he was a Henry fellow at the University of Cambridge, he has been at Harvard since 1947; he obtained a bachelor's degree there in 1951 and a doctorate in 1954. He has served as Chairman of the Harvard Computing Center and as President of the Association for Computing Machinery. Currently he is the Chairman of the Computer Science and Engineering Board of the National Academy of Sciences, and Director of Project TACT (Technological Aids to Creative Thought), sponsored at Harvard by the National Science Foundation. He is also a consultant to the Office of Science and Technology, Executive Office of the President. In addition to numerous papers on the computer sciences and their applications, he is the author of two books.

Bibliography

Coulter, C. L. 1964. "Computing Problems and Methods in X-Ray Crystallography." In Franz L. Alt and M. Rubinoff, eds., *Advances in Computers*, vol. 5. Academic Press.

Gelernter, H. 1965. "Data Collection and Reduction for Nuclear Particle Trace Detectors." In Franz L. Alt and M. Rubinoff, eds., *Advances in Computers*, vol. 6. Academic Press.

Kuno, Susumo. In press. "Computer Analysis of Natural Languages." In Jack Schwartz, ed., *Mathematical Aspects of Computer Science*. American Mathematical Society.

Miller, G. A., E. Galanter, and K. H. Pribram. 1960. *Plans and the Structure of Behavior*. Holt, Rinehart, & Winston.

Oettinger, Anthony G. 1965. "Automatic Processing of Natural and Formal Languages." In Wayne A. Kalenich, ed., *Proceedings of the 1965 IFIP Congress*, I, 9–16. Spartan Books.

Oettinger, Anthony G. 1966. "A Vision of Technology and Education." *Communications of the Association for Computing Machinery*, **9**, no. 7 (July 1966), 487–490.

Oettinger, Anthony G. 1971. "Communications in the National Decision-Making Process." In Martin Greenberger, ed., *Computers, Communications, and the Public Interest*. Johns Hopkins Press.

Oettinger, Anthony G. 1969. *Run, Computer, Run: The Mythology of Educational Innovation*. Harvard University Press.

Sass, Margo A., and William D. Wilkinson. 1965. *Computer Augmentation of Human Reasoning*. Spartan Books.

INDEX

Adams, John Couch, 266
Adder, 19, 148
Address, 4, 21, 28
Addition, 11, 19
Aiken, Howard H., 9
Algorithm, 136
American Airlines, 249
Analogy, reasoning by, 125
And, 11, 17, 145
Anfinsen, Christian B., 175
Arbuckle, Timothy, 109
Aristoxenus, 114
Artificial Intelligence, 90, 95, 104, 123, 172, 268
Assignment Statements, 77

Babbage, Charles, 9, 134, 153
Bartok, Bela, 118
Bell Telephone Laboratories, 9, 48, 56, 116, 141, 263
Belsky, M. A., 109
Bernstein, Alex, 91, 108
Bigelow, Julian H., 123
Binary system, 10, 145
Bit, 9, 28
Block diagram, 70, 191, 205
Bobrow, Daniel G., 91, 129
Boeing Company, 241
Bolt, Beranek, and Newman, Inc., 79, 252
Boole, George, 17
Boundary conditions, 198, 221
Brahms, Johannes, 115
Bunker, Don L., 267
Burroughs Corporation, 17, 44, 216
Buxton, J. N., 230

Cage, John, 116
California Computer Products, Inc., 245
California Institute of Technology, 177
California, University of, 44, 159, 252, 266
Cambridge, University of, 123, 173
Capablanca, José, 112
Cards, punched. See Input-output
Carnegie Institute of Technology (Carnegie-Mellon University), 95, 123
Carroll, Arthur B., 218
Challis, James, 266
Channel. See Data channel
Characters
    coding, 10
    generating in display, 51
    recognizing printed, 90, 95

Checkers, 70, 123
Chess, 90, 95, 108, 123, 140
Children's Cancer Research Foundation, 182
Chip, 7, 26, 38, 219
Chopin, Frederic F., 115
Circuits, 17
    combinatorial, 19
    integrated, 2, 7, 25, 28, 219
    sequential, 20
Clipping, 60
Combinatorial circuit. See Circuits
Computability, 136, 145
Control Data Corporation, 27, 42
Coons, Steven Anson, 13, 229, 233
Corbató, F. J., 5, 12, 76, 79, 135, 179, 239, 248, 251, 264
Core memory. See Memory
Corey, Elias J., 64
Corey, Robert B., 177
Cost of computers, 2, 9, 21, 34, 42
Craik, K. J. W., 123
CRT (cathode ray tube) See Displays
CTSS (Compatible Time-Sharing System), 79
Culler, Glen, 269

Dalton, John, 266
Data channel, 46
Davidon, William, 183
De Groot, A. D., 106
Debugging, 76, 80, 198
Debussy, Claude A., 115
DENDRAL, 93
Digital Equipment Corporation, 64, 80
Disk memory. See Memory
Display, 3, 42, 53, 80, 123, 162, 179, 199, 233, 239, 253, 265
    calligraphic, 53
    head-mounted, 61
    hidden lines in, 51, 130
    hidden surfaces in, 63
    as input, 201, 267
    raster, 53
    of text, 53, 90
    See also Light pen, RAND Tablet
Display file, 57
Display processor, 56
Domino problem, 136
Dorodnitsyn, A. A., 195
Douglas Aircraft Company, 243
Doyle, Worthie, 100
Dreyfus, Hubert L., 91
Drum memory. See Memory
Duffield, A. M., 93

Eckert, J. Presper, 9, 153
Education, 13, 76, 230, 251, 270
Einstein, Albert, 194
Ellis, Thomas O., 51
Engineering, 229, 233
ENIAC (Electronic Numerical Integrator And Computer), 9, 134, 153
Euclid, 134, 136
Evans, David C., 2, 11, 17
Evans, Thomas G., 124
Evans and Sutherland Computer Corp, 62
Executive. See Operating system

Fabri-Tek, Incorporated, 24
Fairchild Corporation, 7, 54, 219
Fan-in, 148
Fano, R. M., 5, 12, 76, 79, 135, 179, 239, 248, 251, 264
Fateman, R. J., 93
Fermi, Enrico, 194
FIDAC (Film Input to Digital Automatic Computer), 201, 267
Flip-flop, 19, 38
Florida State University, 252
Florida, University of, 116
Flow chart. See Block diagram
Fluid dynamics. See Hydrodynamics
Ford Motor Company, 240
Fromm, Jacob E., 171, 194, 267

Galileo, 194
Galle, John, 266
Games, 90, 104, 139
    See also Checkers, Chess, Nim
Gauss, Karl Friedrich, 157
General Electric Company, 86, 245, 250
General Motors Corporation, 243
General Problem Solver, 123
General Research Corporation, 185
Gold, Bernard, 95
Graphic output. See Display
Greenberger, Martin, 229, 245
Greenblatt, R., 92

Halting problem, 144
Hamilton, William F., II, 171, 185
Harlow, Francis H., 171, 194, 267
Harmon, Leon D., 69
Harvard University, 9, 64, 141, 182, 248, 263
Haverford College, 183
Hebrew University of Jerusalem, 150
Herzog, Bertram, 243

Heuristic, 124
Hilbert, David, 141
Hiller, Lejaren A., Jr., 92, 113
Huygens, Christian, 265
Hydrodynamics, 155, 171, 194, 227

IIT Research Institute, 237
ILLIAC, 113, 171, 216
Illinois, University of, 113, 123, 216, 252
Infinity lemma, 140
Information theory, 113
Input-output, 3, 7, 42
    formatted, 48
    of punched cards, 42, 263
    of punched tape, 45
    See also Display
Institute for Advanced Study, 153, 209
Instructions, 4, 7, 45, 76
    See also Machine language
Instruction counter, 4
Integrated circuits. See Circuits
International Business Machines
    Corp., 23, 48, 54, 70, 79, 92, 95,
    108, 123, 150, 153, 196, 204, 233,
    250, 252, 267
Interrupt, 42
Issacson, L. M., 116
Iteration, 161, 189, 224

Julesz, Bela, 263

Kemeny, John G., 134, 170, 208
Kendrew, John C., 173, 263
Keydata Corporation, 249
Knowlton, Kenneth C., 69
Knuth, Donald E., 135
Kuno, Susumo, 269

Langridge, Robert, 182, 264
Language
    natural, 91, 104, 129, 231, 268
    programming. See Programming
        languages
Ledley, Robert S., 172, 201, 265
Lehmer, D. H., 159
Leibniz, Gottfried Wilhelm von, 153
Leverrier, Urbain, 266
Levinthal, Cyrus, 48, 83, 170, 173, 232,
    264
Licklider, J. C. R., 233
Light pen, 51, 58, 253
Lipetz, Ben-Ami, 13
Lipscomb, William N., Jr., 263
LISP, 76, 126, 270
Lockheed Corporation, 243, 249
Los Alamos Scientific Laboratory,
    153, 164, 268
Louis Berger and Associates, 238
Lovelace, Augusta Ada, 10
Lubs, Herbert A., Jr., 202
Lucretius, 266

MAC, Project. See Project MAC
MacEwan, Andrew A., 182
MACHACK-6, 92
Machine language, 4, 105
    See also Instructions
Machine tools, computer-controlled,
    237
MADAM, 109
MACSYMA, 93
Management. See Organizations
MANIAC (Mathematical Analyzer,
    Numerical Integrator And
    Computer), 153, 209
Marceau, Ian W., 224

Mark I, 11
Markoff approximation, 93, 120
Martin, W. A., 93
Massachusetts Institute of Technology,
    48, 60, 79, 92, 95, 123, 173, 210,
    233, 239, 248, 264
    See also Project MAC
Mathematics, 77, 136, 153, 195
Mathews, M. V., 93
Mauchly, John W., 9, 153
MAUDE (Morse AUtomatic
    DEcoder), 95
McCarthy, John, 2, 7, 80, 123, 270
McCracken, Daniel D., 135, 164
McCulloch, Warren S., 123, 210
Mead Corporation, 236
Meaning. See Semantics
Memory, 2, 7, 17, 28, 209
    core, 9, 22, 31
    data cell, 27
    disk, 23, 38, 46, 221
    drum, 23, 38, 45
    monolithic ferrite, 34
    photographic, 25
    random-access, 21, 39
    tape, magnetic, 12, 23, 42
    thin-film, 17, 34
    virtual, 25
    wire, 34
Memory snatch. See Data channel
Mesh, 196, 221, 194, 219
Meyer, Leonard B., 116
Michigan, University of, 243, 252
Microelectronics. See Circuits,
    integrated
Miller, James Grier, 232
Minsky, Marvin L., 11, 70, 91,
    123, 268
Model, 53, 170, 185, 194, 227, 231,
    53, 168, 183, 192, 225, 229
Modulus, 149
Monte Carlo method, 117, 135, 156,
    164
Morse code, 90, 95
MOS (Metal-Oxide-Semiconductor),
    2, 38
Motorola Semiconductor Products,
    Inc., 27
Mozart, W. A., 115
Music, 92, 113

Nance, Dana K., 171, 185, 169, 183
Nand, 17
National Biomedical Research
    Foundation, 206
National Institutes of Health, 175
Neisser, Ulric, 90, 95
Network analysis, 188
Newell, Allen, 95, 123
Newton, Issac, 266
Nim, 139
Noll, A. Michael, 15
Nor, 17
Not, 11, 17

Oettinger, Anthony G., 231, 245, 263
Operating system, 47, 76, 83, 248
Or, 11, 17, 145
Organizations, 229, 245, 271, 227,
    243, 269
Output. See Input-output
Oxford, University of, 195

Page, 85
Palestrina, Giovanni Pierluigi da, 116
Pandemonium, 100
Papert, Seymour, 91, 231

Pascal, Blaise, 9, 153
Password, 81
Pattern recognition, 90, 95, 201
Pauling, Linus, 177
PDP (Programmed Data Processor).
    See Digital Equipment
    Corporation
Pennsylvania State University, 252
Pennsylvania, University of, 9, 156
Personalization, 9, 252
Perspective projection, 65
Perutz, M. F., 173, 263
Pierce, John R., 116
Pinkerton, Richard C., 116
Pitts, Walter H., 123, 210
Pittsburgh, University of, 252
Planning, 129
Poe, Edgar Allan, 104
Precision Instrument Company, 223
Princeton University, 208
Privacy, 81
    See also Social implications of
        computing
Programming, 3, 70
    linear, 224
Programming languages, 3, 42, 70,
    237
Project MAC, 79, 127, 179, 233, 242,
    248, 264
    See also Massachusetts Institute of
        Technology

Rabin, M. O., 150
Radio Corporation of America, 8, 23, 41
Rajchman, Jan A., 2, 28
Ramanujan, Srinivasa, 157
RAND Corporation, 51, 95, 123
RAND Tablet, 42, 64
Randell, B., 230
Random sequences, 114, 135, 165
Random-access memory. See Memory
Raphael, Bertram, 91
Recursive, 73
Registers, 4, 17, 38
Relaxation, 223
Reliability, 84, 260
Reproduction
    of chromosomes, 201
    of machines, 213
Roberts, Lawrence G., 51, 64, 91, 123
Roberts, Michael De V., 91, 108
Romney, Gordon, 68
Rosenblueth, Arturo, 123
Rosler, L., 93
Ross, Douglas T., 243
Ruddle, Frank H., 172, 201, 265
Russell, Bertrand, 95

SABRE, 249
SAGE, 248
Samuel, Arthur L., 70, 92, 95, 123
Sanders Corporation, 54
Scanner, 51
Schönberg, Arnold, 117
Schwartz, Judah L., 60
Segment, 85
Selfridge, Oliver G., 90, 95
Semantics, 77, 91, 260, 269
Sequential circuits. See Circuits
Service Bureau Corporation, 109
Shannon, Claude E., 91, 104, 109, 239
Shannon, John P., 268
Shaw, J. C. (John Clifford), 95, 123
Simon, Herbert A., 95, 123
Simulation. See Model
Sketchpad, 239
Slotnick, D. L., 171, 216

Smith, Adam, 248, 250
Social implications of computers, 12, 87, 131, 226, 250
Solomon, 216
Spectra 70, 8, 23
Speed of computers, 2, 7, 21, 34, 45, 145, 208, 216
Sperry Rand Corporation, 27, 40
  See also UNIVAC
Standard Oil Company (New Jersey), 250
Stanford University, 92, 123, 251
Stein, P. R., 162
Steiner, Jakob, 160
Stibitz, George R., 9
Stockhausen, Karlheinz, 117
Store. *See* Memory
Stotz, Robert, 181
Strachey, Christopher, 3, 11, 70, 231
Stravinsky, Igor, 114
Stretch, 153, 196
Strings of characters, 11
Structure, hierarchical, 74
Student, 129
Subroutines
  for central processors, 246
  for display processors, 59
Superconductivity, 39
Supervisor. *See* Operating system
Suppes, Patrick, 14, 228, 230, 249, 251, 268, 270
Sutherland, Ivan E., 3, 42, 53, 135, 239

Sutherland, William R., 49, 241
Syntax, 77, 91, 206, 231
System Development Corporation, 79, 252
Systems analysis. *See* Programming

Tablet. *See* RAND tablet
Tape, magnetic. *See* Memory
Tape, punched. *See* Input-output
Texas Instruments, Incorporated, 22, 219
Texas, University of, 252
Theory. *See* Model
Thin-film memory. *See* Memory
Thom, Alexander, 195
Thompson, Fred B., 91
Tillman, Coyt, 233
Time-sharing, 5, 42, 76, 79, 135, 179, 239, 248, 251, 264
Torres y Quevedo, L., 104
Transistors, 25
Traveling-salesman problem, 160
Triad Oil Company, 245
Turing, Alan M., 7, 109, 134, 136, 170, 210, 268
Turing machine, 138, 210
TX-2, 239

Ulam, Stanislaw M., 134, 153, 164
UNIVAC, 10, 23, 153, 245
Universal machine, 7, 28, 170, 210
Utah, University of, 62

Venn diagrams, 18
Von Kármán, Theodor, 196
Von Kempelen, Wolfgang, 104
Von Neumann, John, 10, 153, 164, 208

Wagner, Richard, 113
Wang, Hao, 134, 136
Ward, John E., 181
Warnock, John, 65
Watkins, Gary, 67
Watson, Herman, 183
Weather Bureau, U. S., 163
Weather prediction, 227
Weaver, Warren, 114
Weizenbaum, Joseph, 91
Wells, Mark B., 158
Westinghouse Electric Corporation, 155, 217, 246
Whitehead, Alfred North, 70, 95
Wiener, Norbert, 123, 208
Window, 60
Winograd, Shmuel, 134, 145
Wipke, W. Todd, 64
Word, 4, 20, 28

Yale University, 202
Yngve, Victor H., 129

Zajac, E. E., 48
Zwick, Martin, 183